The Development of the British Economy

Third Edition
1914–1980

Sidney Pollard

Professor of Economic History, University of Bielefeld, West Germany

Edward Arnold

First published 1962 by
Edward Arnold (Publishers) Ltd,
41 Bedford Square, London WC1B 3DQ
Reprinted 1963, 1967
Second edition, revised 1969
Reprinted 1970
Reprinted as a paperback 1973
Reprinted 1976, 1979
Third edition 1983

Edward Arnold (Australia) Pty Ltd
80 Waverley Road
Caulfield East
Victoria 3145

First published in the United States of America 1983 by
Edward Arnold
300 North Charles Street
Baltimore
Maryland 21201

British Library Cataloguing in Publication Data
Pollard, Sidney
    The Development of the British economy.—3rd ed.
    1. Great Britain—Economic conditions—20th century
    I. Title
    330.941   HC256

ISBN 0-7131-6395-X

Text set in 10/11 pt English Times Compugraphic
by Colset Private Limited, Singapore
Printed and Bound in Great Britain by R Clay (The Chaucer Press) Ltd, Bungay,
Suffolk

Contents

Preface

The difficulties of writing recent history are well known. Much of the material is not yet available, the monographs and autobiographies have not yet been written, and many of the actors are still alive, to refute the most ingenious theories. Above all, we are still too close to the events, and too emotionally involved, to see them in their historical perspective.

But the pitfalls of writing recent history are as nothing compared with the pitfalls of teaching it, for it is here that the gap between the generations is at its most unbridgeable. What are everyday events and terms to the teacher are strange mysteries to the student, who finds the nuances, the background, the flavour of events, so familiar to the teacher as to be not worth making explicit, lost on him in a welter of unrecognizable references. The teaching of recent economic history has its own special difficulties, for it enters into the subjects of complex theoretical debate of yesterday, much of which is still unfinished. Yet teaching there must be, if the student is not to carry away with him a blank in his mind regarding the period when 'history' ends and when 'current economic problems' begin – precisely the period in which the minds of his elders were formed, and which some of them, alas, have never succeeded in leaving.

This book arose out of my desire to teach present-day students something about the no-man's land between history and applied economics or current affairs, and my difficulty in finding suitable general introductions, as distinct from specialist treatises and polemical works, of which there are probably too many. The usual tributes paid by the author in his Preface in this case must go to my students who unwittingly, and most likely unwillingly, forced me to write it. It is intended primarily for University students of Economics, Modern History and related subjects, and it assumes a modicum of knowledge of economic terms and institutions, such as any regular reader of the more intelligent weekly press could also command. It is hoped that it may also be of some use to their teachers and, further, to those interested members of the public, graduates, perhaps, in the subjects named here, and now active in business or public affairs, who require some knowledge of recent events to make up their own minds, believing with the author that the infallibility of our professional economic Oracles is by no means assured, even though they conform to their Delphic ancestor's habit of speaking in riddles, and regularly improve on it by speaking with several different voices at once.

A special word needs to be said about the bibliography. Traditionally, books designed mainly as textbooks have their reading lists either at the end of each chapter or at the end of the volume. Both suffer from similar limitations, for while the earnest student will be exasperated by not finding further reading hints on the pages on which his subject-matter occurs, the idle one will be too discouraged by the length of the reading list to make a start at all. Here, therefore (apart from a few general works mentioned at the end), the bibliography occurs in the form of footnotes to the text. These notes, even where they have the ostensible object of referring to the origins of quotations, statistics or unusual views, are all primarily intended as hints to further reading. It follows that the student's reading should extend beyond the page or chapter of the work quoted, according to the demand of his interests.

Each sectional chapter division has been treated as self-contained for the purposes of the bibliography, in the sense that full references are given again, even if the work has been mentioned in earlier sections or chapters. The statistical examples have been chosen deliberately from a wide range of sources, and conflicting series are occasionally given side by side in order to teach a healthy scepticism about economic measurement. The literature has been chosen so that the sum of the footnote references to each section forms the complete bibliography of the section and the sum of the references in each chapter, the bibliography of that chapter. It has, further, been chosen so as to make the student familiar with a wide selection of reading matter available, including books, reprints of documents, articles in learned journals and other periodicals, and official papers and statistics.

S. P.

In this second impression, the bibliography has been brought up to date, and some minor corrections to the text have been made. For some of the latter I am much indebted to Dr Walter Stern and Mr C. G. Hanson.

S. P.

7 August 1963

The enlarged edition brings the present volume virtually up to date. The new final chapter runs an even greater danger of showing all the weaknesses of writing on contemporary history, for not only may it stand too close to the events to recognize all the facts, but it may also fall into the trap of taking sides in the controversies. Yet to leave a widening gap between itself and the present would progressively diminish the value of the rest of the book. Amendments and additions to the rest of the book have been kept to a minimum, and mostly concern the literature published since the last revision.

S. P.

31 May 1968

In this third edition, the book has once more been brought up to date, ending formally in 1980 but extending in some respects to 1982. The final chapter of the last edition, which covered 17 years, would have had to cover 30 years in this, and it has therefore been split into three by topics, each covering the whole period, in parallel with the chapters covering the inter-war period. To preserve the same total length, the earlier chapters have been correspondingly shortened, and have been largely re-written to incorporate the literature and some of the controversies that have appeared in the course of the past 20 years or so. As before, the most recent events have been the most difficult to describe, and in the face of an economics profession split down the middle between monetarists and Keynesians, each of several different hues, a bland neutrality would have been even more difficult to attain than on former occasions, and has not been attempted.

S. P.

31 October 1982

Abbreviations used in Footnote References

Amer.Econ.Rev.	*American Economic Review*
B.of Eng.Qtly.Bull.	*Bank of England Quarterly Bulletin*
Bull.Oxf.Inst.Stat.	*Bulletin of the Oxford Institute of Statistics*
Bus.Hist.Rev.	*Business History Review*
Econ.Hist.Rev.	*Economic History Review*
Econ.J.	*Economic Journal*
Expl.Econ.Hist.	*Explorations in Economic History*
Geog.J.	*Geographical Journal*
J.Econ. and Business History	*Journal of Economic and Business History*
J.Econ.Hist.	*Journal of Economic History*
J.Royal Soc.of Arts	*Journal of the Royal Society of Arts*
J.R.Stat.S.	*Journal of the Royal Statistical Society*
J.Transport History	*Journal of Transport History*
Manchester School	*Manchester School of Economic and Social Studies*
Nat.Inst.Econ.Rev.	*National Institute Economic Review*
Oxf.Bull.Econ.Stat.	*Oxford Bulletin of Economics and Statistics*
Oxf.Econ.P.	*Oxford Economic Papers*
QJE	*Quarterly Journal of Economics*
Rev.Econ.Studies	*Review of Economic Studies*
Rev. of Econ. and Statistics	*Review of Economics and Statistics*
Scot.J.Pol.Econ.	*Scottish Journal of Political Economy*
Yorkshire Bulletin	*Yorkshire Bulletin of Economic and Social Studies*
HSWW	*(Official) History of the Second World War*
NS	*New Series*
RC	*Royal Commission*
SC	*Select Committee*
2nd S.	*Second Series*

Note: In references to articles in journals the convention has been followed where possible of separating volume and issue numbers by an oblique stroke: thus 3/13 means Volume 3, Number 13. The date afterwards refers to the date of the number, not necessarily of the whole volume.

In accordance with the practice which has become increasingly common in recent economic literature, the word 'billion' is used throughout in the American sense of a thousand million, and *not* in the traditional British sense of a million million.

1

The End of the Long Peace and the First World War, 1914–1918

1 British Industry and its Position in the World

The popular ideas about a country and an age, the ideas which are so all-pervasive that men find it largely unnecessary to express them on paper, take a long time to mature, and they take a long time to eradicate. The ideas which the British citizen imbibed in the last years of the century of peace which came to a close in 1914, as he watched the areas of red spread across the map, and saw fresh technical marvels introduced every year, were based on the experiences of the past two or three generations. These contained a dual promise of progress: the promise that science and industry would continue to improve material conditions of living, and the promise that Britain would continue to be at the head of this march of improvement.

Yet there were misgivings. The 'Great Depression' of the 1870s and 1880s had emphasized the inability to avoid the periodic crises which brought with them heavy unemployment and business losses, even without the financial panics that had previously been thought responsible for them, and it had also, for the first time, raised a serious fear of foreign competition in manufactures in which Britain had been dominating world markets for a century. There had also been occasional scares about the exhaustion of British coal reserves, or the world shortage of nitrogenous fertilizers.

Possibly the chief doubt about the prospects of progress arose not so much out of its general direction, but largely out of the glaring inequalities in income and wealth: in 1911–13, it has been estimated, 170,000 persons, or 0·85% of the population, owned 65·5% of the capital in the country, while at the other extreme, over $16\frac{1}{3}$ million, or 87·4% of the property-owning population, owned only 8·5% between them.[1] But inequality, of at least the same or even greater extent[2] had existed before. What was new was the fact that real wages were no longer rising, as they had been to 1900; the realization that in the midst of the much-boasted wealth of Britain, poverty was no longer necessary; and the diversion of much of the new wealth to classes who had not learnt the 'double bluff' of pre-war society noted by Keynes,[3] that capitalists were allowed to appropriate a large part of the nation's wealth, in the face of bitter poverty among the rest of the population, only on condition that they did not enjoy it, but re-invested it in their concerns.

Change and proposals for change were in the air. It was as if the age of

[1] H. Campion, *Public and Private Property* (Oxford, 1938).
[2] Peter H. Lindert and Jeffrey G. Williamson, *Revising England's Social Tables, 1688–1867*, Department of Economics, University of California, Davis, Working Paper No. 176, 1981.
[3] J. M. Keynes, *Economic Consequences of the Peace* (New York, 1920), pp. 18–22.

peace and progress had lasted too long. Men who had little to lose, and men who had a great deal, seemed to crave change for its own sake. A spirit of restlessness appeared to pervade the last years of the Long Peace.[4]

From the vantage-point of later years, it is not difficult to point to weaknesses in the British industrial structure before 1914, but they would not have been easy to prove to contemporaries. Total industrial production was still growing and 1913 was a peak year on any reckoning. Between 1900 and 1913 gross domestic product (GDP) of the United Kingdom at factor cost was still growing at the rate of 1·7% a year, and even output per head was rising at an average of 0·7%.[5] This was below the growth rates of the mid-nineteenth century and below contemporary American or German rates, but might be explained by the high absolute level already achieved in Britain. Exports were also rising, but at no more than 0·93% per head p.a.[6] and they showed a dangerous concentration on a narrow range of industries: thus in 1911–13, textiles still accounted for 51·2% of exports (they had been 67·9% in 1857–9). Other consumer goods accounted for 10·6%, producer goods for 33·7% and other goods for the remaining 4·5%.

Altogether, the old 'staple trades' coal, iron and steel, machinery and vehicles, ships and textiles between them contributed two-thirds of all exports in 1911–13. The buoyancy of some of them in export markets was misleading even then, as they showed signs of real stagnation. Thus the output of coal per miner had been falling since the early 1880s, and in the Lancashire cotton and Cleveland pig iron industries real costs had not been reduced at all since 1885,[7] while the costs of our chief competitors were still falling.

Coal mining, the most basic of industries, providing the fuel and determining the location of the others, was still expanding. From 223 million tons at the turn of the century, production had increased to 287 million tons in 1913, of which over 94 million tons was for export and bunkering. The coalfields were still being extended, notably the difficult, but prolific South Wales field, the rich seams of the Yorkshire-North Midlands area which were followed eastwards as they dipped deeper below the surface, and the newly discovered field in Kent.[8] However, technically the industry was falling behind other countries. Only 8% of the coal was cut mechanically in 1913, and even less was mechanically conveyed underground; in the use of electricity, concrete, even steel, British pits seemed backward, though the geography of the British fields and the nature of the seams might explain the delay in the introduction of methods which were not yet fully proved.

Employment in the pig iron and steel works, at little over 100,000, was far

---

[4] The atmosphere of those years is captured most aptly in Geo. Dangerfield, *The Strange Death of Liberal England* (1936), a book to be recommended more for its intuitive perception than its historical accuracy. Also G. D. H. Cole and R. Postgate, *The Common People, 1746–1938* (1938), chapter 37.

[5] C. H. Feinstein, *National Income, Expenditure and Output of the United Kingdom 1855–1956* (Cambridge, 1972), T. 18.

[6] C. K. Harley and D. N. McCloskey, 'Foreign Trade, Competition and the Expanding International Economy', in Roderick Floud and Donald McCloskey (eds.), *The Economic History of Britain Since 1700*, Vol. 2, *1860 to the 1970s* (Cambridge, 1981), p. 51.

[7] G. T. Jones, *Increasing Return* (1933). The paradox of the export successes of the 'staple' industries in the face of the loss of their relative efficiency is discussed in pp. 10–11 below.

[8] H. Stanley Jevons, *The British Coal Trade* (1915).

smaller than in the mines, but its basic importance for an industrial country was equally evident. Here a considerable growth in British output had been overtaken by the faster growth of Germany and the USA. In 1913 the USA produced 31 million tons, Germany 16·5 million, and Britain 10·3 million of pig iron; in steel production, by 1913 the American output was of the order of 13 milion tons, the German of 7 million, and the British of 5 million.

As in the case of coal, home output could not be said to be stagnating; but while blast furnaces hardly changed in this country, abroad new building and replacement constantly enlarged their size and raised their efficiency, and the same could be said of the steel furnaces and converters. Britain adopted the cheaper basic processes only very slowly, and the final change-over even from puddled iron to steel took place long after it had been completed elsewhere.[9]

In general engineering and shipbuilding Britain was also losing her early lead. In some respects she was paying the penalty for being the pioneer. Thus the early excellence of the British marine steam engine and, at the turn of the century, of the steam turbine designed by Charles Parsons, was the direct cause (together with the abundance of steam coal) of the neglect of the oil-fired marine engines and motors in Britain, and it was these which turned out to be the engines of the future. Further, the period of Britain's supremacy was one in which success in industry, whether in coal mining, iron puddling, steel rolling, in textile spinning and weaving, in building or in engineering, depended to a large extent on the skill of craftsmen, their use of tools and machinery, their knowledge of their materials. Britain had a race of craftsmen second to none, and it was precisely the lack of such craftsmen in sufficient numbers in the USA which forced American employers to pioneer automatic and foolproof machinery, mass-produced articles, using interchangeable parts as well as 'scientific management'. These, again, turned out to be the methods of the future, but they were resisted here both by masters and men,[10] and adopted only slowly, if at all, before 1914. The lag behind Germany in electrical engineering, as well as in chemicals, pointed to another hangover from earlier days: the neglect of university-trained scientists.[11]

As a result of these and other factors, British achievements in the engineering branches were mixed. In motor cars, office equipment, most machine tools, agricultural machinery and electrical machinery the record was poor; clock making was almost wiped out. By contrast, British did well in the older manufactures of steam engines, textile machinery and heavy machine tools, and the newer manufacture of bicycles. In shipbuilding, the United Kingdom still built 60% of the world's mercantile tonnage over the whole period 1900–14.[12] This was the sort of proportion that had been familiar in other

[9] Peter Temin, 'The Relative Decline of the British Steel Industry, 1880–1913', in H. Rosovsky (ed.), *Industrialization in Two Systems*, (New York, 1966).

[10] E. H. Phelps-Brown, *Growth of British Industrial Relations* (1959), pp. 94–6.

[11] J. H. Clapham, *An Economic History of Modern Britain*, Vol. 3 (Cambridge, 1938), chapters 1 and 3; A. P. M. Fleming and H J. Brocklehurst, *A History of Engineering* (1925), chapters 9–11.

[12] S. Pollard, 'British and World Shipbuilding', *J. Econ. Hist.*, 17/3, 1957; *Report on Engineering Trades after the War* (1918, Cd. 9073); S. B. Saul, 'The Market and the Development of the Mechanical Engineering Industries in Britain, 1860–1914', *Ec. Hist. Rev.*, 20/1, 1967; idem, 'The Engineering Industry', in D. H. Aldcroft (ed.), *The Development of British Industry and Foreign Competition 1875–1914* (1968); R. A. Church, 'Nineteenth-Century Clock Technology

industries 50 years earlier. All told, engineering exports by 1911–13 had increased threefold in value since the early 1880s. In 1907 about half the output of the main sectors of engineering was exported. Engineering output is notoriously difficult to measure, but one estimate put the British share of world machinery production in 1913 at 11·8%, compared with the USA, 50%, and Germany, 20·6%.

The textile industries formed the remainder of the old staple trades, which Britain had pioneered and on which her exports still largely depended. Of these, the cotton trade was still by far the most important exporter. In the years 1911–13, it accounted for an average of £123 million, compared with £54 million for all other textile exports combined. Both output and exports (especially of piece goods) were still on the increase, and there were some signs of technical improvement, but British firms failed to adopt the key cost-reducing innovation, the ring spindle.[13]

The woollen and worsted industries were still registering a steady growth. The linen and silk industries had shrunk to relative insignificance, and the output of silk thread and silk goods was actually declining in absolute terms. The numbers employed in all these textile trades were declining at a faster rate than in any other occupation between 1891 and 1911.

There was one other old staple industry, though it had long since ceased to figure in the export statistics: this was agriculture, the chief victim of the Free Trade policy of the nineteenth century. Cheap freights and unrestricted imports reduced the home output of wheat, but meat production found growing home markets, and since 1870, the proportion of cultivated land under permanent pasture had risen from 42% to 53%. Market gardening was another occupation which made economic sense, in a population now largely urban, and the crisis in agriculture may be said to have been over by 1910.[14] The rising world prices for food in the early years of the century largely contributed to the strength of British, and foreign, agriculture.

By contrast with these old staples, some newer industries promised well for the future by their rapid rate of growth, though they were still relatively insignificant. Among them, electrical engineering and supply were based to a considerable extent on British inventions and discoveries, but Britain lagged sadly behind Germany and even America in their development. The gas engine, and the motor car industry, its chief user, were equally the fruits of foreign, rather than British, enterprise. The British chemical industry also appeared increasingly unable to keep pace, despite its early lead, being handicapped by the lack of scientists and by being wedded to older processes, e.g.

in Britain, the United States, and Switzerland', *Ec. Hist. Rev.*, 28/4, 1975; A. E. Harrison, 'The Competitiveness of the British Cycle Industry', ibid., 22/3, 1969; S. B. Saul, 'The Motor Industry in Britain to 1914', *Business History*, 5, 1962.

[13] Lars G. Sandberg, 'American Rings and English Mules: The Role of Economic Rationality', *Q.J.E.*, 83, 1968; William Lazonick, 'Factor Costs and the Diffusion of Ring Spinning in Britain Prior to World War I', *ibid.*, 96, 1981; *idem*, 'Production Relations, Labor Productivity and Choice of Technique: British and US Cotton Spinning', *J.Econ.Hist.*, 41/3, 1981.

[14] A. D. Hall, *A Pilgrimage of British Farming* (1912); Lord Ernle, *English Farming, Past and Present* (4th ed., 1927), chapters 18 and 19; T. W. Fletcher, 'The Great Depression of English Agriculture, 1873–1896', *Ec. Hist. Rev.*, 13/3, 1961.

the Leblanc, rather than the Solvay, process of making soda. The war quickly showed up the serious shortcomings in the making of organic chemicals, such as high explosives, the shortage of oleum, one of their basic raw materials, and the neglect of the recent methods of producing fertilizer.[15]

Though perhaps relatively backward, these industries were among the most rapidly expanding ones, together with the allied rubber,[16] oil refining, airplane, artificial silk and scientific instruments industries. There was progress in other industries also, especially in glass, pottery, paper-making and printing, food preparation and boot and shoe making, all of which contributed not a little to the rising standards of comfort in Britain.

The industries enumerated so far employed some 40% of the occupied population between them. Changes in other sectors, including commerce, distribution, building, the professions, and central and local government, contributed equally to the growth in consumption and living standards, though they were usually less spectacular and less easy to capture in the statistics.

Larger companies in all sectors had now accepted the joint-stock form of organization, and following an Act of 1907 which made special provisions for the smaller companies, smaller businesses could also gain advantages by doing so. By 1911 over three-quarters of all companies, whether registered as 'private' or not, were in fact private companies which did not come before the public for capital.

By the standards of the mid-twentieth century or those of contemporary USA[17], industrial amalgamation and combination in the last years of peace had not proceeded very far. There were, in effect, two distinct, even if related, movements: a simple growth in size, and an attempt to restrict competition. The two were often confused, but while the former usually took place in order to obtain economies in working, administration, marketing or finance, the latter was, more often than not, directed towards raising prices to consumers. Both tended to occur in slack times when markets were difficult.[18]

Combinations of this kind began to be viewed with apprehension wherever they obtained control over a significant share of their markets; thus in the case of railways, from the 1850s, and the banks in 1918,[19] official policy became expressly opposed to permitting any further reduction in the small

---

[15] Cf. S. B. Saul, *Studies in British Overseas Trade, 1870–1914* (Liverpool, 1960), pp. 37 ff.; T. I. Williams, *The Chemical Industry* (1953), chapter 6; L. F. Haber, *The Chemical Industry during the Nineteenth Century* (Oxford, 1958), chapter 9; idem, *The Chemical Industry 1900–1930* (Oxford, 1971), pp. 135 ff.; Peter H. Lindert and Keith Trace, 'Yardsticks for Victorian Entrepreneurs', in Donald N. McCloskey (ed.), *Essays on a Mature Economy: Britain After 1840*, (1971).

[16] Wm. Woodruff, *The Rise of the British Rubber Industry during the Nineteenth Century* (Liverpool, 1958).

[17] Alfred D. Chandler, Jr, 'The Development of Modern Management Structures in the US and UK', in Leslie Hannah (ed.), *Management Strategy and Business Development* (1976).

[18] Leslie Hannah, 'Mergers in British Manufacturing Industry, 1880–1918', *Oxf. Econ. P.*, 26, 1974, p. 9; Lance Davis, 'The Capital Market and Industrial Concentration: The US and UK, a Comparative Study', *Ec. Hist. Rev.*, 19/2, 1966, p. 266.

[19] Treasury Committee on Bank Amalgamations, *Report* (1918), in T. E. Gregory, *Statutes, Documents and Reports Relating to British Banking*, vol. 2 (Oxford, 1929).

number of competing units. The authorities did not, however, intervene to curb the activities of private combinations to restrict competition.

In some industries the typical form of organization was an association of independent producers, agreeing on common prices, and often developing common sales organizations and restriction schemes on output in order to protect their prices. These associations were most notable in the iron and steel industry. Some, like those of the steel rail makers from 1904, the screw makers in the 1890s and again from 1905, and the wire-netting makers, were international. By 1914, some 80 associations were in operation in the industry, each controlling one or a related group of products. Another group of trades in which this type of association was prominent, side by side with single-firm monopolies, was the building materials industry. It was calculated that in 1914 one-quarter of the cost of a cottage was fully price controlled, and a second quarter partially so; some of these monopolistic costs, however, were represented by the wages of skilled workers.[20] The shipping conferences or 'rings' which had been flourishing since the 1870s were normally limited to liner companies which stood to lose heavily if their ships sailed empty at their advertised times, and they brought to perfection a weapon adopted later by other associations: the deferred rebate.[21]

Some associations took the ultimate step of a complete merger to obtain monopolistic powers in this period, especially in the chemical and the textile industries. Among chemical firms the Salt Union (1888), the United Alkali Co. (1891), Brunner Mond & Co. (1881), Borax Consolidated (1899) and the Nobel Dynamite Trust were the most prominent. In textiles, J. & P. Coats (1890), the English Sewing Cotton Co. (1897) stood out, together with the following associations, each formed of numerous small constituent companies: Fine Cotton Spinners' and Doublers' (1898), Calico Printers' (1899), Bleachers' (1900), Bradford Dyers' (1898), and Woolcombers' (1900). In other industries were found Imperial Tobacco (1901–2), British Oil and Cake Mills (1899), the Distillers' Company (1907) and Associated Portland Cement (1900).[22]

A different method of organization making remarkable progress in the years before 1914 was that of the co-operative society. With a membership of 3 million, the 1,385 societies had total sales of nearly £90 million, and had been transformed from insignificant local associations to a major factor in retail distribution and a few related fields. A significant share of the basic weekly shopping by the working-class housewife in the north was done in the local 'co-op' branch, still working on the 'Rochdale principles' of paying dividends on purchases, not on shares, and keeping to 'one member, one vote'. A few producer societies, and some agricultural societies, notably in Ireland, also worked on co-operative principles. In this period co-operative trading was an important factor in the pioneering of large-scale enterprise in retailing, in promoting the campaign for wholesome and unadulterated food,

---

[20] *Report of the Committee on Trusts* (1919. Cd. 9236). Some of the unpublished material on which this Report was based was used by Clapham, *op. cit*, chapter 5.

[21] *S.C. on Shipping Rings* (1909. Cd. 4668, 4669, 4670, 4685).

[22] Hermann Levy, *Monopolies, Trusts and Cartels in British Industry* (2nd ed., 1927); F. W. Hirst, *Monopolies, Trusts and Kartells* (1905); Henry W. Macrosty, *The Trust Movement in British Industry* (1907).

and in providing convenient facilities for working-class savings.[23]

While there were modern traits to be found in industrial and commercial organization, the skill and enterprise of the British entrepreneur of that period have been called in question. In particular, the failure of the economy to grow at the rate of the USA, of Germany and most other continental countries, and the failure to modernize certain key industries and to develop others, have been seen as part of a general decline in enterprise. Against this, it has been argued in several detailed studies, the British entrepreneur behaved rationally in obeying the market signals that he met. In many fields he stayed indeed on top of the world; in others, he was not to be blamed if the market misled him into actions which, in the long run, turned out to be inhibiting for British progress. The debate is still unresolved, and it turns largely on the functions and range of the entrepreneur. How many years ahead should he plan for? Which among the economic data surrounding him should he consider as given, and which should he endeavour to change if necessary?[24] How far was he to blame for the British 'over-commitment' to slow-growth industries?[25]

2 The Banks, the Money Market and Foreign Investment

Among the many changes in the forms of economic organization in the generation before 1914, those in the field of banking were among the most significant. The swallowing up of the private banks by the joint-stock bank engaged in branch banking, 'a trickle in the middle decades of the century, . . . had become a headlong rush as the century neared its end. In the new century amalgamations continued to follow one upon the other, and they were now amalgamations between banks already greatly enlarged by earlier absorptions.'[26] This process was all but completed by 1914, when the several hundred private banks had shrunk to fewer than a score, but there now were 20 joint-stock banks with over 100 branches each (the largest, the London City and Midland, having over 700), besides 20 or so with fewer than 100 branches each and local connections only. Between them, they maintained about 7,000 offices in England and Wales. In Scotland, where joint-stock banking had a longer tradition, there were eight banking companies in 1914, with just under 1,200 branches between them. In the 'race' of amalgamations, the objective was increasingly seen to be national coverage for each firm. In the process, any existing gaps were filled by opening new offices and sub-offices, which increased in number year by year.[27]

[23] C. R. Fay, *Great Britain from Adam Smith to the Present Day* (4th ed., 1937), chapter 20; G. D. H. Cole, *A Century of Co-operation* (1944).

[24] D. H. Aldcroft, 'The Entrepreneur and the British Economy 1870–1914', *Ec. Hist. Rev.*, 17/1, 1964; Donald N. McCloskey, 'Did Victorian Britain fail?', *ibid.*, 23/3, 1970; Donald N. McCloskey and Lars G. Sandberg, 'From Damnation to Redemption: Judgements on the Late Victorian Entrepreneur', *Expl. Ec. Hist.*, 9 (1971); D. H. Aldcroft, 'Technical Progress and British Enterprise, 1875–1914', *Business History*, 8, 1966; William H. Phillips, 'Induced Innovation and Economic Performance in Late Victorian British Industry', *J. Econ. Hist.*, 42/1, 1982.

[25] H. W. Richardson, 'Over-commitment in Britain Before 1930', *Oxf. Econ. P.*, 17, 1965.

[26] R. S. Sayers, *Lloyd's Bank in the History of English Banking* (Oxford, 1957), p. 241.

[27] J. F. Ashby, *The Story of the Banks* (1934); P. W. Matthews, *The Banker's Clearing House* (1921), chapter 7; J. Sykes, *The Amalgamation Movement in British Banking, 1825–1924* (1926).

The process bespeaks an increasing banking habit of the population: between 1906 and 1914 alone, bank deposits per head of population rose from £18·8 to £23·4, and clearings from £292 to £359. Its consequences were far-reaching. The circulation of private bank notes virtually disappeared, except for Scotland, the cheque system became all but universal, and Bank of England notes were mainly used for wage payments and small retail purchases only,[28] while inland bills were rendered largely obsolete:[29] bills were now used mostly for foreign traffic only.

A further result of amalgamation was to make banking much safer as resources and reserves were immeasurably increased. At the same time the individual banks obtained more power in the money market: just as the decline of the inland bill tended to squeeze the discount houses out of home markets, so the opening of branches or agencies abroad by the joint-stock banks made inroads into the work of other specialist firms. The accumulation of 'private' gold reserves by the banks (the Midland alone held £8 million by 1914, and the others probably £16 million between them) made it more easy for them to defy the central bank, had they so desired,[30] though in fact collaboration with the Bank of England became closer, and a liaison committee was set up in 1911 and justified its existence during the early days of financial panic after the outbreak of war.

The strengthening of the English banking structure by amalgamation also altered the role of the Bank of England as the central bank and banker of last resort. An internal drain having become unlikely since there were very few country banks with their own note issue left, it would appear, to judge from the evidence given to the US Monetary Commission, that the Bank was almost exclusively concerned with the foreign exchanges, and with safeguarding the gold reserve against the dangers of a drain abroad.

The Bank's two main weapons in carrying out its obligations as a central bank were the bank rate and open market operations. The former could sometimes be accompanied by greater selectivity in the kind of paper the Bank would accept for rediscounting; the ideal, however, was to lend freely, but at high rates, in times of need. A rise in the bank rate achieved its primary object if it led to a general rise of interest rates in London. These were then expected to call forth an influx of foreign funds including gold, on the one hand, and to discourage enterprise, lead to a reduction of stocks and to general deflation at home on the other, thus reversing the outflow of gold which was the usual ground upon which the high bank rate policy had been put into operation. 'Open market operations' covered a variety of actions with which the Bank experimented in this period to supplement its bank rate policy by making money scarce or plentiful in the City. They ranged from purchases and sales of securities to influencing market rates (as distinct from

[28] Evidence of Governor and Directors of the Bank of England to US National Monetary Commission in 1910, reprinted in T. E. Gregory (ed.), *Selected Statutes, Documents and Reports Relating to British Banking, 1832–1928* (Oxford, 1929), vol. 2, p. 309; also First Report of Cunliffe Committee, quoted in *ibid.*, pp. 335–6.

[29] W. T. C. King, *History of the London Discount Market* (1936), pp. 271–5.

[30] E. Victor Morgan, *Theory and Practice of Central Banking, 1797–1913* (Cambridge 1943), pp. 210–12.

bank rate) and the gold market, and included the increasingly effective 'hint from headquarters' to the clearing banks.[31]

Several circumstances combined to turn the imperfect control of the Bank of England over the market which existed in 1890 into the smooth and perfect instrument of the last years before 1914.[32] In the first place, the gold reserve rose after the mid-1890s, when the vast quantities from the new goldfields of Alaska and South Africa began to arrive in London. In the years before 1914, the reserve fluctuated around the comfortable level of £30 million, creeping up to £40 million.[33] Secondly, the Bank could count on the support of other strong institutions, including foreign central banks, and the joint-stock banks and it could use the growing funds of Colonial Governments and British local authorities to back up its policies.

Above all, the powers of the Bank over the City depended on the growth of London as the leading money market in the world. Most of the world was on a gold standard by the end of the nineteenth century, but the premier position of London ensured that an attractive rate would bring gold from the four corners of the earth. This power of a high rate to attract gold was demonstrated in 1907, when, after a serious loss of gold to America, a 7% bank rate brought in speedily £19 million in gold from 24 countries.

In the years before 1914, the facilities in London for raising capital for British industry were limited and badly co-ordinated. Local authorities, Railways and public utilities could use the London money market, and their securities were freely quoted on the Stock Exchange. For the rest of the domestic capital needs, however, the Stock Exchange was of little help: in the years before the war, only 10% of real investment in this country was made by issues of industrial firms through the London Stock Exchange, and only 3% by new industrial firms. Neither were the banks, which were quite content to finance the growing volume of Stock Exchange speculation, prepared to finance industry. As a result, capital for industry had to be found largely by personal connections, in provincial centres, and by ploughing back the firms' own profits.[34]

By contrast, the market for investing abroad was extremely well organized. Particularly active were the merchant banks which floated foreign loans,

[31] R. S. Sayers, *Bank of England Operation, 1890–1914* (1936), and 'Open Market Operations in English Central Banking' in his *Central Banking after Bagehot* (Oxford 1957); idem, *The Bank of England 1891–1944*, 3 vols. (Cambridge, 1976), vol. 1, chapter 3; P. Barrett Whale, 'The Working of the Pre-War Gold Standard', *Economica*, 1937, reprinted in T. S. Ashton and R. S. Sayers (eds.), *Papers in English Monetary History* (Oxford, 1953); A. G. Ford, 'Notes on the Working of the Gold Standard before 1914', *Oxf. Econ. P.*, NS, 12/1, 1960; Donald N. McCloskey and J. Richard Zecher, 'How the Gold Standard Worked 1880–1913', in Donald N. McCloskey, *Enterprise and Trade in Victorian Britain* (1981).

[32] W. E. Beach, *British International Gold Movements and Banking Policy, 1881–1913* (Cambridge, Mass., 1935), chapters 7–9.

[33] R. G. Hawtrey, *A Century of Bank Rate* (1938), pp. 46–8.

[34] A. K. Cairncross, *Home and Foreign Investment 1870–1913* (Cambridge, 1953), chapter 5; F. Lavington, *The English Capital Market* (1921); and the controversy in A. R. Hall, 'A Note on the English Capital Market as a Source of Funds Before 1914', *Economica*, NS, 24/93, 1957; A. K. Cairncross, 'The English Capital Market Before 1914', *ibid.*, 25/98, 1958, pp. 142–6; A. R. Hall, 'The English Capital Market Before 1914 – a Reply', *ibid.*, 25/100, pp. 339–43. But see Lance Davis, 'The Capital Markets and Industrial Concentration: The US and UK, a Comparative Study', *Ec. Hist. Rev*, 19/2, 1966, p. 262.

acted as agents for foreign governments and public corporations, accepted foreign bills and engaged in foreign exchange operations. In consequence, foreign investment in the last years of peace had reached an astonishing level. According to Imlah, capital assets abroad owned by British citizens amounted to about £2·4 billion at the turn of the century; by the outbreak of war, they had risen to £4 billion.[35] More recent estimates have reduced this to perhaps £2·8 billion, still an enormous sum. Further, the pace of foreign investment tended to increase from an average of under £50 million per annum in 1901–5 to about £150 million per annum in 1907–10 and £200 million per annum in 1911–13. From 1907 on, annual investment abroad appears to have exceeded the total of real net investments at home.

How was this vast capital export, amounting in the last years to about one-third of the total export trade, financed? Britain, it must be remembered, showed a substantial unfavourable balance on merchandise trade of the order of £150 million annually. This negative balance, to which must be added (net) bullion imports and tourist expenditure abroad of about £20 million, was almost exactly counterbalanced by large and rising credit terms for net invisible exports: banking, insurance and shipping earnings. The surplus was provided by dividends and interest rising from about £100 million to £200 million between 1900 and 1913, and it was these which allowed Britain to increase her foreign investments at an equally rapid rate. This was not merely a statistical coincidence: a large part of the foreign investment was, in fact, direct re-investment of earnings abroad.[36]

In the wave-like movements of this long-term trend, booms in capital exports coincided with booms in the exports of capital goods and with a high tide of emigration from the United Kingdom, particularly to the countries which received a large share of the British capital, alternating with periods of an exactly opposite character.[37] The years before 1914 formed the second half of the last, and perhaps most powerfully marked, of these cycles, in which the other advanced countries of Europe also registered exceptionally large exports of capital.[38] At the same time British investment, as well as British migration, went increasingly to areas within the Empire. Thus in 1901–10 an annual average of 85,000 migrated from the United Kingdom to Canada, and 23,000 to Australia and New Zealand. In 1911–13, the figures were 189,000 and 85,000 respectively. The proportions of British emigrants making for

[35] A. H. Imlah, 'British Balance of Payments and Export of Capital, 1816–1913', *Ec. Hist. Rev.*, 5/2, 1952; reprinted in *Economic Elements in the Pax Britannica* (Cambridge, Mass., 1958). Other broadly similar estimates are summarized in E. Victor Morgan, *Studies in British Financial Policy, 1914–1925* (1952), p. 328; J. H. Lenfant, 'Great Britain's Capital Formation, 1865–1914', *Economica*, NS, 18/70, 1951; C. H. Feinstein, *National Income, Expenditure and Output of the United Kingdom 1855–1965* (Cambridge, 1972), p. 205. But see D. C. M. Platt, 'British Portfolio Investment Overseas before 1870. Some Doubts', *Ec. Hist. Rev.*, 33/1, 1980, pp. 14–16.
[36] A dissenting view will be found in A. G. Ford, 'The Transfer of British Foreign Lending, 1870–1913', *Ec. Hist. Rev.*, 11/2, 1958.
[37] Brinley Thomas, *Migration and Economic Growth* (Cambridge, 1954); Cairncross, *op. cit.*, chapter 8; P. L. Cottrell, *British Overseas Investment in the Nineteenth Century (1975)*, chapters 5 and 6.
[38] C. K. Hobson, *The Export of Capital* (1914).

territories within the Empire were 28% in the 1890's, 63% between 1901 and 1912, and 78% in 1913.

When we note, further, that the years before 1914 were also marked by a general rise in world prices, in which food and raw materials, the main British imports, tended to rise faster in price than the manufactured goods which Britain exported,[39] it may now be possible to discern a distinct pattern in the unhealthy reliance of the staple industries on exports, the export boom in capital goods, the lag behind other countries in technical equipment and progress, the concentration of the City of London on foreign lending, and the downward pressure on real incomes (except for profits), in the last years of peace. Do they all add up to the statement that Britain invested too much abroad, to the detriment of her own industrial future?

The question admits of no easy answer. The direction of the British investment programme was not the outcome of a deliberate decision, but of the choices of innumerable investors. It has long been assumed that they invested abroad because the returns were higher, but even that seems no longer certain, particularly when the risks are added in. It may well have been that the smoothness of the City operations channelled funds abroad that might have earned more at home.[40] Even if foreign returns were higher, it mattered for Britain's future whether they were earned in equipping complementary economies, supplying raw materials and food, as had largely been the case earlier, or whether they were equipping competing economies with such items as textile machinery, as was increasingly the case in the early twentieth century. Moreover, even if it were true that small marginal investments at home would bring only low returns, the massive re-equipment which investment at German or American rates would have made possible would most likely have taken Britain on a distinctly steeper growth path, enjoying rising instead of stagnating real wage levels.

The destination of the funds thus sent abroad was significant.[41] By 1910, when foreign investments totalled some £3$\frac{1}{4}$ million, about £1,550–£1,650 million was invested within the Empire, virtually all of it in four regions,

---

[39] H. A. Imlah, *Economic Elements*, pp. 87–8; also 'Terms of Trade of the United Kingdom 1798–1915', *J. Econ. Hist.*, 10/2, Nov. 1950; Cairncross, *op. cit.*, p. 206; W. W. Rostow, 'The Terms of Trade in Theory and Practice', *Ec. Hist. Rev.*, 3/1, 1950, and 'The Historical Analysis of the Terms of Trade', *ibid.*, 4/1, 1951.

[40] F. W. Taussig, 'Great Britain's Foreign Trade Terms after 1900', *Econ. J.*, 1925; John Saville, 'Some Retarding Factors in the British Economy before 1914', *Yorkshire Bulletin*, 13/1, 1961; Lance E. Davis and Robert A. Huttenback, 'The Political Economy of British Imperialism: Measures of Benefits and Support', *J. Econ. Hist.*, 42/1, 1982, p. 125; Michael Edelstein, 'Realized Rates of Return on UK Home and Overseas Portfolio Investment in the Age of High Imperialism', *Expl. Ec. Hist.*, 13, 1976; *idem*, UK Savings in the Age of High Imperialism and After', *Amer. Econ. Rev.*, Papers and Proceedings, 67, 1977; *idem*, 'Rigidity and Bias in the British Capital Market, 1870–1913', in D. N. McCloskey, *Essays on a Mature Economy*; W. P. Kennedy, 'Foreign Investment, Trade and Growth in the United Kingdom 1870–1913', *Expl. Ec. Hist.*, 11, 1974; *idem* 'Institutional Response to Economic Growth: Capital Markets in Britain to 1914', in Leslie Hannah (ed.), *Management Strategy and Business Development* (1976), pp. 151–83; *idem*, 'Economic Growth and Structural Change in the United Kingdom 1870–1914', *J. Econ. Hist.*, 42/1, 1982, pp. 105–14, and McCloskey in discussion, pp. 117–18.

[41] For recent summaries, see Morgan, *Studies*, p. 328; Saul, *op. cit.*, chapters 8 and 9; Matthew Simon, 'The Pattern of New British Portfolio Foreign Investment 1865–1914', in A. R. Hall (ed.), *The Export of Capital from Britain 1870–1914* (1968).

Canada, Australia–New Zealand, Africa, and India–Ceylon, holding just under £400 million each. The United States and the rest of America came next, with over £600 million each, and other areas shared the remainder. By 1913, 47% of British overseas investment was in the Empire. The importance of the Empire stands out, particularly, since, with South America,[42] it formed the area of the fastest increase of investments.

Modern Imperialism has many roots. It was fed by nationalism and jingoism, perhaps the most potent beliefs in the advanced countries of the West before 1914; it owed much to the inspiration of soldiers, poets, missionaries and explorers; and often colonies were sought for their strategic value. But the main root of Imperialism was economic. As far as there were economic roots, these did not lie so much in the search for trade: the proportion of British overseas commerce that went to the colonies had been stationary or declining in the half-century to 1900, despite the growth in their wealth and number. The chief economic significance of the New Colonial Empire is to be found, first, in the promise of relatively protected investment opportunities,[43] and second, in the promised relief for social and economic pressures at home.[44]

Thus much of the overt political drive for Empire was associated with a growing, if still sporadic, protectionism in the name of 'fair trade', which aimed at creating jobs at home by a tariff and mutual preferences within it between Britain and her colonies. The powerful advocacy of Joseph Chamberlain converted the Conservative Party to this policy, but it failed to persuade the nation. Nor had Chamberlain's forward policy at the Colonial Office much effect on colonial trade or colonial development. The only effective protectionist measure was the prohibitive export duty on Malayan tin ore in 1903, which kept the smelting capacity within the Empire.[45]

3 Pre-War Incomes and the Standard of Living

In the second half of the nineteenth century it became one of the unspoken tenets of all classes that total national output per head would rise in the long run and that those performing some useful economic function would normally share in the increased wealth. Long-term upward movements do not, however, exclude movements in the opposite direction for substantial periods of time, and in the first 14 years of this century, while the total national product increased as before, the real wages of labour remained stationary or declined.

[42] J. Fred Rippy, *British Investments in Latin America, 1822–1949* (Minneapolis, 1959), chapter 4.
[43] J. A. Hobson, *Imperialism* (1st ed., 1902; 3rd ed., 1938); also V. I. Lenin, *Imperialism, the Highest Stage of Capitalism* (1916, repr. in *Selected Works*, vol. 5, 1936); Clive Day, *A History of Commerce* (New York, 1907), chapters 37, 38, 53; W. Ashworth, *A Short History of the International Economy, 1850–1950* (1952), chapter 6; D. K. Fieldhouse, *Economics and Empire 1830–1914* (1973).
[44] P. J. Cain and A. G. Hopkins, 'The Political Economy of British Expansion Overseas, 1750–1914, *Ec. Hist. Rev.*, 33–4, 1980.
[45] S. B. Saul, 'The Economic Significance of "Constructive Imperialism" ', *J. Econ. Hist.*, 17/2, 1957.

According to Hoffmann, the index of industrial production rose from 77·1 to 100·0 between 1900 and 1913, both of these being peak years; Feinstein's more recent figures show a rise from an index of 80·1 to 100, or by 24·8%. 'Unearned' income in the form of interest and dividends from abroad rose even faster. Total national income at constant prices, according to Prest, grew by 20·3% between 1900 and 1913.[46] In view of a population increase from 41·2 million in 1900 to 45·7 million in 1913, or of 11% real national income per head rose by about $8\frac{1}{2}$%,[47] and productivity per worker employed rose by 7% in those years.

This increased national output was not necessarily reflected in increased personal consumption, for the price rises occurred largely in food and textile raw materials, the bases of consumers' expenditure, while the relative prices of capital goods fell. Thus the volume index of total consumers' expenditure stood at 111·4 in 1911 and 111·7 in 1912, 1900 being 100, so that it was only just keeping pace with the growth in population.[48] Food consumption, in fact, was falling behind the population figure. Wage-earners stood to lose most by the relative movement of prices, since about seven-tenths of their incomes were spent on food and clothing.

To make matters worse, wages were falling relatively to other incomes, declining as a proportion of total incomes, from 41·3% in 1900 to a bare 36·2% in 1913.[49] Thus real wages experienced an absolute fall of about 5%.[50] For the whole of the period 1902–12, real wages were well below the levels reached in 1899–1901, and in some years, especially 1909–11, they were less than 90% of the earlier figures.[51] The failure of wages to rise with the country's prosperity, against all expectation, was bound to cause unrest and bitterness in the ranks of labour, without necessarily understanding the reason.

Statistics of this kind should not be credited with too great an accuracy, but the general trend of real wage indices is established beyond doubt. Within these general figures of wage changes, however, three developments stand out: differences in the payments for different jobs, differences as between families of varying sizes, and the incidence of unemployment and cyclical variation of employment.

The difference between the nominal weekly wage rates of skilled and unskilled men was exceptionally wide in this period. The unweighted average of unskilled wages in five industries (coal, cotton, engineering, building and railways) was 60% of the skilled wage in 1886 and $58\frac{1}{2}$% in 1913. It was to rise

---

[46] C. H. Feinstein, *National Income, Expenditure and Output in the United Kingdom, 1855-1965* (Cambridge, 1972), T. 24–5; W. G. Hoffmann, *British Industry 1700-1950* (Oxford, 1955); J. Kuczynski, *A Short History of Labour Conditions in Britain, 1750 to the Present Day* (1946 ed.), p. 121; A. R. Prest, 'National Income of the United Kingdom, 1870-1946', *Econ. J.*, 58/229, 1948.

[47] Prest's figures as corrected by C. H. Feinstein yield an increase of 4% only: 'Income and Investment in the United Kingdom, 1856-1914', *Econ. J.*, 71/282, 1961.

[48] A. R. Prest and A. A. Adams, *Consumer Expenditure in the United Kingdom, 1900-1919* (Cambridge, 1954).

[49] Feinstein's figures are: 41·5% and 37·8% respectively. Cf. also A. L. Bowley, *The Change in the Distribution of the National Income, 1880-1913* (Oxford, 1920).

[50] W. T. Layton and G. Crowther, *An Introduction to the Study of Prices* (3rd ed., 1938).

[51] A contemporary calculation produced these index figures for real wages: 1895—163; 1900—179; 1910—161. J. A. Hobson, *Gold, Prices and Wages* (1913), chapter 7.

to 77·7% in 1902, and then settle around the 67% mark in the inter-war years.[52] Artisans' wages were in the region of 40s. to 50s. per week in all but the smallest towns, and labourers' still round the 25s. mark.[53] Women's industrial wages were around one-third to one-half of a man's wage.

The differences in the wage rates between the skilled and the unskilled were widened by the fact that it was often the labourers' jobs that were the most irregular, employers preferring to keep their skilled crews together. Further, a wage of £1 per week or under might provide all the necessities of life for a single man or a couple, but would cause hardship and want for a family with several children. Families were getting smaller: from a normal family of 5–6 children, the average for marriages contracted in 1900–7 had fallen to just over 3, and in 1910–14 to under 3. But there were growing class differences, the lower the social status of the family, the larger being the number of its children. The life of householders who belonged to that half of the labour force which brought home an average of 20s. or less per week, or who had an unfavourable ratio of dependants, was bound to be a life of economic hardship or distress.

Charles Booth found in London that about one-third of the population lived below a standard which kept them physically efficient, later called the 'poverty line'. This discovery, in the richest city of the world, was soon confirmed by the recruiting sergeants and by other inquiries, made in York in 1899 by B. S. Rowntree, and in the four towns of Northampton, Warrington, Stanley and Reading, undertaken in 1912–13 by A. L. Bowley and A. R. Burnett-Hurst.[54] Among the men who in 1911 received less than 25s. if in regular work, there could not have been fewer than 2 million who were married and who would have dependent families, numbering 8 million souls all told. All of them were 'underfed, under-housed and insufficiently clothed. The children among them suffer more than the adults. Their growth is stunted, their mental powers are cramped, their health is undermined.'[55]

Unemployment fluctuated round an average of 4% among trade union members, but in the very worst years it rose up to 11%; in 1908 and 1909, for example, it was over $8\frac{1}{2}$%. In such years, standards of consumption would deteriorate still further and debts would have to be incurred.[56] Mass unemployment, like poverty, was not, of course, a new phenomenon in the early twentieth century, but it was the new interest in social conditions, the rising flood of Socialist propaganda, and, not least, the remarkable growth of cities which brought this long-standing evil to inescapable public notice.

[52] K. G. J. C. Knowles and D. J. Robertson, 'Differences Between the Wages of Skilled and Unskilled Workers, 1880–1950', *Bull. Oxf. Inst. Stat.*, 13/4, 1951, p. 111.

[53] J. F. W. Rowe, *Wages in Practice and Theory* (1928), chapters 1, 2 and 3 and Appx. 1: Board of Trade, *Report on Earnings and Hours of Labour* (1911. Cd. 5814).

[54] E. H. Phelps-Brown, *Growth of British Industrial Relations* (1959), pp. 19–20; Ch. Booth, *Life and Labour in London* (1904 ed.); B. S. Rowntree, *Poverty, a Study of Town Life* (1902); A. L. Bowley and A. R. Burnett-Hurst, *Livelihood and Poverty* (1915); *Report of Inter-Department Committee on Physical Deterioration* (1904. Cd. 2175).

[55] (Mrs) Pember Reeves, *Round About a Pound a Week* (1913), p. 214. Also see Standish Meacham, *A Life Apart: the English Working Class 1890–1914* (Cambridge, Mass., 1977).

[56] A. C. Pigou, *Unemployment* (1913); W. H. Beveridge, *Unemployment, a Problem of Industry* (1909, repr. 1930 as Part I of a new edition).

Unemployment relief was a local responsibility, but the basic Poor Law provision, administered by the elected Guardians of local 'Unions' of parishes, had been found increasingly ineffective in dealing with the bulk of cyclical unemployment. As a result, local authorities, subject to increasing pressure from their working-class voters, had begun to supplement the work of the Guardians by supporting Public Relief Committees and providing public works in slack periods. The Unemployed Workmen Act passed in 1905 by the Conservative administration attempted to regularize such aid by establishing Distress Committees in all the large towns of over 50,000 inhabitants and by encouraging local labour exchanges and the provision of work, but it merely added to the confusion of principles, authorities and funds by which poor relief and unemployment relief were granted or refused. The appointment of the Royal Commission on the Poor Laws and the Relief of Distress at the end of 1905 symbolized the widespread conviction that a new approach to this, as to several other social problems, was now required: 'measures which only 10 years ago would have been dismissed as impracticable were now (1906) debated seriously'.[57]

Most of the causes of this change have been mentioned already: the discovery of widespread poverty by the new social science, the stagnation of real wages, the realization that unemployment was beyond the power of the individual to avert. There was also the cumulative effect of the power of civil servants, health and factory inspectors, and local government officers, who had a professional interest in further reform. Their influence must not be underrated, as 'England was becoming bureaucratic': employment in local and central government rose from 104,000 in 1891 to 226,000 in 1911.[58] Overriding all these was the workmen's suffrage, granted by the Reform Acts of 1867 and 1884, which the working classes had learnt to manipulate after about a generation.

The vote was not used by working men to ensure that their majority in the country was reflected by a majority in Parliament, since the main political divisions were conceived to run on different lines. The Labour Party, which was indeed founded in those years, was established only as a minority pressure group, with no agreed policies of its own other than those relating to the interests of labour. Nevertheless, politicians of all parties began more consciously to address themselves to the new electorate, knowing the balance of forces and the ingrained allegiance of the old. Above all, labour was to be propitiated by welfare provisions. This preoccupation subtly and imperceptibly changed the attitude of Governments: the initial drive may have been the concern to secure votes, but the effect was nonetheless that for the first time in British history 'the poor' were considered to be full citizens, deserving as much consideration as the more fortunate classes. What had been a matter of charity to one's inferiors was becoming a matter of rights to one's equals.[59]

---

[57] E. H. Phelps-Brown, *Growth of British Industrial Relations* (1959), p. 253.

[58] E. Halévy, *A Short History of the English People in the Nineteenth Century*, vol. 6, *The Rule of Democracy*, Book 1 (1952 ed.), p. 262. On a different calculation, excluding 'industrial' employment, such as in dockyards, post office, gas and water works, but including teachers, the central and local authorities employed 632,000 persons in July 1914.

[59] See, in general, Gertrude Williams, *The State and the Standard of Living* (1936), esp. chapters 1 and 4.

In 1897 the Workmen's (Compensation for Accidents) Act as passed, as one of the fruits of Joseph Chamberlain's attempts to win the Conservative Party for social reforms,[60] which were also to include pensions and arbitration in labour disputes. Though limited in scope, the Act introduced a new principle. Hitherto, compensation for accidents at work was still based on the degree of liability by the employer; the novel principle of 1897 was, according to Chamberlain, 'that the right to compensation of any person injured in the ordinary course of his employment is a public right and a national obligation'.[61] Thus what had been a private contractual relation was transformed into one of public concern. In 1899 agriculture was brought in, and by a further Act in 1906 virtually all employments, including now also many very small firms, while compensation for certain industrial diseases was also enacted. The Act of 1906, which added 6 million workers to the $7\frac{1}{4}$ million encompassed by the existing legislation, was one of the earliest of that complex of social welfare Acts passed by the Liberals in the last nine years of peace.

Another one of their early subjects for legislation was the relief of the old. As a rule old age held the terror of destitution for all those who earned their bread by manual work. The existing Poor Law and its institutions were so feared and detested among respectable workmen, that the greatest hardship was suffered before resort was had to them. By 1905, when the Royal Commission on the Poor Laws met, national relief for the destitution of old age had secured general approval.

The Old Age Pensions Act, passed in 1908, provided for non-contributory payments, since under any sound contributory scheme at least 20 years would have had to elapse before the first pension was actually paid. All respectable persons over 70 years of age whose income did not exceed £21 a year were to receive 5s. a week (7s. 6d. for a married couple), and those with incomes of £21 to £31, proportionally smaller pensions. The 'tests' of respectability were inevitable relaxed, and by 1913 three-fifths of the population over 70 was in receipt of pensions.

In contrast with old age pensions, the two main welfare provisions embodied in the two parts of the National Insurance Act of 1911 caused considerable controversy. The disagreement was in part about principles. At one extreme was the view of Sidney and Beatrice Webb, expressed in the Minority Report of the Royal Commission on the Poor Laws and the Relief of Distress (of which Beatrice was a member), favouring the 'break-up of the poor law', i.e. the provision of separate and functionally different institutions for the able-bodied unemployed, the sick, the old, the orphans and the lunatics. It also favoured a 'national minimum of civilized life', open to all, provided by the State, a kind of safety net to offer security in the face of every conceivable calamity. At the other extreme were members of the Charity Organization Society and others who feared that payments as of right would destroy the character and self-reliance of the poor, and therefore opposed them.[62]

---

[60] W. C. Mallalieu, 'Joseph Chamberlain and Workmen's Compensation', *J. Econ. Hist.*, 10/1, 1950.

[61] Quoted in Gertrude Williams, *op. cit.*, p. 145.

[62] Beatrice Webb, *Our Partnership* (1948), pp. 341–2, 383, 418, 482.

Beside the opponents on principle, there were also the vested interests. Trade unions and Friendly Societies wanted to keep their benefit functions; doctors were afraid of losing their poor law practices and the 'industrial' insurance companies threatened to kill by a whispering campaign of their ubiquitous agents any scheme that would harm their interests. The debate, necessarily, was about means as well as about principles, and the two could not be separated. The resulting Act was a compromise.

Both parts of the National Insurance Act had in common tripartite contributions, by employee, employer and the State, but otherwise there were great differences between them. Part II, dealing with unemployment insurance, included in the scheme seven industries only, mainly those considered most liable to cyclical fluctuation, with about $2\frac{1}{4}$ million workers in 1911, or one-sixth of the total industrial labour force. It was administered by the Labour Exchanges, and by those trade unions which adapted their existing out-of-work benefits to it. The benefit was 7s. a week, payable for up to 15 weeks in a year only.[63]

Part I, dealing with health insurance, by contrast, was well-nigh universal, affecting about 13 million workers. It was based on the German model, but was modified by the claims of the existing entrenched institutions, which became 'approved societies'[64] under the Act, the societies were required to pay for certain basic medical services, but they could add various additional benefits for their members if their funds permitted. Both schemes were thus run nominally on insurance principles, with accrued benefits as of right, and both paid out their first benefits in January 1913.[65]

The two Acts of 1908 and 1911 were central to the welfare legislation of those years, but they were flanked by many other measures conceived in the same spirit. Thus the belief that much of the existing unemployment was 'frictional' led to an Act authorizing the establishment of Labour Exchanges in 1909, on the model of the (London) Central Unemployment Body, set up under the Act of 1905. Under the Trade Boards Act of 1909, four Trade Boards were to be set up in the sweated trades of ready-made tailoring, paper-box making, lace making and chain making, and there were powers to make orders establishing Boards for other industries. Each Board consisted of an equal number of employers' and workers' representatives together with some official 'appointed' members, and had powers to lay down minimum time and piece wages, which were then enforceable at law. In 1913, when four more trades were added, altogether half a million workers were covered by this minimum wages legislation.[66] It represented a remarkable break with the

---

[63] W. H. Beveridge, *Power and Influence* (1953); Sir Frank Tillyard and F. N. Ball, *Unemployed Insurance 1911–48* (Leigh-on-Sea, 1949), chapters 1 and 2.

[64] The 'Approved societies' were made up as follows in 1912: industrial life offices, 41·5%, friendly societies without branches, 22·8%, friendly societies with branches, 23·7%, trade unions, 11·5%, and employers' provident funds, 0·5%, of the membership of 12,390,000. Sir William Beveridge, *Social Insurance and Allied Services* (Beveridge Report) (1942. Cmd. 6404), para 53.

[65] H. N. Bunbury (ed.), *Lloyd George's Ambulance Wagon* (1957); R. W. Harris, *National Health Insurance in Great Britain, 1911–1946* (1946), chapters 2–4; M. Bruce, *The Coming of the Welfare State* (1961), pp. 156–89.

[66] *Report of Committee on Trade Board Acts* (1922. Cmd. 1645); Stephen Gwynn and G. M. Tuckwell, *Life of Dilke*, vol. 2 (1917), chapter 52.

past, and was followed quickly by the minimum wage legislation for coal miners in 1912.

Balfour's Education Act of 1902, which made a beginning with the provision of secondary education, was not only an important measure of social reform[67] in itself, but was also used as a basis for public health and other reforms. Thus school medical inspection, made permissive in 1902, became obligatory on local authorities in 1907 and in 1906 school meals for needy children were permitted. At about the same time, in 1908, a Children's Act made various acts of cruelty to children illegal, and in 1914 the Government undertook to subsidize milk depots, local welfare centres and other similar institutions of progressive local authorities.[68] An energetic attack on infantile mortality, one of the most serious problems of the early twentieth century, began effectively with an Act of 1902 providing for the training of midwives and the exclusion of the unqualified.

Medical interests secured two further sets of measures of far-reaching social significance. The first was a provision of the Factory and Workshops Act of 1891 under which the Home Secretary was empowered to enforce safety regulations for occupations he considered dangerous: by 1910, elaborate precautions had been enforced in 22 industries, and certain dangerous occupations prohibited altogether.[69] The other was the Housing and Town Planning Act of 1909, representing for the first time a positive, rather than a restrictive, approach to the building of towns and cities.[70]

Hours of work were regulated by Shop Acts in 1904 and 1911, and in the mines by the Miners' Eight Hours Act of 1908.[71] Lastly, the previously ineffective legislation to provide for small holdings for agricultural workers and others was replaced by the Small Holdings and Allotments Act of 1907, which enabled the Board of Agriculture to induce County Councils to use their compulsory powers to acquire land for small holdings. By 1914, 14,000 small holdings had come into existence under the Act.[72]

Views on the new social legislation did not as a rule differ along party lines: the political battle was fought out over the raising of the necessary finance. From 1908 onward, the Liberals attempted to use the growing tax burden itself as a weapon to redistribute income in favour of the poorer classes, but it was the budget for 1909/10, the first to be presented by Lloyd George, that was the basis of the most bitter party strife, and of a major constitutional crisis, two General Elections and the Parliament Act of 1911.

To pay for the enlarged navy and the welfare legislation, income tax was increased to 1s. 2d. in the pound, the grading was made steeper, and a supertax, to yield £2·3 million in a full year, was put on incomes over £5,000 a year. At the same time, death duties were made heavier, stamp duties were raised,

[67] G. A. N. Lowndes, *The Silent Social Revolution* (1937).

[68] W. M. Frazer, *History of English Public Health, 1834–1939* (1950), Part III and Part IV, sections 1 and 2; J. M. Mackintosh, *Trends of Opinion about the Public Health, 1901–1951* (1953), sections 1 and 2.

[69] H. A. Mess, *Factory Legislation and its Administration, 1891–1924* (1926), chapters 2–9.

[70] W. Ashworth, *The Genesis of Modern British Town Planning* (1954), chapter 7.

[71] B. McCormick and J. E. Williams, 'The Miners and the Eight-Hour Day, 1863–1910', *Ec. Hist. Rev.*, N. S., 12/2, 1959.

[72] Hermann Levy, *Large and Small Holdings* (Cambridge, 1911), chapter 8; W. Hasbach, *History of the English Agricultural Labourer* (1908), chapters 5 and 6.

and an additional £3·5 million was to be raised by increasing tobacco and spirit duties. The most controversial issue, however, in this 'People's Budget' was the imposition of the 'land taxes', designed to tax part of the 'unearned increment' in land values – a stock proposal of Radical reformers for decades, but bitterly opposed by the 'landlords' House of Lords which attempted for the last time to throw out a money bill. It was not until 1911 that normal budgeting was resumed.[73]

These budgetary reforms represented a not insignificant transfer of purchasing power from the rich to the poor. Direct taxation, as a proportion of revenue, was raised steadily from about 50% in the years 1901–1905 to 57·5% in 1912/13, at a time when the working classes were virtually excluded from its incidence. The stormy last years of peace saw not only the foundations laid for the present Welfare State, but also the faint beginnings of the use of the budget, not merely to provide the means of the Government's expenditure, but also as an instrument of social policy.

4 Economic Control and the Effects of War on British Industry

When Britain declared war on Germany and her allies in August 1914, it was almost a century since a major war had been fought by this country and its lessons had long since been forgotten. In spite of some relevant parallels in the Boer War,[74] there was no experience of the economic stresses and the industrial efforts involved in a modern full-scale struggle. Moreover, there was the belief, common at the outbreak of all wars, that it would be short.

In so far as the economic problems were considered, they were thought of as specific, not general. It was recognized, for example, that recruitment for the army would have to be greatly expanded, and, indeed, so effectively was this done that before long the volunteers outran the supplies to clothe and arm them. Further, wars had never in the past been financed out of current revenue, and the Government prepared to borrow heavily. Foreign trade and the foreign exchanges were likely to be affected, and special provision had to be made for them. But these and a few minor actions of a specific nature were thought to exhaust the list of economic actions of the Government, and as for the rest, there would be 'business as usual'.[75]

In practice, until Lloyd George's Ministry of December 1916, which formed a watershed in the conduct of the war, the apparatus of Government control was limited almost entirely to such specific examples of intervention, though they were more extensive than had at first been assumed. Thus the railway companies were placed at once under Government control, though the actual management was left in the existing hands, shareholders receiving fixed returns. The supply of sugar, some two-thirds of which had come from the Central Powers in peace-time, was placed under an (executive) Royal Commission on Sugar Supplies. The Government also began to build up a secret reserve of wheat and assumed control over the food crops of India.

[73] J. F. Rees, *A Short Fiscal and Financial History of England, 1815–1918* (1921), chapter 7.
[74] Clive Trebilcock, 'War and the Failure of Industrial Mobilisation: 1899 and 1914', in J. M. Winter (ed.), *War and Economic Development* (Cambridge, 1975).
[75] Samuel J. Hurwitz, *State Intervention in Great Britain, A Study of Economic Control and Social Response, 1914–1919* (New York, 1949), chapter 2.

The War Office, seeking to procure its necessary supplies, began as early as October 1914 to purchase meat abroad, and before long, turning to other commodities, it found itself forced to assume responsibility for competing civilian supplies also, by the need to prevent speculative price rises. Thus the sandbag shortage, felt in 1915, led it ultimately in August 1916 to undertake the buying and control of the whole jute crop just as it was obliged to buy, as sole agent, the Russian flax crop in March 1916, Indian kips (for army boots) in May 1916, and the home wool clip, for blankets, in November 1916. Some strategic stocks were wholly requisitioned, the beginning being made with toluol in November 1914. Beside the need to control financial markets and labour supplies, which will be treated separately below, the control over shipping appeared in the early stages of the war as a specific problem, namely the requisitioning of a certain number of ships for use by the Admiralty.

In general, in order to obtain the necessary supplies of war materials in the early months of the war, 'it was thought preferable to rely on private enterprise and the laws of supply and demand'; 'a prosperous state of trade, regular employment at good wages and high profits for the Revenue to tax and the Treasury to borrow, were regarded with good reason as essential conditions for the successful prosecution of the war'.[76]

This attitude failed to reckon with the sheer magnitude of the military demand in an all-out war against a European power under modern conditions, and with the distortions that this would impart to the civilian part of the economy. What appeared at first as a specific need or shortage often quickly became a sympton of a much wider alteration in supply and demand relationships. Some relatively minor control, to deal with an immediate issue, often had repercussions which required Government intervention further and further back, until the State found itself directing a major part of the country's industries, and controlling or licensing most of the remainder. Thus a sudden demand for blankets would set up an immediate rise in the price and lead to the hoarding of wool tops, which would affect other sectors of the woollen and worsted industries; and this, in turn, might affect British agriculture or imports from Australia, and so on in unending progression. This lession was learnt slowly, because it was learnt reluctantly. It was driven home, first of all, in the 'munitions' industry, the industry most immediately affected.

'Munitions' included arms and ammunition, transport of all kinds, including aircraft, and optical instruments used by the Forces. Deficiencies in their supply appeared with the very first recruiting drive of the war. The pre-war system of army contracts, which allowed only a limited number of firms to tender, made the shortage even more acute than it need have been, for it disregarded the productive capacity of the firms not on the official lists of suppliers. Nevertheless, all that was done to meet the sudden flow of demand was to give the Service Departments virtually unlimited spending power, and it was hoped that by offering sufficiently high prices, the supplies would be forthcoming.

The normal price mechanism was, however, quite unable to bring about the switch in resources of the required vast magnitude. The need for physical

---

[76] E. M. H. Lloyd, *Experiments in State Control* (Oxford, 1924), pp. 22, 23, 261.

controls was all the more easily accepted in this field, since the main shortage, that of shells, was causing serious losses at the front and was turned into a major political issue as the 'Great Shell Scandal'.[77]

Greater powers given to the Government under the Defence of the Realm Act (DORA) in March 1915 to take over any existing factory or workshop making munitions failed to speed the supply of shells. More comprehensive and far-reaching powers were needed, and were provided in May 1915, with the creation of a new Ministry of Munitions under Lloyd George, increasingly the strong man in the Government.

From the very beginning, the new Minister found that he had to cast his net of control and direction very wide indeed. One of the first necessities was an expansion of the labour force in the industry. This was done, first by blocking the enlistment of skilled engineering and metal workers by a system of exemption 'badges', later converted into a list of 'starred occupations', and next by organizing a large-scale recruiting drive of workers from outside the industry to provide for expansion.

For this, the consent of the trade unions concerned had first to be obtained. In the Treasury Agreement of March 1915, later incorporated in his Munitions of War Bill, which became law early in July, the unions were to permit 'dilution', i.e. the substitution of skilled labour by unskilled or semi-skilled men and women; they agreed to abolish other cherished trade union practices which had the effect of restricting output and to renounce the right of the individual worker to leave his employment without the permission of his firm; and lastly, they were prepared to forgo the right to strike, and accept arbitration instead, for the duration of the war. In return, the trade unions obtained a guarantee that their practices would be restored at the end of the war, that the concessions would apply to munitions firms only, and that profits in these 'controlled' firms would be limited to the pre-war level plus an excess of one-fifth. By September 1915, 715 of the main engineering establishments were thus 'controlled'.

This Munitions Act was to lead to much labour unrest later in the war; its immediate result, however, was a considerable extension of the Government's powers of economic control. It formed the beginning of a system of Government-directed production of the weapons of war, which quickly included Government-owned shell factories, the purchase and control of the supply and distribution of certain metals and chemicals, and a whole network of regulations stretching back to the raw material supply.[78]

From a beginning of 20 clerks in the Army Contracts Department in August 1914, the Ministry of Munitions had grown to employ a staff of 65,000 by November 1918; it controlled the employment of 2 million workers directly, and 3·4 million all told; it managed 250 Government factories, quarries and mines and supervised operations in 20,000 'controlled' establishments; and between June 1915 and March 1919 it disbursed £2,000 million.

[77] D. Lloyd George, *War Memoirs*, vol. 1 (1933); *History of the Ministry of Munitions*, vol. 1 (1922).

[78] J. Hurstfield, 'The Control of British Raw Material Supplies, 1919–1939', *Ec. Hist. Rev.*, 14/1–2, 1944, p. 2.

Munitions formed only one particular case of growing strains and stresses in the economy. By the end of 1916 it had become abundantly clear that the free price mechanism had failed to serve the country at war. The symptons were many. The Government could not get the deliveries it ordered, while resources were diverted to private luxury consumption or lay unused.[79] Price rises led to profiteering, but did not bring forth increased supplies. Distribution of commodities as well as of incomes was erratic and unjust, and caused unrest among workers. It began to be dimly understood that the diversion of millions of men and of commensurate resources to the unproductive activities of war had created real shortages for which unco-ordinated measures of price control, or allocation, or rationing, or profit limitation alone would not work. What was required was a comprehensive system of control, using all available means together.[80]

The apparatus of control, as perfected in 1917 and 1918, used many different methods. There was direct control of productive capacity, either by taking over the management of firms, as in the case of the railways, the National Shell Factories, the collieries, the flour mills and the Irish distilleries, or control by requisitioning of output or by licensing; there was State purchase of raw materials, especially abroad; there were restrictions of dealings, especially of imports and exports, by licensing and other means, and similar restrictions of capital expenditure. There was also price fixing, usually on a cost-plus basis, after a thorough check of accounts; control of distribution, both of consumer goods and of raw materials; and control of labour, including military conscription, first undertaken with selected groups in March 1916. By the end of the war, the Government had direct charge of shipping, railway and canal transport; it purchased about 90% of all the imports and marketed over 80% of the food consumed at home, besides controlling most of the prices. Direct or indirect control over industry and agriculture was virtually all-pervasive. Reasons of space forbid a detailed description of its development after December 1916, but it will be illustrated by two examples: shipping and food consumption.

At the outbreak of hostilities, Britain possessed about 42% of the world's ocean-going steamer tonnage, much of which was unemployed. There therefore, appeared to be little cause to fear a shortage of shipping.

Some 4 million tons were at once requisitioned out of the total sea-going tonnage of 19 million gross tons in 1914, and by 1916 the requisitioned vessels, for British and Allied Governments, rose to 37% of the total. By then, some pressures had made themselves felt. Some 4 million tons were immobilized in enemy ports and elsewhere. Certain ports were closed to mercantile vessels, and ships were re-routed for reasons of safety, thus making journeys longer, while the remaining ports became congested and turn-round was slowed down. Ships as well as docks and railways lost men by enlistment, and crews were further depleted by the departure of foreign sailors. Enemey submarines, at first of minor significance, increased their effectiveness, and by August 1916 had sunk a total of 1·7 million gross tons under the British

[79] E. Crammond, 'The Cost of the War', *J. R. Stat. S.*, 78/3, 1915,.p. 399.
[80] The best concise discussion will be found in E. V. Morgan, *Studies in British Financial Policy, 1914–25* (1952), chapter 2.

flag, while British shipyards were obliged to work almost exclusively for the Admiralty, and mercantile launchings, averaging over 1·8 million gross tons in the years 1911–13, had fallen to a third of that figure in 1915 and 1916. Against this, as compensating factors, a large tonnage of enemy shipping was impounded at the outbreak of war, and more was captured; from November 1915 a Port and Transit Executive Committee speeded turn-round, and in 1916 shipping began to be co-ordinated to much greater effect; ships were withdrawn from overseas routes and used on the home trade routes, while export restrictions, from 1915 on, reduced the demand for tonnage still further. Altogether, until about August 1916 these two tendencies roughly cancelled out, and the supply and demand for tonnage were not seriously out of step.

Nevertheless, because of the piecemeal or specific form of Government control in its requisitioning and re-directing of an ever larger share of the tonnage the Government had so depleted the 'free' shipping available that in a market of notoriously inelastic demand, freights rocketed in some cases to four or five times their peace-time level, profits soared, and large capital gains were registered in mergers and purchases. To the outcry caused by this profiteering was added a real major shipping crisis, as with unrestricted U-boat warfare from 1 February 1917, annual sinkings reached 3,730,000 gross tons of British shipping alone. Neutral shipping was driven away from British ports; convoy sailings and other precautions reduced the efficiency of the remaining fleet; and the failure of the North American harvest in 1916 forced Britain to divert ships to the longer Australian run for the home wheat supply.

Under the new Shipping Controller in the spring of 1917 all available liners were put on the North Atlantic track, to collect grain, the whole of the liner tonnage was requisitioned, imports were restricted by licence, and in January 1918 coastal vessels came under much closer direct control. These vigorous measures kept the supply lines to Britain open, even though the tonnage 'deficit' had risen to 3 million tons by February 1918, while a further 20% was tied up in direct military service. The total losses were $7\frac{3}{4}$ million tons (38% of the tonnage under the British flag in 1914), and the tonnage available at the armistice was 18% less than at the declaration of war.[81]

Among the most complex schemes of control relating to foodstuffs was that evolved for meat, since it had to cover both imports and home-grown meat for both military and civilian use. As long as supplies were sufficient to meet effective demand, the only direct Government action was the bulk purchase of imported meat for the use of the Forces; by early 1917, however, the sinkings by submarines, the growing demands by the Allies, and the fact that army rations were much higher than the quantities consumed by many of the men as civilians, caused a shortage which led to immediate price rises, without any evident parallel rises in costs. The first measure taken was a price control on retail butchers, who, it was hoped, would be forced to lower their own bids for meat and thus reduce prices all down the line to the farmer or stockbreeder. This policy worked for a time, but towards the end of 1917, the

[81] C. E. Fayle, *The War and the Shipping Industry* (1927), and *History of the Great War: Seaborne Trade*, 3 vols. (1920, 1923, 1924); Sir Arthur Salter, *Allied Shipping Control* (1921).

Government had to step in by ordering heavy slaughtering and purchasing all meat from the farm from December–January 1917–18 onwards. All the firms engaged in slaughtering and wholesaling were turned into agents of the Government by April 1918 and finally meat was rationed to consumers.[82]

Food control in general was largely seen in terms of its effects on industrial unrest. The conjunction of shortage of supply, unwarranted price increases ('profiteering') and maldistribution was liable to touch on a peculiarly sensitive spot in the morale of the working population, since 50–60% of the typical working-class household budget was still being spent on food and drink, and it was the workers whose consumption was reduced first when shortages pushed up prices. In 1917, the Commission of Enquiry into Industrial Unrest found that its 'eight panels [were] unanimous in regarding the opinion of the working classes, that they have been exploited by the rise of food prices, as the universal and most important cause of unrest'.[83] Positive action over food followed at once. A prominent labour leader, J. R. Clynes, was appointed to the post of Food Controller, and his advisory 'Consumers' Council' was made up almost entirely of representatives of labour organizations. In July 1917, the prices of wheat, sugar and meat were fixed. Within the next six months, a food crisis of major proportions had enlarged the scope of the Ministry beyond all expectation.

Britain was at no time in actual danger of starvation or even malnutrition. Total consumption in terms of calories per adult male even in the worst year of 1917 amounted to 3,320 per day, compared with 3,300 as the minimum laid down by the Allied Scientific Commission, and within these totals, distribution was probably much more equitable in war than in peace. Of some foods there was never a shortage: the supply of flour, of potatoes, of bacon and ham and of margarine and lard increased throughout the war years, and some of these acted as substitutes for meat, butter, milk and sugar, the consumption of which declined. The food crisis of November 1917 to February 1918 was, in fact, largely psychological: fear of shortages set up a tendency to hoard and created the conditions of highly inelastic demand in which a slight shortfall was translated into a substantial price rise.

By November 1917 all the main categories of food were price-controlled, control reaching back in some cases through several earlier stages of production, and the bread subsidy began on 1 September. The first commodity to be rationed was sugar, the supply of which began to decline seriously. Some 2,000 local Food Control Committees were apointed to deal with sugar rationing, and the system adopted was essentially one of 'registration' with certain shops.

By December 1917 shortages appeared in meat, butter, margarine, tea, bacon and cheese, caused partly by losses at sea, but in part by the panic buying itself. Queues collected in all large towns with surprising speed: in London, $1\frac{1}{2}$ million people stood in queues weekly, and in Sheffield and Coventry munitions workers threatened to queue in working hours. Rationing was adopted generally after that, but there was no national uniformity: thus by mid-march there were 31 million persons rationed for butter

[82] E. M. H. Lloyd, *Experiments in State Control* (Oxford, 1924).
[83] E. Cannan, 'Industrial Unrest', *Econ. J.*, 27/108, 1917, p. 456.

and margarine, 16 million for tea and meat, 2 million for cheese and 1·2 million for lard, and there was the 'national' sugar scheme on a parallel basis.

Food rationing proved difficult to abolish after the war: the milk control scheme only *began* in the winter of 1918–19. However, control was exercised increasingly in the interests of and under pressure from the producers rather than the consumers, except in so far as it was used to reduce working-class unrest by keeping prices down. The attempt to placate both producers and consumers could be met only by subsidies, and these were paid in growing amounts. With the collapse of world prices in the second half of 1920 food control and subsidies were no longer necessary and the Ministry of Food itself was wound up in March 1921.[84] There were few other war-time controls which survived long into the early disturbed post-war years.' "Back to 1914" became a common cry',[85] and by the middle of 1922 virtually the whole machinery of Government control was dismantled.

As far as British industry in general was concerned, its total output had hardly declined at all in the years of war, in spite of the mobilization of 5,700,000 men in the fighting services, of shortages of materials and of losses at sea. According to Hoffmann, the index of industrial production (excluding building) declined from 100 in 1913 to the lowest point of 80·8 in 1918, but 1913 had been an exceptional year and the decline was hardly steeper than that in any ordinary trade cycle; according to Ridley's more recent statistics, industrial production fell only from 57·3 in 1913 to 53·7 in 1918.[86] These results were achieved largely by longer hours of labour and more intensive work, by better organization, better equipment and better management. Pressure of war needs, urgent appeals and direct aid by Government departments had created a new outlook and a more active approach. Even those who had been most critical of Britain's competitive position before 1914 had to admit that the stimulus of war had infused a fresh spirit of enterprise into British industry.[87]

Scientific research, for example, unduly neglected by British industrialists, was stimulated by the Government which set up in July 1915 a department to promote scientific research in industry. In 1916 it became the Department of Scientific and Industrial Research, sponsoring research not only directly in universities and elsewhere, but also encouraging industry to set up its own research associations.[88] The discovery of applied science by British industry

[84] W. H. Beveridge, *British Food Control* (1928).

[85] R. H. Tawney, 'The Abolition of Economic Controls, 1918–21', *Ec. Hist. Rev.*, 13/1–2, 1943, p. 14; S. M. H. Armitage, *The Politics of Decontrol of Industry: Britain and the United States* (1969); A. T. Lauterbach, 'Economic Demobilization in Britain after the First World War', *Political Science Quarterly* 57, 1942; A. C. Pigou, 'Government Control in War and Peace', *Econ. J.*, 28/112, 1918, p. 363; also *Aspects of British Economic History, 1918–1925* (1948 ed.), Part IV.

[86] W. G. Hoffmann, *British Industry, 1700–1950* (Oxford, 1955), Table 54; T. M. Ridley, 'Industrial Production in the UK, 1900–1953', *Economica*, 22/85, 1955.

[87] E.g. the articles in the *Economic Journal*, reprinted in J. W. Lea, *Britain's Decline* (Birmingham, 1922).

[88] R. S. Sayers, 'The Springs of Technical Progress in Britain, 1919–1939', *Econ. J.*, 60/238, 1950, pp. 279–80; R. S. Edwards, *Co-operative Industrial Research* (1950), chapter 4; Sir Harry Melville, *The Department of Scientific and Industrial Research* (1962), chapter 2.

may be said to have dated from those years, though it was still in an embryonic stage.

Some industries had hardly existed at all in this country before the war and had to be established in war-time to maintain supplies formerly drawn from Germany. They included the making of scientific instruments, of ball bearings, of chemical and laboratory glassware, of tungsten and of chemical products including benzol, toluol and ammonia liquor.[89] Others, again, had been in infancy in 1914 and grew to manhood only because of military demands, the most important being the aircraft industry.

In general, improved processes, the saving of labour and material, the use of scrap metal, the standardizing of components, the re-planning of factory layouts were encouraged by war conditions in the best firms, and often imposed by the Government in others. The 'practical application (of control) to munitions and non-munitions industries, aided by the control of materials and the operation of the priority principle, resulted in an enormous increase in output, more efficient industries, and great economies in production'.[90] Again, the need to provide figures for cost-plus contracts, as well as for Excess Profits Duty, introduced up-to-date accounting practices into many firms. Problems of large-scale management were often tackled systematically for the first time. In its turn, the Government was obliged to collect new sets of statistics which could be of assistance to industrial management.[91]

Further, the controls and allocation and rationing schemes 'stimulated organization, advertised rationalization'; and broke 'down trade jealousies and secrecies'.[92] Among major industries, engineering was changed most. Before the war, British engineering firms had tended to undertake too many different jobs, and had failed to get long enough 'runs' of repetition work. They were able to do this by using highly skilled labour, and relatively little specialized machinery: 'It would probably be true to say that no country in the world could show such a high level of workmanship, or so much out-of-date machinery.'[93] Under the stress of the voracious demands for arms, ammunition, motor vehicles and machinery for other war-important industries, the Government was soon forced to impose rationalization.

Much of the war-time capacity in engineering could be scrapped after the war with little hardship on capital or labour. What remained was new methods such as automatic welding, or the use of limit gauges by unskilled labour, as well as new techniques of management. Above all, some sections, particularly the building of motor vehicles and aircraft and of machine tools, faced a promising future in a world eager for improved capital equipment and hoping to progress by mechanization. Apart from the products for industries which themselves suffered contraction, such as textile machinery,

---

[89] E.g. C. M. Whittaker, 'The British Coal-Tar Colour Industry and its Difficulties in Times of War', *J. Royal Soc. of Arts*, 65/8 Dec. 1916; Roy and Kay MacLeod, 'Government and the Optical Industry in Britain, 1814–18', in J. M. Winter (ed.), *War and Economic Development* (Cambridge, 1975); H. and S. Rose, *Science and Society* (1969), chapter 3.

[90] *History of the Ministry of Munitions* (1922), vol. 7, Part 1, p. 87.

[91] E. M. H. Lloyd, *Experiments in State Control* (Oxford, 1924), pp. 389–92.

[92] R. H. Tawney, 'Abolition of Economic Controls, 1918–21', *Ec. Hist. Rev.*, 13/1–2, 1943, p. 8; *Ministry of Munitions*, vol. 7, Part 1, p. 102.

[93] *Ministry of Munitions*, vol. 7, Part 1, p. 94.

railway locomotives or marine engines, in the engineering industry no permanent reduction was necessary from the inflated war-time capacity.

Shipbuilding was less fortunate. The heavy sinkings beginning at the end of 1916 had forced an enlargement of the mercantile building programme, while the provision of new tonnage became one of the chief contributions of the United States to the Allied cause. Japan, Holland and Scandinavia, deprived of British ships, also enlarged their building capacity. When the transport difficulties and dislocations of 1919 simulated a world shipping shortage much greater than actually existed[94] shipyards rapidly converted from building warships to building merchant vessels and world output reached almost $5\frac{1}{2}$ million tons in 1919, 7 million in 1920 and nearly 6 million in 1921 and afterwards collapsed. Thus the main legacy of the war was a greatly inflated building capacity, which had to compete against an even more inflated capacity elsewhere.

The war-time demand for armaments and ships quickly outran the capacity of the existing steelworks, denuded as they were of labour by heavy recruiting. Ultimately the steelmaking capacity of the country was enlarged by 50%, though much of this was completed only in the years 1919–20, when the war demand was past and costs of construction were at their highest. Capacity in the rest of the world was also greatly and permanently enlarged in war-time, particularly in the United States, where it rose by 15 million tons, or 50%, to produce over two-thirds of the world output of steel in 1918. The subsequent decline in world demand and in output was less steep than in shipbuilding, but it was still sufficient to make over-capacity a permanent feature of the inter-war years.[95]

In this period of Government-stimulated growth, some major technical changes were taken in hand. By far the most important was the long-overdue expansion of basic open-hearth capacity to make use of the extensive ore fields of the East Midlands in place of the high-grade ore from overseas, at a time of shortage of shipping tonnage and of foreign currency. This change to open-hearth furnaces also allowed steelmakers to use more scrap and waste, and during the war years the steel scrap ratio was raised from 15% to 50%. The new works were more efficient than much of the existing capacity in other respects also.

War conditions gave the industry 'a taste of collective research'.[96] New alloys for aircraft and tanks were developed; metallurgists were learning to improve the tensile strength of steel, were perfecting manufacturing methods of cupro-nickel, were learning to build up worn mechanical parts by electro-deposit methods, and were introducing extrusion processes for brass rod and copper tubing.[97] However, since the expansion of capacity during the war was carried out under the control of the industry itself, it largely took the form of extensions to existing works: this had the immediate result of reducing the

[94] Fayle, *The War and the Shipping Industry*, chapters 21, 25; p. 23 above.

[95] T. H. Burnham and G. O. Hoskins, *Iron and Steel in Britain, 1870–1930* (1943); M. S. Birkett, 'The Iron and Steel Trades during the War', *J. R. Stat. S.*, 83/3, 1920.

[96] D. L. Burn, *The Economic History of Steelmaking, 1867–1939* (Cambridge, 1940), pp. 350, 369.

[97] *Ministry of Munitions*, vol. 7, Part 1, chapter 6, and vol. 7, Part 2.

burden on the transport system, but it prevented a major shift in favour of the areas with the lowest costs.

Beside the munitions industry and the metallurgical and chemical industries associated with it, the sectors of the economy most affected by the war were agriculture, coal mining and rail transport. At the outbreak of war, Britain imported from abroad four-fifths of the cereals consumed, two-fifths of the meat, three-quarters of the fruit, besides all the sugar and colonial products and substantial proportions of other foodstuffs. Yet no special attention was paid to the food supply of the country in the first two years of the war. By the time that shipping losses and a poor harvest in North America drew attention to the need to increase home food supply towards the end of 1916, the farmers had been denuded of labour and of horses, and fertilizer and feeding stuffs, being largely imported, were in short supply. It was possible to increase the proportion of the population living on the produce of British acres by only one method, and that was to plough up pasture land for potatoes and, above all, grain, and thus reverse the slow process which had continued since the 1870s: it was calculated that 100 acres would maintain only 9 persons if used as meat-producing pasture, and 41 if used as milk-producing pasture; but they would maintain 172 persons if planted with oats, 208 if planted with wheat, and 418 with potatoes.[98]

For the harvest year of 1917 about one million acres were added to tillage and for 1918, some 3 million acres more than in 1916 were ploughed up. Compared with the average harvests of 1904–13, the wheat production increased from 1·56 million to 2·58 million tons, oats from 3·04 to 4·46 million, barley from 1·52 to 1·56 and potatoes from 6·59 to 9·22 million tons in 1918.[99] This was achieved at the cost of reducing the grassland by $3\frac{1}{2}$ million acres and decreasing the home output of milk and meat.[100]

To help the British farmer in these efforts, the Food Production Department of the Board of Agriculture distributed and allocated scarce fertilizer and equipment; it supplied 22,000 men, including prisoners of war, 300,000 part-time women workers and a women's land army which at its maximum numbered 16,000, this special labour being responsible for 2·2 million out of the 3 million extra arable acres; and it spread knowledge of improved methods. Above all, it sent out several thousand tractors to open up a new era in British farming. The tractor remained a permanent feature of British agriculture, but the distribution of land between pasture and the different crops reverted quickly to the pre-war proportions and the crops of 1924–8 (excluding the Irish Free State) bore a striking resemblance to the crops grown in 1909–13.[101]

In coal mining, after a decline of 11% of output, and a loss of a quarter of a million men in the first year of war, there was built up a most complex system of control, beginning with price control and export licensing in 1915 and

[98] G. P. Jones and A. G. Pool, *A Hundred Years of Economic Development* (1959 ed.), chapter 16.

[99] T. H. Middleton, *Food Production in War* (Oxford, 1923), pp. 112, 154, 192, 241.

[100] E.g., Sir R. Henry Rew, 'The Progress of British Agriculture', Pres. Address, *J. R. Stat. S.*, 85/1, 1922.

[101] A. W. Flux, 'Our Food Supply Before and After the War', Pres. Address, *J. R. Stat. S.*, 93/4, 1930.

ending, in 1918, with a state of virtual nationalization of the mines. Though the former managers were still in charge of individual pits, the Government had taken over control of the mines of South Wales in December 1916 and all the other mines in February 1917. Under an Act of February 1918, the Coal Controller received 15% of the excess profits of the industry as a fund to pay the guaranteed dividends to high cost companies, and only 5% was to be kept by the owners; the remaining 80% was to be paid in tax. During the period of control, the State determined capital investment, it 'zoned' all coal supplies to save transport, and it allocated scarce resources, in particular pit props, by central direction.

The reason for the close official control of the coal mines was only in part the need to maintain the supply of a basic fuel and raw material; in large measure it sprang from the desire to keep down the price of coal to consumers while permitting miners' wages to rise in line with other wages and the cost of living. Wages were subsidized out of the very high prices secured by that part of the coal output that was exported, and after the armistice, with most of the western European coalfields damaged or out of action, and an insatiable demand for coal the Government benefited by soaring export prices to the extent of £170 million in one financial year. As soon as the boom collapsed – export prices fell from 80s. to 40s. a ton in one month, December 1920 – and industrial relations deteriorated into bitter hostility, the Government withdrew and handed the mines over to the former owners in March 1921. The legacies of the war were, therefore, a capacity larger than normal peace-time exports could warrant, and a bitter hostility between employers and workers on principles as well as on day-to-day wage rates and working conditions.[102]

The British railway companies were taken over by the Government on the outbreak of war, and administered as a single unit by a Railway Executive Committee, consisting of the General Managers of 10 of the main lines. Returns to shareholders were guaranteed at the very generous level of 1913 out of a pool, shared among the 130 companies taken over. Detailed administration, as in the case of the coal mines, was left in the hands of the former managers, but the ending of competition permitted many economies to be introduced, such as the closing of duplicated services over rival lines and the pooling of rolling stock.

Rates and fares, like coal prices, were held down in order to stabilize the cost of living, but a bitter rail strike forced the Government to allow wages and rates to rise at the end of 1919. A Select Committee of 1918 reported in favour of ultimate unification with nationalization as one of the possible forms it might take. To avoid nationalization, the Railway Act of 1921 forced all existing lines, apart from some suburban and some light railways, into four companies, to be privately owned and run for profit.[103]

In contrast with the industries enumerated so far, cotton may be taken as

---

[102] R. A. S. Redmayne, *The British Coal Mining Industry During the War* (Oxford, 1923); W. H. B. Court, 'Problems of the British Coal Industry Between the Wars', *Ec. Hist. Rev.*, 15/1–2, 1945; M. W. Kirby, *The British Coalmining Industry 1870–1946* (1977), chapters 2 and 3.

[103] E. A. Pratt, *British Railways and the Great War*, 2 vols. (1921), esp. chapters 8, 9, 11, 47, 48, 49, 74; C. E. R. Sherrington, *The Economics of Rail Transport in Britain*, vol. 1 (1928), chapter 12.

an example of an industry which was not considered of importance to the war, and in which recruitment for the Forces proceeded apace, unhindered by badges or starred lists, though much of the labour force was female and remained. Throughout the war, 'Egyptian' cotton was at no time in short supply, but from 1916 onward supplies of raw cotton from the United States were restricted.

A Cotton Control Board was set up by the Board of Trade in June 1917 with the objective of rationing out the limited supplies of American cotton. Restriction of output was achieved by limiting the proportions of spindles and looms that could be worked, and collecting a levy on those worked in excess. Those at work, mainly the spinners and weavers of 'Egyptian' cotton, could recoup themselves by charging higher prices, while the price of raw cotton was kept down simply by limiting its demand. The workers, most of whom agreed to be stood off a week at a time on a 'rota' system, received unemployment benefit out of the levies so collected.[104]

Until wage disputes broke out in the summer of 1918, the scheme satisfied the employers, the workers and the unions, though it could be held against the industry that it was wantonly hoarding labour desperately needed elsewhere. Its temporary success was largely due to the fact that the reduction was in the supply of the raw material, not in the demand, so that its costs could be borne by the public who were charged higher prices.

Thus the war taught British industry collaboration and organization: trade associations for raw material allocation, common research projects, price control or other purposes were formed in many industries for the first time.[105] The war also taught the country to look at its national equipment in a new light, not as private property alone, but as the capital helping to provide the national income. This was particularly so in industries administered nationally, like shipping, the railways or the coal mines, and it was no accident that it was under the influence of war that compulsory amalgamation of collieries and nationalization of coal royalties, unification of all internal transport, including roads and canals, and a reorganization of the building industry, as well as a national electricity grid were first seriously considered,[106] or that protection of 'key' industries found general favour.

5 Finance and Trade During the War

At the outbreak of war it was assumed that the task of the Chancellor of the Exchequer would simply be the collection of sufficient funds, both by taxation and by borrowing, to allow the Government to bid in the open market, in competition with others, for such commodities and services as it required. By early 1917 it had become clear that there was a dual objective of taxation in war-time: the provision of funds for Government departments, *and* the removal of funds from private hands in which they would have helped to raise prices and divert resources to inessential uses. The fiscal theory of the second

---

[104] H. D. Henderson, *The Cotton Control Board* (Oxford, 1922).

[105] J. M. Rees, *Trusts in British Industry, 1914–21* (1922), p. 27.

[106] R. H. Tawney, 'Abolition', p. 11; Redmayne, *op. cit.*, pp. 81–2; *Ministry of Munitions*, vol. 8, Part 3, chapter 4.

World War was not fully developed in the first – the relation between savings and the contributions to government loans, in particular, was by no means wholly understood – but from early 1917 onwards enlightened opinion had an adequate grasp of the main principles of fiscal policy in war-time.[107] 'In the face of extravagance and inflation', wrote the *Economist*,[108] 'the only cure was surely taxation or compulsory borrowing which alone could have taken out of the hands of thoughtless and ignorant people the power to warp the economic energy of the country from the war work on which it should be concentrated.'

Faced with the need to enlarge revenue at once, the first reaction of the Chancellor of the Exchequer was to increase the burden evenly over all the different groups of taxpayers. Thus in November 1914, the income tax and supertax rates were doubled, at the same time as the rates of duty on beer and tea were raised.[109] In the long run, however, such simple apportionment could not bear the strain of tax levels at several times their peace-time values. In particular, the taxes on consumption, falling mainly on the poor, would merely lead to demands for higher wages. Customs and excise revenue likewise arose from commodities the consumption of which had to be limited for various reasons in the later stages of the war.

Thus the main additional burden of taxation had to fall on the direct taxes. The 'normal' rate of income tax was raised, by steps, from 1*s*. 2*d*. in the pound in 1913–14 to 6*s*. in the two years 1918–19 and 1919–20, while the exemption limit was lowered from £160 to £130 in 1915. Since, at the same time, prices and wages were rising to about double the pre-war level by 1918, and treble by 1920, the total numbers of incomes actually paying the tax rose from 1·13 million in 1913–14 to 3 million in 1917–18 and 3·9 million in 1919–20.[110] Supertax rates were similarly raised.

To these direct taxes was added the Excess Profits Duty, beginning with the second budget of 1915. Like the Munitions Levy, which preceded it, EPD was designed in part to meet the popular complaints of profiteering, and was levied on firms, not on individuals – an innovation of considerable importance in British taxation practice. Its average rate over the period was 63% of the excess profits made, but the actual amount collected has been estimated to have been but 34%; it was subject to much evasion, delay and fraudulent practices. Yet it yielded, until its repeal in 1921, £1,154 million, or one-quarter of the total tax revenue in this period.[111]

By these means, as well as the simple effect of the inflation, the yield from direct taxes was raised from £94 million in 1913–14 to £508 million in 1917–18 and £721 million in 1919–20, or as a proportion of total tax revenue, from 57·5% in 1913–14 to about 80% in the last two years of war, to fall again to 68·2% in 1920–1. Indirect taxes, therefore, increased relatively much less and

---

[107] E.g. Hartley Withers, *Our Money and the State* (1917); A. W. Kirkaldy (ed.), *Industry and Finance* (1917), Preface; cf. also A. C. Pigou, *The Economy and Finance of the War* (1916).

[108] *The Economist*, 5 May 1917.

[109] D. Lloyd George, *War Memoirs*, vol. 1 (1933), pp. 116–19.

[110] Sir Bernard Mallet and C. Oswald George, *British Budgets (Second Series), 1913–14 to 1920–21* (1929), pp. 324–5; T. J. Kiernan, *British War Finance and the Consequences* (1920).

[111] J. R. Hicks, U. K. Hicks and L. Rostas, *The Taxation of War Wealth* (Oxford, 1941); A. W. Kirkaldy (ed.), *British Finance, During and After the War, 1914–21* (1921), chapter 7.

barely kept pace with the rise in prices to the end of the war, showing a real rise only in the boom years of 1919 and 1920. Their sources were mostly traditional: in 1920–1, four-fifths of the indirect taxation came from alcohol and tobacco and one-seventh from the 'breakfast table' duties; new war duties raised less than 7%. They included the entertainments duty, easy to collect and acceptable as taxing a 'luxury', and the so-called 'McKenna Duties' introduced in 1915. These were a tax of $33\frac{1}{3}$% *ad valorem* on such luxuries as motor cars and cycles, watches and clocks and musical instruments, and a specific duty on film.

The strong concentration of the additional taxation on direct taxes tended to increase somewhat the redistributive effect of the tax system, at least in the higher ranges. The percentages of incomes paid in taxes compared as shown in Table 1·1:[112]

Table 1·1:   Percentages of incomes paid in taxes

		1913–14	1918–19
Earned:	£100	6·0%	13·8%
	£500	5·8%	13·1%
	£10,000	8·1%	42·6%
Unearned:	£10,000	15·1%	50·3%

This shift towards greater equality was mainly based on the belief that there was little additional taxable capacity left among the poor, so that all the additions had to come from the pockets of the rich.

By these means, revenue was increased fourfold to 1918–19 and sixfold to 1920–1, the peak year; in real terms, it was more than doubled. Expenditure, however, grew at a vastly greater rate, as shown in Table 1·2.

Table 1·2:   Revenue and expenditure, United Kingdom

Financial year	Revenue £m.	Expenditure £m.	Surplus or deficit	
1913–14	198·2	197·5	+0·7	—
1914–15	226·7	560·5	—	−333·8
1915–16	336·8	1,559·2	—	−1,222·4
1916–17	573·4	2,198·1	—	−1,624·7
1917–18	707·2	2,696·2	—	−1,989·0
1918–19	889·0	2,579·3	—	−1,690·3
1919–20	1,339·6	1,665·8	—	−326·2
1920–21	1,426·0	1,195·4	+230·6	—

It will be noted that revenue did not fully meet expenditure until almost two years after the armistice. Further, it is evident that had taxation been as vigorous in the early years as it became later in the war, borrowing could have

---

[112] Rt Hon Herbert Samuel, 'The Taxation of the Various Classes of the People', Pres. Address, *J. R. Stat. S.*, 82/2, 1919; Mallet and George, *op. cit.*, Table XXI.

been kept down to more manageable proportions, especially before 1917.[113]

It was a mixture of motives which induced successive Chancellors to be gentle with taxpayers in the first three years of the war. At first, the duration, the cost, and the price rises of the war were greatly underestimated, nor would the public have been ready for higher taxation in the early years. Moreover, the Government was not, apparently, averse in principle to raising most of its war expenditure by borrowing, and it appeared in 1916 that the Chancellor was satisfied as long as the sums raised in taxation were sufficient to meet the interest and the sinking fund for repayments on the debts outstanding, besides the normal peace-time expenditure. The total deficit on the war budgets amounted to £7,186 million, and the national debt was increased by about the same sum. This increase completely dwarfed the pre-war national debt of £650 million.

Contemporaries were much preoccupied with the 'burden' of this vast national debt created during the war. By 1917–19, much of the borrowing was made in depreciated pounds and at high rates. The average interest on the war debt was 4·65%, but several loans had been issued at less than par. Only in September 1917 did the Government begin its continuous issue of War Bonds, which had the advantage of withdrawing savings regularly as they were made, in place of the earlier fixed subscription period loans involving extensive temporary bank loans.[114] Had the Government taken firmer measures to discourage other forms of investment, it could have secured far more favourable rates. This large deadweight debt, together with a floating debt which rose from £16 million at the outbreak of war to a maximum of £1,570 million in June 1919, created most serious problems for the Treasury in the post-war years.

More important, perhaps, was the question how far the fiscal policy of successive Chancellors succeeded in diverting the necessary resources to the Government's war effort with the greatest possible efficiency and the least possible disturbance.[115] Deducting loans to Dominions and Allies, and certain capital transactions, Government expenditure on internal current account rose from one-twelfth of the national income to over half in 1918–19: this was much more than could have been financed out of normal savings. With private capital issues still running at an average of £52 million per annum in the years 1915–18, Government borrowings in 1914–17 were at about three times the pre-war level of savings,[116] and the deficit alone amounted to one-third of the national income in 1915–16 and to 40% of the national income in 1917–18. Budget policy was clearly the major factor in the war-time rise of prices.

Owing to the concentrated nature of the British banking system, Government credit creation over and above taxation and genuine savings translated easily into inflation. Borrowings from the Bank of England which were then spent by the Government appeared in the recipients' bank as credit with the

---

[113] J. M. Keynes, *A Treatise on Money* (1930), vol. 2, pp. 170–6; W. Ashworth, *An Economic History of England, 1870–1939* (1960), pp. 270–3.

[114] Frank L. McVey, *The Financial History of Great Britain, 1914–1918* (New York, 1918).

[115] The best account will be found in E. V. Morgan, *Studies*, pp. 99 ff.

[116] Morgan, *op. cit.*, pp. 41–2, 264.

Bank of England. This was then treated as cash reserve by the banker and could be used, to the extent of 80–90%, to make advances to customers, with which Treasury Bills and Government securities were bought, and so on in ever widening circles. Before the war, this would have led to a rise in the discount rate; in war time, it was fed by an unlimited issue of currency notes.[117]

In place of the pre-war bank notes backed by a highly sensitive gold reserve, there were now 'currency notes' in circulation, created by the Treasury early in August 1914, in denominations of £1 and 10s. as Britain come off the Gold Standard. The Treasury issued these notes freely to the public *via* the Bank of England and the joint-stock banks. The Bank was obliged to open a 'Currency Note Redemption Account', which became, in effect, a lender to the Government and a direct means of creating credit.

The direct inflationary effect of these notes was, however, small. The value of the notes in circulation, taking the average of the last quarter of the year, rose from £34 million in 1914 to £299 million in 1918 and to a peak of £354 million in 1920, after which it declined, but about half of this was merely replacing the gold in circulation before the war and now withdrawn or hoarded. Much the largest share of the rise in the quantity of money, £1,130 million out of £1,560 million was accounted for by the rise in commercial bank deposits,[118] and there were increases also in savings banks and Bank of England deposits, and in notes issued by Scottish and Irish banks; the only decline was registered in the quantity of gold in the hands of the public.[119] Most of the gold was absorbed by the Bank of England, the holdings of which rose from about £30 million before the war to £87 million at the end of 1914, £107 million in 1918 and a peak of £155 million in 1920. The share of the financial system in the price rise during the war was thus largely the creation of sufficient liquidity to allow the inflationary budgeting to proceed unchecked.

In addition, there occurred a real cost inflation from the middle of 1915 to the middle of 1917, aided by such outside factors as shortage of materials and labour, losses at sea and consequent rises in freight and insurance costs, and rising costs of imports. From June 1917 until the middle of 1919, price control kept rises in the cost of living again to a minimum.[120]

Altogether the banking system had become highly liquid at the end of the war, with rises in 'investments' (mainly in Government stock), in 'discounts' (largely in the form of Treasury Bills) and in cash and money at call and short notice. It was ready to support a rapid expansion of credit the moment controls were taken off. At the same time, the volume of short-term debt (Treasury Bills) outstanding would make the Government quite incapable of checking that expansion, even if it had the desire to do so.

If the consumer was considered only very belatedly, the financial institutions of this country were protected by a large number of comprehensive

[117] Committee on Currency and Foreign Exchanges after the War, *First Interim Report* (1918), para. 10, reprinted in T. E. Gregory, *Banking Statutes and Reports*, vol. 2.

[118] Cf. also Mallet and George, *op. cit.*, p. 374.

[119] A. W. Kirkaldy (ed.), *Industry and Finance* (Supplementary Volume) (1920), p. 144.

[120] Morgan, *op. cit.*, pp. 291 ff.; S. E. Harris, *Monetary Problems of the British Empire* (New York, 1941), Part II, Book 4.

measures from the very beginning of the war. At the outbreak of war, London was a long-term and probably also a short-term creditor to the rest of the world, besides being its main foreign exchange market. The actual declaration of war by Britain had been preceded, at the end of July 1914, by financial panic in many continental cities. When London houses attempted to call in their loans, the frantic search on the Continent for sterling to meet obligations turned all foreign exchanges (except that of Paris, which was in a short-term creditor position) in favour of London. There was thus no question of a foreign exchange crisis, or a gold drain, in London itself: on the contrary, in the critical days of late July and early August 1914, the world was engaged in attempting to make payments to London.

What strain there was, was internal and had several causes, but perhaps the most important was the fear that foreign debtors would be unable to meet their obligations on the bills of exchange. There were about £350 million outstanding, of which some two-thirds were payable by foreign firms in London, but while the payments by the foreign houses remained uncertain, the accepting houses were committed to find payment for those bills which were falling due at a rate of £3 million per day. The joint-stock banks, in anticipation of demands for accommodation by the acceptance houses, called in their loans, and tried to strengthen their own position with the Bank of England. As a result, between 22 July and 1 August, the Bank of England's reserve fell from £29·3 million to £10 million.[121]

On 1 August, the Bank raised its discount rate to the panic level of 10%, but in the then state of the City, this was not considered sufficient. A Bank Holiday was declared to Thursday, 6 August inclusive, in order to give five clear days for emergency measures. On 1 August, the Government authorized an increase in the fiduciary issue if necessary; in the next few days the decision to issue £1 and 10s. Treasury notes, mentioned earlier, was taken, and Scottish and Irish notes and postal orders were made temporary legal tender, while a moratorium was imposed on bills. The exchange market was assisted by a Government guarantee on losses, and Bank of England loans at 2% on easy terms. Other early measures to steady the money market included a general debt moratorium on 6 August, a scheme to allow joint-stock banks to advance money on new bills with a Government guarantee in November, and a scheme, announced on 31 October, to help those who held shares on margins and might be hit by the expected price falls. Altogether, the Government guaranteed about £500 million of securities, many of them enemy securities.[122]

These elaborate and costly defences of the financial system at a time when the greatest sacrifices were demanded from the rest of the nation, turned out to have been largely unnecessary. There was no sign of a run on banks, no drain of gold abroad; most of the internal drain seems to have been to the coffers of the joint-stock banks.

[121] This account, as much else in this section, is based on Morgan, *op. cit.*

[122] E.g. A. W. Kirkaldy (ed.), *British Finance, 1914–21*, chapters 1 and 2, and *Credit, Industry and the War* (1915), p. 197; R. G. Hawtrey, *A Century of Bank Rate* (1938), p. 125; R. S. Sayers, *Central Banking After Bagehot* (1957), p. 67; D. Lloyd George, *War Memoirs*, vol. 1 (1933), pp. 101 ff.

But careful measures of protection continued, and the financial institutions survived the war with few outward changes. The most important was the virtual completion of the process of amalgamation among the large banks. By 1920, there were only 20 independent banks left in England and Wales, having 7,257 branches between them, but of these, the five largest companies controlled 83% of the deposits. Out of the amalgamations of the war and the years immediately following had emerged the 'Big Five'.

> The economic and financial changes associated with the war indirectly influenced the banking structure and are the ultimate explanation of the rapidity of the amalgamation movement which characterized the war period, particularly the last twelve months, and which in a relatively short space of time altered British banking, it may almost be said, from top to bottom.[123]

Public disquiet about the elimination of competition led to the appointment of a Treasury Committee which reported in 1918.[124] On balance, the Committee held that the dangers of further amalgamation outweighed the possible benefits, and recommended legislation to require Government sanction for any future amalgamation, such sanction to be withheld where it would tend to eliminate local competition, or where it would make a single bank overwhelmingly strong. A Bill to that effect was withdrawn on the undertaking given by the banks to follow the recommendations of the Committee. Thus banking in this country has remained an oligopoly, yet strongly competitive in some respects.

In its external relationships the British economy had entered the war in a strong position; even against the USA the annual claims of interest, dividends and service charges brought in a sum approaching $400 million in dollar exchange. Elsewhere, as country after country closed its Exchange and declared a moratorium, British firms called in their loans and refused to discount new foreign bills, and the world was left searching for sterling to meet its short-term obligations. Only New York had remained open, and the debtors of several continents turned to it to use their dollar securities and holdings as means of payment to London. American houses, obliged to make these remittances to London, could not offset them because of the moratoria, 'so that New York, as the centre of American finance, was called to pay one side of a running account for the whole world'.[125] For a time, the rate on London rose from its normal $4·90 to $6·50.

By early 1915, however, the dollar exchange had not only recovered its pre-war gold parity; it was beginning to push up beyond it. As British productive capacity was switched from exports to war production, and as exports of merchandise, as well as of shipping and financial services, consequently began to fall off, while imports held up to supply the booming war factories, the balance of payments began to turn heavily against Britain. The USA, in particular, became a source of imports of all kinds for which no equivalent goods or services could be exported, directly or *via* another country. Gold was transferred to America by the Bank of England and from Ottawa, and

[123] T. E. Gregory, *The Westminster Bank Through a Century*, vol. 2 (1936), p. 10.
[124] The Report is reprinted in Gregory, *Statutes and Reports*, vol. 2.
[125] F. L. McVey, *The Financial History of Great Britain, 1914-1918* (New York, 1918), p. 62.

some dollar securities were sold, but the exchanges kept falling from $4·86 in January to $4·76$\frac{1}{4}$ in July, $4·55$\frac{1}{2}$ in September and $4·49 in October. It became clear that the British deficits on current account with the USA were of an order of magnitude which was beyond the power of the gold reserve to sustain.

The monetary reserves, which in 1914 amounted to $165 million in central gold reserves and $600 million other monetary gold for all purposes, could be supplemented by dollar securities worth $2,600 million.[126] At first, at the time of the visit of the Anglo-French Commission to the USA to raise a $500 million loan in September-October 1915, it had been intended to use British-held dollar securities as collateral for loans only. By the end of 1915, however, it had become clear that some might have to be sold in order to maintain payments to America and to stabilize the exchange rate. To operate effectively it was necessary to unify the control over the British-held dollar securities, and after the voluntary 'Mobilization of Securities Scheme' of 1915 to transfer privately held American securities to the Treasury, which brought in about half of them, powers were given in January 1917 to conscript the remainder.[127]

The actual sales of dollar securities were minimal, amounting to only £207 million in 1915–19, plus perhaps another £54 million of sterling and other securities:[128] but by a judicious use of loans, gold payments, high interest rates, direct operation on the sensitive exchange markets, and American loans, obtained at a high cost of lost independence[129] the Government successfully held the dollar exchange at between $4·76 and $4·77 from January 1916 to February 1919, while at the same time financing large and growing purchases from the USA and acting as an exceedingly generous lender to her Allies. From the outbreak of war until the end of the financial year 1918/19, Britain had lent some £1,741 million, including £171 million to countries within the Empire, £434$\frac{1}{2}$ million to France, £568 million to Russia and £412$\frac{1}{2}$ million to Italy. As against this, she had, in turn, received loans to the amount of £1,365 million, of which £1,027 million came from the USA, £135 million from Canada and the remainder mostly from neutral countries. British loans, therefore, exceeded British borrowings by some £350 million, and American loans had, in a sense, been transmitted to other Allies, the British Government acting, as London finance houses had often done before, as intermediaries. The position may be made clear by Table 1·3.[130]

Britain will be seen to have fought the war out of her own resources, the sale of foreign securities (Column F) roughly balancing the net loans to the Allies (Columns G + H).

This conclusion emphasizes the comfortable balance of payments position of Britain, in spite of the buoyant demand for imports in the war years at a time of severe cuts in exports. In values, exports (including re-exports)

[126] US Federal Reserve, *Bulletin*.

[127] Kirkaldy, *British Finance, 1914–21*, pp. 183 ff.

[128] Morgan, *Studies*, pp. 327 ff.

[129] Kathleen Burk, 'J. M. Keynes and the Exchange Rate Crisis of July 1917', *Ec. Hist. Rev.*, 32/3, 1979.

[130] Based on Morgan, *op. cit.*, p. 341.

Table 1·3:   Estimated balance of payments of the UK, 1914–19 (£ m.)

Year	Deficit on merchandise account A	Government payments abroad B	Credit on invisible items C	Miscellaneous* D	Balance before Government loans, etc. (A + B + C + D) E	Sale of foreign investments F	Government borrowing abroad G	Government lending abroad H
1914	− 170	− 20	+ 315	− 125	0	0	0	0
1915	− 368	− 50	+ 395	+ 225	+ 202	+ 43	+ 53	− 298
1916	− 345	− 50	+ 520	− 24	+ 101	+ 110	+ 319	− 530
1917	− 467	− 80	+ 575	− 57	− 29	+ 60	+ 532	− 563
1918	− 784	−	+ 580	+ 97	− 107	+ 23	+ 381	− 297
1919	− 663	−	+ 605	+ 109	+ 51	+ 29	+ 57	− 139

* Short-term loans, gold movements, etc.

remained fairly stable, the average for 1914–18 being £547 million, compared with £578 million in 1911–12. Retained imports, however, rose roughly in proportion with prices, from £601 million in 1914 to £1,285 million in 1918.

To some extent, the British position was eased by an improvement in the terms of trade, aided, no doubt, by the bulk purchase of raw materials by the Ministry of Munitions and the War Office. There were gains also in the growth of the 'invisible exports' in Table 1·3 (Column C), referring to shipping, banking, insurance and similar services, which showed a substantial increase in monetary terms in the war period, while they must have shrunk in volume. Finally, the balance of payments was strengthened by reducing overseas long-term investment to a mere trickle, an average of some £20 million annually in 1915–18.

Much of the trade with the Central Powers was diverted to North America, and the adverse trade balance with the USA remained after the war. There was also a sharp increase in the American share of world production, and the USA changed within a short span from a major debtor to a major creditor nation. This expressed one of the most significant permanent economic changes wrought by the war.

6 Labour and the War

By 1914, the working men's main defence organization, the trade union, was rapidly, if erratically, achieving official recognition. In the few employments in which trade unions were not 'recognized', the railways and the Shipping Federation being the outstanding examples, industrial disputes before the war largely took the form of attempts to enforce such recognition. Trade union membership, reaching over 4·1 million in 1913–14, covered perhaps 30% of the eligible working force, but, as always, this average hid a very high percentage of membership in a few sectors, such as the skilled grades in engineering, printing, textiles, transport and the mines, and an almost complete absence of organization elsewhere, as in agriculture and among shop-assistants.

The adverse legal decision of the House of Lords in the Taff Vale Case of

1901, which cost the Railway Servants' union £23,000 in damages and a similar sum in other costs, had appeared to trade unionists to shatter at one blow their power of striking, and thereby their bargaining power, built up over a long period.[131] Most of the leaders of the large unions were, in politics, Liberals and some were Conservatives, but the need to reverse the Taff Vale judgement by legislative action and to strengthen the Labour pressure group in Parliament generally, induced them to flock to the recently formed 'Labour Representation Committee', an organization made up of trade unions and various small Socialist societies with the object of securing the election of 'labour' representatives to Parliament and local government bodies.

In the General Election of 1906, which registered a Liberal landslide, the LRC, soon re-named the 'Labour Party', secured 29 seats, and there were a dozen or more working men returned as Liberals, many of whom adhered to the Labour group later. Labour, finding itself in alliance with the Government Party, could exert some influence on legislation. One result was the Trade Disputes Act of 1906, passed without serious opposition, which freed the trade unions from liability for civil actions in respect of any wrongful act committed by or on behalf of the union.

The immediate pre-war years saw a series of extensive and often violent industrial disputes. Possibly universal education since 1870, which had created the first generation of fully literate wage-earners, had contributed to a feeling of discontent and to industrial tension.[132] There may have been special factors in certain industries to cause unrest, and it was noticeable that the main disputes took place within only a handful of industries. Further, the disregard for established authority, manifesting itself in the years before 1914 among upper-class suffragettes, and Conservative leaders plotting mutiny and insurrection over Irish Home Rule, may also have transmitted itself to industrial disputes. The tendency of the Government to settle major disputes by enforcing unpalatable decisions on employers, on the apparent grounds that large firms could be coerced while numerous workmen could not, was also a source of bitterness among some powerful employers' associations.[133]

Basically, however, there can be little doubt that the virulence of the years between 1908 and 1914 was engendered by the failure of real wages to rise and by the actual decline of some of them, at a time when the wealthy classes were evidently becoming richer. Several of the disputes arose behind the backs of the official trade union leadership, others brought out many non-unionists, and in a few cases there were strikes without any discoverable trade union at all. Strikes of this nature are normally the sympton of a background of dissatisfaction, rather than the result of a disagreement over any specific issue. By 1911–13 some 20 million working days were lost every year in disputes.

The main industries affected were the railways, the docks and coalmining. Although there were major strikes and lock-outs also in other industries, as

---

[131] S. and B. Webb, *The History of Trade Unionism, 1666–1920* (1920 ed.), chapters 9–11; G. D. H. Cole and R. Postgate, *The Common People 1746–1938* (1938), chapters 38, 39; Pauline Gregg, *A Social and Economic History of Britain, 1760–1950* (1950), chapter 19.

[132] This is the argument strongly put forward by Phelps-Brown, *Growth of British Industrial Relations* (1959).

[133] R. V. Sires, 'Labor Unrest in England, 1910–1914', *J. Econ. Hist.*, 15/3, 1955.

for example in the Lancashire cotton industry in 1910 and 1911, among the London builders in 1914, among woollen and worsted workers in 1911, and among the boilermakers in 1908 and 1910, the unions in the railways, transport and mining did, in a sense, act as pacemakers for the others, and in 1914 they combined in a 'Triple Alliance'. Originally intended to ensure that all their contracts were terminated, and all their claims made, at the same time, it was quickly looked upon as an undertaking to call sympathetic strikes by the other two if any one of them was under attack.[134] There was clearly a powerful threat to the economy, and thus in the last resort to the Government, implied in an alliance of the workers in these three basic industries.

This movement received some impetus from a new outlook, called 'Syndicalism'. Its intellectual origins lay in France and America, but its concrete base was the depression of wages, together with the apparent apathy and ineffectiveness of the official Labour Party and trade union leaders and the mounting violence of both sides in conducting industrial disputes. Beside Syndicalism, there were also the closely related programmes of Industrial Unionism, and Guild Socialism. The Syndicalists opposed both the bourgeois State and the State-Socialist parties within it. They believed in 'direct action', the political strike, using the trade unions to capture political power and administer the new society, especially its industries, and they distrusted any class collaboration as a stratagem designed to keep labour in subjection.

Under Tom Mann, the most influential Syndicalist leader, the Transport Workers' Federation had been formed in 1910. The Miners' Federation of 1908 and the railwaymen's union in 1913 were other approaches to industrial unionism. In South Wales, an official committee had issued *The Miners' Next Step* in 1912, in which the new policy was preached, and in 1913, Larkin, the Irish leader, raised large audiences for other 'forward policies'. There was the Triple Alliance and in 1914, there began an unofficial movement even among the building workers, perhaps the most scattered among all the craft unions, to combine in one industrial union.[135]

Syndicalism did not survive in any strength after 1914, while Guild Socialism, always more a movement of intellectuals than of trade union members, experienced a brief efflorescence after the war, and then also sank into insignificance. There was, however, one other relic of the disturbed industrial scene of 1910–14 which was destined to grow into major importance. This was the 'machinery' for settling disputes and for conciliation and

[134] G. A. Phillips, 'The Triple Industrial Alliance in 1914', *Ec. Hist. Rev.*, 24/1, 1971; Henry Pelling, 'The Labour Unrest, 1911–14', in *Popular Politics and Society in Late Victorian Britain* (1968).

[135] For information on the trade union development in this period, see the works quoted above by E. H. Phelps-Brown, S. and B. Webb, Pauline Gregg (chapter 19) and Cole and Postgate. Also Elie Halévy, *A Short History of the English People in the Nineteenth Century* vol. 6, *The Rule of Democracy*, Book 1 (1952 ed.); G. D. H. Cole, *A Short History of the British Working-Class Movement, 1900–1927*, vol. 3 (1927), chapters 4 and 5, and *The World of Labour* (1913); Branko Pribićević, *The Shop Stewards' Movement and Workers' Control, 1910–1922* (Oxford, 1959), chapters 1, 4, 7; B. C. Roberts, *The Trades Union Congress, 1868–1921* (1958), chapter 7; George Dangerfield, *The Strange Death of Liberal England* (1936), Part II, chapter 4; Kenneth D. Brown, *Labour and Unemployment, 1900–1914* (1971); E. H. Hunt, *British Labour History 1815–1914* (1981); John Lovell, *British Trade Unions 1875–1933* (1977), chapter 4.

arbitration, strongly supported by the Labour Department of the Board of Trade and its Chief Industrial Commissioner, Sir George R. (later Lord) Askwith. Until 1906, the machinery of the Conciliation Act had been used only about 20 times per annum; in 1907–9 it was used on over 50 occasions, and in 1911–13 on over 300 occasions a year. At the time it was of particular importance in enabling employers and men to meet round the table on a basis of equality.[136]

The war began with unemployment, mainly caused by uncertainty and the collapse of certain specific markets,[137] but this quickly gave way to a labour shortage which continued to intensify as the war progressed. The voracious demands both of the army and of the munitions industries for manpower soon denuded the rest of industry and created an overriding shortage which dominated the history of labour in the war.

Initially, the cry was for volunteers, but it soon became evident that there were more men in uniform than there were arms available to equip them, and there was a still greater shortfall in the stocks of ammunition to keep them supplied at the front. The Ministry of Munitions was established essentially to rectify this serious error of over-recruitment, and quickly realized that the manpower budget of a country at war had to extend further back than the recruiting sergeant.

Some of the early mistakes were beyond repair. Key personnel of engineering works, coal mines and elsewhere, once they had been accepted into the fighting forces, were virtually impossible to retrieve, though many of them naturally drifted to the repair depots set up overseas, or did other work in which their skills were used. Within twelve months, the workers in all war-important skilled crafts were exempt from recruitment, but complex problems for staffing the home industries remained. Available supplies of manpower had to be distributed between industries which could well afford to contract their employment, others which had to make good any losses of manpower by recruitment, and others still which had actually to increase their labour force, while furnishing some men for the forces.

This policy was not always carried out smoothly, and at the worst time, after the beginning of compulsory military service in 1916, some men found themselves shuttled backwards and forwards between industry and the front. Again, the German spring offensive of 1918 caused a temporary panic in which military commanders disrupted the careful plans of attaching key workers to such vital industries as coal mining, agriculture and even engineering, in order to fill the depleted battalions with the last reserves of able-bodied men.

In general, after the initial pool of unemployment men had been used up in the early weeks of 1915, the only substantial reserve of labour was to be found among the women who could be induced to enter industry for the first time. There was some substitution of female labour for male everywhere, and in the munitions industry there was, in addition, substitution of unskilled labour for skilled, known as 'dilution', because of the impossibility of training skilled men requiring several years' apprenticeship fast enough to fill

---

[136] G. R. Askwith, *Industrial Problems and Disputes* (1920).
[137] G. D.H. Cole, *Labour in War Time* (1915).

the rapidly expanding munitions works. In the end, the extent of the transfer carried through was remarkable. Several occupations in which women had begun to replace men to a slight extent before 1914, were turned permanently into female preserves. These included work in shops and offices, in hotels, theatres and cinemas, and to some extent on public transport. On the other hand, in many factories the male labour was easily re-absorbed in the course of 1919, and much of the female labour which had replaced it left industry again.

One by-product of this shift in employment was a revolutionary advance in the economic position of women, whose new-found economic independence was rewarded with the vote after the war with virtually no opposition. Another important by-product was a greater concern for workers' welfare in industrial work, including the provision of works canteens and enquiries into fatigue,[138] hours and conditions of factory work. By November 1918, about 1,000 women supervisors had been appointed to observe and regulate the conditions of work of women, at a time when some 1,600,000 were employed, directly or indirectly, by the Government.[139]

400,000 temporary women war workers were drawn from domestic service, but most others had taken up paid employment for the first time and total female employment in industry, transport, commerce and the professions increased from 3,280,000 in July 1914 to 4,950,000 in November 1918, or by over $1\frac{1}{2}$ million. This compared with a loss of $2\frac{1}{2}$ million men in the same occupations in this period. Total employment was thus reduced, but in the munitions industry, including the metals and chemical industries and the Government industrial establishments, the number of men employed rose from 1,869,000 to 2,309,000, and of women from 212,000 to 945,000, a total net increase of nearly 1,200,000 workers.[140] It was there that the chief labour problems of the war were bound to occur.

The general scarcity of labour might have been expected to push up wages; instead, workers seemed content to allow the value of their real wages to be whittled away by the creeping inflation of 1915–17. Most money wages were raised slightly in the course of these years, but not nearly as much as prices, until by July 1917 real wages had dropped by one-fifth compared with their immediate pre-war level: Bowley's wage index of those in full-time employment stood then at 135–140, with the cost of living at 160–180 (July 1914 = 100); according to Kuczynski, real wages had dropped from 97 to 74 (1900 = 100), and according to Layton and Crowther, from 174 to 142 (1850 = 100).[141]

There were several causes of this paradoxical behaviour of wage-earners. First, trade unions never fight as hard against a drop in real wages caused by rising prices as against a cut in money wage rates. Secondly, in the early

[138] E.g. *Memorandum* No. 12 (1916. Cd. 8344), and *Industrial Efficiency and Fatigue* (1917. Cd. 8511); also, Henry Carter, *The Control of the Drink Trade* (1918).

[139] D. Lloyd George, *War Memoirs* (1933), vol. 1, pp. 292, 341 ff.; Asa Briggs, *Social Thought and Social Action* (1961), chapter 5.

[140] A. W. Kirkaldy (ed.), *Industry and Finance* (1920), p. 96.

[141] J. Kuczynski, *A Short History of Labour Conditions in Great Britain, 1750 to the Present Day* (1946 ed.), p. 120; A. L. Bowley, *Prices and Wages in the United Kingdom, 1914–1920* (Oxford, 1921), p. 106.

months the war was generally expected to be of short duration, and the loss in real wages was felt to be an appropriate sacrifice on the part of those who stayed behind, to match that of the volunteers. Thirdly, the replacement of men by women (paid at 50–60% of men's rates even when doing a man's job) greatly reduced the pressure on the labour market. Fourthly, the trade unions were hamstrung by the Treasury Agreement of March 1915, later incorporated in the first Munitions of War Act. But above all, the decline was in real wage *rates* only; earnings, with secure full employment, overtime, night work, and bonus or piece payments, roughly kept in step with the rises in the cost of living. According to Feinstein's recent estimates, earnings for 1918 stood at 209 (1914 = 100) while the cost of living, July to July, stood at 210. The total wages bill, including forces' pay, stood at 250.[142]

There were some signs of dissatisfaction from an early date. The miners, for example, refused to accept any curb on their right to strike, and the South Wales miners actually went on strike, defying the Act within a few days of its passing, and emerged victorious. On the Clyde, much influenced by the Socialist Labour Party and the ILP, trouble was brewing in the engineering trades from early 1915 onwards. By and large, however, despite falling wage rates, more intensive work, and many inconveniences, the working classes showed no serious signs of dissatisfaction in the first two and a half years of the war.

It was in the course of 1917 that all the factors which had kept wage claims within narrow limits seemed to break down at once. The impotence of the official trade union leadership was neutralized by the shop stewards on the one hand, and a more complete system of arbitration on the other. New members flocked into the trade unions, whose membership was doubled in the course of the war, from 3,959,000 in 1913 to 8,023,000 in 1919. Feelings of patriotism and self-sacrifice were giving way to disillusionment at the sight of the uninhibited profiteering and luxury spending of the rich, when it contrasted with the food shortages and queues, and occasional complete breakdowns in supplies of tea, sugar, meat, fats or potatoes in the working-class quarters. There was growing dissatisfaction with the capriciously high earnings of unskilled men on piecework by the side of the fixed datal rates of skilled men.

Also, prices were getting out of hand. Taking July 1914 as 100, controlled food prices stood at 202 in August 1917, when they were stabilized for about a year, before being allowed to rise to 233 in November 1918. Uncontrolled foods stood at 213 in July 1917 and 384 in November 1918, textiles at 234 and 307, and soap at 133 and 233.[143] Other grievances noted by the commissions on industrial unrest and the Select Committee on National Expenditure were the inability of workers in some industries to make up earnings by piecework and overtime, the restrictions on liberty, especially the licensing laws affecting the sale of alcohol, the powers of employers over the mobility of

---

[142] J. A. Dowie, '1919–20 is in Need of Attention', *Ec. Hist. Rev.*, 28/3, 1975, pp. 442, 449; C. H. Feinstein, *National Income and Expenditure*, T. 55.

[143] W. H. Beveridge, *British Food Control* (1928), pp. 322–3.

their workers by the withholding of the leaving certificates, and compulsory arbitration.[144]

There set in a serious decline in morale, particularly in the centres of the munitions industry, the Clyde, Sheffield, Barrow and Coventry. The March Revolution in Russia, and signs of revolt among other belligerents, had alerted the British Government. A separate Ministry of Labour was created, and $1\frac{1}{4}$ million additional munitions workers were brought within the scope of the unemployment insurance provisions. Special commissions reported on 'industrial unrest'. Much of the control apparatus, including food rationing and subsidies, excess profits duties, exemption schemes from conscription, and wage arbitration awards as well as the plans of the newly established Ministry of Reconstruction were drawn up very much under the shadow of the threat from the war-weary and rebellious working classes.

The problem was most acute in the munitions industries, which may be taken to epitomize the difficulties of adaptation to the war conditions, and the critical importance of morale. Here the key section was the engineering industry, where 550,000 men were organized in trade unions, about one-third of the work force, and of these 161,000 were in the Amalgamated Society of Engineers (ASE).[145]

The engineering industry had been in the throes of some painful changes and readjustments at the time of the outbreak of war. There was, on the one hand, the new, semi-automatic, specialized machinery which made it possible to subdivide the work and replace skilled men by 'semi-skilled' workers at appropriately lower wages. There was also, in combination with the first change, the growing movement to introduce 'scientific management' as established in the USA, involving time and motion study, reallocation of work and complex premium bonus systems designed to get the maximum of work out of each worker. The ASE as the chief spokesman of the skilled crafts was opposed to both trends and had fought the costly 1897–8 strike over the issue of piecework. The strike had been settled on the employers' terms, but the ASE was gradually trying to win back some of the ground given up then. Superimposed on this potentially explosive situation was a series of wage claims and disputes, based on the rising prices since 1908, and a movement for an 8-hour day.[146]

The Treasury Agreement of March 1915, and the Munitions Act which incorporated it, had obliged the unions to give up precisely the main points of contention of peace-time. It is true that there was a Government promise that all the pre-war conditions would be restored at the end of the war, but few men believed that the march of history could be reversed in this way. At the centre of the agreement stood the division of jobs so as to allow 'dilution'.

Dilution itself proceeded by several stages. In March 1915, the Shells and

[144] *Select Committee of HoC on National Expenditure*, 167 (1917); E. Cannan, 'Industrial Unrest', *Econ. J.*, 27/108, 1917; Cole and Postgate, *The Common People* (1938), chapter 41; M. B. Hammond, *British Labor Conditions and Legislation during the War* (New York, 1919), chapter 9.

[145] Branko Pribićević, *The Shop Stewards' Movement and Workers' Control 1910–1922* (Oxford, 1959), p. 27.

[146] J. B. Jefferys, *The Story of the Engineers, 1800–1945* (1945), chapters 7 and 8.

Fuses Agreement permitted women and young persons to work special single-purpose machines, involving virtually no skill, while the Treasury Agreement, of greater potential significance, permitted the employment of semi-skilled workers on tasks and on machines hitherto solely the preserve of fully-skilled men. By the dilution scheme of October 1915, formerly skilled work could be further subdivided and rearranged. About a year later, in September 1916, followed a general substitution scheme, as the inflow of semi-skilled men ceased and many of them were called up to the forces, and more and more machines were manned by unfit men, cripples and women, who could be up-graded at will. The last stage began in the summer of 1917, when even skilled men began to be called up; there was now no limit to substitution and up-grading. Friction increased when the mixed Dilution Commissions on the Tyne and Clyde were disbanded and the Ministry undertook to apply the policy directly.[147]

These changes occurred while new sets of payments by results and bonus rates had to be negotiated shop by shop, including minimum wages for women, and while extension of premises, or moves to newly established works, brought fresh problems. Before the war, employers had negotiated separately with representatives of the various craft and other unions represented in their shops. Now, the unions had largely abdicated their role, and many leaders were engaged in speeding war work and in enforcing national agreements; at the same time the problems which multiplied in the works were not those of just one craft, but those affecting the workmen as a whole, whatever their divided union allegiance.

These conditions favoured the rise of the shop stewards as the representatives and leaders of the men in the engineering shops, shipyards and arsenals irrespective of which union they belonged to or, indeed, of whether they belonged to a union at all. Before the war the shop stewards' main tasks had been the collection of union dues, the checking of membership cards and the negotiations over the settlement of piece rates, but now they became the obvious authority to settle many immediate questions. The shop stewards forming their factory works committees, with chief shop stewards or conveners at their head, came to be taken, by employers and Government alike, as the accredited spokesmen of the munition workers.[148]

The shop stewards and the works committees developed spontaneously, without any central direction or initial planning, and they did not conform to a single pattern. In large munitions centres representatives from all works formed a district Workers' Council, as in Coventry or Sheffield. Many of the leading shop stewards had a background of Syndicalism, and under the leadership of J. T. Murphy of Sheffield, the workers' councils began to grope for a philosophy and national organization of their own. At the same time it was evident that some of the outrage of the craftsmen who invariably took the lead in this movement arose from the violation of their craft exclusiveness.[149] The power of the shop stewards' movement waned as soon as the war was over; the National Workers' Committee Movement, established

---

[147] G. D. H. Cole, *Trade Unions and Munitions* (Oxford, 1923).

[148] G. D. H. Cole, *Workshop Organization* (Oxford, 1923).

[149] James Hinton, *The First Shop Stewards' Movement* (1973).

with a new constitution in 1921, represented their last flicker of independent life.[150]

Meanwhile, however, the shop stewards' organizations bore the brunt of the war-time disputes. The Clyde Workers' Committee was the first, being formed out of the strike of February 1915. In November of that year it led the 'rent strike', which persuaded the Government to take the momentous decision of keeping rents down to near their pre-war level by the Rent Restriction Act. A renewed strike flared up on the Clyde in March 1916, in the teeth of opposition by the official union leadership, after the arrest of some of the leaders and repeated suppression of the local workers' paper, and several of the leaders were deported from the Clyde without charge or trial. At the same time, the Government began to treat the Clyde with particular care and circumspection, and there were no further major interruptions of work there for the rest of the war.

Elsewhere there was mounting indignation towards the end of 1916 at the growing number of skilled men called up in breach of the Government's specific pledges of exemption. As a result of a strike of munition workers in Sheffield on this issue, organized by the local shop stewards' committee, the 'trade card' scheme of exemption for skilled men was instituted by the Government. The scheme, in effect, handed over completely to the trade unions the task of certifying who were the skilled men who should be exempt from military service. It was badly organized and had, indeed, little to recommend it. But the announcement by the Government in April 1917 that the mounting labour shortage required its scrapping, and a scheme of wholesale volunteer industrial enlistment, sent up a wave of protest. It was the proposal to extend dilution to private work which caused the most bitter opposition, and when a small firm near Rochdale tried to apply dilution to private work without even waiting for the promised Government sanction, there broke out the most widespread engineering strike of the war in May 1917. These strikes were exclusively organized by the shop stewards.

The first reaction of the Government was to arrest the strike leaders, but the men ultimately won their point. The dilution clause was withdrawn, the 'leaving certificate', the most resented aspect of earlier Munitions Acts, was also abolished, and by the new Munitions Act of 1917 national wage advances were to apply to non-federated as well as federated firms. The trade card scheme, however, was replaced by a 'schedule of protected occupations', under which wholesale recruitment of skilled men in April–December 1917 was carried through in spite of bitter opposition on the part of the engineering workers. An attempt in 1918, under DORA 8A, to prevent certain firms from employing men with certain scarce skills by 'labour embargoes' was defeated by a strike in Coventry.

Perhaps the most important result of the labour unrest in 1917–18 was the belated upward revision of wage scales. In the munitions industry, where the Committee on Production, as arbitration tribunal, had powers to make legally binding awards, wage awards were to be national by an agreement in February 1917. In May 1917 the Committee on Production was re-grouped in several panels to get through its work more quickly. It became the Court of

---

[150] Pribićević, *passim*.

Arbitration under the Wages (Temporary Regulation) Act of 1918, and in 1919 it became the Industrial Court under the Industrial Courts Act of that year. The system of changing wages uniformly over the whole country and the whole industry by arbitration continued into 1920.

One of the most striking changes wrought by the war of 1914–18 was the relative rise in the wage of the unskilled, as compared with that of the skilled men. Thus in the engineering and shipbuilding trades, representative wage rates moved as shown in Table 1·4:[151]

Table 1·4: Movement of wage rates in engineering and shipbuilding trades (July 1914 = 100)

	Skilled fitter and turner	Skilled plater	Unskilled labourer
July 1917	134	130	154
July 1918	173	169	213
July 1920	231	223	309

This difference may, to some extent, be ascribed to the simple effect of granting flat-rate increases, which in turn, could be justified on the grounds that during emergencies the real wages of the unskilled men at the margin of subsistence should not be lowered. But an important trend of this kind was bound to have a deeper cause. It represented the underlying reality in most industries of the declining importance of manual skill of the old type, and the growing predominance of semi-skilled or virtually unskilled machine-minders.

The tensions created by this process even before the war were aggravated in the munitions industry in war-time by the fact that skilled engineers were often on time rates, while the dilutees worked on piece rates and bonus work which might give them earnings in excess of those of the skilled men, who often set up or maintained the machines they worked on. Moreover, dilution often meant that the lucrative, repetitive jobs went to the unskilled dilutees, while the skilled men were permanently on the intricate and difficult jobs, yielding lean earnings only. A series of strikes in the munitions industry between October and December 1917 originated from those grievances.

These developments in the engineering and allied industries were mirrored, more or less faithfully, in many others. The practice of industry-wide, in the place of local, collective bargaining, which first emerged in 1914–18,[152] was destined to spread in the inter-war years, while the Trade Board Act of 1918, extending the original Boards in the sweated trades to wherever 'no adequate machinery exists for the effective regulation of wages throughout the trade', further emphasized the trend towards national wage bargaining. Lastly, the war-time shop stewards' movement furnished much of the drive behind the giant amalgamation of the early 1920s, of which the Amalgamated Engineering Union, created out of the ASE and nine other societies, was the earliest.[153]

[151] Bowley, *Prices and Wages*, p. 131.
[152] S. and B. Webb, *History of Trade Unionism* (1920 ed.), chapter 9; B. C. Roberts, *The Trades Union Congress, 1868–1921* (1958), chapter 8.
[153] Jefferys, *op. cit.*, pp. 189 ff.

7 'Reconstruction' and Post-War Planning

As early as December 1914 the Board of Trade considered that there was an 'urgent need' to discuss the problem of unemployment after the war.[154] By the end of 1916 the labour unrest was lending new poignancy to this view, while the sustained sacrifices demanded of all classes of the population during the war were giving birth to the widespread feeling that victory should bring more than a mere return to pre-war conditions. The later phrase of 'homes fit for heroes' expressed a general hope that out of the horrors and deprivations of the war there should emerge a society more worthy of the sacrifices it had demanded in its defence. 'Government emphasis on reconstruction grew out of the sufferings and the low spirit of the citizens during the three bitter years beginning in 1914.'[155]

The Government did not remain unaware of this mood, and it was also conscious of the post-war problems that were likely to arise out of the violently changed trading and financial conditions.[156] It set up a Reconstruction Committee in 1916 which was turned, in July 1917, into the Ministry of Reconstruction under Dr Addison.[157] The Ministry did its work through committees, some of which had been sub-committees of the earlier organization, the two most important being those discussing demobilization and machinery for dealing with labour questions.

Demobilization plans were drawn up with some care, and included transitional unemployment pay, housing, and provisions for both munition workers and soldiers and sailors. In the event, the carefully worked-out scheme broke down after November 1918 as soldiers refused to wait their turn and made their own way home, but their re-absorption into civilian posts caused much less trouble than expected. After a short rise of unemployment in January–February 1919, the able-bodied men found employment very quickly, while within a year, three-quarters of a million women workers left paid employment with hardly a trace, and others returned to domestic service.

Labour questions were discussed by a committee under J. H. Whitley, later Speaker of the House of Commons. Its first report in 1917, the 'Whitley Report', proposed standing joint industrial councils, made up of representatives of employers and workers, on national, district and works level, as a peaceful means of resolving differences on labour questions and others. These proposals, although by no means new,[158] excited much attention in view of the existing labour unrest, but turned out to be of little practical significance; their only really successful application came to be in the Government service, including the Civil Service, the dockyards and the Post Office,

---

[154] W. H. Beveridge, *Power and Influence* (1953), p. 136.

[155] S. J. Hurwitz, *State Intervention in Britain. A Study of Economic Control and Social Response, 1914–1919* (New York, 1949), pp. 286–7; Arthur Marwick, *The Deluge* (Harmondsworth, 1967), pp. 296 ff.

[156] W. H. Dawson (ed.), *After-War Problems* (1917).

[157] Ch. Addison, *Politics From Within, 1911–1918*, 2 vols. (1924), vol. 2, chapters 14, 15, 18.

[158] E.g. A. W. Kirkaldy (ed.), *Labour, Finance and the War* (1916), pp. 42 ff., and *Industry and Finance* (1917), pp. 160 ff.; M. B. Hammond, *British Labor Conditions and Legislation during the War* (New York, 1919), pp. 272–9.

when the Cabinet could at last be persuaded to permit them.

The Ministry of Reconstruction also considered the post-war supply of raw materials for Britain, the Empire and the Allies, as well as industrial capacity and demand, and organized special inquiries into several industries. By March 1918, there were also in existence committees on education, on scientific and industrial research, on Empire settlement and on civil air transport, among others. There was a rash of new departments and authorities: the Ministry of Transport (1919), the Ministry of Health (1919), the Ministry of Pensions (1917), the Forestry Commission (1919), the Medical Research Council (1920) and the Electricity Commissioners (1919), but not all of these derived from a spirit of 'reconstruction'.

In the immediate post-war years, the willingness to carry through significant reforms derived largely from the fear of a revolt from below,[159] just as the failure to hold on to many of the war-time gains, and the indecent haste with which most controls were abolished, owed something to the weakness of Labour in the centres of power that really counted.[160]

The Labour Party had been given a new constitution in 1918[161] which allowed individual membership and also accepted a Socialist programme, embracing in its four main points the 'universal enforcement of a National Minimum', the old demand of the Webbs, 'democratic control of industry', including nationalization, as well as proposals for a capital levy and further redistributive taxation.

Labour (together with the independent, non-Coalition Liberals), it is true, was badly defeated in the General Election immediately following the war, but that 'khaki election' had been won by the Coalition Government largely by appealing to the passions of hatred of Germany, rather than by a reconstruction programme at home: the question of reconstruction was still open in 1919–21. Labour's policy of nationalization had much widespread support because of the war time experience and while the Socialist demands for a widely planned economy[162] were soon pushed aside by the overwhelming desire of businessmen for freedom to profit from the incipient boom, a few Government-controlled industries and services, notably coal mining, shipping and the railways, could not be so easily disposed of. The main battle was fought over coal, especially since the miners themselves were insistent that it be nationalized.

The immediate post-war years, with their frequent strikes, both for political and economic aims, their unsettled markets, the confident demands of Labour and the apparent weakness with which employers and the Government were prepared to give in to them, have sometimes been considered years

[159] E.g. Paul Barton Johnson, *Land Fit for Heroes. The Planning of British Reconstruction 1916–1919* (Chicago, 1968), pp. 301, 374, 403. Also see P. Abrams, 'The Failure of Social Reform, 1918–1920', *Past and Present*, 24, 1963.

[160] S. and B. Webb, *History of Trade Unionism* (1920 ed.), chapter 11.

[161] R. H. Tawney, 'The Abolition of Economic Controls 1918–21', *Ec. Hist. Rev.*, 13/1–2, 1943; P. Abrams, 'The Failure of Social Reform: 1918–1920', *Past and Present*, 24, 1963; Albert T. Lauterbach, 'Economic Demobilization in Great Britain After the First World War', *Political Science Quarterly*, 57, 1942; Arthur Marwick, 'The Impact of the First World War on British Society', *Journal of Contemporary History*, 3 (1968), p. 61.

[162] E.g. Sir Leo Chiozza Money, *The Triumph of Nationalization* (1920).

of potential revolution. The example of Russia was feared to be infectious, and indeed it was on the issue of arming the enemies of the young Soviet State that the Labour Movement most directly defied and defeated the Government. According to this view, it was Lloyd George's skilful delaying tactics, especially by calling the Industrial Conference and by appointing the Sankey Coal Commission, until the appetite for nationalization had evaporated, which preserved the free enterprise system in this country.[163]

This view exaggerates the revolutionary mood of the Labour Party. All that can be said is that the period of 1918–21 was one high point of Socialist endeavour – organization, membership and propaganda being at a higher level than ever before, while the comforts of office and the frittering away of energies in piecemeal reforms had not yet set in.

Though the danger was small, the delaying tactics were undoubtedly effective. It has now been shown that a damaging coal strike was averted in March 1919 only on the promise that there would be some form of nationalization of the coal mines.[164] That promise was broken, but meanwhile the Sankey Commission of 1919 produced a report which kept the parties talking and thus prevented a change in ownership of the coal mines. The National Industrial Conference of employers' and trade union representatives failed to establish a permanent peaceful meeting ground of capital and labour, and, having met its objective of delay, was allowed to expire quietly in 1921. At the same time, the inflationary price rises of 1918–20, which forced the unions to spend most of their energies on raising wages, did as much as any deliberate action to divert interests from grand schemes of nationalization.

Something remained of the high hopes and militant actions of the years 1917–21. The Industrial Courts Act of 1919, one of the results of the Whitley Report, extended the Ministry of Labour's power of conciliation and inquiry, without power of compulsory arbitration.[165] There was progressive legislation in many fields, such as the Housing and Town Planning Act of 1919, and the extension of insurance by the Unemployment Insurance Act of 1920. The number of Trade Boards was multiplied. Less widely noted was the general reduction in working hours in 1919, a result of post-war trade union power as well as of studies in industrial fatigue. In virtually every industry, the working day was reduced from 9 hours[166] to about 8, and $46\frac{1}{2}$–48 hours became the standard working week, at no loss of wages; even in the steel works, when two shifts of 12 hours average had been worked, the change was to three 8-hour shifts.[167] This reduction in hours of work became firmly established, and remained perhaps the most valuable permanent gain from all the high hopes of post-war 'reconstruction'.

[163] Charles Loch Mowat, *Britain Between the Wars, 1918–1940* (1956 ed.), chapter 1, sect. 9; G. D. H. Cole and R. Postgate, *The Common People 1746–1938* (1938), pp. 535 ff.

[164] S. M. H. Armitage, *The Politics of Decontrol of Industry: Britain and the United States* (1969), p. 120.

[165] R. Charles, *The Development of Industrial Relations in Britain 1911–1939* (1973). Rodney Lowe, 'The Failure of Consensus in Britain: the National Industrial Conference, 1919–1921', *Historical Journal*, 21 (1978).

[166] In contemporary terminology, a 9-hour day meant a 54-hour week, usually $9\frac{1}{2}$ hours on weekdays, $6\frac{1}{2}$ on Saturdays.

[167] A. L. Bowley, *Prices and Wages*, Appx. III.

2
British Industry and Transport between the Wars

1 Production and Productivity

The inter-war years bear a dual character in the minds of those who lived through them, and this is reflected in much of the historical writing about them. On the one hand, there were to be found growing wealth, greatly improved amenities, a widening of horizons and a downward spread to new social groups of many benefits of civilization which had been available hitherto to only a small minority. On the other there existed prolonged and at times massive unemployment combined with privation, social stagnation and the personal hopelessness associated with it. 'Poverty in the midst of plenty', and the 'two nations' were concepts that were frequently used to describe these apparently contradictory trends. This chapter and the following two will explore these two themes further, as well as the relationship between them.

Statistics of the Gross Domestic Product (GDP) and of industrial and manufacturing output show at once the ambivalent nature of British economic progress. Peak to peak, there were satisfactory rates of growth that compared well with earlier periods, even if deflated for rising population.[1] Thus GDP grew by an annual 1·9% between the peaks of 1920 and 1929, and 1·8% in 1929–39; manufacturing output rose by 2·8% and 3·3% a year in 1920–29 and 1928–37 respectively. The increase was spread among all major sections, and in most cases represented also a rise in output per employee and per hour (see Table 2·2).[2]

Yet at the same time the losses of output between those peak years, not to mention the sharp drops from 1919 and after 1937, give an indication of the waste incurred by idle capital and idle manpower, quite apart from the immeasurable psychological costs borne by men and women without work. Industrial production was at least 22% below its former peak in 1921 and 11% below in 1931, and the losses were larger still when measured against the rising trend line.

The figures in Table 2·1 show clearly two distinct cycles after the post-war disturbances to 1920: they have high points in 1929 and 1937, and troughs in 1922 and 1931–2. Most statistics support the further conclusion that of these cycles, the second showed a more satisfactory and consistent growth than the first. This contrast between the decades is heightened by the comparison

[1] D. H. Aldcroft, 'Economic Growth in Britain in the Inter-war Years: A Re-assessment', *Ec. Hist. Rev.*, 20/2, 1967.
[2] A. Maddison, 'Output, Employment and Productivity in British Manufacturing in the Last Half-Century', *Bull. Oxf. Inst. Stat.*, 17/4, 1955.

Table 2·1:   GDP and industrial production, 1919–1939* (Index: 1913 = 100)

Year	GDP at constant factor cost	Industrial production	Manufacturing
(1919)	(100·9)	(89·8)	(92·2)
(1920)	(94·8)	(99·8)	(101·5)
1920	91·3	97·9	99·7
1921	83·9	79·7	77·6
1922	88·2	92·2	90·3
1923	91·0	97·6	96·7
1924	94·8	108·4	106·5
1925	99·4	112·7	109·8
1926	95·7	106·6	106·3
1927	103·4	122·8	117·5
1928	104·7	119·5	117·2
1929	107·8	125·5	122·0
1930	107·0	120·1	116·8
1931	101·5	112·3	108·8
1932	102·3	111·9	109·4
1933	105·3	119·3	117·5
1934	112·2	131·3	128·2
1935	116·5	141·2	138·8
1936	121·8	153·9	152·8
1937	126·1	163·1	162·1
1938	127·6	158·7	157·4
1939	128·9	—	—

* C. H. Feinstein, *National Income, Expenditure and Output of the United Kingdom 1855–1965* (Cambridge, 1972), T. 19 and T. 112. Items in brackets include Southern Ireland. Also see K. S. Lomax 'Growth and Productivity in the United Kingdom', *Productivity Measurement Review*, 38, 1964.

Table 2·2:   Output in manufacturing in 1935 (1907 = 100)

	Total manufacturing output	Manufacturing output per employee year	Manufacturing output per employee hour
Iron and steel	147·9	139·6	154
Engineering, shipbuilding, vehicles	271·5	177·6	196
Non-ferrous metals	135·2	121·0	131
Chemicals	222·6	157·7	174
Textiles	109·1	134·6	155
Clothing	125·3	125·3	146
Leather	131·8	120·9	136
Food, drink, tobacco	129·6	96·8	108
Timber	176·0	132·0	147
Paper, printing, publishing	262·6	192·7	208
Clay and building materials	213·3	160·3	180
Miscellaneous	362·0	207·8	228
Total Manufacturing	176·6	151·9	171

with other major countries, particularly the USA, since there the development was reversed, the 1920s being the decade with the sustained growth, while the 1930s not only suffered a more severe depression, but also developed only a weak recovery. In fact, both in manufacturing production and productivity, the USA and Germany performed far worse in the 1930s than the British economy.[3] Any explanation of the causes of the British growth and the British trade cycle will have to bear those differences in mind.

It is possible, though it has not recommended itself to many, to take overall growth, such as is expressed in the figures presented here, as the dominant theme, and see the whole period as essentially one of expansion.[4] By concentrating on the middle years of the period, 1924–1937 which were undisturbed by war and rearmament, and had the advantage for purposes of comparison that the three peak years 1924, 1929 and 1937 had similar rates of unemployment (10·3%, 10·4% and 10·8%), this even rate of growth becomes even more evident.

The similarity is seen in rates of change of input as well as output (see Table 2·3):

Table 2·3: Annual rates of growth:

	1924–9	1929–37
total output	2·2 %	2·3 %
total employment	1·3	1·3
total capital stock	1·6	1·7
population	0·34	0·43

Overall, a considerable part of the growth, around an average annual increase of 0·9% of GDP, was due not to additional inputs of labour and capital, but to rising productivity, sometimes known as the 'residual'.[5]

However, if measured by capacity utilization, 1924, at 94·8%, is not comparable with 1929 and 1937, both of which may be put at 100%,[6] so that what emerges is a much faster growth of capacity in the second cycle than the first. The view that, after a poor performance in the 1920s, the 1930s saw a genuine breakthrough, is indeed widespread and finds support not only in the output statistics but also in the quality of the modern investment and the structuring of British industry towards the growth-oriented sectors in the second phase;[7]

---

[3] L. Rostas, 'Industrial Production, Productivity and Distribution in Britain, Germany and the United States', *Econ. J.*, 53, 1943, p. 49.

[4] Aldcroft, *loc. cit.*, and *idem*, 'Economic Progress in Britain in the 1920s', *Scot. J. Pol. Econ.*, 13, 1960, and *The Inter-War Economy, Britain 1919–1939* (1970).

[5] J. A. Dowie, 'Growth in the Inter-War Period: Some More Arithmetic', *Ec. Hist. Rev.*, 2181, 1968, p. 100; Aldcroft, 'Economic Growth', p. 317; E. H. Phelps-Brown and B. Weber, 'Accumulation, Productivity and Distribution in the British Economy, 1870–1938', *Econ. J.*, 63/256, 1953; R. C. O. Matthews, 'Some Aspects of Post-War Growth in the British Economy in Relation to the Historical Experience', *Transactions of the Manchester Statistical Society*, 1964–5, pp. 14, 20.

[6] Neil K. Buxton, Introduction to Neil K. Buxton and Derek H. Aldcroft (eds.), *British Industry Between the Wars. Instability and Economic Development 1919–1939* (1979), p. 13.

[7] H. W. Richardson, 'The Basis of Recovery in the 1930's: A Review and a New Interpretation', *Ec. Hist. Rev.*, 15/2, 1962; *idem, Economic Recovery in Britain 1932–9* (1967); N. K. Buxton, 'Economic Progress in the 1920s: A Reappraisal', *Scot. J. Pol. Econ.*, 13, 1960.

at last, it seemed then, Britain was beginning to catch up on the more advanced countries after years of falling behind.

Others observers still have tended to differentiate between the declining old staple and the expanding 'new' industries, and the gradually growing weight of the latter over the former in the economy.[8] However, the distinction between 'new' and 'old' industries and their performance, attractive though it seems at first sight, is not always a clear one: thus engineering contained both 'old' and 'new' sections, and one of the industries which are most frequently held responsible for the recovery of the 1930s, the building industry, is one of the oldest. Moreover, several of the 'new' industries failed to show any growth in productivity, their expansion being due largely to a growth in inputs only, and many of them were small. It is therefore difficult to place the whole weight of the expansion on them.[9] One is on safer ground with the assertion (though it has little explanatory value) that there were some industries which grew faster than the rest, while others stagnated and even declined, and that it was the former which carried the expansionary drive of the British economy. The so-called 'Verdoorn's Law', according to which the productivity of growing industries grows more satisfactorily that that of stagnating industries, also fits the British inter-war experience fairly well.[10]

Despite these ambiguities in the concept as well as the role of the 'new' and 'old staple' industries, there is some value in the distinction. Thus the new industries showed a much higher rate of investment in the 1920s, though the distinction largely disappeared in the depression of the 1930s. Again, in terms of net output, the new industries showed persistently better results in both decades (see Table 2·4).[11]

Table 2·4: Rates of change of gross domestic fixed capital formation (% per annum)

	'New' industries	Old staple industries
1924–29	+ 11·4	− 2·2
1929–32	− 6·4	− 5·7
1932–37	+ 20·9	− 20·4

Contribution to the value of total net output (in % of net output of all Census of Production trades)

	'New' industries	Old staple industries
1924	14·1	37·0
1930	15·9	29·6
1935	21·0	27·8

[8] H. W. Richardson, 'Over-Commitment in Britain Before 1930' *Oxf. Econ. P.* 17, 1965; *idem*, 'The New Industries Between the Wars', *ibid.* 13, 1961; B. W. E. Alford, *Depression or Recovery? British Economic Growth 1918–1939* (1972). But see N. K. Buxton, 'The Role of the New Industries in Britain During the 1930s: A Reinterpretation', *Bus. Hist. Rev.* 49 (1975).

[9] Buxton and Aldcroft, pp. 17–18; B. W. E. Alford, 'New Industries for Old? British Industries Between the Wars', in Roderick Floud and Donald McCloskey (eds.), *The Economic History of Britain Since 1700*, vol. 2 (Cambridge, 1981), pp. 316–7.

[10] J. A. Dowie, *op. cit.*, p. 105.

[11] Neil K. Buxton, 'Role of the New Industries', p. 221; Aldcroft, 'Economic Growth', p. 320.

Indices of the output of the major new industries compared as shown in Table 2·5.

Table 2·5: Indices of the output of major new industries

	1924	1930	1935
Electrical goods	55	67	100
Electricity supply	45	71	100
Automobiles and cycles	42	61	100
Aircraft	23	65	100
Silk and rayon	20	47	100
Hosiery	70	69	100
Chemical and allied goods	67	69	100
Share of above, plus scientific instruments[12]	12·5%	16·3%	19·0%

The changing weight of different industries was an inevitable concomitant of economic progress:

> The shift of emphasis from one area within the productive system to another in addition to knowledge, new technology, and innovation means changes in the identity of the new and rapidly growing industries. By the same token there is a tendency towards retardation in the rate of growth of older industries, as the economic effects of technical progress and innovation within them slacken and as they feel increasingly the competition of the newer industries for limited resources. To put it differently, a sustained high rate of growth depends upon a continuous emergence of new inventions and innovations, providing the bases for new industries whose high rates of growth compensate for the inevitable slowing down in the rate of invention and innovation, and upon the economic effects of both, which retard the rates of growth of the older industries. A high rate of over-all growth in an economy is thus necessarily accompanied by considerable shifting in relative importance among industries, as the old decline and the new increase in relative weight in the nation's output.[13]

If the replacement of one set of industries by another is a normal aspect of economic progress, why, in this period, was it associated with persistent mass unemployment? Why did the new industries not absorb more rapidly the resources, especially the labour, released by the declining staple trades? In part, the explanation lies in an overall failure of demand beyond the structural misallocation at the beginning of the period; in particular, the new industries were unable to capture the export markets lost by the old staples. It was the tragedy of British industry that the shift had to be made too quickly, and had to be carried out in the midst of a world depression, in conditions made more difficult by a change in the terms of trade, a restrictive monetary policy until 1931 and an open home market to the same date, in the midst of rampant protectionism abroad. Secondly many of the new industries were less labour-intensive than the old. Finally, the labour made redundant in the older industries, frequently consisting of men brought up to certain skills or to hard physical labour, could not be integrated in the new industries calling

---

[12] In 1907, it had been 6.5%.

[13] Simon Kuznets, *Six Lectures on Economic Growth* (Illinois, 1959), p. 33.

for different skills and located in the different parts of the country.[14] These points will be discussed further in later sections of this and the next chapter. However, the shifts that did occur were not insignificant (see Table 2·6)[15]:

Table 2·6:   Numbers employed in the United Kingdom (000)

	Average 1920–1	Average 1937–8	Change
Agriculture, forestry, fishing	1,112	762	− 350
Mining and quarrying	1,204	791	− 413
Manufacture	6,668	6,539	− 129
Building and contracting	840	1,159	+ 319
Gas, water, electricity	185	291	+ 106
Transport and communication	1,482	1,513	+ 31
Distribution, insurance, banking	2,120	2,897	+ 777
National, local government	1,381	1,222	− 159
Professional services	721	950	+ 229
Miscellaneous services	2,025	2,755	+ 730
Grand Total	17,738	18,879	+ 1,141
Salaried workers	3,758	4,810	+ 1,052

To this economic recovery, exports contributed but little. Exports of goods and services at constant (1938) prices averaged £730 million in 1920–1, £970 million in 1928–9 and £783 million in 1937–8; exports and re-exports of goods, as a proportion of GDP at market prices, fell from 22·8% to 18·2% and 10·8% respectively. Investments fluctuated widely and in total rose from an average of £305 m. to £450 m. and £588 in those years, at constant (1938) market prices, or from 8·5% to 10·35 % and 11·5% of GNP.[16] Most of the inter-war expansion was, however, associated with a growth in domestic consumer demand. According to one calculation, 46·7% of the increase in GDP between 1932 and 1937 was accounted for by the rise in consumers' expenditure, against 14·1% by public authorities' current expenditure, 20·1% by gross domestic investment and 19·1% by exports.[17] Once again, the paradox of rising welfare in the midst of unemployment and industrial depression turns out to form an important aspect of the period.

One aspect of the economic growth, as we have seen, was the high value of the 'residual', that part of the extra output not due to extra input of labour and capital. It largely represents improved technology, and better industrial organization and distribution. There is indeed no doubt that in the inter-war

[14] Aldcroft, 'Economic Growth', pp. 324–5; W. Ashworth, *An Economic History of England, 1879–1939* (1960), p. 321 also pp. 331–5, 414–16.

[15] Agatha L. Chapman and Rose Knight, *Wages and Salaries in the United Kingdom, 1920–1938* (Cambridge, 1953), p. 18; cf. also Marks Abrams, *The Condition of the British People, 1911–1945* (1945), p. 63; Sir William Beveridge, *Full Employment in a Free Society* (1945 ed.). pp. 316–20; Phyllis Deane and W. A. Cole, *British Economic Growth 1688–1959* (Cambridge, 1962), chapters 4, 5 and 9, sec. 3.

[16] Feinstein, *op. cit.*, T. 11, 15–16, 38–9, 48–9; T. Barna, 'Investment in Industry – Has Britain Lagged?', *The Banker*, April 1957, pp. 226–9; H. W. Richardson, *Economic Recovery*, pp. 103 ff., 124 ff.

[17] Sean Glyn and John Oxborrow, *Interwar Britain: a Social and Economic History* (1976), p. 30.

years it was mainly technological progress which changed the structure of many existing industries and created others by introducing new products and services, materials or processes. While the rate of technical progress is diffi-cult to measure, it seems safe to say that in the inter-war years the consumer was offered more new products, and the industrialist more new machinery and materials, than at any comparable period in history.

There was still a considerable time lag between invention and application. The major new industries which emerged into full maturity in 1919–39[18] were all based on inventions or discoveries made in the generation before 1914, if not earlier, just as the major discoveries of the inter-war years (e.g. television, penicillin, the jet engine and nylon) were turned to practical use only after 1939. Yet it would be true to say that it was in this period that at least some part of British industry became interested for the first time in technological discovery itself. It was significant that in a country which had so long main-tained an industrial superiority by the skill of its artisans, and in which indus-trialists (not to mention dons) were content to rest in ignorance of the natural sciences,[19] this consciousness for the need of scientific training and research arose first because of military needs.

With the aid of the Department of Scientific and Industrial Research, set up in 1916 to provide Government support for scientific research with possible industrial applications, much research work was carried out by independent institutions, such as Universities, and 13 successful grant-aided co-operative research associations for whole industries were established in the period 1918–21, 8 in 1923–38, and 4 in 1941–4. In 1918–23, 24 research associations altogether were licensed by the Board of Trade.[20] The Medical Research Council (1920), the Agricultural Research Council (1931) and several research stations, of which the National Physical Laboratory (1900) was the earliest, also received Government funds.

Apart from Government sponsorship, which declined in importance after the early 1920s, private industry was itself turning increasingly to research and systematic control techniques to improve its methods and products and discover new ones. The efforts were most uneven, and well below those of comparable firms in the USA and Germany[21]: perhaps half the industrial research expenditure was incurred in three industries only, electrical engin-eering, chemicals and aircraft, each with strong military associations.

Yet, compared with the pre-war years, progress had been rapid. Partly with official sanction,[22] a quiet revolution in the relative status of scientific and technical education was beginning,[23] and technical colleges and research laboratories in firms increased steadily and unobstrusively in number and standing.[24] Interest in the technical marvels of the new age, such as radio,

[18] Including electrical engineering, chemicals, rayon, radio, motion pictures, aircraft and motor engineering.

[19] E.g. R. F. Harrod, *The Prof.* (1959), pp. 17–27, 53.

[20] Sir H. Frank Heath and A. L. Hetherington, *Industrial Research and Development in the United Kingdom* (1964), chapter 32 and Appx. II.

[21] Committee on Industry and Trade (Balfour Committee), *Survey of Industries*, vol. 1 (1927), pp. 318–20.

[22] *Natural Science in Education* (1918. Cd. 9011).

[23] IAAM and SMA, *The Teaching of Science in Secondary Schools* (1958 ed.) pp. 8–9.

[24] Balfour Committee, *Report*, vol. 1, pp. 178 ff.

aircraft, photography and film, more powerful telescopes and faster means of land transports, helped to popularize science from the 1920s onwards among wide sections of the population.[25]

Even in the industries most tenaciously clinging to 'practical experience', as distinct from scientific training, in coal, iron and steel, engineering and shipbuilding, it could be said at the end of the 1920s that

> the scientific spirit in these days is a vital factor in manufacturing success. Its importance cannot be exaggerated. It is not too much to say that in the research laboratory lies the source of prosperity in the future to labour and capital alike. Research secures the means of reducing costs and increasing output, but it goes far beyond this . . . and scientific research is now regarded with respect by even the most conservative of our industrial leaders.[26]

In some key industries later to be known as 'science-based', research came to be undertaken on a large scale, involving the collaboration of scientists of various disciplines, a measure of planning and co-ordination, and the much more costly work of 'development'. In the twentieth-century invention, 'the origin of the idea may have been far back, perhaps in the genius of some inventive individual: but it has no significance for investment until it has passed, in some firm or institution, through the difficult and costly stage of development or design'.[27] This, in turn, helped to intensify two existing tendencies: the growing participation of the Government in industrial research, and the concentration of production in the hands of very large firms in all the industries which relied heavily on scientific or technological innovation.

Beside the spectacular brainwaves, it was the gradual adaptation and improvement, often of only humble parts of machines or materials; the linked development of one new process waiting for improvements in others before it can be applied; and the constant pressure on the average firm to reach the level of the best which contributed to industrial growth. Examples were such new techniques as the extension of welding to many aspects of shipbuilding, new alloy metallurgy, precision control[28] and cellulose spray painting.

Last, but by no means least, science and research invaded the very citadel of entrepreneurship itself. The management of men, the layout of plant, the grouping, selecting, training of staff, work study and study of fatigue, besides many others, became aspects of 'scientific management' which were being introduced from across the Atlantic in at least a few large and progressive firms, and developed to fit the native soil.[29]

2 New and Growing Industries

One of the most critically important of the new industries was electrical engineering, together with the supply of electricity. It could be taken as the

[25] C. L. Mowat, *Britain between the Wars* (1956 ed.), pp. 219–22.

[26] Lord Aberconway, *The Basic Industries of Great Britain* (1927), pp. 353–4.

[27] C. F. Carter and B. R. Williams, *Investment in Innovation* (1958), p. 138.

[28] R. S. Sayers, 'The Springs of Technical Progress in Britain, 1919–1939', *Econ. J.*, 60/238, 1950.

[29] L. Urwick and E. F. L. Brech, *The Marketing of Scientific Management* (1957 ed.), esp. vol. 2; E. F. L. Brech (ed.), *The Principles and Practice of Management* (1958 ed.), pp. 56–64.

symbol of the new industrial Britain, freeing other industries from dependence on the coalfields of the north and west and setting in motion a vast migration to the Midlands and the southeast. Backward technically until 1918, and behind other countries in consumption per head in the 1920s, by the late 1930s the industry was close, if not equal, to its foreign rivals, while the British 'grid' constituted a method of distributing electric power which had no equal anywhere in the world.[30]

The early haphazard and scattered development had led to much technical inefficiency in an industry such as electricity generation. In 1925 there was still a bewildering variety of voltages and, in the case of AC, of cycles in use. Although larger stations were much more economical than smaller ones, in 1925 28 stations generated 50% of the power between them, and another 88 generated 39%, but the remaining 11% was shared between 322 suppliers.[31] Each carried its own surplus capacity for meeting the heavy peak demands, and at less than peak demand, the efficient stations ran at less than full capacity, while the inefficient stations were kept going also.

The Electricity (Supply) Act of 1919 which attempted to encourage amalgamations remained a dead letter, but following the Weir Committee Report of the Ministry of Transport in 1925, the Electricity (Supply) Act of 1926 introduced more effective changes. A Central Electricity Board was set up and given the right to monopolize all the wholesaling of electricity. With funds derived from powers to borrow money at fixed interest, it successfully pursued a policy of concentrating all output in a small number of base load stations and new super-stations (144 by 1935), while closing down large numbers of the smaller, inefficient ones. The whole system was connected by means of a ñational 'grid' of high-tension transmission cables which incidentally employed about 100,000 people at the bottom of the slump, and total output rose from 6,600 million units in 1925 to 26,400 million units in 1939.[32]

Improved technical and thermal efficiency, the falling price of coal, and the 'grid', allowing the closing of high-cost stations and a reduction in the proportion of idle capacity, all helped to lower costs, and as electricity became cheaper, it came within reach of new classes of the community. There were 730,000 electricity consumers in 1920, 2,844,000 in 1929 and 8,920,000 in 1938; in the late 1930s, consumers were being added at a rate of 700,000–800,000 a year.[33] With the spread of new electrical consumer durables, cookers, radios, refrigerators, washing machines, vacuum cleaners and electric irons, each of these households increased its consumption of

[30] *Committee on the Position of the Electrical Trades after the War, Report* (1918. Cd. 9072); M. E. Dimock, *British Public Utilities* (1933), p. 197; R. A. S. Hennessy, *The Electrical Revolution* (Newcastle, 1972), pp. 19 ff.

[31] H. H. Ballin, *The Organization of Electricity Supply in Great Britain* (1946), chapter 8.

[32] J. G. Crowther, *Discoveries and Inventions of the 20th Century* (1955 ed.), pp. 95–8; Sir Henry Self and Miss Elizabeth Watson, *Electricity Supply in Great Britain* (1952), chapter 4; Lincoln Gordon, *The Public Corporation in Britain* (1938), chapter 3; Leslie Hannah, *Electricity Before Nationalisation. A Study of the Development of the Electricity Supply Industry in Britain to 1948* (1979), pp. 95 ff.

[33] British Association, *Britain in Recovery* (1938), p. 265; Richard Stone, *Measurement of Consumers' Expenditure in the United Kingdom, 1920–1938* (Cambridge, 1954), p. 418; Alfred Plummer, *New British Industries in the Twentieth Century* (1937), chapter 2/1.

electricity, while the new industries established away from the coalfields, electric street lighting, and the conversion of some railway traction added further important sources of demand. Thus, with falling marginal costs and an elastic demand, the growth in the output of electricity was not reversed even in the slump, and in the 1930s its rate of growth in Britain exceeded that in the rest of the world.

These conditions offered great opportunities for electrical engineering. Employment rose particularly fast in the 1930s, and the number of insured workers grew from 173,600 in 1924 to 367,000 in 1937. Their contribution to the value of gross output rose from 1·9% in 1924 to 3·0% in 1935, and of net output of all manufacturing, from 3·9% to 4·8%. The export record of the industry was good, and although there were large imports of various electrical goods from Germany and of lamps and valves from Holland, the British industry kept control of its home market, aided as it was by protective measures in 1921 and 1926.[34] There were several innovations that originated in Great Britain.[35]

A high degree of specialization allowed innumerable small firms to survive, but, as in other countries, the industry came to be dominated by a few large firms. Further, in an industry so dependent on constant inventions and patents[36] it was perhaps not surprising that restrictive associations of producers were particularly rampant. Most of these, including, for example, the Electric Lamp Manufacturers' Association, which was perhaps the best known,[37] had international links, and so had some of the leading firms, such as EMI (Electrical and Musical Industries), a combine formed in 1931.

Comparable in importance with electricity in the inter-war years was the motor industry. The motor car changed people's habits of living, shopping, travelling and holidaying; it affected the layout of towns and of suburbs; it created the first true conveyor-belt factories and stimulated innumerable ancillary industries, some of them of major importance in their own right, including oil refining, rubber, electrical goods, glass, metallurgy, both ferrous and non-ferrous, and mechanical engineering.

Before the war, motor vehicles had been made singly or at best in batches; 34,000 motor vehicles of all kinds were built in 1913, but among the cars alone there had been 198 different models.[38] During the war, motor engineers benefited greatly by the experience of building military trucks and engines,

---

[34] Balfour Committee, *Survey of Industries*, vol. 4, chapter 3; Plummer, *op. cit.*, chapter 2/II; Lord Aberconway, *The Basic Industries* (1927), pp. 317 ff.; A. E. Kahn, *Great Britain in the World Economy* (1946), pp. 43–120; R. E. Catterall, 'Electrical Engineering', in Buxton and Aldcroft, *British Industry*, p. 241.

[35] Crowther, *op. cit.*, p. 372; S. G. Sturmey, *The Economic Development of Radio* (1948), p. 179.

[36] Thomas Wilson, 'The Electronics Industry', in Duncan Burn, *The Structure of British Industry*, vol. 2 (Cambridge, 1958), pp. 132–49.

[37] Monopolies Commission, *Report on the Supply of Electric Lamps* (1951. 287), esp. chapter 2; cf. also *Report on the Supply of Insulated Electric Wires and Cables* (1952. 209), chapter 4; *Report on the Supply of Electric Valves and Cathode Ray Tubes* (1956. 16), chapters 2–4; *Report on the Supply and Export of Electrical and Allied Machinery and Plant* (1957. 42), chapter 1.

[38] PEP, *Engineering Reports II: Motor Vehicles* (1950), p. 5.

though the output of luxury cars had to be suspended. The war also left the McKenna duty of $33\frac{1}{3}$ *ad valorem* on imported cars.

After 1918 the industry grew quickly out of its pre-war methods. By 1922 Austin had started on the production of his first 'mass car', the Austin 7 and in 1924 had introduced 'continuous flow production', and by 1925 Morris, who had also introduced a production line, made 41% of the total output of British cars in his class.[39] By the end of the 1920s all the large motor firms were reaping the advantage of mass production, mass markets and of new manufacturing techniques. Omitting motor cycles, the annual output of motor vehicles rose from 95,000 in 1923 to a peak of 511,000 in 1937; employment rose more slowly, from 220,000 insured workers in 1924 to 380,000 in 1939 (including aircraft); and the average factory value of private cars made in Great Britain fell from £308 per car in 1912 to £259 in 1924 and £130 in 1935–6.[40] Falling costs and an elastic market thus went together as in the case of electricity, and by the early 1930s were beginning to tap an extremely elastic section of the market. Exports and imports were not of much importance, but the motor-cycle industry, which had exported over 40% of its output in the 1920s, suffered serious contraction when the foreign demand declined in the 1930s.[41]

In this period, the number of makers fell from 96 in 1922 to 20 in 1939. By 1929, 75% of the output (by numbers) was accounted for by three firms, 60% being accounted for by the two largest alone. By 1939 the market was shared more evenly among the 'Big Six'.[42] There was also a geographical concentration in Birmingham, Coventry and the London region. In the production of commercial vehicles, concentration went less far, though most of the large private car producers also made commercial vehicles. Several motor firms survived by catering for narrowly specialized markets in the luxury car and sports car range.

Closely linked with the development of the motor car engine was the development of aircraft production. From 1930 onwards the needs of the RAF provided a backbone of orders as well as research, and in the early 1930s some 30,000 people were employed in aircraft manufacturing. Rearmament, and the erection of 'shadow' factories from 1936 onward, drew several of the larger motor firms into the production of aircraft.[43]

Some new industries were based on advances in the science of chemistry and in chemical engineering. One of the most significant of them was the man-made fibre industry, limited, before 1939, almost entirely to rayon and

---

[39] P. W. S. Andrews and Elizabeth Brunner, *The Life of Lord Nuffield* (Oxford, 1955), p. 112; Roy Church, *Herbert Austin. The British Motor Car Industry to 1941* (1979), pp. 73, 98; R. J. Overy, *William Morris, Lord Nuffield* (1976), pp. 29 ff.; M. Miller and R. A. Church, 'Motor Manufacturing', in Buxton and Aldcroft, p. 180; Kenneth Richardson, *The Motor Industry 1896–1939* (1977), pp. 83–88.

[40] G. C. Allen, *British Industries and their Organization* (1959 ed.), p. 204; Plummer, *op. cit.*, p. 87.

[41] G. Maxcy and A. Silberston, *The Motor Industry* (1959), chapter 1; L. F. Duval, 'The Motor Industry', in *Britain in Recovery*, Part II, chapter 7.

[42] G. Maxcy, 'The Motor Industry', in P. L. Cook (ed.), *Effects of Merger* (1958).

[43] Peter Fearon, 'The British Airframe Industry and the State, 1918–35', *Ec. Hist. Rev.*, 22/2, 1974, and discussion in *ibid.*, 28/4, 1975, pp. 648–662; *idem*, 'Airframe Manufacturing', in Buxton and Aldcroft, *op. cit.*

rayon staple, based on cellulose derived from wood-pulp or cotton linters. In 1913, the output had been something over 6 million lb. of rayon filament. By 1927 Britain produced 53 m. lb. of filament and 2 m. lb. of staple, the figures rising to 115 m. lb. and 58 m. lb. respectively by 1939, representing 7·7% of the world output. The rate of growth of output and investment in this new industry was thus very rapid, but even in 1939 all man-made fibres together only accounted for 8–9% of the fibres used in the world's textile industries.

In the early stages, the thin continuous filament with its smooth, lustrous surface suggested its use as a substitute for silk, and rayon became widely known as 'artificial silk'. In the 1920s, improvements made possible the production of mixed fabrics, and even the substitution for cotton and finally for wool and linen: in 1934 spinning of rayon staple began in a Rochdale mill and weaving in another demonstration plant, and a similar plant was opened in Bradford; high-tenacity types of viscose rayon could be used in the industrial field, e.g. for tyre cords. Nevertheless, the chief successes were scored in replacing silk and in opening wider markets for goods formerly made of silk, helped by the marked decline in its costs and prices. By 1936, the total number employed in the rayon industry was about 100,000.[44]

The industry was from the beginning dominated by a small number of large firms. Before 1914, Courtauld's, an old-established silk-throwing firm which acquired the various British patents and factories in 1904, had not only a virtual monopoly in Britain, but also a large share of the total world output. Several other firms were established in the 1920s, but even in 1939, while the issued capital of Courtauld's was £32 million, and that of British Celanese £13.5 million, that of the other nine firms combined only came to £5.2 million.[45] The hegemony of the two leading firms was assisted by price agreements in the 1930s, by disguised protection since 1925, by international links with the main producers abroad, and by maintaining a high rate of technical improvement.[46]

At the centre of the 'chemical industry' proper stood Imperial Chemical Industries Ltd., formed in 1926 by a merger of four companies. One of these, British Dyestuffs Corporation Ltd, had been set up in 1918 largely with Government financial support and protection by licensing (for synthetic dyestuffs) and by a $33\frac{1}{3}$% duty (for other organic chemicals). The other constituent firms were Brunner-Mond Ltd, a combine that had put up the first large-scale British plant for fixing nitrogen from the air at Billingham, Stockton-on-Tees, in 1923; United Alkali; and Nobel Industries, dominating the explosives industry. The company had an initial capital of £65 million.

[44] R. Robson, *The Man-made Fibres Industry* (1958), pp. 19–29; D. C. Hague, *The Economics of Man-made Fibres* (1957), p. 86; Plummer, *New Industries,* chapter 4/II, 'Rayon'; D. C. Coleman, *Courtaulds. An Economic and Social History*, 3 vols., vol. 2 (Oxford, 1969), pp. 245–50, 319–20.

[45] Hague, *op. cit.*, p. 78. Courtauld's and British Celanese, the main producers of acetate yarn, merged in 1957. G. C. Allen, *British Industries*, p. 288; J. Harrop, 'The Growth of the Rayon Industry in the Inter-War Years', *Yorkshire Bulletin*, 20/2, 1968; *idem*, 'Rayon', in Buxton and Aldcroft; D. C. Coleman, *Courtaulds*.

[46] Balfour Committee, *Survey of Industries*, vol. 3, chapter 3, 'The Artificial Silk Industry'; H. A. Silverman, 'The Artificial Textile Industry', in *Studies in Industrial Organization* (1946), ed. H. A. Silverman, pp. 307 ff., 334.

Several other chemical firms were absorbed soon after,[47] and the company joined international cartel and exchange of information agreements with foreign firms. After some initial mistakes, the very scale of the enterprise helped to raise the technical efficiency of the British industry to the level of its chief foreign rivals.[48]

Few sectors of the chemical industry remained outside the control of ICI, exercised by agreements, by control of patents or ingredients, by control of subsidiaries and by other methods. The soap industry, however, was dominated by the vast Lever combine, which joined with its chief Dutch rivals, Jurgens' and Van den Bergh (the Margarine Union of 1927), in 1929 and had interests in other industries also.[49] Oil refining was another related industry, dominated from the beginning in this country by large firms. Thermal cracking began in 1913, and catalytic cracking plants were developed just before the Second World War. In the 1930s, however, an increasing proportion of motor spirit was imported, while the output of British refineries actually fell from 604 m. gallons in 1929 to 455 m. gallons in 1938.[50]

Another industry which showed remarkable technical progress and came to be dominated by a single large firm was glass making. Between the wars, sheet glass making was revolutionized by Pilkington's adaptation of the Slingluff process of the Pittsburgh Plate Glass Co. in 1930. Plate glass making, in turn, was changed into a continuous flow process between rollers; continuous polishing and grinding was also perfected at Pilkington's. During the First World War, the formerly neglected production of optical glass and chemical and heat-resisting glassware had been established, and in the inter-war years laminated and armour plate or toughened glass were developed from a pre-war British discovery.[51] These developments occurred at a time when demand was rising by leaps and bounds by the needs of motor vehicles, by the building boom and by the rapidly growing sales of light bulbs, glass containers used in food perservation, milk bottles, etc. Flat glass making, including plate and window glass, came to be dominated by a single firm, Pilkington's, who had bought out most of the other large makers.[52]

If glass making was typical of the old industries which were being revolutionized by new techniques, the working of aluminium, rubber and plastic

[47] W. B. Reddaway, 'The Chemical Industry', in Duncan Burn (ed.), *The Structure of British Industry*, vol. 1 (Cambridge 1958), pp. 223 ff.; Stephen Miall, *History of the British Chemical Industry* (1931), pp. 61–2; A. F. Lucas, *Industrial Reconstruction* (1937), pp. 178–90.

[48] Plummer, chapter 6/1, 'Synthetic Dyestuffs'; W. J. Reader, 'Chemical Industry', in Buxton and Aldcroft, *op. cit.*; *idem, Imperial Chemical Industries: A History*, vol. 2: *The First Quarter Century 1926–1952 (Oxford, 1975);* L. F. Haber, *Chemical* Industry 1900–1930 (Oxford, 1971), esp. chapter 10.

[49] Charles Wilson, *The History of Unilever*, 2 vols. (1954); Ruth Cohen, 'The Soap Industry', in P. L. Cook (ed.), *Effects of Mergers* (1958).

[50] Duncan Burn, 'The Oil Industry', in *Structure of British Industry*, vol. 1; PEP, *The British Fuel and Power Industries* (1947), pp. 199–209.

[51] Heath and Hetherington, chapter 10; L. M. Angus-Butterworth, *The Manufacture of Glass* (1948), chapters 16–19.

[52] Working Party Reports, *Hand-blown Domestic Glassware* (1947); T. C. Barker, *Pilkington Brothers and the Glass Industry* (1960); P. L. Cook, 'The Flat-Glass Industry', in P. L. Cook (ed.), *Effects of Mergers* (1958); T\ C. Barker, 'A Family Firm becomes a Public Company: Changes at Pilkington Brothers Limited in the Interwar Years', in L. Hannah (ed.), *Management Strategy and Business Development* (1976).

typified the new industries based on new materials. While world output of aluminium rose by 330% between 1913 and 1929, and by 165% between 1929 and 1939, British production of virgin aluminium increased from 10,000 to 25,000 metric tons between 1913 and 1939, and consumption from 16,000 metric tons in 1925 to 90,000 metric tons in 1939. Economies of scale led to an early concentration in large firms: in 1923 an international cartel agreement protected the European market, and after 1929 it was extended also to America and Canada.[53]

Rubber was used for rainwear and other purposes in the nineteenth century, but the rubber industry became of importance only with the motor vehicle of the twentieth. By 1937, two-thirds of the world's rubber supplies were used for motor tyres and tubes.[54] Rubber tyre making in Britain was dominated by the largest firm, Dunlop's,[55] and there were price agreements and far-reaching international links among the leading firms, particularly after a $33\frac{1}{3}$% tariff in 1927. Rubber footwear was similarly organized.[56]

Lastly, there was a whole range of consumer goods and services which expanded with the rising standards of living. Among those which typically showed steady increases in productivity without any spectacular technical changes were boots and shoes, and hosiery. Both had lost exports, but could more than make up for it by the buoyant home demand.[57]

Flour-milling, an industry once to be found in every village, had moved to the ports in large and efficient units before 1914 in order to deal with imported grain. During the war, many inland mills were revived to cope with the increased home wheat production so that by the early 1920s there was much surplus capacity. This was aggravated by technical improvement at a time when the consumption of flour hardly rose at all. The enormous technical advantages of size led to domination by a handful of firms, and at the end of 1938, Rank's, Spiller's and the Co-operative Wholesale Societies between them controlled 65–70% of the industry's capacity. Under the leadership of the former two the industry was 'rationalized' in 1929, by the purchase and removal of much redundant capacity by the 'Purchase Finance Co. Ltd', owned by the seven largest firms. Prices and profits were then effectively maintained by a quota system, organized by the 'Millers' Mutual Aid Association'.[58]

The canning of food, by contrast, faced a rapidly expanding market in the inter-war years. The consumption of canned vegetables is estimated to have

[53] Plummer, *New Industries*, chapter 4/1; J. D. Edwards, F. C. Frary and Z. Jeffries, *The Aluminium Industry* (New York, 1930), vol. 1, pp. 43–7.

[54] G. Rae, 'The Statistics of the Rubber Industry', *J. R. Stat. S.*, 101/2, 1938, p. 340; Audrey G. Donnithorne, *British Rubber Manufacturing* (1958), chapter 3.

[55] In 1951–2, the company accounted for 47% of British sales. Pre-war figures are not available, but were similar. Monopolies Commission, *Supply and Export of Pneumatic Tyres* (1955. 133), p. 82.

[56] Monopolies Commission, *Rubber Footwear* (1956. 328).

[57] Working Party Reports, *Boots and Shoes* (1946), section 5; H. A. Silverman, 'The Boot and Shoe Industry', in *Studies in Industrial Organization* (1946), ed. Silverman; H. A. Silverman, 'The Hosiery Industry', in *ibid.*; F. A. Wells, 'The Hosiery Trade', in *Britain in Depression* (1935); Working Party Reports, *Hosiery* (1946), esp. chapters 2, 7, 8.

[58] H. V. Edwards, 'Flour Milling', in *Further Studies in Industrial Organization* (1948), ed. M. P. Fogarty.

risen from an average of 24,000 tons p.a. in 1920–2 to 193,000 tons in 1937–8, and the home production of canned and bottled fruit from 30,000 cwt to 180,000 cwt in the same years. The industry, established during the war with the aid of the Ministry of Agriculture, found it difficult to stand up to American competition. The Metal Box Co., a firm with international links established in 1921, controlled 90% of the British output of cans, but imports, especially of canned fruit and vegetables, still accounted for the bulk of consumption.[59]

One of the industries most disorganized during the First World War was building, since nearly all private work had been stopped and the labour force dispersed: from 920,000 in July 1914 it fell to 438,000 at the time of the armistice and by July 1920 had recovered only to 796,000.[60] From then on a series of public programmes and favourable conditions for private building kept the industry booming throughout the inter-war years, except for a brief interval in 1928–30. The housing boom of the early 1930s saw the most rapid rate of house building in British history and was widely believed to have helped to pull the country out of the slump,[61] yet at the time house building accounted for only about one-third of the output of building and con-tracting, including repair. There was little rise in productivity, so that most of the increased output was achieved by increased employment. There were few large firms, and these mostly in civil engineering. By contrast, the suppliers of many building materials, following in the footsteps of the Portland Cement industry before the war, became strongly cartellized in this period.[62]

The new or growing industries were thus of several types. Some were directly replacing an old industry, including artificial silk, motor cars, alumi-nium and canned food. Others represented genuinely new products or ser-vices: among them were radio, aircraft and electrical goods. Others still were long-established industries for which the home market was growing: these included building, boots and shoes, and hosiery.

Some of the new industries, such as electrical and motor engineering, had substantial export sales, but fundamentally, unlike the old staples, they were based on a buoyant home market. Similarly, most of the prosperous indus-tries were 'sheltered' from the competition of foreign makers, by costs of transport, tariffs or by the nature of their supply. Many of the new industries depended on State support, encouragement or sponsorship; many required a high degree of scientific knowledge, and a surprisingly large number of them were dominated by a single large firm, or a few firms strongly cartellized, often with international links.[63]

[59] Richard Stone, *The Measurement of Consumers' Expenditure* (Cambridge, 1954), Tables 36, 40; Plummer, *New Industries,* chapter 5, 'Canning of Foodstuffs'; W. E. Minchinton, *The British Tinplate Industry* (Oxford, 1957), pp. 178–80.

[60] Quoted in G. C. Allen, *British Industries,* p. 304.

[61] pp. 152–3 below.

[62] Alfred C. Bossom, 'The Building Industry since the War', in *Britain in Depression;* Sir Harold Bellman, 'The Building Trades', in *Britain in Recovery;* Monopolies Commission Reports, *Cast Iron Rain Water Goods* (1951. 136); P. L. Cook, 'The Cement Industry', in P. L. Cook (ed.), *Effects of Mergers* (1958).

[63] Plummer, *op. cit.,* chapters 1, 6 and 7; H. Clay, *The Post-War Unemployment Problem* (1929), p. 108.

Again, few of the new and growing industries were tied to the coalfields or even to the ports. In consequence, many settled in the Midlands, to benefit from the old-established skills in working metals, or farther south, round the largest single market, the metropolis. Thus the industries in the new industrial suburbs to the north and west of London which formed an important part of the national output were the motor industry, the electrical industry, engineering, chemical engineering, and the manufacture of foodstuffs, furniture, musical instruments and office equipment and stationery.[64] The geographical shift was distinctly away from the centres of the old staple industries in certain regions in the north and west.

3 The Old and Declining Industries

Coal had been the symbol of the old industrial Britain. It had driven her industries and it determined their location since the days of the Industrial Revolution. The decline in the output of coal after the peak of 1913 was equally symbolic. The coal industry was buffeted by all the storms which drove the other old staple trades before them in this period, and was dragged down by them into depression and secular decline.

Prior to 1914, the traditions and organization of this industry had been geared to a steadily expanding market, and excess demand continued to 1919–20. Thereafter a series of fortuitous events helped to prolong the illusion of a continuing sellers' market in coal, including the strike of April–July 1921, the American coal strike of 1922, and the French invasion of the Ruhr in 1923. Up to the end of 1924, in fact, unemployment in coal was below the national average.[65] It was not until 1925 that the industry was brought up against a sharp fall in demand, and it took some years longer before it recognized that the reduction in the aggregate demand for coal was permanent and would become its dominant theme.

That part of the demand for coal which came from the home market ceased to grow for the first time in centuries: home consumption, including coastwise bunkers, was estimated at 183.8 million tons in 1913 and at 185 million tons in 1937–8.[66] Exports, which were at a level of about 100 m.t. in 1913 and again in 1923 because of freak market conditions, reached only about 50 m.t. even in the relatively good years of 1937–8. The shortfall of demand as against capacity was thus of the order of 40–50 m.t. yearly and was basically due to the loss of overseas markets, to the lower-cost producers in Germany, Poland and the Netherlands.

Technically, the British industry fell behind its foreign competitors after 1918. Output per man-shift rose, between 1913 and 1936, by 117% in Holland, 81% in the Ruhr, 73% in Poland, 50–51% in Belgium, 22–25% in France and 10% in Britain.[67] There was some progress: in 1913 8% of the coal

[64] D. H. Smith, *The Industries of Greater London* (1933), pp. 131, 154.

[65] Cf. J. M. Keynes, *The Economic Consequences of the Peace* (New York, 1920), p. 93; W. H. B. Court, 'Problems of the British Coal Industry between the Wars', *Ec. Hist. Rev.*, 15/1–2, 1945, p. 8; Henry Clay, *The Post-War Unemployment Problem* (1929), p. 41.

[66] R. Stone, *Measurement of Consumers' Expenditure* (Cambridge, 1954), p. 235; A. M. Neumann, *Economic Organization of the British Coal Industry* (1934), p. 98.

[67] A. Beacham, 'Efficiency and Organization of the British Coal Industry', *Econ. J.*, 55/218–19, 1945, p. 207.

was cut by machine, in 1929 28%, in 1934 47% and in 1939 61%, while mechanical conveyance was used on 12% of the coal in 1928, 37% in 1934 and 54% in 1938.[68] Improvements were concentrated in the large modern pits sunk in the eastward extensions of the coalfield in Yorkshire, Nottinghamshire and Scotland.[69]

The organization of the industry made it hard for it to put its house in order. The typical British colliery was too small to be efficient[70] and there were too many independent and competing firms to form effective voluntary associations. Reorganization was bedevilled by the strongly felt demand, among miners and others, for the nationalization of the coal mines.

The Sankey Commission of 1919 was the first of a series of official bodies which attempted to deal with the problem of organization in the coal industry in this period. Composed of owners' and miners' representatives in equal numbers with a judge as chairman, an agreed set of recommendations was most unlikely to emerge. In the event, the chairman appeared to use his casting vote in favour of nationalization, mainly on technical grounds, and virtually all members agreed on a recommendation to nationalize the coal royalties. Both suggestions were ignored by the Government, and the only permanent result, apart from the miners' Welfare Fund financed by a levy of 1*d.* per ton of coal, was the lasting suspicion of the miners that they had been tricked by the Government by means of the Commission into delaying their demands until their post-war economic and political strength had been dissipated. In March 1921, when prices and profits were tumbling, the Government handed the industry and its problems back to its private owners.

The newly found 'freedom' was ushered in by one of the most costly and bitter strikes in the history of coal mining,[71] ended by a complex agreement on the division of the surplus profits and wages, on a regional basis, but this broke down as soon as over-production and heavy unemployment began to affect the industry in 1925–6. A temporary Government subsidy of £23 million enabled the owners to cut prices while keeping up wages in 1925–6, but in the end they insisted on cutting wages, increasing hours from 7 to 8 and making regional in place of national wage agreements. The miners resisted in a seven-months strike, ushered in by a General Strike called in sympathy by the TUC, but ultimately had to give in.

Meanwhile, following the Samuel Commission of 1925, the Mining Industry Act of 1926 attempted to encourage colliery amalgamation schemes, but since the initiative had still to come from the industry, the Act had negligible results. Such amalgamations as took place were the results of purely private initiative. In 1920–9, there were 20 amalgamations, involving

---

[68] PEP, *Report on the British Coal Industry* (1936), p. 2; G. C. Allen, *British Industries* (1959 ed.), p. 70; E. C. Rhodes, 'Labour and Output in the Coal Mining Industry in Great Britain', *J. R. Stat. S.*, 94/4, 1931. Cf. also Balfour Commission, *Survey of Industries*, vol. 4, chapter 5; Neil K. Buxton, 'Coalmining', in Buxton and Aldcroft, pp. 56–61.

[69] E. C. Rhodes, 'Output, Labour and Machines in the Coal Mining Industry of Great Britain', *Economica*, NS, 12/46, 1945.

[70] For a discussion, see Neil K. Buxton, 'Entrepreneurial Efficiency in the British Coal Industry between the Wars', *Ec. Hist. Rev.*, 23/3, 1970, and debate in *ibid.*, 25/4, 1972, pp. 655–73.

[71] A. R. Redmayne, *Coalmining During the War* (Oxford, 1923), chapters 14–16.

over 200 pits, and there were further significant combinations in South Wales and in Lancashire in 1929–30.[72] Of regional cartel schemes, the most effective was the Midland scheme which embraced Lancashire, Yorkshire, Nottinghamshire and Derbyshire and had a large and secure home market as base: for two years from 1928 it was fairly successful in restricting output, subsidizing exports and controlling the Humber Coal Exporters' Association. Its success seemed to point to a way to prevent further price falls, losses and industrial disputes.[73]

The Coal Mines Act of 1930, the most important measure affecting the industry in the inter-war years, attempted to apply the lessons of the 1920s. Part I of the Act set up a compulsory cartel scheme. A Central Council was to determine the allocation of sales quotas between the 17 districts and the districts, in turn, allocated quotas to individual collieries. But this quota system was not backed by an effective national price maintenance scheme, and price competition, particularly between districts, continued with undiminished bitterness.[74] Nevertheless the cartel scheme established by Part I of the Act of 1930 helped to reduce output and keep up prices and profits, and since quotas were transferable, it led to some concentration of production.

These cartel powers were designed to raise the price of coal temporarily. Part II of the Act was to effect a permanent cure. It set up the Coal Mines Reorganization Commission, charged with the task of reorganizing the industry mainly by amalgamations and concentration of production. In the face of the determined opposition of the industry, however, the Commission was unable to carry out its task.[75] Its powers were transferred to the Coal Commission by the Coal Act of 1938, which also authorized the nationalization of coal royalties, ultimately completed in 1942 at a cost of £66$\frac{1}{2}$ million.

The history of the coal industry has been described at some length since it illustrates better than any other the fundamental problems of the declining staple industries in the inter-war years. Largely because of the fall in exports, there was a drop in output from an annual average of 268 millions tons in 1907–14 to 228 million tons in 1934–8. Even these figures were only achieved by drastic price cuts. In 1929, perhaps the best inter-war year, it was estimated that one-quarter of the German industry, one-quarter to one-third of the British, and one-half of the Polish were surplus to requirements. Employment fell drastically from 1,226,000 in 1920 to 702,000 in 1938. After 1925, unemployment was seldom under 20% and generally well above this figure, while at least 200,000 miners drifted out of the industry.[76]

[72] Neumann, *op. cit.*, pp. 152 ff.; Lord Aberconway, *The Basic Industries of Great Britain* (1927), p. 22.

[73] J. H. Jones, G. Cartwright and P. H. Guénault, *The Coal-mining Industry* (1939), chapter 6; W. M. Kirby, *The British Coalmining Industry 1870–1946* (1977), chapter 6. But see: Neil K. Buxton, 'Entrepreneurial Efficiency and the British Coal Industry between the Wars', *Ec. Hist. Rev.* 23/3, 1970.

[74] J. H. Jones *et al.*, *Coal-mining Industry*, pp. 127–33.

[75] Ivor Thomas, 'The Coal Mines Reorganization Commission', in W. A. Robson (ed.), *Public Enterprise* (1937); M. W. Kirby, 'The Control of Competition in the British Coalmining Industry in the Thirties', *Ec. Hist. Rev.*, 26/2, 1973.

[76] G. C. Allen, *British Industries*, chapter 3; J. H. Jones, G. Cartwright, and W. Prest, 'The Coal Industry', in *Britain in Depression*; J. H. Jones, 'The Coalmining Industry', in *Britain in Recovery*; PEP, *Report on the British Coal Industry* (1936), pp. 23–5.

The iron and steel industry was another of the basic staple trades which suffered a decline in exports. Moreover, the war had created a large surplus capacity and the post-war boom of 1919–20 burdened it with much watered capital, and this hung like a millstone round its neck until the re-armament of the late 1930s. After a period of decline, steel output rose from the earlier peak of $9\frac{1}{2}$ m.t. in 1917–18 to 13 m.t. in 1937.[77] These figures may be compared with a capacity of 12 m.t. after the war.[78] There was thus, throughout, much redundant capacity and a high level of unemployment, generally fluctuating around the 20% level.

The British industry lost much of its competitive edge in the 1920s. While tariffs abroad and foreign cartels reduced exports, the home market was flooded with cheap foreign steel. In 1911–13 the average annual excess of exports of iron and steel over imports had been $2\frac{3}{4}$ million tons; by 1921–2, it had shrunk to about $1\frac{1}{4}$ m.t. and in 1927–9 to a mere $\frac{3}{4}$ m.t. At the same time, while the world output of steel had risen from 75 m.t. in 1913 to 118 m.t. in 1929, the British output had increased by only 2 m.t.[79] Significantly, domestic consumption, which was just over 5 m.t. of steel a year in 1910–14, rose to 7·6 m.t. in 1927–31 and 10·6 m.t. in 1935–8.

In the post-war period Britain's capacity was still geared too much towards puddled bar iron and acid steel instead of basic steel, and, besides, her steelworks were antiquated, the furnaces too small, mechanical aids insufficient, and the layout of works dictated by history rather than technical needs. Blast furnaces were particularly backward and inefficient.[80] Some improvements did take place.

There was a geographical shift was towards the Lincolnshire and East Midland ore fields, which produced 18·7% of the pig iron in 1920 and 37·4% in 1932. In North Lincolnshire large integrated works were set up on the ore field, about 20 miles from the coal, but there was much expansion also in Sheffield, badly sited from almost every point of view, but containing 80% of the British electric furnace capacity, as well as in Consett and the Lancashire Steel Corporation, both away from the coast and the ore. If there was no clear move to better sites, there was little progress made towards regional self-sufficiency either, and millions of tons of ore, coke and coal had regularly to be transported over long distances.[81] There were several amalgamations in the industry in the 1920s, including South Durham and Cargo Fleet, Dorman Long and Bolckow-Vaughan, Cammell-Laird and Vickers, Guest, Keen & Nettlefold and Baldwin, Colville and Beardmore, the Lancashire Steel

[77] H. G. Roepke, *Movements of the British Iron and Steel Industry, 1720–1951* (Urbana, Ill., 1956), p. 111.

[78] E. D. McCallum, 'The Iron and Steel Industry', in *Britain in Depression*.

[79] T. H. Burnham and G. O. Hoskins, *Iron and Steel in Britain, 1870–1930* (1943), Tables 91, 93; M. S. Birkett, 'The Iron and Steel Industry since the War', *J. R. Stat. S.*, 93/3, 1930, p. 373.

[80] E.g. Burnham and Hoskins, pp. 190–3; D. L. Burn, *The Economic History of Steelmaking, 1867–1939* (Cambridge, 1940), pp. 362–70, 408–13, 427; J. C. Carr and Walter Taplin, *History of the British Steel Industry* (Oxford, 1962), parts 4 and 5; Balfour Committee, *Survey of Industries*, IV, pp. 21–32; K. Warren, 'Iron and Steel', in Buxton and Aldcroft; Neil K. Buxton, 'Efficiency and Organization in Scotland's Iron and Steel Industry during the Interwar Period', *Ec. Hist. Rev.*, 29/1, 1976.

[81] Roepke, pp. 115–16; IDAC (May Committee): *Report on the . . . Iron and Steel Industry* (1936. Cmd. 5507), p. 61.

Corporation and the United Steel Companies.

The world depression hit the iron and steel industry with particular force because of its dependence on capital goods. The production of pig iron dropped by 53% between 1929 and 1932, and of steel by 45%. A large part of the industry's capital had to be written off, £42 million being thus wiped off among 37 firms in 1927–36.[82] The subsequent recovery was equally remarkable, assisted by a $33\frac{1}{3}$% tariff in 1932, which however raised costs to consumers like the motor industry.[83] By 1934 output returned to the level of 1929, and continued to expand. If iron and steel did worse in Britain than in the rest of the world in the 1920s, it did better in the 1930s: the country's share of the world's steel output rose from 7·6% in 1931 to 9·7% in 1937.

Like Part I of the Coal Mines Act of 1930, the tariff on iron and steel in 1932 was granted on the understanding that reorganization was to follow. The Government looked for the benefits of monopoly, tempered by planning in the national interest. Accordingly, the British Iron and Steel Federation was formed in April 1934, and was given fairly strong powers. In 1935–6 it took over the price-fixing functions of earlier sectional associations, and it negotiated with foreign cartels to impose quantitative restrictions on imports, after establishing a position of strength by getting the tariff on steel raised temporarily from $33\frac{1}{3}$% to 50%; it bought foreign scrap and pig iron for the industry as a whole and sold them cheaply to home producers, financing the transaction with a levy. BISF's planning, however, tended to be restrictive, and the location of new plants, such as the Richard Thomas works ultimately sited at Ebbw Vale, was bedevilled by political wire-pulling.[84]

Under pressure from the banks, there were further mergers and schemes of 'rationalization' and integration after 1928. In 1932, 10 vertical combines had 47% of the pig-iron capacity and 60% of the steel capacity between them.[85] These mergers and the officially supported cartel policy certainly kept up prices and profits but it is not certain that they contributed greatly to economic efficiency. It was the moderate boom beginning in 1935, and the rearmament orders which followed, which led to a phenomenal increase in the output of steel in the late 1930s[86] from 5·2 million tons in 1931, to 9·85 m.t. in 1935, 13·0 m.t. in 1937 and, after a relapse in 1938, to 13·2 m.t. in 1939.

Shipbuilding suffered even more than steelmaking in the depression from the declining demand for capital goods. The combined result of the war and the post-war boom was that in 1919–20 the world shipbuilding capacity was more than doubled, while the world's shipping tonnage, and thus the potential demand for ships, hardly increased at all. From 1920 onwards the tonnage under construction fell, though the years 1927–30 were relatively good years, British launchings then running at about 75% of the level of 1911–13. In the slump, with millions of tons of shipping laid up, the building of new tonnage virtually came to a standstill: in 1933 the launchings from British yards fell to 7% of the pre-war figure. Throughout the early 1930s a large part

[82] P. W. S. Andrews and E. Brunner, *Capital Development in Steel* (Oxford, 1951), p. 85.

[83] B. W. E. Alford, 'New Industries for Old?', in Roderick Floud and Donald McCloskey (eds.), *The Economic History of Britain Since 1700* vol. 2 (Cambridge, 1981), p. 311.

[84] Roepke, chapter 6; Burn, pp. 461–4.

[85] G. C. Allen, *British Industries*, p. 115.

[86] E. D. McCallum, 'The Iron and Steel Industry', in *Britain in Recovery*.

of the industry was idle, and its unemployment rate was among the highest in the country.

The expansion of building capacity abroad in 1915–19 had lowered the British share of world output from 58·7% in 1909–13 to about 40%, reaching 64% in 1924 and being well over 50% in 1927–30, launchings for foreign owners continuing to form a substantial proportion of the output, though a lower one than in the case of some foreign countries.[87] Britain was slow in adopting some newer types of ship: thus in 1927–30 British yards built 65% of the world's tonnage of steamships, but only 41% of motor vessels.[88] Yards were older, sites often restricted, steel prices and labour costs higher here than elsewhere, but the problem of the industry was not so much its relatively high costs – it held its own quite well with other countries – as the low level of the world's needs compared with the available capacity. Surplus ships, laid up after 1920, but capable of being brought into use again, and estimated at 11 million tons in 1922 and 6 million in 1925–6, kept down freight rates and orders for new tonnage, except for new types of ships, such as motor vessels and oil tankers. In Britain, a capacity estimated at between 3 m.t. and 4 m.t. p.a. in the 1920s,[89] compared with an output which fluctuated between 640,000 and 1,540,000 tons.

There was a heavy decline of the labour attached to the industry, and large financial losses were incurred. Some firms went out of business, others saved themselves by mergers, like Harland & Wolff of Belfast and the Clyde, Palmer's and the Northumberland Shipbuilding Co. on the Tyne, Hawthorne – Leslie and Vickers-Armstrong.[90] When the disastrous collapse of markets in 1929–33 threatened to obliterate much of the industry altogether, 'National Shipbuilders' Security Ltd.' was formed in 1930 with the support of nearly the whole of the industry, and aided by the 'Bankers' Industrial Development Co.', an organization set up by the Bank of England and the clearing banks. It could raise funds, to be repaid by a 1% levy on the sales of participating firms, in order 'to assist the Shipbuilding Industry by the purchase of redundant and/or obsolete shipyards, the dismantling and disposal of their contents and the resale of sites under restriction against further use for shipbuilding'. By 1937, 28 firms with a capacity of over 1 million tons out of a total of perhaps $3\frac{1}{2}$ m.t. had been bought up and destroyed, while a number of others, less fortunate, had been forced into liquidation.

There was also the so-called 'scrap and build' scheme of Part II of the British Shipping (Assistance) Act of 1935, to help the builders of cargo tramp vessels. In return for an undertaking to scrap 2 tons of existing tonnage for every ton newly built, the Treasury offered loans on favourable terms to owners. Tramp ship owners availed themselves of this offer only to a limited

[87] Leslie Jones, *Shipbuilding in Britain* (Cardiff, 1957), p. 64; J. R. Parkinson, 'Shipbuilding', in Buxton and Aldcroft, p. 95.

[88] G. R. Henning and Keith Trace, 'Britain and the Motor Ship: A Case of the Delayed Adoption of New Technology?', *J. Econ. Hist.*, 35, 1975.

[89] Balfour Committee, *Survey of Industries*, vol. 4, chapter 4; Jones, *op. cit.* p. 124.

[90] H. M. Hallsworth, 'The Shipbuilding Industry', in *Britain in Depression*, pp. 255–6, and 'The Shipbuilding Industry', in *Britain in Recovery*, p. 358.

extent, however, not least because of Part I of the same Act which gave them subsidies on sailings and thus discouraged the scrapping of tonnage.

Little was achieved also in enforcing specialization, lowering costs or recapturing markets. Instead, from 1934 onwards attempts were made to raise prices. Launchings for export orders failed to pick up in the face of foreign subsidies and protection. On the contrary, in the mid-1930s even some British owners began to place their orders abroad,[91] deriving some indirect benefits from foreign subsidy payments.

In the engineering industry, some sections, such as motor engineering and electrical engineering, were expanding rapidly and absorbing much capital and labour from the declining sectors. Among the latter were some that had been part of Britain's strength before 1914, notably steam engine making, including locomotive and marine engineering, and the building of textile machinery.

Engineering in the widest sense had expanded faster than any other occupation during the war: the Census figures showed an increase in employment from 1,779,000 in 1911 to 2,491,000 in 1921, and the insurance figures, calculated on a different basis, registered an increase from 1,028,000 in 1913–14 to 1,647,000 in 1919–20.[92] The necessary reductions were less painful than they might have been because of the large numbers of women workers involved, but in some sectors male workers were affected also. According to the Census of Production, engineering output in 1924 was only slightly higher than in 1907. It then rose to 121 in 1929 (1924 = 100), dropped heavily in the depression, then rose quickly after 1933. By 1937, it was perhaps 60% above the 1924 level, employing 30% more workers, the increases being largely due to motor and electrical engineering, while general engineering and other sections showed substantial reductions in employment.[93]

Though there were some large specialist firms in the industry, e.g. Babcock & Wilcox, boilermakers, or Platt Bros. Ltd, textile machinery makers, most firms in general engineering were of small or medium size.[94] It was not at all certain that large size necessarily promoted efficiency, which depended largely on technical innovation; good progress was being made particularly in mass-production and in accepting standard specifications for components, in association with the British Standards Institution which had arisen out of the British Engineering Standards Association. Technical progress still depended largely on improved mechanical aids and on efficient prime movers, that is, on engineering. Direct comparisons of efficiency with other countries can only be made separately for each subsection of the engineering industry, if at all. Until 1929, world trade in engineering products was growing so fast that even British exports were increasing in absolute terms, though they declined as a proportion of world exports. This picture changed radically in the 1930s, when export markets collapsed. The industry then came to rely increasingly

[91] G. C. Allen, *British Industries*, p. 155.

[92] Balfour Committee, *Survey of Industries*, vol. 4, pp. 132–3; H. Clay, *Unemployment*, pp. 84–6.

[93] E. Allen, 'Engineering', in *Britain in Depression*.

[94] PEP, *Agricultural Machinery* (1949), p. 10; T. R. Gourvish, 'Mechanical Engineering', in Buxton and Aldcroft, pp. 146–7.

on the home market, largely protected by the tariff of 1932 and increasingly prosperous after 1933.

The cotton industry had grown up as an export trade, and despite the rapid growth of competing industries in other countries in the generation before 1914, Britain's share in the international trade of cotton yarns and piece goods was still 65% in 1909–13.[95] 75% of the British output was exported in 1913, and 70% in 1920–6, the proportion of piece goods being 85% in both periods, and cotton goods accounted for 25% of total British exports by value in 1910–13.

During the war, the output of cotton textiles had been curtailed. As a result of the pent-up demand created thereby, prices rose excessively in the boom years 1919–20, and many cotton firms were lured into over-capitalization by bonus issues of shares at inflated values.[96] When the bubble was pricked, the highly competitive spinning and weaving sections suffered a disproportionate fall in prices, since the monopolistic finishing sections succeeded in maintaining their margins fairly well.

The decline in the cotton industry which followed, especially in the case of piece goods, was wholly due to the fall in exports; home sales, in fact, were rising.[97]

Table 2.7: The decline in the cotton industry

	Yarn (million lb.)		Piece goods (million sq. yds.)		Machinery		
	Pro-duction	Exports	Pro-duction	Exports	Spindles (m. mule equiva-lent)	Looms (000)	Labour in spinning, doubling, weaving (000)
1912	1,982	244	8,050	6,913	61·4	786	621·5
1930	1,047	137	3,500	2,472	63·2	700	564·1
1938	1,070	123	3,126	1,494	42·1	495	393·0

The fall in exports could not be ascribed to a fall in the world's cotton goods consumption, but was due to the rise of newly established competitors abroad. Lancashire was inclined to blame this loss entirely on the cheap labour of the East, but other Western countries showed that it was possible, by operating with high wages and first-class equipment, to stand up to low wages competition. The British industry remained technically backward[98]

[95] G. C. Allen, *British Industries*, p. 217.

[96] Balfour Committee, *Survey of Industries*, vol. 3, pp. 36–8, 123–7; G. W. Daniels and J. Jewkes, 'The Post-War Depression in the Lancashire Cotton Industry', *J. R. Stat. S.*, 91/2, 1928, pp. 170–80.

[97] Working Party Reports, *Cotton* (1946), p. 6; R. Robson, *The Cotton Industry in Britain* (1957), Appendix. The piece goods figures for 1912 are in millions of linear yards, but the difference is negligible: in millions of linear yards, the export figure for 1930 would have been 2,490 instead of 2,472. The figures for 1930 and 1938 include small quantities of spun rayon and mixtures. Imports were negligible, except in 1930, when they reached 10% of home consumption. Cf. also A. C. Pigou, *Aspects of British Economic History 1918–1925* (1948 ed.), Part III, chapter 4.

[98] William Lazonick, 'Industrial Organization and Technical Change: The Decline of the British Cotton Industry', *Bus. Hist. Rev.*, 1982; J. H. Porter, 'Cotton and Wool Textiles', in Buxton and Aldcroft, pp. 35–6.

and was unable to reorganize at a time when markets, prices and profits were falling away. Output per man-hour rose very slowly compared with such countries as Japan or the USA.[99] Its proportion of the world's mill consumption of cotton fell from 20% in 1910–13 to 9% in 1936–8, and its share of the world's cotton goods exports, from 58% to 28%. The producers of finer counts suffered less than the makers of coarser yarns and fabrics, but competition became effective in increasingly higher levels of quality.

Up to 1930, some attempts were made to improve efficiency in the industry, but after that the world depression turned the emphasis away from technical improvements to a panic reduction in capacity. Both methods, according to the official Clynes Report of 1930,[100] required reorganization in the industry. There had been some amalgamations in the post-war boom, but most firms remained small and agreement was difficult to reach among the hundreds of independent producers. A Cotton Yarn Association was established in 1927 to keep up prices, but failed within a few months, as was inevitable in an industry consisting of so many small units. A new approach was required, and with the help of the Bankers' Industrial Development Corporation, the Lancashire Cotton Corporation was set up in 1929 for the American section of the industry. It quickly acquired 9 million spindles, which it reduced to $4\frac{1}{4}$ million by 1939, at the same time modernizing the property it retained. In the smaller Egyptian section, the banks set up the Combined Egyptian Mills Ltd in 1929, which bought up 3 million spindles capacity. The Quilt Manufacturers' Association was formed in the same year. These 'voluntary' actions were reinforced by the Act of 1936, which set up the Spindles Board, with powers to raise a compulsory levy, used to acquire and scrap, by 1939, 6 million spindles out of the $13\frac{1}{2}$ million still thought to be redundant. The Cotton Industry (Reorganization) Act of 1939 created machinery for fixing compulsory minimum prices by setting up a Statutory Cotton Industry Board.[101] The State, having ensured the reduction of capacity, thus created a compulsory cartel to raise prices. The outbreak of war prevented the functioning of the Cotton Board as originally intended, and its powers were modified by an Act of 1940.

Structurally, the woollen and worsted industry was not dissimilar from the cotton industry. It consisted of large numbers of small firms, though in the woollen section vertical integration was common and most firms engaged in both spinning and weaving. Since it had always relied less on exports and more on the home market than cotton, it suffered less by the general decline in the former and benefited more by the buoyancy of the latter in the 1930s. Moreover, the British woollen and worsted industry did not lose its share of world exports, but suffered only from the decline in total world trade, caused by crippling tariffs in some countries and growing self-sufficiency in others. This was largely due to the continued importance of the quality trade, in which the traditional skill of British labour continued to be an advantage. As

[99] Working Party Reports, *Cotton*, pp. 8–9, 50, chapter 6; L. Rostas, 'Productivity of Labour in the Cotton Industry', *Econ. J.*, 55/218–19, 1945, p. 199; A. J. Brown, *Applied Economics* (1947), chapter V/3.

[100] *Report of the Committee on the Cotton Industry* (1930. Cmd. 3615).

[101] H. G. Hughes and C. T. Saunders, 'The Cotton Industry', in *Britain in Recovery*, pp. 448–9.

far as the mechanical equipment was concerned, however, too much of it was antiquated, and output per man-hour or per spindle was only a fraction of the American figure.[102]

After 1929, the more serious drop in exports was not fully made up by the growing home market of the 1930s, though the tariff of 1932 had reduced imports at once from 50 million to 7 million square yards of cloth. Employment declined steadily in the inter-war period, and unemployment was above the average, reaching 36·4% in 1931, the worst year. Schemes of control were being considered more seriously in the 1930s,[103] mainly with a view to ending price cutting in the home market, but were not implemented.

The pottery industry was smaller than those considered so far, yet it has occupied an important place in British industrial production and exports since the Industrial Revolution, and like the other old staples, it is highly localized so as to form the main livelihood of a substantial region of the country, the 'Potteries'. In some sectors of the industry, notably electrical porcelain accessories, there was growth rather than decline, but the industry as a whole, especially domestic pottery, suffered from falling sales at home, while tariffs abroad reduced export sales by half between 1924 and 1935. The British industry received protection under the Safeguarding Act from 1927 on.[104]

Technical progress was not negligible, even though many of the innumerable small firms were chronically short of capital and the installation of automatic or semi-automatic machinery for table-ware was far behind. Tunnel kilns, perfected in 1910, gradually spread in the inter-war years, replacing the beehive kilns, and firing by gas or electricity became more common. The production of tiles and electric fittings was mechanized in the 1920s.[105] These improvements led to further declines in employment, and the industry had a high level of unemployment in the inter-war period, reaching 38·8% in 1931 and about 45% in 1932.

The staple industries which were in a state of depression or in absolute decline in the 1920s and 1930s were thus, to a large extent, victims of the same set of circumstances. There was, first, the contraction of vital foreign markets, largely because of self-sufficiency or tariffs abroad. Secondly, the British share of world trade was shrinking, as the British industries appeared antiquated, yet in a period of low profits unable to modernize their equipment, preferring, instead, restrictive and monopolistic schemes. Thirdly, the staple export industries on which Britain had concentrated in the past were no longer the growth sectors in world demand. With greater purchasing power in western countries, 'instead of demanding fine, durable British cottons and woollens, china, or cutlery, consumers in protected markets, subjected to high-pressure salesmanship, turned to new mass-produced cheap luxuries – silks and rayons, radios, automobiles, household gadgets, movies, phonographs – and to the home market goods and services – electric light, newspapers and books, sports, housing and leisure'.[106] Fourthly, after 1925

[102] Working Party Reports, *Wool* (1947), pp. 66–7, chapter 8.
[103] A. N. Shimmin, 'The Wool Textile Industry', in *Britain in Recovery*, p. 467.
[104] Working Party Reports, *Pottery* (1946), pp. 1, 36–7.
[105] John Thomas, 'The Pottery Industry', in *Britain in Depression*, p. 413.
[106] A. E. Kahn, *Great Britain in the World Economy* (1946), p. 74.

the relative loss of markets was aggravated by the over-valuation of the pound.

In addition, there were often specific causes for the depression in particular industries. Thus steel, shipbuilding and engineering suffered from the unhealthy over-expansion during the war; coal from being replaced, in part, by oil and hydro-electric power; and cotton from the ease with which backward low-wage countries could install up-to-date machinery.[107] Finally, the more the world's governments turned for remedies to autarchy, restrictions or bilateral agreements, the more they were bound to injure the industries which depended for the health on free access to the world's markets.

4 The Changing Location of Industry

The interaction between the declining staple industries and the new and expanding trades was a determinant in the changes in foreign trade and home consumption. It was also responsible for a decisive shift in the geographical location of British industry and population between 1920 and 1939.

Some of the declining industries including railways, shipping and agriculture were widely scattered geographically, but mostly they were highly concentrated in small and clearly defined areas. Some of these held concentrations of two or three of these old basic industries and were utterly dependent on their prosperity. These original locations had been determined largely by easily accessible coal and iron deposits, by water power available from mountain streams, and by other materials, such as salt in Cheshire, fireclay near Stourbridge, and grindstones near Sheffield. Once established, an industry would call into being others of an ancillary or complementary nature, as well as a large labour force, a canal and railway network, and these would in turn attract yet other industries by a snowball effect, the whole depending ultimately on steam power based on coal. Thus, by 1914, much of Britain's basic staple industry was to be found in a few areas in South Wales, Lancashire and the West Riding, the industrial West Midlands, the northeast coast and Clydeside.

The effects of the decline and depression of the old staple industries on employment and prosperity generally were naturally felt with particular force in these narrowly limited areas, and they were not compensated by a parallel

Table 2·8a: Percentage of net output of industry in regions, 1924–35[108]

	1924	1930	1935
Old Industrial Regions*	49·6	42·4	37·6
New Industrial Regions**	28·7	33·4	37·1
Rest of Great Britain	21·7	24·2	25·3
Total Great Britain	100	100	100

* Lancashire and Cheshire, West Riding, Northumberland and Durham, South Wales and Monmouthshire and West Central Scotland Regions of the Census of Production.
** Greater London, Warwickshire etc. Regions of the Census of Production.

[107] W. A. Lewis, *Economic Survey 1919–1939* (1949), pp. 42, 87.
[108] PEP, *Report on the Location of Industry in Great Britain* (1939), p. 44.

establishment of the new industries. In general, these settled in new areas, mainly in the Midlands and the south. This is illustrated in Tables 2·8a and 2·8b.

Table 2·8b: Percentage of total population and insured population in regions, 1921–37[109]

	Total population		Insured population	
	1921	1937	1923	1937
1 Lancashire	11·6	10·9	15·7	13·8
2 West Riding, Notts and Derby	10·9	10·8	13·0	12·2
3 Northumberland and Durham	5·2	4·8	5·7	4·9
4 Mid-Scotland	6·2	6·0	7·3	6·6
5 Glamorgan and Monmouth	4·0	3·4	4·2	3·3
6 London and Home Counties	23·5	25·7	22·4	26·0
7 Midland Counties*	9·5	9·7	11·2	11·7
Old industrial areas (1–5)	37·9	35·9	45·9	40·8
New industrial areas (6–7)	33·0	35·4	33·6	37·7
8 Rest of Great Britain	29·1	28·7	20·5	21·5
Total Great Britain	100	100	100	100

* Industrial Midland Counties, except Notts and Derbyshire.

In June 1923, the four southern Divisions of the Ministry of Labour (London, South-East, South-West and the Midlands) contained 46·6% of the insured population, and the rest of the United Kingdom (including Northern Ireland) the remaining 53·4%: in June 1938 these figures had been almost exactly reversed, the south now having 53·9% and the north 46·1% of the insured population. There was a still larger shift when measured by net industrial output.

This shift was not so much the result of a southward 'migration' of industry, as the result of its original distribution, as it was the south and east which contained mainly industries which were destined to expand, while the typical industries of the north and west were declining. The extent of that factor is illustrated in Table 2·9, which should be compared with Table 2·8b.[110]

To some extent, however, every industry showed rather better results in the expanding areas than in the declining ones,[111] the multiplier effect of local prosperity being particularly evident in 'local', as distinct from 'basic', industries, such as local transport, distribution, hotels and entertainment services and above all, building.[112]

[109] *Report of the Royal Commission on the Distribution of the Industrial Population* (Barlow Commission) (1940. Cmd. 6153). Based on the Ministry of Labour Regions. Cf. also Mark Abrams, *The Condition of the British People, 1911–1945* (1945), p. 22.

[110] M. P. Fogarty, *Prospects of the Industrial Areas of Great Britain* (1945), p. 16.

[111] R. C. Tress, 'Unemployment and the Diversification of Industry', *Manchester School,* 9/2, 1938; D. G. Champernowne, 'The Uneven Distribution of Unemployment in the United Kingdom, 1929–36', *Rev. Econ. Studies,* 6/2, 1938; A. M. Carr-Saunders and D. Caradog Jones, *A Survey of the Social Structure of England and Wales* (Oxford, 2nd ed., 1937), p. 43.

[112] S. R. Dennison, *The Location of Industry and the Depressed Areas* (1939), pp. 40–1, 158; J. H. Jones, in Appx. II to Barlow Commission, *Report,* pp. 274–6.

Table 2·9:   Change of employment in regions, 1923–37

	Percent of insured workers in each region employed in:				Total change in employment, %	Hypothetical change if employment in 21 industries had changed alike in all regions
	16 expanding industries		5 declining industries			
	1923	1937	1923	1937		
1 Lancashire	9	16	36	24	+ 8	+ 11
2 West Riding, Notts, Derby	9	14	43	32	+ 15	+ 9
3 Northumberland, Durham	6	9	49	33	+ 5	+ 4
4 Mid-Scotland	10	13	24	15	+ 10	+ 18
5 Glamorgan and Monmouth	4	6	59	41	– 4	+ 1
6 London and Home Counties	21	25	1	1	+ 43	+ 40
7 Midland Counties	26	30	12	7	+ 28	+ 29
Great Britain	14	19	23	14	+ 22	+ 22

There was substantial migration involved in this geographical shift, as shown by the following *annual* gains and losses by migration in the years 1931–6:[113]

Table 2·10:   Migration of labour, 1931–6

London and Home Counties	+ 71,600	North West	– 6,900
South East	+ 18,300	Wales	– 22,100
South West	+ 11,400	North East	– 24,200
Midlands	+ 5,500		
Scotland	+ 1,300		

This was entirely voluntary, induced by the classic economic forces of supply and demand. The pull of higher wages was relatively unimportant here: it was the comparative levels of unemployment – as well as the distance – which were the most powerful factors affecting the decision to migrate.[114] Yet the resistance to migration was high also, for to the end of our period the northern and Welsh unemployment figures remained obstinately at double the southern rates, migration having been quite insufficient to level them out. The July proportions of the insured population unemployed in the eight years 1929–36 averaged 11·0% in the four regions of South Britain, and 22·8% in North Britain and Wales. The difference was even more marked in the case of protracted unemployment, of 12 months or over: in June 1936, for example, this ranged from 9% in London and the southeast to 37% in Wales.[115] Moreover the declining parts of the country had more underemployment and a markedly smaller percentage of the population seeking employment: Where most of the men were out of work, women, youths and old men did not even trouble to sign on at the Labour Exchange.[116] Lastly, for a man on the

[113] H. W. Richardson, *Economic Recovery in Britain, 1932–9* (1967), pp. 279–82.
[114] H. Makower, J. Marschak and H. W. Robinson, 'Studies in Mobility of Labour', *Oxf. Econ. P.*, 1/1, 1938.
[115] H. W. Robinson, 'Employment and Unemployment', in *Britain in Recovery* (1938), p. 97.
[116] J. H. Jones, in Appx. II to Barlow Commission, *Report*, pp. 264–5; S. R. Dennison, 'The Effects of Recovery on the Various Regions', in *Britain in Recovery*, p. 109; Board of Trade and Scottish Office, *Distribution of Industry* (1948. Cmd. 7540), p. 7.

unemployment register, the chances of reabsorption into industry were much higher in the prosperous than in the depressed areas.[117] None of these differences was ironed out by migration; they remained as strongly marked at the end of our period as at the beginning.

The new industries of the southern half of Britain differed from the old staples not only by the fact that they were growing instead of declining. They were also industries of a different character. The main precondition of the southern industrial renaissance was the fact that the new industries were no longer tied to any particular area by bulky fuel or raw material needs. In place of localized coal for steam power and heat, electricity was available everywhere, especially after the completion of the grid. Likewise, few of the new industries were troubled by high transport costs of bulky raw materials. The raw materials either formed only a very small item in total costs, or they were imported, and any port could become a good location. At the same time, the development of road transport made industry altogether less dependent on the old rail and canal networks and forced down railway rates to 'exceptional', i.e. lower rates, while 'tapering' charges on the railways made long distances less disadvantageous. Industry was thus more footloose and had greater freedom of choice of location than in the nineteenth century. In 1924, 55% (or including cotton and wool, 70%) of the declining industries were tied to their location by heavy transport costs, and in 1934 the proportion was still 50% (65%). By contrast, among the growing industries the proportion was only 10% in both years.

Moreover, in place of skilled or brawny male labour, most of the new industries required adaptable but essentially unskilled labour, much of it female. In place of the capital goods and foreign markets of the old staples, the new industries were largely mass-producing consumer goods for the home market. Proximity to the market often became the decisive consideration, and the relaxation of the old localizing restrictions permitted industry to follow it.[118] As a result, London, forming the largest concentration of home consumers, became the main location for new industries: in 1932–7, it accounted for five-sixths of the net increase in the number of factories, two-fifths of employment in new factories and one-third of all factory extensions undertaken, even though it had only one-fifth of the population. Birmingham and its conurbation formed another large market attracting the new industries. Even in the depressed parts of the country, the large cities were exempt from the worst effects of industrial decline. In following the market as the main factor in location, industry was concerned not so much with transport costs as with speed and regularity of supplies, and immediate knowledge of changes in markets, tastes and fashions.

In many cases, however, the rationality of the geographical shift can easily be exaggerated.[119] In preferring the south to the north, industrialists moved into areas of higher rents and higher wages; they left areas with well developed public utilities and plentiful labour for districts in which good

[117] H. W. Singer, 'Regional Labour Markets and the Process of Unemployment', *Rev. Econ. Studies*, 7, 1939–40.

[118] P. G. Hall, *The Industries of London since 1861* (1962).

[119] G. D. H. Cole, *Building and Planning* (1945), p. 23.

roads and other services had still to be laid out, and where labour was scarce and untrained. Nor was it true that trade unions were more restrictive in the north;[120] in fact, the only clear-cut case in this period of an industry driven out by high wages and trade union power was the printing industry, which migrated out of Central London to such places as St Albans, Cheltenham and Ipswich. Constricted space, high rents and traffic jams forced other industries also to move out of London into the suburbs, to make the outer ring of London the fastest growing area in the country: between 1901 and 1938, the population of the County of London declined by 150,000, but that of Greater London grew by 1,600,000.[121] There may have been a few industrialists who consciously preferred the climate or the amenities of the south, and there may have been a few others who worked out comparative costs in some detail. But largely, industry moved south because the south was expanding and prosperous.[122]

This left the north with a double burden. As the staple industries contracted, the populations of whole districts were thrown out of work, without hope of alternative employment. Ancillary trades and finally local service trades suffered, and as the most energetic workers left, the areas affected became caught up in a vicious circle of depression and decline. In the depression of the early 1930s the problem had grown to such dimensions that Governments could no longer ignore it. In some areas, up to 80% of the insured population was out of work: even after recovery had begun, in May 1934, 74·1% of the insured males were unemployed in Brynmawr, 73·4% in Dowlais, 69·1% in Merthyr and 65·7% in Ferndale,[123] while high unemployment rates even in 'prosperous' areas robbed migration of its purpose.

Regional surveys in 1931–2[124] showed that with the collapse of export markets and, in some areas, the exhaustion of the coal or other mineral deposits, there was little hope of rehabilitating the local staple industries which had formed the mainstay of employment in those districts. After further reports, published in November 1934,[125] four of these areas were officially designated 'depressed', quickly renamed 'special areas' in 1934, by the Special Areas (Development and Improvement) Act, 1934.

[120]*First Report of Commissioner for the Special Areas* (*England and Wales*) (1935. Cmd. 4957), pp. 14–16.

[121] PEP, *Location of Industry*, p. 47, map on p. 171; D. H. Smith, *The Industries of Greater London* (1933); Fogarty, *Prospects*, chapters 14, 15; Mowat, *Britain between the Wars*, p. 225; Brinley Thomas, 'The Influx of Labour into London and the South-East, 1920–36', *Economica*, NS, 4/15, 1937.

[122] PEP, *Location of Industry*, chapter 3; Dennison, *Location of Industry*, pp. 30–2; R. C. on the Geographical Distribution of the Industrial Population (Barlow Commission), *Minutes of Evidence* (1937), *passim*.

[123] Ministry of Labour, *Reports of Investigations into the Industrial Conditions in Certain Depressed Areas* (1934. Cmd. 4728), p. 136.

[124] *Industrial Surveys* of: *South Wales* (University College of South Wales and Monmouth, 1932); *Lancashire Area, excluding Merseyside* (University of Manchester, 1932); *Merseyside* (University of Liverpool, 1932); *North East Coast Area* (Armstrong College, 1932); *South West of Scotland* (University of Glasgow, 1932); J. Jewkes and A. Winterbottom, *An Industrial Survey of West Cumberland* (1933); also see Neil K. Buxton, 'Economic Growth in Scotland Between the Wars: the Role of Production Structure and Rationalisation', *Ec. Hist. Rev.* 33/4, 1980.

[125] Cmd. 4728, quoted above.

Under the Act, two Commissioners were appointed, one for the Scottish Special Area, and one for England and Wales, responsible for the other three Special Areas of South Wales and Monmouth, West Cumberland and Tyneside with part of Durham. At first their powers were very seriously limited as they were not simply to give relief, nor were they to supplement the grants of other departments, e.g. for roadmaking, or to give direct grants to concerns working for profit. As a result, though nearly £17 million had been spent on grants by September 1938, the benefits were negligible.

By then it had become clear that the old industries of the Special Areas would not revive, while the loss of the social capital represented by houses, public utilities and local communities through mass emigration could not be contemplated. The only feasible solution was the introduction of new industries into the Special Areas, and this became the official policy on the basis of two further Acts, the Special Areas Reconstruction (Agreements) Act of 1936, and the Special Areas (Amendment) Act of 1937. Further help was given by the Finance Act of 1937, which permitted the Treasury to remit the defence contribution of firms in the Special Areas.

Under the Act of 1936, Special Area Reconstruction Associations were set up, with a Treasury guarantee, to finance firms settling in those areas. This financial aid was supplemented in 1936 by the Nuffield Trust, and by the outbreak of war £$\frac{3}{4}$ million had been spent by SARAs and £2·2 million by the Trust. The Act of 1937 gave the Treasury authority to provide direct assistance to firms, and £1·1 million had been loaned under this part of the Act by 1939. The Commissioners, at the same time, were permitted to make contributions towards the rent, rate and tax payments of firms settling there, and to provide factories for letting.

This last was perhaps the most valuable of the powers granted, and led to the establishment of industrial estates. These had proved themselves in other parts of the country since the creation of the Trafford Park estate in 1894, which by 1939 had 200 works, employing 50,000 people. Other large and successful estates were at Slough and in Welwyn and Letchworth garden cities, all three in the outer ring of London suburbs, and Manchester and Liverpool Corporations were on the point of launching their own at Wythenshawe and Speke, respectively. On these and other estates the owners provided the land, the buildings and all services, such as power, light and roads. Industrialists renting a factory on an estate thus saved much of their capital costs, and had the further advantage that if their business expanded or declined, there were other factories of different sizes available. The Commissioners laid out large trading estates of this type in the Special Areas at Hillington, Treforest and Team Valley, providing by the outbreak of war employment for 1,600, 2,500 and 3,300 respectively, though they were still largely in the building stage. There were also minor schemes at Pallion (Sunderland), St Helens Auckland, Larkhall and Cyfarthfa, and employment for a total of 12,000 had been found by 1939.

These results, while gratifying, could scarcely be said to have made much impression on a surplus population in the Special Areas, variously estimated at between 200,000 and 400,000 insured workers with their families. Similarly, the transfer (assisted migration) scheme of the Ministry of Labour, undertaken on the recommendation of the Industrial Transfer Board in 1928, and the preference in placing Government orders, or the compulsory diversion of firms set up by foreigners, made only a negligible difference. In 1938, the gap in the unemployment percentages between them and the rest of the country was, if anything, wider than in 1934. It was only the re-armament boom of 1938–9, and the war-time and post-war revival of many of the staple industries, which brought new employment opportunities for the older centres of industry.

5 Agriculture

In the war years, agriculturists had found themselves in a sellers' market, and when unrestricted U-boat warfare began to threaten the food supply of these islands, the depleted labour force on the land was stretched to the utmost to produce the largest quantity of foodstuffs that the soil would yield. The Corn Production Act of 1917 gave farmers and farm workers the necessary security of prices and wages beyond the war years,[126] and the policy of deliberate encouragement of a high level of corn production was continued, largely for strategic reasons, by the Agriculture Act of 1920. This aided the farmers by guaranteeing minimum prices for wheat and oats, and the tenants by greater security of tenure, and spread some benefits to farm workers also by continuing the machinery of fixing agricultural wages. Since home supplies, even with the campaigns of 1917–19, still only formed a small proportion of food grains available to the British housewife, substantial aid could be given to British farmers at a relatively low cost to the consumer.

No sooner was the Agriculture Act on the statute book, however, than world grain prices began to crash down from their inflated post-war height. The emergency which the Act was designed to meet had arrived much sooner than expected. The wheat harvest sold at an average of 86s. 4d. a quarter in 1920, 49s. in 1921 and 40s. 9d. in 1922,[127] and it was estimated that the State would have to meet a bill of some £20 million under the guarantee laid down by the Act.[128] At this the Government took fright, and within a few months of their enactment, the price guarantees were repealed by the Corn Production (Repeal) Act of 1921. Wage fixing by the Agricultural Wages Board was also abolished and wage levels were reduced at once.

As world prices of foodstuffs continued to fall rapidly to 1923, and after an interval, again from 1926 onwards, British agriculture reverted to its pre-war trends. More and more farmers gave up their arable farming and concentrated on the products in which their proximity to the home markets outweighed the disadvantages of high rents and small fields: fruit, dairy produce and meat. With a rising standard of living, the consumption in the United Kingdom of all types of meat rose from an average of 48·6 m. cwt a year in 1920–2 to an average of 58·3 m. cwt in 1937–8, of eggs from 3,915 million to 9,385 million, of milk from 849 to 1,000 m. gallons and of butter from 4·1 to 10·0 m. cwt[129] These increases represented a considerable growth potential

---

[126] R. J. Hammond, 'British Food Supplies 1914–1939', *Econ. Hist. Rev.*, 16/1, 1946, p. 2.

[127] Jones and Pool, *A Hundred Years of Economic Development* (1959 ed.,) pp. 327–8.

[128] C. S. Orwin, *A History of English Farming* (1949), p. 84. Cf. p. 28 above.

[129] Richard Stone, *Measurement of Consumers' Expenditure* (Cambridge, 1954); Viscount Astor and B. Seebohm Rowntree, *British Agriculture* (1938), p. 3.

for British farming, but falling costs abroad and more efficient methods of packing, grading and preserving ensured that these former strongholds were now also under attack. The proportion of imported meat, dairy produce and vegetables was growing,[130] and agriculture again turned into a declining, and generally depressed, industry.

There were some scattered Government aid in the 1920s. After the heavy war fellings, the Forestry Commission was set up as early as 1919 to speed afforestation by buying or leasing land for planting and by assisting private and local authority owners, and by 1939 about 1 million acres had been acquired, including 120,000 acres of Crown land.[131] The pre-war encouragement of small holdings was continued, first by the Land Settlement (Facilities) Act of 1919, under which 17,000 ex-servicemen were settled on small farms, and then by the Small Holdings and Allotment Act of 1926 and the Agricultural Land (Utilization) Act of 1931.

In 1928 agricultural land and buildings were relieved of local rate burdens, and more generous credits were made available under the Agricultural Credit Act of 1928. The Agricultural Mortgage Corporation was established, financed by the banks, including the Bank of England, and by the Treasury; for Scotland, a similar Act was passed in 1929. These schemes, however, came up against the farmers' objection against mortgaging his property, and as they did not come into operation until 1930, when an agricultural slump of calamitous proportions had set in, while their money was raised at high rates just before the introduction of cheap money, they were not very effective. Lastly, the Agricultural Holdings Act of 1923 gave the tenant freedom of cropping and greater security of tenure, though it permitted his eviction for bad husbandry.[132]

The most significant Government gesture of the 1920s in aid of agriculture was the creation of a beet sugar industry, following continental models. In view of the large surplus capacity of the cane sugar plantations in the colonies and of the subsidized and experienced beet sugar industry in Europe, the British Sugar Subsidy Act of 1925 was passed, granting a subsidy for ten years, but of declining value, in the hope that at the end of the period the industry would be able to stand on its own legs. As a result, the acreage under sugar beet rose from virtually nothing to well over 350,000 over most of the 1930s,[133] while the crop provided employment for an additional 32,000 men in agriculture, beside others in the factories, and became a valuable source of cash to many farmers in the depression.

The costs, however, were substantial. The subsidies in the original ten years' period of 1925–34 amounted to £30 million, to which has to be added the sum of £10 million in abatement of excise duty; on renewal, the annual cost of the subsidy was about £3$\frac{1}{4}$ million. To justify this, the Government amalgamated the existing 18 factories into the British Sugar Corporation Ltd

---

[130] A. W. Flux, 'Our Food Supply Before and After the War', *J. R. Stat. S.*, 93/4, 1930, p. 541; E. M. Ojala, *Agriculture and Economic Progress* (1952), pp. 203, 209.

[131] E. P. Stebbing, 'The Forestry Commission in Great Britain', *Quarterly Review,* 256/508, 1931; Sir R. G. Stapledon, *The Land Today and Tomorrow* (1944 ed.), chapter 7; John Parker, 'The Forestry Commission', in W. A. Robson (ed.), *Public Enterprise* (1937).

[132] Aston and Rowntree, *op. cit.*, pp. 378 ff.

[133] Noel Deerr, *The History of Sugar*, vol. 2 (1950), pp. 481, 497.

in 1936, with a nominal capital of £5 million. Its chairman and two members of the Board were Government nominees, and while the subsidy continued, the profits of the Corporation were limited to 4% plus a declining proportion of any surplus beyond that level, the remainder to benefit the Treasury. The total subsidy was limited to 560,000 tons of white sugar, estimated to represent 375,000 acres. There was also a Sugar Commission appointed, to supervise research, education and other matters.[134]

Compared with this Government-sponsored development, the voluntary schemes organized by the farmers remained singularly ineffective or, like the hop growers', collapsed after only a short period.[135] These failures strengthened the growing belief that in agriculture, where innumerable producers competed freely with each other and usually with importers as well, organized marketing could survive only with the help of statutory compulsion.

Agricultural co-operation also made very little headway in Great Britain. The Agricultural Organization Society, founded in England in 1900 (a separate AOS was set up in 1905 in Scotland), was wound up in 1924 when it lost its Government subsidy. It was left to the National Farmers' Union to take English agricultural co-operation under its wing, a task which it performed without much enthusiasm.[136] The Welsh section of the AOS, which had separated from the mother society, survived, and even in England the demise of the AOS did not destroy the co-operative societies. By 1935 there were, apart from the small holding and allotment societies, about 230 co-operative societies in England, 81 in Wales and 88 in Scotland, with total sales of £12.6 million. Most of them were purchasing societies. Many of the remainder were organized to pack and sell co-operatively their members' produce, mainly eggs, dairy produce and meat.[137]

As the world depression spread in the early 1930s, most of the world's food, produced by farmers and peasants in conditions of inelastic supply, fell drastically in price and huge stocks accumulated in the food exporting countries, threatening further price falls and hampering any possibility of relief by curtailing production. Fertile overseas areas made productive in the war years were flooding the world with unwanted grain. The world stocks of wheat, which had averaged 635 million bushels in 1922–8, rose to a record of 900 million in 1931 and finally to 1,140 million in 1934. The index of wheat prices in Britain, taking 1911–13 as 100, fell from 130 in 1929 to 76 in 1931, that of barley from 125 in 1929 to 96 in 1932, and of oats from 125 in 1929 to 80 in 1933.[138]

In 1931 the Government abandoned free trade. Agriculture was turned into a highly protected, organized and subsidized sector of the economy, mainly by the Wheat Act of 1932, the Import Duties Act of 1932 and the Agricultural Marketing Acts of 1931 and 1933.

The Wheat Act provided the most direct subsidy. Producers were assured

---

[134] Heath and Hetherington, chapter 8; Plummer, *New Industries*, chapter 6/II.

[135] C. S. Orwin, 'Agriculture: Grain and other Crops', in *Britain in Depression*, pp. 100–1.

[136] C. R. Fay, *Co-operation at Home and Abroad*, vol. 2 (2nd ed., 1948), chapter 13.

[137] M. Digby, *Producers and Consumers* (1938), chapters 6–8; Horace Plunckett Foundation, *Agricultural Co-operation in England* (1930).

[138] Royal Institute of International Affairs, *World Agriculture* (1932).

of the 'standard guaranteed price' of 10s. a cwt, equivalent to 45s. a quarter, and if the market price fell below it the Government made up the difference to the growers in the form of a subsidy, up to a maximum of 27 m. cwt. By an ingenious provision, each grower was to be paid the average shortfall in price per cwt sold, so that those who sold at a higher than average price would keep their differential advantage. At the same time it was hoped that the limitation on the total crop to be subsidized would prevent a large expansion of wheat production in an overstocked world.

After 1933 wheat prices gradually began to rise from their slump levels, so that the deficit payments to British farmers declined sharply. The hope of limiting the acreage under wheat was not, however, fulfilled; it rose from 1·2 million acres to over 1·7 million in 1934 and the limit of 27 m. cwt was exceeded nearly every year; the Agriculture Act of 1937, in fact, raised the limit of the subsidized crop to 36 m. cwt.

Import duties under the Act of 1932 and under a special Act were at first applied to horticultural produce only, but were soon extended to oats and barley also. In view of the prosperous home market on his doorstep, protection was a particular boon to the farmer, and in 1937 it was supplemented by subsidies to growers.

The Agricultural Marketing Act of 1931 enabled two-thirds of the producers of any agricultural commodity to prepare a scheme for organized marketing, and with Parliamentary approval, this became compulsory on all. The only price control scheme set up under this Act was that of the Hop Marketing Board. Others found that the powers of collective marketing given under the Act of 1931 were insufficient. The Agricultural Marketing Act of 1933 added two new sets of powers. The organized producers were now authorized to control output as well as prices of their commodities, while the Government could add protection to any scheme that required it. On the basis of this formidable battery of powers, several schemes were organized with some differences of detail, but on the same basic principles.

The Potato Marketing Board, set up early in 1934, dealt with a crop which had little to fear from imports, except for 'earlies', but had suffered in the past from a highly variable yield as against a most inelastic demand. Of all the marketing schemes it was the most successful. It succeeded in stabilizing the acreage grown by a penal levy on excess acreage, it administered a quantitative control of imports from 1934 onwards, and it regulated the seasonal variations in supply by a simple method of control, the 'riddle': by varying the gauge of the riddle through which all potatoes had to pass before sale, it could vary the share of the crop sold for human consumption.

The Milk Marketing Boards, for England and Wales and for Scotland respectively, formed at the end of 1933, could build on earlier unofficial scheme organized since 1922 by the Permanent Joint Milk Committee. It had little to fear from imports, and could discriminate by charging more to liquid milk consumers, but the fall in world prices for dairy products in 1930 led farmers who had hitherto sold to manufacturers to invade the liquid milk market and threaten the dual scheme. In 1932 high tariffs were put on dairy products, but as imports from Empire countries were exempt, the British farmer was not much benefited thereby, and compulsory organization by the Milk Marketing Boards was thought necessary. The Boards controlled the

sales of all registered producers and maintained the dual price, or discriminatory monopoly, system. In 1933–4, for example, the average price for
liquid milk in England and Wales was 13·6*d.* per gallon, and for milk to
manufacturers, 5*d.* per gallon. The farmers, however, received uniform
prices according to the total sale of the regional 'pool'. The Boards were also
active in stimulating consumption and in grading and attesting 'accredited'
and 'attested' herds.[139]

The Bacon and Pig Marketing Boards, established in 1933, were the least
successful. Attempting to stimulate home production at the expense of
imports, they provided temporary Government loans but were unable to fill
the gap between rising demand and curtailed imports. Total bacon supplies,
for example, fell from 13·7 m. cwt in 1932 to 10·0 m. cwt in 1938. The main
result was a marked rise in prices to consumers. By 1936 the original scheme
had virtually broken down. Marketing schemes for other livestock proved to
be even more difficult to execute and had to be abandoned. Instead, severe
and diminishing quota restrictions were imposed on imports of meat from
non-Empire countries, and by the Cattle Industry (Emergency Provisions)
Act of 1934 large subsidy payments were made to home producers. In the
three years 1934–7 £11·4 million was paid out under this head.[140]

The massive State intervention in agriculture in the 1930s sketched here
reversed a policy of *laissez-faire* which was nearly a century old. It was criticized for keeping food prices needlessly high, for adding to the world glut in
food production, and for wasting money. The annual costs of agricultural
subsidies and protection in the 1930s were variously estimated at between £32
and £41 million;[141] including the additional costs of raising food at home
which could more cheaply have been bought abroad, it might well have been
£100 million. Even then, prices barely rose to levels at which British farmers
could make a profit: the index of agricultural prices, taking 1927–9 as 100,
fell as low as 77 in 1933, but even by 1937–9 had only crept back to $90–90\frac{1}{2}$.[142]
The Marketing Boards were criticized as mere elaborate excuses for protection and import restriction. Lastly, it was evident that Britain could not
simultaneously hope to benefit her home farmers and the Empire growers
whom she was pledged to support under the Ottawa Agreement of 1932.[143]

Even if it be accepted that in a world of rising tariffs, international commodity schemes, bilateral trade agreements and managed currencies, such as
the world of the 1930s had become, British agriculture alone could not be left
unprotected, it might, nevertheless, be pertinent to ask what results were
achieved by the drastic revision of British agricultural policy. It did not
change the general downward trend in British farming since the 1870s. The

---

[139] A. W. Ashby, 'The Milk Industry', in *Britain in Depression*, and 'The Milk Industry', in
Britain in Recovery; C. R. Fay, *Co-operation at Home and Abroad*, vol. 2 (2nd ed., 1948),
chapter 14. See, in general, H. T. Williams, *Principles for British Agricultural Policy* (1960),
chapter 2.

[140] A. W. Ashby, 'The Livestock and Meat Industry', in *Britain in Depression*, and 'The
Livestock and Meat Trade', in *Britain in Recovery*.

[141] R. J. Thompson, 'State Expenditure on Agriculture in Great Britain in 1938–9', *J. R.
Stat. S.*, 101/4, 1938, p. 737; Sir A. Daniel Hall, *Reconstruction and the Land* (1942), pp. 41–2.

[142] R. J. Thompson, 'The Future of Agriculture', *J. R. Stat. S.*, 106/1, 1943.

[143] Cf. esp. Astor and Rowntree, *passim*; R. J. Hammond, *op. cit.*, pp. 4–10.

flight from the land continued: employment in agriculture and forestry in the United Kingdom fell from an average of 1,004,000 in 1920-2 to an average of 735,000 in 1937-8, or from 6·3% to 3·9% of total employment, parallel with the decline of the contribution of agriculture to the national income from 6·1% to 3·5%.[144] Workers left the industry at the rate of 10,000 a year, and the exodus of the young men was particularly marked: the number of young male workers under 21 declined by 44% between 1921-4 and 1938.[145] By contrast, the number of farmers and members of their families working on their own farms declined but little.

The drift from the land had various causes. Low wages formed one of them. The Agricultural Wages (Regulation) Act introduced by the Labour Government in 1924 had succeeded in raising the relative level of agricultural wages, but in absolute terms they were still far below the industrial: thus in 1924 agricultural workers were paid an average of 28s. a week, builders' labourers 55s. 6d. and bricklayers 73s. 5d., while in 1936 the figures were still 32s. 4d., 52s. 2d. and 69s. 4d. In Scotland, statutory minimum wages had to wait until the Agricultural Wages (Regulation) (Scotland) Act of 1937.[146]

In addition to low wages, agricultural workers complained of long and irregular hours of work, poor opportunities for advancement, poor housing, the system of tied cottages, poor schools and few amenities. In 1939 it was estimated that only 25,000-30,000 of the 366,000 agricultural homesteads were served with electricity. The rural water supply was deficient in many areas, and as late as 1939 there were at least 5,186 parishes without a sewage system.[147]

Gross agricultural output in the 1920s was around the pre-war level and rose in the mid-1930s beyond it, stimulated by subsidies, protection and the buoyant home market.[148] This output was maintained in the face of a shrinking labour force by rising labour productivity: the output per person engaged in agriculture over the country as a whole was estimated to have risen by 20% between 1921 and 1941, or 1% per annum.[149] Partly these results were achieved by mechanization, such as the employment of combine harvesters, milking machines and tractors: there were 55,000 of the latter on British farms by 1939.[150] Agricultural research, starting with the Development Fund of £2 million in 1910, was greatly expanded.[151] Yields, pest control and farm management generally were greatly improved, though crop yield per acre (as

[144] Agatha L. Chapman and Rose Knight, *Wages and Salaries in the United Kingdom, 1920-1938* (Cambridge, 1953), pp. 18, 20; C. H. Feinstein, *National Income, Expenditure and Output of the United Kingdom, 1855-1965* (Cambridge, 1972), T. 26-7.

[145] *Report of the Committee on Land Utilization in Rural Areas (Scott Report)* (1942. Cmd. 6378), p. 16; Edgar Thomas, *Introduction to Agricultural Economics* (1949), p. 65.

[146] Astor and Rowntree, p. 313; Thomas, pp. 91-4.

[147] *Scott Report*, pp. 16-19.

[148] Astor and Rowntree, p. 53; C. H. Feinstein, T. 24-5; Leo Drescher, 'The Development of Agricultural Production in Great Britain and Ireland from the Early Nineteenth Century', and T. W. Fletcher, 'Drescher's Index, a Comment', in *Manchester School*, 23/2, 1955; E. M. Ojala, *Agriculture and Economic Progress* (1952), pp. 208-9.

[149] R. M. Carslaw and P. E. Graves, 'The Changing Organization of Arable Farms', in *Econ. J.*, 47/187, 1937; Thomas *op. cit.*, pp. 86-7.

[150] PEP, *Agricultural Machinery* (1949), p. 6.

[151] PEP, *Report on Agricultural Research in Great Britain* (1938).

distinct from output per worker) in England and Wales rose but little between the 10-year periods 1886–95 and 1926–35 while much marginal land had gone out of production in the interim. In Scotland, progress were more marked.[152]

The trend in the size of holdings was downward. Among all holdings in Great Britain over 5 acres, holdings over 300 acres in 1924–5 accounted for 3·9% and for 3·3% in 1939; those of 50–300 acres, for 38·6% and 34·4% respectively, and small holdings of 5–50 acres, for 57–5% and 62·3% respectively. It was not, in fact, certain whether large holdings were necessarily more efficient than small. It could not be denied that the yield per acre was much higher on the smaller holdings.[153]

The main trend of the pre-war years, the decline of arable, continued after the interruption of the war years. For Great Britain as a whole, it fell from 14·44 million acres in 1921–5 to 11·86 million in 1938, while permanent grass increased from 16·2 to 17·4 million acres and rough grazing, etc., from 14·5 to 16·1 million acres.[154] Livestock and livestock products remained by far the most important products of farming in Britain, accounting in 1937–8 for 70·5% of the value of output, with farm crops valued at 16·1% and horticultural products at 13·4%.[155] There was a considerable increase in market garden produce in the inter-war period to supply the growing and still sheltered markets of the cities, but even at the end of the period there were scarcely more than $\frac{1}{4}$ million acres under green vegetables.

There was one important respect in which a pre-war trend was reversed. The number of owner-occupied holdings rose substantially, from 10% in 1914 to over 20% in 1921 and 37% in 1927 in England and Wales, and there was a corresponding change in Scotland. The reasons included tax changes in war-time which favoured owner-occupancy compared with tenancy, a buying spree in 1919–20, and, after a lull in sales, renewed transfers to tenants in 1924–5, when a slight improvement in agricultural prices persuaded tenants that now was the time to buy, and landlords that now was the time to sell.[156] After 1925 the buying of land by tenants ceased. This was one of the most significant symptoms of decline, and of the deep depression which even the Government apparatus of protection and support of the 1930s could not fully stem.

6 Transport and Communications

The Railway Act of 1921 was a political compromise. Denying the clamour for nationalization after the war, it was designed to preserve the unified rates and charges over the whole country. The four main lines which emerged as a result of the Act were grouped partly with the aim of ensuring that each had its due share of revenue-earning and losing lines. The existing capital, including the compensation payable for neglected repairs and replacement,

[152] Hall, *op. cit.*, p. 93.

[153] R. L. Cohen, *The Economics of Agriculture* (1940), chapter 4; A. W. M. Kitchin, 'Small Holdings and the Agricultural Structure', *Econ. J.*, 44/176, 1934.

[154] L. Dudley Stamp and S. H. Beaver, *The British Isles* (1937 ed.), p. 153.

[155] Thomas, *op. cit.*, p. 11.

[156] S. G. Sturmey, 'Owner-Farming in England and Wales, 1900–1950' *Manchester School*, 23/3, 1955.

fixed at £60 million, was all converted into the new railway stock.

The four systems, the London and North Eastern Railway, the London Midland and Scottish Railway, the Great Western Railway and the Southern Railway, each covered a large region within which all competition ceased. To prevent the exploitation of this monopoly by the main lines, the Act laid it down, in the second place, that the railways were to provide reasonable service and that rates were to be fixed so as to secure to the companies a net revenue equivalent to the earnings of their constituent lines in 1913, plus an allowance for the capital invested since: the total sum thus arrived at was about £51 million per annum, allocated in fixed proportions among the companies. A Railway Rates Tribunal was set up to control rates on the new principle of securing this agreed total net revenue,[157] as well as keeping to the former principles of equity as between traders. At the same time Part III of the Act gave greater flexibility of charging by creating 21 classes of goods in place of the former eight.

In the third place, the Act established a permanent system of negotiation and conciliation with all grades of staff, in notable contrast with the pre-war refusal of the companies even to recognize the unions. There was a court of appeal in the form of the National Wages Board which included outside neutral nominees: 'Parliament', it was said, 'has definitely asserted the right to intervene to secure in the public interest harmony and co-operation in railway management.'[158] The system broke down in 1933, however, over a demand by the companies for a 10% reduction in pay, and new machinery was set up in 1935.

Lastly, the amalgamation of lines was expected to lead to great economies in running, and the Minister of Transport was authorized by Part II of the Act to require the companies to standardize their equipment and collaborate by common working, common use of rolling stock and similar means in the interest of economy. Estimates of possible economies varied from £4 million a year to £45 million.[159]

In sum, the Act of 1921, which dominated the history of railways in Britain until the outbreak of the Second World War, marked the end of an epoch. After almost a century of retreat from its original anti-monopoly position, the State had at last granted the railways the right to monopoly of transport in the interest of efficient working, but with the most stringent measures of control to protect the public at the same time. It was ironic that at the very moment when the long campaign for railway amalgamation and monopoly had at last been won, it should turn into a hollow victory by the rise of the motor vehicle, which represented more dangerous competition than ever one railway line had offered another.

[157] Sir Hubert Llewellyn Smith, *The Board of Trade* (1928), p. 142; C. I. Savage, *An Economic History of Transport* (1959), pp. 98–114; E. A. Pratt, *British Railways and the Great War* (1921), chapters 47, 48; C. E. R. Sherrington, *The Economics of Rail Transport in Great Britain*, vol. 1 (1928), pp. 251 ff.; Derek H. Aldcroft, *Studies in British Transport History 1870–1970* (Newton Abbot, 1974), pp. 125 ff.

[158] Sir W. M. Acworth, 'Grouping under the Railways Act, 1921', *Econ. J.*, 33/129, 1923, p. 19.

[159] Acworth, *loc. cit.*, p. 35; M. E. Dimock, *British Public Utilities and National Development* (1933), p. 80; H. J. Dyos and D. H. Aldcroft, *British Transport. An Economic Survey from the Seventeenth Century to the Twentieth* (Leicester, 1971), pp. 293–7, 308.

As a result, much of the Act became pointless if not directly harmful. The new system of fixing actual rates proved far too rigid in a period of falling costs and prices. Before long, 'exceptional' rates became the rule: by 1935, 84% of the tonnage carried, and 68·4% of gross receipts, came from exceptional rates; and in 1936 only 7% of passengers paid standard fares, the remainder travelling at reduced rates. The 'standard net revenue' of £51 million, beyond which the public was to share the benefits, was in fact never reached between the wars. Though there was no labour unemployment, the railways became a seriously depressed industry. In 1932, £260 million of their capital went without any dividend. While passenger traffic barely held its own, goods traffic fell from over 300 million tons in 1919–20 to 250–280 m.t. in most years in the 1930s.[160]

Apart from the vast nominal capital of the constituent companies, amounting to £1,085 million, which bore no relation to present or future earning power, and the special statutory restrictions to prevent the exploitation of their crumbling monopoly, the railways had three other sources of weakness in the inter-war years: their own inability to lose the monopoly mentality and to modernize and improve their working; the falling off of heavy mineral traffic, including coal and iron ore, owing to the depression; and the competition of the motor vehicle. These will be examined in turn.

The Royal Commission on Transport made one of the most severe criticisms on the first head. While making allowances for the grave post-war problems facing railway staffs, it believed

> that in the days of their monopoly the railways had in some way, insufficiently studied the needs of the public, and their policy had become utterly conservative. Although between the most important centres of population there were excellent services of trains . . . the passenger services generally were unnecessarily slow and often inconveniently timed . . . It is certainly remarkable that there has been practically no improvement in locomotive speed in this country during the last 80 years.[161]

Such a sweeping indictment was hardly fair. For one thing, there was some competition even between railways. For another, the railways' record of innovations was by no means negligible. Containers were introduced, easing the transport of fragile goods; railhead facilities were greatly improved; door-to-door services inaugurated. Electrification speeded up suburban services in the Manchester, Newcastle, Liverpool and London areas. The Southern Railway electrified its main line to Brighton and Worthing in 1933 and to Portsmouth, Reading, Maidstone and Chatham later in the 1930s. Diesel engines were put on shunting services and some passenger railcars were used by the GWR. From 1935 onward the main line companies began to introduce faster non-stop long-distance services, often with specially named trains: by 1938 there were 107 daily trains with average speeds of over

[160] H. M. Hallsworth, 'Rail Transport', in *Britain in Depression*, p. 193, and *Britain in Recovery*, pp. 286, 292; Savage, *op. cit.*, p. 114; Philip S. Bagwell, *The Transport Revolution from 1770* (1974), p. 255.

[161] Royal Commission on Transport, *Final Report: The Co-ordination and Development of Transport* (1931. Cmd. 3751), pp. 37–8.

60 m.p.h., compared with 25 in 1934 and 4 in 1914.[162] All this in spite of the difficulty of raising capital for a declining industry from the market or its own surpluses, leading to actual disinvestment on the railways in the inter-war years.[163]

The falling off in mineral traffic, caused by the decline in the production of coal, iron and steel, was bound to hit the railways more than any other means of traffic. In 1936, for example, coal accounted for $177\frac{1}{2}$ million tons of the total railway goods traffic of 281 million tons; in 1913 the railways had still carried $225\frac{1}{2}$ m.t. of coal and coke, and as late as 1929 it had still been 207 m.t.[164] Road transport did not compete in this field, and did not suffer by this decline.

Basically, however, the railways were in decline because of the rise of road motor transport, growing particularly fast from about 1926 onward: indeed, much of the traffic lost in the strike of that year was lost permanently. By 1933–5, the main lines had lost an estimated one half of their traffic to the roads.[165] Among the railways' weaknesses imposed by law was a rigid and publicized rate structure: their competitors' rates were neither, and when in competition, could always be reduced just below the railway rates. The railways were obliged to charge so much a mile to passengers; bus and coach fares tapered with distance, and thus became the more attractive, the longer the journey. In the case of goods, the railway charges depended in part on the value of the cargo, while road haulage charges depended only on size and ease of handling; thus the more valuable cargoes tended to travel by road, and for both passengers and goods the roads skimmed off the cream and the railways were left with the less desirable traffic. Further, they had to run services between the less populous centres, and they had to accept all traffic, while the road haulier, knowing the railway rate, could overcharge for any load he did not want to carry.

As difficulties increased, the railways were relieved of some of their handicaps. In 1928, they were given powers to run road passenger vehicles, and within two years had invested $£9\frac{1}{2}$ million, mostly in joint omnibus undertakings with road companies. In 1934 they absorbed Carter Paterson and Pickford's, the leading road cartage contractors. The derating of railway property to the extent of 75% provided the companies with a freight rebates fund. In 1930 and 1933, the competing road vehicles were also restricted by legislation; and finally, in 1939 they were promised the repeal of many of their rate restrictions.[166] In spite of the triumphant advance of road transport, the railways were still by far the most important conveyers of good and merchandise; in 1939, they carried 265 million tons of freight, compared with 100 m.t. by road and under 50 m.t. by canal and coastal shipping; and though the 4,526 million passengers carried by road greatly outnumbered the 1,237 million carried by rail, they were carried over shorter distances.[167]

[162] Hallsworth, in *Britain in Recovery,* pp. 294–5; Jones and Pool, *A Hundred Years of Economic Development*, p. 354.

[163] The disinvestment has been estimated at £125 million in the 19 years 1920–38. Bagwell, *Transport Revolution*, p. 255.

[164] Gilbert Walker, *Road and Rail* (1947 ed.), p. 20.

[165] *Ibid.*, p. 128.

[166] Gilbert Walker, *op. cit.*, p. 233; M. R. Bonavia, *The Economics of Transport* (1954 ed.), pp. 200–1.

[167] Savage, *op. cit.*, p. 175.

The motor vehicle, however, had captured a firm place in modern society. As a goods vehicle, it was more flexible in door to door deliveries and in supplying the distributive trade. In the case of public passenger service, motor vehicles rapidly replaced all other forms of the town omnibus, the 'stage carriage' of official terminology, and were also turned into 'express carriages', i.e. long-distance coaches, and 'contract carriages', or coaches hired as a whole. Meanwhile, the private motor car and motor cycle gave a new freedom of movement to its owners and diverted traffic from both trams and buses, as well as creating much new traffic. All these had been in their infancy in 1914; they appeared to sweep all before them in the inter-war years.

In 1914, the total number of motor vehicles licensed was 389,000. By 1939 there were over 3 million motor vehicles on the road, of which 2 million were private cars.[168] The motor car had become the normal means of transport for the middle classes, just as the motor goods vehicle had become indispensable to many businesses. Both vehicles and their fuel became large-scale sources of taxation: direct taxation yielded £1$\frac{1}{2}$ million in 1920 and £34$\frac{1}{2}$ million in 1937, while net fuel tax and import duty receipts rose from £5 million to £46$\frac{1}{2}$ million in the same period. Expenditure on the roads rose from £26$\frac{1}{2}$ milion in 1920 to £65$\frac{1}{2}$ million in 1930. The mileage of class 1 and 2 roads rose from 38,000 in 1924 to 44,000 in 1937, but the mileage of unclassified roads fell in the same period by some 4,600, so that the net addition was only 1,600 miles. The Trunk Roads Act of 1936 transferred the trunk roads outside London and the County Boroughs and large Burghs wholly to the Ministry of Transport. The number of motor vehicles per mile of road rose from 0·8 in 1909 to 7·5 in 1924 and to 16·4 in 1937.[169]

Legislation to cope with this kind of traffic increase limped behind in the 1920s. The three main statutes affecting road traffic were passed in the 1930s. The Road Traffic Act of 1930 included the abolition of general speed limits for private cars and compulsory insurance against third party risks. The Road Traffic Act of 1934 introduced provisions for a 30 m.p.h. limit in built-up areas, a driving test, and powers to establish pedestrian crossings, amending also the Act of 1933.

The remainder of the Act of 1930 dealt with the regulation of road passenger transport, largely on the lines laid down by the second report of the Royal Commission on Transport.[170] Up to that time, the bus and coach services outside London had grown up virtually without control. In rural areas, some 5,000 operators of one or two vehicles each continued to function, having in 1931 20% of the existing buses between them. At the other end of the scale, the Tillings Group together with the two other large 'associated' groups, British Electric Traction and Scottish Motor Traction, controlled some 40% of the buses in the country. Tillings' came to an agreement in 1929 with the railway companies to share any bus company in which both were

---

[168] Savage, *op. cit.*, pp. 96, 142; L. F. Duval, 'The Motor Industry', in *Britain in Recovery*, p. 317.

[169] Duval, *loc. cit.*, pp. 312–15; K. G. Fenelon, 'The Road Transport Industry', in *Britain in Depression*, p. 213.

[170] R. C. on Transport, *Second Report, The Licensing and Regulation of Public Service Vehicles* (1929. Cmd. 3416).

interested, in equal holdings. Many municipalities had also acquired powers to run their own bus services, either jointly with private companies or alone, and in 1929 there were 100 such, operating 4,700 buses.[171]

The Act of 1930 introduced a strict system of control of public service vehicles with the dual objective of providing full and co-ordinated public regular services, and of protecting existing operators against competition by newcomers. The newly established Traffic Commissioners had powers to grant licences to bus operators and to regulate conditions of service, including the fares to be charged. In addition, vehicles had to meet various safety and other requirements before receiving a licence. In the event, the Commissioners interpreted their duties rigidly, giving preference to the 'prior' service and strongly discouraging new services. As a result, broadly speaking, the general structure and even the fare system of road passenger transport were frozen in the position they had reached in 1930, except that amalgamations still remained possible.[172] The Act also laid down conditions of service for drivers and conductors, including a system of licensing of drivers, maximum hours of work, and a 'fair wages clause'. While the regulation of hours was fairly well enforced, the attempt to control wages was not successful.

The other important measure relating to road transport was the Road and Rail Traffic Act of 1933, which regulated the carrying of goods on the road, and attempted to co-ordinate road and rail traffic. Part I established a licensing system for goods vehicles, operated by the existing Traffic Commissioners. The granting of 'A' and 'B' licences (for carriers wholly or partly for reward) was handled perhaps even more restrictively than the licensing of passenger vehicles, so that existing operators were even more secure from competition, and the numbers of vehicles on 'A' and 'B' licences actually fell in the years following the Act. 'C' licences for firms carrying their own goods continued to increase very rapidly.

There were also, as in the earlier Act for passenger vehicles, regulations as to speed limits and the condition of vehicles, and there were clauses relating to the hours of work of drivers and to their wages. Ultimately, joint boards were established and the Minister of Labour was given power to determine wages by order under the Road Haulage Wages Act of 1938. Part II of the Act referred to railway rates.[173] Unlike the public service companies, firms in the road haulage industry remained small: even in 1938, the average number of vehicles among 'A' licence holders was three, and 85% of operators had fewer than five.[174]

The only thoroughgoing scheme of co-ordination was that applied to the passenger transport of the Metropolis. London was served by main line and suburban railways, by Metropolitan and underground railways, by trams, buses and, later, trolley buses, belonging to many different companies. From 1922 onward more intense competition and the practices of 'chasing', racing

[171] Savage, *op. cit.*, chapter 6.

[172] D. N. Chester, *Public Control of Road Passenger Transport* (Manchester, 1936), pp. 50, 87; Aldcroft, *British Transport History*, pp. 187–207.

[173] J. R. Sargent, *British Transport Policy* (Oxford, 1958), p. 43.

[174] Savage, *op. cit.*, p. 136; Alfred Plummer, *New British Industries in the Twentieth Century* (1937), chapter 3/I.

and boxing in buses of rival companies had become an inconvenience, as well as a danger, to the public. There were by 1924 nearly 500 independent vehicles running in London, besides those of the London General,[175] while outlying districts were left without any service at all.

The London Traffic Act of 1924, following a strike of tramwaymen and omnibus workers, created a powerful apparatus of control by the Minister and the licensing authority over London buses. As a result, most of the independent bus proprietors combined and in 1927 formed the London Public Omnibus Company, which quickly came to an agreement with the dominant firm, the London General. Lord Ashfield, the forceful chairman of the Underground Group, itself an amalgamation which included the London General Omnibus Co., pointed to the need for the extension of the electric and underground systems to the suburbs, but before these were built, demanded an assurance that no duplicate lines would be permitted. In 1928 the Underground, the Metropolitan and the main line railways decided to pool their London revenues, and complete unification followed the Act of 1933.

Under it, the London Passenger Transport Board took over the property of 5 railway companies (excluding the main lines), 17 tramway undertakings (including 14 municipally owned) and 66 bus companies, plus parts of 69 other companies, to run them as a unified service and as a monopoly in London and a region about 30 miles from Charing Cross, except for the four main line railway companies, with which all the Metropolitan revenues were pooled. The members of the Board were appointed by a panel of trustees of public standing, and were thus made as far as possible independent of outside influence, except that the stockholders (many of whom were private persons) had the power to put in an official Receiver if certain minimum rates on the capital were not paid. The LPTB stock amounted to £109 million on inception, and in 1936 the Board employed some 72,000 persons.[176]

British shipping suffered from the shortage of world demand in relation to supply. Within the world total, the British share fell, in part because British owners tended to be conservative, and were less willing than owners in other high-wage countries, like the Netherlands, Germany or Scandinavia, to switch to oil-firing or diesel motors which could reduce costs.

Even in the 1920s freights tumbled from an index of 374 in 1920 to 166 in 1921, falling further to 115 in 1929. Tramp freights fell even faster, from 602 in March 1920 to 141 in 1921 and 106 in 1929.[177] World tonnage was expanding, while trade rose but little and between 1929 and 1932 actually fell from 130 to 97 (1913 = 100). As a result British tonnage laid up rose from 630,000 g.t. in 1929 to 3,610,000 g.t. in 1932, and large fleets were sold to foreign flags, presumably to compete with the remaining British tonnage either with the aid of subsidies, or lower wage costs, or both. Tramp freight rates suf-

---

[175] London Transport (publ.), *London General – The Story of the London Bus, 1856–1956* (1956).

[176] T. C. Barker and Michael Robbins, *A History of London Transport*, vol. 2, *The Twentieth Century* (1974), chapter 15.

[177] C. E. Fayle, *The War and the Shipping Industry* (1927), chapter 25 and Table 2, p. 415; L. Isserlis, 'Shipping', in *Britain in Depression*, p. 239; Dyos and Aldcroft, *British Transport*, pp. 376–96.

fered particularly heavily, falling in 1933-5 to somewhere below three-quarters of the already low level of 1929.[178] As a counter-measure, the British Government introduced subsidies to tramp vessels in Part I of the British Shipping (Assistance) Act of 1935. A Tramp Shipping Subsidy Committee was to administer this part of the Act; at the same time, the Tramp Shipping Administrative Committee was to encourage the industry to reorganize and eliminate competition. It was successful to the extent of aiding the setting up of minimum freight schemes, including foreign tonnage, for the grain trade from Australia, Canada and the Argentine to Europe. The 'scrap and build' subsidy under Part II of the Act was noted above.[179]

Liner companies with their large resources, and the regular incoming payments of mail and other contracts, as well as their well organized 'rings' to keep up freights, found it easier than tramps to withstand the slump; nevertheless, several groups only survived by amalgamation. About one-quarter of the British tonnage, i.e. one-half of the liner tonnage, came under the control of the 'Big Five' – the P & O, Royal Mail, Cunard, Ellerman and Furness-Withy groups.[180] Of these, the Royal Mail group, an £80 million concern controlling the largest merchant fleet in the world, collapsed early in 1931, the whole of the ordinary capital of the company being lost.[181] Only the Cunard Company received a subsidy, on condition that it amalgamated with the White Star line (which in 1927 had been acquired by the Royal Mail group). It took the form of a loan on very easy terms to finance the construction of two new giant liners for regular transatlantic service, the *Queen Mary*, on which work had begun and had been suspended, and the *Queen Elizabeth*.

From 1936 onward freight rates began to rise. British and world tonnage had been allowed to run down, and prosperity at home raised the weight of imports, which had fallen from $60\frac{1}{2}$ million tons in 1929 to 52 m.t. in 1932, again to over 75 m.t. by 1937. Exports, however, did not recover, largely because of the lagging sales of coal, and this, in turn, forced British shipping to make outward journeys in ballast and deprived it of one of its main competitive advantages.[182]

The heavier-than-air craft had proved itself in military missions during the war, and in August 1919 two air services to Paris began in tiny ramshackle planes. Several other companies followed, but apart from providing the main airports and navigational aids under the Air Navigation Act of 1920, the British Government refused to subsidize these services. Unable to withstand the competition of the heavily subsidized foreign aircraft, the British companies folded up one by one, and for a time, in 1921, there was not a single commercial airline left in this country. The strategic importance of civil aviation could not, however, be ignored for long, and there followed subsidies to ultimately four companies amalgamated into a single company,

[178] L. Isserlis, 'Tramp Shipping Cargoes and Freights', *J. R. Stat. S.*, 101/1, 1938, pp. 78–9, 94.

[179] p. 71 above.

[180] C. E. Fayle, *A Short History of the World's Shipping Industry* (1933), p. 298.

[181] *Economist*, 7.2.1931, pp. 299–300.

[182] Peter Duff, *British Ships and Shipping* (1949), p. 21.

'Imperial Airways', in 1924.[183] Starting with 13 small aircraft with a total seating capacity of 112, and a staff of 260, it quickly proved technically successful, and opened up new routes to India, the Far East, South Africa and Australia, experimenting, in 1937–9, with transatlantic flights also. By 1939, it had a fleet of 77 aircraft of 191,000 h.p. and a staff of 3,500, but financially it was still dependent on the Government.[184]

Services to Europe were neglected by Imperial Airways and by 1935, 19 private companies operated 76 services within the British Isles, though that number was later reduced.[185] In that year, British Airways, a merger of three companies, was also given a subsidy, together with a monopoly of services to Berlin and Scandinavia and a share in the lucrative London–Paris route. With rising subsidies both companies soon showed high profits, and the British Overseas Airways Act, passed in August 1939, bought out the former shareholders and nationalized the property. BOAC came into operation after the outbreak of war, in November.

Telephones had been slow to get off the ground in Britain. There was much muddle and inefficiency, and with only 700,000 subscribers in 1912, when the system was nationalized and handed over to the Post Office, the proportion of the population linked up was far smaller than in most other civilized countries. The number of subscribers reached 1 million at the beginning of 1922, 2 million in 1932 and $3\frac{1}{4}$ million in 1939. The only special effort made to extend the service was the offer of subsidized terms to rural subscribers, and these greatly encouraged the spread of the telephone into the countryside.[186] By contrast, the British Post Office letter service remained second to none and was enormously expanded in 1919–39. Among its technical innovations in this period were the special electric underground railway, authorized in 1913 but completed only in 1927, linking six sorting offices and two main line stations by $6\frac{1}{2}$ miles of line below some of London's busiest streets, and the air mail service. The first regular air mail contract began in 1926 (on the Egypt-Karachi section of the Indian route), and by 1935, 19 million letters were sent by air mail.[187] The telegraph service, however, declined to about half its volume between 1920 and 1940, driven out by the telephone on the one hand, and wireless communication on the other.

The original commercial application of wireless telegraphy, following Marconi's first English radio patent of 1896, was to link ships with the shore and with each other. The Marconi International Marine Communication Co. Ltd, formed in 1900, dominated the field here by controlling most of the necessary patents, though there were some rival companies.[188] There followed radio communication between fixed points which was of similar

[183] A. J. Quin-Harkin, 'Imperial Airways, 1924–40', *J. Transport History*, 1/4, Nov. 1954; E. Birkhead, 'The Financial Failure of British Air Transport Companies 1919–24, *ibid.*, 4/3, May 1960.

[184] Sir Osborne Mance and J. E. Wheeler, *International Air Transport* (1944), pp. 45–6;

[185] Plummer, *New Industries*, chapter 3/II; Aldcroft, *British Transport History*, pp. 208–25.

[186] Sir Evelyn Murray, *The Post Office* (1927), chapter 8; Arthur Hazlewood, 'The Origin of the State Telephone System in Britain', *Oxf. Econ. P.*, NS, 5/1, 1953.

[187] Howard Robinson, *The British Post Office, a History* (Princeton, N J, 1948), chapter 30.

[188] S. G. Sturmey, *The Economic Development of Radio* (1958), chapter 3; H. E. Hancock, *Wireless at Sea* (1951).

potential strategic importance. The contract to link up various parts of the Empire was also ultimately award to Marconi's in 1913, but no stations had been built by the outbreak of war.

The need of war called forth important technical improvements, and innumerable signallers were trained who were, in the 1920s, to play a major part as 'hams' or amateur radio enthusiasts. After the war, imperial radio links were demanded more urgently than ever but Britain remained without intercontinental radio links as late as 1924. In that year, Marconi's announced a revolutionary discovery, the 'beam', or directed short wave transmission. The invention forced the hands of the Post Office. Marconi's received the Imperial contract and, by 1928, 'beam' links had been established with Canada, South Africa, India and Australia. At the same time, the Post Office opened its own valve transmitter at Rugby, then the most powerful in the world, for radio telephony.

The two separate services, the cable systems and the wireless stations, were compulsorily amalgamated after the Imperial Wireless and Cable Conference of 1928, and the Post Office was forced to lease to the resulting organization its own beam station, which it finally made over in 1938. Cables and Wireless had some of the attributes of a Public Corporation: its rates and services were scrutinized by an official Advisory Committee, its distribution of profits was limited in the public interest, and two of the directors, including the chairman, had to be approved by the Government. But compared with other Public Corporations formed at that time, the shareholders' interests were more powerfully represented, and the deals shaping its financial structure more doubtful.[189]

Wireless broadcasting, as distinct from point-to-point communication, was entirely a post-war development. The idea of public information and entertainment arose in the USA as a by-product of an advertisement campaign by the Westinghouse Company in Pittsburgh. By the time broadcasting was considered in Britain in 1922, the adverse American experience made with unregulated competing stations, and the Post Office preference for monopoly ensured general approval for the decision that broadcasting, when established in this country, would be a monopoly controlled in the public interest.[190]

It was handed over to a consortium of the six principal wireless equipment makers, united as the 'British Broadcasting Company', which other manufacturers ultimately also joined. The BB Co. was given all the manufacturing patent rights and its income was derived from the heavy royalties charged on each receiving set sold and from a share of the receiving licences, issued by the Post Office. The large manufacturers were additionally rewarded with the restriction of receiving licences to British-made sets only, at a time when foreign-made sets were generally both cheaper and better. The BB Co., using some of the existing stations of the Marconi Co., which had begun regular broadcasting in 1922, started its regular services in 1923. At the end of 1922

---

[189] Sturmey, *op. cit.*, chapters 4–6; Dimock, *op. cit.*, chapter 4; H. F. Heath and A. L. Hetherington, *Industrial Research and Development in the United Kingdom* (1946), pp. 209 ff.
[190] Lincoln Gordon, *The Public Corporation in Great Britain* (1938), chapter 4.

there had been 36,000 licences issued; at the end of 1924, there were 1,130,000; at the end of 1926, when the BB Co.'s existence ended, the number had risen to 2,178,000.

From the first, the broadcasting company and its programmes were dominated by the General Manager, J. C. W. (later Lord) Reith, who imposed on it a distinct shape which also influenced the structure and objectives of other Public Utility Corporations in this country. In Reith's view, the company was to be a monopoly established under the auspices of the State, but not subject to day-to-day public control; it was not to be run to make profits, but to provide a public service, with a conscious social purpose. It held a stewardship to contribute 'constantly and cumulatively to the intellectual and moral well-being of the community', with idealism playing a part, 'perhaps a determining part'.[191]

Reith succeeded in imposing his conceptions on the two official committees of inquiry into broadcasting, the Sykes Committee of 1923 and the Crawford Committee of 1925. When the extended licence of the BB Co. expired at the end of 1926, the British Broadcasting Corporation, formed according to the new conception of a Public Corporation, took it over. Its Governors, though appointed by the Government, were not responsible to it; and operating within a secure income of licence fees, it was not in need of revenue from advertisers or others. 'Those directing the policy of the Corporation were not influenced by the profit motive. They were not interested in the material welfare of the Corporation; their interest was in the intellectual and ethical welfare of the listeners'.[192]

Broadcasting did indeed become a major influence on the information, on the political and other views, the culture and entertainment of modern nations. By the end of 1929, there were almost 3 million licence holders in Britain and at the end of 1938 nearly 9 million, or the large majority of homes in this country. The Corporation ultimately broadcast two complete sets of programmes, one national and one for the seven regions.[193]

Television was based on scientific discoveries made before 1900, especially the reactions of the selenium cell and the cathode ray tube, but it was not until the 1920s that television broadcasting was seriously considered as a commercial proposition. In Britain the main initiative came from J. L. Baird and his sponsoring companies. The system ultimately adopted was based on the experiments made with a cathode ray tube by V. K. Zworykin in America in 1931 and developed here by the Marconi-EMI combine. The BBC turned to it in 1937, providing the only regular television broadcasts anywhere before the war, received by an estimated 20,000 sets by 1939.[194]

7 New Forms of Industrial Organization

The earlier sections of this chapter contain numerous references to new forms of business organization and to a greatly extended range of functions of the

[191] M. E. Dimock, *Public Utilities,* p. 268; R. H. Coase, *British Broadcasting, a Study in Monopoly* (1950), chapter 3.

[192] Coase, *op. cit.*, p. 118; Asa Briggs, *The History of Broadcasting in the United Kingdom,* vol. 1 (1961); J. C. W. Reith, *Into the Wind* (1949), Part 2.

[193] Sturmey, *op. cit.*, chapters 8, 9.

[194] Sturmey, *op. cit.*, chapter 10.

Government and other public authorities in industry, agriculture and transport. These developments were evidence of a new attitude towards economic policy and represent a distinct phase in the economic development of this country.[195]

The paid-up capital of registered joint-stock companies with limited liability, the typical form of industrial enterprise, rose from £$2\frac{1}{2}$ billion in April 1914 to £4·1 billion at the end of 1921 and to over £6 billion in 1938.[196] The large increase between 1914 and 1921 reflected in part the share boom of 1919–20 in which capital was increased by watering, by the ploughing back of the results of war-time profiteering and by speculative promotion[197] but throughout the inter-war period the expansion of genuine joint-stock enterprise continued and many of the remaining individually owned firms and partnerships were converted to the joint-stock form of organization. By 1938 the partnership or the individual trading on his own had become very exceptional in industry, though they still persisted in retail distribution, in agriculture, in the professions and in a few other sectors. The share of joint-stock enterprise in the economy is difficult to estimate: according to the tax returns, it obtained about 85% of the profits of manufacturing industry in the late 1930s.[198]

The number of public joint-stock companies on the register actually declined in this period, but at the same time there was a large increase in the number of private companies, the typical form of organization of the family firm. In 1938, while the private companies outnumbered the public companies by ten to one, they had an aggregate capital of only £1,900 million, compared with the £4,100 million of the latter.[199]

A large share of industry and transport was, even in the 1920s, not controlled by private enterprise at all, but by various types of public or non-profit-making organizations, and their growth is one of the most significant aspects of the period. Among the most important of them were the co-operative societies, registered under the Industrial and Provident Societies Acts, and the building societies, registered under the Building Society Acts; enterprises administered by charitable, educational and similar bodies; local authorities, administering over one-third of the gas works, two-thirds of electricity supplies, four-fifths of water supplies and of tramway mileage, virtually all the trolley-bus systems as well as a large proportion of omnibus and other services. There were, further, *ad hoc* authorities such as dock and harbour boards, including those of London, Liverpool and Glasgow, and the Metropolitan Water Board, established in 1902; companies established by Act of Parliament, mainly in the public utility field, including the railways; enterprises administered directly by the State, including the Post Office, the dockyards, and the Crown Lands; and the Public Corporations. In 1928 the Liberal Industrial Inquiry found that the capital administered by these

---

[195] W. Ashworth, *An Economic History of England, 1870–1939* (1960), chapter 15.

[196] Balfour Committee, *Survey of Industries*, vol. 1 (1927), p. 125; A. Beacham, *Economics of Industrial Organization* (3rd ed., 1955), p. 6.

[197] H. W. Macrosty, 'Inflation and Deflation in the United States and the United Kingdom, 1919–1923', *J. R. Stat. S.*, 90/1, 1927, pp. 70–2.

[198] P. Sargant Florence, *The Logic of British and American Industry* (1953), p. 170.

[199] A. B. Levy, *Private Corporations and their Control*, vol. 1 (1950), sections 18 and 20.

authorities came to about £4 billion (including £1¼ billion for roads and £1·15 billion for railways) and was thus of the same order of magnitude as the aggregate capital of all joint-stock companies. Public property as a proportion of total property was estimated to have risen from 6–8% in 1911–13 to 8–12% in 1932–4.[200]

The extension of the joint-stock type of organization was, from the beginning, associated with the need for large sums of capital, and it proceeded fastest in industries composed of large firms and using much capital per worker. Technical needs and market conditions favoured the large unit in this period, and the typical form of organization changed with the increase in the typical size of the firm. In one industry after another the family firm gave way to the registered company with its numerous and anonymous shareholders and its elected Board of Directors.

By the end of the 1930s, one of the consequences of this development, the divorce of ownership from control, had become very marked. In most of the larger companies the proportion of the shares held by any single holder (or indeed by the Board) had become insignificant and there were thousands, and even tens of thousands of shareholders; large holders were often found to be not individuals but other companies. Thus a relatively small holding might dominate a company in view of the scattered nature of the rest of the holdings, and this might mean 'government by bloc-holder', but more commonly left control in the hands of a self-perpetuating Board of Directors who were administering an institution rather than their own property.[201] As Keynes noted

> When this stage is reached, the general stability and reputation of the institution are more considered by the management than the maximum of profit for the shareholders . . . .This is particularly the case if their great size or semi-monopolistic position renders them conspicuous in the public eye.[202]

Moreover, as was noted in 1939,

> The increasing dominance of industry by combines and cartels has given a further twist to the meaning of ownership. It is becoming less a right to draw a share in the profits, and more a right to draw dividends in perpetuity – the factor of risk, the short-term risk at least, is declining. Absentee ownership, as Veblen has called it, is no longer at the mercy of competition.[203]

In Britain that development might have been slower than elsewhere[204], but even here an increasing proportion of workers was to be found in large firms. By 1935 there were three industries in which more than half the workers

---

[200] Liberal Industrial Inquiry, *Britain's Industrial Future* (1928), chapter 6; Balfour Committee, *Survey of Industries*, vol. 2 (1928), chapter 8; H. Campion, *Public and Private Property in Great Britain* (1939), chapter 5.

[201] E.g. P. Sargant Florence, 'The Statistical Analysis of Joint-Stock Company Control', *J. R. Stat. S.*, 110/1, 1947; also his *Logic*, pp. 176 ff., and *Ownership, Control and Success of Large Companies* (1961).

[202] J. M. Keynes, 'The End of Laissez-Faire' (1924), in *Essays in Persuasion* (1931), pp. 314–15.

[203] M. Compton and E. H. Bott, *British Industry* (1940), p. 128.

[204] Alfred D. Chandler, 'The Growth of the Transnational Industrial Firm in the United States and the United Kingdom: A Comparative Analysis', *Ec. Hist. Rev.* 33/3, 1980, pp. 401–2, 408–9.

employed worked in *plants* employing 1,000 workers or more (electrical machinery, motor and cycle manufacturing and iron and steel rolling and smelting) and in a further four industries (silk and art silk, newspaper production, shipbuilding and sugar and sugar confectionery) over 40% did so. The proportions of workers in plants employing 500 and over varied from 58·4% to 83·5% in these seven industries. All told, of about 5·2 million workers in the industries enumerated by the Census of Production, 21·5% worked in *plants* employing 1,000 and over, and another 13·9% in plants employing 500–999 workers. The proportion working in *firms* employing 1,000 and over was 31·2% in 1935; and those in firms employing 500–999, 13·3%, i.e. nearly half the labour force was to be found in firms employing 500 workers and over.[205]

Even this does not show fully the extent of industrial concentration, for many firms, while nominally independent, were being combined frequently in their own, but sometimes even in quite different industries in complex ways inadequately described as 'lateral' or 'diagonal' integration. The links between the firms forming a group were sometimes economic or technical, but often they were little more than financial. Holding companies or subsidiaries were the most common means of control, but there were also interlocking capital holdings, frequently unknown to the public, and interlocking directorates. In 1936 it was found that among a sample of 623 directors of large firms with capitals of over £500,000 each, only 25% held single directorships. No fewer than 81 (13%) held 10 or more.[206]

In their pioneer study[207] Leak and Maizels, using the Census of Production of 1935, found that 55% of all workers enumerated, or just under 4 million, worked in 'units' (i.e. industrial groups) employing 500 men or over. Among the most highly concentrated trade groups were mining and quarrying (89%), public utilities (78%), engineering, shipbuilding and vehicles (67%), iron and steel, chemicals (both 59%), food, drink and tobacco (50%) and textiles (49%). Sub-groups with specially high proportions of employees in units of 500 and over included blast furnaces (92%), aircraft (91%), coal mines (94%), tramways (94%), tobacco (88%), biscuits (82%), iron and steel rolling and melting (87%) and railways (100%). Nearly 1·7 million workers worked in the 135 largest units employing 5,000 each or over and producing 44·5% of the gross output. Equally telling was the share held by the three largest units in any one industry, as a measure of concentration: there were no fewer than 33 trades in which the largest three units accounted for 70% of the total employment or more.[208] According to a different calculation, the share of the largest 100 companies in manufacturing net output rose from 17% in 1919 to 23% in 1939.[209]

[205] Florence, *Logic*, pp. 24, 34.

[206] Florence, 'Joint-Stock Company Control', p. 14, and *Ownership*, chapter 4; J. M. Rees, *Trusts in British Industry, 1914–1921* (1922), pp. 28, 31, 71 ff.; H. Levy, *The New Industrial System* (1936), § 20.

[207] H. Leak and A. Maizels, 'The Structure of British Industry', *J. R. Stat. S.*, 108/1–2, 1945.

[208] P. E. Hart and S. J. Prais, 'The Analysis of Business Concentration: A Statistical Approach', *J. R. Stat. S.*, 119/2, 1956.

[209] Leslie Hannah, *The Rise of the Corporate Economy* (1976), p. 216.

Concentration of industry has often been equated with monopolistic control. The mere growth in the size of firms need not, however, by itself restrict competition, nor was the motive of the organizers necessarily the monopolistic control of markets. In part, it derived from the technical and economic advantages of size, aided also by the contemporary revolution in office equipment and administrative techniques. In part it was the new mass consumers' markets and efficient means of transport and distribution to supply them, which called forth mass production by single large firms. New industries especially, including electrical engineering, rayon, aluminium, motors, films and chemicals, were dominated by a few giant concerns, but new techniques or marketing opportunities also led to concentration in older industries, such as brewing.[210] In part, concentration was the result of the growing control of companies by financial interests which looked for extensions, or it was defensive, in which case the mergers frequently failed.[211]

In the main, however, growing concentration was associated with restriction of competition and the creation of monopolistic markets. The logical conclusion of this development was the creation of a single large monopolistic firm dominating an industry by controlling, say, 70% or more of its capacity. Several of these survived from the period before 1914;[212] among the new combines established to dominate their markets as monopolists or quasi-monopolists were those in chemicals (1926), whisky distilling (1925), soap and margarine (1929), matches (1927), glass bottles, yeast and seed crushing.[213] In almost every case, increased prices and profits were easier to find as a result of mergers, than increased efficiency.[214]

Apart from the single firm, the most widespread form of monopoly organization to arise in the inter-war years was the trade association. At the end of the war, the Committee on Trusts enumerated 93 associations in many different industries which had had dealings with the Ministry of Munitions, mostly with price-fixing functions, in a list which was stated not to be exhaustive.[215] John Hilton, the Secretary of the Committee, estimated that over 500 associations were then in existence. The Federation of British Industries had been formed in 1916 with 50 affiliated organizations and by 1918 it had 129, mostly of the trade association type, claiming a membership of 16,000 firms;

---

[210] Hermann Levy, *New Industrial System, passim*; A. Plummer, *New Industries of the Twentieth Century* (1937), chapter 7; J. E. Vaizey, 'The Brewing Industry', in P. L. Cook (ed.), *Effects of Mergers* (1958), pp. 413–19; and *The Brewing Industry 1886–1951* (1960), pp. 25–45, 149–55.

[211] H. A. Marquand, *The Dynamics of Industrial Combination* (1931), chapters 7–11; Leslie Hannah, 'Managerial Innovation and the Rise of the Large-Scale Company in Interwar Britain', *Ec. Hist. Rev.* 27/2, 1974, pp. 267–8.

[212] Cf. chapter 1, section 1 above.

[213] P. L. Cook (ed.), *Effects of Mergers*; H. Levy, *Monopolies, Trusts and Cartels in Britain To-day* (1927 ed.), chapter 9.

[214] E.g. A. F. Lucas, *Industrial Reconstruction and the Control of Competition* (1937), chapter 8; G. C. Allen, 'An Aspect of "Industrial Reorganization" ', *Econ. J.*, 55/218–19; 1945; Ernest Davies, *National Capitalism, The Government's Record as a Protector of Private Monopoly* (1939).

[215] Min. of Reconstruction, *Report of the Committee on Trusts* (1919. Cd. 9236).

the National Union of Manufacturers also evolved at the same time, in 1917, out of the British Manufacturers' Association of 1915.[216]

Many of these trade associations collapsed in the slump of 1921–2, but in the 'rationalization' movement of 1924–9, much of it Government-supported, others were formed. By the late 1930s there were probably 1,000–1,200 in existence in manufacturing alone, with a similar number to be found in distribution and other spheres.[217] Most of them were driven sooner or later to concern themselves with price fixing and control. Where the power of these associations was bolstered either by the power of a quasi-monopolistic firm acting as price leader, as in soap making, rayon, tyres or matches, or by patents, as in electric lamps, pharmaceutical products or shoe making machinery, the fixed price was virtually unchallengeable.[218]

Some trade associations went further and approached those of the German-type cartel by controlling not only prices, but also output quotas or capacity. They included the Sulphate of Ammonia Federation, the National Benzol Co., the Nitrate Producers' Association, and the Cable Makers' Association, and similar methods were in use among large building and civil engineering contractors. Government-sponsored Marketing Boards and the coal industry operated ˙in a similar way in the 1930s. The Shipping Conferences continued to exclude competition by their well-tried methods of deferred rebates. Finally, some associations sponsored subsidiary companies which systematically bought up and destroyed excess capacity. This occurred in shipbuilding, grain milling, wool combing, and among licensed houses, as well as (with Government assistance) in cotton spinning.

Some cartels shared out international markets according to prearranged quotas, including the international rail cartel, revived in 1926, and the associations among makers of electric lamps, chemicals, minerals, tobacco and glass bottles, among others. The oil industry was dominated by a few competing giant international concerns with price agreements and understandings.[219] On the other hand, the international cartels of such raw materials as tin, rubber, coffee and sugar had only temporary effects at best.[220] Finally, some large monopolistic firms spread networks of agreements across many frontiers: among them were Courtauld's, Unilever, the Swedish Match Co., Dunlop, J. & P. Coats, Nestlé, the International Nickel Co., the Amalgamated Metals Corporation Ltd., EMI, ICI, Ford's, General Motors, the Singer Sewing Machine Co., and the (American) General Electric Co.[221]

Monopolistic combination of one kind or another became much more common during the inter-war years, to the the extent that by the end of the period restrictive practices had become the normal framework of economic

[216] R. F. Holland, 'The Federation of British Industries and the International Economy, 1929–39, *Ec. Hist. Rev.* 34/2, 1981; Wyn Grant and David Marsh, *The Confederation of British Industry* (1977), pp. 19–20.

[217] PEP, *Industrial Trade Associations* (1957).

[218] Lucas, *op. cit.*, chapter 9.

[219] Patrick Fitzgerald, *Industrial Combination in England* (1927), chapter 19.

[220] PEP, *Report on International Trade* (1937), pp. 102 ff., gives some details of 28 international cartels and mentions 28 others.

[221] Alfred Plummer, *International Combines in Modern Industry* (3rd ed., 1951); E. Hexner, *International Cartels* (1946).

life, buttressed as they were by associations, agreements and Acts of Parliament. Trade 'was the subject of the most extensive, though not always co-ordinated, control instituted by the producers, distributors, and consumers'. 'As a feature of industrial and commercial organization', wrote an observer in 1937, 'free competition has nearly disappeared from the British scene.'[222]

At least as striking as the extension of monopolistic market conditions was the reversal of the public attitude towards it. The Committee on Trusts, at the end of the war, took it for granted that monopoly was undesirable. In 1919, also, the Treasury enforced a gentlemen's agreement on the banks to abstain from further amalgamation, and as late as 1923 and 1925, there were abortive private members' bills against restraint of competition, and the report of the Royal Commission on Food Prices of 1925 was equally hostile.[223]

These, however, were the last symptoms of a dying era. The drive towards the 'rationalization' of industry, introduced in this country from Germany about 1924, was perhaps the first sign of change. It began as a movement to improve techniques, but it was soon mainly looking for savings by structural and economic, rather than technical, reorganization, 'the right arrangement of the relations of producers to each other'.[224] This often required the collaboration of firms to provide common services, or, more commonly, to provide a full load for the more up-to-date plant while scrapping the less efficient. Such measures were more logically applied to the whole of an industry, and thus rationalization led directly to schemes of control and monopoly. The height of the 'rationalization' movement was passed in 1929, for the slump created the fear that 'over-rationalization' would lead to higher output and more unemployment,[225] and the problem became less that of reducing real costs than that of reducing total capacity. Thenceforward 'planning' became the favoured term. Meanwhile, however, the former attitude to competition and monopoly had been largely reversed.

The first straw in the wind was the official blessing, by a Departmental Committee, of the co-operative selling of coal in 1926.[226] More significant was the cautious support given to industrial control schemes by the influential Balfour Committee on Industry and Trade in its Final Report in 1929.[227] By 1931 the Macmillan Committee added its powerful voice to the clamour of industry for organization and association and expressed its 'strong opinion that sectional interests should not be allowed to stand in the way of reorganizations which are in the national interest'.[228] In the same

[222] J. Hurstfield, 'The Control of British Raw Material Supplies, 1919–1939', *Ec. Hist. Rev.*, 14/1–2, 1944, p. 1; A. F. Lucas, *op. cit.*, p. 64.

[223] PEP, *Industrial Trade Associations* (1957), chapter 1; G. C. Allen, 'Monopoly and Competition in the United Kingdom', in E. H. Chamberlin (ed.), *Monopoly and Competition and their Regulation* (1954).

[224] D. H. MacGregor *et al.*, 'Problems of Rationalisation', *Econ. J.*, 40/159, 1930, p. 352; cf. also L. Urwick, *The Meaning of Rationalisation* (1929), and Walter Meakin, *The New Industrial Revolution* (1928).

[225] T. E. Gregory, 'Rationalisation and Technological Unemployment', *Econ. J.*, 40/160, 1930.

[226] *Report of the D. C. on Co-operative Selling in the Coal Industry* (1926. Cmd. 2770).

[227] Balfour Committee, *Final Report* (1929), pp. 297, 304, 308.

[228] *Report of the Committee on Finance and Industry* (Macmillan Report) (1931. Cmd. 3897), para. 385.

year, the Greene Committee on Restraint of Trade (in retailing) was equally emphatic that monopolistic practices should be tolerated in the name of 'freedom of contract'.

The new Labour members of the Committee on Trusts had as early as 1919 emphasized their belief that evolution towards combination and monopoly was 'both inevitable and desirable',[229] as long as it was controlled in the public interest. Conservative opinion by the early 1930s was equally strongly in favour of regulation and control. Some Conservatives were even prepared to go further, and plan industry as a whole.

> Such a policy [wrote Mr Harold Macmillan in 1932][230] is impossible without the co-operation of industry. Production cannot be planned in relation to established demand while industries are organized on competitive lines. *In present circumstances there are no channels through which any economic policy at all can be effectively administered throughout the field of productive effort* [H. M. italics]. It is for this reason that I regard it as a matter of primary importance to produce an orderly structure in each of our national industries amenable to the authority of a representative directorate conducting the industries as self-governing units in accordance with the circumstances of the modern world.

Even the Liberal Industrial Inquiry of 1928 was prepared to see free competition in industry displaced. In many industries, it reported, public enterprise had proved itself superior and there 'the *ad-hoc* Public Board points to the right line of evolution'. Elsewhere, they were averse to restoring

> the old conditions of competition, which often involve waste and [? of] effort, the uneconomic duplication of plant or equipment, and the impossibility of adopting the full advantages of large-scale production. In modern conditions a tendency towards some degree of monopoly in an increasing number of industries is, in our opinion, inevitable and even, quite often, desirable in the interest of efficiency. It is, therefore, no longer useful to treat trusts, cartels, combinations, holding companies and trade associations as inexpedient abnormalities in the economic system to be prevented, checked, and harried. . . . We believe that there is still room . . . for large-scale enterprises of semi-monopolistic character which are run for private profit and controlled by individuals.

As for trade associations,

> we think that cases may arise in which it is in the legitimate interests of a trade or industry that a small minority shall be required to conform to the rules which the majority have decided to impose upon themselves . . . we suggest, therefore, that, where an Incorporated Association can show that 75 per cent of those affected are in favour of a trade rule or instruction . . . the Association shall have the right to apply for powers to issue an order enforcing the rule in question on all members of the trade or industry or of the appropriate section of it, whether within the Association or not.[231]

Even the *Economist* believed that 'a very wide measure of public control

[229] *Report of the Committee on Trusts* (1919. Cd. 9236), p. 13.

[230] Harold Macmillan, *Reconstruction, A Plea for a National Policy* (1933), pp. 9–10. Also see R. Boothby *et al., Industry and the State* (1927), pp. 157–8.

[231] Liberal Industrial Inquiry, *Britain's Industrial Future* (1928), pp. 77, 93–4, 99.

will be necessary if the badly needed work of rationalization is ever to make any real progress.'[232]

A Committee of the FBI in 1935 strongly urged legislation to strengthen trade associations, and in 1934 Lord Melchett on behalf of the Industrial Reorganization League, sponsored a Bill in the House of Lords giving compulsory powers to the majority of producers in any one industry to enforce schemes of reorganization on the rest, 'with the general object of promoting greater efficiency, eliminating wasteful competition, and facilitating production, manufacture and supply of the products of that industry'.

These bills were stillborn, but the Government was acting in the same sense. The compulsory railway amalgamation of 1921 was the first specific step. In 1930 came the Coal Mines Act with its compulsory cartel scheme and Reorganization Commission, and in 1931–3 the Marketing Boards. In 1930 and 1933 competition in road transport was restricted by Traffic Commissioners, in 1934, a Herring Industry Board was set up, and in 1936 the Spindles Board was established to restrict competition in cotton spinning. Subsidies were made the occasion by the State to restrict or end competition in beet sugar production, civil aviation and transatlantic passenger shipping, and tariffs were used to restrict competition in iron and steel making, among others. In the Finance Act of 1935 the Government provided that 'if a scheme of organization covering the majority of an industry had been certified by the Board of Trade as being of assistance in reducing excess capacity, contributions to it might be deducted from income for tax purposes'.[233]

In the course of the 1930s, the State thus played an active part in the cartellization of industry and it intervened directly to provide a monopolistic framework where firms were too weak or too scattered, as in the old staples of coal, cotton, iron and steel, shipbuilding and agriculture. For a third type of industry, the public utility, the country groped its way through to a new and significant form of organization, the Public Corporation.

Public Corporations had been pioneered by Dock and Harbour Boards before 1914. Between the wars the most important new authorities were the Forestry Commission (1919), the Central Electricity Board (1926), the British Broadcasting Corporation (1926), the London Passenger Transport Board (1933) and the British Overseas Airways Corporation (1939). In addition the Post Office was modelled more closely on that of the Public Corporation.

The Public Corporation was an attempt to cope with the problem of the administration of large or nationally important industries, mostly requiring large capital sums, a secure control of their market and a strong interest in general or social, as distinct from sectional, welfare. It was a compromise, to avoid both the exploitation of the public by a private monopoly, and the day-to-day political interference to which ordinary Departments of State are normally subjected. The capital might be held by the State or by former owners, including private shareholders, but there was the most complete separation possible between ownership and control. Despite its decisive rejec-

---

[232] *Economist*, 21 July 1934, 25 Aug. 1934. Cf. also Arthur Salter, *Recovery* (1932); and *The Next Five Years, an Essay in Political Agreement* (1935), written by 152 professional people of all parties.

[233] PEP, *Industrial Trade Associations* (1957), p. 29.

tion by the Haldane Committee in 1918,[234] the Public Corporation enjoyed general support and roused widespread interest as a new administrative device.[235]

The manifold new developments of industrial organization described here implied a fundamental change in thought. The nineteenth-century belief in an unlimited extension of markets was shattered by the experience of declining export markets in the 1920s and world-wide deficiency of purchasing power in the 1930s. Technical and organizational problems were thus transformed, and the main task was, not how to supply ever-extending markets at the lowest cost, but how to cater for a stagnant demand without an excess of unemployment. For the manufacturer, the limits and capacity of his own industry thus acquired a new significance as it had to be measured against a known static demand. 'The whole reorganization movement is premised upon a common purpose, a unified policy, and concerted action'.[236] It seemed as though the country was moving inexorably into a corporate economic structure, the solution tried in several fascist countries.

In the event, the extremes were avoided. Large sectors of the economy still remained unorganized, dominated by small units, or at least subject to bitter oligopolistic competition. Associations and agreements, as long as they were not State-supported, were not always permanent. The economy proved more flexible than had been allowed and changes from old to new industries were carried through with greater speed in the 1930s. In retrospect, it seems that much of the organizational, anti-competitive phase of history in 1919–39 was directly derived from the world economic depression. Its character was all the more easily forced into a restrictive mould, because of the existence of a long-term trend, making necessary ever larger agglomerations of capital for maximum productive efficiency, and providing at the same time the administrative, transport and distributive means to manage them. This trend was evident before 1914, as it had continued after 1939.

---

[234] *Reports of the Committee on the Machinery of Government* (1918. Cd. 9230).

[235] See esp. W. A. Robson (ed.), *Public Enterprise* (1937); T. H. O'Brien, *British Experiments in Public Ownership and Control* (1937); Lincoln Gordon, *The Public Corporation in Great Britain* (1938); J. F. Sleeman, *British Public Utilities* (1953); M. E. Dimock, *British Public Utilities and National Development* (1933); Balfour Committee, *Survey of Industries*, vol. 2, chapter 8 (2); Ernest Davies, *National Enterprise: The Development of the Public Corporation* (1946), chapters 2, 3, 9.

[236] Lucas, *Industrial Reconstruction*, p. 43.

3
Commercial and Financial Developments

1 The Changing Pattern of Retail and Wholesale Trading

The main theme of the last chapter was industrial change; above all the decline of industries producing for export and the growth of production and services for domestic use. This trend was bound to reduce the relative volume of international trade of the United Kingdom but the causal connection was by no means all one way: it was often developments abroad which forced the changing industrial pattern on Britain. At the same time, the striking differences between the industrial history of the 1920s and the 1930s were at least in part due to the differences in financial policy. The history of these commercial and financial developments, and their interaction with the changing pattern of industry, will be the theme of this chapter.

The industrial revolution of the eighteenth century had mainly transformed the production of capital goods and semi-manufactures. The making of many consumer goods entered the phase of mass-production much later and it was only in the inter-war years that this change was greatly speeded up and virtually completed, while at the same time a whole host of new factory-made consumer goods appeared on the market, from electrical goods to patent polishes and cleaning powders, and from plastic containers to artificial silk stockings and photographic apparatus. The rise of the new industries, both a cause and a consequence of a prosperous home market, particularly in the late 1930s, was an aspect of the opening of the era of mass-consumption.

One of the sectors most immediately affected was retail distribution. It had begun to change slowly even before 1914, but after 1919 its changes were greatly accelerated. The old-established boundaries between retailers were being broken down. New goods called forth new retailing specialists, and some of these, like electrical goods suppliers, had to undertake the new function of after-sales services. In other cases the change was in the opposite direction, as manufacturers increasingly performed many of the traditional functions of the retailer, such as weighing, packing and pricing, in the factory, and then substituted their own reputation for that of the retailer in the eyes of the consumer.

Information and salesmanship by the shopkeeper was increasingly replaced by advertising by the manufacturer. In this period, the mass-production of consumer goods for a national market and the rise of new media such as mass-circulation newspapers, radio and film afforded new opportunities for the advertiser. By 1938, it was estimated that about £106 million a year was being spent on advertising. Press advertising alone, according to another calculation, had risen from £22 million in 1907 to £60 million in 1930.[1] Much of this derived from manufacturers who succeeded in turning all kinds of consumption goods into 'household words' by advertising, free gift schemes and similar methods. Cosmetics, cigarettes and medicaments were still among the most heavily advertised, 20–50% of the retail price being accounted for by advertising costs; but other commodities, including alcoholic drinks, manufactured foods and fountain pens, had now joined this group of highly advertised commodities.[2]

Motor transport also exerted great influence on retail distribution. From the early 1920s onward, motor vans and lorries permitted direct delivery from manufacturer or importer, or from depots to multiple branches, and they also replaced the errand-boy. At the same time the rural motor bus brought villagers regularly into the market towns and transformed their shopping centres. In the 1930s, the acquisition of private motor cars by large sections of the middle classes allowed many of them to live in the country or in a residential suburb, the third important influence on retailing in the inter-war period. Estates generally had their own shopping centres, and the creation of new housing estates was one of the most potent causes of the increasing number of shops in this period.

Lastly, there was the effect of the general rise in living standards, bringing an enlarged spending power to a middle class rapidly growing in numbers, and even allowing greater freedom to spend to the working classes in the prosperous industries and districts in the 1930s. Broad groups of the population began to demand better shops, greater choice, style, and fashion, and other improvements, and a different collection of goods. The weighting of the official cost-of-living index bears eloquent witness to the changes in the consuming habits of the working classes, though the earlier figures are not too reliable (see Table 3·1).

Table 3·1: Working-class expenditure

Proportions spent on:	Budget of 1904 (1914 cost-of-living index)	Budget of 1937–8 (1947 cost-of-living index)
Food	60%	35%
Rent and rates	16	9
Clothing	12	9
Fuel and light	8	7
Other items in 1904 Budget	4	16
	100	76
Items not in 1904 Budget	—	24
	100	100

For the whole population of the United Kingdom, proportions of retail sales have been estimated as shown in Table 3·2.[3]

[1] N. Kaldor and R. Silverman, *A Statistical Analysis of Advertising Expenditure and of the Revenue of the Press* (Cambridge, 1948), pp. 7 ff.; F. P. Bishop, *The Economics of Advertising* (1944), pp. 54–5; Ralph Harris and Arthur Seldon, *Advertising in a Free Society* (1959), pp. 5–11, 25, Appx. C.

[2] Kaldor and Silverman, *op. cit.*, Table 75, pp. 144–7.

[3] J. B. Jefferys, *Retail Trading in Britain, 1850–1950* (Cambridge, 1954), pp. 44–5.

Table 3·2:　Proportions of retail sales, 1910–1939

	1910	1920	1939
Food	57·7%	50·7%	46·6%
Clothing	18·8	24·6	19·4
Reading, writing materials, confectionery, tobacco	8·8	9·3	14·4
Other goods	14·7	15·4	19·6
Totals, in £ million	892	2,863	2,302

One effect of all these influences on retail was the growth of capital and employment, absolutely and in relation to other trades. Few reliable statistics exist, but what was not in dispute, was that the number of shops was increasing. One estimate put the annual increase in the years 1924–32 at about 6%, at a time when the population increased by 0·55% per annum, though other estimates put the rate of increase rather lower.[4] Wherever official figures existed for licensing or other purposes, as among tobacconists or vendors of medicines,[5] they confirmed a rapid rise. Furniture, hardware, electrical goods and other 'non-essential' types of shops were growing even faster in numbers.

The number of workers engaged in distribution (including wholesaling) grew from an average of 1,661,000 in 1920–2 to 2,436,000 in 1937–8, or from 10·4% to 12·9% of total employment. There was an actual increase even in such areas as the four depressed counties of South Wales[6] which lost population in this period.[7] Including owner-managers and working proprietors, distribution employed about 3 million people in 1939, mostly in the retail field.

The increase in resources devoted to distribution was natural, in view of the fact that the economies of mass-production automatically threw greater burdens of costs on the distributive network (though the saving on the one greatly outweighed the additions to cost of the other);[8] that further, there were few improvements in the technical equipment of shops; and lastly, that distribution required personal services at a time when a rising standard of living implied that the cost of labour rose as compared with that of goods. Nevertheless, it could be held that the increase was quite out of proportion to any increases likely on those grounds, and that the main cause of the growth of the resources devoted to the distributive trades was the decline of price competition in ever wider fields of retailing, and its replacement by competi-.tion in ever more lavish services. As in industry,[9] these 'imperfections' were

[4] Henry Smith, *Retail Distribution* (2nd ed., 1948), pp. 35–7, 90–106; P. Ford, 'Competition and the Number of Retail Shops, 1901–31', *Econ. J.*, 45/179, 1935, and 'Decentralisation and Changes in the Number of Shops, 1901–1931', *ibid.*, 46/182, 1936; also P. Ford and G. V, White, 'Trends in Retail Distribution in Yorkshire (West Riding), 1901–1927', *Manchester School*, 7/2, 1936.

[5] Hermann Levy, *The Shops of Britain* (1948), pp. 31–43, 50, 56, 71; Jefferys, *op. cit.*, p. 53.

[6] Henry Smith, *op. cit.*, p. 106; A. L. Chapman and Rose Knight, *Wages and Salaries in the United Kingdom, 1920–38* (Cambridge, 1953), p. 18.

[7] British National Committee, International Chamber of Commerce, *Trial Census of Distribution in Six Towns* (1937).

[8] Sir Arnold Plant, 'The Distribution of Proprietary Articles', in *Some Modern Business Problems* (1937), p. 313.

[9] Cf. chapter 2, section 7 above.

fostered by monopolistic associations, and these, in turn, were related to the increase in the size of firms.

The proportions of trade held by different types of retailer changed as shown in Table 3·3.[10]

Table 3·3: Proportions of trade by types of retailer, 1915–1939

	1915	1939	Change
Co-operative societies	$7\frac{1}{2}$–9%	10–$11\frac{1}{2}$%	+$2\frac{1}{2}$%
Department stores	2–3	$4\frac{1}{2}$–$5\frac{1}{2}$	+$2\frac{1}{2}$
Multiple shops	7–$8\frac{1}{2}$	18–$19\frac{1}{2}$	+11
'Independents', owning 1–9 shops each, by difference	$79\frac{1}{2}$–$83\frac{1}{2}$	$63\frac{1}{2}$–$67\frac{1}{2}$	–16

The growth of the 'multiple' shops retailer, owning 10 or more shops, was the most outstanding of these developments. Between the wars, this type of organization spread to virtually every trade, and to all price and quality ranges.[11] Only the chains of variety stores or bazaars continued to rely mainly on their price appeal.

Among the multiple firms, in turn, the growth occurred largely among the larger chains. Between 1920 and 1939, the number of branches of firms owning 25 shops or more increased from 20,602 to 39,013; among these, the number of shops in firms with 200 branches or more grew from 10,942 to 21,283. Variety chain stores grew from 300 to 1,200 in the same period. Some of the growth was accounted for by mergers among the larger chains, but other firms grew rapidly without amalgamations: thus Boots' had 200 branches in 1900 and 1,180 in 1938, while Marks & Spencer had 140 in 1927 and 230 in 1938. Many chains were linked with manufacturing or importing organizations, either by the forward integration of manufacturers, or the backward integration of the stores.[12] In the inter-war years, the large chains, additionally, began to exert considerable influence on their suppliers, without actually owning them. Some department stores also combined, and by 1939 there were four large groups, controlling 200 stores between them.

Co-operative retail societies remained in this period the only significant and successful examples of co-operation in Britain. Their main strength lay in Lancashire and the West Riding, north-eastern England and Scotland, but in the inter-war years they spread rapidly into the co-operative 'deserts' of the south.[13] Their trading pattern remained that of the basic needs of working-class households. About two-thirds of the societies' sales was still in groceries and other food. In many non-essential articles and services they were negligible. The growth in the total share of co-operative retailing is shown in Table 3·3.

Membership, however, increased much more rapidly, from 3 million in 1914 to $4\frac{1}{2}$ million in 1920 and $8\frac{1}{2}$ million in 1939. The fall in the average sales

[10] J. B. Jefferys, *The Distribution of Consumer Goods* (Cambridge, 1950), pp. 29, 73.

[11] Jefferys, *op. cit.*, pp. 120–2.

[12] Hermann Levy, *Retail Trade Associations* (1942), pp. 29–34; H. Compton and E. H. Bott, *British Industry* (1940), chapter 6.

[13] J. A. Hough, *Co-operative Retailing, 1914–1945* (1949); S. M. Bushell, 'The Relative Importance of Co-operative, Multiple and Other Retail Traders', *Economica*, 1/1, Jan. 1921, Table 1.

per member was to some extent a reflection of the increase in the number, and fall in the size, of families.[14] In 1919, with 4·1 million members, co-operative societies held 10·7 million sugar registrations, while in 1940, with 8·5 million members, they only held 13·5 million registrations.

Among co-operative retail societies the large organization also made headway against the small. The average membership of all societies rose from 3,054 in 1914 to 8,643 in 1939: by 1935, $56\frac{1}{2}$ % of the members were in large societies of 20,000 members and over.[15]

In retail distribution, the decline of price competition, mainly by the spread of 'resale price maintenance', depended basically on the existence of branded, identical goods with a very wide, and preferably a national, market. Thus it was that price maintenance was first found in bookselling as early as the eighteenth century, and by the 1890s had begun to spread to groceries and proprietary medicines.[16] The latter were protected by the 'Proprietary Articles Trade Association' (PATA), established in 1896, which became a model for other associations and exerted great power. In 1938 it had 3,000 different articles on its protected list. Price maintenance itself covered about 3% of the domestic consumer's expenditure on goods in 1900; by 1938, this had grown to 30%.[17] Other methods of control included stop lists, boycotts, deferred rebates, distance limits, the most successful being newspaper vendors and sellers of photographic goods, and licensing, as in the case of pharmacists and motor and cycle dealers. The official Committee on Restraint of Trade, reporting in 1931,[18] deplored the propping up of prices and the restrictions of entry practised by many associations, but it felt that there was no 'compelling reason' for intervention by the State.

The small shop managed to survive in large numbers, in the absence of important technical advantages of size, because of the personal qualities of the shopkeeper, advantages of site, inertia on the part of the housewife, and the relatively small capital required. At the same time, advertising, packing, weighing and branding by manufacturers or wholesalers reduced the necessary skill of keeping many types of shop. Thus retail distribution became one of the last refuges of the small entrepreneur. By 1938, of an estimated 747,000 shops, all but 90,000 were still in the hands of small firms with 1–9 branches, the overwhelming majority being single shops managed by working proprietors.

The decades before 1914, which had seen the widespread replacement of producer-retailers by large-scale manufacturers or bulk importers, had greatly favoured the development of wholesaling, and to some extent this tendency continued into the post-war period. The main changes of the period, however, worked in the opposite direction. Packing, blending and breaking bulk, even selection and pricing, were increasingly carried out by the manufacturer. Manufacturers of branded and advertised goods began to

---

[14] G. D. H. Cole, *A Century of Co-operation* (Manchester, 1944), pp. 371–2.

[15] A. M. Carr-Saunders, P. Sargant Florence, Robert Peers *et al.*, *Consumers' Co-operation in Great Britain* (1938), pp. 45–6.

[16] B. S. Yamey, *The Economics of Resale Price Maintenance* (1954), chapters 7 and 8.

[17] *Report of the Committee on Resale Price Maintenance* (Lloyd Jacob Committee) (1949. Cmd. 7696), p. 1; Jefferys, *Retail Trading*, pp. 53, 96–7.

[18] *Report of the Committee appointed . . . to Consider Certain Trade Practices* (1931).

send their travellers and delivery vans direct to retailers, cutting out the wholesaler completely, and this was particularly so in commodities in which condition at the time of sale, or after-sale service and guarantee, were important, including biscuits, flour, meat, soap, books, electrical goods, photographic and sports goods and furniture. The large chains, at the same time, did their own wholesaling, and their growth thus further reduced the scope of the specialist firm. By 1938, there were some 25,000–30,000 wholesaling firms left, and a further 20,000 wholesaler-retailers, handling about 40% of the consumer goods sold.[19]

The scope of the merchant firms trading overseas was reduced by similar factors as well as by the decline in Britain's international trade, and the artificial barriers put up by many countries against foreign imports.[20] Britain's entrepôt trade fell from £110 million in 1913 to £62 million in 1938, when prices were higher.

British merchants also suffered from the direct competition of foreign firms, often enjoying stronger financial and other support by their home Governments and banks than the British house, as well as a more adaptable joint-agency system and more go-ahead staff.

> British overseas trade [it was being said] has been conducted in the past too much, as it were, in the English Club, in the seaports and with a 'take it or leave it' attitude to the 'dagoes' who are the inhabitants of the country and the customers of British trade. Individual instances of failures on the part of British manufacturers to meet local requirements occur almost daily. Most of these are relatively trivial, but they typify an ignorance of, and lack of contact with, foreign markets which are symptomatic of fundamental shortcomings.

In this, British manufacturers were not without blame, for in their packaging, style and language of instructions accompanying their goods they took less account of local wishes than competing manufacturers from other countries.[21]

In the changing nature of trade with formerly backward, but now rapidly developing parts of the globe, the better technical training of foreign representatives became more important than the knowledge of the international market for raw materials which was the *forte* of the British merchant. He was squeezed not only by foreign houses, but also by the large British manufacturers. For if he succeeded in opening a region to large sales, the manufacturer was tempted to send out his own representative and keep the merchanting profits for himself; tariff regulations might also force him to open branch factories. If, on the other hand, the merchant failed to sell the product, the manufacturer was equally tempted to by-pass him and try other channels. The shift from merchant to manufacturers' agent was detrimental to British trade as a whole, since the latter, unlike the former, had no interest in return cargoes. At the same time the British merchant, who had often acted

[19] Jefferys, *Retail Trading*, pp. 47–9, and *Distribution of Consumer Goods*, pp. 21–9, 46–8, 117–18; D. C. Braithwaite and S. P. Dobbs, *Distribution of Consumable Goods* (1932).

[20] J. Hurstfield, 'The Control of Raw Material Supplies, 1919–1939', *Ec. Hist. Rev.* 14/1–2, 1944, pp. 19–20.

[21] PEP, *Report on International Trade* (1937), pp. 140–1; cf. also A. E. Kahn, *Great Britain in the World Economy* (1946), p. 79.

as local banker and shipper was weakened by the decline in British overseas investment, or pushed out altogether by developing native or Government-sponsored firms, reducing further the demand for British financial and shipping services.[22] A long phase of the history of British overseas commerce was coming to a close in the inter-war years.

2 The Course of Overseas Trade

The decline in the position of the British overseas merchant was linked to the fall of the share of British trade. After the upheavals of war, the boom of 1919-20 and the runaway inflations of several countries in the early 1920s further dislocated established trade connections, but world trade as a whole recovered remarkably quickly and soon began to grow beyond its pre-war level. In this growth the industrial progress and rising national incomes of the advanced countries played a major part, but the exports of primary producers were lagging. This was probably due to the decline in the rate of population increase in Europe, and to a tendency to protect the over-large peasantry, and to substitute home-produced commodities for imports.[23] At the same time, the continued high rate of population increase in overseas areas made it easier to keep much of the primary production in the country of origin.

These factors, together with the over-stimulation of the production of primary products during the war, caused a certain weakness in the world demand for them even in the 1920s. In the depression of the early 1930s it suffered a disastrous collapse. As a result, the primary producing countries, which were generally also international debtor countries, found it impossible to service their debts or pay for imports from the advanced countries. Here was one of the main causes of a vicious circle of shrinking world trade in the 1930s.[24]

Before 1914, Great Britain, by a free market for gold as well as for imported commodities, and by large overseas investment operations, had held the balance between the world's raw material and manufactured exports. After the war, this role should have fallen to the United States by virtue of her economic strength and her emergence as the world's main lender. Long-term foreign investments had changed as shown in Table 3·4.[25]

Table 3·4: Long-term foreign investment (in £ million)

	1914	1929
Great Britain	4,004	3,737
France	1,766	719
Germany	1,376	226
USA	513	3,018

[22] PEP, *ibid.*, pp. 12–14, 131 ff.

[23] W. A. Lewis, *Economic Survey, 1919–1939* (1949), pp. 149 ff., 196, and 'World Production, Prices and Trade, 1870–1960', *Manchester School*, 20/2, May 1952. F. Benham, 'The Muddle of the Thirties', *Economica*, NS, 12/45, 1945.

[24] A. E. Kahn, *Great Britain in the World Economy* (1946), pp. 42–3, 63; A. J. Brown, *Industrialization and Trade* (1943), pp. 11, 56–71; D. C. Corner, 'Exports and the British Trade Cycle: 1929', *Manchester School*, 24, 1956.

The USA, however, was unable to play her role in world trade quite as Britain had played it.

There were several reasons for this. For one thing, the USA retained her high tariff and in any case had far less need of imports than had the British economy in its days of economic leadership. Britain, in fact, remained the world's chief free market for most raw materials and food products, the 'dumping ground of foreign exporters',[26] before 1931 and the largest market even after that date, while becoming too weak to stand the financial strain which such a position involved.

Secondly, the USA had become the world's chief lender at a time when international capital movements and indebtedness were being bedevilled by war loan repayments and reparations of vast dimensions. As for Germany, her annual reparations instalments, even after they were scaled down by the Dawes Plan of 1924 and the Young Plan of 1929 were largely advanced by the USA. As far as the war loans among the Allies were concerned, moratoria and standstill agreements lightened the burdens of the weaker nations, but the USA insisted on *some* repayments, based on ability to pay, so that Britain actually repaid more to the USA than she could collect from the financially weaker allies whom she had helped during the war. These payments also gained little for the creditors,[27] but caused much harm to the debtors and to the vanquished nations, they disrupted the flows of international payments, and they created a new phenomenon, the highly industrialized debtor nation, of which Germany, Japan and Italy were the leading examples. These countries were forced by their position into ever tighter control and artificial restriction over foreign trade and payments, including the creation of several artificial exchange rates by which they hoped to extract forced loans from abroad.[28]

Thirdly, American lending differed greatly in character from the overseas investments of Britain before 1914. It arose out of the war rather than out of normal trade relations, or it was speculative. Much of it, also, was politically directed, but without effective political control. Above all, for the American investment market foreign investment was marginal, and was easily jettisoned, as in 1928, when the boom in American home securities diverted all funds to Wall Street. Yet for the rest of the world, the reversal of the outflow of American investments to become an inflow appeared to be of staggering proportions.[29] Similarly, there was a flight of short-term funds into the USA from 1934 onwards, converting a net export of short-term capital into a net import.

Nor was this all, for with the onset of the American slump in 1929, imports into the USA fell off drastically and were further reduced by the tariff of 1930:[30] payments on merchandise import account fell from \$4,399 million in

[25] Colin Clark, *Conditions of Economic Progress* (1951 ed.), p. 514.

[26] PEP, *Report on International Trade* (1937), p. 63.

[27] H. W. Arndt, *The Economic Lessons of the Nineteen-Thirties* (1944), p. 28.

[28] PEP, *International Trade*, pp. 19–20; Sir Arthur Salter, *Recovery* (1932), pp. 51 ff., also 100–7 and chapter 3.

[29] Hal B. Lary *et al.* (US Dept. of Commerce), *The United States in the World Economy* (Washington, 1943, London, 1944), pp. 89 ff., Appx., Tables I–III.

[30] J. K. Galbraith, *The Great Crash* (1955), pp. 162–3.

1929 to $1,323 million in 1932. The amount of dollars thus made available to the rest of the world by American lending and purchases fell from $7,400 million a year to $2,400 million in the course of three years, 1929–32, or by 68%, and if the fixed debt payments which had to be met out of these totals are deducted, the dollars available to foreigners for other purposes were cut by an even greater percentage margin.

A cut of such magnitude, caused by sudden reversals of the trade and lendings flows, created an overpowering dollar shortage, related to, though not quite of the same nature as, the more prolonged dollar shortage of the post-war years.[31] It forced other countries to deflate and ultimately to go off the gold standard, while as part of the large-scale capital inflows, $10 billion of gold was sent to America in 1934–9 and duly re-interred there without being allowed to affect the value of the dollar. Thus, the United States, instead of acting as a buffer, and using its vast gold reserves to stabilize world trade when threatened by the dislocations of the slump, tended by its policy to make matters worse.

The reduction of American overseas trade to less than a third in value in the depression was accompanied by reductions in world trade between other countries in the 1930s. Currency and trade restrictions, Government-sponsored autarchy, bilateral and regional agreements, all tended to reduce still further the flow of goods across frontiers, already affected by the depression. In the recovery which followed, world trade expanded again, but it failed to reach the levels of 1929, and in 1938 there began a renewed cyclical downward turn in world trade which was interrupted by the outbreak of war.

In the 1920s, Britain's volume of imports was steadily increasing, and her exports steadily declining.[32] In the slump, Britain suffered rather less than many other countries. Her share of the world export trade in manufactured goods fell from 27·5% in 1911–13 to 23·8% in 1921–5 and 18·5% in 1931–8, and as a proportion of national income, overseas trade declined as shown in Table 3·5.[33]

Table 3·5: Decline in overseas trade as a proportion of national income

Ratio of exports to national product		Ratio of imports to national income	
1907	33%	1913	31%
1924	27%	1929	25%
1938	15%	1938	16%

With a strongly rising volume of imports, and an equally marked fall in the volume of exports, Britain would have been faced with a rapidly widening

[31] A. J. Brown, 'Dollars and Crises', *Ec. Hist. Rev.*, 2nd S., 12/2, Dec. 1959; Donald MacDougall, *The World Dollar Problem* (1957), pp. 35–42, Appx. 1A; M. E. Falkus, 'United States Economic Policy and the "Dollar Gap" of the 1920s', *Ec. Hist. Rev.* 24/4, 1971.

[32] H. S. Booker, *The Problem of Britain's Overseas Trade* (1948), chapter 3; H. W. Macrosty, 'The Overseas Trade of the United Kingdom, 1924–31', *J. R. Stat. S.*, 95/4, 1932; G. D. H. Cole, *British Trade and Industry* (1932), chapter 9.

[33] W. A. Lewis, *op. cit.*, pp. 82, 85. For slightly different figures, see G. D. A. MacDougall, 'General Survey, 1929–37' in *Britain in Recovery* (1938), p. 13.

unfavourable trade gap, if it had not been for a remarkably favourable trend of relative prices.[34] The improvement in Britain's terms of trade as shown in Table 3·6 was one of the outstanding characteristics of the whole period.

Table 3·6: Terms of trade, exports/imports, 1908–1937

	Quantum of trade		Terms of trade	
	Quantum of imports	Quantum of exports	Export prices import prices 1913 = 100*	Net terms of trade 1938 = 100**
1908–13	92	91	97	143
1921–9	104	79	127	115
1930–7	115	64	138	103

* Lewis, Appx., Table XV, p. 202.
** B. R. Mitchell and Phyllis Deane, *Abstract of British Historical Statistics* (Cambridge, 1962), p. 332.

It was this change in the terms of trade which permitted, and in part caused, the rising standard of living in Britain while condemning the export industries to unemployment and decline. In 1929 it was estimated that the unemployment in the six leading staple export trades caused by the fall in exports since 1913 alone amounted to 700,000–800,000 workers, or virtually the whole of the intractable core of the unemployment of the 1920s.[35] Meanwhile the low prices of primary products on the world markets were ruining many of the primary producers who had been the chief customers of Britain.

In the 1930s Britain had some success in transferring resources from the old export industries and benefiting by the favourable trade terms, and in increasing the exports of the growth industries.[36] Rising incomes and standards of comfort led to an expansion of employment in the service trades, building and other sheltered industries, and the nature of import demand also changed. After 1929, virtually the whole of the increase in imports was in the form of consumption goods, mainly food, drink and tobacco.[37]

Compared with pre-war trade the 1920s saw a growth in the trade with Commonwealth countries, and a corresponding decrease in the trade with Western European nations and with Russia. As far as trade with North America was concerned, exports showed a substantial decline, while imports were rising. The resultant strain on sterling was aggravated by the fact that other European countries also had an unfavourable trade balance with the USA, covering it by American loans and investments, and by running a surplus with Britain which was its surplus with her colonies. A large quadrilateral world trade thus had to be kept in balance by the dollar earnings of the British overseas territories which were members of the sterling bloc.[38]

[34] Elliott Zupnick, *Britain's Postwar Dollar Problem* (New York, 1957), pp. 24–7.
[35] E. V. Francis, *Britain's Economic Strategy* (1939), pp. 55–6.
[36] W. A. Lewis, p. 78; for a different tabulation for 1927–8 see F. H. Awad, 'The Structure of the World Export Trade, 1926–1953', *Yorkshire Bulletin*, 11/1, 1959, p. 35.
[37] G. N. Butterworth and H. Campion, 'Changes in British Import Trade' *Manchester School*, 8/1, 1937.
[38] A. E. Kahn, *op. cit.*, chapters 12 and 13; Zupnick, pp. 37–8.

In the 1930s this complex system of trade virtually broke down. One limb, the dollar earnings of the colonies, shrank disastrously with the price fall of primary commodities and the decline in the American demand for industrial raw materials in the slump. A second limb, the European (and American) surplus with Britain, was reduced in size by Britain's new policies of protection, currency manipulation and more direct aids. In the same period, she allowed her sales and purchases with the Commonwealth and South America to decline and the deflationary effects of these tendencies further aggravated the two main problems, the unemployment in the British export industries and the low income of the overseas trading partners.

The favourable price trend was approximately of the right order of magnitude to counteract the unfavourable volume movements and keep the visible trade gap in the inter-war years on a fairly even keel. It averaged £225 million in 1921–4, rose to an average of £396 million in 1925–31, fell to £276 million in 1932–5 and then showed a strongly rising tendency again, increasing to well over £400 million by 1937.[39] To meet this adverse merchandise trade gap of £200–400 million a year, Great Britain relied largely on her income from overseas investments, and on the 'invisible' earnings from shipping, banking, insurance and similar services.

These invisible earnings, apart from the income from gilt-edged securities expressed in sterling, were all dependent on prosperity abroad and a high level of international trade. As long as world prosperity held up reasonably well, they were more than sufficient to cover the visible trade gap. With the onset of the depression, however, both exports and imports fell away, but there was a far more drastic fall in net invisible earnings which had accounted for about a third of the balance of payments in the 1920s. Shipping incomes dropped to a nadir of £65 million in 1933, investment income to £150 million in 1932, and commissions and miscellaneous incomes to a bare £40 million: a fall for these three items together by £200 million. The small regular surplus available for foreign investment disappeared in 1930, and in 1931 became a deficit, leading to a repatriation of capital on balance to the extent of £104 million. The drastic steps taken in that year, including protection and depreciation of the currency, reduced the unfavourable balance (including 'invisibles') to £51 million in 1932 and to much smaller amounts later, but throughout the 1930s repayments of capital slightly exceeded foreign lending[40] for the first time since the Industrial Revolution.

What little lending occurred in the 1930s was made almost entirely within the Empire. New capital issues indicate the trend[41] (see Table 3·7).

---

[39] Annual figures will be found in e.g., E. V. Morgan, *Studies in British Financial Policy, 1914–25* (1952), p. 341; A. E. Kahn, *Great Britain in the World Economy* (1946), p. 126, also chapters 9 and 10. Recently revised figures in R. G. Ware, 'The Balance of Payments in the Inter-War Period: Further Details', *B. of Eng. Qtly. Bull.* 14/1, 1974, pp. 47–52.

[40] Sir Robert Kindersley, 'British Overseas Investments, 1938', *Econ. J.* 49/196, 1939, p. 694. His main figures are summarized in A. E. Kahn, *op. cit.*, p. 187; Royal Institute of International Affairs, *The Problem of International Investment* (1937); Tse Chun Chang, 'The British Balance of Payments, 1924–1938', *Econ. J.*, 57/228, 1947.

[41] J. H. Richardson, *British Economic Foreign Policy* (1936), p. 73 and chapter 3.

Table 3·7:   Trends in investment, 1911–36 (in £ million)

	1911–12	1925–9	1932–6
Home investment	38	165	124
Overseas investment: Empire	67	67	28
'' '' elsewhere	95	48	3
Totals	200	280	255

This switch was partly due to growing Treasury control of foreign lending from 1931 on.[42] Control was transferred in 1936 to the Foreign Transactions Advisory Committee, which later became the Capital Issues Committee.

With these capital repayments and large-scale defaults, the nominal value of British overseas investments fell from £4,100 million in 1927 to £3,490 million in 1939;[43] the fall in the real value, in terms of earning power, was certainly greater, since over £1,900 million of this investment was in the form of equity and loan capital of companies. Holdings within the Empire accounted for 47% in 1913, 59% in 1929 and 61% in 1936.[44]

3 Great Britain Under Protection

One of the emergency measures taken by Britain in 1931 to rectify the unfavourable trade balance was the imposition of protective tariffs. This decision represents such a complete reversal of traditional economic policy that it deserves separate treatment.

The continued free-trade policy in Britain in the face of the protectionism of all the other leading industrial states had had the support of the electorate, which had decisively defeated the Conservative Party on the two occasions when it made protection an important electoral issue, in 1906 and in 1923, and even in 1931 could scarcely be said to have given the 'National' Government a mandate for ending free trade. Economists and economic advisers were also all but united in opposing protection, and their views were summarized in the brilliantly argued *Tariffs: the Case Examined*,[45] which appeared in the year in which protection was finally to triumph.

There had been many digressions from the narrow path of free trade even before 1931, but they could all be deemed to have been measures dealing with particular issues which still left the main principle intact. During the war, in 1915, the so-called 'McKenna duties' were imposed, consisting of a duty of $33\frac{1}{3}$% *ad valorem* on some imported luxury goods. Their original object was the saving of foreign exchange and of shipping space, but they were not repealed after the war, except briefly by the Labour Government of 1924, and when re-imposed, they were extended in 1926 to commercial vehicles and parts. They allowed such industries as motor manufacturing to grow to maturity behind a substantial tariff wall which was high enough to keep out most imports.[46]

---

[42] For control before 1931 see John Atkin, 'Offical Regulation of British Overseas Investment, 1914–1931', *Ec. Hist. Rev.* 23/3, 1970.

[43] Bank of England figures; Kindersley's are slightly higher throughout.

[44] Series of articles by Sir Robert Kindersley in the *Economic Journal* in the 1930s.

[45] W. H. Beveridge *et al.*, *Tariffs: The Case Examined* (1931).

[46] PEP, *Engineering Reports, II: Motor Vehicles* (1950), p. 75.

In the later years of the war, the prohibition of imports, except under licence, was extended to a wide range of commodities until September 1919, and was kept on afterwards for the products of certain 'key industries', such as dyestuffs and other chemicals, scientific instruments, laboratory glassware and magnetos, for all of which the country had depended mainly on imports before the war. When the High Court declared this continued prohibition to be illegal, it was re-imposed in two new Acts.

The Dyestuffs (Import Regulation) Act, 1920, prohibited the import of dyestuffs for 10 years, except under licence, allowing a vigorous growth of the industry in Britain. The second measure, the Safeguarding of Industries Act of 1921, was more complex. It protected the other 'key industries' by a tariff of $33\frac{1}{3}\%$ *ad valorem*, but by Part II it also permitted the extension of such protection to other industries (which could make no claim on grounds of military importance), provided they could show that foreign products undersold them either by selling below costs of production or by the depreciation of a foreign currency. Under the currency depreciation clause, a few minor manufactures, including fabric gloves, glassware, hollow-ware and gas mantles, were protected by tariffs. The German Reparation (Recovery) Act of 1921 permitted the Treasury to impose duties of up to 50% *ad valorem* on German imports in part payment of reparations, and despite a complex and ingenious machinery devised to prevent this, the duties were in fact protective, to the extent of 26% *ad valorem* on the average.[47]

In 1925 the Safeguarding Act was somewhat extended: industries might be granted protection if imports enjoyed unfair advantages by virtue not only of currency depreciation, but also of subsidies or bounties, or by inferior conditions of employment abroad. Under these clauses, protection was extended to cutlery, pottery, lace, buttons, wrapping paper and some very minor industries. There were also silk duties and hop duties imposed in 1925, which in spite of their complex provisions had a clear, if limited, protective effect, as had the petrol and sugar duties. The McKenna duties were re-imposed in the same year.[48]

A special type of protection was extended to the film industry. The Cinematograph Films Act of 1927 established a compulsory minimum quota of British pictures, rising from $7\frac{1}{2}\%$ for renters and 5% for exhibitors, by steps of $2\frac{1}{2}\%$ to reach 20% for both in 1936-8. The quota system was an undoubted success, and by 1936 the British film industry had by its own efforts exceeded the minimum quota at home, and had established a growing export market for its products.[49]

All these measures together did not constitute a protectionist policy. In 1930 only 17% of imports by value were dutiable, mostly by revenue duties only: protective duties did not affect more than 2-3% of imports. This was altered drastically in the economic blizzard of 1931, which drove Britain off the gold standard, created a large unfavourable balance of payments and

[47] E. B. McGuire, *The British Tariff System* (1939), chapter 17.

[48] G. P. Jones and A. G. Pool, *A Hundred Years of Economic Development in Great Britain* (1959), pp. 317-23; J. H. Richardson, 'Tariffs, Preferences and other Forms of Protection', in *Britain in Recovery* (1938), p. 126; Sir Hubert Llewellyn Smith, *The Board of Trade* (1928), pp. 185-8.

[49] Alfred Plummer, *New British Industries in the Twentieth Century* (1937), chapter 6/IV.

brought in, by the snap election of October, a vast Conservative majority under the guise of supporters for the 'National' Government,[50] eager to impose protection. While protection was being debated, a temporary Abnormal Importations (Customs Duties) Act was passed at once, to stop the rushing in of imports in anticipation of later duties. The Act permitted *ad valorem* duties of up to 100%, though only 50% was generally imposed in practice on a wide range of manufactured goods. Another early protective measure was the Horticultural Products (Emergency Duties) Act, also passed before the end of the year.

In February 1932, the Import Duties Act inaugurated the protectionist era in Britain. The Act was not to apply to Empire goods for the time being, nor to the commodities covered by earlier protectionist legislation. There was also a specific free list, including wheat, meat and other foodstuffs, as well as all important industrial raw materials. On other commodities, a general tariff of 10% *ad valorem* was imposed and an Import Duties Advisory Committee (IDAC) was appointed, to suggest alterations in that general tariff. Following its report in April 1932,[51] duties on manufactured goods in general were increased by 10% to a total of 20% *ad valorem*, on luxury goods to 25% or 30%, on bicycles and some chemicals to $33\frac{1}{3}$% and on certain industrial raw materials and semi-manufactures to 15%. After the alterations agreed to at Ottawa later in the year, the total effect was to leave about one-quarter of imports duty free (many of them, however, restricted by other methods), one-half paying 10–20%, 8% paying new duties of over 20% and the remainder of imports paying the old McKenna and Safeguarding Duties.[52] In the following years innumerable alterations of specific duty rates were suggested by IDAC and put into force; of these, the most important was the duty of $33\frac{1}{3}$% imposed on steel imports on condition that the industry was reorganized, and the temporary raising of the steel tariff to 50% in 1935 in order to force the European steel cartel to grant better terms to the British industry.[53] Of the other protectionist measures introduced in the 1930s, the most important ones were those relating to agricultural products, noted in chapter 2, section 5 above.

As noted above, imports from Empire countries were exempted from the original tariff of 1932. Britain's new system of protection made it possible for her to build up a system of imperial preferences and to this end an Imperial Economic Conference assembled in Ottawa in July–August 1932, hoping to expand trade among the members of the British Commonwealth in a world of shrinking commerce and rising trade barriers. These hopes were to be largely disappointed, for in fact neither Britain nor the Dominions had much room to manœuvre.

In the first place, there was no hope of making the Empire economically self-sufficient. In 1924–9, about 60% of the exports of Britain, India and Canada, about 50% of the exports of Australia, and 36% of the exports of

---

[50] C. L. Mowat, *Britain Between the Wars* (1956 ed.), pp. 409–12.

[51] (Cmd. 4066). Also see *Recommendations of the IDAC*, 45 pts., Parliamentary Papers, 1932–3, XVI.

[52] J. H. Richardson, in *Britain in Recovery*, p. 129. Also F. Benham, *Great Britain Under Protection* (New York, 1941), chapter 2.

[53] D. Abel, *A History of British Tariffs, 1923–1942* (1945).

South Africa had gone to countries outside the Empire,[54] and the Empire countries could not replace these markets. If they depended on sales to outsiders, they must needs allow foreigners to import goods in return, and their exports could not be sold in preferential Empire markets at prices higher than the ruling world level.[55]

In the second place, the mercantilist conception of an industrialized mother country linked with primary producer colonies, had become grossly anachronistic by 1932. The Dominions had infant industries, which they were determined to protect even against the United Kingdom, while Great Britain had at last decided to protect her farmers. As a result, all that could be achieved, after weeks of bitter wrangling, was a series of bilateral treaties,[56] according to which Britain would use a system of quotas and licences to ensure that Empire imports would increase at the expense of foreign importers and not British farmers, while the Dominions granted their preference in return, not by lowering tariffs to British exporters but by raising them still higher against other countries. British tariffs on imports from the rest of the world were also raised in the aggregate by the Ottawa agreement as shown in Table 3·8.[57]

Table 3·8:   British tariffs before and after the Ottawa agreements

		1930	1932 Before Ottawa	1932 After Ottawa
% of imports free of duty		83·0	30·2	25·2
% of foreign imports subject to new duties at:	10%	—	32·9	28·3
	11–20%	—	15·3	21·8
	over 20%	—	4·6	7·7
		83·0	83·0	83·0

The network was completed by the imposition, in the months which followed, of imperial preference on the Colonies also. Only the Irish Free State stood out, being engaged in a tariff war with Great Britain, largely of political origin.

The imperial preference system was followed by a diversion of part of the trade formerly conducted with outside regions towards Empire regions,[58] but it is not certain how far Ottawa was responsible for it, since it was in line with a long-term trend, and with the trend of investments, as well as being furthered by the exchange stability within the sterling bloc in contrast with the exchange uncertainties in the rest of the world. As Table 3·9 shows, the rest of the Empire benefited more from Ottawa than the United Kingdom, but Britain had started in a more favourable position:[59]

[54] PEP, *Report on International Trade* (1937), p. 66.

[55] Benham, *op. cit.*, pp. 80–1.

[56] *Imperial Economic Conference at Ottawa, Summary of Proceedings and Copies of Trade Agreements* (1932. Cmd. 4174).

[57] Francis, *Britain's Economic Strategy* (1939) p. 203; J. H. Richardson, *British Economic Foreign Policy* (1936), p. 128.

[58] PEP, *International Trade*, pp. 66–74.

[59] Richardson, in *Britain in Recovery*, p. 138; F. C. Benham, *Great Britain Under Protection*

Table 3·9: UK trade with Empire countries (excluding Irish Free State)

	% of UK imports from Empire	% of UK exports to Empire
1913	25·0	32·9
1924–9 (average)	26·8	35·2
1931	24·5	32·6
1933	34·3	36·0
1937	37·3	39·7

The new tariffs and quotas also permitted Britain to offer concessions, or threaten retaliation, to other countries. Normally Britain insisted on the most-favoured-nation clause, which tended to have a general downward effect on tariff rates, but in an increasingly restrictive world, commercial agreements became strictly bilateral, the proportion of world trade condusted bilaterally or by barter rising to 12%. Britain made 20 such agreements in 1933–8.[60] These allowed her to insist that countries with which Great Britain had large unfavourable balances, like the Baltic countries and the Argentine, would take more of her own goods, such as coal. Specially high retaliatory duties, apart from the Irish case, were used by Britain only twice, in 1934, against France and against Japan, but once the system had got going, there were few downward revisions. The most important was the trade agreement between Britain and the USA made in November 1938 after three years of delicate negotiations, but there was no opportunity of developing it before the outbreak of war; a treaty with Germany in 1939 was similarly thwarted by political events.

It is not easy to summarize the total effects of protection in the 1930s on Britain's trade and prosperity. The traditional claim that free trade will ensure the most efficient use of resources was irrelevant when 20% of the national resources or more were idle; the doctrine of comparative costs had to be greatly modified when applied in a context of exchange manipulation, tariffs, quotas and subsidies abroad and international or foreign cartels which could and did freely engage in dumping or in discriminatory pricing. The structural alterations required of British industry were too great to be carried out satisfactorily without State aid, including protection. Lastly, it was felt that at a time when all countries were attempting to export their unemployment, the multiplier effect of deflation and increasing unemployment could be cut off by cutting off imports, though the problem was not put in such terms at the time.

The arguments actually used in 1931 were far less sophisticated. Statesmen appeared to be looking for the more direct effects of protection – the salvaging of individual industries, the prevention of undercutting by ill-paid labour – of the kind which in normal times economic theory had little difficulty in showing up as illusory or mistaken. Some hoped for rising prices as a possible cause of a cyclical upswing, others wanted simply to stop the unfavourable trade balance by the crudest method available, or to raise revenue. The British 'National' Government had a 'doctor's mandate' to try

(1941), pp. 256–7; Ian M. Drummond, *British Economic Policy and the Empire 1919–1939* (1972), pp. 102–4.

[60] McGuire, chapter 19.

any remedy in 1931 and prescribed protection as a nostrum for a variety of ills and with a variety of motives.

It may be doubted whether protection helped greatly to pull Britain out of her exchange difficulties, still more out of the slump. When she used her economic power to force her coal on Scandinavia, Polish and German coal, squeezed out of that market, turned south and drove British coal out of Italy and France, so that little was gained by that manœuvre. If British manufacturers enjoyed a preference over Americans in Canada, the Americans retaliated by opening branch factories in Canada which then enjoyed preference over imports from Britain. On the other hand, the ill effects of protection feared by orthodox economists were equally hard to find. Apart from the special case of agriculture, it would be hard to point to a single industry fostered in Britain by the tariff which was obviously uneconomic or inappropriate for this country. Again, the British consumer would have benefited little if foreign imports in the 1930s had been allowed to ruin British steelmaking, agriculture or shipbuilding. Continued free trade, while it would have driven prices down still further for the consumer, might well have robbed him of the purchasing power to make use of his opportunity. Even increasingly sophisticated modern techniques have been unable to show how far individual industries benefited, though it seems clear that the cotton industry, which had little influence on British recovery, was among those which benefited most, and building and steel, which had great influence, benefited least or may even have been harmed.[61]

There was, certainly, an immediate sharp reduction in imports, and in the sequel home production rose much faster than imports, pointing to a possible replacement of one by the other. At the same time, however, there was also an even larger fall in exports, and the fall in total foreign trade as a proportion of home production was part of a secular trend, and may well not have been caused by the tariff as such. Similarly, protection did not seem to have led to any noticeable rise in prices: these continued to fall to 1932–3, and then rose slowly as the cyclical upswing began, as might have been expected (see Table 3·10).[62]

Table 3·10:   Price indices 1919–39

	Consumers' goods and services (1913 = 100)	Total final output (1913 = 100)	Retail prices all items (1958 = 100)
1931	168·6	158·0	35
1932	164·3	153·3	34
1933	160·9	150·7	33
1937	168·6	162·1	36
1938	171·2	163·4	37
1939	182·1	172·1	38

[61] Forrest Capie, 'The British Tariff and Industrial Protection in the 1930s', *Ec. Hist. Rev.* 31/3, 1978 and discussion in *ibid.* 34/1, 1981, pp. 132–42.

[62] C. H. Feinstein, *National Income, Expenditure and Output of the United Kingdom, 1855–1965* (Cambridge, 1972), T. 133; London and Cambridge Economic Service, *The British Economy, Key Statistics 1900–1966*, Table E.

In the last resort, protection in Britain was only one in a long chain of measures, and by itself it could neither reverse nor speed up the world's march to economic disruption and stagnation evident in the Great Depression of the 1930s. Its imposition in 1932 was motivated at least as much by politics as by economics. It arose out of the desire of the Government to be seen to make a gesture and take some novel action to stave off economic disaster, and at the same time to please some of its friends, rather than out of a careful balancing of economic advantages. In this, it resembled other economic policies of Governments more closely than is commonly allowed.

4 The Changing Role of the Budget

The dislocation of the public finances caused by the war, as described in chapter 1, section 5 above, could not be ended immediately by the armistice. The budget continued to be unbalanced for a further two years;[63] the budget of 1920-1 was the first to achieve a surplus, and it may thus be considered to have been the first 'normal' peace-time budget.

However, there could be no simple return to the pre-war type of budget. On the expenditure side, the changes, in Morgan's 'adjusted' terms, were as shown in Table 3·11.[64]

Table 3·11: Budgetary changes, 1913–45 (in £ million)

	1913–14	1920–1	1924–5
Consolidated fund services	37	378	394
Fighting services	86	354	138
Munitions	—	33	—
Revenue departments	30	76	64
Other civil departments	55	466	257
	208	1,306	853
Less appropriations in aid*	12	150	54
	196	1,156	799

* Sales by Departments to other Departments or to the private sector.

It will be noted that the main changes occurred in the course of the war: bearing in mind the temporarily high prices, the budget of 1920-1 was, broadly, representative of the inter-war budgets which were to follow.

Among the changes since 1913–14, the striking increase in the 'Consolidated Fund Services' stands out, representing mainly the national debt. In money terms, its burden increased tenfold, and unlike the other items of expenditure, it could not be reduced when prices and costs fell. Compared with pre-war, the national debt increased from $\frac{1}{40}$ to $\frac{1}{4}$ of the total private property in the country; the annual interest payments, negligible

---

[63] E. V. Morgan, *Studies in British Financial Policy, 1914-25* (1952), p. 98. On Professor Morgan's 'adjusted' figures, showing the sums actually collected and spent in the economic, rather than the administrative sense of the official figures, there was, in fact, a surplus of £110 million in 1919/20, p. 104.

[64] *Ibid.*, p. 101.

before the war, rose to over 40% of the budget, and as prices fell in the early 1920s, the real burden of this debt, as a payment from mainly the active part of the population to mainly the inactive, became distinctly heavier.

The total national debt was at its maximum in March 1920, when it stood at £7,830 million. Of this, only £315 million was funded, £1,230 being external, and the rest consisting of a 'floating' debt of some £1,250 million and of other unfunded debt of nearly £5,000 million with varying repayment dates and terms. The floating debt was tackled first, and within three years the Treasury Bills outstanding were reduced from over £1,100 million to little more than half this sum, while Ways and Means advances, standing at over £200 million in March 1920, were almost wiped out at the end of the decade.[65] The funding of this part of the floating debt, in the then existing market conditions, could only be done at great cost. The reduction of £440 million in short-term debt in the four financial years 1921–5 was achieved only by raising the nominal value of long-term issues by £1,000 million and forcing up long-term interest rates.

As it was, most critics were agreed that the war debts had been contracted at too generous a rate.[66] Moreover, with £2,100 million of the unfunded debt in 1920 falling due for repayment in 1–7 years, and £2,900 million in 8–10 years from the date of issue, repayments and renewals followed each other so closely in the 1920s that the whole tended to coagulate into one single mass of war debt, to be dealt with together. Actual repayments out of budget surpluses, often needlessly disguised as 'sinking funds', reached £583 million in 1925–6, but the nominal national debt fell by less than this, partly because of unfavourable conversions. The nominal total was brought down by £300 million, to £7,530 million, in 1931, and by 1935, of the £5,590 million of public debt held outside the Departments, £4,483 million was over 15 years or undated.[67]

The burden on the economy, however, was still high. The debt service fluctuated round 7% of the national income and rose to $8\frac{1}{4}$% in 1932 with the fall of incomes in the depression. Relief came only with the great War Loan Conversion of 1932, and the associated fall in short-term rates. The debt service burden then fell to 5·45% of national income in 1933, 5·00% in 1934 and 4·65% in 1935.

Next to the increase in the Consolidated Fund Services, the most striking increases occurred in the expenditure on the social services (see Table 3·12), though part of these were derived from special contributions under the insurance schemes.[68]

[65] A. T. K. Grant, *A Study of the Capital Market in Post-War Britain* (1937), pp. 86 ff; F. W. Paish, 'The Floating Debt, 1914–1939' in T. Balogh, *Studies in Financial Organization* (Cambridge, 1947).

[66] Ursula K. Hicks, *The Finance of British Government, 1920–1936* (1938), p. 317; E. V. Morgan, *op. cit.*, p. 139, also 94–7, 115–51; A. W. Kirkaldy (ed.), *British Finance During and After the War, 1914–21* (1921), pp. 161–2.

[67] *Report of the Committee on the Working of the Monetary System* (Radcliffe Committee) (1959. Cmnd. 827), Table 26.

[68] G. D. H. and M. Cole, *The Condition of Britain* (1937), pp. 328–9; C. L. Mowat, *Britain Between the Wars*, p. 497.

Table 3·12: Social services expenditure, 1913–34 (in £ million)

Payments made:	Area covered	1913–14	1921–2	1933–4
Poor relief	GB	16½	46	47
Health insurance	GB	14½	24½	32
Old-age pensions	GB	10	22	58½
Widows', etc., pensions	GB	—	—	22½
War pensions	UK	—	88½	44
Unemployment insurance	UK	½	53	88½
Totals		41½	234	292½
Contributions levied				
Health insurance	GB	17	25	26
Pensions	GB	—	—	23
Unemployment insurance	UK	2	30½	39½
Totals		19	55½	88½

Housing and education were other costly services, both of which also derived some share of their incomes from local authorities. As a result, the budgets of the local authorities were rising as rapidly as those of the Central Government[69] (see Table 3·13).

Table 3·13: Local Authorities expenditure and revenue (£m.)

Current expenditure (excl. trading)	1913–14	1938–9	Revenue	1913–14	1938–9
Education	36	118	Rates	82	215
Health	9	86	Current grants	27	164
Roads	23	68	Trading and		
Other	54	114	other	12	19
Totals	122	386	**Totals**	121	398
Capital expenditure (incl. trading)					
Housing	0	67			
Roads	4	16			
Trading	5	37			
Other	16	52			
Totals	25	172			

Most of this expansion occurred during the war or in the immediate post-war years, as a response to the claims or threats of Labour, but substantial increases were also voted in 1924 and 1925. Measured as a proportion of national income, social expenditure by the public authorities, national and local, increased from 5·5% in 1913 to 10·3% in 1924 and 13·0% in 1938; in the depression, when national income declined while relief payments kept up, it had risen even further, to 15·8% in 1932. Total Government expenditure as

[69] A. R. Prest, *Public Finance in Theory and Practice* (1960), pp. 181–2.

a proportion of GNP rose from 12·4% in 1913 to a peacetime peak of 29·4% in 1921, then levelled off around 24%, but with peaks at 28·8% in 1931 and 30·0% in 1938.[70]

A permanent increase in expenditure of such magnitude was bound to call forth major changes also in the methods of raising revenue. In broad outline, the total changes are summarized in table 3·14.[71]

Table 3·14:   Sources of revenue, 1913–39 (in £ million)

	1913–14	1924–5	1932–3	1938–9
Inland Revenue	88	419	411	520
(of which Income Tax)	(44)	(274)	(251)	(336)
Customs and Excise	75	234	288	341
Miscellaneous	10	64	45	66
Totals	173	717	744	927

Again, the main alterations occurred in the war years, the only important change after 1920 being the imposition of the tariff in 1932. Income tax, standing at 6s. in 1920–1, never fell below 4s. in the pound in the inter-war years. To mitigate some of its effects, more generous allowances for dependent relatives, and a differential in favour of earned incomes, suggested by the Royal Commission on the Income Tax in 1920,[72] were adopted, and were largely responsible for the form which the British tax structure assumed in the inter-war years. The war time Excess Profits Duty was abolished in 1921 and Corporation Profits Duty was repealed in 1924.

Among indirect taxation, the duties on tobacco and alcoholic drinks were retained at a high level after the war, and to these the hydrocarbon oil taxes and motor duties were added. New sources of taxation needed from 1925, largely in order to finance the growing social programme, were, apart from entertainments duty and the abortive betting tax of 1926, derived largely from protection. The tariff, even in the depression, yielded £40 million a year, and artificially raised food prices constituted a further large burden on the poor.

Before the war, 57·5% of the revenue had been in the form of direct taxes. This rose to a peak of 82·7% in 1917–18 and then settled at about 66% in the 1920s. It fell somewhat with the imposition of protective duties in 1932. The lowering of real wages by taxing the consumption of the working classes was, in fact, one of the aims of the protectionists. The high war-time taxes had been levied mainly on the rich, but owing to the expanded welfare services not all the redistributive effects were lost, particularly since Snowden's budgets of 1924 and 1930 were designed to benefit the lower income groups.

The examples in Table 3·15 show the changing burden of total taxation, including the estimated shares of indirect taxes, etc., expressed as a

[70] Ursula K. Hicks, *Public Finance* (1947), p. 32. Also Alan T. Peacock and Jack Wiseman, *The Growth of Public Expenditure in the United Kingdom* (1967), p. 166.

[71] Prest, *op. cit.*, pp. 157–8; *Statistical Abstract of the UK*, Annual.

[72] *Royal Commission on Income Tax, Report* (1920. Cmd. 615), paras. 126–40.

percentage of income, on a family of two adults and three dependent children, living on earned income only at different levels of income:[73]

Table 3·15:   Taxation as a percentage of income, 1913–38

	Income of £100	£200	£500	£1,000	£10,000
1913–14	5·4	4·0	4·4	5·2	8·0
1918–19	9·9	7·9	10·2	16·9	42·5
1923–4	14·1	11·8	8·0	14·1	37·1
1925–6	11·9	10·2	6·2	11·0	31·2
1930–1	11·0	9·6	4·5	9·7	35·8
1937–8	10·4	8·4	5·6	11·8	39·1

British taxation, it will be observed, was not as 'progressive' as is often supposed. Taxes on smaller families, and local rates, were even more regressive over a wide range. Medium incomes between £250 and £1,000 a year enjoyed the lowest percentage burden. The heaviest burdens on the poorer families were duties on tea, sugar, tobacco, alcohol and, latterly, taxes on production, such as wheat and coal.[74] On the other hand, death duties and profits taxes, which fell more heavily on the rich, are omitted from the table.

As far as the allocation of expenditure was concerned, it also worked in the direction of redistribution in this period. According to one estimate, while in 1913 the working classes received less in social services than they paid in taxes, by 1925 they contributed only 85% of the cost (receiving the excess of £45 million from other classes) and in 1935 they contributed but 79%, receiving an excess of £91 million.[75] For 1937 it was found that, on various assumptions, the sums redistributed to the poorer income groups (receiving under £125 a year) were in the range of £193–274 million. The total redistributed amounted to 5–6% of the national income.[76] Other calculations put the amount of redistribution lower than this.

These figures may seem disappointingly small. There were several causes for it. In the first place, a large proportion of the welfare schemes was financed by the working classes themselves: the employees' weekly insurance payments alone rose from 1·9% of average earnings in industry in 1912 to 2·3% of the higher earnings in 1938. Further indirect taxation, including protective tariffs, added by 1938 an average of 7·2% to the prices of all goods. The percentage was particularly high for tobacco (49·4%) and alcoholic drinks (37·8%), widely consumed by the poorer classes.[77]

Secondly, not all the benefits of social welfare provisions went to the

[73] G. Findlay Shirras and L. Rostas, *The Burden of British Taxation* (Cambridge, 1942), p. 58; cf. also Sir Bernard Mallet and C. Oswald George, *British Budgets* (*Second Series*), *1913–14 to 1920–21* (1929), Appx. Table XXI.

[74] Shirras and Rostas, p. 37; Hicks, *Finance of British Government*, chapter 16.

[75] Mowat, *Britain Between the Wars*, p. 492; Colin Clark, *National Income and Outlay* (1937), pp. 145–8.

[76] T. Barna, *The Redistribution of Incomes through Public Finance in 1937* (Oxford, 1945), pp. 229–30.

[77] Prest, *Public Finance*, p. 360.

poorer families. The housing subsidies, for example, benefited chiefly the better-off manual workers and the white-collar workers and lower middle classes. The benefits of public provision for education were greatest for families still higher on the income scale. One estimate puts the incidence of divisible benefits in 1937 at the annual rates *per capita* (£)[78] as follows:

Table 3·16: Social welfare benefits per capita (£) in 1937

Income class	Education	Public health	Health insurance	Assistance and unemployment insurance	Pensions	Housing
Under £125	2·1	1·2	0·7	4·2	5·1	0·4
£125 and under £250	3·1	1·2	0·4	0·8	1·1	0·7
£250 ″ ″ £500	3·7	1·3	—	—	0·3	—

Lastly, the large annual national debt payments added a further strong regressive element to the tax system.

The budget, originally designed merely to meet the necessary expenditure of the Government, had even before 1914 acquired the secondary duty of assisting in carrying out other desirable social and economic aims, by the nature of the taxes collected and the expenditure disbursed. Now, given the size of Government transactions, (e.g. public gross fixed capital formation, running at £312 million in 1938, represented over 30% of the total of some £1,000 million) the support of official monetary policy, and above all the maintenance of the value of the currency, became a third task to be placed upon the budget between the wars. In the century of peace before 1914 the value of the pound sterling had been maintained in terms of gold by the free convertibility at the Central Bank. However, since the abrogation of the gold standard, in practice in 1914 and legally in 1919, there had occurred a considerable measure of inflation, which could plausibly be blamed on the over-expansion of the currency by the Government. As the restoration of the pound to its pre-war parity with gold became an aim of policy from 1919 onward, the Government was bound to accept the responsibility of playing itself a major part in the necessary deflation. The runaway inflations which occurred in the early 1920s in several countries, also seemed to point to the conclusion that sound currency could only be achieved by 'orthodox' finance, which consisted in balancing the budget. In turn, this affected the parallel attempts to prevent, or cure, industrial fluctuations leading to mass unemployment. These turned, after years of debate, into yet a fourth task of the budget.

This new aspect of economic policy had several roots. It derived from the proposals of the Swedish economists in the late 1920s, from the budding 'national income' approach of economists, and the doctrines on money, interest, investment and saving propagated by J. M. Keynes.[79] It received its

---

[78] U. K. Hicks, *Public Finance*, p. 298.
[79] J. M. Keynes, *A Treatise on Money*, 2 vols. (1930), and *The Means to Prosperity* (1933); also R. F. Kahn's fundamental contribution, 'The Relation of Home Investment to Employment', *Econ. J.*, 41/162, 1931.

most complete exposition in Keynes's *General Theory*,[80] and it is with his name that it is generally associated.

In the narrow sense, the new doctrine asserted that in depressions it was the duty of the Government to expand its activities and to create additional incomes by programmes of public works and other inflationary actions,[81] as well as to encourage investment by low interest rates. This was in direct contrast to the current 'Treasury view', described by the then Chancellor, Winston Churchill, in the House of Commons in April 1929 as 'the orthodox Treasury doctrine which has steadfastly held that, whatever might be the political or social advantages, very little additional employment and no permanent additional employment can, in fact, and as a general rule, be created by State borrowing and State expenditure'.[82] The official view did not change throughout the depression years.[83]

In the wider sense, the new doctrine held that it was the duty of the Government, by budgetary as well as other means, to control the economy so as to keep it at a steady and high level of activity. Sweden, Australia, New Zealand and, to some extent, the USA carried out policies which, however unconsciously, were in line with the new economics; but in Britain the pragmatic efforts of the Labour Government of 1929–31 to foster public works by the Development (Loan Guarantee and Grants) Act and the Colonial Development Act of 1929 were a failure. Although Keynes made many converts among academic economists, it was not until the early years of the war that the new economics received official sanction in budgetary policy and elsewhere.[84] It followed from the new, and now widely accepted doctrine, that British budgetary policy in the inter-war years was of a nature to aggravate the ill effects of the trade cycle.

In the financial year 1919–20, when all the Government's efforts should have been directed to restraining inflation, it added to it by a budget deficit. From 1920–1, by contrast, the Government determined to achieve a surplus and reduce the floating debt in order to regain control over the market and prepare the way for the ultimate return to gold at the old parity. The consequent immense deflationary pressure, applied by the Government from April 1920 onwards, when the boom began to sag, greatly aggravated the effects and extent of the slump. Budgetary policy was similarly ill-timed in the recurring crises and difficulties of the remainder of the inter-war years.[85]

Deflationary policies were maintained in all the budgets of the early 1920s, and throughout the decade it proved possible to devote regularly, year by year, a sum averaging £50 million for debt redemption. Meanwhile, however, the severe depression continued, and the accepted doctrine for a rigidly

---

[80] J. M. Keynes, *General Theory of Employment, Interest and Money* (1936).

[81] R. F. Bretherton, F. A. Burchardt, R. S. G. Rutherford, *Public Investment and the Trade Cycle* (1941), chapter 1.

[82] Quoted in S. H. Beer, *Treasury Control* (1956), pp. 1–2.

[83] U. K. Hicks, *Finance of British Government*, chapter 13; A. D. Gayer, *Monetary Policy and Economic Stabilisation* (1935), chapter 10; Richard W. Lyman, *The First Labour Government, 1924* (London, 1957), chapter 9; K. J. Hancock, 'The Reduction of Unemployment as a Problem of Public Policy, 1920–29', *Ec. Hist. Rev.*, 2nd S., 15/2, 1962, pp. 335–8.

[84] U. K. Hicks, *Public Finance*, chapter 17; H. W. Arndt, *The Economic Lessons of the Nineteen-Thirties* (1944), chapters 2 and 8. Also chapter 5 section 3, below.

[85] Cf. also sections 5, 6 and 7 of this chapter.

orthodox Chancellor in such a case was to reduce taxation, but only if he could impose equivalent cuts in expenditure. Some tax remissions were made in 1922–3, while the fall in incomes would clearly reduce the yield from all existing taxes: the problem was to find the reductions in expenditure. A committee of businessmen, headed by Sir Eric Geddes, was therefore set up to suggest economies, and in three reports[86] recommended cuts totalling £87 million, quickly dubbed the 'Geddes axe'.

Few departments escaped the axe. Some large savings were to be achieved on the military service votes, but the most severe cuts were reserved for the social services, including education and tuberculosis, maternity and child welfare services. Among others, the Ministry of Transport, the Mines Department, the Electricity Commissioners, the Department of Overseas Trade, the Ministry of Labour and the Employment Exchanges were to be abolished. These destructive proposals were not accepted in their entirety by the Chancellor; nevertheless, some of the social services, above all education, took over a decade to recover from the cuts imposed in 1922. As it turned out, there was a large surplus of over £100 million achieved in 1922–3, used for debt redemption. In the next year, revenue was down by £77 million, largely owing to cuts in income tax, profits tax and beer duties, but as expenditure was also down by £24 million, there was still a sizeable surplus.

Snowden's budget of 1924 represented a partial reversal of the trend to wipe out the egalitarian legacies of the war. He made substantial reductions in indirect taxation, notably among the (revenue) customs duties, and the McKenna duties were also repealed, with the thorough approval of the Liberals on whom the Government depended in the House. The result was virtually to wipe out the surplus of earlier years and to end the era of surpluses of the early 1920s: henceforth budgets were more closely balanced, and over the rest of the inter-war years, surpluses and deficits roughly cancelled out.

Winston Churchill's budget of 1925 was the second important budget of the decade. Apart from the re-introduction of the gold standard, the budget speech was notable for reversing the previous deflationary emphasis. The new Widows', Orphans' and Old Age Contributory Pensions Act laid extra burden on the Exchequer, particularly in years to come. Churchill's budget of 1928 added further expenditure and so did Neville Chamberlain's Local Government Act of 1929, which, among other reforms, included a major measure of derating for agricultural land, industry and the railways. The Treasury was to make up the losses of rates to local authorities, estimated at £30 million, by 'block' grants, which, unlike earlier grants, favoured the authorities with the poorer incomes and higher costs.[87]

While expenditure was thus increased in 1925, income tax rates were cut. Inevitably, the year 1925–6 ended with a deficit and so did the next year, and Churchill balanced his budgets only by short-term manipulation. These inflationary budgets were introduced just at a time when the re-establishment of the gold standard forced deflationary policies on the monetary authorities.

Snowden's budget of 1930 was introduced in an atmosphere of worsening

[86] *Committee on National Expenditure, Reports* (1922. Cmd. 1581, 1582, 1589).

[87] C. L. Mowat, *Britain Between the Wars*, pp. 199–200, 339–42; P. J. Grigg, *Prejudice and Judgment* (1948), pp. 194–209.

trade and mounting unemployment. Forced to find additional revenue to meet the shortfall expected because of declining incomes and mounting pension and relief payments, the Chancellor added heavily to direct taxes, including 6*d*. on the income tax, while allowing a whole series of safe-guarding duties to lapse. No important changes were made in the budget of 1931; the threatening deficits were to be met by raids, anticipations and transfers on Churchillian models. Proposals for reducing expenditure expected from a Committee presided over by Sir George May, however, had a large share in bringing down the second Labour Government and setting thereby the political course for the 1930s.

Technically, the May Report was concerned with the narrow problem of making an estimate of the budget deficit to be expected, and suggesting means of meeting it. Within this relatively narrow framework, however, it is difficult to avoid the conclusion that the Report was designed to thwart and damage the Labour Government and its social welfare programme, especially the increased unemployment payments which it had authorized. The Committee's estimates rested on the most pessimistic assumptions,[88] and the expenditures singled out for special comment were those with a welfare content. The Unemployment Insurance Fund, which had kept solvent throughout the heavy unemployment of the 1920s, but was now running a deficit, received particular attention, and defaults on its existing rates of payments were among the Committee's strongest recommendations, while reductions in the national debt payments, then at close on £300 million a year, were not even considered, though they were recommended by the Macmillan Committee reporting at about the same time,[89] and in the event were carried out without a hitch in the following year. By such means, it was possible for the May Committee to forecast a total budget deficit of £120 million a year. This the Committee proposed to meet by raising another £24 million in taxes and cutting expenditure by £96 million, of which two-thirds was to be accounted for by slashing unemployment pay.

Several members of the Cabinet were not prepared to see relief cut to the extent demanded, but after the Labour Government had split on this issue, and a 'National' Government formed in August 1931, many of the May Committee suggestions were adopted by Snowden in his autumn budget.[90] Direct and indirect taxes were heavily increased, and unemployment contributions raised. On the expenditure side, there were reductions in the appropriations to the sinking fund, in salaries of civil servants, police, teachers and others, and a 10% cut in unemployment benefit rates and other reductions in benefits.

Salary cuts and rigid economy at the centre were backed up by the enforcement of the most severe retrenchment in local government. Economy circulars of an almost mandatory tone were sent round. Public works grants were abruptly discontinued. An (unofficial) embargo was placed on local borrowing on the stock

[88] P. J. Grigg, *op. cit.*, p. 255.
[89] *Committee on Finance and Industry, Report* (1931. Cmd. 3897), Addendum, I, paras. 28–30.
[90] C. L. Mowat, *op. cit.*, pp. 379–412.

exchange. The fall in rate-receipts due to the depression and the activities of local economy committees, their nerves completely shattered by the magnitude of the disaster, caused an even greater collapse of local than of central spending.[91]

In the event, the budget balanced almost exactly, at £851 million.

From 1932 onwards, Chancellors operated in a less restrictive environment, helped by the successful conversion of some £1,970 million of War Loan from 5% to $3\frac{1}{2}$% in the course of 1932, the revenue of the newly imposed tariff and the easing of the balance of payments by going off gold. However, Britain was alone among major Western nations not to resort to budget deficits to promote recovery and, according to the more accurate constant employment budget balance calculations, it appers that the budgets of the 1930s until 1936 were even more restrictive and therefore more harmful than had once been thought.[92]

Table 3·17:   Central government accounts, calendar years 1920–38* (£ million)

	Taxes on income	Taxes on expenditure	Total receipts (incl. other items)	Total expenditure	Deficit/ surplus
1920	609	334	1053	964	+89
1925	344	289	816	794	+20
1931	328	312	874	908	−32
1932	352	348	912	886	+26
1933	310	346	881	836	+45
1936	288	396	921	907	+14
1938	383	415	1036	1145	−109

* C.H. Feinstein, *National Income*, T. 31–2.

In 1934, expecting a surplus, Neville Chamberlain restored unemployment rates and half the cuts in Government salaries, the rest being made good in 1935–6; at the same time, the standard rate of income tax was reduced by 6*d*, from 5*s*. to 4*s*. 6*d*. in the pound. The 1936 budget was the first in which defence expenditure rose significantly, by £50 million to £187 million. Like the budget of the following years, it was met in part by a rise in income tax rates. Even so, the budget of 1938–9 made provision for borrowing £90 million, and the budget of 1939–40 £380 million for defence expenditure. The last budget was not destined to survive the financial year. A September budget, after the outbreak of war, increased income tax from 5*s*. 6*d*. to 7*s*. 6*d*. in the pound and introduced an excess profits tax of 60%, besides making other changes.

5 Economic and Financial Policy in the 1920s

The war ended with wholesale prices 140%, and the cost of living 120–125%, above the level of July 1914. Technically, deflation might have been possible in 1919, but politically it was unthinkable.[93] As demobilized soldiers returned

[91] U. K. Hicks, *Finance of British Government*, pp. 361–2.

[92] Roger Middleton, 'The Constant Employment Budget Balance and British Budgeting Policy, 1929–1939', *Ec. Hist. Rev.* 34/2, 1981.

[93] C. H. Feinstein, *National Income*, T. 31–2. J. M. Keynes, *A Treatise on Money* (1930), vol. 2, pp. 176–7.

to civilian employment by the million, the fear among members of the Government and their advisers was of widespread unemployment, not of runaway inflation. Instead of restricting credit, Britain went formally off gold in March 1919 (having been *de facto* off gold since the outbreak of war) and allowed the credit expansion of the war years to go on into 1920.

On this swelling stream of easy credit, employment picked up rapidly in the summer of 1919, the demand coming from the backlog of necessary consumer goods restricted during the war years, translated into demands for stocks and capital goods, also run down during the war. Prices rose sharply, a speculative element in the boom feeding on itself to keep inflation going. Thus the boom of 1919–20 was largely one of prices, not output: at no stage did industrial output approach, let alone exceed, that of 1913.[94] An important element here was the substantial reduction in working hours enforced in most industries after the war, which raised labour costs without raising real earnings.[95] However, wages and other costs, while rising, rose less than prices, and there was a shift in the distribution of incomes in favour of profits, used in part to carry through a substantial programme of capital investment and re-equipment of British industry, and this in turn led to the over-capitalization which was to burden several major British industries with top-heavy capital structures for the next two decades.

Before long, the Government's main preoccupation was the inflation.[96] In April 1920, a deflationary budget and determined action to reduce the floating debt was accompanied by a rise in bank rate, and there followed one of the most precipitous declines in British industrial history, unemployment rising from 2% to 18%, and the index of industrial activity falling from 117·9 to 90·0 in the space of one year.[97] Almost overnight, the Government had turned from unemployment as a major preoccupation to callous disregard for it altogether, as soon as the social peace was no longer threatened.[98]

Some months before this reversal of policy, in December 1919, the influential Cunliffe Committee on Currency and Foreign Exchanges after the War had reported to recommend the restoration of the gold standard at the earliest possible opportunity.[99] It was content to retain notes for small payments in place of the gold sovereigns of pre-war years, and therefore was prepared to enlarge the fiduciary issue by amalgamating the Treasury notes, in circulation since 1914, with the Bank of England note issue of which up to then only some £17 million had been fiduciary. For large transactions, however, the cheque and the bank deposit system was to be brought back to gold by restoring the power of the Central Bank to force the joint-stock banks to vary the aggregate of their deposits in accordance with the state of its gold reserve. But in 1919 Britain was still far from such equilibrium. In order to

[94] A. C. Pigou, *Aspects of British Economic History, 1918–1925* (1947), p. 62.

[95] J. A. Dowie, '1919–20 is in need of attention', *Ec. Hist. Rev.* 28/3, 1975.

[96] Susan Howson, 'The Origins of Dear Money, 1919–20', *ibid.* 27/1, 1974; *idem*, 'A Dear Money Man?: Keynes on Monetary Policy, 1920', *Econ. J.*, 83, 1973; *idem*, *Domestic Monetary Management in Britain 1919–1938*, (Cambridge, 1975), p. 28.

[97] W. H. Beveridge, *Full Employment in a Free Society* (1944), p. 313.

[98] Rodney Lowe, 'The Erosion of State Intervention in Britain 1917–24', *Ec. Hist. Rev.* 31/2, 1978.

[99] Reprinted in T. E. Gregory, *Select Statutes, Documents and Reports Relating to British Banking, 1832–1928* (Oxford, 1929), pp. 366 ff.

regain a 'currency upon a sound basis', a stringent financial policy was necessary. The budget would have to be balanced, foreign lending suspended (except to borrowers who were capable of repaying their loans), foreign trade brought into balance, and the large surplus of bank notes reduced. On the latter point, the Committee suggested that the minimum note issue of one year should become the maximum issue of the next.

This programme was accepted by the Government in principle and in detail.[100] The severe deflation induced from April 1920 onward became the first step in a consistent policy which had one over-riding aim: the restoration of the gold standard at the old parity at the earliest possible moment.[101] Neither the heavy unemployment, nor the obstinate inability of production or exports to return to their pre-war figures, was to divert the authorities from their course. The efficacy of the gold standard which, once established, would restore British trade, prosperity and prestige, became a Sorelian myth in the City. It was happily convenient for City interests that their own prosperity, security and comfort, at no matter what cost to other sectors of the economy, was the only way to benefit the British economy as a whole.

Imbued with these ideas, the Government pursued its deflationary policy with consistent ruthlessness. A bank rate of near panic level, at 7%, was kept on for a year, until April 1921, at a time of disastrous unemployment, and even afterwards the rate was reduced but slowly. The 'Geddes axe' became a by-word for callous meanness. Agricultural price support, in spite of a statutory guarantee for four years, was overthrown with indecent haste as soon as it became operative.[102] But, within its limits, the policy began to work.

The budget was balanced, and a favourable foreign balance of payments restored. The short-term debt, which had destroyed the power of the Bank over the market, was greatly reduced. So was the note issue, and bank deposits fell from over £2,000 million in December 1920 to £1,800 million in June 1925.[103] Above all, prices came down almost as fast as they had climbed: wholesale prices, which had risen from about 210 in March 1919 (1913 = 100) to a peak of 310–340 in mid-1920, were down to 190–210 in March 1921 and 160–170 in February 1922. Wage rates, which did not reach their peak until early in 1921, proved very flexible also (quite a number had been tied to the cost-of-living index) and fell from 275 in the winter of 1920–1 (July 1914 = 100) to 173 in the winter of 1923–4, rising slowly to 181 in March 1925.[104] From 1922 onwards it was even possible to pursue more normal policies appropriate to a slump, such as a lower bank rate, and a slight recovery was nursed up in 1922–4, though the preparations of the authorities for the return to gold helped to hold it back well below the recovery of other countries.

---

[100] Treasury Minute of 15 December 1919 (Cmd. 485), reprinted in Gregory, *loc. cit.*, p. 371.

[101] A. C. Pigou, *Aspects of British Economic History, 1918–1925* (1947 ed.), Part V, chapter 1; S. E. Harris, *Monetary Problems of the British Empire* (New York, 1931), Part II, Book 5; Lawrence Smith, 'England's Return to the Gold Standard in 1925', *J. Econ. and Business History*, 4, 1931–2, p. 230.

[102] W. Philip Jeffcock, *Agricultural Politics* (Ipswich, 1937), p. 6.

[103] E. V. Morgan, *Studies in British Financial Policy, 1914–25* (1925), pp. 73, 155–6, 220–31. Also p. 126 above.

[104] *Ibid.*, pp. 73, 271–86.

Substantial as this deflation in prices and costs was, however, it had just not gone far enough to match American prices and permit an easy return to gold at pre-war parities. The dollar rate of exchange, which had fallen to below $3·50 in the autumn of 1920, rose to about $4·70, or near parity, in the winter of 1922–3,[105] and then fluctuated, not about a mean of the pre-war gold equivalent rate of $4·86, but about a rate around $4·40 or $4·50, i.e. 10% less. Home prices, costs and wages, were stuck at a level about 10% too high, and in spite of the 'capitalist offensive' fought from 1921 on to bring them down,[106] wages could not be reduced any further especially since wages in export industries had been sharply lowered already, while wages in the 'sheltered' home industries remained immune to pressure.[107] Combinations of capital and cartel agreements made other prices increasingly sticky downwards, and high taxes added further rigidities.[108]

If the stickiness of home costs was one reason for making the return to gold difficult, the level of the gold reserve was another. It had stood at about £150 million when the Cunliffe Committee reported, and this became accepted, for no very sound reason, as the safe minimum, but it was no easy task to keep the reserve at that level. With a weakened balance of trade, and a restored City machinery to send capital abroad in spite of the unofficial embargo on foreign loans by the Bank of England,[109] there was a tendency for gold to flow out, avoided only by attracting short-term funds to London, sources of trouble later.

From the middle of 1924 on the authorities began to push up the exchange rate of the pound to a level which would make free convertibility possible. London rates of interest were raised substantially above those ruling in New York, and funds began to flow in. The belief that an attempt would be made to restore the pound to its old parity in the course of 1925, before inconvertibility would lapse automatically at the end of the year, attracted further funds. By April 1925 the pound had virtually reached its pre-war parity with the dollar, and Mr Churchill, the Chancellor of the Exchequer, announced the return to gold. Britain could claim to have made a major contribution to the stabilization of the foreign exchanges after the stress of wars and revolutions, and a large number of other countries returned to gold in the next year or two, though not all at pre-war parities.

Nevertheless, the decision to return to gold at the old parity was one of the most controversial of the period. It called forth a large volume of criticism, among the most intelligent and far-sighted of which was that associated with the name of J. M. Keynes.[110] Although Keynes had most of the orthodox

[105] A. J. Youngson, *The British Economy, 1920.1957* (1960), p. 29.

[106] W. A. Lewis, *Economic Survey, 1919.1939* (1949), pp. 43.4.

[107] Henry Clay, *The Post-War Unemployment Problem* (1929), p. 93.

[108] E. Nevin, *The Mechanism of Cheap Money, a Study of British Monetary Policy, 1931.1939* (Cardiff, 1955), pp. 23, 32; A. D. Gayer, *Monetary Policy and Economic Stabilisation* (1935), chapter 3; J. M. Keynes, *A Treatise on Money* (1930), vol. 2, pp. 180 ff.

[109] Sir Henry Clay, *Lord Norman* (1957), pp. 144.5.

[110] J. M. Keynes, *Tract on Monetary Reform* (1923) and *The Economic Consequences of Mr. Churchill* (1925). Cf. also André Siegfried, *England's Crisis* (1931), chapter 2, §1; K. J. Hancock, 'Unemployment and the Economists in the 1920s', *Economica*, NS, 27/108, 1960, pp. 308.11; D. E. Moggridge, *British Monetary Policy 1924.1931. The Norman Conquest of $4·86* (Cambridge, 1972).

economic opinion against him at the time, there would be few today who would deny that Keynes's misgivings were warranted.[111]

Keynes's criticism ran along two lines. The first was concerned to show that at the old parity the pound would be over-valued to the extent of about 10%. This was borne out by the internal price levels: with pre-war at 100, British internal prices even in the favourable month of April 1925 stood at 176 compared with 165 in the USA. The hopes of the authorities that world prices were about to rise up to the British price level and thus remove the handicap they had put on British industry, were misplaced; world prices fell after 1925 and several other countries, including France, Belgium and Germany, returned to gold at lower parities, thus making the competitive disability of British prices greater still. The decision to return had taken appalling risks with British industry. It was a City decision, emphatically not a decision of the industrialists: 'had their views been given as much weight as those of the City, it is unlikely that the change would ever have been made'.[112]

The forecasts of the critics as to the consequences of returning to gold at too high a level soon began to come true with fateful precision. A price differential of around 10%, while encouraging imports, formed a most severe handicap to the export industries in their most difficult period, when Britain was falling most calamitously behind other industrial countries. According to one calculation, a return to gold at the correct parity would, in a 'normal' year like 1928, have reduced unemployment by more than half, from 1,290,000 to 561,000 and allowed the authorities freedom to carry out most of the rest of their policies.[113]

The ill-effects of the high interest rates which the Bank of England was forced to maintain to prevent the loss of gold as a result of the weaker trade balance were more pervasive still. They kept up the burdens of the national debt charge, and thus of taxation. They attracted speculative funds of dangerous instability into London. Above all, dear money was designed to depress enterprise directly, and to preserve the foreign exchanges by creating deflation and unemployment at home. This high structure of interest rates in a period of depression was to be described later as 'putting on the brake when going uphill'.[114]

These issues were debated at length in the evidence and in the Report of the Macmillan Committee which sat in 1929–31;[115] most dramatically, they came up in the exchanges between Montagu Norman, Governor of the Bank of England throughout this period, and a key figure in the working of the gold

[111] For a rare recent contrary view, see Youngson, *op. cit.*, chapter 7; also R. S. Sayers, 'The Return to Gold', in L. S. Pressnell (ed.), *Studies in the Industrial Revolution* (1960), and T. E. Gregory, *The First Year of the Gold Standard* (1926), and *The Gold Standard and its Future* (3rd ed., 1934), chapters 3 and 4.

[112] Alan Bullock, the *Life and Times of Ernest Bevin*, Vol. 1 (1960), p. 267, cf. also pp. 428–9, and F. E. Gannett and B. F. Catherwood, *Industrial and Labour Relations in Great Britain* (1939), p. 283; S. Pollard, Introduction to *The Gold Standard and Employment Policies between the Wars* (1970); N. H. Dimsdale, 'British Monetary Policy and the Exchange Rate 1920–1938', *Oxf. Econ. P.*, 33, 1981, Supplement, p. 315.

[113] Moggridge, *British Monetary Policy*, pp. 100–6, 249–50; and *The Return to Gold, 1925* (Cambridge 1969) pp. 94–6.

[114] R. G. Hawtrey, *The Gold Standard in Theory and Practice* (5th ed., 1947), pp. 108, 119.

[115] *Report of the Committee on Finance and Industry* (1931. Cmd. 3897); *Minutes of Evidence*, 2 vols. (1931).

standard, and his questioners, above all Keynes and Ernest Bevin. The Governor at first denied that the high bank rate he was forced to impose to maintain the gold standard was responsible for creating unemployment (Questions 3328, 3334–8, 3343–51); he was then driven to concede that his high bank rate was designed directly to create unemployment (Qq. 3492–3). The burden of his evidence to the Macmillan Committee was that he was under such constant pressure to keep up rates to prevent a drain abroad that he could not, even had he wished, consider the effects on industry, but that until 1930, at least, he had not greatly troubled about them.[116]

In retrospect, it seems impossible to deny that the preparations and the return to gold at too high a rate contributed to the depressed conditions of British industry in 1925–9, at a time when the rest of the world enjoyed a prolific boom, just as the removal of the handicap in 1931 was responsible for the sudden spurt of British exports relatively to other countries.

Keynes's second line of criticism was that in post-war conditions the international gold standard would not be allowed to work as freely as the idealized pre-war standard was said to have done. The large gold hoarders, the Bank of France and the Federal Reserve Board of the USA, would not play the game according to the rules, but would 'manage' their currency in spite of compensating gold flows, thus rendering impossible the task of a country like Great Britain with a gold reserve of barely £150 million to maintain stability in the sterling area as well as among several minor currencies[117]. Britain could stabilize either price levels or exchange rates, but could not do both; and she would do better to concentrate on stabilizing prices.

This forecast, also, was abundantly justified by later events.[118] In Britain, changes in the banking structure and in the money market further interfered very seriously with the automatic regulative function of the gold reserve of the Bank of England, described with such great confidence by the Cunliffe Committee.[119] For one thing, by 1925 a high bank rate did not bring in any provincial funds, as in former periods, for there were none. Instead, it merely attracted short-term foreign funds, which left again the moment the London rate was reduced, without effect on the general price level. If, on the other hand, a high bank rate did succeed in compressing incomes and creating deflation in Britain, with the consequence of a rise in exports and an influx of gold or funds, this would, under existing conditions, merely spread deflation abroad and thus counteract the British deflation.[120] It was an essential part of the mechanism of the pre-war gold standard that there was a single credit centre, London, which could enforce its monetary policies on the rest of the world. After the war, there were two major centres, London and New York,

[116] *Minutes of Evidence*, 18th Day. Even then, Norman's evidence as published was doctored: his own words showed even less concern with industry. A. Boyle, *Montagu Norman* (1967), p. 258; T. Gregory; 'Lord Norman: A New Interpretation', *Lloyds Bank Review*, 88 (1968), p. 38.

[117] For some of these external burdens on the sterling reserves, see L. S. Pressnell, '1925: The Burden on Sterling', *Ec. Hist. Rev.* 31/1, 1978.

[118] A. D. Gayer, *Monetary Policy and Economic Stablisation* (1935), chapter 2; W. A. Morton, *British Finance 1930–1940* (Madison, 1943), pp. 87, 97–101.

[119] *First Interim Report*, Cd. 9182 paras. 4–7.

[120] R. G. Hawtrey, (5th ed., 1947), pp. 124–5; A. E. Kahn, *op. cit.*, pp. 20–1; Keynes, *Treatise on Money*, pp. 309–15; Gayer, p. 23.

and several minor ones, and the mechanism was, therefore, likely to show very different responses.[121]

Secondly, the large quantities of Treasury Bills still outstanding even after the conversion and funding of 1921-5 and a weekly issue of £40 million of Treasury Bills to be absorbed, nullified the former power of the Bank of England to influence the lending policies of the joint-stock 'banks via the latter's credit with it, treated by them as part of their cash reserve: the banks and the money market had the power of maintaining their cash in spite of losses of gold by abstaining from buying Treasury bills',[122] and the Bank of England was forced to take up these bills and render its own restrictive policy nugatory. The Macmillan Committee failed to note this development, though it found that one-half of the short-term assets of the clearing banks consisted of Treasury Bills even in the 1920s,[123] but it was discussed by Lord Bradbury, in a dissenting Memorandum.[124] The official recognition of this mechanism had to wait for the Radcliffe Report of 1959,[125] which at last killed the concept, 'given an extra thirty years' lease of life by the Macmillan Report, that the effective basis of credit resides in the cash reserves of the banks',[126]

Lastly, a true international gold standard assumes that changes in the foreign exchange position would be rectified by changes in home prices, but industry in Britain (and elsewhere) in the 1920s was too rigid to stand this flexible price system. The City, ill-informed as it was of industrial affairs, remained ignorant of this inflexibility, and thus 'fundamentally economic policy and structural conditions were out of phase with each other'.[127]

The gold standard, re-established at too high a parity by Britain, would have been difficult to work at the best of times, in view of the permanent structural changes; as it happened, it set out on its course in the most unfavourable circumstances. Some countries returned to gold on a 'gold exchange' basis, basing their convertibility on reserves held in the form of balances in London or New York which could be turned into gold, thus putting a dangerous burden on London, especially since the 'gold exchange' countries got their London balances, not by foreign trade surplus, but by short-term loans.[128] In the pre-war days the Bank of England had held sufficient short-term claims by London on foreign centres to balance roughly the foreign short-term claims on London, and to make the effects of a change

[121] W. A. Brown, Jr, *The International Gold Standard Re-interpreted, 1914-34*, 2 vols. (New York, 1940).

[122] Hawtrey, *Century of Bank Rate*, pp. 136, 257.

[123] *Committee on Finance and Industry, Report* (1931. Cmd. 3897), paras. 22, 29, 72-87, Appx. I, Table 3, pp. 296-7; also see Keynes, *Treatise on Money*, chapters 2, 25, 32; T. Balogh, *Studies in Financial Organisation* (Cambridge, 1947), pp. 39-40, 56 ff.; Nevin, *Cheap Money*, pp. 118-20; *Radcliffe Report*, paras. 506-11.

[124] Cmd. 3897, *Memorandum of Dissent* by Lord Bradbury, paras. 19-22.

[125] *Report of the Committee on the Working of the Monetary System* (1959. Cmnd. 827).

[126] W. Manning Dicey, 'Treasury Bills and the Money Supply', *Lloyd's Bank Review*, NS, 55, 1960, p. 1, and *Money under Review* (1960), p. 11, also pp. 52-63; cf. also R. S. Sayers, *Central Banking after Bagehot* (1957), p. 21.

[127] David Williams, 'Montagu Norman and Banking Policy in the Nineteen-Twenties', *Yorkshire Bull.*, 11/1, 1959, p. 55. For a full-scale study see Sir Henry Clay, *Lord Norman* (1957).

[128] W. A. Lewis, *op. cit.*, p. 47.

in bank rate felt quickly in all parts of the globe; but in the 1920s, foreign short-term holdings in London greatly exceeded the sterling bills on foreign account and other similar assests by a margin estimated by the Macmillan Committee at £250–300 million.[129]

Moreover, several countries, including Japan, Poland, and France, returned to gold at rates which under-valued their currencies, thus giving their exporters an additional advantage over those of Britain, while others including Italy, Belgium and France, stabilized their currency at high home price levels, allowing their industrialists to preserve their inflation gains of lower real wages and other fixed charges.[130] The slow fall of world prices after 1925 made the task of the export industries more difficult still.[131]

High rates to prevent gold drains dampened incipient economic expansion in the late 1920s. The burden of high interest rates and restrictive bank policies could not be eased as long as internal costs stayed up,[132] and it proved impossible to lower these: wages in 1929 stood at 99·5 (1924 = 100). By the end of the decade the harmful effect of British monetary policy on industry and exports was widely understood, but short of allowing home prices to rise, which would mean jettisoning the gold parity, there seemed to be no practicable policy to solve the dilemma of the British economy.

6 The Years of Crisis: 1929–1931

Up to 1929, Britain had been labouring under the special difficulties of over-large export industries and an over-valued currency, but the rest of the world had witnessed something akin to the orthodox cyclical sequence: a speculative and inflationary boom in 1919–20, followed by collapse and depression in 1921–2, and succeeded, in turn, by a rise to general conditions of prosperity in the later 1920s, including a rapid increase in output, profits and incomes, and a boom in share prices which ended, after an orgy of stock exchange speculation, in a financial crash, signalizing the onset of yet another depression.

In conformity with the new distribution of economic power, the crash actually occurred in New York, in October 1929.[133] It was, to begin with, a purely financial phenomenon, but soon transmitted itself to the productive sectors, and as production and incomes contracted in the USA, the supply of dollars to the rest of the world fell drastically, as described in section 2 above, and depression spread quickly to the rest of the world.

It proved to be far more severe and protracted than any previous slump. In the worst-affected countries, industrial output fell by one-half in three years. Prices and overseas trade also showed falls of unprecedented dimensions, and the unique severity of the depression was underlined by the inability of the world to pull out of it in the manner of the pre-1914 trade cycles. The

---

[129] Cmd. 3897, paras, 92–3, 260, 347–9; I. Drummond, 'Britain and the World Economy', in Roderick Floud and Donald McCloskey, *The Economic History of Britain Since 1700*, vol. 2 (Cambridge, 1981), p. 296.

[130] Henry Clay, *The Post-War Unemployment Problem* (1929), p. 76.

[131] J. H. Jones, in *Britain in Depression* (1935), pp. 8–13; p. 138 above.

[132] E.g. L. Robbins, *The Great Depression* (1934), chapter 5.

[133] The best account is in J. K. Galbraith, *The Great Crash* (1955).

onset of the depression in 1929 was further distinguished by a series of severe financial and foreign exchange crises. The background to these crises, the war debt and reparations obligations, the calamitous fall of primary product prices, and the maladjustment of the currencies of the leading countries, have been noted in earlier sections of this chapter. There was also no single financial centre to play London's part of the nineteenth century, to act as buffer and smoothe the flow of international payments.[134] We may now turn to observe how they affected the United Kingdom in the crisis years.

The difficulties began, in fact, as early as 1928, with the abrupt cessation of American lending, when dollar funds were diverted to New York to participate in the stock exchange speculation. When, at the end of 1929, the cessation of American lending was followed by the abrupt fall in American purchases, triggering off a general decline in world trade, each country tried to reduce its imports and increase its exports[135] by means of tariffs, restrictions and currency barriers, and this hit the British capacity to earn foreign exchange particularly hard.

In London, bank rate was raised to $6\frac{1}{2}$% late in September 1929, though it was reduced again with the inflow of funds from New York after the collapse there. But by now the world depression, carrying unemployment to industrial countries and loss of incomes to primary producing countries, had begun its inexorable march. Prices, employment and production all turned down sharply. The British figures are given in Table 3·18.

Table 3·18:   Prices, employment and production, 1929–33

	Wholesale prices	Registered unemployed (Ministry of Labour)		Index of industrial activity*
	(Board of Trade) 1929 = 100	%	Numbers (000)	
1929	100	10·4	1,249	118·7
1930	87·5	16·1	1,975	107·4
1931	76·8	21·3	2,698	86·8
1932	74·9	22·1	2,813	81·1
1933	75·0	19·9	2,221	89·3

* W.H. Beveridge, *Full Employment in a Free Society* (1944), p. 313.

Elsewhere, the reduction was far greater. While British industrial production (1929 = 100) fell to 84 in 1932, it fell to 72 in France, and 53 in Germany and the USA.[136]

In the course of 1930, a drain of gold to Berlin was added to the earlier

[134] C. P. Kindleberger, *The World in Depression 1929–39* (1973), pp. 291–2, 305; *idem, Manias, Panics and Crashes. A History of Financial Crises* (1978), pp. 4–6; D. E. Moggridge, 'Financial Crises and Lenders of Last Resort: Policy in the Crises 1920 and 1929', *Journal of European Economic History* 10/1, 1981; Sean Glyn and John Oxborrow, *Interwar Britain: a Social and Economic* History (1976), pp. 62–3.

[135] A. J. Youngson, *The British Economy, 1920–1957* (1960), pp. 79–80; Herbert Heaton, *The British Way to Recovery* (Minneapolis, 1934), p. 7.

[136] H. W. Richardson, 'The Economic Significance of the Depression in Britain', *Journal of Contemporary History*, 4, 1969.

drain to Paris. The Bank of England was further weakened by the fall of share prices on the London Stock Exchange at the end of 1929 and other pressures, and to make matters worse, Paris added £95 million and New York £64 million to their gold reserves in the course of the year.[137] In 1930 the Bank of England succeeded in withstanding the strain by drawing gold from South Africa and Australia, but in 1931 it had to raise its rate well above those of New York and Paris, attracting funds which were to add to the embarrassment of London when the European financial crisis set in.[138]

It began with the threatened collapse of the Austrian Kredit-Anstalt in May 1931, an institution controlling the majority of the banking and much of the industry of the country. Disaster was staved off, but meanwhile the crisis had spread to Germany, and then also to Hungary and Romania. Germany had been denuded of working capital by inflation, and it had operated on short-term loans from abroad, including Britain, drawn there by exceptionally high interest rates. These funds were frozen by international moratorium as the crisis worsened later in the year, adding materially to the problems of London,[139] while Germany, having exhausted her aid from the Bank for International Settlements, was not precluded from continuing to draw on London. 'British short-term borrowing came to an abrupt end while its lending became indefinitely prolonged.'[140]

Unlike the pre-war days, London no longer had large commercial bill claims on the rest of the world to balance this withdrawal of foreign short-term funds. Instead, the Bank's gold reserve had to stand most of the strain and quickly dropped to £130 million. The level of unemployment inhibited the raising of the bank rate to panic heights; it would, in any case, at best only bring back some 'hot' money which would leave again at the first opportunity, and meanwhile scare off many fund holders.[141] The only alternative was to raise a loan of £50 million in New York and Paris.

The irony was that New York and Paris, bloated with gold, experienced no drain at all. In a financial system which left the economic fate of the world to be decided by international bankers and exchange speculators, as soon as any centre showed signs of weakness, withdrawals began which turned the dreaded weakness into reality.[142] In the summer of 1931, the holders of these mobile funds, mentioned several times already, the undesirable, but essential

---

[137] *Committee on Finance and Industry* (Cmd. 3897), paras. 163-6, 311; Hawtrey, *Gold Standard*, pp. 115-18; H. F. Fraser, *Great Britain and the Gold Standard* (1933); G. Cassel, *The Crisis in the World's Monetary System* (1932).

[138] *Committee on Finance and Industry*, para. 295; J. G. Smith and G. J. Walker, 'Currency and Banking', in *Britain in Depression* (1935).

[139] Sir Arthur Salter, *Recovery* (1932), pp. 43 ff.; Royal Institute of International Affairs, *Monetary Policy and the Depression* (1933), pp. 10-12; A. E. Kahn, *Great Britain in the World Economy* (1946), p. 38; W. A. Morton, *British Finance, 1930-1940* (Madison, 1943), pp. 30-7; Edward W. Bennett, *Germany and the Diplomacy of the Financial Crisis, 1931* (Cambridge, Mass., 1962), pp. 221 ff.

[140] U. K. Hicks, *Finance of the British Government, 1920-1936* (1938), p. 348.

[141] H. V. Hodson, *Slump and Recovery, 1929-1937* (1938), p. 67; Nevin, *Cheap Money*, p. 16; D. Williams, 'London and the 1931 Financial Crisis', *Ec. Hist. Rev.*, 2nd S., 15/3, 1963; D. E. Moggridge, 'The 1931 Financial Crisis – a New View', *The Banker*, 120, April 1970.

[142] *Second Annual Report* of the Bank for International Settlements (Basle, 1932), quoted in Gayer, p. 27; cf. also N. F. Hall, *The Exchange Equalisation Account* (1935), p. 19.

buttresses of sterling under an over-valued gold standard, began to attack London. In three weeks, Continental holders withdrew £41 million, and over the whole period of crisis, some £200 million of this 'hot' money was withdrawn.

The belief of the financiers in the weakness of London, which originated in the increasingly unfavourable trade balance of the United Kingdom and the threat to the gold reserve of the Bank of England, was further strengthened by the fact that it was a Labour Government which held office; by the emphasis of the Macmillan Report, which appeared on 14 July, on the unhealthy dependence of London on short-term funds; and by the threatened budget deficit, highlighted by the 'highly coloured account of the national finances'[143] of the May Committee Report presented on the last day of July.[144] To cap it all, a case of insubordination at Invergordon over cuts in naval pay was exaggerated in the world press as that final indignity, a mutiny in the Royal Navy. When the drain on London continued into August and the Treasury sought a further loan of £80 million in Paris and New York, the British Government was told bluntly that it must carry through at least some of the May Committee's recommendations, especially the severe cut in unemployment pay, before its application would be considered. Once again, as in 1914 and in 1925, the interests of bankers and financiers were to come first.

Those who characterized the outcome as a 'bankers' ramp'[145] were, however, misdirecting their criticism: bankers and speculators could not be blamed for seeking the best possible terms for themselves. As long as it was believed that the sole function of Government in an economic crisis was to establish a favourable financial framework, the City could not be blamed for interpreting this as a framework favourable to itself. Significantly in 1939, when it was war, not unemployment, that threatened, 'the authorities in America, France and Holland co-operated with the British in suppressing activities of the cosmopolitan speculator whose only concern is profit'[146]

Faced by the ultimatum of the bankers over the £80 million loan in August 1931, the Labour Government split on the issue of how far to cut back unemployment relief at their behest, and several of its members, led by the Prime Minister, Ramsey MacDonald, joined by Conservative leaders and by some Liberals, formed a 'National' Government on 24 August to save the country from its financial perils.[147] The ousting of the Labour Government at once reduced the speculative pressure on sterling, even before the new Government had taken any action. Thus favoured, it obtained the foreign loan that had been refused its predecessor, and, confirmed in office by an overwhelming vote in the snap election of October 1931 by voters who fondly

---

[143] Smith and Walker, p. 36.

[144] p. 133 above.

[145] Cf. the excellent discussion on this point in C. L. Mowat, *Britain Between the Wars* (1956 ed.), chapter 7, section 6. A detailed partisan account will be found in R. Bassett, *Nineteen Thirty One, Political Crisis* (1958).

[146] L. Waight, *The History and Mechanism of the Exchange Equalisation Account* (Cambridge, 1939), p. 143.

[147] Philip Viscount Snowden, *An Autobiography* (1934), chapters 76–80; Ramsay Muir, *The Record of the National Government* (1936), chapters 3–9.

hoped it intended to cure depression when it merely wished to cause more effective deflation, stumbled into all the disasters which the Labour Government was ousted to prevent. The trade balance remained highly unfavourable, the payments to the sinking funds for debt redemption were partly suspended and, above all, the pound was driven off gold. Even in its decision to come off gold, the Bank of England's 'chief concern was not to gain advantages for British export trade by exploiting the new situation, but to conserve the international utility of the London money market'.[148]

This action, taken on 20 September 1931, followed a renewed drain of gold. It afforded instant relief, and was accompanied by the raising of the bank rate to 6%. Within 10 days sterling had depreciated by 18% and at the end of the year it was down to $3·40.

A large number of other countries inside and outside the sterling bloc followed Britain off gold in the course of the next few months, but since the USA, Germany, France, Belgium, Holland, Italy and Poland, among others, remained on gold for the time being, sterling goods enjoyed a sudden price advantage, reversing directly the unfavourable position of 1925–31.[149] Most of the countries adversely affected reacted by raising tariffs against British goods, but since Britain also introduced protection, the favourable impact on the trade balance remained for a time.

There was also relief in other ways. Foreign borrowers found repayment in sterling easier. Home prices kept very steady, so that confidence in sterling was quickly restored and funds began to flow in again. The panic loans of £130 million from France and America were repaid with surprising ease.[150] The vast resources of the large joint-stock banks which had emerged from earlier amalgamations, ensured that Britain, unlike other countries, suffered no bank collapses or defaults.

By April 1932, with the pound stabilized, a balanced budget and effective protection, the financial crisis was over. Bank rate was steadily reduced, reaching 2% in June. The industrial depression was at its worst in the third quarter of 1932, but thenceforward all indices showed a strong upward trend, leading up to the boom of 1937.

7 Financial Policy and Institutions in the 1930s

The 'cheap money' policy of a 2% bank rate ushered in a period of stable prices, stable interest rates and stable exchange rates. Stability in the foreign exchanges was achieved by means of the Exchange Equalization Account, established in April 1932, and its supporting measures.[151] It was one of the major innovations introduced into the British financial scene in the age of

---

[148] W. A. Brown, Jr, *The International Gold Standard Re-interpreted, 1914–1934*, 2 vols. (New York, 1940), vol. 2, p. 1093. Robert Skidelsky, *Politicians and the Slump. The Labour Government of 1929–1931* (1967).

[149] W. A. Lewis, *Economic Survey, 1919–1939* (1949), pp. 63–5; H. W. Arndt, *The Economic Lessons of the Nineteen-Thirties* (1944), pp. 96–9.

[150] J. H. Richardson, *British Economic Foreign Policy* (1936), pp. 36 ff.

[151] J. G. Smith and G. J. Walker, 'Currency and Banking', in *Britain in Depression* (1935), p. 45; John Redmond, 'An Indicator of Effective Exchange Rate of the Pound in the Nineteen-Thirties', *Ec. Hist. Rev.* 33/1, 1980.

'managed' currencies. Originally launched with a sum of £175 million in Treasury Bills, it began operations at a period when sterling was very strong and it was thus able quickly to acquire a large quantity of foreign currency in exchange for its sterling bills. Its financial basis was enlarged by £200 million in May 1933, and a further sum of £200 million was added in 1937.

The duty of the fund was to counteract, by suitable purchases and sales, any temporary divergence from the stabilized exchange rates without affecting their long-term level.[152] In practice, the Account appeared deliberately to depress the value of the pound below its natural level in order to favour the British balance of payments.[153] In the process it accumulated a large gold hoard, which stood it in good stead when a heavy drain to France set in in 1938.[154]

The USA, one of the worst sufferers in the depression, went off gold in April 1933, and the dollar was ultimately stabilized at 50% of the old gold parity, the pound being then closely linked with it at the old ratio. With the dollar and sterling blocs devalued, and Germany's foreign trade tightly controlled at several different artificial exchange rates, France and the other gold bloc members were left alone at a higher price level. The resulting unemployment and outflow of capital, forced France to devalue also in 1936.[155] The three main currencies, the pound, dollar and franc, were thus all off gold, but were tied, in practice, to each other by the Tripartite Agreement not to alter exchange rates without prior consultation.[156]

The currency areas covered by the Tripartite Agreement formed the only important region in which international trade in the old sense was still carried on, but even there it proved possible to isolate each country from changes occurring in the others. Thus the collapse of the American prosperity in 1937 had far less effect on the rest of the world than the crash of 1929.[157] The currency systems of Germany and the countries in its orbit, pursuing their different policies of rearmament and autarchy, were even more immune from the effects of alterations in world trade, gold movements or exchange rates.[158]

After the financial strains of 1931, Britain was thus able to sail into calmer waters of protection, a managed currency, a balanced budget and cheap money. Before following out the consequences of these policies, it will be advisable to trace the main changes of the financial institutions of the United Kingdom between 1913 and the 1930s.

At the centre, with bank rate left unaltered for seven years at 2%, the Bank

[152] W. Manning Dacey, 'The Technique of Insulation', *The Banker*, 48/153, Oct. 1938; L. Waight, *The History and Mechanism of the Exchange Equalisation Account* (Cambridge, 1939), p. 11; N. F. Hall, *The Exchange Equalisation Account* (1935).

[153] N. F. Hall, 'The Foreign Exchanges, 1932–1937', in *Britain in Recovery* (1938); A. E. Kahn, *Great Britain in the World Economy* (1946), pp. 202–3; Redmond, p. 89.

[154] A. E. Kahn, pp. 196–8; R. G. Hawtrey, *The Gold Standard in Theory and Practice* (5th ed., 1947), p. 221.

[155] H. V. Hodson, *Slump and Recovery, 1929–1937* (1938), chapters 6, 10, 11; R. G. Hawtrey, *Gold Standard*, pp. 161—73.

[156] Ian M. Drummond, *The Floating Pound and the Sterling Area 1931–1939* (1981), chapters 8 and 9.

[157] W. A. Lewis, *Economic Survey, 1919–1939* (1949), pp. 67–72.

[158] Royal Institute of International Affairs, *Monetary Policy and the Depression* (1933) Appx. IV.

of England could no longer operate an interest rate policy, and instead manipulated cash supplies and exercised 'quality control'. The cash supply could safely be expanded as long as the American cash base was enlarged still faster under the 'New Deal' policies.[159] The responsibility over the foreign exchanges was transferred to the Exchange Equalization Account.

The joint-stock banks had, by the early 1930s, fully completed the process of amalgamation that was all but consummated by 1920.[160] Between 1922 and 1924, the number of banks was further reduced by eight. In 1927–8, the Liverpool-based Martin's Bank was established out of a merger of three firms, having a large regional coverage, and in 1935 a similar merger created the District Bank, based on Manchester, as the eleventh member of the London Clearing House in 1936. At the end of 1938, there remained independent only four London clearing banks, four Scottish and three Irish banks, besides the 'Big Five'. The dominance of the latter, the Midland, Barclay's, Lloyd's, the National Provincial and the Westminster Banks, is shown by the following comparison of deposits, capital and reserves on 31 December 1938:[161]

'Big Five' banks	£2,299 m.
Other English banks	239
Scottish banks	248
Northern Irish banks	151

Fundamentally, the policy of British banks remained unchanged in this period. Their loans, as far as they were made to industry or agriculture, were intended to be self-liquidating or short-term, and direct investment in the share or loan capital of industry continued to be shunned.[162] Compared with pre-war, the scope of overseas investment was much reduced, and at the same time the rate of saving had markedly decreased. Possibly the increase in the propensity to consume was associated with the relative decline in the incomes of the rich, by higher taxation and by the normal tendency of the share of profits to fall in all great depressions. According to one estimate, gross investment fell from 25% to 16%, and net investment from 17% to 6–7% of national income between 1911 and 1938.[163]

In view of this diminished stream of savings, it became more important than ever to improve the defective channel of funds[164] from the money market to industry. This problem was noted by the Balfour Committee, but it received its first important public recognition in the Report of the Macmillan

[159] R. S. Sayers, *Central Banking After Bagehot* (1957), pp. 29–31; G. D. H. Cole, *Money, Trade and Investment* (1954), p. 84.

[160] Joseph Sykes, *The Amalgamation Movement in English Banking* (1926).

[161] T. Balogh, *Studies in Financial Organisation* (Cambridge, 1947), pp. 14–15, 114–18; H. Compton and E. H. Bott, *British Industry* (1940), p. 171; R. J. Truptil, *British Banks and the London Money Market* (1936), Part I, chapters 2 and 6.

[162] F. Lavington, *The English Capital Market* (1921), chapters 31–3.

[163] A. E. Kahn, pp. 137–8; T. Balogh, p. 277; Colin Clark, *National Income and Outlay* (1937), pp. 185, 250–3; W. H. Beveridge, *Full Employment in a Free Society* (1944), pp. 104–5; J. B. Jefferys and Dorothy Walters, 'National Income and Expenditure of the UK 1870–1952', *Income and Wealth*, Series V, 1955, p. 17.

[164] A. B. Levy, *Private Corporations and Their Control* (1950), vol. 1, pp. 164–5; A. T. K. Grant, *A Study of the Capital Market in Post-War Britain* (1937), chapter 8.

Committee. Its terms of reference, provided by the Labour Government, to 'inquire into banking, finance and credit . . . and to make recommendations calculated to enable these agencies to promote the development of trade and commerce and the employment of labour', were a sign of the new preoccupation with the welfare of industry. In its Report, the Committee strongly recommended a closer, and more continuous, interest of the banks in industry. In particular, it approved of the German practice of associating a bank with several competing firms in one industry, which led to 'rationalization' and the strengthening of the industry by the elimination of competition:

> British companies in the iron and steel, electrical and other industries [it reported] must meet in the gate their great American and German competitors who are generally financially powerful and closely supported by banking and financial groups, with whom they have continuous relationships. British Industry, without similar support, will undoubtedly be at a disadvantage. But such effective support cannot be obtained merely for a particular occasion. It can only be the result of intimate co-operation over years during which the financial interests get an insight into the problems and the requirements of the industry in question.[165]

There was also particular reference to medium-term finance extended over 1–5 years; to long-dated industrial capital; and to small and medium-sized firms, needing capital in sums of up to £200,000, for which the City made very inadequate provision – the 'Macmillan gap'.[166] A greater concern for the long-term rate of interest, including presumably industrial investment, was also urged on the Bank of England.[167]

In practice, several banks had become reluctant holders of shares or bonds in various enterprises in the collapse of 1920–1, and others had taken an interest in restrictive control schemes. The Bank of England itself had formed a separate agency, Securities Management Trust, in 1929 to administer the large and varied industrial property which had fallen into its lap, and this was enlarged in 1930 into the Bankers Industrial Development Co.[168] That concern was launched with a capital of £6 million, of which the Bank of England provided one-quarter, other large banks providing the rest. It was instrumental in financing reconstruction schemes concerned with destroying surplus capacity, including National Shipbuilders Security Ltd and the Lancashire Cotton Corporation, and with providing loans for the steel industry. The Bank of England also took part in the flotation of the United Dominions Trust with its various subsidiaries one of which, Credit for Industry Ltd (1934), was specifically designed to help smaller firms with long-term loans.[169]

These developments, however, could scarcely be said to have met the recommendations of the Macmillan Committee in full. The 'Macmillan gap'

[165] *Report of the Committee on Finance and Industry* (1931. Cmd. 3897), para. 384, also paras. 378–83, 386; R. F. Harrod, *John Maynard Keynes* (1951), pp. 413–16.

[166] Cmd. 3897, paras. 392–404. Also see S. E. Thomas, *British Banks and the Finance of Industry* (1930), chapters 4–6; U. K. Hicks, *The Finance of the British Government, 1920–1936* (1938), p. 259.

[167] Cmd. 3897, para. 306 (iv).

[168] Sir Henry Clay, *Lord Norman* (1957), chapter 8; p. 71 above.

[169] T. Balogh, *op. cit.*, pp. 199–201; A. Beacham, *Economics of Industrial Organisation* (3rd ed., 1955), pp. 22–4; Grant, pp. 215–17.

remained unbridged in the 1930s.[170] The banks, far from increasing their participation in industry, found in the 1930s that their industrial holdings of the slump years were being wiped out as soon as the recovery began.[171] As a result, the banks, though willing to hold 55–60% of deposits in the form of 'advances' to industry, could seldom manage to place more than 40%, and were obliged to hold the rest in the form of 'investments', i.e. Government securities which rose from £264 million in February 1932 to £610 million in October 1936. As this was such an appreciable part of the total, precipitate sales would have forced down the price and caused capital losses, so that bank 'investments', formerly considered fairly liquid, in practice became far less so.[172] The banks, however, contributed indirectly to the necessary outside financing of growing firms in the recovery period by their participation in Investment Trusts, Finance Companies and Hire-Purchase Finance Firms.[173]

It was a reflection of the general rise in incomes that an increasing share of the national savings came from 'small' and institutional savers, mainly the Building Societies and the Insurance Companies. Both were benefiting from the increase in freely disposable incomes and the rise in numbers of the lower middle classes, and the insurance companies in particular began to place a larger share of their investments in debentures and even in equities of industry.[174]

These 'small' savings which had amounted to only £32 million a year, or 13·2% of net accumulation, in 1901–13, had risen to £110·3 million a year, or over half the total net investment, in 1924–35. Of this latter sum, the Insurance Companies were responsible for £57$\frac{1}{2}$ million, Building Societies for £51$\frac{1}{2}$ million, and Post Office and Trustee Savings Banks for £1$\frac{1}{2}$ million. The typical working-class savings represented by the last figure thus remained small.[175] The distribution of total assets changed as shown in Table 3·19.[176]

Table 3·19: Financial assets, 1920–1939

	Total £m.	% Shares held by: Banks and discount co's	Life insurance co's	Building societies	P.O. and other savings banks	Other
1920	4,552	59·5	16·4	1·9	17·5	4·7
1929	5,553	48·2	22·5	5·6	17·1	6·2
1939	8,126	41·3	23·2	9·5	17·1	8·4

[170] (Radcliffe) *Committee on the Working of the Monetary System* (1959. Cmnd. 827), paras. 229–34, 932.

[171] Sir Arthur Salter, *Recovery* (1932), pp. 90–1.

[172] Truptil, *op. cit.*, p. 306; also *Radcliffe Report*, paras. 139–40; T. Balogh, pp. 73–4.

[173] T. Balogh, pp. 158 ff., 256–9, 278–88.

[174] Nevin, *Cheap Money*, pp. 264–5; Sir Harold Bellman, *Bricks and Mortals* (1961), chapters 7–9.

[175] John Hilton, *Rich Man, Poor Man* (1944, 3rd imp. 1947), chapter 2; Colin Clark, 'Determination of the Multiplier from National Income Statistics', *Econ. J.*, 48/191, 1938, p. 436.

[176] E. H. Phelps-Brown and Bernard Weber, 'Accumulation, Productivity and Distribution in the British Economy, 1870–1938', *Econ. J.*, 63/250, June 1953; T. Balogh, p. 96; David K. Sheppard, *The Growth and Role of UK Financial Institutions 1880–1962* (1971), p. 3.

In contrast with the rising opportunities of these new institutions, the older types of financial houses, notably the Acceptance House (merchant bankers) and the Discount Houses, found many of their pre-war markets closed or shrinking,[177] the former because of the shrinkage in international trade and lending, and the latter because of the decline of the inland bill. The yearly average of all commercial bills outstanding, both inland-drawn and foreign-drawn, was within the range of £400–650 million in the 1920s; it fell to well below £300 million in the 1930s,[178] and of the foreign acceptance business the clearing banks had captured a large share.[179] Since the supply of Treasury Bills also showed signs of drying up, because of successful funding operations at a time of cheap money on the one hand, and large increases in the holdings of Government departments and of foreigners on the other,[180] there was a 'bill famine', which drove down the rate on Treasury Bills issued by tender from about 4–5% in the years 1925–32 to 0·6% from 1933 onward, i.e. nearly $1\frac{1}{2}$% below bank rate. The decline in the quantity and the interest rate of both commercial and Treasury bills severely restricted the scope of the traditional business of the discount market.

With these changes in the institutional framework in mind, we may now turn to the course of the cheap money policy itself. In the beginning, in 1932, the policy was not the result of deliberate decision: rates were pulled down by a 'tangled mass of forces'.[181] The advantages of cheap money, which led to its retention for 19 years, until 1951, became apparent and acceptable only gradually. Market rates had been falling, and the prices of Consols and other gilt-edged securities rising, from September 1931 onward, without official action, and this allowed the authorities, as soon as the foreign loans of £130 million, raised during the crisis, were paid off to begin to reduce the bank rate in March 1932[182] to reach 2% in June, where it remained. Around it, the structure of other rates also settled down to exceptionally low levels, bill rates, in particular, staying round $\frac{1}{2}$% until 1939, as noted above, and even long-term rates being distinctly lower than in the 1920s.

There were at least four major reasons which launched, and kept, the Government on its cheap money course. First, low rates in London would keep away foreign 'hot' money. This consideration may have weighed heavily in the early period of this policy. Secondly, low rates were a simple device for reducing Government expenditure without causing social unrest. This, also, was an early motive, and was triumphantly vindicated by the great conversion of 1932, although low market rates were not the only precondition of success. The conversion and funding operations were also assisted by the growth of departmental funds, as well as the funds of the Exchange Equalization Account, all of which gave the Treasury much greater freedom over the timing of its issues, compared with the constant stream of renewals

[177] *Macmillan Report*, paras. 88–95; Truptil, *op. cit.*, chapters 3 and 4, pp. 307–9.
[178] T. Balogh, pp. 167, 177–82.
[179] J. Sykes, *op. cit.*, p. 171.
[180] A. J. Youngson, *The British Economy, 1920-1957* (1960), pp. 194–5; T. Balogh, pp. 61 ff., 133, and Appx. I to Part II by F. W. Paish; Nevin, *Cheap Money*, pp. 134–43, 179.
[181] Nevin, *Cheap Money*, pp. 107–8, also 57–8.
[182] E. Nevin, 'The Origins of Cheap Money', *Economica*, NS, 20/77, 1953.

which tied the Government's hands in the 1920s.[183] Thirdly, there may have been the desire to favour by low interest rates the active as against the passive members of the community: a step in the direction of what Keynes came to call the 'euthanasia of the rentier'.

Lastly, the authorities also began to look on cheap money as a method of increasing the total level of activity in the economy. This motive became operative, at the earliest, in 1933, but was later responsible for the continuation of the policy in the face of many changing circumstances. Whether low rates actually stimulated the economy in the 1930s is in some doubt. They were certainly accompanied by a large increase in the quantity of money,[184] but as noted above on p.149 there were few industrial borrowers in the early 1930s in the face of willing lenders – a circumstance which helped to keep down rates. In the later 1930s the net effect of the Government's policy was in the opposite direction. The shortage of bills made the banks illiquid and unwilling to lend, and in the incipient boom of 1936–7 the authorities induced a distinct cash shortage, which went directly and deliberately, though only temporarily, against the overall expansionary effect of cheap money.

How far Government policy as a whole, including other measures, could be held responsible for the industrial recovery has been subject to much debate, but few would give it much weight today. Low rates might, according to Hawtrey, have had directly beneficial effects in 1931, but by 1932 it was too late, and the recovery had to wait for other, more general factors.[185] Home capital issues, which one would have expected to be among the first indices to show the benefits of cheap money, did not begin to rise until some 18 months after the beginning of the upswing. Moreover, even the cheap money policy of 1932 was directly counteracted by deflationary budgets until 1934, and by the decision taken in 1931, at the depth of the depression, to work off the accumulated deficit of £115 million of the Unemployment Fund by collecting more in contributions than was paid out in benefits. The investments by the public utilities were all timed to begin much too late to affect the recovery, except for the electricity grid which by sheer accident rose to the peak of its constructional work in the depression.[186] More positive was the contribution made by the tariff. It is possible to argue that apart for direct sectoral benefits, by reducing imports it reduced the extent by which British incomes had to decline by virtue of the decline in exports, i.e. that the downward multiplier was cut off. Further, by taxing imports (as well as by banning foreign capital issues) the protectionist policy encouraged expenditure in such sectors as building and the service trades at home, which were undoubtedly connected with the onset of the recovery.[187]

---

[183] U. K. Hicks, *Finance of the British Government*, pp. 364–9.

[184] Truptil, p. 298; H. W. Arndt, *The Economic Lessons of the Nineteen-Thirties* (1944), chapter 4; Sheppard, *Financial Institutions*, p. 18.

[185] Hawtrey, *Gold Standard*, pp. 149–52.

[186] U. K. Hicks, *Finance of the British Government*, pp. 280–95, 376–7; also E. Nevin, pp. 229 ff.; R. F. Bretherton, F. A. Burchardt, R. S. G. Rutherford, *Public Investment and the Trade Cycle in Great Britain* (1941), p. 407; Roger Middleton, 'The Constant Employment Budget Balance', *Ec. Hist. Rev.* 34/2, 1981.

[187] A. E. Kahn, pp. 154–6, 262–4; W. A. Morton, *British Finance, 1930–1940* (Madison, 1943), p. 82, also chapters 14–17.

Basically, the claim that the Government's cheap money policy assisted the economic recovery must rest on the claim that it helped to bring about the building boom of the 1930s.[188] The building boom was at once the symbol and a main carrier of British industrial recovery from the Great Depression. It began largely as a boom in the building of private dwellings, as distinct from local authority building.[189] Starting from the relatively high level of building of the 1920s, when an average of 150,000 dwellings a year of all kinds was completed, output stayed around the 200,000 mark in 1930–3, and then rose rapidly to well over 350,000 dwellings a year. In those totals, the figure of dwellings completed by local authorities remained fairly constantly at about 75,000 a year. From 1934 on, the boom was further boosted by industrial and commercial building which showed the usual accelerator effects during the upswing of a trade cycle.[190]

Building employed only 6–7$\frac{1}{2}$% of all insured workers in the 1930s, but it accounted for 30% of the increase in employment in 1932–5 if the increase in the indigenous building materials industry is included. If to this are added the usual multiplier effects and the increased demand for furniture, as well as the fact that the building indices were leading the others in the upswing, it is clear that here was a critical mechanism for stimulating British recovery at work.[191]

The connection between the building boom and low interest rates was not clear-cut. Most of the building, and 75% of the dwelling houses, were financed by building societies, the phenomenal growth of which was one of the most striking aspects of the boom, their total balances out on mortage rising from £316 million at the end of 1930 to £706 million at the end of 1939. But it took eight years for their mortgage rates to fall by 1%, from an average of 5·87% in 1931 to 4·80% in 1939;[192] the average reduction by 1933, when building was in full swing, was only 0·3%. Local authority building was affected by Government policy rather than by the falling mortgage rates of the 1930s.[193] In sum, the direct effect of cheap money could not have been large. On the other hand, the fact that building societies kept up their rates on shares and deposits while others dropped, diverted increasing funds to them. Moreover, a large proportion of building was for investment, and it was clear that it was low interest rates at a time when rents showed no disposition to fall which made returns on housing investment so attractive.[194]

The other main factor at work on the supply side was the reduction in cost: a house costing £350 in 1931 fell to well below £300 in 1933–4,[195] and despite a

[188] H. W. Richardson, *Economic Recovery in Britain, 1932–9* (1967), pp. 142 ff.; R. M. MacIntosh, 'A Note on Cheap Money and the British Housing Boom, 1932–37', *Econ. J.* 61, 1951.

[189] G. D. H. Cole, *Building and Planning* (1945), pp. 96–7.

[190] Figures in E. Nevin, *Cheap Money*, p. 269; cf. B. Weber and J. Parry Lewis, 'Industrial Building in Great Britain, 1923–38', *Scot. J. Pol. Econ.,* 8/1, Feb. 1961.

[191] G. D. A. MacDougall, 'General Survey, 1929–1937', in *Britain in Recovery* (1938), pp. 46–8, also Sir Harold Bellman, 'The Building Trades', in *ibid.*; W. A. Lewis, *Economic Survey, 1919–39* (1949), p. 87; A. P. Becker, 'Housing in England and Wales during the Business Depression of the 1930s', *Ec. Hist. Rev.*, 2nd S., 3/3, 1951, p. 325; H. W. Richardson and D. H. Aldcroft, *Building in the British Economy Between the Wars* (1968).

[192] Becker, p. 335.

[193] U. K. Hicks, *Finance of the British Government*, p. 131.

[194] Nevin, *Cheap Money*, pp. 272 ff.

[195] L. R. Connor, 'Urban Housing in England and Wales', *J. R. Stat. S.*, 99/1, 1936, p. 39.

rise in the general price level, its price did not increase again until 1937. For this both materials and labour were responsible: building materials showing a sharp reduction in price, and labour a marked increase in output per head after the low level of the early post-war years.[196]

Of at least equal importance were the changes on the demand side. The well-known 'building cycle', which was held back from its expected upswing in the 1920s because of the generally depressed condition of the country and the effects of rent restriction,[197] began to operate with full force in the 1930s. A shortage of houses, estimated at 600,000–1,000,000 in 1920, increased to an estimated peak of 1·2 to 2 million in 1930. This was accentuated by the migration of population to new regions and suburbs.[198] Rising standards of consumption and of housing by-laws which condemned many houses as unfit to live in, contributed to this further demand in the 1930s.[199]

Higher incomes also called forth substantial increases in many service trades, entertainments, and other 'sheltered' industries. They were the kind of goods and services which the bulk of the lower middle classes and skilled workers demanded with their increased real incomes, and the rise in their real wages or salaries, in turn, was achieved, not by rising money payments, but by falling prices, pulled down by falling prices of imports. In all this, Government action, even cheap money, played a relatively minor part. The impetus came from a rising demand, which was based in the final analysis on the greatly improved terms of trade and on lowered real costs of production, and the main positive action of the Government consisted in channelling the additional demand into home-produced goods and services rather than imports.

The trade cycle began to turn down in 1937, long before it had reached full employment levels. However, rearmament took up the slack,[200] and with building still booming, the recession of 1938–9 was milder than that following 1929, and was short-lived. The needs of war soon led to the full employment of all available resources.

---

[196] I. Bowen, 'Building Output and the Trade Cycle (UK, 1924–38)', *Oxf. Econ. P.*, 3, 1940, p. 116; R. L. Reiss, *Municipal and Private Enterprise Housing* (1945), pp. 24–6.

[197] W. A. Lewis, *Economic Survey*, p. 86.

[198] J. B. Cullingworth, *Housing Needs and Planning Policy* (1960), chapter 2.

[199] Herbert W. Robinson, *The Economics of Building* (1939), pp. 119–22; W. F. Stolper, 'British Monetary Policy and the Housing Boom', *Quarterly Journal of Economics*, 56/1, Part II, Nov. 1941; Reiss, *passim*; C. L. Mowat, *Britain Between the Wars*, pp. 458/61.

[200] H. V. Hodson, *Slump and Recovery, 1929–1937* (1938), chapter 12.

4

Social Conditions between the Wars

1 The Age of Mass Unemployment

Industrially, the main development in Britain between the wars was the enforced shift of resources from the old to the new industries, from the export trades to the sheltered home industries. The last chapter traced the consequences of this shift on the trading and financial position of Britain in the world economy. This chapter will follow out its consequences on the well-being of different sections of the population, and in particular, the contrast between the high and rising incomes among those in full employment in the expanding sectors, and the poverty and long-period unemployment of many of those in the declining sectors. Unemployment of men and of resources occupies a central place in the history of the inter-war years.

At the end of the war, some transitional unemployment was expected as soldiers and war-workers were being demobilized and fitted into their normal peace-time occupations, but the actual transfer from the forces to civilian occupations was accomplished with remarkable smoothness. Between the armistice and April 1920, 2,900,000 men were added to civilian employment, while the number of females in civilian employment dropped by 500,000 and numbers in the Forces were reduced by 3,600,000. Throughout this period of gigantic changes, unemployment remained generally below the half million mark. A maximum of 1,093,000 were paid out-of-work donation in April 1919,[1] but it is doubtful how many of them were truly unemployed; a year later there was an acute labour shortage in most areas.[2]

Then the boom collapsed, and by March 1921 unemployment in the insured trades reached 15%. The coal stoppage of April to June raised the figure to 22%, but even after the dispute was over, the proportion remained obstinately at 16–17%. Employment improved in 1924, and was at a high level again in 1927–9, but even in the best months, the official unemployment rate stood at 9–10%, or over a million unemployed. Before the war, the maximum rate over a period of 60 years or more had been 11%, and the average $4\frac{1}{2}$% (and the insurance scheme had been built on the actuarial assumption of such a rate). Now, fluctuations in unemployment similar to those of the pre-1914 era seemed to be superimposed on an irreducible 'hard core' of close on a million unemployed men.[3]

The 'Great Depression' of the early 1930s brought with it a level of unemployment that put even the 1920s in the shade. The official unemployment

---

[1] A. C. Pigou, *Aspects of British Economic History, 1918–1925* (1947), pp. 36–40.
[2] E. V. Morgan, *Studies in British Financial Policy, 1914–25* (1952), pp. 70–2.
[3] Henry Clay, *The Post-War Unemployment Problem* (1929), pp. 24, 28.

rate reached a peak of 23% or nearly one-quarter of the insured population in August 1932, and stayed above 20% for over two years. In terms of numbers, this meant a figure of nearly 3 million people without work, but there were in addition several important sections of the population outside the field of insurance, and therefore excluded from the official statistics. Among them were agricultural workers, domestic servants, self-employed persons, persons employed by members of their immediate family, and most salaried employees, besides civil servants, police, armed forces and railwaymen. Further, in the bad years of the slump, many had ceased to register with the Ministry of Labour, as they had exhausted their unemployment insurance benefits and considered it unlikely that they would ever be found work again. For these groups, the proportions out of work were lower, but they added to the total numbers which they brought up to an estimated 3,289,000 in 1931 and 3,750,000 in the peak period of September 1932.[4] Some 6–7 million people were living on the dole.

Improvement set in in 1933, and while the numbers out of work fell to a minimum of 9% (1,400,000 on the official register) by September 1937, the numbers in employment rose faster still. Some 2 million persons were added to the employed population between 1933 and 1937, of whom fewer than $1\frac{1}{2}$ million came from the ranks of the registered unemployed.[5] The position worsened in 1938–9, when 1,800,000–1,900,000 persons (12%) were on the official unemployment registers, in spite of re-armament, but this deterioration was interrupted by the outbreak of war in September 1939.

General unemployment percentages hide very great differences between industries, areas, workers of different skills, ages or sex. In the years before 1914 old staples were still expanding, and as late as 1919 it was assumed that industries such as coal and cotton would have so little unemployment compared with other occupations, that they would want to establish their own 'special' insurance schemes at more favourable rates.[6] In the event, it was the old industrial areas and the old staple export trades which suffered most.

In the early 1920s, the heaviest unemployment rates were recorded in the industries which had been over-expanded during the war: shipbuilding, engineering and the metal industries generally. After 1925, coal and cotton came to the forefront, but by the end of the decades it was becoming clear that it was the staple export trades, above all coal mining, but also cotton, wool, tin-plate, iron and steel and pottery, which fared the worst in the general depression.[7] By contrast, industries which were rapidly expanding, like electrical engineering or motor engineering, or which catered largely for the home market, like distribution or motor transport, had relatively low rates of unemployment.

In 1929–31 the effects of a general world economic depression were added to the special problems of the export industries, and there were further changes. The new industries and services continued to enjoy the lowest

---

[4] Colin Clark, *National Income and Outlay* (1937), p. 31; H. W. Robinson, 'Employment and Unemployment', in *Britain in Recovery* (1938), p. 95.

[5] R. C. Davison, *British Unemployment Policy since 1930* (1938), p. 49.

[6] W. H. Beveridge, *Unemployment, a Problem of Industry* (1930), pp. 291, 405.

[7] Clay, *op. cit.*, pp. 27–8, 41–52, 81–4, 92–5, 108; Pigou, *op. cit.*, pp. 46–50.

unemployment figures until 1931, but they failed to show the same rate of recovery as the rest of the country in the next few years. The reason was that as soon as trade improved, there was an influx from the declining sectors in such numbers as to overstrain their capacity of absorbing labour[8] (see Table 4·1). Some capital goods industries, which are usually subject to much greater cyclical fluctuations than those producing consumer goods, had a much more than normally rapid expansion in the 1930s,[9] having been held back for almost 20 years, first by the war and then by the 'doldrums' of the 1920s.

Table 4·1:   Unemployment percentages in selected industries

		1932	1937
(A)	Expanding Industries:		
	Building	29·0	13·8
	Motor vehicles, etc.	20·0	4·8
	Electrical engineering	16·3	3·1
	Food industries	16·6	12·4
	Hotel, etc., service	17·3	14·2
	Distributive trades	12·2	8·8
(B)	Declining Industries:		
	Coal mining	33·9	14·7
	Woollen and worsted	20·7	10·2
	Cotton	28·5	11·5
	Shipbuilding	62·2	23·8
	Jute	42·2	26·8
	Pig-iron making	43·5	9·8

Within industry it was, as ever, the unskilled workers who bore the brunt of the unemployment, and the salaried employees and managers who suffered least. According to the calculations of Colin Clark, based on the Census of 1931, there were in that year 30·5% of unskilled labourers unemployed and 14·4% of skilled and semi-skilled industrial workers, but only 5–8% of white-collar workers, and a bare $\frac{1}{2}$ – 2% of working proprietors of businesses or shops, and farmers.[10] If persons temporarily stopped were included also, the differences between these groups would be greater still.

In view of the strong localization of most of the basic and staple industries, the incidence of high unemployment in them was reflected in high local rates of unemployment in certain areas.[11] As late as 1934, most of the industrial towns in the Welsh valleys, and many towns on the Tyne and in Durham, had unemployment rates of over 50%, and some well over 70% of the total workers insured. In West Cumberland there were towns like Frizington, where a bare 33 men were on unemployment insurance benefit, while 515

---

[8] W. H. Beveridge, *Full Employment in a Free Society* (1944), pp. 49–59, 83, Table 33 (pp. 316–20), based on his series of three articles, 'An Analysis of Unemployment', *Economica*, NS, 3 and 4, Nos. 12–14, 1936–7, esp. No. 12, Nov. 1936, p. 374.

[9] E. H. Phelps-Brown and G. L. S. Shackle, 'British Economic Fluctuations', *Oxf. Econ. P.*, No. 2, 1939.

[10] Colin Clark, *National Income and Outlay*, p. 46, and *The Conditions of Economic Progress* (1951 ed.), p. 470.

[11] See above, chapter 2, section 4.

had been unemployed for so long that they had exhausted their insurance claims and were kept on 'Transitional Payments'.[12]

Unemployment of such extent and durations was a social, as well as an economic problem. The man who was on the dole for a long period lost some of his skill and his self-respect, and often also the will to work, and some permanent damage to his personality was only too likely.[13] Men became bitter, cynical and disillusioned, and less sure of their moral bearings when they were denied work and found themselves and their families in poverty in the midst of a rich society.

There were also special problem groups among them. There were boys and girls, shunted into dead-end jobs when leaving school and then thrown on the labour market when old enough to claim full wages, without skill and without a trade, and there were the youths who never secured a steady job at all, even for a time.[14] There were the older men who found it impossible, once they were dismissed, ever to gain new employment; there were labourers with large families who secured almost as much, if not more, on the dole, because of the family allowance element in it, as when they were working, and who had therefore no incentive to seek work; and there were craftsmen, proud of their skill, who refused inferior jobs and failed to realize that their craft had become out-of-date.

In the relatively prosperous districts unemployment was often felt as a stigma and kept secret, and men out of work preferred isolation. In the depressed areas, where unemployment was the common lot of many or most workers, there was often comradeship in distress, but it tended to sap the overriding desire to be at work again. There were, further, often local or perhaps even national differences in attitude: the proud families of Crook Town, keeping up an outward appearance of serenity and respectability, contrasted with the gregarious families of the Welsh valleys, only too eager to exaggerate their distress and dramatize their ill-luck.[15] Whatever the area, however, much personal suffering has to be added to the economic loss of output, of skill and of willingness to work, as the costs of prolonged periods of unemployment.

Among applicants for benefit or allowances in 1929, only 4·7% had been unemployed twelve months or more. But the proportion rose to 16·4% in August 1932, 25·0% in August 1936 and (after a change in the classification) 22·6% in August 1939.[16] In some of the badly hit areas, the proportions were very much higher. In September 1936, while only 0·4% of the insured fell into this category in prosperous Deptford, the proportion was 18·8% in Crook

[12] Ministry of Labour, *Reports of Investigations into the Industrial Conditions of Certain Depressed Areas* (1934. Cmd. 4728), pp. 27, 106, 136.

[13] H. W. Singer, *Unemployment and the Unemployed* (1940), chapter 12. Cf. also M. Bruce, *The Coming of the Welfare State* (1961), pp. 228–40; H. L. Beales and R. S. Lambert (eds.), *Memoirs of the Unemployed* (1934).

[14] W. R. Garside, 'Juvenile Unemployment and Public Policy between the Wars', *Ec. Hist. Rev.* 30/2, 1977, and discussion in *ibid.* 32/4, 1979, pp. 523–32.

[15] (Pilgrim Trust), *Men Without Work* (Cambridge, 1938) is a report of six typical urban areas in 1936, including Crook and the Rhondda. Cf. also C. L. Mowat, *Britain Between the Wars* (1956 ed.), pp. 480–90; A. J. Lush, *Disinherited Youth* (Edinburgh, 1943).

[16] Beveridge, *Full Employment*, Table 8, p. 64. Cf. also Clark, *National Income and Outlay*, p. 48.

and 28·1% in the Rhondda, in both these places forming over one-half of the unemployed population.[17]

By contrast, the proportion in continuous unemployment for three months or less was 78·5% of those registered in 1929, 59% in August 1932 and it fluctuated around this proportion in the later 1930s. This high proportion gave rise to the phrase of the 'stage army' of the unemployed, but in depression years the spell of work consisted often of a few days' or a few weeks' employment only, perhaps as relief drivers or postmen, interrupting years of general unemployment, so that a high proportion of those nominally on the register for a short period only were in fact long-period cases.[18]

After years of such experiences, a certain fatalism made itself felt. Sir William (later Lord) Beveridge recognized three main groups in 1937: (*a*) short-period, frictional or seasonal unemployment, amounting to 6–8% of the insured population, or 800,000–1,000,000 people and accepted as inescapable; (*b*) long-period hard-core unemployed in contracting industries and regions or handicapped by old age, numbering 4%, or 500,000, who might be reduced in numbers in the long run; and (*c*) cyclical unemployment of workers temporarily thrown out of work of whom there might be up to 6%, or 800,000, at the bottom of a slump. The numbers referred to insured persons only; there would be others outside the insurance scheme. The pre-war long-term average of $4\frac{1}{2}$% unemployment could never be attained again because of structural changes in industry. There were indeed many causes and types of unemployment;[19] but in view of the experience of the economy in 1939–79, such pessimism turned out to be misplaced, and most of all the view which deemed unemployment to be largely voluntary, attributing it to a generous dole.[20]

The pre-war insurance scheme in certain industries was extended in 1916 to cover some 4 million workers. In November 1918, when the Government was in fear of rebellion, a non-contributory Out-of-Work Donation scheme was started as a temporary measure. It carried the burden of the transitional months and allowed the more permanent Act of 1920 to be introduced at leisure. The civilian scheme ended in November 1919 and the service scheme in 1921, and their total cost of £66 million[21] seemed a small price to pay for social peace at a critical time.

The Unemployment Insurance Act of 1920 contained all the main prin-

[17] *Men Without Work, passim.* The Report deals largely with those unemployed for 12 months or more.

[18] H. W. Singer, *op. cit.*, chapter 1.

[19] Sir William Beveridge, 'An Analysis of Unemployment, III', *Economica*, NS, 4/14, 1937, pp. 180–2. Cf. also R. C. Davison, *The Unemployed, Old Policies and New* (1929), chapter 6; Susan Howson, 'Slump and Unemployment', in Roderick Floud and Donald McCloskey, *The Economic History of Britain since 1700*, vol. 2 (Cambridge, 1981), p. 270; Alan E. Booth and Sean Glyn, 'Unemployment in the Interwar Period: A Multiple Problem', *Journal of Contemporary History*, 10, 1975.

[20] Daniel K. Benjamin and Lewis A. Kochin, 'Searching for an Explanation of Unemployment in Interwar Britain', *Journal of Political Economy*, 87, 1979.

[21] Karl de Schweinitz, *England's Road to Social Security*, p. 218; E. M. Burns, *British Unemployment Programs, 1920–1938* (Washington, 1941), p. 7. Miss Burns's work, together with the works by Davison and Lord Beveridge quoted earlier in this section, form the main sources for the study of unemployment insurance and assistance in this period.

ciples of the Act of 1911, but extended its scope to virtually all employments.[22] Eleven million workers were included, rising gradually over the period to 15·4 million in 1938,[23] and all official unemployment statistics were based on that category of insured persons. Contributions and benefit rights were much as they had been in the earlier, more limited scheme, and so was the assumed unemployment rate of about 4%.

The Act had hardly been put into effect when the slump set in, raising unemployment rates to well over 10% for the decade instead of 4%. This soon wiped out the accumulated surplus of £22 million, and presented the Government in 1921 with the dilemma which was to dog all administrations for the next two decades: how to preserve the 'insurance' principle of the original scheme, while at the same time preventing the hundreds of thousands who had exhausted their benefit entitlement from being treated as paupers. It was to solve this that a third type of benefit was interposed, neither insurance nor charity, but with some of the characteristics of both, changing in detail several times in the inter-war years, but remaining in essentials the same.

The 'insurance' scheme was based on compulsory statutory contributions, in return for which there was a contractual right to certain benefits, though the exact terms were changed from time to time. For the other types of benefit there was no such right; they were subject to some form of means or needs test.

These 'intermediate' schemes, being neither insurance nor Poor Law, were improvisations, and there were no fewer than 18 amending Acts to the Unemployment Insurance Act between 1920 and 1930 and more in the 1930s. At first the intermediate scheme, called 'uncovenanted benefit' in 1921–4, then 'extended benefit' in 1924–8 and 'transitional benefit' in 1928–31, was paid out of the Insurance Fund, but since this destroyed its solvency, its cost was transferred to the Treasury. Even so, to prevent too many persons falling out of benefit, conditions of drawing and rates of benefit were eased several times, especially by the Labour Government in 1924, and this in turn plunged the Fund into debt to the tune of £25 million by 1928, while there were almost as many unemployed who had exhausted their benefit and were on the supplementary scheme as there were on the full insurance scheme. Another group, numbering 120,000–140,000 insured, and making with their dependants some half million persons, had slipped through the meshes of both and had to be looked after by the Poor Law Guardians.

In both the Poor Law and the supplementary schemes, relief was given according to needs, and local administration and interpretation differed widely. By 1926 three Poor Law Unions had gone bankrupt, having exhausted their borrowing powers, and were replaced by Ministry nominees. In general, 'the level of assistance has varied with the political complexion, the social theories, and the financial status of the individual relief authorities'.[24]

Following the Blanesburgh Departmental Committee on Unemployment

---

[22] The main groups exempted are listed on p. 155 above.
[23] Alan T. Peacock, *The Economics of National Insurance* (1952), p. 15.
[24] E. M. Burns, p. 28.

Insurance, which reported in 1927,[25] the Unemployment Act of 1927, operative in 1928, set out to abolish 'extended benefit' by granting drawing rights to all who had 8 contributions in the past two years, or 30 weeks' contributions at any time.[26] Contributions and benefits were lowered, in order to render the scheme financially sound.

But this scheme also went gravely astray in its actuarial estimate of financial burden and return. Being launched in what was probably the least depressed year of the 1920s, it assumed an average unemployment rate of 6%, or 1,160,000 persons out of work; in fact, the rate rose from 9% in 1927 to 13·6% in March 1930, 19·6% in December of that year, and then stayed above 20% for over two years. The heavy outpayments which plunged the Fund deeper into nominal debt helped to precipitate the economic and political crisis of 1931, as described in chapter 3 above. It also forced the Government to consider anew the principles of unemployment insurance.

Meanwhile, the burden of unemployment was also undermining the old Poor Law. Throughout the 1920s a minimum of 350,000–450,000 persons out of work received out-door relief in Great Britain, and at certain times these numbers were very much higher: there were 1,244,000 persons in June 1922, for example, and over $1\frac{1}{2}$ million during the prolonged coal strike of 1926. The local system of Poor Law Guardians was not designed and was unable to take such strains, and the Poor Law had to be entirely re-cast.

The new law, the Local Government Act of 1929 (and a similar Act for Scotland), confirmed by the Poor Law Act of 1930, abolished the traditional Poor Law and the Guardians as from 1930, and transferred their work to Public Assistance Committees of County Councils and County Borough Councils. Perhaps the most significant change was the turning of the labour 'test' for the able-bodied from a deterrent into the 'primary objective . . . to maintain the employability of those able and willing to work, so that when opportunity offers, these men may have no difficulty in resuming their places in industry'.[27] The 'genuinely seeking work' clause, dating from 1924, was also abolished, since the notion of 'voluntary unemployment' had become patently unhelpful in existing conditions.

In 1930 a Royal Commission on Unemployment Insurance was set up to consider the thorough reconstruction of the original scheme, which by 1931 'was hardly recognizable through the tangled mass of opportunist legislation'.[28] Its report of 1932 was the basis of the more permanent legislation of 1934. Meanwhile, however, the deficits of the Unemployment Fund mounted to new heights in 1931, even though the Treasury had taken over the total current costs of the 'transitional' benefits. It led to drastic cuts in benefits and increases in contributions. The total weekly contribution per adult male worker was raised from $22\frac{1}{2}d$. to 30*d*. and the benefit rates were cut by about one-tenth, in line with the cost of living. The terms on which benefit was

[25] *Report of the Departmental Committee on Unemployment Insurance* (1927).

[26] G. P. Jones and A. G. Pool, *A Hundred Years of Economic Development in Great Britain* (1959 ed.), pp. 392–5.

[27] E. M. Burns, *op. cit.*, p. 26, quoting from a Ministry of Health circular of 1930.

[28] David C. Marsh, *National Insurance and Assistance in Great Britain* (1950), p. 44, quoting PEP, *Report on British Social Services* (1937).

granted were tightened up to the extent of reducing by some 700,000 the numbers receiving insurance benefits, matched by a rise of only about 250,000 in the numbers receiving transitional payments. Within a year about 180,000 persons were removed from the register altogether.[29]

Once a person had exhausted his insurance benefit, now reduced to a maximum of 26 weeks, he was forced to turn to the intermediate scheme, now called 'transitional', with a searching needs test, and the widespread bitterness resulting from reductions in the 'dole' because of earnings of other members of the family, or some small property, dates mainly from those years. The local standards of needs tests differed widely in practice, while many deplored, with Sir Henry Betterton, the Minister of Labour the 'complete divorce between the responsibility of the central authority, which is providing the money, and that of the local authority which disburses it'.[30] But with all its faults, this was the system which saw Britain through the worst of the depression from 1931 to 1934, until a more permanent solution could be devised.

The Holman Gregory Commission of 1930, noted above, reported in 1932, and on its Reports[31] was based the new Unemployment Act of 1934, which was to put the unemployment scheme at last on a sound and permanent footing. It was in two parts, dealing with insurance and assistance respectively. The insurance scheme was to remain actuarially sound, and watched over by an Unemployment Insurance Statutory Committee. In the event, with better trade leading up to the boom of 1937, and rates of unemployment much below the calculated break-even rate of $16\frac{3}{4}\%$ (the rate of 1934), the Fund succeeded not only in staying solvent, but could also afford to raise benefits and lower contributions, while paying off much of the accumulated debt. In 1936 agricultural workers were catered for by a new parallel scheme, and in 1937 several other groups formerly excluded were brought in.

For those whose spell out of work exceeded the limit of 26 weeks, and for many of those outside the insurable classes altogether, the transitional benefits were to be replaced by a new scheme, administered by a central Unemployment Assistance Board, with its own staff of full-time officers, in place of the local Committees. It was given fairly wide latitude in granting claims as long as 'capacity to work', 'availability for work' and 'need', less narrowly defined, were proved. It was to take over most able-bodied but uninsured persons from the Poor Law, and it was to pitch its benefits high enough to avoid any need for supplementation by it. In this way it was hoped to reduce the burden on the Poor Law, now administered by the Public Assistance Committees of the local authorities.

In the event, its rates turned out to be too low, and it was not until the 'second appointed day', 1 April 1937, that the Board took over about 100,000 Poor Law cases, mostly able-bodied persons, and began everywhere to pay its own rates.

---

[29] G. D. H. and Margaret Cole, *The Condition of Britain* (1937), chapter 4; Sean Glyn and John Oxborrow, *Interwar Britain: A Social and Economic History* (1976), p. 256.

[30] HoC, 30.11.1933.

[31] *Interim Report of the Royal Commission on Unemployment Insurance* (1931. Cmd. 3872), *Final Report* (1932. Cmd. 4185).

In the next few years, those who drew benefit under insurance and assistance schemes were about equal in numbers, and there were still some 150,000 unemployed, plus 250,000 dependants, thrown on the Poor Law until March 1937. From April 1937 on (the second appointed day), their numbers shrank to 30,000 and 40,000 respectively.

Public authorities also originated other measures of relief, besides direct benefit payments. Local schemes to help the depressed areas have been noted in chapter 2, section 4, above,[32] and the aid to land settlement was noted in the same chapter, section 5. Industrial Transfer Boards, established in 1928, helped individuals and whole families in their removal in search of work, though in practice voluntary migration achieved much more than assisted transfer. Until 1929 there were also substantial sums expended in assisting migration overseas.[33] The establishment of Government Training Centres, of residential Instructional Centres, and other means of training[34] were of some help to young persons and to those returning from the armed services after the war.

Public works, as noted on p. 131 above, as measures of relief enjoyed little official support. They were of some importance in the 1920s. From 1921 on, local authorities undertook construction schemes, and there were some Government grants for the maintenance of public buildings and for afforestation, partly with the unemployed in mind. But the Central Government's contribution to road building in the 1920s came largely out of the Road Fund, and the important trunk road programme and five years' programme of 1929 were cut in 1931, for reasons of economy, when they might have been of the greatest use. The Unemployment Grants Committee itself spent £69·5 million between December 1920 and January 1932 assisting local authorities with public works, but this compared with the £600 million paid out in the same period in benefit and relief. A maximum of 60,000 men worked on these schemes in 1931, when total unemployment was over $2\frac{1}{2}$ million. Even this grudging aid was suspended in 1931, and though public opinion became more favourable towards public works from 1935 on,[35] little was done before the war.

2 Housing, Health and Other Welfare Provisions

The nineteenth century believed that the housing of ordinary families could safely be left to the forces of unfettered demand and supply. The sorry results of this policy of *laissez-faire* in house building are with us still. Even the nineteenth century was forced to deal with the worst consequences of this unchecked town building for profit, from the 1840s onwards, on grounds of health, and from the 1890s on, also on grounds of the loss of amenities for the urban population as a whole.[36] The Housing and Town Planning Act of 1909

---

[32] A brief list will be found in the *Report of the Royal Commission on the Distribution of the Industrial Population* (Barlow Report) (1940. Cmd. 6153), pp. 146 ff.

[33] pp. 181–2 below.

[34] R. C. Davison, *Unemployment Policy*, chapter 6, and *The Unemployed*, chapter 7.

[35] J. H. Richardson, *British Economic Foreign Policy* (1936), p. 44.

[36] W. Ashworth, *The Genesis of Modern British Town Planning* (1954).

was the latest attempt to take account of the amenity value to the community lost or gained by private building, but the public provision of housing for the poorer classes before 1914 was still little more than experimental, and was limited to some slum-clearance schemes of a few progressive town councils.

The war completely revolutionized the market for houses for letting. Rent control, imposed as a result of protests by Glasgow munition workers in 1915 to keep down the cost of living, reduced the real level of rents in a period of rising prices, though ultimately an increase of 40–50% on pre-war rents was permitted. After the war, the housing shortage caused by the interruption of building would have raised rents so much beyond the pre-war figures as to cause widespread hardship and unrest. Hence rent control was kept on after 1918 and was, in fact, extended to more expensive property in 1919 and 1920.

In view of rising expectations of civilized minima for working-class houses, well expressed by the recommendations of the Tudor Walters Committee of the Ministry of Reconstruction in 1917–18, the rising costs of new houses would drive their economic rents far above the level of the old controlled rents. As a result of these developments, three interrelated conditions came to determine the housing market from 1919 onward. First, there remained an intractable shortage of working-class dwellings to let at current (controlled) rents; secondly, the level of rents of a large proportion of dwellings was artificial, being either controlled below its market level or subsidized; and thirdly, a gap had opened between the weekly rent which wage-earners were prepared to pay, and the costs of the sort of accommodation which they (and society) as a whole were coming to expect as a minimum.

The shortage of houses in 1919 has been variously computed at between 600,000 and 1 million,[37] mostly in the cheaper range of houses. Since private investment in houses built for letting had been made unprofitable, it was decided to encourage it by a Government subsidy, believed in the face of the evidence[38] to be temporary only. In the event, housing needs grew faster than new dwellings and subsidized housing became one of the cornerstones of public welfare provision.

Under the first measure, the Housing and Town Planning Act of 1919 (the 'Addison Act') the building of houses was made obligatory on the local authorities rather than permissive, and they were to receive a subsidy to the extent of the entire loss beyond the proceeds of a penny rate. Subsidies were available also for Housing Associations and non-profit-making Housing Trusts. Private enterprise was excluded, but could claim a capital subsidy of £260 a house under certain easy conditions.

The Ministry of Health had certain powers over the building and the rents charged, and this ensured that subsidized houses were indeed built for those in most urgent need, irrespective of the rent they could afford. But since there was pressure to proceed quickly and the Act gave no incentive to local authorities, who were in immediate charge of the building, to practise economy at a time of shortages and rising prices in the boom of 1919–20, the building under

---

[37] p. 153 above; W. F. Stolper, 'British Monetary Policy and the Housing Boom', *QJE*, 56/1, part II, Nov. 1941, p. 90; Seymour J. Price, *Building Societies, Their Origin and History* (1958), pp. 292–3.

[38] *Royal Commission on Housing of the Industrial Population in Scotland* (1917. Cd. 8731).

the Addison Act were completed on the most extravagant terms. A large part of the subsidies flowed directly into the pockets of profiteering builders, to the tune of £1 a week per house. In March 1921, tenders for a non-parlour type of house reached £838 a house, compared with £371 in January 1923. Building under the Addison Act was suspended in 1922 as part of the economy campaign of that year. By March 1923, the houses built in England and Wales under the legislation of 1919 totalled 155,000 by local authorities, 44,000 by private enterprise with subsidy, and 54,000 without. The additional need since 1919, because of the net increase in the number of families, was estimated at 460,000 in the same period, so that the shortage had increased by some 200,000 dwellings, in spite of the extravagant spending.[39]

New principles of subsidizing building were introduced by the ('Chamberlain') Housing Act of 1923. Local economies were encouraged by limiting the subsidy for each house to £6 a year for 20 years, all the remainder of the loss to be borne by the local authority. This method ensured local economy in housing management; but the Act failed to encourage the building of working-class housing (if that, indeed, was its object), for under the high rate of interest then ruling, the subsidy was too low to permit rents which working-class families could afford. On the other hand, the Act was used by private enterprise builders, and nearly 400,000 of their houses ultimately claimed and received subsidies under it, mostly built for sale to the middle classes.

The tendency of the Chamberlain Act to use the taxpayers' money to subsidize the housing of those who needed it least, while leaving the large working-class demand unfulfilled, was redressed to some extent by the Labour Government in the following year. Its ('Wheatley') Housing (Financial Provisions) Act of 1924 raised the subsidy per house to £9 a year for 40 years, provided that the house was built for letting and that the rent did not exceed the 'appropriate normal rent' of the district.[40] Local authorities were stimulated thereby to provide large numbers of houses for the better-off artisan classes, but since the rates were calculated so as to leave little or no profit to the house owner, private enterprise was not attracted and preferred the Chamberlain scheme, the two schemes continuing side by side, one used by local authorities, the other by private builders. In 1927 the rates of subsidies on both were drastically reduced, and in 1929 the Chamberlain Act subsidies were ended, the Wheatley subsidies being abolished by the Housing Act of 1933.

The total number of houses built under the two schemes in England and Wales was nearly 960,000, of which 580,000 were provided by local authorities (358,000 of them by 1930) and 378,000 by private enterprise, nearly all of them by 1930. Including some 536,000 houses built since the end of the war without subsidy, the total of new houses built in England and Wales by the end of 1930 was almost $1\frac{1}{2}$ million, and from 1926 onwards the rate of construction had been 200,000 dwellings a year. Official opinion began to believe

[39] R. L. Reiss, *Municipal and Private Enterprise Housing* (1945), pp. 32 ff.; Marian Bowley, *Housing and the State* (1945), chapter 2; C. L. Mowat, *Britain Between the Wars* (1956 ed.), p. 44.

[40] Richard W. Lyman, *The First Labour Government, 1924* (1957), chapter 8.

that the basic housing needs were now being met, and the general subsidy schemes began to wound up, the subsidies of the 1930s being designed for particular purposes, such as slum clearance and the abolition of over-crowding.

At the same time, rent control was also eased. The Act of 1923 had per-mitted the decontrol of rents on changes of tenancy and the Housing Act of 1933 freed all large houses from rent control. The Housing Act of 1938, however, after six years of building boom, maintained rent control for the smaller buildings, reflecting the fact that, in spite of the repeal of the general housing subsidies, the housing shortage was by no means over for the poorer classes of the community: the general subsidies had been cut off too soon.[41] The number of separate families, a rough guide to the housing needs of the community, was still growing more rapidly than the number of dwellings until 1930. But in this total housing market, the demand for the more expen-sive accommodation was now being met. A private-enterprise housing boom developed in the 1930s[42] which provided almost 3 million new houses, vir-tually all for better-off owners and tenants. Those who occupied the cheaper houses could, in theory, find accommodation by 'filtering up' into dwellings thus vacated,[43] but mobility was low, partly as a result of rent control, and by the end of the 1930s there developed strong signs of an over-supply of expen-sive houses, while the shortage of cheap accommodation was as acute as ever.

The legislation of the 1930s dealt with special cases only. The first of the new Acts, the ('Greenwood') Housing Act of 1930, offered Government sub-sidies to local authorities for slum clearance schemes.[44] Up to then, it was esti-mated that only 11,000 slum houses in England and Wales had been pulled down and replaced, largely because of the absolute shortage of dwellings, but the new Act started from the assumption that the shortage was beginning to wane, and that replacement of slum property could begin. With the repeal of the existing general subsidies in 1933, it became the main effective subsidy scheme.

The Greenwood Act had the novel feature that subsidies varied, not with the number of houses, but with the number of people displaced and rehoused. The local authorities thus had a strong incentive to tackle the most populous areas first, and to provide new houses as fast as the old slums were pulled down. Further, all authorities with populations of over 20,000 were required to prepare five-year schemes for slum clearance, and continue them until all slums had been removed. Actual plans envisaged the scrapping of only 250,000 houses (out of at least 750,000 unfit), the building of 285,000 and the re-housing of $1\frac{1}{4}$ million people.

In 1935 a further Act extended subsidies to building designed to abate over-crowding, especially if high-cost flats were required. By then, according to the Report on Overcrowding in England and Wales, published by the Ministry of Health in 1936,[45] only 3·8% of dwellings were judged to be 'over-

---

[41] G. D. H. and M. I. Cole, *The Condition of Britain* (1937), chapter 3.

[42] pp. 152–3 above.

[43] A. P. Becker, 'Housing in England and Wales during the Business Depression of the 1930s', *Ec. Hist. Rev.*, 2nd S., 3/3, 1951, p. 323.

[44] E. D. (Lord) Simon, *The Anti-Slum Campaign* (1933), esp. chapter 13.

[45] Ministry of Health, *Report of Overcrowding Survey of England and Wales* (1936).

crowded', but this figure hid large regional concentrations, especially on Tyneside, where working-class flats were still typical, and in Scotland (not covered by this Report) where 22·6% of working-class dwellings were over-crowded in 1935. In any case, 'overcrowding' depends on the standards adopted, and a slightly more rigorous standard produced an average of 9·5%.[46] The consolidating Housing Act of 1936 gave local authorities power to clear slum property without compensation, in default; subsidy rates were reduced for general cases, and raised for special cases, like urban flats and agricultural areas, by the Housing Act of 1938. The total number of houses built in England and Wales under the legislation of the 1930s was 289,000 by local authorities and 8,000 by private enterprise.

By 1939 much of the overcrowding of 1936 had been abolished. Of the $1\frac{1}{4}$ million persons to be rehoused, only 239,000 were left in·their old quarters, nearly half of them in five cities – London, Leeds, Liverpool, Manchester and Sheffield. In many areas the five-year plans had been completed, and in others they were all but complete on the outbreak of war. But elsewhere slums were newly developing: in 1939, some 550,000 dwellings were still left which were fit for destruction under the slum clearance Acts, and 350,000 'marginal' dwellings, likely to become slums in a few years' time.

In Scotland, where housing needs were far greater and conditions far worse, more houses were built by local authorities and fewer by private enter-prise than in England and Wales. The total number of dwellings completed between the wars in Great Britain compared as shown in Table 4·2.[47]

Table 4·2:   Dwellings completed between the wars (in 000)

	England and Wales	Scotland	Great Britain
By local authorities	1,163	230	1,393
By private enterprise with subsidy	433	43	476
By private enterprise without subsidy	2,596	63	2,659
	4,192	336	4,528

New building thus amounted to $4\frac{1}{2}$ million *dwellings*, of which over two-thirds were built by private enterprise. Virtually all of these, except for 48,000 built by Housing Associations, were for letting to middle-class tenants or for sale to owner-occupiers, again for the middle classes and the top group of artisans. Many of the remainder, built by local authorities, were also let at rents which could be afforded by the better-off workers only.

Bearing in mind that about 700,000 dwellings were pulled down or con-verted, the net addition was of the order of 3·8 million.[48] Since the number of families was estimated to have risen by 3·3 million, the gap was closed, mainly in the late 1930s, to the extent of half a million dwellings since 1919, or

[46] Mowat, p. 507; G. D. H. Cole, *Building and Planning* (1945), pp. 102–3.
[47] Reiss, p. 15; Miss Bowley's figures vary slightly from these, *op. cit.*, Table 2, p. 271, and Appx. I.
[48] Richard Stone, *The Measurement of Consumers' Expenditure and Behaviour in the United Kingdom, 1920–1938*, vol. 1 (Cambridge, 1954), Table 92 and chapter 15.

not quite enough to meet the estimated shortage of 1919. Between 1914 and 1939, while the share of housing privately rented had fallen from 80% to 46% of the total, local authority rented housing had risen from 1% to 14% and owner-occupied from 6% to 31%.[49] There was still a considerable shortage of cheap accommodation in 1938, besides the slum property condemned and waiting to be cleared and replaced.[50]

Nevertheless, there had been substantial improvements. Over one-third of the stock of houses in existence had been built in the past 20 years, to much higher standards than pre-war working-class dwellings. Compared with pre-war years, 'the majority of those who benefited by the increase in the national income and by the more equal distribution of this income, tended to enjoy the bulk of their gains in terms of better housing conditions'.[51] Virtually all those with weekly incomes of under £3, and most of those with incomes £3–5, were now in old controlled accommodation or in new housing provided by the public authorities. Housing, like public health and education, was increasingly recognized to be an important public service.

Health insurance had a wide coverage from its beginnings in 1911. By 1921, over 15 million persons were included, and by 1938 the numbers insured had increased to nearly 20 million. Only the numbers of those insured under the Widows', Orphans' and Old-Age Pensions scheme exceeded those insured by the health scheme (by about 1 million) in 1938.[52] In this period the basic principles of health insurance, including the central position of the 'approved societies', remained unchanged, in spite of much criticism of the wasteful and uneven administration of the latter.

There was little attempt made to integrate the insurance scheme with the public health legislation, in spite of the establishment of the Ministry of Health in 1919, responsible for both, but there were other changes.[53] The abolition of the Poor Law Unions, and the transfer of their duties and property (including the hospitals) to County and County Borough Councils were accomplished by Chamberlain's Local Government Act of 1929. By contrast, thoroughgoing reforms proposed by the Lawrence Commission of 1926 were postponed for economy reasons.[54] The voluntary hospitals could be persuaded neither by the critique by the Dawson Committee of 1920 and the Cave Committee of 1921, nor by Government financial aid, to act on the variety of standards and the lack of co-ordination among them. Only after the Council (ex-Poor Law) hospitals in 1930 provided some direct competitive spur in the 1930s were standards gradually raised, and some collaboration between the local authority hospitals and the voluntary hospitals in their regions established. Hospital contributory schemes increased greatly, and by

---

[49] Sean Glyn and John Oxborrow, *Interwar Britain: A Social and Economic History* (1976) p. 221.

[50] M. J. Elsas, *Housing Before the War and After* (1942).

[51] Mark Abrams, *The Condition of the British People, 1911–1945* (1945), p. 44.

[52] Alan T. Peacock, *The Economics of National Insurance* (1952), p. 15; D. C. Marsh, *National Insurance and Assistance in Great Britain* (1950), chapter 3; PEP, *Report on the British Social Services* (1937), p. 123.

[53] Sir George Newman, *The Building of a Nation's Health* (1939), chapter 4.

[54] *Royal Commission on National Health Insurance* (1926. Cmd. 2596); Hermann Levy, *National Health Insurance* (Cambridge, 1944), chapters 3, 5; J. S. Ross, *The National Health Service in Great Britain* (1952), pp. 41–56.

1937 there were at least 5 million voluntary contributors, paying for at least 10 million persons, including dependants, but since the voluntary hospitals could not enlarge the number of beds, many contributing patients were treated in Council hospitals.[55]

Infectious diseases had been the responsibility of the local health authorities since the nineteenth century, and many of them maintained extensive isolation hospitals, tuberculosis sanatoria and similar institutions. In 1918, the Maternity and Child Welfare Act gave local authorities greater power to extend their facilities in this field, including the provision of clinics, and the Midwives Act of 1936 required them to provide trained midwives. In a little over 20 years, the number of Infant Welfare Centres had risen from a handful to 3,580 in 1938, and the number of ante-natal clinics to 1,795 in England and Wales.[56] The Venereal Diseases Act of 1917 and the Mental Treatment Act of 1930 opened up new fields in the public health services. The Blind Persons Act of 1920 made Counties and County Boroughs responsible for the welfare of the blind, and granted them non-contributory pensions at the age of 50, lowered to 40 in 1938. Meanwhile, the Nurses Registration Act of 1919 gave an enhanced status to the nursing profession.

Thus at the end of the 1930s, there had been substantial progress made in many separate fields, without bringing the different aspects of public health administrations any closer together, except, perhaps, in the hands of the Local Medical Officer of Health. The insurance scheme covered only about half the adult population; it excluded some 15 million wives of insured persons except when they were child-bearing, and it failed to provide most types of specialist and hospital treatment even for those it covered. Youths of 14–16 years of age were brought in only in 1938, and children between one and five not at all.

The local authorities were entirely separate from those administering the insurance scheme, yet they gave medical and dental inspection, but not always treatment, to schoolchildren.[57] They were also responsible for medical services such as the treatment of infectious diseases, venereal diseases and insanity, as well as for more general legislation as to building, sewage, slaughter houses, food adulteration, and so forth. The Acts relating to most of these functions were consolidated by the Public Health Act of 1936, extended by the Food and Drugs Act of 1938 which adopted clauses found useful in local Acts. Since taking over the functions of the Poor Law Guardians in 1930, the Public Assistance Committees of the larger local authorities also controlled many hospitals, and were responsible for all medical assistance required by paupers. The other public hospitals, including the teaching hospitals, continued to be managed by yet a third set of authorities, the voluntary committees. Of the 3,029 hospitals in existence in Great Britain, 1,013 were voluntary, 116 were general public hospitals, 523

[55] Levy, pp. 167–71; W. M. Frazer, *A History of English Public Health, 1834–1939* (1950), pp. 390–3; PEP, *The British Health Services* (1937), p. 16; Harry Eckstein, *The English Health Service* (Cambridge, Mass., 1959), chapter 5.

[56] R. M. Titmuss, *Birth, Poverty and Health* (1943), p. 33.

[57] H. and M. Wickwar, *The Social Services, an Historical Survey* (2nd ed., 1949), p. 120.

were Poor Law hospitals, and the rest was made up of special hospitals and sanatoria managed by the local authorities.[58]

Efforts to unify these various services were, however, becoming more numerous. In 1930 the BMA and in 1937 the authors of a most comprehensive report on the British Health Services, published by PEP, favoured major reorganization.[59] The Cathcart Committee on Scottish Health Services, which sat from 1933 to 1936[60] demanded an extension of insurance benefits and a comprehensive national health policy, to aim at 'the fitness of the people', including preventive as well as curative measures. Thus public opinion before the war was being prepared for the changes that were to occur after it.

The third pre-1914 benefit scheme, the non-contributory old-age pension, was not changed in principle in this period, but payments were raised to 10s. a week and the income limits (above which no payments were made) were raised periodically also. Superimposed on this scheme were the new contributory pensions which would, in due course, be paid out as a right and without a needs test, and begin at the age of 65 instead of 70. They were linked with several other benefits in the comprehensive Widows', Orphans' and Old Age Contributory Pensions Act of 1925. Apart from old-age pensions for insured men (at 10s. a week), there were to be pensions for widows, children's allowances for widows, and payments for orphans of insured persons. An Act of 1937 opened this scheme, on a voluntary basis, to independent workers of small means.[61]

The war and the brave hopes for the post-war world brought major changes in the field of public education also. The Fisher Education Act of 1918 gave the Board of Education, and the Counties and County Boroughs, as local education authorities, strong encouragement and greater power to develop a comprehensive system of education from the nursery school to the evening class. The Board's financial aid to the local authorities was increased to at least 50% of expenditure. Full-time education to the age of 14 was made compulsory by revoking all concessions to part-timers and early leavers. Local authorities were permitted to raise the school-leaving age to 15, or, in default, to provide day continuation schools for youths aged 14 to 16 for one day a week. Finally, the noble aspiration was written into the Act, that 'adequate provision shall be made in order to secure that children and young persons shall not be debarred from receiving the benefits of any form of education by which they are capable of profiting through inability to pay fees'.

The hopes which had inspired the Act were largely disappointed. The Geddes axe and the general spirit of economy after 1921 killed all continuation schools except the one at Rugby. The school-leaving age remained at 14, and measures to tackle the overcrowding, the poor equipment, the lack of staff in so many of the ordinary Council schools were deferred for yet

[58] C. L. Mowat, *Britain Between the Wars* (1956 ed.), p. 497.
[59] PEP, *op. cit.*, p. 25.
[60] *Report of the Committee on the Scottish Health Services* (1936. Cmd. 5204).
[61] Marsh, *op. cit.*, chapter 6; Charles E. Clarke, *Social Insurance in Britain* (Cambridge, 1950), pp. 7–9.

another decade. Yet some impetus remained from the Fisher Act, particularly in the field of secondary education. The Hadow Report,[62] the work of a committee appointed by the Labour Government of 1924, proposed the ending of 'elementary' education at 11, and the provision of separate curricula beyond that age to children of differing abilities. In addition to the existing grammar schools and the junior technical and trade schools with their strong vocational bias, there should also be so-called 'modern' schools, selective and non-selective, which should combine practical teaching with a liberal approach, and should thus fill a gap between the other two types, while claiming staff and equipment comparable with those of grammar schools. 'Senior' classes should be provided preferably away from the 'primary' school for children under 11, and transfer between the different types of school should be made possible.

The Report was adopted, and reorganization proceeded throughout the rest of the inter-war period, though progress was slow in rural areas and among the 'voluntary schools' controlled by the churches.[63] By 1938, 63·5% of all children over 11 were in reorganized ('modern') schools.[64] The influential Spens Committee, appointed in 1933 and reporting in 1938,[65] further elaborated the idea of a type of school having parity of esteem with the grammar school, but giving a more practical education in place of the stress on classics and the preparation for a university: the 'Technical High Schools'.[66]

The extension of schooling to 15, planned by the Labour Government for 1931, was thwarted largely by the opposition of the churches, but was re-enacted in 1936, when the churches were appeased by large grants. Timed to come into effect in September 1939, it was again held up, by the war. Throughout the period, education expenditure rose as a proportion of net national income, from 1·2% in 1920 to 2·4% in 1935 for the public sector, plus a rise of from 0·15% to 0·21% for the private sector.[67] Children from poorer homes, however continued in practice to be denied the opportunity of higher education in all but the most exceptional circumstances.[68] Higher education was still mainly for the rich.

Taken all in all, the more generous impulses and the more ambitious social demands of the war years had not been entirely rendered nugatory by the reaction of the early 1920s. There was a considerable expansion of the public services into new fields; there was, at the same time, a gradual abandonment

[62] Board of Education Consultative Committee, *Report on the Education of the Adolescent* (1927).

[63] H. and M. Wickwar, *The Social Services*, pp. 73–82; G. A. N. Lowndes, *The Silent Social Revolution* (1937), p. 101.

[64] A. M. Carr-Saunders and D. Caradog Jones, *A Survey of the Social Structure of England and Wales* (Oxford, 2nd ed., 1937), chapter 11.

[65] Board of Education Consultative Committee, *Report on Secondary Education* (1938).

[66] John Graves, *Policy and Progress in Secondary Education, 1902–1942* (1943), chapters 16–22.

[67] John Vaizey and John Sheehan, *Resources for Education. An Economic Study of Education in the United Kingdom, 1920–1965* (1968), p. 139.

[68] K. Lindsay, *Social Progress and Educational Waste* (1926); R. M. Titmuss, *op. cit.*, pp. 63–4.

of comprehensive poor relief based on destitution, and its replacement by contractual insurance benefits. Administratively, also, there was a distinct movement away from *ad hoc* bodies, and the transfer of functions to the normal local authority, supported by Exchequer grants. These tendencies appeared to meet with general approval; and the last years before the war saw numerous proposals, made by official and unofficial bodies of influence, to proceed farther in the same direction.

3 The Trade Unions and the Politics of Poverty

The war had brought about a remarkable increase in the power, status and size of trade unions. The peak of their membership was reached in 1920, when it stood at 8·3 million; after that it declined to 4·4 million in 1933, to recover again to 6·3 million in 1939. The membership of the unions affiliated to the Trades Union Congress in these years was 6·5 million, 3·5 million and 4·7 million respectively.[69] Several factors accounted for the war-time growth. There was the unions' success in raising wages and improving conditions, applied to all workers, including non-unionists. The growth of the community spirit, fostered during the war, and the knowledge of common hardships, helped to claim adherence and loyalty. Full employment removed the former fear of the blacklisting of union members. The momentous political leftward impetus further focused attention on the unions and on the role they might play. Conversely, the inability of the unions to hold their high money wage level after 1920 (though adequately explained by the general deflation), the mass unemployment, the disillusionment with the political impotence of Labour, and the return of the spirit of individualistic self-seeking were not without influence on the decline of trade-union membership after 1920.

In their appearances before manpower boards, arbitration tribunals and various public authorities in the war, the trade unions within each industry had been forced to collaborate closely, and this encouraged a movement towards amalgamation. The Trade Union (Amalgamation) Act of 1917 made amalgamation easier, and the widespread support for industrial unionism given by many of the shop stewards' committees during the war[70] worked in the same direction. The outcome was a series of major amalgamations establishing the very large unions which have dominated the union world to the present day. Among them was the amalgamation of the ASE with nine smaller societies in 1920 to form the Amalgamated Engineering Union, the National Union of Foundry Workers formed in the same year, the NU of General and Municipal Workers in 1924, the Transport and General Workers' Union in 1922, the Amalgamated Union of Building Trade Workers in 1921, the Amalgamated Society of Woodworkers in 1921, and the Iron and Steel Trades Confederation in 1917.[71] Other amalgamations formed

[69] N. Barou, *British Trade Unions* (1947), Appx. XIV.

[70] Branko Pribićević, *The Shop Stewards' Movement and Workers' Control, 1910–1922* (Oxford, 1959).

[71] J. B. Jefferys, *The Story of the Engineers, 1800–1945* (1945), pp. 191–4; H. J. Fyrth and Henry Collins, *The Foundry Workers, a Trade Union History* (1959), pp. 151–8; H. A. Clegg, *General Union* (Oxford, 1954), Part I; V. L. Allen, *Trade Union Leadership* (1957), chapter 3

in the years 1920–2 led to the formation of the NU of Textile Workers, the NU of Distributive and Allied Workers, the NU of Printing, Bookbinding and Paper Workers, the Union of Post Office Workers, the Tailors' and Garment Workers' Union, the Civil Service Clerical Association, the NU of Sheet Metal Workers and the NU of Blastfurnacemen.

These amalgamations and others like them gave an appearance of greater strength to the unions concerned. But quite apart from the inevitable teething troubles, size was not necessarily an advantage even in the longer run. There developed a large full-time bureacracy, while the power of the local branch diminished, and apathy grew; unofficial strikes showed that communication with the union leadership had broken down. The leaders themselves, instead of having spent their younger years battling for their society, came increasingly to be men who had worked their way up inside a safe, strong, hierarchical and generally recognized organization, more concerned to preserve peace with employers and to safeguard their benefit funds than to sanction adventurous drives to recruit new members or raise wages.

This tendency to settle down to respectable and responsible trade union policies became more evident after 1926, the year of the General Strike. By contrast, before about 1906 a policy of caution had been obligatory on many unions because of their weakness. The years in between, forming an interlude of stationary real wages in the secular upward movement of working-class living standards,[72] and interrupted by the war which gave its own strong impetus to trade union militancy, formed a unique period in which trade unions were both strong enough, and militant enough, to challenge their employers repeatedly and persistently, both in narrow skirmishes and on a broad front. There were four main issues in the strikes of this watershed of trade union history: first, the recognition of trade unions by employers; secondly, increases in wages in the era of rising prices up to 1920, and resistance to the attempts to cut wage costs ahead of prices in the slump years afterwards; thirdly, the integration of new types of skilled or semi-skilled work, from machine minding to bus driving, into the old-established categories of skilled, apprenticed crafts; and fourthly, the permanent retention of some of the gains in working conditions achieved in the period of labour shortage, 1915–20, above all, the shorter working week without loss of pay, introduced in most industries in 1919–20.[73] In addition, there were the political demands: 'Labour is challenging the whole structure of capitalist industry as it now exists', wrote one group of moderate leaders in 1919; 'it demands a system of industrial control which shall be truly democratic in character.'[74]

The earlier of the important post-war strikes took place on the Clyde, the storm centre of the war years, and in Belfast, where the engineers, led by their shop stewards, came out for a 40 and 44-hour week respectively in January

and Appendices; Alan Bullock, *The Life and Times of Ernest Bevin*, vol. 1 (1960), pp. 153ff.; (Arthur Pugh) *Men of Steel* (1951), chapter 13; R. W. Postgate, *The Builders' History* (1923), chapter 18; S. Higgenbottam, *Our Society's History* (1939); G. D. H. Cole, *Organised Labour* (1924), Part 4; PEP, *British Trade Unionism* (1948), pp. 97, 103–4.

[72] E. H. Phelps-Brown, *The Growth of British Industrial Relations* (1959), p. 354.

[73] See p. 50 above.

[74] D. F. MacDonald, *The State and the Trade Unions* (1960), p. 98.

and February 1919. They were defeated, but not without violent street battles and many arrests. Perhaps more significant for the unsettled conditions of the times was the police strike, in July 1919, following a successful action a year earlier, but ending in the defeat of the strikers and legislation outlawing the union.[75] The miners' threat to strike for the nationalization of coal in February 1919 had been staved off by the appointment of the Sankey Commission, and by its report in favour of nationalization, but in June there was a strike of cotton workers, and in July of Yorkshire miners. The national railway strike of September–October 1919, to enforce a wage settlement, was important for being, in effect, conducted against the Government which was then still administering the railways, and for the large amount of sympathy it roused among many other transport workers and the public at large.[76]

There were other disputes, concerned mainly with purely industrial questions. In 1920 a Special Court of Inquiry was set up under the Industrial Courts Act to hear the case of the Transport Workers' Federation for higher wages and decasualization in the docks. The union's case was brilliantly presented by Ernest Bevin, who earned the title the 'Dockers' KC' by his advocacy, and the court awarded a national minimum wage as well as proposing a scheme for regulating the labour market at the docks, though this latter was ignored by the employers. The largest of the post-war disputes outside the coal mining industry began in March 1922, when the engineering employers locked out all members of the AEU and of 47 other unions in their industry in order to enforce unlimited overtime working at the discretion of the employers. The struggle went on until June when the men, having exhausted their funds, returned to work on the employers' terms.

The high incidence of strikes in the post-war years is brought out in Table 4·3.[77]

Table 4·3: Incidence of Strikes, 1911–39

Average of years	No. of strikes beginning in year	Workers involved in strikes beginning in year (million)	Working days lost by strikes during the year (million)
1911–14	1,034	0·88	17·9
1915–18	775	0·68	4·2
1919–21	1,241	2·11	49·1
1922–26*	568	0·63	38·8**
1927–39	570	0·31	3·1

* Excluding the General Strike.
* * Average 1922–5; 11·7 million.

[75] V. L. Allen, 'The National Union of Police and Prison Officers', *Ec. Hist. Rev.*, 2nd S., 11/1, 1958.
[76] G. D. H. Cole, *A Short History of the British Working-Class Movement, 1789–1947* (1952 ed.), pp. 392–3; G. W. Alcock, *Fifty Years of Railway Trade Unionism* (1922).
[77] K. G. J. C. Knowles, *Strikes – A Study in Industrial Conflict* (Oxford, 1952), Appx. Table 1.

The industrial unrest illustrated by these strike statistics was combined with much political activity on the part of labour. The war had left a relic of class hatred, and with the example of the Bolshevik Revolution and other Continental revolutions before them, the working classes took to more revolutionary politics. 'Nationalization of the mines, the railways, and the land; workers' control of industry; a capital levy; work or maintenance; an end to class distinction; the abolition of poverty and riches – these were the slogans which captured a considerable section of the working classes'.[78] The high point of activity, perhaps, occurred in August 1920, when a 'Council of Action' was set up by the Labour Party and the TUC to stop the sending of military aid by the British Government to the armies trying to destroy the young Soviet Union. This campaign was successful, and in the same year a Communist Party was formed, but was refused affiliation to the Labour Party.

In 1920–1 the organization of the TUC was overhauled, and the Parliamentary Committee replaced by a 'General Council', more fully representative of all important sections of workers and with far wider industrial powers and duties. In 1924, further steps in the same direction were taken when Congress voted in favour of the 'Industrial Workers Charter', proposing to form one single union for each industry, with the object of maximizing its power. Congress also demanded the nationalization of the key industries, and the General Council was strengthened.[79] At the same time federations and industrial alliances of several unions were established or discussed.

The militancy of both the political and the industrial wings of the Labour Movement was met by the Government by some temporary expedients, like the Wages (Temporary Regulations) Act of November 1918, which prohibited any reduction of wages in the course of the next six months, the 'out-of-work donation', described in the last section, and the Industrial Conference. Some gains were of permanent benefit, including legislation to promote arbitration, conciliation and the fixing of wages.

The scheme of joint industrial councils based on the reports of the Whitley Committee of the Ministry of Reconstruction[80] was, after its initial widespread acceptance, not as successful as had been hoped. The high point of the movement was reached at the end of 1920, when there were 75 JICs, covering $3\frac{1}{2}$ million workers, and 33 'Interim Industrial Reconstruction Committees' but little of this survived except what was established in the Civil Service and by statutory authority elsewhere, as on the railways under the Railway Act of 1921 and in agriculture under the Agricultural Wages (Regulation) Act of 1924.[81]

The scope of Trade Boards was extended by an Amending Act in 1918 and between 1919 and 1921, 33 new boards were set up. After 1922, when the immediate need to pacify Labour had passed, and until 1939 only about 10

[78] Alan Bullock, *The Life and Times of Ernest Bevin*, vol. 1 (1960), p. 99.

[79] W. Milne-Bailey, *Trade Union Documents* (1929), No. 83. Also see Rodger Charles, *The Development of Industrial Relations in Britain 1911–1939* (1973), Part III.

[80] Cd. 8606 (1917), Cd. 9001, 9002, 9099, 9153 (1918).

[81] J. B. Seymour, *The Whitley Councils Scheme* (1932); J. H. Richardson, *Industrial Relations in Great Britain* (Geneva, 1933), chapter 4.

new industries were added, apart from 18 in Northern Ireland. The total number of workers covered was about $1\frac{1}{2}$ million.[82]

The third organization to emerge from the recommendations of the Whitley Committee was the Industrial Court, set up under the Industrial Courts Act of 1919. Composed of members drawn from three sections, employers, employed and 'independents', its decisions were not binding, but out of 1,700 awards in the 19 years to 1939, only four were questioned by one or the other party to the dispute.[83] In 1936 the Civil Service Arbitration Tribunal, working to much the same rules, was set up to deal with all Civil Service cases. The Industrial Court was also given additional jurisdiction from time to time, such as powers to arbitrate on hours and conditions under the Road Traffic Act, 1930 (amended 1933), under the Sugar Industry (Reorganization) Act of 1936, the Air Navigation Act of 1936, and the Road Haulage Wages Act of 1938. This latter Act also included the unusual principle, first introduced by the Cotton Manufacturing Industry (Temporary Provisions) Act of 1934, of giving statutory sanction to wages arrived at by collective bargaining, and making them applicable to all firms.

In the period of the post-war unrest, the cockpit of the industrial struggles was the coal industry. While forming only 6·2% of the industrial population, the miners furnished 41·8% of all strikers between 1911 and 1945, and if the General Strike of 1926 is excluded, in which the other trades were striking in support of the miners' demands, the miner was eight times as likely to strike as the average worker; the only other major industries above the average were textiles (2·2 times), metal working, etc. (1·4) and transport (1·5).[84]

Among all the groups of workers demanding the nationalization of their industry after the war, the miners were the most insistent, and enjoyed the most widespread support. In view of the great coal shortage in Europe, and the ugly temper in many mining districts, the Government felt constrained to appoint the Sankey Commission early in 1919 to stave off a threatened miners' strike on this question. Its disregard of the recommendation of Lord Sankey for nationalization persuaded the miners that they had been tricked into calling off their strike when it stood the greatest chance of success, in February 1919, in order to enter into a period of procrastination in which their industrial power would steadily diminish. To the distrust of the coal owners, dating from pre-war years, there was added distrust of the Government.[85]

Meanwhile, in 1920, the industry was still riding the high wave of prosperity and selling its exports at unprecedented prices. The miners struck for higher wages in October, and in spite of the failure of the Triple Alliance to

[82] J. J. Mallon, 'Trade Boards', in G. D. H. Cole, *British Trade Unions To-day* (1939); Dorothy Sells, *The British Trade Boards System* (1923); Milne-Bailey, Nos. 116–18; Paul Barton Johnson, *Land Fit For Heroes. The Planning of British Reconstruction 1916–1919* (Chicago, 1968), pp. 459 ff.

[83] F. E. Gannett and B. F. Catherwood, *Industrial and Labour Relations in Great Britain* (1939), p. 18; G. P. Jones and A. G. Pool, *A Hundred Years of Economic Development in Great Britain* (1959 ed.), pp. 386–9.

[84] Knowles, *Strikes*, p. 203.

[85] A. Hutt, *The Post-War History of the British Working Class* (1937), chapter 1, and *British Trade Unionism* (1952 ed.), chapter 7; also p. 67 above.

support them, achieved a partial victory after a three weeks' strike. A wage increase was granted, but made conditional upon increased output, the so-called 'datum line', and permanent terms were to be worked out by the end of March 1921. Meanwhile, despite its failure on this occasion, the threat of the Triple Alliance had led the Government to introduce the Emergency Powers Act of 1920, which empowered the Government to declare a 'state of emergency' and govern by decree, on threat of any action 'of such a nature and on so extensive a scale as to be calculated, by interfering with the supply and distribution of food, water, fuel, or light, or with the means of locomotion, to deprive the community, or any substantial portion of the community, of the essentials of life'.[86] It was put into force and used with some effect in the mining disputes of 1921 and 1926.

Before the new permanent rate of mining wages could be worked out, a sharp slump of coal export prices reduced the surplus available (home coal price having been kept down throughout this period) and the Government announced its intention of handing the industry back to the owners on 31 March 1921. The owners at once determined on drastic wage reductions and locked out the miners while the Government declared a State of Emergency and made even more extensive military preparations than in the strikes of 1919 and 1920. There followed a series of manœuvres and negotiations behind the scenes in which the Triple Alliance first appeared to be willing to back the miners, but later, on 15 April, 'Black Friday', withdrew their support. Whether betrayed, as sometimes alleged, or unable to agree where the decision-making power in the Triple Alliance should lie, the Alliance broke up, in effect, in 1921.[87]

Left in the lurch by their allies, the miners suffered a crushing defeat and had to return to work on the owners' terms in June 1921, when their funds were exhausted. They had to submit not only to a wage cut, but also swallow the bitter pill of a return from the national wage agreements of war-time to the earlier district agreements.[88] There followed large-scale wage reductions and a mass defection of membership in many industries. The bargaining positions in the labour market had radically changed with the change in the economic climate, from boom to slump.

The first Labour Government did not, in its short span of office in 1924, come up to the fears of its enemies, nor did it fulfil the hopes of its more revolutionary supporters, who had assumed that Socialist measures might be introduced.[89] When it was defeated, by the combined action of a press stunt and its own pathological fear of being labelled 'revolutionary', it became clear that the post-war settlement of the labour question, the more permanent equilibrium of forces after the disorientation of the war years, would be decided in the industrial field, not the political. Again it was the coal mining industry which became the scene of battle.

In the summer of 1925, coal prices and sales had begun a further rapid and

---

[86] Emergency Powers Act, 1920, 10 & 11 Geo. V, ch. 55, sec. 1.

[87] Francis Williams, *Magnificent Journey* (1954), chapter 21.

[88] J. W. F. Rowe, *Wages in the Coal Industry* (1923); J. R. Raynes, *Coal and its Conflicts* (1928).

[89] G. D. H. Cole, *History of the Labour Party Since 1914* (1948); Richard W. Lyman, *The First Labour Government, 1924* (1957).

permanent decline, and the owners demanded, not only a return to the wages of 1921–4, but also the repeal of the Seven Hours Act of 1919 and its replacement by eight-hour shifts. In view of the unfavourable market situation and their own depleted finances after the stoppage of 1921, the miners felt unable to resist these demands unaided, and turned for help to the General Council of the TUC, recently provided with authority which seemed to fit the new situation. Trade union rates were under attack all along the line, especially in the export industries, which were desperately anxious to reduce costs, and there was little doubt that the outcome of the miners' dispute would largely determine other wage levels. In July 1925, the Trades Union Congress pledged its full support to the miners, to the extent of being prepared to call a general sympathetic strike.

Faced with this threat, the Government (which collaborated with the mine owners throughout this dispute) climbed down on 'Red Friday'. It decided to offer a temporary subsidy to enable the mine owners to continue to pay existing wage rates, and to appoint a Royal Commission. The Report of the Commission, presided over by Sir Herbert Samuel, the fourth official body to inquire into the industry since 1918, was subsequently ignored, but the subsidy had given a breathing space of nine months. This the Government used to prepare for an all-out struggle with the miners' union and the TUC. Large coal stocks were built up, the country was divided into 10 areas under Civil Commissioners provided with wide powers, an Emergency Committee for Supply and Transport was appointed, and an Organization for the Maintenance of Supplies was set up on private initiative, to marshal volunteer strike breakers. By contrast, the General Council of the TUC made no preparations whatever.

The subsidy expired at the end of April, the miners were locked out, and the General Council called a 'general strike' in support of the miners' case for midnight, Monday, 3 May. The 'first line' of trades, including transport, iron and steel, printing, building and electricity and gas workers, was called out at once, and the 'second line' of engineers and shipbuilders was called out on 11 May.

Despite the lack of preparation, the response of the rank and file exceeded all expectations. The strike, in the trades called out, was virtually complete. As most of the fuel supplies and transport were affected, local trades councils or other *ad hoc* bodies took over some of the functions of local government to provide necessary services to hospitals, etc., and others attempted, in the absence of newspapers, to counter the information and propaganda of the BBC, which was wholly under the influence of the Government, by information sheets of their own.

The strike brought forth much capacity for organization, enthusiasm and solidarity of the ordinary membership, but these were wholly nullified by the attitude of its leaders. 'For the rank and file the strike was a triumph: for most of its national leaders a humiliation.'[90] The General Council itself

---

[90] C. L. Mowat, *Britain Between the Wars* (1956 ed.), p. 313. Other good accounts of the General Strike will be found in: Julian Symons, *The General Strike* (1957); W. H. Crook, *The General Strike* (1931); A. J. Cook, *The Nine Days* (1927); Hamilton Fyfe, *Behind the Scenes of the Great Strike* (1926); Alan Bullock, *op. cit.*, pp. 299–344; Milne-Bailey Nos. 141–52; John Lovell, *British Trade Unions 1875–1933* (1977), pp. 56–8.

virtually disintegrated as a directing organ. Whatever positive directive was given from the centre, was due to individuals, above all Ernest Bevin, though most of the initiative seemed to come from below.

The members of the General Council, having intended a gesture of sympathy and solidarity with the miners found themselves driven by the deliberate decision of the Government, to challenge the Government and the constitution. Unwilling to win, they could not compromise either, since the Cabinet, temporarily under the sway of its more ebullient members led by Winston Churchill, was determined to achieve complete victory. In the end, using the pretext that a compromise formula suggested by Sir Herbert Samuel might be adopted, the General Council called off the strike on 12 May, after nine days, without any conditions or promises on the part of Government or owners. The strikers, who had only begun to get into their stride, were unable to understand this submission, but discipline again prevailed and most of them returned to work.

The miners' leaders had scarcely been consulted, and they stayed out. Their funds had been low, and the subscriptions to their aid, totalling £1·8 million, a large part of which had come from the Russian miners, were insufficient for a prolonged struggle. After nearly eight months, the men were starved into submission, and agreements were made district by district, in each case involving major reductions in wages and increases in hours to $7\frac{1}{2}$ or 8 per shift.[91]

The immediate cost of the coal strike was the loss of 28 million tons of coal for export; the total losses, including losses of wages, have been put at £175–270 million. Among trade union leaders, the main consequence was the determination to avoid at all costs a repetition of the head-on clash with the Government. There were very few full-scale national strikes after 1927: disputes remained local and short and were often unofficial.[92] The years beginning in 1927 were among the most peaceful in recorded history, as trade union leaders showed signs of 'exhaustion, disillusionment and recognition of the futility of industrial stoppages following the disastrous experiences of 1926'.[93] Only the cotton industry showed an upsurge of industrial disputes in 1929, 1931 and 1932, losing in those three years $15\frac{1}{2}$ million working days, or over 70% of the number lost in all industries.

The leading trade unionists turned to collaboration with the owners and managers of their own industries. They were met more than half-way by those employers who were coming to look for a solution to the grave industrial problems of the age in rationalization, association or a corporate form of industrial organization in which the workers' representatives would play a part.[94] 'We realize', wrote Sir Alfred Mond (later Lord Melchett) and 20 other large employers to the Central Council of the TUC in November 1927, 'that industrial reconstruction can be undertaken only in conjunction with

[91] R. Page Arnot, *The Miners: Years of Struggle* (1953), chapters 12–14; D. H. Robertson, 'A Narrative of the Coal Strike', *Econ. J.*, 36/143, 1926.

[92] Knowles, pp. 155–7; H. A. Clegg and R. Adams, *The Employers' Challenge* (Oxford, 1957), chapter 1; G. D. H. Cole, *An Introduction to Trade Unionism* (1953), chapter X/1.

[93] J. H. Richardson, 'Industrial Relations', in *Britain in Depression* (1935), pp. 59–60; also his 'Industrial Relations' in *Britain in Recovery* (1938), pp. 115–17.

[94] E.g. Sir Alfred Mond, *Industry and Politics* (1927); Bullock, *op. cit.*, chapter 15.

and with the co-operation of those entitled and empowered to speak for organized Labour.' They initiated the so-called 'Mond-Turner' conversations, with the full official support of the General Council of the TUC which told the 1928 Congress that it was

> for the trade union movement to say boldly that not only is it concerned with the prosperity of industry, but that it is going to have a voice in the way industry is carried on . . . the unions can use their power to promote and guide the scientific reorganization of industry.[95]

Although the conversations were never officially supported by any employers' organization, they helped to give trade unions a breathing space after their defeat of 1926, and to allow industry to reap the benefit of the boom of 1927–9 without being subject to claims for increased wages.

The General Strike also closed an epoch which began in 1907, in which unions relied on putting pressure on the public at large in order to induce the Government to mediate and enforce some concessions on the employers. Henceforward for many years to come no trade union leader would dare to challenge the intervention of the Government. Henceforward also those favouring gradual reform would swamp trade unionists who were in favour of State Socialism or Guild Socialism. Finally, the fiasco of the General Strike destroyed the 'myth' of the efficacy of this ultimate weapon in the armoury of the working classes, which had haunted them since the days of Syndicalism before 1914.

The strike also left its mark on the Statute Book: the employers' victory was embodied in the Trade Disputes and Trade Unions Act of 1927. This made general strikes illegal, mainly by outlawing all sympathy strikes which were held by the Courts to be designed to coerce the Government either directly or by inflicting hardship on the public. It forbade State employees to belong to societies or federations not consisting wholly of State employees. Further, it restricted picketing and gave the Government the power, by injunction, to attack trade union funds, the worst aspect of these sections of the Act being their vagueness and consequent uncertainty. Finally, it substituted 'contracting in' for 'contracting out' of the political levy, and thus at once reduced sharply the trade union contributions to Labour Party funds.

This measure, widely deplored as a needless act of vengeance, contributed to the General Election result of 1929, which returned Labour as the largest party in the House. Labour took office again under James Ramsay MacDonald, with Liberal support, but the second Labour Government did little to further the cause of the trade unions or of its own Socialist supporters. It split over measures to deal with the effects of the great depression and worsening unemployment and, following an ignominious defeat at the polls at the end of 1931, decimated the party in the House and wiped out its chances of office for the next decade.

Yet the political and industrial struggles of the 1920s had by no means been in vain. After the worst of the slump was over, the more generous

---

[95] Quoted in A. Hutt, *Post-War History of the British Working Class*, p. 178. Also Ben Turner, *About Myself* (1930); G. W. McDonald and H. F. Gospel, 'The Mond-Turner Talks 1927–1933', *Historical Journal* 16/4, 1973; Rodger Charles, *Industrial Relations*, Part IV.

welfare provisions described in the last two sections were enacted. In the trade unions, which began to register large increases in membership, the conversatism of their leaders did not go unchallenged. The National Unemployed Workers' Movement remained active, and was largely instrumental in forcing the Government to postpone and finally abandon the cuts in the dole which were to operate under Part II of the Unemployment Act of 1934, even though the official trade union leadership opposed its policies and hampered its actions. There were numerous unofficial strikes, directed against the union leadership as much as against the employers. In a few cases, as among the London busmen, breakaway unions were formed. By and large, however, the trade unions maintained their character of solidity, and forming a steadying, conservative influence on the Labour Party itself.

4 Changes in Population and Social Structure

The population increase which had accompanied the industrialization of this country continued between the wars, the United Kingdom figures rising from 43·74 million in the middle of 1920 to 47·49 million in the middle of 1938,[96] but the rate of increase had begun to decline sharply in the second decade of the twentieth century. It contracted further in the 1920s and 1930s at such a headlong rate that fears began to be expressed about the ultimate decline of the population of the United Kingdom.[97]

In absolute terms, the natural increase of population in Great Britain was at its highest in 1901–11, when births exceeded deaths by nearly 4·6 million and despite heavy emigration, the net increase in the home population was 3·8 million in 1901–11.[98] In the following decade, 1911–21, the natural increase fell to 2·8 million (net, 1·9 million) and there were further drops after the war, the increase for 1921–31 being only 2·6 million (2·0 million) and in 1931–41 1·2 million, though there was a net increase of 1·8 million then, because of some net immigration. As the total population was rising throughout this period, the proportionate decline in the rate of increase was faster than these figures suggest; and since the death rate was falling it follows that the fall in the birth rate was precipitate.

The population increase between the wars was associated with a geographical shift, closely associated with the changing location of industry (see Table 4·4).[99]

The growth of the inter-war period was also accompanied by further urbanization, and it was still largely the rural areas that acted as population reservoirs for the growing towns. The main growth occurred in the smaller towns with growing industries (e.g. Oxford, York, Leicester and Norwich)

[96] Richard Stone, *Measurement of Consumers' Expenditure and Behaviour in the United Kingdom, 1920–1938* (Cambridge, 1954), Table 116, p. 414.

[97] E.g. D. V. Glass, *The Struggle for Population* (1936).

[98] *Report of the Royal Commission on Population* (1948. Cmd. 7695), Table IV, p. 9; most of this section is based on this report.

[99] Chapter 2, section 4 above. Also Mark Abrams, *The Condition of the British People, 1911–1945* (1945), p. 22. Cf. also A. Beacham, *Structure of British Industry* (1955 ed.), p. 150; G. D. H. Cole and R. Postgate, *The Common People, 1746–1938* (1938), pp. 612–13.

Table 4·4: Distribution of the population in Great Britain

Regional distribution (R = largely rural)	Population in 1938 (million)	% Change 1921–38	Multiplication of population 1801–1921
Southeast	14·49	+ 18·1	5
Midlands	7·21	+ 11·6	4
West Riding	3·46	+ 6.0	5½
Eastern counties (R)	1·85	+ 3·7	2
Lancashire and Cheshire	6·16	+ 3·5	7
Southwest (R)	2·08	+ 3·3	2
Northern rural belt (R)	1·29	+ 3·1	3
Scotland	4·99	+ 2·1	3
Northumberland and Durham	2·20	− 1·0	7
North and Central Wales (R)	0·68	− 4·8	2
South Wales	1·78	− 8·1	9
Great Britain	46·20	+ 8·0	4

and in the expanding coal and iron ore fields of the east Midlands.[100] The conurbations remained stationary or declined in population, with the exception of London and Birmingham,[101] whose unrestricted sprawl created some of the main social and transport problems of the age.

There was some emigration in the first post-war decade, mainly to Empire countries, but it was at an average rate of about 130,000 a year, or a mere 40% of the immediate pre-war rate,[102] and even then it had to be officially supported to a much larger extent than before 1914. It was not only that there were fewer potential emigrants: most receiving countries had reversed their attitude, and among the causes of the new restrictiveness were unemployment in the towns and the weakness of primary product prices. Even Britain became less liberal: the Aliens Act of 1914 and 1919 led to the Aliens Order of 1920, under which immigrants were admitted only if they could prove their ability to maintain themselves and their families.

The Dominions at first formed an exception, for they were eager to have British immigrants, even though in part at least this was due to their anxiety to avoid having to admit others. In 1919 the Government's free passage scheme for ex-service men and their families assisted 86,000 persons to emigrate within three years. When it had become clear that there would be very little unaided migration on the pre-war scale, the Imperial Conference of 1921 proposed further assistance, and the Empire Settlement Act of 1922 authorized an expenditure of up to £3 million a year, provided the receiving Governments matched it by at least equal sums. 400,000 migrants in the next nine years benefited from aid under this Act, but most of them only by small sums, and it is doubtful how far these actually contributed to their decision to emigrate. Special schemes of settlement, as for example one designed to open

[100] PEP, *Report on the Location of Industry in Great Britain* (1939), p. 197, map on p. 171 and Appx. III, pp. 294–9.

[101] David C. Marsh, *The Changing Social Structure of England and Wales, 1871–1951* (1958), chapter 4; Mark Abrams, *op. cit.*, p. 35.

[102] W. A. Carrothers, *Emigration from the British Isles* (1929), Appx. I and IV.

up new land in Western Australia, failed dismally. In 1925, a more ambitious agreement made with Australia to settle 450,000 immigrants from Britain in 10 years, was also a failure and was terminated in 1932 after £4·3 million had been spent.[103] An official report in May 1938 pronounced against any further programmes of this kind.[104]

Long before this, however, the conditions relating to migration had changed. As the Great Depression began to affect overseas countries, the doors of even the Dominions were closed almost completely. Meanwhile the wish to emigrate had evaporated even faster than the official encouragement. There was, in fact, in the 1930s for the first time since figures were recorded a *net* annual immigration at a rate of 35,000 a year in 1931–4, and 13,000 a year in 1935–8,[105] though it should be noted that the net increase was confined to England. Scotland and Wales continued to lose population.

Not only migration, but the birth rate and the death rate too, were greatly influenced by economic and social conditions. The death rate had been falling steadily for over a century, and the fall had been particularly marked since the 1890s.[106] The 'standardized' death rate for England and Wales had fallen from 13·5 per thousand in 1911–14 to 9·3 in 1937, though it was still 13·3 in Scotland in that year.[107] The expectation of life for men increased from 43·7 years in 1881 to 61·8 years in 1938, and for women from 47·2 to 65·8 for the corresponding years.[108]

More significant as a measure of social conditions was the fall in the maternity and the infantile death rate. 'Infantile mortality is the most sensitive index we possess of social welfare and of sanitary administration, especially under urban conditions.'[109] While the infantile death rate (deaths in the first year of life per 1,000 live births) fell from 110 in 1911–15 to 58 in 1937 in England and Wales (but standing at 80 in Scotland in the latter year), the differences between classes and between regions tended even to widen (see Table 4·5).[110]

Table 4·5:   Infant mortality per 1,000 legitimate live births (by social class of father)

Social Class		1911	1930–2
I	(Upper and middle)	76	33
II	(Between I and III)	106	45
III	(Skilled labour)	113	58
IV	(Between III and V)	122	67
V	(Unskilled labour)	153	77

[103] N. H. Carrier and J. R. Jeffery, *External Migration, a Study of the Available Statistics, 1815–1950* (1953).

[104] *Report of the British Overseas Settlement Board* (1938. Cmd. 5766).

[105] Julius Isaac, *Economics of Migration* (1947), Table 6, p. 64.

[106] *Report of the Royal Commission on Population*, pp. 18–20.

[107] C. L. Mowat, *Britain Between the Wars* (1956 ed.), pp. 513–14.

[108] Eva M. Hubback, *The Population of Britain* (1947), p. 23.

[109] Sir Arthur Newsholme, quoted in R. M. Titmuss, *Birth, Poverty and Wealth, a Study of Infant Mortality* (1943), p. 12. Cf. also Fred Grundy, *The New Public Health* (1957), pp. 136–45.

[110] Titmuss, *op. cit.*, p. 26.

The labourer's infant mortality rate was double the best rate in 1911, but more than double in 1930–2; where they could be isolated more exactly than in this crude general tabulation, the class differences were greater still.

The differences between regions were equally startling. Thus in 1935, the infant mortality rate was 57 for England and Wales and 77 for Scotland, but it was 32 in Coulsdon and Purley and 114 in Jarrow. There were similar differences in child mortality and maternal mortality, as shown in Table 4·6.[111]

Table 4·6:   Child mortality and maternal mortality, 1935

	Deaths at ages		Maternal mortality per 1,000 births, 1936
	1–2	2–5	
	(per 1,000 living, 1931–4)		
North I (Durham and Northumberland)	22·05	6·57	5·29
Wales I (4 Southern Counties)	15·44	5·34	4·78
Southeast England	10·94	3·80	2·57
Greater London	12·55	4·25	2·16

Comparisons between smaller areas, such as towns or urban districts, showed still greater differences, and more detailed analysis pointed to the conclusion that it was poverty and unemployment which thwarted the better sanitary conditions, better nutrition and better care that benefited the better-off.[112]

If the death rate was falling, the birth rate was falling faster still. The crude birth rate declined from 23·6 per thousand in England and Wales in 1911–15 (25·4 in Scotland) to 15·1 (17·7) in 1938. The annual number of births fell from about 1 million before 1914 to a minimum of 580,000 in 1932 and hovered around 700,000 for most of the 1930s, in spite of a larger total population. The excess of births over deaths fell to about $2\frac{1}{2}$ per thousand, or a mere 110,000 a year,[113] but on the basis of the 'net reproduction rate' of the number of girls born and likely to survive to child-bearing age to replace the existing female population of the same age group,[114] England and Wales failed to reach a rate of 1 (i.e. a long-run stationary population) from 1922 onward; in 1933 the rate fell to 0·75.

The causes for the fall in the birth rate were complex.[115] In part they lay in improved technical means and wider knowledge of methods of birth control, and in the relaxation of obedience to religious prohibition of their use; in part they were to be found in the improved status of women; in part they were the

[111] Richard M. Titmuss, *Poverty and Population* (1938), pp. 80, 102–3, 144.

[112] E.g. A. Hutt, *The Condition of the Working Class in Britain* (1933), pp. 41–2, 164; Charles Webster, 'Healthy or Hungry Thirties?', *History Workshop*, 13, 1982.

[113] A. M. Carr-Saunders, D. Caradog Jones and C. A. Moser, *A Survey of Social Conditions in England and Wales* (Oxford, 1958), chapter 2.

[114] Hubback, pp. 18–25.

[115] The best brief discussion will be found in *Royal Commission on Population. Report* (1949), chapters 4 and 5. Cf. also Hubback, *op. cit.*, Part II; Sean Glyn and John Oxborrow, *Interwar Britain: a Social and Economic History* (1976), pp. 193–204.

effects of the 'social example' of the upper classes which throughout this period had, on average, smaller families than the lower, and were thus ahead of them in the downward march. To a large extent, however, the causes were economic: on the one hand, the Education Acts ensured that children had ceased to be a source of income to their families until they were near marriageable age; on the other, rising incomes made the alternatives that were available if the family size was kept down relatively more attractive.

The economic effects of these population changes worked mainly through the declining size of families, and the changed age structure of the population. The average number of live births per married woman born in 1841–5 was 5·71, and in 1861–5 it was 4·66; women married in 1900–9 had only an average of 3·37 live births, and those married in 1925–9 only 2·19.[116] As the span of life lengthened at the same time, the proportion of the lifetime spent with the children living at home was falling also, and the average family household size was falling even faster than the birth figures would indicate. Thus between 1911 and 1939, the number of families consisting of 1 or 2 persons almost doubled, from 1·9 million to 3·7 million, while the number of large families, of 5 persons or more, actually fell from 3·7 to 3·1 million.[117] Throughout this period, the size of family still increased however, as one descended the social scale.

Thus for any given size of population there was an increasing number of families, demanding their separate households and contributing to the housing shortage and the building boom. For every adult wage-earner there was a smaller number of dependants – a potent cause of the improvement in living standards. With smaller families, married women found it easier to go out to work and could do so for a larger proportion of their married lives. The working housewife and the relative decline in the number of domestic servants for households of equivalent standing were, in turn, contributing factors to the great increase in the production of tinned foods, household gadgets, ready-made clothes, and other mass-produced consumption goods, as well as of services like laundries and restaurants.

There was a growing proportion of older people in the population, but there were even fewer children, so that the population of working age could increase from 63·9% to 67·7% of the total population, or in absolute numbers, from 26·1 to 32·3 million. This contributed materially to the rising standard of income per head.[118] Meanwhile, among the consequences of the changing age structure were the growing burden of old-age pensions and, because of rising standards and expectation of life, the growth of private and company pension schemes, as well as the increasing rigidity which this ageing process of a whole society imposed on the economy.

These changes in population were inextricably interwoven with changes in the social structure of Britain. The decline in the birth rate, in particular, was closely connected with the relative growth in numbers of the professional and lower middle classes who tended to have smaller families than the manual working classes. The outstanding social change in this period was, in fact, the

[116] *Royal Commission on Population*, Tables 15, 16 and 17.
[117] Mark Abrams, *op. cit.*, p. 41; Marsh, chapter 3.
[118] p. 187 below.

growth of the 'white-collar' workers. This change, in turn, was a compound of two closely connected factors, the growth of the 'salariat' in industry and elsewhere, and the growth of the kind of occupations, like retail distribution, local government and entertainments, which employed a very high proportion of salaried persons.

The growth of the salaried personnel in industry is difficult to measure. One estimate puts the increase of salaried personnel in private industry between the Census years 1911 and 1931 at 1,170,000 (from 1·04 million to 2·21 million), and in public administration (including teaching) at 200,000 (from 489,000 to 687,000), or a total increase of nearly 1·4 million persons, of whom 650,000 were women.[119]

There are more reliable estimates available for the growth in the service industries and in tertiary industries generally. Table 4·7 reproduces some of the best estimates.

Table 4·7: Industrial distribution of the working population, 1920–39

	Changes in numbers employed (000)			(Chapman & Knight)††		
	1921–31 (Marsh)*	1931–9 (Frankel)**	Total change 1921–39†	Average employment		Change 1920–2 to 1937–8
				1920–2	1937–8	
Primary industries	−466	−419	−885	2,135	1,586	−549
Secondary industries	−491	+1,050	+559	8,099	9,448	+1,349
Tertiary industries	+873	+1,210	+2,083	5,301	7,336	+2,035
All employment	−74	+1,841	+1,767	15,535	18,370	+2,835

* Marsh, *op. cit.*, p. 105; excludes defence and 'Miscellaneous'.
** H. Frankel, 'The Industrial Distribution of the Population of Great Britain in July 1939', *J. R. Stat. S.*, 108/3–4, 1945, pp. 420–1.
† A combination of the previous two columns; as they are not drawn up strictly on the same basis, this total should be taken as approximate only.
†† Agatha L. Chapman and Rose Knight, *Wages and Salaries in the United Kingdom, 1920–1938* (Cambridge, 1953), p. 18. Excludes armed forces. Cf. also Colin Clark, *National Income and Outlay* (1937), p. 38, Table 13, and *The Conditions of Economic Progress* (2nd ed., 1951), pp. 316–25; G. D. H. and M. I. Cole, *The Condition of Britain* (1937), pp. 45–9; C. W. McMahon and G. D. N. Worswick, 'The Growth of Services in the Economy I', *District Bank Review*, No. 136, Dec. 1960.

This tendency of the growth of the service industries, and of the growth of the 'salariat' within each industry,[120] was common to all advanced countries. It contributed a certain factor of stability to incomes, since their rate of unemployment was much lower than that of manual workers and their salaries also kept up better in the depressions (though they rose slower in the recovery, also),[121] and without it the depression would have been even worse.

[119] J. G. Marley and H. Campion, 'Changes in Salaries in Great Britain, 1924–1939', in A. L. Bowley, *Studies in the National Income, 1924–1938* (Cambridge, 1942), p. 86; also P. S. Florence, *The Logic of British and American Industry* (1953), Table IVA, p. 139; L. Rostas, 'Industrial Production, Productivity and Distribution in Britain, Germany and the United States', *Econ. J.*, 53/20, 1943, p. 51.

[120] E. H. Phelps-Brown, *Growth of British Industrial Relations*, (1959) p. 61; also David Lockwood, *The Blackcoated Worker* (1958), p. 36; D. Caradog Jones, 'Some Notes on the Census of Occupations for England and Wales', *J. R. Stat. S.*, 1915, 78/1; Elie Halevy, *A History of the English People* (1926), vol. 6/1, pp. 262–5.

[121] Marley and Campion, *loc. cit.*, pp. 92–4.

Moreover the growing salaried and professional groups also added to the social stability of the country, for with a birth rate below the average, they invariably largely recruited from below, offering opportunities for advancement to many ambitious and capable working-class children who would have otherwise joined the most rebellious ranks of Labour.[122]

5 The Rise in the Standard of Living

It is time to draw together the many strands of information available and weave out of them a picture of general economic progress. The statistics of national income have been widely used as the most general measuring rod of economic welfare since the pioneer work by Bowley, Stamp and Colin Clark. A. R. Prest's and C. H. Feinstein's more recent figures are summarized in Table 4·8.[123]

Table 4·8:   National income statistics, 1912–38

Average of years	Net national income of the UK at factor cost, £m.	Index of national income at constant (1900) prices, 1900 = 100		Net national product at 1938 factor cost	
				1921–4 = 100	
		National income	Income per head	Total	Per head
1912–14	2,301	118·4	106·6	(117·0)*	113·9*
1919–20	5,562	124·7	113·8	(109·4)*	104·3*
1921–4	4,020	110·6	102·4	100	100
1925–6	3,947	117·9	107·5	108·9	107·3
1927–9	4,159	130·1	117·5	116·6	113·9
1930–2	3,730	129·7	115·8	114·5	110·5
1933–5	4,006	143·1	126·1	126·5	120·5
1936–8	4,558	155·1	134·9	135·3	127·3

* Including Southern Ireland.

In spite of some apparent increases in the post-war boom, real national income (as well as income per head) had barely reached the pre-war level by 1924. Total output probably exceeded the best of the years before 1914, but it was neutralized by the loss of income from abroad owing to the sale of assets during the war. From 1925 onward a remarkable and sustained rise set in, barely held back by the depression. From the beginning of the recovery onward the rate of increase was speeded up, the late 1930s showing as much increase as the whole of the period between 1913 and the mid-1930s. This was

[122] Lockwood, *passim*, esp. chapter 4; F. D. Klingender, *Clerical Labour in Britain* (1935).

[123] A. R. Prest, 'National Income of the United Kingdom 1870–1946', *Econ. J.*, 58/229, 1948; A. L. Bowley, *Studies in the National Income, 1924–1938* (Cambridge, 1942), esp. Table IX, p. 81; Colin Clark, *The Conditions of Economic Progress* (1951 ed.), esp. p. 63; A. L. Bowley and J. C. Stamp, *The National Income, 1924* (1927); Colin Clark, *National Income and Outlay* (1937), Table 37, p. 88, also pp. 267–9; J. B. Jefferys and D. Walters, 'National Income and Expenditure of the UK, 1870–1952', *Income and Wealth*, Series V, p. 19, Table VIII; C. H. Feinstein, *National Income, Expenditure and Output of the United Kingdom, 1855–1965* (Cambridge, 1972), T. 15–16, 121; H. W. Richardson, *Economic Recovery in Britain, 1932–9* (1967), pp. 36 ff.

true both of total national income, and of income per head, in real terms.

Within these totals of all incomes, real wages also rose substantially, though their rise was more evenly spread between the 1920s and the 1930s. The main changes are summarized in Table 4·9 (1930 = 100):[124]

Table 4·9: Rise in real income of wage-earners, 1920–38

	Cost-of-living index	Index of intra-industry real earnings of wage-earners	Net real wages per full-time week (Kuczynski)	Real wage rates
1920	157·6	90·9	97·1	94·7
1924	110·8	91·3	88·3	91·9
1929	103·8	97·2	93·2	96·7
1932	91·1	105·9	102·9	106·1
1937	97·5	105·9	101·0	105·2
1938	98·7	108·7	103·9	107·0

It should be noted that these figures of real earnings depend heavily on the cost-of-living index, which was itself the subject of much debate. After stagnation in the early 1920s,[125] real wages rose by about 10% to 1930 and continued to rise in the depression years, remaining almost stationary for the rest of the 1930s.

This picture would be strongly modified by the incidence of unemployment. It is, in particular, to a large extent the improved employment position which caused the national income to rise in the late 1930s while real wages per head of employed worker remained constant. Further, if the earnings of the men in work were spread over the whole of the working class, including those out of work, the date at which the high wages of 1913 were being earned again would be postponed from 1927 to 1930, and would put the post-war peak of 1937 at a bare 5%, instead of 13%, above the 1913 real wage rate.[126] Some observers, however, expressed the more optimistic view that 'the British (working-class) consumer, in fact, has for several years been getting the best of both worlds. From 1929 to 1932 the fall in prices outweighed to his advantage the fall in employment. And from 1933 to 1937 the rise in employment outweighed to his advantage the rise in prices.'[127] Most estimates put the increase in real weekly wages between the pre-war years and 1937–8 at

[124] A. L. Chapman and Rose Knight, *Wages and Salaries in the United Kingdom, 1920–1938* (Cambridge, 1953), Tables 11, 14, pp. 30–3; J. Kuczynski, *A Short History of Labour Conditions in Great Britain, 1750 to the Present Day* (1946 ed.), p. 120; last column based on E. C. Ramsbottom. 'The Course of Wage Rates in the United Kingdom, 1921–1934', *J. R. Stat. S.*, 98/4, 1935, 'Wage Rates in the United Kingdom, 1934–1937', *ibid.*, 101/1, 1938, and 'Wage Rates in the United Kingdom in 1938', *ibid.*, 102/2, 1939.

[125] E. V. Morgan, *Studies in British Financial Policy, 1914–25* (1952), pp. 284–6.

[126] J. Kuczynski, *A Short History of Labour Conditions in Great Britain, 1750 to the Present Day* (1946 ed.), p. 120; cf. also G. D. H. Cole and R. Postgate, *The Common People, 1746–1938* (1938), chapter 49.

[127] *Economist*, 1.1.1938, p. 14; also in G. D. A. MacDougall, 'General Survey, 1929–1937', in *Britain in Recovery* (1938), pp. 26–7.

between 20% and 33%, while the working day was shorter by about one hour.[128]

The rise in living standards, and especially in real incomes of the working classes, was the outcome of several factors, some of which have been discussed already. Among them was the increase in output per man-hour,[129] the improvement in the terms of trade,[130] and an increase in the proportion of the national product consumed.[131] Other relevant factors were a change in the age structure,[132] an increase in the proportion of salaried, i.e. higher-paid, employees, and a slight tendency towards greater equality in incomes. The main factor working in the opposite direction, and cancelling a large part of these advantages, was the heavy increase in unemployment.[133]

Before the war, a large part, perhaps one-half, of the long-term increase in real wages had been due simply to a shift of wage-earners into better jobs, but in the inter-war years this effect was negligible.[134] Instead, there was a marked shift into salaried occupations, and in spite of their low remuneration in some cases,[135] this shift normally meant both an increase in weekly pay, and a reduction in the incidence of unemployment.

Lastly, real wages rose because of a redistribution of income in favour of wage-earners. The constancy of the wage bill as a proportion of total national income around the 40% mark has often been noted; but in view of the fact that wage-earners formed a steadily falling proportion of the total occupied population, from 78·0% in 1900 to 74·1% in 1913, 73·0% in 1924 and 71·4% in 1938, according to Phelps-Brown and Hart,[136] their constant share of the total national income clearly represents a relative rise in their income.

The parallel long-run egalitarian tendency in the distribution of property, however, was so slight as to be hardly perceptible. Heavy progressive death duties and direct taxation did little more than counteract the tendency of the economic system to work in favour of those owning capital. According to estate duty returns, in 1911–13, 96·9% of persons owning property owned under £1,000 each, and in 1936–8 the figure was still 93·0%. At the other end of the scale, 0·4% of property owners owned 55·6% of the total capital in 1911–13, and in 1936–8, 0·95% of owners owned 55·68% of the capital,[137]

[128] E. H. Phelps-Brown, *The Growth of British Industrial Relations* (1959), p. 345; W. A. Lewis, *Economic Survey, 1919–1939* (1949), p. 139; J. A. Dowie, '1919–20 is in Need of Attention', *Ec. Hist. Rev.*, 28/3, 1975.

[129] p. 52 above.

[130] p. 117 above.

[131] p. 147 above.

[132] *Report of the Royal Commission on Population* (1949. Cmd. 7695), p. 112.

[133] Section 1 of this chapter. Cf. also A. E. Kahn, *Great Britain in the World Economy* (New York, 1946), p. 265.

[134] A. L. Bowley, *Wages and Incomes in the UK since 1860* (Cambridge, 1937), Appx. C; Chapman and Knight, *op. cit.*, pp. 33–4.

[135] A. Hutt, *The Condition of the Working Class in Britain* (1933), chapter 8.

[136] E. H. Phelps-Brown and P. E. Hart, 'The Share of Wages in the National Income', *Econ. J.*, 62/246, 1952, pp. 276–7; Clark, *National Income*, pp. 94, 100–1, 125; Bowley, *Studies in the National Income*, pp. 56–8; Chapman and Knight, pp. 18–23; Feinstein, *National Income*, T. 45.

[137] H. Campion, *Public and Private Property in Great Britain* (1939); Kathleen M. Langley, 'The Distribution of Capital in Private Hands, 1936–1938 and 1946–1947', *Bull. Oxf. Inst. Stat.*, 12/12, 1950. Table on p. 355 and 13/2, 1951, pp. 45–7; G. W. Daniels and H. Campion, *The*

and even then much of the apparent redistribution was clearly caused by precautions taken against the incidence of death duties.

In sum, there was in this period an appreciable rise in the standards of comfort and welfare of working-class families, particularly those in which the wage-earners were in regular employment. This conclusion is supported by the remarkable increase in small savings, including working-class savings.[138] It is also supported by the significant change in the pattern of working-class expenditure, as shown in the budgets used by the Ministry of Labour, after large-scale sample inquiries, for its cost-of-living index.[139]

These budgets show that in 1937–8, as compared with before 1914, the 'average' working-class family had fewer people between whom the larger income was divided, and that there were consequent reductions in the shares of income expended in food, clothing and rent, leaving quite large increases in expenditure for non-necessities and semi-luxuries. These were often the very items which could be cheapened by mass-production. Moreover, statistics fail to take full account of the difference made by electricity instead of candles, and gas cookers instead of coal or coke ranges, as standard equipment in working-class homes; of improved housing, including indoor water and sanitation; or of radio, the cinema and newspapers within almost everybody's reach. A most significant pointer was the adoption, in 1938, of one week's paid holiday as standard practice, after the report of Lord Amulree's Committee on Holidays with Pay,[140] in all the industries in which conditions were governed by Trade Boards or Agricultural Wage Boards. Up to 1937, only $1\frac{1}{2}$ – $1\frac{3}{4}$ million wage-earners received paid holidays by collective agreement, though the total receiving paid holidays was nearer 4 millions out of the $18\frac{1}{2}$ millions earning £250 a year or less; in 1939 it was 11 millions, or the large majority, though few of these had the resources or experience as yet to spend their holidays away from home.[141]

Within the basic food bill itself, there was a decline in the consumption of the cheap filler and substitute foods, while the consumption of foodstuffs of which the demand was highly elastic with respect to incomes, or which were considered semi-luxuries, increased rapidly. The consumption of wheat, for example, fell from 4·28 lb. per head per week in 1910–14 to 4·05 lb. in 1924 and 3·77 lb. in 1938. Other foods are shown in Table 4·10.[142]

The improvement in the general standard of nutrition is shown in the increase in the consumption of calories per head from 3,057 a day in 1901–13

Distribution of the National Capital (Manchester, 1936); G. D. H. and M. I. Cole, *The Condition of Britain* (1937), p. 75; C. L. Mowat, *Britain Between the Wars* (1956 ed.), p. 494.

[138] p. 149 above, also G. D. H. Cole, *Money, Trade and Investment* (1954), pp. 220–1; Esme Preston, 'Personal Savings Through Institutional Channels (1937–1949)', *Bull. Oxf. Inst. Stat.*, 12/9, 1950, Table 7, p. 252; Henry Durant and J. Goldmann, 'The Distribution of Working-Class Savings', *ibid.*, 7/1, 1945.

[139] *Min. Labour Gazette*, Dec. 1940.

[140] Cmd. 5724 (1938).

[141] C. L. Mowat, *Britain Between the Wars* (1956 ed.), pp. 500–1; Phelps-Brown, *op. cit.*, pp. 347–8; Elizabeth Brunner, *Holiday Making and Holiday Trades* (1945), pp. 9, 13–15; J. A. R. Pimlott, *The Englishman's Holiday* (1947), pp. 214–15.

[142] Stone, *Consumers' Expenditure*, Tables 10, 21, 35, 45, 53, 109, 116; H. V. Edwards, 'Flour Milling', in *Further Studies in Industrial Organisation* (1948), ed. M. P. Forgarty, p. 77.

Table 4·10:   Changes in food consumption, 1920–38

	Annual consumption	
	1920–2	1937–8
Potatoes (tons per head)	0·083	0·074
Fresh milk (mn. gall.)	848	1,000
Cream (mn. gall.)	3·22	9·19
Eggs (mn.)	3,915	9,385
Soft drinks (mn. gall.)	1·72	5·79
Sugar, chocolate, confectionery (mn. tons)	1·06	1·53

Table 4·11:   Nutrients available per head per day in the UK

	Average 1920–2	Average 1937–8
Protein (g.)	87·2	90·55
Fat (g.)	127·1	152·9
Carbohydrates (g.)	413·0	414·95
Calcium (mg.)	754	815
Vitamin A (i.u.)	3,616	4,749
" B_1 (mg.)	1·31	1·375
" C (mg.)	118·0	135·5
Riboflavin (mg.)	1·71	1·90

to 3,139 in 1924–8 and 3,398 in 1937–8. Other indices compared as shown in Table 4·11.[143]

Yet, in the face of all this indubitable progress, there were still enormous areas of poverty left, much preventible misery and illness and many premature deaths. In part, it was the greatly enlarged and more detailed knowledge of the poor and their problems which brought these tasks more urgently before the public eye. Apart from the official statistics, the best-known social surveys in this period were those for London, Merseyside, Southampton, York, Tyneside, Becontree and Dagenham, Brynmawr, Bristol and Sheffield.[144] The inquiries in York and London could be directly compared with the pre-war surveys, and this was also the case in the less ambitious survey made by A. L. Bowley in five Midland towns.[145]

'Primary poverty', poverty so great that the lack of the necessary food and shelter actually impaired health and efficiency, occurred in York, in 1899, among 15·46% of the working classes, and in 1936 among 6·8%. In practice,

[143] Stone, *op. cit.*, Table 61; John Boyd Orr, *Food, Health and Income* (2nd ed., 1937), pp. 24–5.

[144] H. A. Mess, *Industrial Tyneside: a Social Survey* (1928); Sir H. Llewellyn Smith (Director), *The New Survey of London Life and Labour* (9 vols., 1930–5); P. Ford, *Work and Wealth in a Modern Port: an Economic Survey of Southampton* (1934); B. Seebohm Rowntree, *Poverty and Progress* (1941); D. Caradog Jones, *Social Survey of Merseyside* (3 vols., Liverpool, 1934); Terence Young, *Becontree and Dagenham* (1934); Hilda Jennings, *Brynmawr: A Study of a Distressed Area* (1934); Herbert Tout, *Standard of Living in Bristol* (Bristol, 1938); A. D. K. Owen, *Housing Problem in Sheffield* (Sheffield, 1931), *Unemployment in Sheffield* (Sheffield, 1932), *Juvenile Employment and Welfare in Sheffield* and *Standard of Living in Sheffield* (Sheffield, 1933); and, in general, A. F. Wells, *The Local Social Survey in Great Britain* (1935).

[145] A. L. Bowley and A. R. Burnett-Hurst, *Livelihood and Poverty* (1915), and A. L. Bowley and M. H. Hoggs, *Has Poverty Diminished?* (1925).

human psychological needs would demand more than this bare physical minimum,[146] and a realistic standard would require a rather higher income level to meet some non-necessities as well as the minimum physical needs – the 'poverty line'. In York in 1936, 31·1% of working-class families (or 17·7% of the total population) fell below this line, and in Bristol in 1937 (a boom year), 10·7% of working-class families fell below it. In the other surveys, the 'poverty standard' differed. The London Survey used a lower figure, according to which 9·8% of the London working-class families lived in poverty in 1928, another good year. On the same standard, the proportion on Merseyside (1929) was 17·3%, in Liverpool (1929) 16·1% and in Southampton (1931) 20·0%. On the Rowntree standard, the Merseyside proportion would have been about 30%. On a different, even more rigorous physical needs standard, the Pilgrim Trust found 30% of the long-term unemployed to be in poverty, and another 14% just above it.[147]

A different study in this field was made by John (Lord) Boyd Orr in 1936,[148] who showed that as much as half the population was bound to have diets deficient in some respects even in the most prosperous years of the 1930s: the food consumption of the lower-income groups would have to rise by 12–25% before it became sufficient for maintaining perfect health.[149]

The size of families still mattered. 'The incidence of poverty', stated the Report to the Pilgrim Trust,[150] 'is progressively greater according to the number of children under working age in the family concerned:' this meant that a far larger proportion of children than of adults lived in poverty. In York, Rowntree found that while only 31·1% of the working-class population lived below the poverty line, 52·5% of the children under one and 49·7% of the children from one to five did so. Similarly, in Birmingham, in a sample survey in 1939, it was found that 14% of the families, but 30% of the children, had insufficient food.[151] It was out of considerations of this kind that a strong movement, led by Eleanor Rathbone, demanded family allowances for all, including those in work, in order to reduce the economic burdens of children in working-class households.

The causes of poverty were essentially the same as before 1914: the interruption of the earning power of the main breadwinner owing to illness, to casual type of work, or, above all, to unemployment; an inadequate wage; and a large family of dependants. Several of these causes could be present at the same time. There had been progress, but there was still much poverty. It was not the least of the consequences of the Second World War that the hopes and dreams of the small minority with the most sensitive social conscience in the 1930s became acceptable as social legislation to the large majority after 1945.

---

[146] G. D. H. and M. I. Cole, *Condition of Britain*, pp. 134–8.

[147] Pilgrim Trust, *Men Without Work* (Cambridge, 1938), p. 109.

[148] J. Boyd Orr, *Food, Health and Income* (1936, 2nd ed. 1937); also Sir George Newman, *The Building of a Nation's Health* (1939), pp. 352–9.

[149] *Op. cit.*, p. 11.

[150] Mark Abrams, *The Condition of the British People, 1911–1945* (1945), pp. 99 ff.

[151] See esp. E. F. Rathbone, *The Disinherited Family* (1924, new ed. 1949), and Mary Stocks, *Eleanor Rathbone* (1949), chapter 8.

5

The British Economy in Total War, 1939–1945

1 The War Economy and Economic Planning

The outbreak of the Second World War in September 1939 found the British Government prepared to a much greater extent for the policies of economic control than it had been in 1914. The experience of 1914–18 had not been entirely forgotten. From the early 1930s on, several Government departments had been engaged in preparing elaborate war plans, and some of the necessary legislation was passed within a few days of the declaration of war. Some of the very officials chosen to implement economic war policy in 1939–40 were the same persons who had administered the controls of 1917–18. As a result, the war economy shifted into gear more quickly in the Second World War than the First, and many of the earlier errors were avoided.

Unlike 1914 it was also understood in 1939 that the apparatus of control would have to reach back far beyond the munitions industry.[1] The second main lesson digested was the need to enlist the voluntary support of labour, particularly in the munitions and other essential industries, and the Ministry of Labour in particular, mindful of the costly strikes of 1914–18, fell over backwards to retain the goodwill of workers and their leaders. Other lessons of value carried over from the first war to the second included the methods of civilian food rationing, and the Schedule of Reserved Occupations evolved in the 1930s, on the basis of the Schedule of Protected Occupations of the earlier war, to prevent the call-up of key workers.[2]

Nevertheless, it seems in retrospect that many lessons that ought to have been learnt had been forgotten, or were applied too late after great and unnecessary cost. The control of civilian trade and consumption, the control over the foreign exchanges and capital movements, the control over labour demand and supply, rationing of food and the expansion of munition-making and machine tool capacity all appeared as belated measures forced on the Government by the march of events rather than as orderly stages of the creation of a war economy. Even some specific errors of the First World War were repeated, including a rash over-recruitment from the mines, resulting in

---

[1] E.g. I. Bowen and G. D. N. Worswick, 'The Controls and War Finance' (1940), in Oxford Institute of Statistics, *Studies in War Economics* (Oxford, 1947).

[2] W. K. Hancock and M. M. Gowing, *British War Economy* (1949), pp. 48 ff. The present section is based largely on that work, which forms the central volume in the Official History of the Second World War, United Kingdom Civil Series (HSWW), as well as on the other volumes in that series. An excellent summary of Hancock and Gowing will be found in the form of chapter 5 of A. J. Youngson, *The British Economy, 1920–1957* (1960).

a fuel shortage later, an agricultural expansion programme neglecting the importance of saving the bulkiest imports, and an over-optimistic assessment of shipping needs and resources which seriously endangered military operations and civilian supplies at several critical points during the war.

There was a certain basic similarity between the two World Wars, as far as British economic strategy was concerned. Both wars were fought against a well-prepared Germany at the head of a continental coalition, while Britain and her Allies, entering the war far less prepared, depended on their command of the world's resources outside Europe to build up gradually a power superior to Germany's with which to crush her after weakening her by means of an economic blockade. But here the similarity ends, for not only were there technical changes, such as the vulnerability of Britain to serious air attacks, but whereas in the First World War the position of the chief belligerents in the west was never seriously threatened, the Second World War, besides the much greater part played in it by non-European battlefields, witnessed several startling reverses of fortune, including the fall of France and the successive entry of Soviet Russia, the USA and Japan into the war. Each of these imposed major changes of economic policy, so that the economic history of this period is best treated in the light of the needs of these successive phases of the war, rather than as a gradually emergent controlled economy, as in 1914–18.

Four main phases of the war may be distinguished. The first period, the 'phoney war', was essentially a period of waiting and preparation by the Allies, apparently secure behind the Channel and the Maginot line. It was shattered by the German invasion and occupation of Norway, Denmark, Holland, Belgium and part of France, and the period ended with the evacuation of the British Expeditionary Force from Dunkirk. The second period ran from the summer of 1940 to the Japanese attack on Pearl Harbor in December 1941. It began with the air 'Battle of Britain' which thwarted a German invasion of these shores, and continued as a war of attrition by air attacks and attacks on British merchant shipping. Germany also consolidated her power in the Mediterranean and seriously threatened the British positions in the Middle East. This was the period when Britain virtually stood alone and prospects seemed bleakest. Even the German attack in the east in the summer of 1941, which was ultimately to prove so disastrous to the Axis powers, gave no immediate relief to Britain who, on the contrary, made some of her scarce resources available to her new Russian ally.

With the entry of the USA into the war in December 1941 ultimate victory for the Allies seemed again a reasonable hope, but meanwhile the third phase of the war, which lasted until the invasion of Normandy in June 1944, had opened disastrously with the sinkings at Pearl Harbor, withdrawals in the Middle East, the loss of much of South-Eastern Asia to the Japanese and severe shipping losses in the Atlantic. Further, in the first year the entry of America increased rather than relieved the pressure on the British economy, for American Lend-Lease shipments were reduced in favour of American mobilization, and much valuable British tonnage was diverted to the use of the American services. It took some time for the vast productive potential of the USA to be converted into actual munitions, but when these began to come off the production lines, North Africa was invaded and cleared of the enemy, and Allied landings in Italy were paralleled by the Russian counter-offensives in the east and victorious American actions in the Pacific.

The fourth phase was ushered in by the invasion of Normandy by British and American forces after the Allies had established complete superiority at sea and in the air. Despite the successful establishment of a bridgehead in the west, and the advance of the Red Army in the east, the war against Germany, contrary to expectations, dragged on until May 1945, causing great strain on the Allied transport system. By contrast, the fighting against Japan, estimated to take 12–18 months after 'VE-day', was over in a few weeks, thanks largely to the grim destruction wrought by the atom bombs on Hiroshima and Nagasaki.

In the late 1930s actual preparations for the war, as distinct from paper planning, had been negligible with the single and possibly decisive exception of aircraft building capacity under the programmes of 1936 and after.[3] Even the eleventh-hour suggestion by Sir Arthur Salter of stockpiling certain strategic raw materials, and the bulk-purchasing agreements for Australian and New Zealand wool, were made too late to bring tangible results before the declaration of war on 3 September 1939.[4]

This declaration, it is true, was accompanied by a formidable array of legislation, prepared beforehand. The Emergency Powers (Defence) Act, 1939, had been passed on 24 August and gave the most far-reaching powers to the Government; in addition, some 60 other statutes were passed in the early weeks of the war. By 1 September several new Ministries had been created, including the Ministries of Supply, of Economic Warfare, of Home Security, of Information, of Food and of Shipping, united in May 1941 with Transport to become the Ministry of War Transport. Recruitment was added to the duties of the Ministry of Labour, which thus became the Ministry of Labour and National Service and as such played one of the central parts in the combined economic and military strategy of the war. There were also innumerable co-ordinating, planning and emergency committees and boards established at an early date.

The crucial role of translating the needs of the Services into orders for industry, and converting industry to a war footing to supply them, was intended for the Ministry of Supply. In the event, since the Admiralty hung on to its control over shipbuilding[5] and the RAF over aircraft, the Ministry of Supply was restricted to supplying the Army, and a limited range of arms and stores to the other two Services. In 1940 the Ministry of Aircraft Production was set up, occupying the centre of the stage in the critical summer months of 1940, and continuing as the third supply department thereafter.[6]

There was thus a great deal of administrative activity, but there was as yet little to show for it. Government expenditure ran at £20 million a week at the outbreak of war and was still only £33½ million weekly in the sixth month, and

---

[3] P. W. S. Andrews and E. Brunner, *Life of Lord Nuffield* (Oxford, 1955), Part IV, chapter 6; PEP, *Engineering Reports II: Motor Vehicles* (1950), pp. 39–40.

[4] J. Hurstfield, *The Control of Raw Materials* (HSWW, 1953), p. 79, Appx. I, pp. 427–30, also his 'Control of Raw Material Supplies, 1919–1939', *Ec. Hist. Rev.*, 14/1–2, 1944, pp. 25–6.

[5] J. D. Scott and Richard Hughes, *The Administration of War Production* (HSWW, 1955), pp. 140–7, 213–16.

[6] Scott and Hughes, Part IV.

much of that increase was due to price rises. The production of munitions was nowhere near the limits of physical capacity. Control over foreign exchange was still lax. While British holdings of foreign securities had to be registered, foreign holders of sterling balances could still engage in exchange dealings, and there was still freedom of payments within the Sterling Area until May 1940.[7]

The numbers in the Services had risen from 480,000 in June 1939 to 1,850,000 at the end of March 1940, but there were still 1 million unemployed in April 1940, and little consideration was as yet given to a planned allocation of manpower. Similarly, there was no serious rationing of shipping space, so that in the first eight months of war there was actually a fall in some of the most vital stocks, including fats, sugar, timber, oil and iron ore. At the same time the production of many inessentials continued unhindered.[8]

Since so many resources were still not fully employed, there appeared to be as yet no need of general economic planning, and departments pursued their own policies, even competing for the same scarce resources without co-ordination with their neighbours. Only the pace of mobilization was co-ordinated: soldiers were conscripted only at the leisurely rate at which they could be equipped.[9] 'Reflecting upon this first period of the war, the historian finds himself oppressed by a feeling of lost opportunity.'[10]

One main preoccupation of the Government at this stage was the rise in the cost of living, which actually proceeded faster in the early months of the Second World War than it had done in the first, and conjured up dangers of similar labour troubles. In the official index, certain foods were heavily over-weighted, so that it was possible by food subsidies on some of these items to make a considerable impact on keeping down the cost-of-living *index*.[11] From this beginning was gradually built up a consistent policy of large-scale subsidy for items within the working-class cost-of-living index, and of heavy taxation of goods outside it. In the early months, however, subsidies, combined with the limitation of profit margins, operating from 1 January 1940, merely served to create an irrational price structure.

By April – May 1940 the growing impact of mobilization was beginning to affect the economy at several points at once. The engineering industry, as the basis of the munitions industry, began to feel a shortage of skilled workers as well as of machine tools, a large proportion of which had to be imported; there was a drain on the foreign exchange reserves and a consequent need to divert resources to exports; there was need to build up stocks, in the face of a growing shipping shortage. These and other pressures were on the point of enforcing their own logic of a more thorough-going system of economic control, when the German offensive, ending in the collapse of France,

---

[7] T. Balogh, 'The Drift Towards a Rational Foreign Exchange Policy', *Economica*, NS, 7/27, 1940, and 'Foreign Exchange and Export Trade Policy', *Econ. J.*, 50/197, 1940; R. F. Harrod, *The Life of John Maynard Keynes* (1951), pp. 494 ff.

[8] E. L. Hargreaves and M. M. Gowing, *Civil Industry and Trade* (HSWW, 1952), pp. 16–18.

[9] M. M. Postan, *British War Production* (HSWW, 1952), p. 102.

[10] Hancock and Gowing, p. 149.

[11] H. M. D. Parker, *Manpower, a Study of War-Time Policy and Administration* (HSWW, 1957), p. 82; R. S. Sayers, *Financial Policy, 1939–1945* (HSWW, 1956), pp. 63–4.

completely shattered the long-term timetable to which the British war economy had been geared.

The debacle in the west led to the replacement of Chamberlain's Conservative Ministry by a Coalition Government led by Winston Churchill, which could pursue and enforce policies of a harshness which its predecessor would not have dared to contemplate. The British people as a whole had been shocked into a willingness to work and to bear privations inconceivable before May 1940. The isolation of Britain in Europe brought the realities of the war home to the American people to a sufficient extent to permit President Roosevelt to authorize aid culminating in Lend-Lease in March 1941.[12] At the same time, Britain benefited by the end of the need to supply France with scarce coal, and the addition to shipping tonnage under British control as Norwegian, Dutch and other masters sought refuge in ports in Allied hands.

All these, however, were minor advantages compared with the strategic and economic problems posed by the devastating military reverse. Britain lay open to German bombing by air, especially of communications and war industries, and the production drive was thus severely hampered by delays, precautions, dispersals, as well as by direct damage. The dangers to shipping were immeasurably increased, and the east coast ports had to be closed to the larger vessels, blocking up still further the bottlenecks at the west coast ports. The supply of several important raw materials, including high-grade iron ore, was cut off at once. The hope of strangling Germany by blockade was converted into an immediate danger of a blockade of this country, carried out by U-boats, mines and aircraft.[13] Meanwhile, contrary to Britain's tradition of providing ships and material to aid an allied Continental army, she had for the first time to build up a large army herself, while strengthening the equipment of the other two Services also. The sudden increases of demand on home industry, resources and manpower drove Britain to a hasty improvisation of innumerable economic controls. They were only slowly built up into an integrated system in the following years.

In the midst of the air Battle of Britain, the building of aircraft became number one priority, by the orders of the new Minister of Aircraft Production, Lord Beaverbrook, and in view of the threatening invasion, the projects that could be completed quickly had overriding priority claims to all resources. The air battle was won by such means, but only at the expense of disrupting long-term mobilization plans. From the autumn of 1940 onward, however, great strides were made in techniques of planning as well as in methods of financial control. By 1941, the economy as a whole began to be planned, rationed and allocated, and integrated with the flow of money payments by the new statistical analysis contained in the first white paper on national income and expenditure.[14]

Economists and statisticians in favour of the national income approach were employed in increasing numbers in key departmental posts. Keynes him-

---

[12] R. D. Hall, *North American Supply* (HSWW, 1955), p. 127.

[13] W. N. Medlicott, *The Economic Blockade*, vol. 1 (HSWW, 1952), chapter 12.

[14] Hancock and Gowing, p. 152. See pp. 212–4 below.

self had become economic adviser to the Treasury in 1940.[15] One of the earliest lessons they taught was the interchangeable nature of scarce resources. Thus, for example, food could be brought in from North America, a short trip using little tonnage, but costly in hard currency, or it could be brought in from Australia, using only sterling currency, but much more costly in tonnage. Scarce shipping and scarce foreign exchange were thus substitutes for one another up to a point, and since both could be saved by employing more labour in home agriculture to raise British home output, scarce labour could be used as a substitute for either.

A second principle was also established as a result of the experience of the aircraft programme of the summer of 1940. 'Priorities' as a method of control had proved utterly unsuitable, except for the occasional crash programme, for often the higher-priority product was produced only at great cost in terms of another product, only slightly less essential, and a system of relative priorities ultimately left the decision to the individual manufacturer and his ability to secure his own supplies of components, raw materials and labour. Instead, a system of allocation was evolved, which ensured to each department, and each manufacturer, a designated quantum of supplies, the total allocation being equivalent to the total quantity available.[16]

Such a system could work only if there was a basis of knowledge of the resources available, and if there was some supreme authority, capable of deciding between different claims on scarce resources, including those of strategic needs against civilian goods to maintain morale and efficiency at home.[17] It was in this period that many new statistical services and methods were evolved, and that the Production Executive, a Committee of the War Cabinet under the Lord President of the Council, emerged as the main arbiter on planning.[18] From it radiated the lines of command and communication which ultimately made up the economic planning machine. In February 1942, the Ministry of Production was created as a further co-ordinating agency.

There was, in all this, little direct control of industry, though powers existed for it. Apart from the State-owned Royal Ordnance factories, which at their peak employed 300,000 workers,[19] the dockyards and the 170 'agency' factories, the Government did not own any enterprises itself. It had immediate direction of some basic industries and services, such as the railways or the ports, and it gave some detailed directives elsewhere, as in the 'concentration' schemes for less essential industries, organized by the Board of Trade in 1941.[20] But by and large private managements were left in control

[15] U. K. Hicks, *Public Finance* (1947), p. 41; Harrod, *Life of Keynes*, pp. 501–3; D. N. Chester, 'The Central Machinery for Economic Policy', in *Lessons of the British War Economy* (Cambridge, 1951).

[16] Hurstfield, *op. cit.*, pp. 89 ff; Postan, pp. 159–61.

[17] Hargreaves and Gowing, chapter 13.

[18] Postan, pp. 142 ff., 248 ff., Scott and Hughes, Part 5; also Gilbert Walker, *Economic Planning by Programme and Control in Great Britain* (1957), chapter 3; E. A. G. Robinson, 'The Overall Allocation of Resources', E. Devons, 'The Problem of Co-ordination in Aircraft Production', R. Pares, 'The Work of a Departmental Priority Office', in *Lessons of the British War Economy*.

[19] William Hornby, *Factories and Plant* (HSWW, 1958), p. 89; P. Inman, *Labour in the Munitions Industries* (HSWW, 1957), p. 180.

[20] Board of Trade, *Concentration of Production* (1941. Cmd. 6258); Hargreaves and

of their firms, being made to conform to central plans indirectly, by allocations of raw materials[21] and labour, by licensing of capital equipment and maintenance, by controlled prices and by taxes.

Similarly, in spite of the unrestricted powers of conscription of workers, and in spite of the fact that the manpower budget and allocation became the central planning tool, labour, while directed in some isolated cases (the selective coalmining scheme of August 1943, yielding 22,000 as 'Bevin boys' to the mines, being perhaps the most spectacular), was not normally individually conscripted. Under the Essential Works Order and the Registration for Employment Order, SR & O (1941), Nos. 302 and 368, workers could be sent to, or kept in, essential industries or occupations, according to their age, sex and skill, but their actual employers and their right to move was left to their own choice as far as possible.

Finally, there were no full and self-consistent economic plans made for each period *ab initio*, as was attempted in the USA: instead, the system was to 'allocate upon the user basis for preceding periods, modified where necessary by changes in the requirements or supply situations'.[22] Some sectors, retail distribution being perhaps the most important, could not be controlled at all for the purpose of yielding up resources (other than labour) for the war effort, in spite of several determined attempts to do so.[23]

Nevertheless, the mechanism evolved was capable of mobilizing the British economy to an extent unmatched by any other belligerent.[24] As far as manpower was concerned, for example, Britain mobilized between mid-1939 and the peak period of September 1943, no fewer than $8\frac{1}{2}$ million insured persons (18% of the total population) for the Forces, the auxiliary Forces, and the munitions industries, beside some 400,000 workers past insurable age, 160,000 from Ireland (North and South), many thousands of other immigrants and refugees, and ultimately 224,000 prisoners of war. $4\frac{3}{4}$ million were drawn from civilian industries, $1\frac{1}{4}$ million from among the unemployed, and $2\frac{1}{2}$ million from formerly non-industrial classes, mainly housewives and domestic workers.[25] These shifts, in turn, caused other complex shifts and replacements, from jobs of lesser war importance to jobs of greater importance. There were also the special schemes of allocating scarce craftsmen, the geographical transfer of factories from scarce labour areas to areas of surplus

Gowing, chapter 10; G. D. N. Worswick, 'Concentration in the Leicester Hosiery Industry', *Bull. Oxf. Inst. Stat.*, 3/6, 1941, and 'Concentration, Success or Failure?' *ibid.*, 3/16, 1941; G. C. Allen, 'The Concentration of Production Policy', in D. N. Chester (ed.), *Lessons of the British War Economy*.

[21] W. Ashworth, *Contracts and Finance* (HSWW, 1953), pp. 41 ff.

[22] Hurstfield, *op. cit.*, p. 95.

[23] Henry Smith, *Retail Distribution* (2nd ed., 1948), p. 145, chapter 6; J. B. Jefferys, *Retail Trading in Britain, 1850–1950* (Cambridge, 1954), chapter 3; H. Levy, *Retail Trade Associations* (1942), chapter 19; Board of Trade, *Reports of the Retail Trade Committee* (1941–42).

[24] C. T. Saunders, 'Manpower Distribution 1939–1945: Some International Comparisons', *Manchester School*, 14/2, 1946, p. 19; A. J. Brown, *Applied Economics* (1947), p. 23.

[25] Ministry of Labour and National Service, *Report for the Years 1939–1946* (1947. Cmd. 7225), pp. 4, 54–7; Sir Godfrey Ince, 'The Mobilisation of Manpower in Great Britain for the Second World War', *Manchester School,* 14/1, 1946; M. Kalecki, 'Labour in the War Industries of Britain and the USA' (1943), in Oxford Inst. of Statistics, *Studies in War Economics*; Alan Bullock, *The Life and Times of Ernest Bevin II: Minister of Labour 1940–1945* (1967).

labour, the dilution of skills and re-designing of jobs, and many other adjustments.[26]

Similarly, with a shipping tonnage scarcely above the pre-war level,[27] and far less effective because of the convoy system and congestion at the ports, Britain succeeded in supplying the booming munitions and other industries with raw materials, in transporting and supplying troops to distant theatres of war, in sending convoys to Russia, in transporting American troops and their supplies to this country, and in launching the sea-borne invasions of North Africa, Italy, Southern France and, finally, Normandy, while feeding the home population better in many respects than it had been fed before the war.[28]

Again, rationing required a major planning effort in itself, and extended to food and clothing, as well as furniture and furnishing,[29] the total calculated not to exceed available supplies. It was supported by agricultural planning on the one hand, and by the unique British 'utility' scheme for clothing and furniture on the other, the latter begun under SR & O (1941), No. 1281, and quickly spreading, to permit control of standards, of prices and of supplies of materials to the producers.[30]

The entry of America into the war in its third phase did not permit any relaxation of the tight control over the British economy. Ultimately, from the middle of 1943 onward, it proved possible to co-ordinate and specialize to some extent the production and use of resources of the two countries. Thus the USA increasingly produced merchant ships for both, while Britain's productive potential could be used to most effect in building, e.g., warships or airfields and hutments for American troops stationed in Britain and in freeing men for the Armed Forces.[31] By 1943–4, the USA supplied about one-quarter of the munitions need of the Empire, the United Kingdom still supplying well over 60%.[32]

This co-ordination was not without its own difficulties for Britain. The method of Lend-Lease put Britain in a position where she could not order, merely request, and her requests were subjected to disconcerting amendment as a result of simultaneous demands by the American Services. As far as shipping was concerned, while in 1942 the losses were sustained by the British mercantile marine, the additions were made to the American, and the summer months of 1942 saw the most serious shipping crisis of the war. American

---

[26] P. Inman, *Labour in the Munitions Industries; Statistics Relating to the War Effort of the United Kingdom* (1944. Cmd. 6564), section 1.

[27] E.g. Central Statistical Office, *Statistical Digest of the War* (HSWW, 1951), Table 70.

[28] C. B. A. Behrens, *Merchant Shipping and the Demands of War* (HSWW, 1955), chapters 12–17.

[29] L. Robbins, *The Economic Problem in Peace and War* (1947), pp. 7–8; W. B. Reddaway, 'Rationing', in *Lessons of the British War Economy*, p. 191.

[30] H. E. Wadsworth, 'Utility Cloth and Clothing Scheme', *Rev. Econ. Studies,* 16(2)/40, 1949–50; E. L. Hargreaves, 'Price Control of (Non-food) Consumer Goods', *Oxf. Econ. P.,* No. 8, 1947; M. Kalecki, 'Rationing and Price Control', *Bull. Oxf. Inst. Stat.,* 6/2, 1944 (also in *Studies in War Economics*); P. Ady, 'Utility Goods', *ibid.,* 4/15, 1942; H. A. Silverman, 'The Boot and Shoe Industry', in *Studies in Industrial Organisation* (1946), p. 230.

[31] H. D. Hall and C. C. Wrigley, *Studies of Òverseas Supply* (HSWW, 1956), chapters 4–6.

[32] R. G. D. Allen, 'Mutual Aid Between the US and the British Empire, 1941–5', *J. R. Stat. S.,* 109/3, 1946, p. 268.

agencies, therefore, found it difficult to appreciate on what narrow margins British economic planning had to operate.

From the autumn of 1943 onward, in the last phase of the war, the Allied output of aircraft, ships, tanks, vehicles and guns had become so vastly greater than that of the Axis powers, that production had ceased to be a problem, and the main problem was to come to grips with the enemy to make the superiority effective. In Britain there could still be no relaxation, however. Manpower began to be transferred from industry to the Forces, and production and strategic allocations were afoot to deal with Japan, as well as with the reconstruction and export needs of the first years of peace, particularly their expected critical foreign exchange position. The manpower budget for the first year after Victory in Europe, for example, calculated that there would be an estimated shortfall of 800,000 workers.

2 Industry in the War Years

Britain being within easy reach of German aircraft and missiles, there was much direct damage to industry caused by bombing, and indirect damage caused by the necessary air raid precautions and salvaging operations. But beyond these, and in the long run more decisive, was the enforced consumption of capital. Total war demanded all the resources that could be spared, and among those spared most easily in the short run were those normally used for the replacement and upkeep of capital.

According to official estimates, annual net non-war capital formation in the United Kingdom fell from £214 million in 1938 to about £ − 1,000 million (capital consumption) in 1940–5, or from 5% of net national income to − 12%.[33] These figures hide the enormous increase in the stock of capital in certain key industries, especially the sums invested by the Government which peaked in 1941–2. Overall, only investment in buildings and vehicles fell substantially: shipbuilding was much higher than in the 1930s, and so was investment in plant and machinery at least until 1942. By 1947, the stock of plant and machinery was equal to, or higher than before the war (see Table 5·1).[34]

Table 5·1:   Plant and machinery in 1947, (£million in constant 1948 prices)

	Gross		Net	
	End 1938	End 1947	End 1938	End 1947
All plant and machinery	6964	7404	3759	3737
Manufacturing and distribution only	4141	4346	2127	2234

The shortfall lay elsewhere and was to be found, beside the housing sector, in the neglect of railway maintenance, the over-felling of timber or the selec-

[33] *National Income and Expenditure of the UK, 1938–1945* (1946. Cmd. 6784), Table 4.

[34] C. H. Feinstein, *National Income, Expenditure and Output in the United Kingdom, 1855–1965* (Cambridge, 1972), T. 89; T. Barna, 'Investment in Industry – Has Britain Lagged?', *The Banker*, April 1957, pp. 219–23; Philip Redfern, 'Net Investment in Fixed Assets in the United Kingdom, 1938–1953', *J. R. Stat. S.*, Series A, 118, 1955, pp. 159, 160.

tive working of the easiest coal seams. Finally, the lack of opportunity of industrial training among the men and women drafted into the Forces must be reckoned an additional capital loss.

War gave a violent twist to the allocation of resources, affecting different industries very differently. Those which catered mainly for civilian demands were cut down drastically despite the decision, after some years of war, to consider a certain minimum output of such goods as furniture, saucepans and crockery, as a necessity for the maintenance of civilian morale. Other civilian supply industries, with scarcely even that justification, like furs or carpets,[35] lost an even larger percentage of their labour force and had their capital run down.

Further, shortages of materials or skilled labour led necessarily to simpler styles and plainer finishes. Official 'utility' schemes introduced methods of mass-production and quality control for clothing and furniture, but elsewhere standards often lapsed haphazardly, without any corresponding benefits. Craftsmen and others came to forget the practices of high-class work, and consumers and producers came to accept the second best and the general attitude of the sellers' market.

Other problems, as they affected the post-war position of many non-munitions industries, are aptly summed up in the following references to building. It should be noted, that they were coloured by the need to explain the poor performance of the building industry, in terms of output per man-hour, even several years after the end of the war.[36]

> During the war, the industry lost a large part of its experienced labour force, and for six years the normal process of recruitment and training was interrupted. Many young craftsmen and apprentices were conscripted for national service before they had gained experience in industry. Other men who left the industry during the war had lost much of their skill by the time they returned while those who remained in the industry throughout the war were employed on work which usually differed markedly from that of peace time. . . . Similar causes affected the efficiency of management. . . . Directing and supervising staff had then to adapt themselves to a situation in which emphasis was no longer laid on speed of construction rather than on costs . . . the Essential Work (Building and Civil Engineering) Order which was in force between 1941 and 1947 left its mark on the industry in the form of relaxed discipline.

The poor performance of industries such as building was, however, counter-balanced by the advances made in others, and manufacturing in particular appeared to have suffered no irreparable permanent damage in efficiency. Between the Census of Production years 1935 and 1948, output *per employee hour* changed as shown in Table 5·2.[37]

[35] Board of Trade, *Working Party Reports; Carpets* (1947), p. 4.

[36] Working Party Report, *Building* (1950), pp. 12–13; also Ministry of Labour and National Service, *Report for the Years 1939–1946* (1947. Cmd. 7225), pp. 87–91; I. Bowen, 'The Control of Building', in D. N. Chester, *Lessons of the British War Economy* (Cambridge, 1951).

[37] Colin Clark, *The Conditions of Economic Progress* (2nd ed., 1951), p. 270.

Table 5·2:   Output per employee hour, 1935–48 (1907 = 100)

	1935	1948
Iron and steel	154	175
Engineering, shipbuilding, vehicles	196	224
Non-ferrous metals	131	190
Chemicals	174	206
Clay and building materials	180	247
Paper, printing and publishing	208	221
Food, drink and tobacco	108	142
Textiles	155	198
Clothing	146	136
Leather	136	141
Miscellaneous	228	278
All manufacturing	171	203

In fact, against the direct damage, the lack of investment, and the loss of skill must be set certain distinctly favourable effects of the war. Among the most important were the scientific and technological advances induced by military and industrial demands, and the direct stimulus to a few industries of great strategic importance, in particular engineering in the widest sense, including vehicles and aircraft, iron and steel and other metals, chemicals and agriculture.

The scientific discoveries of the war years, and those applied on a large scale for the first time during the war, are legion. Among the best known are magnetron valves, centimetric radar and other devices built on them, jet engines and other revolutionary aircraft developments, nuclear fission, electronic computing and control systems, antibiotics, DDT and other insecticides, and, on the other side, ballistic missiles,[38] several of these being developments of a whole series of interdependent discoveries. Many were called forth by military demands, but others were developed to fill new industrial needs or to replace scarce raw materials, such as artificial rubber and nylon and other plastics.

The war also fostered a new attitude to science, and the practice of a massive deployment of scientists and technologists of many specialisms on a broad front, to solve given problems. To the scientists were given not only traditional, 'laboratory' tasks such as the development of a new apparatus or chemical, but also the solution of such logistic problems as the right order and balance of the loading of ships for D-day, an exercise in computation which has since, in principle, been followed in the internal organization of some large firms.

The scientists in Government service in particular developed from isolated and subordinate specialists into members of co-ordinated teams, who in the end had to be allowed to question even the policy and strategy behind the tasks they were set. 'When one compares the freedom and authority enjoyed by the civilian scientists and technicians', noted two historians of the war,[39]

[38] E.g. W. H. G. Armytage, *A Social History of Engineering* (1961), pp. 310 ff.
[39] J. D. Scott and Richard Hughes, *The Administration of War Production* (1955), p. 288, also pp. 327–8.

'both at headquarters and in the establishments, in the period 1943–5 with the isolation and subjection of pre-war days, the change is among the most striking features of the organization of British war production.' Even at the very top, Winston Churchill leaned heavily on Lord Cherwell and a brilliant and unorthodox team of scientists.[40] This enhanced the role of the scientist, and his employment in large teams and with elaborate equipment, has since been adopted by many of the major firms.

Aircraft, electrical and general engineering, chemicals as well as agriculture received the main benefits of expansion and modernization during the war. For example, in one of the most backward British sectors, the machine tool industry, tooling-up for rearmament led to an expansion of production by British makers from 20,000 machine tools in 1935 to 35,000 in 1939 and 100,000 in 1942, and employment in the industry rose from 21,000 in 1935 to a maximum of 68,600 in March 1943; at the same time, imports of American machine tools were expanded from 8,000 in 1939 to a maximum of 33,000 in 1940, many of them being responsible for introducing new methods here. The output of small tools, fine measuring tools and measuring instruments and industrial electrical equipment increased likewise.[41]

Much of the expanded munitions industry had a direct peace-time value, especially the works producing motor vehicles and aircraft. Of the 3·3 million people employed in armaments, excluding chemicals, explosives and iron and steel, at the peak of 1943, 2·2 million were in industries with a civilian base.[42]

The output of aircraft increased from 2,800 in 1938 to nearly 8,000 in 1939, 20,000 in 1941 and over 26,000 in 1943 and 1944. Because of their growing complexity and the growing proportion of heavier aircraft, the structural weight increased even faster, from 9·8 million lb. to 28·9, 87·2 and about 200 million lb. in the same years. The aircraft repaired and engines delivered and repaired rose in the same proportion, and required an industrial effort almost as large as the new building. The capacity of the motor trade was also expanded, though shipbuilding, limited by shortages of labour, of steel and even of berths, after the deliberate destruction of the 1930s, did not expand as much; the output of mercantile tonnage rose to an average of well over 1·1 million g.t. annually in 1941–4, while the launchings of naval and landing craft increased from 94,000 dw. tons in 1939 to 260,000 dw.t. in 1940 and 600,000 dw.t. in 1943.[43] Each of these trades, in turn, depended on large numbers of outside suppliers for materials and components. In the radio, electrical and electronics industry, for example, the output of radio valves rose from under 12 million a year in 1940 to over 35 million in 1944.

[40] M. M. Postan, *British War Production* (1952), p. 144; J. D. Scott, 'Scientific Collaboration between the United Kingdom and North America', in H. D. Hall and C. C. Wrigley, *Studies of Overseas Supply* (HSWW, 1956), chapter 8; G. D. A. MacDougall, 'The Prime Minister's Statistical Section,' in Chester (ed.), *Lessons of the War Economy*; but see C. P. Snow, *Science and Government* (1961).

[41] Postan, pp. 206–7; Wm. Hornby, *Factories and Plant* (1958), chapters 10–13.

[42] Hornby, pp. 28–30.

[43] Central Statistical Office, *Statistical Digest of the War* (1951), Tables 111, 130–1; H. F. Heath and A. L. Hetherington, *Industrial Research and Development in the United Kingdom* (1946), pp. 200 ff.; Asa Briggs, *The History of Broadcasting in the United Kingdom*, 4 vols., vol. 3 (1970) p. 67.

The enlargement of the vital engineering and chemical industries during the war is illustrated in Table 5·3.[44]

Table 5·3:   Growth in chemical and engineering industries, 1939–46

	Insured persons (000)		
	June 1939	November 1946	% Increase
Non-ferrous metal manufacture	55·9	87·8	57·1
Shipbuilding and repair	144·7	219·8	51·9
Constructional engineering	49·0	66·5	35·7
Electric cable, apparatus	195·9	265·5	35·5
Explosives, chemicals	174·3	235·5	35·1
Scientific instruments	48·3	65·0	34·6
Marine engineering	52·2	70·2	34·5
General engineering	704·7	944·3	34·0

The change was not merely one of size. The necessities of war taught new methods of mass-production, of industrial control and management, of design and quality control, and spread this knowledge among a host of sub-contractors. War-time training schemes increased the numbers of key workers, such as draughtsmen and tool-room operators. The capital equipment was greatly enlarged, the Government alone, according to one calculation, investing in 1936–45 over £1,000 million in fixed capital, spread over both Government-owned and agency factories, and capital subsidies to contractors.[45] At the end of the war, machine tools alone worth £100 million were sold from Government factories to private industry, the normal pre-war intake being about £5 million a year.[46] To this have to be added private contractors' investments, which were particularly high in some public utilities, such as electricity generation.

The iron and steel industry was another important sector to be enlarged and modernized. To fill the gap caused by the loss of the high-grade ores after the summer of 1940, the capacity to utilize home ores and steel scrap had to be enlarged. The bulk steel capacity raised to 13 m.t. a year by the schemes of the 1930s proved sufficient for the needs of war, but the sudden increase in the demand for alloy steel could not be met from existing furnaces, and new ones were built to raise output from 500,000 tons (200,000 tons of which from electric furnaces) before the war to $1\frac{3}{4}$ m.t. (half of it in electric furnaces) by 1942. At the same time, the ingot capacity for aluminium, a vital structural material for aircraft, was raised to 31,000 tons in 1939 and increased further to 54,000 tons by 1943; the demand, by that time, had risen to 300,000 tons, of which 100,000 tons were provided from scrap by new plant set up during the war, and the remainder from imports.[47] The capacity for other raw

[44] Postan, p. 385; also C. E. V. Leser, 'Changes in Level and Diversity of Employment in Regions of Great Britain, 1939–47', *Econ. J.*, 59/235, 1949, Table 4.

[45] Postan, p. 448. Hornby, *op. cit.*, chapter 14, puts the Government expenditure in the same years at £425·6 million for aircraft production, and £460·4 million for War Office and Supply. See also p. 200 above.

[46] W. K. Hancock and M. M. Gowing, *British War Economy* (1949), pp. 551–2.

[47] J. Hurstfield, *The Control of Raw Materials* (1953), pp. 335–48; J. Roepke, *Movements of*

materials and semi-manufactures had similarly to be enlarged, *pari passu* with the expansion of the engineering industry.

The other industry to emerge very much strengthened by the war was agriculture. In the late 1930s about 70% of the country's consumption of calories was supplied from abroad, but the proportion was 84% in the case of sugar, oils and fats, 88% of wheat and flour and 91% of butter.[48] As in 1914–18, shipping space for such bulky commodities as grain, and foreign exchange to pay for it, were among the most critical shortages, and agricultural policy was accordingly designed to reduce the dependence on imported food, despite a declining labour force and in the face of shortages of equipment, imported fertilizer and imported feeding stuffs. It succeeded to the extent of saving about half the food imports, while keeping the home population well fed. Measured net of imported feeding stuffs, which were drastically reduced to save shipping space, home output increased from 14·7 billion calories in 1938–9 to 20·0 billion in 1941–2 and 28·1 billion in 1943–4, or by 36% and 91% respectively. Total home food production, by value, rose from 42% to 52% of consumption between 1938 and 1946.[49]

The basic feature of the Government's agricultural policy was the ploughing-up campaign, which raised the area under arable cultivation from just under 12 million to just under 18 million acres.[50] Allowing for land under temporary grass, the actual increase of the land in tillage was over 5 million acres by the end of the war. This increase was obtained at the cost of a corresponding decline in the acreage under permanent grass (the rough grazing remaining constant) and thereby involved a marked shift from animal husbandry to arable: between 1939 and 1945, the number of sheep and lambs, for example, in Great Britain fell from 26 million to $19\frac{1}{2}$ million, pigs from 3·8 million to 1·9 million, and poultry from 64 million head to 45 million. Only cattle were encouraged, and their numbers grew from about 8 million to 8·7 million head, in order to increase the home supply of milk. Imports could thus be converted from bulky cattle feeding stuffs to the more concentrated food values contained in meat, eggs, etc., while British soil was converted to maintain the largest number of people per acre. Up to 1941, the prices of imports were a major consideration. Lend-lease arrangements removed this limitation, and imports were determined thereafter largely on the basis of their use of scarce shipping space.

The increase in the arable acreage was accompanied by remarkable increases in yields per acre. Thus the yield of wheat rose from 17·7 cwt in 1936–8 to 19·7 cwt in 1942–5, of barley from 16·4 to 18·5 cwt and of oats from 15·7 to 16·7 cwt, despite the likelihood that much of the newly ploughed land was marginal. Additional labour could scarcely be credited with this increase, for (allowing for the changing composition of the labour force) the index of

the *British Iron and Steel Industry, 1720–1951* (Urbana, Ill., 1956), chapter 7; P. Inman, *Labour in the Munitions Industries* (1957), p. 158; Duncan Burn, *The Steel Industry 1939–1959* (Cambridge, 1961), chapters 1 and 2.

[48] R. J. Hammond, *Food.*, vol. 1 (HSWW, 1951), Table V, p. 394.

[49] E. F. Nash, 'War-Time Control of Food and Agricultural Prices', in D. N. Chester (ed.), *Lessons of the War Economy*.

[50] *Statistical Digest of the War*, Table 55, p. 57; H. T. Williams, *Principles for British Agricultural Policy* (1960), chapter 5.

agricultural employment in terms of man years stood at 99 in 1939–40 (1937 = 100) and crept up only to 108 in 1943–4 and 109 in 1944–5, working an acreage increased by 50%.[51] The increase in home food production, made up of enlarged yields on a greatly increased acreage, was, in fact, achieved by large-scale mechanization and increased use of fertilizers.

Between 1938–9 and 1945–6 the quantity of fertilizers used on United Kingdom farms (in terms of 1,000 tons) increased as follows: nitrogen, from 60 to 165; phosphate, from 170 to 359; potash, from 75 to 101; and lime, from 1,300 to 2,000. Similarly, between 1939 and 1946 total mechanical horse power on British farms rose from just under 2 million to just under 5 million. The change in these seven years had been greater than in the preceding 14 years of peace.[52] Tractors increased from 56,000 to 203,000 in this period, and the increase of their equipment was as shown in Table 5·4.[53]

Table 5·4:   Increase in farming equipment, 1942–46 (in 000)

	May 1942	April 1944	June 1946
Disc harrows	33·8	58·9	65·2
Cultivators (grubbers)	161·7	191·4	247·8
Binders	131·6	144·0	149·5
Combine harvesters	1·0	2·5	3·8
Milking machines	29·5	37·8	48·3

This transformation was brought about almost entirely by deliberate Government planning and direction, to which was added a whole battery of financial inducements. The Government encouraged capital investment by subsidies for ditching, draining and water supplies, and by grants of between 25% and 75% for approved land reclamation schemes. For current costs, the 50% lime subsidy was continued with subsidies for hill sheep and cattle, and for wheat and potatoes.

All these were additional to the main pre-war incentive, the guaranteed price; agricultural prices under the scheme rose much faster than costs (see Table 5·5).

Table 5·5:   Agricultural prices 1939–45 (1936–8 = 100)

	Official cost of living	Retail food prices	Agricultural prices
1939	104	103	103
1941	130	123	172
1943	130	121	186
1945	133	125	196

The widening gap between farm prices and the prices paid by consumers involved the State in ever-increasing food subsidies, quite apart from the

[51] K. A. H. Murray, *Agriculture* (HSWW, 1955), pp. 85, 273.

[52] D. K. Britton and I. F. Keith, 'A Note on the Statistics of Farm Power Supplies in Great Britain', *The Farm Economist*, 6/6, 1950; Hancock and Gowing, p. 550.

[53] Murray, p. 276; *Statistical Digest of the War*, Table 64; cf. also PEP, *Agricultural Machinery* (1949), p. 95.

direct subsidies and grants rising to £37 million a year in 1943-5, and their results were mainly to raise *net* farm receipts much faster than any other type of incomes,[54] while increased security of tenancy was granted in 1941.[55] Thus fostered, encouraged, cajoled and directed by the Government, agriculture emerged from the war in a healthier and more prosperous state than it had enjoyed for 70 years.

Not all primary production at home was equally fortunate. Elsewhere, the pressure to obtain the largest possible immediate return could lead to a long-run weakening of the industry by the running down of its capital. This may be illustrated by the timber and coal industries.

The shortage of timber was felt only after the Continent became closed to British shipping; then timber became one of the scarcest of materials. The country went to inordinate lengths to reduce its consumption and to find substitutes, often of other scarce materials, such as steel, but at least part of the gap had to be filled by increased home fellings. They rose from an average of 150,000 tons in 1935-8 to a maximum of 1,251,000 tons in 1943 in the case of hardwood, from 180,000 tons to 861,000 tons (1942) in the case of soft-wood, and from 120,000 tons to 1,765,000 tons (1943) in the case of pitwood.[56] The cost of these fellings to the long-term forestry supply of the country was prodigious:

> By the end of 1945 some 60 per cent of Great Britain's softwoods had been taken, and some 40 per cent of the hardwoods. The residue of mature softwoods is miserably small, and though the quantity of mature hardwood is considerably larger, the best had gone. Moreover, the heavy cuttings in the 30-60 year classes has further jeopardized the future prospect. The distribution of age classes . . . is completely out of joint.[57]

The problems of coal mining during the war were more complex. After 15 years of overproduction and unemployment, it was difficult to believe that the coal supply would fall short of needs. It was estimated at first that output some 10% above the peace-time level would be required, but the fall of France and the closure of virtually all other export markets in the summer of 1940 reduced prospective consumption to about 10% *below* prospective output. There was unemployment in the export districts, and the recruitment of miners into the Forces was encouraged. The coal shortage in the winter of 1940-1 was due to transport difficulties, not shortage of supply.[58]

Output, however, was falling. The quantity of total saleable coal had been 231 million tons in 1939, and 224 m.t. in 1940. It fell to 206 m.t. in 1941, and to 204 m.t., 194 m.t., 184 m.t. and 175 m.t. in the following years. Up to 1941, the fall was simply due to the fall in the number of wage-earners on the colliery books, from 766,000 in 1939 to 698,000 in 1941. From then onwards,

---

[54] Murray, *op. cit.*, chapter 11; E. F. Nash, 'War-Time Control of Food and Agricultural Prices', in *Lessons of the British War Economy*.

[55] S. G. Sturmey, 'Owner-Farming in England and Wales, 1900-1950', *Manchester School*, 23/3, 1955, p. 264.

[56] Postan, *op. cit.*, pp. 156, 216; P. Ford, 'The Allocation of Timber', in *Lessons of British War Economy*.

[57] Russell Meiggs, *Home Timber Production* (1949), p. 43.

[58] Hancock and Gowing, chapter XVI (ii).

the numbers remained constant while output per manshift fell, largely because of the ageing of the work force, the deterioration of the fixed equipment, the long-term working out of the best seams, faulty planning and administration and, not least, because of smouldering discontent over wages, the Essential Works Order and the much-publicized campaigns to end absenteeism in the pits. When, in 1942, booming heavy industries and others began to push up the demand for coal there developed a major fuel crisis.

The mines were still haunted by the bad industrial relations of the past. The Government, having contributed to the defeat of the miners in 1926, considered itself duty bound not to permit nationalization by the back door, and its war-time coal control was therefore completely decentralized, the owners' District Executive Boards still determining output and pit-head prices under the cartel scheme. As the coal crisis developed in 1942, this chaotic structure could not stand the strain. A new policy for the mines became urgent, and in June 1942 a new department, the Ministry of Fuel and Power, was created to administer it.[59]

One of its first acts was to take over the Coal Charges Account with its compensating levies scheme from the owners, designed to even out the effects of rising costs and varying prices between districts. Coal control became centralized by Group Production Directors, responsible to Area Controllers, though there was still no question of nationalization, and the new minister set about raising the output of coal.

The most urgent problems related to labour. Though miners' wage and earnings had risen faster than most since the start of the war, they were still, in absolute terms, below the earnings of workers in the munitions industries and in other heavy, unpleasant trades. Voluntary recruitment, either of miners or of others, was therefore a failure, and even the conscripted 'Bevin boys' were recruited only in numbers to make good the wastage, and not to increase the work force. On the advice of a Board of investigation under Lord Greene (the 'Greene Committee'),[60] a substantial wage advance of 2s. 6d. per shift and a national minimum wage were applied at once in 1942. The industry also adopted the National Conciliation Scheme drafted by the Greene Committee, but unrest in the mines was not abated, and in 1943–4 the bad industrial relations in the industry were the nearest approach to the rebellious spirit in the later years of the 1914–18 war.

The capital position of the industry gave equal grounds for concern. As the coal crisis developed, some of the country's scarce engineering capacity was turned over to mining engineering, and with the aid of Government finance, the provision of equipment was greatly increased. The proportion of coal cut by machinery rose from 61% in 1939 to 72% in 1945, and of coal conveyed mechanically from 58% to 71%,[61] but output, both absolute and per manshift, continued to fall year by year. If it had not been for opencast coal, rising from 1·3 million tons in 1942 to $8\frac{1}{2}$ m.t. in 1944, it would have fallen more rapidly still. As it was, stocks were down to dangerous levels in the

---

[59] W. H. B. Court, *Coal* (HSWW, 1951), chapters 9 and 10.
[60] *Report of the Board of Investigation into the Immediate Wage Issue in the Coal-Mining Industry* (1942).
[61] Court, p. 279.

winter of 1944–5. With its equipment run down, and its manpower depleted and in an unco-operative mood, that unhappy industry, after nearly 20 years of sagging demand and excess capacity, emerged from the war with an almost limitless demand, but an utter inability to meet it.

If coal had its own special problems, the running down of capital was nowhere more marked than in inland transport. Ports and railway centres became special targets for enemy bomb attacks, while the public transport system had to carry a load in 1939–45 well above its normal peace-time weight, because of the virtual suspension of private motoring, the enforced residence of millions of people away from home, the military movements, and the disruption or lengthening of the normal supply routes of goods traffic. The increased load on the railways is evident from the figures in Table 5·6:[62]

Table 5·6: Increase in railway traffic, 1938–44

Railways		1938	1942	1944
Net ton-miles (m. tons)	coal	8,104	9,951	9,267
	other	8,162	13,871	15,177
Wagon miles (m.)	loaded	3,003	3,983	4,064
	empty	1,492	1,412	1,427
Passenger miles, main line companies, billion		19*	—	32

* September 1938–August 1939 inclusive.

Apart from the greatly increased traffic, this tabulation shows an increasingly effective control over wagon loads, as full wagon mileage was raised by one-third without any increase in the empty wagon mileage.

In the later years of the war, the Central Transport Committee, set up in 1941, reduced the burdens on the railways to some extent by allocating an increasing quantity of goods to canals and coastal shipping. The traffic on the roads, by contrast, began to be curtailed from 1941 onward, owing to severe shortages of rubber and petrol.[63] Private cars lost their petrol ration completely in March 1942, *C* licence vehicles were severely restricted by zoning and other schemes, and *A* and *B* licence vehicles were gradually diverted from long-distance traffic, which was to be the responsibility of the railways, to short-distance goods traffic especially after bombings and from the congested western ports. Vehicles could be directed to some extent from the beginning by the judicious allocation of the motor fuel ration, but gradually the Government took over complete control of road haulage. By 1943 a special Road Haulage organization was set up under the Ministry of War Transport which came to control 388 large organizations, and all long-distance vehicles, a total of 34,000 goods vehicles.[64] Road passenger vehicles were left under the control of the Regional Transport Commissioners.

As in the First World War, the railways had been placed at once under Government control, the proprietors receiving a guaranteed income, settled

[62] Hancock and Gowing, p. 481.
[63] C. I. Savage, *Inland Transport* (HSWW, 1957).
[64] Gilbert Walker, *Road and Rail* (2nd ed., 1947), p. 230.

at the end of 1940 at £43 million, Government and railways to share war damage costs equally. In view of the greatly increased traffic and the virtual suspension of maintenance, actual net receipts soon exceeded this figure and in 1943, the peak year, reached the total of £105$\frac{1}{2}$ million. But this left the railways near breakdown at the end of the hostilities, and it was to take five years or more to restore them to good working order.[65]

The war, it may be concluded, had profoundly affected British productive capacity, but it left the different branches of manufacturing industry, agriculture, transport and the public utilities, in very different positions. Some important sectors were forced to contract, losing skill, connections and capital equipment; others were forced to expand on a shrinking capital base; but the effects of war were not wholly unfavourable to all. Some industries, notably engineering, metals and chemicals as well as agriculture, expanded and profited greatly, and they were among those that were destined to play a leading part in the post-war reconstruction of Britain.

3 Fiscal and Financial Policy during the War

The mobilization of the British industrial potential for the war was not to be carried through solely by physical controls; fiscal and financial weapons were used also to ensure that resources yielded their highest possible level of productivity. Further, Britain's dependence on imports made it necessary to maintain the foreign value of the pound sterling as well as to husband the limited foreign exchange reserves. Finally, as Government taxation and borrowing were the immediate sources which fed the stream of military expenditure, it was one of the objectives of the fiscal system to distribute the necessary burden fairly between classes and between individuals.[66]

Finance, then, though it had ceased to be the arbiter of military policy, was still one of its major instruments. Provided the physical resources were there, it was a criterion of the efficiency of the financial instruments that it should not stand in the way of their use. 'In the sense that financial obstacles were never allowed to obstruct the war effort, British policy in the Second World War was undoubtedly successful.'[67]

The subordination of finance to strategy was achieved virtually from the start. For this, the experience of the First World War, in which finance had too long and disastrously claimed prime consideration, was as much responsible as the fact that the country's re-armament effort was still small and therefore not too hard to bear. In those early months of 'phoney war', fiscal and financial policy had two main closely interrelated objectives: the prevention of inflationary price rises, which might lead to labour unrest, and the meeting of the costs of the war as far as possible out of increased taxation rather than by borrowing.

The early preoccupation with the level of retail prices may have been somewhat premature. In the first weeks of the war there occurred an inevitable rise

[65] Savage, *Inland Transport*, pp. 634, 638–9.

[66] W. K. Hancock and M. M. Gowing, *British War Economy* (1949), pp. 48 ff.

[67] R. S. Sayers, *Financial Policy, 1939–45* (HSWW, 1956), p. 21. Also M. M. Postan, *British War Production* (1952), p. 82.

in the costs of certain materials in short supply, and of some wages, notably those of miners, accompanied by a corresponding rise in the price of coal. These increases pushed up the cost of living figure by some 10%, but there was clearly as yet no general inflationary pressure in the economy[68] when the Government, as noted above,[69] was stampeded into subsidizing certain foods to keep down the official index. By January 1940 the Chancellor announced the continuation of subsidies on a broad front, though still hedged round with many qualifications,[70] and within six months they had become an integral component of war policy. The budget of April 1941 laid it down that the cost-of-living index would be stabilized in the range of 25–30% above the immediate pre-war level. Later in the war, even some necessities outside the official index were held down in price, though others were deliberately allowed to rise to great heights.

The rising costs of the 'trading' losses incurred by absorbing higher import prices while keeping home prices steady, and for subsidizing home farmers, were borne by the Treasury, but since food accounted for 60% of the weight in the index, the results were considered to warrant the expense. Another item, rent, was held down equally easily by rent control, and the Government also had powers to keep down the price to the consumer of several other goods and services, such as coal and railway fares. In the case of clothing, and what little furniture and other household durables came on the market after 1941, the 'utility' scheme was combined with price control. There were also some general provisions, such as the Goods and Services (Price Control) Act of July 1941, though price control was never quite complete.[71] By contrast, the Government could afford to levy a large part of its revenue by steeply increasing duties on tobacco and alcohol, since their weight in the official index was minute, and even the purchase tax, by careful discrimination, was gradually developed so as to raise the maximum of revenue with the minimum disturbance to the cost-of-living index.

The success of the retail price policy in its objective of limiting the war-time inflation and insulating the home consumer from world price changes may be judged by the statistics given in Table 5·7.[72]

Table 5·7: Wartime price index (first half 1939 = 100)

	Wholesale prices:			Cost of living	Subsidies (£ million)
	Board of trade	Economist	Statist		
1940	140	139	144	121	72
1941	157	151	159	129	138
1942	164	160	169	130	164
1943	167	164	172	129	177
1944	171	168	177	131	215
1945	174	172	182	132	250

[68] Hancock and Gowing, pp. 153–7.

[69] p.195 above.

[70] *HoC Debates*, vol. 356, cols. 1154–9, 31 January, 1940.

[71] E. L. Hargreaves and M. M. Gowing, *Civil Industry and Trade* (1952), p. 122; Hancock and Gowing, pp. 501–4.

[72] G. D. H. Cole, *Money, Trade and Investment* (1954), p. 95; subsidy figures from white

Subsidies for retail commodity prices could only deal with the symptoms of the inflationary problem. Its essence was the fact that the Government was attempting to absorb a much larger share of the national resources than individuals and firms were willing to forgo; and this underlying cause of inflation could ultimately be combated only by a conscious withdrawal of purchasing power from the public by a high level of taxation.

To begin with, however, revenue by taxation was increased for the traditional reason of paying for the war while keeping borrowing to a minimum. The autumn war budget in September 1939 actually over-estimated the total expenditure for the financial year 1939–40 by £116 million. Defence expenditure amounted to only £1,000 million, compared with £382 million in 1938–9. The budget proposals in April 1940 were equally timid, and of the limited sums required, about one-half was raised by taxation, and half by borrowing.

By this time budgetary policy had come under sharp criticism. The critics were led, once again, by J. M. Keynes. In correspondence to *The Times* in November 1939, published as a pamphlet early in 1940,[73] he condemned the traditional assessment of revenue according to the principle of what the taxpayer would bear, which turned out to be about half the required expenditure. By starting at the other end, and calculating the national income and its main components first, it would be possible at once to determine the capacity of war-making available, and the level of taxation necessary to transfer that part of the national income to the Government without creating an inflation. At existing levels of incomes and taxation, for example, he calculated that there was an inflationary 'gap', which could most usefully be viewed as the difference between the proposed Government expenditure and the total of taxes plus savings plus any income or dissaving available from abroad. He therefore proposed increased taxes, sweetened by promises to repay part of them after the war as 'deferred pay' (the later 'post-war credits').

At first, he faced opposition both from Conservative opinion within the Treasury, which distrusted his figures, and from Labour opinion outside, which objected to the heavy taxation of the working classes. But he was swimming with the tide. In April 1940 the *Economist* pointed out that even after its great increase, the British war budget was still well below that of Germany, though it had several years' start to make up.[74] The Chancellor of the Exchequer was becoming impatient with the inability of his Treasury officials to suggest means of stopping the inflation, and in March a war loan of a mere £300 million had been a failure. Above all, it was the shock of the defeats of the summer of 1940 and the change of Government which precipitated the change-over to Keynesian policies, with some support even from within the Treasury.

The new, more vigorous, tax policies allowed war expenditure in the current year to be raised from a prospective £2,000 to £2,800 million. The

paper on *National Income and Expenditure of the United Kingdom 1938 to 1946* (1947. Cmd. 7099), Table 19: these *exclude* housing subsidies.

[73] J. M. Keynes, *How to Pay for the War* (1940); cf. also R. F. Harrod, *The Life of John Maynard Keynes* (1951), pp. 489 ff.

[74] 'A Budget of Delusions', *Economist*, 27 April 1940, pp. 759–60.

income tax was increased, purchase tax was imposed on a broad front, and the Excess Profits Tax was raised from 60% to 100% (i.e. taxing the total increase in profits over a standard pre-war period) though it was later softened by various concessions, including a 20% post-war credit on the tax paid.[75] With Keynes and other leading economists installed at the Treasury by the end of 1940, and others in the Cabinet Office, the transformation was complete.

Kingsley Wood's budget of April 1941 marked the turning point.[76] It was conceived in national income terms, and to symbolize the new approach, was accompanied by a white paper setting out the official estimates of the national income and expenditure,[77] the first of the series which has become, together with other tools developed in war-time, the indispensable guide to economic policy since. According to the official estimates, the 'gap' at existing rates of income and taxation would be of the order of £500 million, of which £200–300 million would be found by increased personal savings, and £250 million by additional taxation, over and above the estimated revenue of £1,636 million. This was to take the form of raising the standard rate of income tax by 1s. 6d. to 10s. in the pound, and other rates in proportion.

The actual figures underlying the budget of 1941 might have been unreliable, as some critics alleged;[78] certainly, the queues at the shops continued, and widespread rationing and price control had to be introduced, after all. But the principle was sound, and the remaining war budgets, 1942–5, showed little change in their mode of calculation or their method of presentation. The only major innovations were 'Pay As You Earn', introduced in September 1943 and applying to about 16 million earners, of whom 12 million were taxable, and the development of the purchase tax as a weapon not only for the raising of revenue, but also to restrict and generally influence consumption.[79] Up to 1942, direct and indirect taxation had roughly increased in step, the former by 177% over 1939, and the latter by 145%. By 1945 the revenue from direct taxes had increased by 300%, while that from indirect taxes had risen by only 160%.

The success of fiscal policy during the war has to be judged against the size of the problem: at the height of the war, about half the current consumption was diverted to the Government, while civilian consumption, in real terms, had to be reduced to something like 80% of the pre-war level[80] (see Table 5·8).

[75] J. R. Hicks, U. K. Hicks and L. Rostas, *The Taxation of War Wealth* (Oxford, 2nd ed., 1942), chapters 11 and 12; A. J. Youngson, *The British Economy 1920–1957* (1960), pp. 150–1; Hancock and Gowing, pp. 327–30.

[76] S. H. Beer, *Treasury Control* (Oxford, 1956), p. 66.

[77] *The Sources of War Finance. An Analysis and an Estimate of the National Income and Expenditure in 1938 and 1940* (1941. Cmd. 6261). Cf. also J. E. Meade and R. Stone, *National Income and Expenditure* (1944 ed.); R. Stone, 'The Use and Development of National Income and Expenditure Estimates', in *Lessons of the British War Economy*; E. F. Jackson, 'The Recent Use of Social Accounting in the United Kingdom', *Income and Wealth*, Series I (1950).

[78] M. Kalecki, 'The Budget and Inflation', *Bull. Oxf. Inst. Stat.*, 3/6, 1941.

[79] Sayers, *op. cit.*, chapter 4.

[80] Statistics based on *National Income and Expenditure of the United Kingdom, 1938–1945* (1946. Cmd. 6784), Tables 4 and 5. Some of the figures have been slightly revised since. Cf. also *Statistics Relating to the War Effort of the United Kingdom* (1944. Cmd. 6564).

Table 5·8:   Comparison of net national product: % distribution

	Personal and Government consumption A	War B	Personal consumption C	Total Government consumption civil and war D	Net non-war capital formation E	Real personal consumption* F
1938	88	7	78	17	5	100
1939	83	15	73½	24½	2	100
1940	72	44	64	52	-16	90
1941	63	54	56	61	-17	83
1942	60	52	52	60	-12	82
1943	56	56	49	63	-12	79
1944	58	54	51	61	-12	83
1945	61	49	54	56	-10	86

* Index, 1938 prices.

In this table, the totals of columns A and B are equal to the totals of C and D. Either pair, together with column E, totals 100, i.e. the Net National Product. According to the A and B columns, it will be seen that at the peak of the war effort, in 1943, armament alone equalled the rest of national consumption. The other division (columns C and D) which forms a more realistic indicator of budgetary policy, shows that the Government share exceeded private consumption for the whole of the period 1941–45 inclusive. Table 5·8 also illustrates the gradual increase of mobilization to its high point in 1943, and the important contribution made by capital consumption to the total war effort.[81]

Government expenditure at such a rate could not conceivably be met entirely out of current revenue. Government borrowing covered, for the whole period 1939–45, about half the expenditure, but significantly its proportion fell progressively in the course of the war[82] (see Table 5·9). Virtually all of that was met by borrowing at home, and with the exception of some £770 million raised by the printing press, i.e. by increasing the fiduciary bank note issue,[83] was derived from savings.

Table 5·9:   Government revenue and borrowing

	Total tax revenue (£m.) A	Total income, incl. income from property after paying National Debt interest (£m.) B	Total deficit on current account (£m.) C	Of which raised by public borrowing at home (£m.) D	Ratio A : D E
1939	980	771	490	352	—
1940	1,382	1,158	2,115	1,550	0·89
1941	2,143	1,905	2,828	2,553	0·84
1942	2,563	2,314	2,909	2,576	1·00
1943	3,052	2,759	2,826	2,972*	1·03
1944	3,262	2,897	2,672	2,792*	1·17
1945	3,265	2,806	2,131	2,442*	1·34

* There was some net lending abroad in these years.

[81] Cf. also U. K. Hicks, *Public Finance* (1947), pp. 110–11; J. Hurstfield, *The Control of Raw Materials* (1953), pp. 106, 126.
[82] Sayers, Appx. I, Tables 4 and 5.
[83] Sayers, p. 223.

Savings were channelled into the hands of the Government partly by what might be called direct controls, and partly by the more normal methods of making attractive offers for them. Among the direct controls were the suspension of opportunities for investment, and pressure on the clearing banks to turn all their available resources over to the Government and to restrict bank advances intended to be used for capital construction.

The methods of raising Government loans showed a degree of subtlety far superior to that of the First World War.[84] Their essence was the exploitation of a discriminating monopoly, i.e. the offer of separate terms to each sector of the market, in each case at the lowest rate necessary to bring forth the loans. The 'cheap money' of the 1930s had lowered general expectations of interest levels, and since there was little hope of attracting foreign lenders to London by high rates, and there were other means available to the Government for inhibiting competing claims for savings, there seemed to be no very good reason for raising the rate structure and thus increasing the interest burden on the Government. The bank rate, after seven years at the 2% level, was raised to 4% on 24 August 1939, but in view of the pointlessness of this gesture, it was lowered again to 3%, and the authorities were able to conduct a '3% war'.

For the small saver, the 'National Savings' movement, which had survived from the First World War, was again made the vehicle of strong patriotic appeals, and savers were offered, besides the Post Office and the Trustee Savings Banks and similar holdings, a series of National Savings Certificates and Defence Bonds. For the larger savers, National War Bonds at $2\frac{1}{2}$% were provided on tap, i.e. as a continuous supply on application, and 3% Savings Bonds were also on offer. At the end of 1941 yet another type of security began to be issued, the Tax Reserve Certificate, to take advantage of the idle funds held by prudent firms in readiness for their tax liability.

Any funds not invested in any of these alternative loans would normally find their way into the banks, and the Government accordingly developed a whole battery of methods to absorb all 'idle' bank balances, including Ways and Means Advances, Treasury Bills and Treasury Deposit Receipts. The first, being considered inflationary, were used as little as possible, and the main weight fell on Treasury Bills. These were at first held mainly by the Departments and later became popular with the general public, being negotiable at the Bank of England; so that the clearing banks' share of assets held in that form fell from 30–40% in the 1930s to 10% in 1944–5.[85]

The banks were obliged to make their contribution to the floating debt by means of a new security issued in the perilous days of July 1940, the Treasury Deposit Receipt. It was rather less liquid than the Treasury Bill, having a currency of six months, and being non-negotiable, though it could be repaid in full for bonds for either the banks or their customers, but its rate, delicately fixed at $1\frac{1}{8}$%, was just above the Bill rate which then stood at a shade over 1%. This meticulous mopping-up of bank liquid reserves was driven to such lengths that occasionally the cash reserves of the clearing banks were actually reduced below the safety level.

[84] The following paragraphs are largely based on Sayers, *op. cit.*, chapter 7.

[85] Edward Nevin and E. W. Davis, *The London Clearing Banks* (1970), pp. 152–3.

At the same time, concrete restrictions placed on individual spending and on business investment, forced businesses and individuals to accumulate their funds in the banks, unless, indeed, they invested them directly in Government paper. For this reason, as well as because of the general inflation, total bank deposits rose from £2,730 million in 1939 to £5,551 million in 1945 (or by 103%), while total bank clearings, indicating the velocity of circulation, only rose from £36·6 billion to £66·9 billion, or by 83%. The London clearing banks alone held average net deposits of £1,257 million in 1939, and £4,035 million at the end of 1945. But of this latter sum, only £1,339 million were private deposits, the rest being business deposits, which had thus risen during the war by over £1,500 million,[86] representing one aspect of the 'forced saving' which consisted of denying firms the real resources for investment in the private sector.

The assets of the London clearing banks were, however, much further distorted by war finance than the liabilities. Commercial advances, as a proportion of deposits, declined dramatically from 44·1% in 1939 to a bare 16·1% in 1945, being smaller even in absolute terms than before the war, and bills discounted fell from 11·3% to 4·0%. Against this, TDRs rose from nil to 38·6%, while 'investments' kept a constant share of the total. In August 1945, Government paper and cash amounted to 83·3% of the deposits of the London clearing banks. They had thus become principally agents for the absorption of funds from the public for the use of the Government. Other financial institutions, for much the same reasons, had their investment portfolios similarly filled with Government paper.

4 The Problem of the Foreign Balance of Payments

Whereas the last years of peace before 1914 had seen large annual surpluses on current account, the balance of payments in the late 1930s had left no margin; and whereas the immediate panic in August 1914 led to a world shortage of sterling, the crisis of the spring of 1938 had led to a *withdrawal* of foreign funds to the extent of £150 million. An actual declaration of war could be expected to lead to a large-scale flight from sterling.[87] If, then, exchange control had been necessary in 1914–18, it was certain to become more so in the Second World War.

The threat to the value of sterling lay largely in the probable adverse balance of payments during the war, though few would have imagined its eventual size. While imports were unlikely to be below their peace-time levels, home industry, diverted to war production, could scarcely be expected to maintain the same level of exports, and Britain's 'invisible exports' were also likely to shrink. Compared with 1914–18, the large buffer of foreign investments which might be sold off to pay for current imports and meanwhile provided invisible earnings had also been severely diminished.[88] Against this, the possible fall in some raw material prices, as Axis purchases were cut off, would afford but little relief.

[86] Ashworth, *op. cit.*, pp. 234–5, Appx. I, Table L, p. 260.

[87] R. S. Sayers, *Central Banking After Bagehot* (1957), p. 65.

[88] Cf. J. M. Keynes, *How to Pay for the War* (1940), Appx., p. 86. Though not very accurate, the figures represent the beliefs current at the outbreak of war.

The trade balance was likely to become particularly adverse with dollar countries. The gold and dollar reserve, estimated at £450 million at the outbreak of war, and planned to be rationed out to last for three years at £150 million a year, was soon being depleted at a much greater rate.[89] Hence a major export drive, particularly to 'hard currency' countries, was undertaken in February 1940, and by April–May it contributed in no small measure to the growing shortage of resources. It had hardly got into its stride, however, before the military collapse in the west and the consequent need for war production at all costs forced the country to sacrifice its exports and its gold and dollar reserve. By late 1940, the hope of meeting all foreign payments necessary to maintain the much enlarged armament programme at home had become plainly illusory. The dollar import problem was solved by 'Lend-Lease', and it became possible to switch exports to areas that provided the most vital strategic materials. In the process, Britain lost many of her traditional markets, which were forced to turn to the USA instead,[90] and the volume of her exports fell to less than one-third of the pre-war figure. At the end of the war, less than 2% of the labour force was engaged on exports, compared with 9·5% before the war.

To the huge adverse balance on visible trade account, shown in Table 5·10, have to be added the expenditure by British troops overseas, and the free deliveries from the dollar area:[91]

Table 5·10: The visible trade balance

	Exports (£m.)	Imports (£m.)	Visible adverse balance (£m.)	Volume index	
				Exports	Imports
1938	471	858	387	100	100
1939	440	840	400	94	97
1941	365	1,132	767	56	82
1943	234	1,228	994	29	77
1945	399	1,053	654	46	62

Taking those additional items into account, over the war period as a whole (September 1939 to December 1945 inclusive), total British current debits amounted to £16,900 million, of which visible imports accounted for £12,200 million. Of this sum, only £6,900 million, or about 40%, was requited by goods and services by the United Kingdom; the rest was financed by sales of capital (£1,200 million), running up debts with other countries (£3,500 million) and *net* grants, mainly from the USA and Canada (£5,400 million).[92]

To keep the pound at a fixed value, settled at $4·03 (some 20% below the old gold parity), under conditions of such strain, two major weapons

[89] W. K. Hancock and M. M. Gowing, *British War Economy* (1949), pp. 112–17; J. Hurstfield, *The Control of Raw Materials* (1953), pp. 108–13; M. M. Postan, *British War Production* (1952), pp. 82–3.

[90] E. L. Hargreaves and M. M. Gowing, *Civil Industry and Trade* (1952), pp. 44 ff., chapters 7–9.

[91] Re-exports and corresponding imports omitted. Central Statistical Office, *Statistical Digest of the War* (1951), Table 142.

[92] R. S. Sayers, *Financial Policy, 1939–45* (1956), Appx. I, Table 10, p. 499.

were used: import controls and financial controls. The import drain was controlled only by degrees, and Britain lost £50 million in foreign exchange in needlessly increased prices,[93] before all imports of food were transferred to the Ministry in March 1940, and private importers were virtually squeezed out. Formal general import control was not imposed until June 1940.

Direct financial controls also took time to evolve. Dealings in gold and foreign exchange, payments abroad and purchases of foreign assets were put under Treasury control at once; holdings of foreign securities had to be registered with the Treasury. But these early controls, like those of imports, left several major loopholes. For one thing, payments within the 'Sterling Area' were left free, and in some parts of it leakages occurred easily; the 'Sterling Area' in its modern sense with its single pool of gold and dollar resources evolved under the lead of the United Kingdom only in 1939–41.[94] Above all, foreign holders of sterling balances could still exchange them for dollars or other 'hard' currency, which then escaped control. The loss of these precious balances in the early months was estimated at $737 million,[95] but was considered necessary in order not to alienate American holders of sterling. Only in May were foreign-held securities blocked, the balances having by then become negligible, and all further leaks were then stopped by bilateral trade treaties. Thus the United Kingdom was able to evolve methods to emerge from the war in the summer of 1945 without being crippled by foreign loans of the 1914–1918 type.

The 'Sterling Balances', i.e. the credits of other countries held in London in blocked accounts, were owed largely, though not wholly, within the 'Sterling Area'. The largest holder was India, whose credit in London rose to well over £1 billion at the end of the war even after more than £300 million of capital assets had been sold off by Britain. 'The main origin [of these credits] was when India was used as the operational basis and arsenal of democracy in the East against Japan.'[96] Other large sums were held by Egypt, Palestine and the Sudan, again on account of the supply and expenditure of Empire troops in their area. Substantial balance also accrued to other Colonial areas, and to South Africa, Australia and New Zealand. Outside the Empire, the Argentine held about £100 million at the end of the war, and Brazil about £40 million, the total of the western hemisphere being over £300 million; and several of the Western European Governments-in-Exile had also accumulated substantial sterling claims, either by transferring their gold to the United Kingdom, or by the active trade balance of their colonies.

The total indebtedness grew at a steady rate of £600 million a year through-

---

[93] T. Balogh, 'The Drift Towards a Rational Foreign Exchange Policy' (1940), in Oxford Institute of Statistics, *Studies in War Economics* (1947), p. 66.

[94] *Report of the Committee on the Working of the Monetary System* (Radcliffe Report) (1959. Cmnd. 827), paras. 647, 723 ff.; A. R. Conan, *The Sterling Area* (1952), p. 52; D. F. McCurrach, 'Britain's US Dollar Problem, 1939–45', *Econ. J.*, 58/231, 1948, p. 356.

[95] H. Duncan Hall, *North American Supply* (HSWW, 1955), p. 270.

[96] H. A. Shannon, 'The Sterling Balances of the Sterling Area 1939–1949', *Econ. J.*, 60/239, 1950, p. 540; H. D. Hall and C. C. Wrigley, *Studies of Overseas Supply* (HSWW, 1956), chapter 9; Sir Dennis H. Robertson, *Britain in the World Economy* (1954), p. 40.

out the later war years, and by mid-1945 had reached the amounts shown in Table 5·11.[97]

Table 5·11: British overseas debts in 1945

Australia, NZ, S. Africa, Eire	384
India, Burma, Middle East	1,732
Colonies and other Sterling Area	607
Total Sterling area	2,723
South and North America	303
European States and Dependencies	267
Rest of the world	62
Grand total	3,355

The sterling balances thus had many origins and many types of owners. Some were owned by populations overseas much poorer than the British; others by European Governments-in-Exile who could claim that their countries, at the end of the war, were in far greater need of rehabilitation than was Britain, and were therefore in no position to provide loans for the latter. While they accumulated, they allowed Britain to fight the war with resources greater than her own, without bankruptcy and without damage to the international value of the pound sterling. At the end of the war, however, they represented a large financial burden, even when not subject to demands of withdrawal. The annual interest and service charge payable abroad, a striking reversal of the old role of Britain as international lender, was hard to bear in the early post-war years; while the need to hold credit balances against them was to lead to serious misunderstandings with the Americans.

By means of external borrowing, and by the sale of capital assets, the United Kingdom obtained from the non-dollar world a total of some £4 billion in 1939–45,[98] a sum of the same order of magnitude as the total British foreign investment at the outbreak of war. Yet it was put in the shade by the contribution of the dollar world (the USA and Canada), which provided £7·5 billion (£6·2 billion net) by gifts and over £1 billion against sales of investments, gold and by accumulating liabilities.

The Canadian contribution, large as it was in relation to the resources of the Dominion, was made with the minimum of friction. Having used up its liquid Canadian resources, the United Kingdom was granted an interest-free loan of $700 million in 1942, and when that was exhausted, the Canadians voted their magnificent 'billion-dollar gift' in 1943. It was followed by two 'mutual aid' appropriations, without strings, totalling $1,800 million in 1943–4, and further credits lasted until 1946. Total gifts and free aids came to $3,468 million, and total supplies and services to the United Kingdom (including those paid for) to $7,441 million, or nearly £2 billion.[99]

[97] Sayers, *Financial Policy*, p. 439; cf. also chapters, 9, 10, 14; T. Balogh, 'The International Aspect', in G. D. N. Worswick and P. H. Ady, *The British Economy, 1945–1950* (Oxford, 1952), pp. 480–3.

[98] R. F. Harrod, *Life of John Maynard Keynes* (1951), p. 606.

[99] Sayers, *Financial Policy*, chapter 11; Hall, *op. cit.*, chapters 1, 2, pp. 483–7; Hall and Wrigley, pp. 46–65.

Very different were the relations with the United States, bedevilled as they were by the strong neutralist and isolationist sector of American public opinion, and by widespread suspicions of Britain's motives. The Johnson Act of 1934 had prohibited loans to foreign Governments which had defaulted on their First World War loans, including the United Kingdom Government, so that all purchases had to be paid for in cash. It was in this period of 'cash and carry', of careful husbanding of gold and dollar reserves, that the British Purchasing Commission (as well as its French counterpart) established itself, to play henceforth a crucial part in economic warfare and in the delicate but vital relationship of the two Anglo-Saxon powers.[100]

Apart from machine tools, the principal British need was for aircraft, and in this period they formed the most important military item ordered in the USA (as well as in Canada). After the fall of France Britain took over the French orders placed there, which alone committed her to an ultimate expenditure of $612 million.

Other British orders both for immediate use and for long-term supply were also stepped up enormously in the second half of 1940, but neither led to any tangible results. The immediate orders failed to materialize because of the sheer inability of American industry, increasingly drawn upon by the American forces also, to meet them quickly enough. It was estimated that at least $200 million of precious British reserves had gone by March 1941, not into buying arms, but into building factories in the USA and in Canada. For all her vast outlay and large future commitments, the United Kingdom had as yet, in the critical months to the end of 1940, received only the minimal actual supplies. Aircraft, for example, from the USA, perhaps the most critical item, only numbered 700 in 1939 and 2,000 for the whole of 1940 (compared with a British home production of 8,000 and 15,000 respectively).[101] Supplies of food, raw materials and other peace-time goods were, however, much more satisfactory; for the whole of 1939–41, their imports from the USA amounted to £667 million, as against £133 million for munitions; only in 1943 did munitions supply begin to exceed the imports of non-war goods.[102]

More disturbing than the short-term delay was the long-term prospect. Though the gold and dollar reserves had been enlarged by current earnings of $2,000 million between September 1939 and December 1940 ($345 by United Kingdom earnings, $670 by Empire commodities and $965 by Dominion gold),[103] the total liquid reserves, including saleable capital assets in the dollar area, were only just sufficient to pay for orders already placed. There was nothing left even to begin to pay the very much enlarged programme for 1941, necessary for the ultimate defeat of the Axis.

As the date of the absolute impoverishment of Britain and her Allies loomed nearer, it was becoming clear that in the last resort the United States would not deny her help. There had been some piecemeal expansion of American aid, as far as her position as a neutral and her Congress and public opinion allowed. The 50 destroyers, for example, handed over in September

[100] M. Jean Monnet of the French Commission was taken on the British staff after the fall of France.

[101] Hall and Wrigley, p. 30.

[102] J. Hurstfield, *Control of Raw Materials*, p. 98.

[103] McCurrach, *loc. cit.*, pp. 358 ff.; Hall, *North American Supplies*, pp. 269–70.

1940 in return for British bases, were a welcome immediate contribution,[104] while the United States co-operated in denying some crucial war materials, such as molybdenum, to Germany and to neutrals within her control.[105] By December 1940 more comprehensive action had become necessary, and President Roosevelt met it by announcing the provision of 'Lend-Lease'.

Lend-lease meant the supply, free of charge, for the duration of the war, of all goods and services needed by Britain and available in the USA; it was granted on the same terms to the other Allies, including Soviet Russia and China. Though lend-lease supplies were, until 1943–4 at least, only marginal to the United Kingdom's war effort, they solved the problem set by the running out of reserves and allowed Britain to dovetail her production with America. Its vast bulk, some $27 billion being made available to the United Kingdom, and $6 billion by the United Kingdom to the USA in 'reciprocal aid' or 'reverse lend-lease', dominated British economic warfare, and its conditions dominated British economic relations with the USA and the rest of the world.[106]

The Lend-Lease Act, though called the 'most unsordid act' in history, had to pass through Congress while America was still neutral and it had to run an annual gauntlet of renewal; and in this process several onerous conditions were exacted. To begin with, Britain had to strip herself bare of dollars and all capital assets in the USA, and great pressure was brought to bear on her to sell even those which could be sold only at a large loss. This reserve gone, the accumulation of a new one, even if desperately required as backing for the 'sterling balances', was viewed with the greatest hostility and suspicion.

Secondly, many months were to elapse before the first substantial lend-lease deliveries actually arrived in Britain, and over two years were to elapse before they exceeded the deliveries paid for in cash. In the interim Britain would, in fact, have been bankrupt if it had not been for a loan of $425 million extended by the Reconstruction Finance Corporation, an American Government agency, against the collateral of British-held American assets valued at $700 million.

Thirdly, lend-lease supplies were, in form, deliveries 'for the defence of the USA', so that, in the last resort, they depended on the wishes of the American Government. Thus, deliveries were liable to sudden cancellation in favour of the American Services, whose shopping lists were usually grossly inflated by British austerity standards.

Fourthly, there were the 'strings' deliberately put in, above all the demand for a prohibition of all British exports containing any raw materials which were also supplied through lend-lease, so that American exporters should not have to compete with the British who were subsidized by the American taxpayer. Somewhat toned down later, the British Government decided to

---

[104] W. S. Churchill, *The Second World War. vol. II. Their Finest Hour* (1949), chapter 20.

[105] Hall, *North American Supplies*, chapters 3–6.

[106] For the history of 'lend-lease', see Edward R. Stettinius, Jr., *Lend-Lease* (New York, 1944); Sayers, *Financial Policy*, chapters 13, 15; Hall, *North American Supplies*, chapters 8–11; Hancock and Gowing, chapter 9; Hall and Wrigley, chapter 3; Hurstfield, chapter 19; A. J. Youngson, *British Economy, 1920–1957* (1960), pp. 152–6.

accept it voluntarily in the Export White Paper of 19 September 1941,[107] before the American entry into the war. By the other main condition, the famous Article VII of the Mutual Aid Agreement of 1942,[108] Britain had to subscribe to the pronouncement against 'discrimination' in international trade after the war, generally understood to be an attack on Imperial preference.

This treatment continued even after Pearl Harbour, when America became a belligerent ally, and after Britain and the Empire granted 'reverse lend-lease' without any strings, representing, though it was much smaller in amount, as high a proportion of the donor's national income, and a greater sacrifice,[109] and provided British scientific knowledge supplied free for such projects as radar, jet engines and nuclear fission.[110] Lastly, the American insistence on unilateral treatment made it impossible for Britain to propose pooling arrangements among her other Allies, so that lend-lease was, in a sense, responsible for the extent of the burdensome Sterling Balances at the end of the war.

When in the later years of the war, American expenditure in Britain and elsewhere in the Sterling Area began to raise the dollar reserve, which the American president, unknown to the British, had determined should not exceed $1,000 million, there began a further series of restrictions to reduce them to that level. Tobacco for civilian consumption was removed from the lend-lease list and in November 1943 capital goods were taken out, at a cost to the sterling area of $200 million. Moreover, Congress was reducing the overall appropriations for lend-lease just as the American troops were leaving Allied soil and the dollar reserves began to fall again, and it was made clear that after the defeat of Germany, lend-lease supplies would be sent only for troops actually fighting the Japanese.

Keynes secured some concessions at the Washington Conference in October 1944 from this intransigent position. The importance of exports to the survival of Britain was recognized and she was allowed to convert some of her export industries even before VE day; as from the beginning of 1945, she was also given greater freedom to export to pay for her raw materials. But the relief was short-lived. VE day, in June, was followed quickly by the surrender of Japan on 14 August. A week later, lend-lease was abruptly stopped, and Britain was faced with the immediate necessity of paying in dollars for goods already in the country or 'in the pipeline' to the tune of $650 million, as well as for continuation orders, if she was not to be starved of necessary food and raw materials.

With her capital equipment run down, more resources devoted to war and needing reconversion to a larger extent than any other Ally, her overseas earnings cut by the loss of one-quarter of her shipping and almost half her investments, Britain was quite unable to earn the necessary dollars, even if the standard of consumption were cut further. The rest of the world, much of

---

[107] Cmd. 6311.

[108] *Treaty Series No. 7* (1942). Cmd. 6391 and Cmd. 6341.

[109] R. G. D. Allen, 'Mutual Aid between the USA and the British Empire 1941–5', *J. R. Stat. S.*, 109/3, 1946; Hancock and Gowing, p. 353, Table 3(c).

[110] Hall and Wrigley, chapter 8.

it devastated and disorganized, was in no position to supply the needs hitherto filled from dollar sources, and was itself in need of dollar aid. The only possible course for Britain was to obtain an American loan of the type which she had succeeded in avoiding throughout the war, and at the end of the war Keynes was sent to Washington once again to negotiate it.

5 Work and Welfare in the War Years

There were several reasons why the costly strikes and the class hatred of the First World War were not repeated in the second. For one thing, the unions and their leaders enjoyed from the outset much greater official recognition, and when, in May 1940, Labour entered the Coalition Government, the outstanding trade unionist of the day, Ernest Bevin, was in charge of policy relating to manpower as Minister of Labour and National Service. Secondly, Labour was politically much more in sympathy with this war and its declared war aims than with the first. Thirdly, the Government made greater efforts to ensure a fair distribution of food and other necessities, and to enlarge social welfare schemes. Finally, unlike the years before 1914, the 1930s had seen very few large strikes, so that, perhaps, it was not surprising that apart from the coal mines, some engineers' strikes in 1940 and a boilermakers' strike in 1944, the war-time strikes were short, small and unofficial.[111]

As prices rose in the early weeks of war, and a shortage of some types of labour made itself felt, it was not possible to hold down wages, and the Government itself, by allowing the very first major wage claim, that of the miners in October 1939, at the cost of raising the price of coal, set a poor example to employers who wished to be intransigent.[112] Under the Coalition Government, with Mr Bevin at the Ministry of Labour manpower policy became more positive, though the Government continued to keep its drastic legal powers in the background, and relied as far as possible on the voluntary co-operation of the unions and the use of peace-time machinery.

As far as collective bargaining was concerned, the basic provision, the Conditions of Employment and National Arbitration Order SR & O (1940), No. 1305, preserved all the existing negotiating machinery, including arbitration and the powers of the Industrial Court. It was only for issues in which agreement could not be reached by existing methods that it established a new National Arbitration Tribunal. Strikes and lockouts were prohibited, unless the Ministry of Labour failed to act; normally the Ministry would refer a dispute either to the National Arbitration Tribunal or to any of the other existing arbitration bodies, and in that case their awards were to have legal force.[113] Altogether, in 1939–45, 816 decisions were handed down by the NAT, 692 by other arbitrators, and there were about 2,150 conciliation

---

[111] Allan Flanders, *Trade Unions* (1952), p. 100; K. G. J. C. Knowles, *Strikes, A Study in Industrial Conflict* (Oxford, 1952), pp. 162–3; Central Statistical Office, *Statistical Digest of the War* (1951), Table 36; A. L. Bowley, 'Labour Disputes in Wartime', *London & Cambridge Economic Service*, No. 103 (1945), p. 8.

[112] W. K. Hancock and M. M. Gowing, *British War Economy* (1949), pp. 164–5.

[113] N. Barou, *British Trade Unions* (1947), pp. 153–4; H. M. D. Parker, *Manpower, a Study in War-Time Policy and Administration* (HSWW, 1957), chapter 25.

settlements. Strikes could not entirely be prevented and against large-scale strikes the Government was as helpless as in 1914–18. In April 1944, the Minister, perhaps remembering with bitterness his struggle with 'unofficial' leaders in his own union, pushed through amendments to the Defence Regulations 1A and Regulation 1AA giving powers to deal severely with incitement to strike, but they were repealed again in the following year.

The direction of labour was based on the drastic Essential Works Order, SR & O No. 302, of March 1941, but its powers were used sparingly for fear of industrial troubles such as accompanied the comb-outs after 1915. Dilution also relied heavily on the experience of 1915–18, and in the engineering industry was negotiated as early as August 1939. It was combined with a system of training, and between mid-1939 and mid-1943 the proportion of women workers in engineering was raised from 10·5% to 31·2%.[114]

Where labour was virtually conscripted into 'controlled' establishments, 'the Minister of Labour was convinced that he could not expect men to give up the right to free choice of employment without guaranteeing them certain conditions of work, including a guaranteed week and the restriction of the employers' right to dismiss them'.[115] This conviction moved him to provide for the expansion of welfare facilities,[116] the strengthening of the 'fair' wages' clause in Government contracts, and the extension of statutory wage determination to trades hitherto poorly organized.

These last received much attention during the war years. Road Haulage had been covered just before the outbreak of war. A Joint Council for the Distributive Trades was set up in 1940, and separate Whitley Councils for different sections of the trade later. In 1943, the Catering Wages Act established the Catering Wages Commission, and Wages Boards to fix pay and conditions of work in the different sections of the trade. The Central Agricultural Wages Board was given powers in 1940 to fix national minimum wage rates for adult male workers. Lastly, in coal mining, owners and miners agreed to a national conciliation scheme, including a National Reference Tribunal of three neutral members. These developments culminated in the Wages Council Act of 1945 which converted the existing Trade Boards and the Road Haulage Wages Board into Wages Councils, gave them additional powers over earnings and conditions, and fostered their extension into other industries. Elsewhere, 56 joint industrial councils were established or re-established in the war years, partly with a view to laying down 'recognized' conditions of employment as stipulated by the Essential Works Order.[117] Mr Bevin's greatest personal triumph was perhaps the decasualization of dock labour, which began in 1941.[118]

As in 1914–18, the trade unions grew greatly in stature and power during the war years. Membership rose from 6¼ million in 1939 to nearly 8 million in

[114] P. Inman, *Labour in the Munition Industries* (HSWW, 1957), p. 80.

[115] Inman, p. 103.

[116] pp. 227–8 below.

[117] D. F. MacDonald, *The State and the Trade Unions* (1960), chapter 9; PEP, *British Trade Unionism* (1948), pp. 39–54; Min. of Labour and Nat. Service, *Report for 1939–46*, pp. 269–94; Allan Flanders, 'Industrial Relations', in G. D. N. Worswick and P. H. Ady, *The British Economy 1945–1950* (Oxford, 1952), pp. 112–15.

[118] Hancock and Gowing, p. 240.

1945. Trade union leaders were increasingly drawn into the machinery of Government. Joint consultation, originated in engineering in 1942, spread to many other industries, and Joint Production Committees, beginning spontaneously in Woolwich in 1940, covered $3\frac{1}{2}$ million workers by the end of 1944.[119] The leaders of the large trade unions, in fact, became so eager to show a sense of responsibility for the economy as a whole, that they laid themselves open to attacks by their own members for neglecting their interests.

If they had exerted their power to the full, like, for example, the farmers,[120] the trade unions could not indeed have been prevented from enforcing wage increases that would have destroyed any hopes of containing the war-time inflation. As it was, real wage *rates* rose more slowly than the cost of living, though faster than the official cost-of-living index, which had its components selectively held down in price (compare columns B and C in Table 5·12). At the same time, overtime, night shifts and week-end work, together with much piecework and up-grading of workers, raised actual *earnings* a good deal more than wage rates:[121]

Table 5·12: Wage rates, earnings and cost-of-living index

	Wage rates*	Official cost-of-living index	Wage-earners' true cost-of-living index	Weekly earnings
	Sept. 1939 = 100		1938 = 100	Oct. 1938 = 100**
	A	B	C	D
1939	104	104	$102\frac{1}{2}$	—
1940	113 – 14	121	120	130
1941	122	128	135	142
1942	131 – 2	129	143	160
1943	136 – 7	129	148	176
1944	143 – 4	130	150	$181\frac{1}{2}$
1945	150 – 1	$133\frac{1}{2}$	—	$180\frac{1}{2}$

* July figures. ** Current weights.

Of the total increase in money earnings of 81%, it was estimated that 32% was due to a rise in wage rates, 9% to changes as between industries, 6% to increases in the hours of work, -1% to changes in the proportion of men, women, boys and girls employed, and 20% to all remaining factors, including overtime and piecework.[122]

Average wages. as always, hide many divergent movements in different

[119] Industrial Welfare Society, *Works Councils and Committees* (1943); N. Barou, p. 170.

[120] p. 206 above.

[121] Ministry of Labour, *Report 1939–46*, pp. 304–5; Parker, *Manpower*, p. 433. J. L. Nicholson, 'Employment and National Income during the War', *Bull. Oxf. Inst. Stat.*, 7/14, 1945, Table 6, and 'Earnings and Hours of Labour', *ibid.*, 8/5, 1946, Table 2; Hancock and Gowing, p. 152; J. Kuczynski, *A Short History of Labour Conditions in Great Britain, 1750 to the Present Day* (3rd ed., 1947), chapter 4.

[122] Nicholson, 'Earnings and Hours'; N. Barou, pp. 159–60.

industries. As soon as full employment conditions permitted, there began an irresistible pressure to raise the wages of the low-paid unskilled and agricultural workers, and of those who received less than others in comparable work, such as miners and railwaymen. Wage rates also had to be boosted in industries which had to attract much new labour quickly, such as engineering and aircraft. The Government accepted several of these grounds in its white paper on *Price Stabilization and Industrial Policy* of July 1941.[123] Thus there were many forces pushing up wage rates, while women's rates rose more than men's, and unskilled rates crept up from about 70% to about 80% of skilled rates in the course of the war.

In view of the profit limitations in force, the freezing of house rents by the Rent and Mortgage Interest Restriction Act of 1939, and the heavy burden of taxation on the rich, rising real wage earnings implied for the second World War, as it did in the first, a substantial redistribution of incomes in favour of wage-earners. While wage incomes (at constant, 1947 prices and after taxation) rose by 18% between 1938 and 1947, and 'social incomes' by 57%, incomes from property fell by 15% and salaries by 21%.[124] The following comparison illustrates but exaggerates slightly the redistribution, since it omits the income from property represented by undistributed profits and capital appreciation[125] (see Table 5·13).

The war also saw a redistribution of property, though it was less marked than that in incomes. For example, the capital owned by owners of £100,000 and over fell from 22% in 1936–8 to 16·1% of the total in 1946–7, and that held by owners of £1,000–£10,000 rose from 29·3% to 32·8%,[126] but allowance has to be made for the changing value of the pound.

Table 5·13:   Redistribution of income

	Post-tax real average incomes in 1949. Index 1938 = 100	Percentage share in post-tax personal incomes at constant (1938) prices	
		1938	1949
Wages	122	37	47
Salaries	83	23	22
Forces' pay	82	2	3
Total work income	—	62	71
Farming income	191 ⎫		
Professional earnings	89 ⎬	12	10
Sole traders' profit	82 ⎭		
Distributed property income	—	20	10
Social income	—	6	9
		100	100

[123] Cmd. 6294. Cf. also B. C. Roberts, *National Wages Policy in War and Peace* (1958), chapter 2.

[124] J. L. Nicholson, 'Employment and National Income', *loc. cit.*, Table 8; *National Income and Expenditure of the United Kingdom, 1938–1945* (1946. Cmd. 6784), Table 9; Dudley Seers, *Changes in the Cost-of-Living and the Distribution of Income since 1938* (Oxford, 1949), p. 64.

[125] Dudley Seers, 'The Levelling of Incomes', *Bull. Oxf. Inst. Stat.*, 12/10 (1950), pp. 278–9.

[126] Kathleen M. Langley, 'The Distribution of Capital in Private Hands in 1936–8 and 1946–7, Part II', *Bull. Oxf. Inst. Stat.*, 13/2, 1951.

The more equitable distribution of war-time was achieved not only by the money flow of incomes, taxation and subsidies, but also by direct control over goods. The luxuries and non-necessities consumed by the rich were reduced most drastically, while many of the non-necessities of the poor, including tobacco, alcohol and cinemas, were maintained deliberately (and heavily taxed) for the combined purposes of maintaining morale, mopping up spending power and providing a broad tax base.

While food consumption as a whole was cut by one-sixth in value,[127] the supplies of many basic foods were maintained at their peace-time levels, and others were even increased. These included liquid milk, flour and other cereals (partly by a higher extraction rate), potatoes, and fats other than butter. The basic foods were rationed in 1940 and consumption per head of meat, of sugar and of tea was cut substantially in the following years.[128] At the end of 1941 there followed the 'points system' rationing for other foods, as well as clothes rationing, and in 1942 'personal points' for sweets. Bread was not rationed at all during the war.[129] Among other goods, the consumption of tobacco and beer, as well as travel, increased most; consumption of fuel and light remained fairly constant; but consumption of clothing was down to less than one-half, and of household goods to less than 40% of pre-war. Private motoring was suspended and restaurant meals limited to 5s. In general, it would be broadly true to state that personal consumption was stabilized at the pre-war skilled artisan level, and that of other classes cut down to approach it.[130]

There was also positive welfare provision, usually on grounds of national efficiency, but also out of the new feeling of common citizenship. For example, school meals were instituted, and they were served to all children, rich and poor alike. In the same way, nurseries were established for working mothers and for others. The cheap milk scheme for young children and expectant mothers began in 1940 and there followed the provision for orange juice, cod liver oil, the special egg allocation and vitamin tablets.[131] By these means there was achieved, after a slight deterioration in 1940 and 1941, a substantial improvement in the health of the country, especially in that of children, in spite of air raids, food shortages, overcrowding, the strain on medical services and other adverse factors. The infant mortality rate, perhaps the most sensitive index, declined substantially from 56 per 1,000 live births in England (77 in Scotland) in 1936–8 to 45 (58) in 1944–6.[132]

Munition workers and those employed in essential industries received

[127] *National Income and Expenditure of the United Kingdom, 1938–1945* (1946. Cmd. 6784), Table 9.
[128] *Statistical Digest of the War*, Tables, 67, 70; *Food Consumption Levels in the United Kingdom* (1947. Cmd. 7203).
[129] A. S. MacNalty, *The Civilian Health and Medical Services*, vol. 1 (HSWW, 1953), chapter 5; Hargreaves and Gowing, *Civil Industry*, chapter 14; W. B. Reddaway, 'Rationing', in *Lessons of the British War Economy*; R. J. Hammond, *Food*, vol. 1 (1951), esp. chapters 8, 14, 15, 22, 23; vol. 2 (1956), Part C.
[130] J. Hurstfield, *The Control of Raw Materials* (1953), Appx. 15, Tables 1–3, Appx. 16; Hancock and Gowing, pp. 324, 492–5.
[131] Sheila Ferguson and Hilde Fitzgerald, *Studies in the Social Services* (HSWW, 1954), chapters 5, 6 and 7; MacNalty, *op. cit.*, chapter 4.
[132] R. M. Titmuss, *Problems of Social Policy* (HSWW, 1950), p. 521, also pp. 509 ff.

special attention. Sometimes it was demanded in the interests of efficiency, and sometimes it was necessary in order to attract and keep workers in factories inconveniently sited; but in part it was, again, called forth by the new spirit fostered by the common experience of the war. There was humanity as well as an intelligent search for efficiency behind the increase from 35 whole-time and 70 part-time factory doctors in the whole country at the outbreak of war to 181 and 890 by 1944, and the increase from 1,500 industrial nurses to 8,000 in 1943. From November 1940 on, factory inspectors had power to make canteens compulsory in the large works, and in these they increased threefold, to 5,000, while in the smaller firms, not subject to the Order of 1940, they grew from 1,400 to 6,800, besides docks' canteens and seamen's welfare centres. The factory inspectorate was also given powers, by an earlier Order of July 1940, to insist on the appointment of welfare officers in large factories of 250 workers and over; their number rose from 1,500 to 5,378 in January 1944. Their employment symbolized the new enlightened attitude to personnel management.[133]

Even outside the factories 'it would, in any relative sense, be true to say that by the end of the Second World War the Government had, through the agency of newly established or existing services, assumed and developed a measure of direct concern for the health and well-being of the population which, by contrast with the role of the Government in the 1930s, was little short of remarkable.'[134] Factory canteens were matched for the general public by the local authorities' 'British Restaurants'.[135] In the face of the danger from bombing, class distinction tended to pall also: provision in shelters, emergency hospitals and evacuation centres was alike for all.

As a result, the association of public welfare with charity and degradation was beginning to fade. Unemployment had been virtually abolished from the middle of 1941 on, but there were still many persons in need, and for them public aid was made more humane. The transfer, in 1940, of pensions, relief of war distress and allowances to families of men in the Forces to the re-named 'Assistance Board' did much also to change the attitude of that institution, and improved the treatment of old-age pensioners who drew supplementary relief under the Act of 1940,[136] and of other paupers.

It was part of the same trend that the committee of officials, set up in June 1941 under the chairmanship of Sir William Beveridge to report on social insurance and allied services after the war, should have been drawn towards one single comprehensive scheme, with similar benefit rates for all kinds of need, available to all as of right. Its report, issued (since its proposals were controversial) under Beveridge's name alone in November 1942, had an immediate and startling popular appeal as the 'Beveridge Report'[137] and became one of the pillars of the country's post-war plans.

---

[133] Inman, chapter 9; Parker, chapter 23; Ministry of Labour, *Report 1939–46,* p. 113.

[134] R. M. Titmuss, p. 506. Cf. also Alan T. Peacock and Jack Wiseman, *The Growth of Public Expenditure in the United Kingdom* (1961).

[135] R. J. Hammond, *Food,* vol. 2, chapters 23–25.

[136] W. H. Beveridge, *Full Employment in a Free Society* (1945 ed.), Part III; D. C. Marsh, *National Insurance and Assistance in Great Britain* (1950), pp. 51–2.

[137] Sir William Beveridge, *Social Insurance and Allied Services* (1942. Cmd. 6404).

6 Plans for Post-war Reconstruction

The common national disaster and triumph of Dunkirk, and the sharing of the hardships and dangers afterwards, had created a new spirit of national consciousness, demanding a new approach to the country's future. In response to 'the strong impulse to fuse the will to victory with aspirations for a better world after victory',[138] Churchill's Coalition Government set up a War Aims Committee of the War Cabinet in August 1940, although it was only in 1943 that a Minister of Reconstruction was appointed. A Minister without Portfolio had been assigned the duty of post-war planning since 1940, and it was as such that Mr Arthur Greenwood invited Sir William Beveridge to report on the insurance services.

The immediate occasion of the appointment of the Beveridge Committee was the protest by the trade unions at the suspension of the work of the Royal Commission on Workmen's Compensation in 1940. This protest, it may be noted in passing, was not the only contribution of the unions to post-war planning. The hopes of the TUC were embodied in its Interim Report of 1944, which proposed joint Industrial Boards for industrial development – the later Development Boards – as well as demanding policies for full employment. Many of the larger unions also made their own post-war plans, the miners, for example, drawing up the twelve-point 'Miners' Charter'.[139]

The Beveridge Report appeared in November 1942. Its main points were embodied in its six 'principles'.[140] The first was its comprehensiveness. It covered all the known causes of the 'giant', Want, by providing for unemployment benefit, sickness benefit, disability benefit, workmen's compensation, old age, widows' and orphans' pensions and benefits, funeral grants and maternity benefit. In addition to these financial provisions, the Report was also based on the assumption that a comprehensive health and rehabilitation service was to be established, and it made the further proposal that children's allowances should be paid to all. These two suggestions, translated into the National Health Service and Family Allowances, became as vital to the fabric of the Welfare State as social insurance itself. Lastly, a system of 'National Assistance' was to be maintained to cover those who despite all forethought did not fit into any of the categories of beneficiaries and those for whom the benefits paid were insufficient. The scheme was to be comprehensive also in the sense of covering the whole population, whether employed, occupied or unoccupied.

The second principle was that of unification of administrative responsibility. Instead of the nine different Government departments, and the multitude of local authorities and 'approved societies'[141] there was to be a single scheme, a single Ministry, and a single weekly stamp to be paid by the insured person and his employer to cover all the insurance provisions.

---

[138] W. K. Hancock and M. M. Gowing, *British War Economy* (1949), p. 534.

[139] N. Barou, *British Trade Unions* (1947), pp. 184–5, chapter 16; PEP, *British Trade Unionism* (1948), p. 147; D. F. MacDonald, *The State and the Trade Unions* (1960), p. 134.

[140] Sir William Beveridge, *Social Insurance and Allied Services* (1942. Cmd. 6404), Paras. 303–9.

[141] W. A. Robson (ed.), *Social Security* (3rd ed., 1948), Introduction, p. 35.

Thirdly, there was classification. The whole population was grouped from the outset in six main classes, and their contribution rates and benefit rights laid down from the beginning. The classes were: wage and salary earners, others gainfully occupied, housewives, others of working age, those below working age and retired persons above working age.

The fourth principle was that of adequate benefits. After careful study, the minimum needs were established and (subject to variations of the cost of living) paid as the standard for all types of benefit, in place of the illogical differences of the rates under existing schemes. Only two exceptions were to be made, a lower rate for old-age pensioners in the early years of the scheme, because of their lower contributions in the course of their working life, and a higher rate in some cases of prolonged incapacity and industrial injury, the former 'workmen's compensation'.

The fifth principle, closely allied to the fourth, was that of flat-rate benefits, according to the size of the family, and irrespective of normal earnings or length of benefit. Corresponding to it was the sixth principle, flat-rate contribution. Of the tripartite income of the Insurance Fund, the Exchequer and local authorities were to contribute about 50%, insured persons (including the self-employed) about 30%, and employers about 20%. The scheme as a whole implied a considerable increase in social security payments. For 1945, for example, these would rise to 10·7% of net national income, compared with 6·4% under the old rates and 7·1% before the war. In future years, this proportion would drop slightly with rising national income, in spite of the heavier burden of the old-age pensions.[142]

Though radical in the changes it proposed, the Beveridge Plan was not revolutionary. It resembled the British educational system in providing a national minimum by the State while allowing those who could afford it to buy better provisions, in the field of superannuation, for example, and, as it turned out, in the medical service also. Moreover, it was the natural culmination of the development of the 1930s and this perhaps explains the remarkable support it received. Its popular appeal was immense, 250,000 copies of the full report and 350,000 of an official abridgement being sold within a few months. Only the Government appeared hostile, though it did not oppose the plan openly.[143]

The hostility of the Government was the less understandable since its most likely ground for misgivings, finance, was taken care of by Beveridge's 'deal' with Keynes representing the Treasury, whereby the additional burdens on the Treasury in the early years were limited to £100 million per annum, largely by postponing the full benefits for old-age pensioners. The Government's own proposals, set forth in two white papers in September 1944,[144] fell short of Beveridge's proposals, especially in respect of the principle of 'adequacy',

[142] R. W. B. Clarke, 'The Beveridge Report and After', and 'Social Security Housekeeping', in *Social Security*; D. C. Marsh, *National Insurance and Assistance in Great Britain* (1950), pp. 65–9; Karl de Sohweinitz, *England's Road to Social Security* (1943), pp. 228–44; Sir W. H. Beveridge, *Pillars of Security* (1942).

[143] Lord Beveridge, *Power and Influence* (1953), chapters 14, 15. For a critical view, see J. W. Nisbet and others, *The Beveridge Plan* (1943).

[144] *Social Insurance*, Part I (1944. Cmd. 6550) and Part II (1944. Cmd. 6551). W. H. Beveridge, 'Epilogue', in *Social Security*, pp. 412–17.

but in many other respects followed them closely. The two parallel proposals for a complete and comprehensive health service after the war, which owed a great deal to the *Draft Interim Report* of the Medical Planning Commission of the BMA and the Royal Colleges in 1942,[145] and for family allowances respectively, were, however, adopted by the Coalition Government during the war, the latter being enacted in June 1945.

Though social security bulked largest in the public eye, the central place in the Government's social reconstruction plan was reserved to the policy for full employment. The Beveridge Report also had made its maintenance one of its basic requirements. It had to assume unemployment at no less than the disastrously high average rate of $8\frac{1}{2}\%$, but Beveridge, with the help of a brilliant team of economists, prepared a second, unofficial report, proposing means of reducing the post-war unemployment rate to 3%.[146] Even before its appearance in November 1944, the Government had brought out its own white paper on Employment Policy[147] in May. Though still hedged with qualifications[148] the white paper marks a decisive turning point in the Government's acceptance 'as one of their primary aims and responsibilities . . . the maintenance of a high and stable level of employment after the war'.

The Government also prepared other social reconstruction plans. The policy for education was outlined in a white paper[149] and incorporated in the Education Act of 1944. This raised the school age to 15 (postponed, in the event, to 1947), foreshadowed its extension to 16, and enacted free secondary education for all. The uses of land and town planning were discussed in three official reports and in a Government white paper in 1944,[150] and in 1943 an independent Ministry of Town and Country Planning was set up. There were also specific plans made for housing after the war,[151] and in 1944 there was a white paper on 'Scientific Research and Development'.[152]

These were long-term plans of reconstruction, but there were the immediate problems of demobilization also. 'The "run-down" of war industry had begun a long time before victory in Europe was in sight and continued long after it had been achieved.'[153] The labour force in the munition industry had begun to be reduced in 1943, permitting some increased recruitment to the Forces, as well as conversion to peacetime and export needs. From the autumn of 1944 on, war contracts were broken on a large scale.[154] When hostilities were actually at an end, a vast controlled demobilization programme as well as tremendous shifts between industries, had to be carried out.

---

[145] *A National Health Service* (Feb. 1944. Cmd. 6502); *British Medical Journal*, 20 June 1942, pp. 743–53.
[146] W. H. Beveridge, *Full Employment in a Free Society* (1944), pp. 21, 126–8.
[147] Cmd. 6527.
[148] U. K. Hicks, *Public Finance* (1947), pp. 325–9, chapter 18.
[149] *Educational Reconstruction* (1944. Cmd. 6548).
[150] *Royal Commission on the Distribution of the Industrial Population* (Barlow Report) (1939. Cmd. 6153); *Committee on Land Utilisation in Rural Areas* (Scott Report) (1942. Cmd. 6378); *Expert Committee on Compensation and Betterment* (Uthwatt Report) (1942. Cmd. 6386); *The Control of Land Use* (1944. Cmd. 6537).
[151] *Housing* (1945. Cmd. 6609).
[152] Cmd. 6514.
[153] M. M. Postan, *British War Production* (1952), p. 371.
[154] W. Ashworth, *Contracts and Finance* (1953), p. 64.

Between the middle of 1945 and the end of 1946, for example, engineering lost half a million workers, mostly women, and building gained over half a million, nearly all men. Much of this transition had been planned well before the end of the war.[155]

Post-war planning also had to consider international economic relationships and policies. They had not been forgotten in wartime negotiations[156] and when the world lay at their feet, the two principal western Allies, Britain and the USA, together with the other Allies, determined the ground plans, not only for the political framework of the United Nations, but also for the operative conditions of post-war economic life.

Governments and peoples alike felt that international economic relations had been among the least satisfactory aspects of the pre-war world. Among the basic weaknesses in the 1930s, inhibiting international trade by a vicious circle of tariffs and restrictions, had been international illiquidity, the shortage in the hands of potential buyers of currencies of the potential sellers. An international bank, holding a generally acceptable currency, could provide the initial liquidity that could carry a much higher level of international trade on the basis of similar national resources. Plans to create such a world authority were first drafted in 1941 by Keynes in Britain and by Harry D. White in the USA, and as both tended to reflect the particular needs of their countries, they found their respective schemes championed by the two Governments. The economic strength of the United States ensured that her proposal was the one which was ultimately accepted, but not before many amendments representing British views had been inserted.[157]

The final scheme, as agreed to at the historic Bretton Woods Conference in July 1944,[158] was in two parts, one dealing with the problem of international liquidity by means of the 'International Monetary Fund, and the other establishing a 'Bank for Reconstruction and Development' for long-term loans. For Britain the Fund was of far greater importance.

By the rules adopted by the IMF, each country paid a contribution to the Fund roughly according to its economic strength, and this was to be made partly in gold and largely in the member's own currency. These quota contributions were held by the Fund, to be available to any member state finding itself short of the currency of another, in exchange for its own, at fixed parity rates. It was clear to all the delegates that the IMF (as indeed the Bank) would in the first instance be used largely to make United States dollars available to

---

[155] E. L. Hargreaves and M. M. Gowing, *Civil Industry and Trade* (1952), pp. 618–27; H. M. D. Parker, *Manpower* (1957), chapter 16; Ministry of Labour and National Service, *Report, 1939–1946*, pp. 73ff., 194 ff.

[156] Cf. p. 222 above.

[157] R. F. Harrod, *Life of John Maynard Keynes* (1951), chapter 13; Richard N. Gardner, *Sterling–Dollar Diplomacy* (Oxford, 1956), chapter 5; J. H. Williams, *Post-War Monetary Plans* (New York, 1947), essays 8–11; Joan Robinson, 'The International Currency Proposals', in *The New Economics* (ed. Seymour E. Harris) (1949); R. Triffin, *Europe and the Money Muddle* (New Haven, 1957), chapter 3; Jacob Viner, 'Two Plans for International Monetary Stabilization', in *International Economics* (Glencoe, Ill., 1951); Brian Tew, *International Monetary Co-operation 1945–1952* (1952), chapters 6, 7; Alvin H. Hansen, *America's Role in the World Economy* (1945), chapters 4–7; A. J. Youngson, *The British Economy 1920–1957* (1960), pp. 155–6.

[158] *United Nations Monetary and Financial Conference, Final Act* (1944. Cmd. 6546).

the rest of the world, and their attitudes to the provisions of the Fund were largely coloured by that fact. Thus the United States insisted successfully on 'limited liability', i.e. a fixed quota, so that there was a clear limit to the total dollars to be contributed, as also on a penalty for being a persistent international borrower on short-term account. It was a measure of British influence on American thinking that there was also a penalty on the country running a persistent surplus – the 'scarce currency' clause, which permitted other members to take protective measures against the country whose currency was in such demand that the Fund's holding of it was running down; in the circumstances, this was most likely to be the American dollar.

The Fund could not, and was not intended to, correct a fundamental and persistent disequilibrium; it was merely to act as a substantial buffer in the case of a temporary unbalance. Member states bound themselves not to devalue their currencies, except under certain conditions to 'correct a fundamental disequilibrium', not to discriminate against other member states and, after a transitional period, not to place restrictions on current international payments. There were, at the time, further negotiations in progress to lower tariffs and other trade restrictions and discriminations, and these ultimately led to the General Agreement on Tariffs and Trade (GATT) in 1947.

Other international obligations undertaken by Britain included the agreement to share in the costs of the United Nations Relief and Rehabilitation Administration (UNRRA),[159] the agency which prevented starvation and diseases from ravaging much of Europe, Asia and other parts of the world after the fighting; the Hot Springs Agreement, establishing the Food and Agriculture Organization (FAO);[160] and the International Labour Organization (ILO) surviving from the days of the League of Nations.[161]

Throughout all the discussions that were to shape the post-war world, Britain's vote tended to be cast for protection and discrimination. The reason was that having lost so many sources of her invisible earnings, and, at least temporarily, her power to produce for export, Britain foresaw the most dire threat to the pound sterling and to her balance of payments if freedom of trade and exchange were to be allowed too quickly. From the viewpoint of mid-1945, before the war had yet ended, the British current balance for 1946, after the end of lend-lease, appeared as shown in Table 5·14.[162]

Table 5·14: The British expected balance of payments, 1946

	1938	1946 estimate
Deficit on visible trade	− 300	− 650
Government expenditure abroad	− 16	− 300
Net invisible income	+ 248	+ 120
Total unfavourable balance (including some other items)	−	− 750

[159] UNRRA, *Resolutions and Reports Adopted by the Council* (1943. Cmd. 6497).

[160] *Final Act of the United Nations Conference on Food and Agriculture* (1943. Cmd. 6451); *Documents relating to the Food and Agriculture Organisation of the United Nations* (1945. Cmd. 6590).

[161] Hansen, chapters 10–13; Sir Frederick Leggett, 'The Contribution of the ILO', in Ministry of Labour and National Service, *The Worker in Industry* (1952).

[162] Hancock and Gowing, p. 549.

Even with the most vigorous export drive and import controls, the adverse balance was unlikely to disappear before 1951, by which time it might have accumulated to a total of £1,250 million. The Treasury experts making these forecasts could not then know that the war against Japan would barely out-last that in Europe, that lend-lease would be abolished at once at its end, and that several other unfavourable factors would combine to make Britain's post-war position far worse than they had dared to imagine in their most pessimistic moments.

6

Reconversion to Peace, 1945–1950

1 The Dollar Problem and the Sterling Crises

The gloomy forecasts about the British balance of payments, with which the last chapter ended, rested on two basic facts. The first was that Britain had for years lived beyond her means by consuming her capital, by borrowing and by gifts from abroad, and that these had to cease in the summer of 1945, leaving a large gap. The second was that the disruption and diversion of British productive capacity during the war had been so violent that, to fill that gap, several years would be needed before it could be restored to its full peace-time efficiency. The years of that restoration form the framework of this chapter.

The year chosen as the end of that period, 1950, is a somewhat arbitrary mark. In some respects 1949 would be a better date, seeing the end, for example, of the period of basic foreign exchange disequilibrium; if the political view is taken, 1951 was the year in which the Labour Government handed over to the Conservatives; and the economic repercussions of the Korean War did not give way to 'normalcy' until 1952 or 1953. In this chapter the artificial limit of the date chosen will be broken whenever events require it. But, broadly, 1950 may be taken as indicating the watershed when the worst of the effects of the war were over and when Britain had returned to a position comparable with that at the outbreak of war.

The war had left several fundamental economic problems, and some of these will be discussed in the next section; but the foreign balance was the most obvious, and appeared the most urgent. Unless large unrequited imports could be brought in to replace lend-lease supplies, the economy was likely to grind to a standstill for lack of fuel, raw materials and food. The only possible sources of supply in a war-ravaged world were in North America, and in order to tap them, Britain had to ask for an American loan.

In the negotiations over this loan, the causes of Britain's foreign trade weakness were put most succinctly.[1] While imports for a larger, more active population could not be cut much below those of pre-war, commodity exports had been reduced to little more than a third in the war, and the sources of invisible exports had also greatly diminished: total merchant shipping, for example, was down from 22·1 to 15·9 million dw. tons (ocean-going vessels of 1,600 tons and over); one-quarter of overseas investments, worth £1,118 million, had been sold off, while the overseas debt was

---

[1] *Statistical Material Presented During the Washington Negotiations* (December 1945. Cmd. 6707); cf. also H. S. Booker, *The Problem of Britain's Overseas Trade* (1948), chapters, 5, 9.

increased by a rise in 'sterling balances' from £476 million to £3,355 million by June 1945 and £3,567 million by the end of the year. To meet this gap, exports would have to be raised by at least 50% in volume above pre-war; to meet at the same time the need of repaying the sterling debt, of building up a shrunken gold and dollar reserve, and of investments in the more backward parts of the Empire, the volume of exports would have to be raised by 75%, at least, and this figure became one of the main 'targets' of economic planning. Even that level was unduly optimistic, for it neglected the import content of increased export goods production (perhaps +15% of imports) and the likely deterioration in the terms of trade.[2] It would take 3–5 years to reach that level of 175% of pre-war exports, and meanwhile an adverse balance of at least £1,250 million would have accumulated. This was the sum which the Americans were asked to cover by a loan.

From the American point of view, however, Britain was only one of many countries seeking aid, and among them she was the least to claim pity on grounds of poverty, and the most to be feared as a potential trade rival. Ultimately a 'line of credit' of $3,750 million was granted to Britain, plus $650 million to pay the outstanding lend-lease debts, and to this the Canadians added a loan, on the same terms, of $1,250 million. The terms themselves were not ungenerous, interest being at 2%, to become payable, together with the capital repayments over 50 years, only in 1951. But there were 'strings'. One was the undertaking by Britain to reduce the sterling balances. Much more serious was the obligation to apply the Bretton Woods terms, not within five years after ratification, as originally agreed, but within a year of the actual granting of the loan, i.e. by July 1947.

This latter condition would inevitably endanger the 'dollar pool' and the pound sterling. It would prevent Britain from using her strong importer position in bilateral trade treaties to the greatest effect, while the Americans did not even undertake to *reduce* their tariff. With the 1930s in mind, Britain was particularly alarmed at being left defenceless against an expected American slump, which would aggravate the dollar payments problem.[3] There was widespread opposition to the acceptance of these onerous terms,[4] but the United Kingdom was not in a position to refuse.

Meanwhile, the high hopes placed on the international institutions designed to ensure a freer flow of trade were being generally disappointed. The International Trade Organization, proposed in December 1945,[5] was stillborn, and the more modest General Agreement on Tariffs and Trade[6] (the Havana Charter), designed to *eliminate* discrimination but only *reduce* tariffs, was being ratified very slowly and came into operation only in 1948.

---

[2] PEP, *Britain and World Trade* (1947), pp. 61 ff.

[3] PEP, *op. cit.*, chapters 7, 9; O. Hoeffding, 'The US, and World Trade', in Mark Abrams (ed.), *Britain and Her Export Trade* (1946).

[4] *Financial Agreement Between the Governments of the United States and the United Kingdom* (1945. Cmd. 6708); Richard N. Gardner, *Sterling-Dollar Diplomacy* (Oxford, 1956), chapters 10, 11; R. D. Hall, *North American Supply* (1955), pp. 477–9; but see R. F. Harrod, *A Page of British Folly* (1946).

[5] *Proposals for Consideration by an International Conference on Trade and Employment* (1945. Cmd. 6709).

[6] 1947. Cmd. 7258.

The International Monetary Fund was, perhaps, even less satisfactory. Its funds proved too small to carry the strain of the vast unbalance in world trade that was rapidly developing; its total transactions amounted to $600 million while American aid outside it (excluding UNRRA and lend-lease) amounted to $20 billion.[7] It had, in fact, been designed to deal with deflationary policies and fears of depression spreading from one country to another, not with persistent dollar shortages: with the problems, in other words, of the 1930s and not of the late 1940s. It could, therefore, do little to cure the world's main economic ailment, which appeared in every country in turn as a dollar shortage or a dollar 'gap'.

The dollar shortage in the rest of the world, as in Britain, was caused by the desperate need for goods and services which could be obtained only in the dollar area – for dollars. In a sense, therefore, it was a transient phenomenon, a consequence of the shattering of productive capacity in the war without a parallel reduction in people's expected real income. Its very universality, however, induced the widespread belief that it was permanent and part of the structure of the world's economy, and even that it had begun in the inter-war years.[8]

Europe's population was rising and its food production falling behind (see Table 6·1).[9]

Table 6·1:   European population and food production

Average of years	Index of population	Index of output, 5 grains	Average of years	Index of output, 7 crops, weighted by value
1912–14	100	100	1909–13	100
1937–9	115	110	1934–8	113
1947–9	113	84	1949–50	103

In addition, many of the European raw materials were nearing exhaustion. The terms of trade were bound to turn against the industrialized countries,[10] and Western Europe was bound to lose her trade surplus even with the non-dollar primary producers. Since, further, American productivity was rising faster than that of the rest of the world, and the USA, unlike Britain in the days of her hegemony, neither allowed imports freely into the country, nor

[7] T. Balogh, 'The International Aspect', in G. D. N. Worswick and P. H. Ady, *The British Economy, 1945–1950* (Oxford, 1952), pp. 504–5; Gardner, chapters 14–17; J. H. Williams, *Post-War Monetary Plans* (Oxford, 1949), essays 5–7; Brian Tew, *International Monetary Co-operation 1945–1952* (1952), chapters 7, 8; Sir Hubert D. Henderson, 'A Criticism of the Havana Charter', *Amer. Econ. Rev.*, 39/3, 1949; Donald B. Marsh, *World Trade and Investment* (New York, 1951), pp. 423–4, chapters 26–29, 32.

[8] p. 116 above; also J. R. Sargent, 'Britain and Europe', in *The British Economy 1945–1950*; Elliott Zupnick, *Britain's Postwar Dollar Problem* (New York, 1957) chapters 5 and 6; G. Crowther, *Balances and Imbalances of Payments* (Boston, Mass., 1957), p. 34.

[9] Ingvar Svennilsen, *Growth and Stagnation in the European Economy* (UK, Geneva, 1954), pp. 236–7, 247, *passim*.

[10] C. P. Kindleberger, 'Industrial Europe's Terms of Trade on Current Account, 1870–1953', *Econ. J.*, 65/257, 1955.

invested her surpluses freely abroad, but, on the contrary, went in for deflationary policies, the dollar gap was growing ever wider.[11] Keynes was almost alone in maintaining, in a posthumous article,[12] that the dollar shortage would be short-lived.

Whether temporary or permanent, Britain had to adjust herself to the dollar shortage for the time being. Considerable successes were achieved in expanding British exports, especially to dollar and other 'hard currency' areas, but the drain on the gold and dollar reserves continued. In July 1946, the dollars of the 'line of credit' became available, and it was intended that they should last until 1951, by which time equilibrium was to be restored but it soon became clear that the loan was drawn on much more rapidly than was safe: in the year to 30 June 1947, purchases from hard currency areas totalled $1,540 million, sales to them only $340 million. A harsh winter was followed by a fuel crisis which held up production and transport and was estimated to have cost £200 million in exports; invisible earnings were disappointing; and the terms of trade turned sharply against the United Kingdom, adding £329 million to the import bill in 1947.[13]

It was in these unpropitious circumstances that the convertibility of sterling had to be permitted on 15 July, under the terms of the dollar loan. The run on the dollar pool was immediate, as almost every country with sterling earnings hurried to convert them into dollars.[14] The drain on the dollar reserve was so alarming that the restrictions had to be put on again after barely one month. The gold and dollar reserves fell in the course of 1947 by over $600 million, or one-quarter. On current balance of payments, there was a deficit of £545 million in the course of the year; with the dollar area alone, of £571 million.[15]

A similar dollar crisis hit the whole of Western Europe in 1947, threatening European recovery and standards of living. Against the background of an emergent 'cold war' between East and West, General Marshall offered massive American aid to Europe in June 1947, provided Europe adopted a measure of economic co-operation. This was eagerly accepted by the governments of Western Europe, who met in September 1947 as the Committee of European Economic Co-operation (CEEC) of 16 nations and prepared a four-year 'plan'. Congress approved 'Marshall Aid' in April 1948, and in September 1948 Western Europe agreed on its distribution. The European Recovery Programme (ERP) provided over $6 billion in its first year (1948–9)

[11] E.g. T. Balogh, *The Dollar Crisis, Cause and Cure* (Oxford, 1950), chapter 1, and 'The Dollar Crisis Revisited', *Oxf. Econ. P.*, NS, 6/2, 1954; J. H. Williams, *Economic Stability in the Modern World* (Oxford, 1952); A. J. Brown, 'Dollars and Crises', *Ec. Hist. Rev.*, 2nd S., 12/2, 1959, pp. 287–90; Seymour E. Harris, *The European Recovery Program* (Cambridge, Mass., 1948), pp. 96 ff.; R. G. Hawtrey, *The Balance of Payments and the Standard of Living* (1950), chapters 4 and 5; Donald MacDougall, *The World Dollar Problem* (1957), esp. chapter 15, Appx. IA and XVc.

[12] J. M. Keynes, 'The Balance of Payments of the United States', *Econ. J.*, 56/222, 1946; cf. also R. F. Harrod, *Life of John Maynard Keynes* (1951), p. 621; R. Triffin, *Gold and the Dollar Crisis* (New Haven, 1960), p. 5.

[13] A. J. Youngson, *The British Economy 1920–1957* (1960), pp. 164–8.

[14] Cf. Paul Bareau, 'The Position of Sterling in International Trade', in Institute of Bankers, *Banking and Foreign Trade* (1953).

[15] *UK Balance of Payments 1946–1950* (No. 2) (1951. Cmd. 8201).

and \$3·8 billion in the next year, plus \$700 million for military aid ('Mutual Defence Assistance'). Thereafter recovery aid tapered off, Britain declining Marshall Aid after the end of 1950, but the Marshall plan had fulfilled its main function of carrying Europe over its critical deficit years.[16] It had also induced closer co-operation among European nations, beginning with the first inter-European payments scheme in October 1948 and ending in the fully-fledged European Payments Union (EPU) of 1950, which encouraged European trade by creating liquidity and mutual credit.[17]

The United Kingdom drew its share of Marshall Aid, while its trade balance also improved impressively in 1948. But at the end of 1948 the relaxation of controls and the booming home demand again made inroads into the precarious balance of payments,[18] while a slight recession in the USA made dollar sales more difficult. A sustained attack on sterling began in international markets[19] and forced the Chancellor to devalue the pound sterling in September 1949, from \$4·03 to \$2·80.

The extent of the devaluation, 30·5%, was far larger than seemed warranted by internal purchasing power or by international markets. Apart from the Sterling Area itself, few of the other countries followed Britain's devaluation to that extreme, Italy, for example, devaluing by 8%, Belgium by 13% and Germany by 20%.[20]

Further, the decision to devalue at all was questionable, nor did it improve Britain's international competitive position[21] for in the existing conditions of import control little could be hoped for from reduced imports, while exports had been held back, not so much by high costs as by sheer inability to produce. After the devaluation, more scarce resources would have to be devoted to exports to buy the identical quantum of imports, and higher import prices would boost inflation.[22] Both the cause of the speculators' attack on sterling and its cure bore a disheartening resemblance to those of 1931.

In many ways, the devaluation was a turning point. It marked the failure of the Government's economic policy, and no alternative was evolved before its defeat at the polls in 1951. It was a flagrant violation of the Bretton Woods Agreement, in spirit if not in letter (the Fund being forced to sanction it as a virtual *fait accompli*), and contributed no little to its weakness and to the

---

[16] J. H. Williams, 'The Task of Economic Recovery', in *Post War Monetary Plans* (Oxford, 1949); H. B. Price, *The Marshall Plan and Its Meaning* (Ithaca, NY), 1955; Robert E. Summers (ed.), *Economic Aid to Europe: The Marshall Plan* (New York, 1948); OEEC, *9th Report. A Decade of Co-operation. Achievements and Perspectives* (Paris, 1958); Triffin, *Europe and the Money Muddle* (New Haven, 1957), chapters 3 and 4; T. Balogh, *Dollar Crisis*, chapter 2.

[17] R. Triffin, *Europe and the Money Muddle*, chapter 5; but see Per Jacobsson, 'Trade and Financial Relations between Countries – the Progress Towards Multilateralism', in Institute of Bankers, *Banking and Foreign Trade* (1953).

[18] Gilbert Walker, *Economic Planning* (1957), pp. 109–29; pp. 247–8 below.

[19] A. A. Rogow, *The Labour Government and British Industry 1945–1951* (Oxford, 1955), pp. 35–6, 121–2.

[20] Tew, *op. cit.*, chapter 9.

[21] M. J. Flanders, 'The Effects of Devaluation on Exports, a Case Study: United Kingdom 1949–54', *Oxford University Institute of Statistics Bulletin*, 25/3, 1963.

[22] Hawtrey, *op. cit.*, pp. 99–111; Triffin, *Money Muddle*, p. 75; R. F. Harrod, *Policy Against Inflation* (1958), pp. 132–51.

general disillusionment with the post-war international institutions. With the ending of the speculative attack, the gold and dollar reserves rose again quickly, from $1,425 million at the end of September 1949 to $2,422 million in mid-1950, and by that time the rapidly rising volume of output and exports was beginning to restore the long-term trade balance. Though the Korean War and the stockpiling crisis associated with it in 1951 caused the third of what threatened to be regular economic crises in alternate years, British economic recovery was by then firmly set.

The main movements are illustrated by the following statistics (£m. except the last two columns)[23] (see Table 6·2).

Table 6·2: The British balance of trade

	Exports A	Balance of visible trade B	Total current balance of payments C	Change in sterling liabilities D	Inter-government transactions, + = receipts by UK − = payments by UK E	Other capital movements F	Changes in gold and dollar reserves G	Board of Trade, 1947 = 100 H	ECA mission,* 1938 = 100
1946	917	− 165	− 295	+ 43	+ 240	+ 99	+ 87	87**	108
1947	1,145	− 415	− 442	− 112	+ 639	− 301	− 216	100	117
1948	1,602	− 192	+ 7	− 346	+ 437	− 167	− 69	102	121
1949	1,841	− 137	+ 38	− 9	+ 160	− 207	− 18	101	122
1950	2,250	− 133	+ 297	+ 340	+ 127	− 81	+ 683	108	133
1951	2,748	− 733	− 419	+ 94	− 36	− 266	− 627	123	159†

* MSA Mission to the United Kingdom, *Economic Development in the United Kingdom, 1850–1950*, pp. 104–5.
** 1938.
† June 1951.

The success of the export drive was quite outstanding, exports increasing even in real terms by 77% between 1946 and 1950. By 1948, the diminished annual dollar deficits were met largely by the net dollar earnings of the raw materials producers of the rest of the Sterling Area.[24] At the same time, British trade with the rest of the Sterling Area also became increasingly favourable.[25]

What was at least as heartening as the 'phenomenal growth of British exports' which 'would have staggered the reconstruction planners of 1943–5 and even the Marshall Aid planners of 1947'[26] was their changed composition. Unlike her balance of the inter-war years, Britain was largely concentrating on the growth sectors of world trade:[27]

[23] *United Kingdom Balance of Payments, 1946–1954* (1954. Cmd. 9291); also *Committee on the Working of the Monetary System* (Radcliffe Report) (1959. Cmnd. 827), p. 234; G. D. H. Cole, *The Post-War Condition of Britain* (1956), chapters 13, 14; *Annual Abstract of Statistics*.

[24] *Radcliffe Report*, paras. 649–56; D. H. Robertson, *Britain in the World Economy* (1954), p. 49; *United Kingdom Balance of Payments 1946–1953* (1953. Cmd. 8976).

[25] J. R. Sargent, 'Britain and the Sterling Area', in *The British Economy, 1945–1950*.

[26] *Radcliffe Report*, para. 402.

[27] P. D. Henderson, 'Britain's International Position', in *The British Economy, 1945–1950*, p. 70; F. H. Awad, 'The Structure of the World Export Trade, 1926–1952', *Yorkshire Bulletin*, 11/1, 1959, p. 35; PEP, *Britain and World Trade* (1947), p. 117, also chapter 8.

Table 6·3: British export composition

Proportion of Exports in 1952–3	United Kingdom	World
Among expanding commodities	65·0%	53·6%
Among stable commodities	4·7	17·5
Among declining commodities	30·3	28·9

The improvement in the current balance of payments (Table 6·2, column C), except for the disastrous Korean War year of 1951, plus the proceeds from loans and aid (column E) were dissipated, not in strengthening the precarious reserves (column G), but in making foreign investments, probably under-estimated in the table;[28] and in paying off some of the sterling balances (columns F and D).[29] Thus the vulnerability of sterling at the beginning of the period was not yet cured at the end. With a reserve of barely £1,000 million, a swing of £200–300 million in any one year, relatively minute in comparison with the total trade of the Sterling Area, of £10,000, would still cause a major crisis.

Critics were not wanting who attacked the order of priorities. Foreign investments at the rate of £1,650 million in six years 1945–51, were considered to be too high. Expenditure on maintaining troops abroad could also have been cut, and a strong case could be made for cutting imports rather than increasing exports, with the incidental merit of turning the terms of trade less sharply against Britain.[30]

The dollar 'gap' and the foreign balance as a whole could not, in fact, be divorced from general economic policy. External unbalance after the war had the same roots as the domestic inflation, namely a rate of incomes and welfare schemes incommensurate with real output and thus a level of *ex-ante* plans of real consumption spending and investment which production did not warrant,[31] but which all classes considered to be their right as victors in a long and weary struggle. Formally, it was the same excess of incomes over output which created the foreign unbalance and the domestic inflationary pressure, and to understand the former fully, it is therefore necessary to turn to a consideration of domestic economic policy.

2 Full Employment Policies in Practice

Economic policy making by the post-war Government was dominated by its inheritance of a large measure of suppressed inflation, i.e. an excess of purchasing power over goods available at current prices, prevented from resulting in open inflation only by price control and physical restrictions. In that sense the war-time Keynesian 'National Income' budgeting had not been harsh enough, for it had been unable to prevent the accumulation of potentially inflationary funds, ready to burst forth as soon as the control

[28] A. R. Conan, *Capital Imports into Sterling Countries* (1960), pp. 82–6; ECE, *Economic Survey of Europe in 1949* (Geneva, 1950), pp. 124–6.
[29] R. F. Harrod, *Policy Against Inflation* (1958), pp. 111 ff.
[30] R. F. Harrod, *Are These Hardships Necessary?* (1947), and *Life of Keynes*, pp. 615–16; H. S. Booker, *op. cit.*, pp. 168–71; S. E. Harris, *European Recovery Program*, pp. 37–41.
[31] Triffin, *Money Muddle*, chapter 2.

barriers were removed. The banks were in a state of over-liquidity which was potentially even more dangerous.[32]

The liquid assets of the personal sector had changed as shown in Table 6·4.[33]

Table 6·4:   The growth of liquid assets

	1938	£ million 1946	1951	% Change 1938–46
Net personal deposits in London Clearing Banks	*c.* 560	1,423	1,675	*c.* +154
Building Society deposits and shares	682	785	1,216	+ 15
Post Office savings bank deposits	495	1,910	1,902	+286
Trustee savings bank deposits	233	643	917	+176
Total liquid assets	*c.* 1,970	4,762	5,710	*c.* +142
Personal disposable income	4,675	7,569	10,389	+ 62
Liquid assets as % of incomes	42%	63%	55%	

Similarly, 'tender' Treasury Bills had risen from £650 million before the war to £1,800 million, the banks held £1,800 million of TDRs, and total money supply as a proportion of national income was 52·4% in 1939, 69·6% in 1945, rising to a peak of 79·2% in 1947.[34] The total excess liquidity in the economy was of the order of magnitude of £3 billion, or a year's tax revenue.[35]

This state of suppressed inflation was highly unstable, but opinion differed widely on the best methods of dealing with it. To follow the model of 1918–19 by removing the controls as quickly as possible was hardly practical politics. More realistic was the proposal of a tax on capital or savings, disguised, perhaps, as a currency 'reform'.[36] The methods used in several continental countries were ably canvassed here,[37] but the Labour Government at no time seriously considered any measure of confiscating capital, apart from the small 'special contribution' of the budget of April 1948. A third group of proposals, favoured by many economists, was for a deflationary policy, including high interest rates, in order to let 'the market', rather than the Government, decide where the necessary cuts were to be made.[38] Apart from

---

[32] Cf., in general, G. D. N. Worswick, 'The British Economy 1945-50', in G. D. N. Worswick and P. H. Ady, *The British Economy 1945-1950* (Oxford, 1952); also R. F. Harrod, *Policy Against Inflation* (1958), pp. 93–106; Edward Nevin and E. W. Davis, *The London Clearing Banks* (1970), p. 149.

[33] *Committee on the Working of the Monetary System (Radcliffe Report)* (1959. Cmnd. 827), Table 22.

[34] W. Manning Dacey, *The British Banking Mechanism* (2nd rev. ed., 1958), p. 176; *Radcliffe Report*, para. 46.

[35] R. G. Hawtrey, *The Balance of Payments and the Standard of Living* (1950), pp. 34–45.

[36] *Radcliffe Report*, para. 45.

[37] E.g. F. W. Paish, 'Planning and the Price System', in *The Post-War Financial Problem and Other Essays* (1950). Cf. also Thomas Wilson, *Inflation* (Oxford, 1961), pp. 153 ff. Keynes, in his essay *How to Pay for the War*, had also suggested a capital levy after the war.

[38] J. E. Meade, *Planning and the Price Mechanism* (1948); John Jewkes, *Ordeal by Planning* (1948).

the fact, however, that to be effective, rates would have to be fantastically high in view of the state of liquidity, this policy was basically only a more sophisticated version of the first, involving unemployment.

In the policy which it eventually adopted, the Government had the advantage of possessing vastly greater economic powers than any peacetime Government had ever possessed before, and it disposed of a larger share of the national income, public revenue (including that of local authorities and the Insurance Funds) amounting to 37·7% of gross national product in 1946 and 34·9% in 1951, compared with 19·0% in 1938.[39] But it had also more objectives to be pursued simultaneously. These included full employment, high and rising productivity, the retention of the more equitable income distribution and the welfare scheme of the war years, a healthy foreign trade balance, the maintenance of the value of the pound, and a speedy dismantling of the more irksome of the war restrictions and controls, among others.[40]

The Labour Government placed the greatest weight on the first two and considered the last two rather less important than some of the critics and this largely accounts for the differences in views.[41] But in pursuing so many objectives at once, it promoted measures which pulled in different directions.

Its main concern was undoubtedly to raise output as fast as possible, particularly of the basic and the export industries, but this brought it up against the shortage of capital. Though the destruction of capital in wartime was exaggerated by contemporaries, and manufacturing industry was better equipped than pre-war, net written down values of fixed assets having actually risen from $9·0 billion (1950 prices) in 1938 to $12·3 billion in 1948,[42] the needs were great to sustain rapid technological progress and substitute capital for imports. Yet savings had already been low in the 1930s and would be reduced still further by the redistribution of incomes, and it was clear that much of the investment would have to be made by the Government itself. Further, a regular budget surplus to remove the threat of the suppressed inflation would require a high rate of taxation, diminishing thereby the source of private savings still further.[43] Accordingly, the Government was torn between opposite taxation policies. In its first budget, it reduced the standard rate of income tax by 1*s*. and made other concessions, but later the need for a budget surplus, disinflation and high revenue to carry through the welfare and investment programme required periodic upward revision of tax rates.

The results of these (and other) conflicting aims behind the budget are summarized in Table 6·5.

---

[39] J. C. R. Dow, 'Fiscal Policy and Monetary Policy as Instruments of Economic Control', *Westminster Bank Review*, Aug. 1960, p. 12.

[40] E.g. *Radcliffe Report*, paras. 53–71.

[41] Hugh Dalton, *High Tide and After, Memoirs 1945–1960* (1962).

[42] F. W. Paish, 'Savings and Investment', *op. cit.*; cf. also C. A. R. Crosland, *Britain's Economic Problem* (1953), pp. 20–3; *Radcliffe Report*, paras. 31–41; F. W. Paish, 'The Post-War Financial Problem', *loc. cit.*; I. Bowen, *Britain's Industrial Survival* (1947), pp. 110 ff; T. Barna, 'Investment in Industry – Has Britain Lagged?', *The Banker*, April 1957, pp. 226, 229; also see p. 200 above.

[43] Findlay Weaver, 'Taxation and Redistribution in the United Kingdom', *Rev. of Econ. and Statistics*, 32/3, 1950.

Table 6·5: Post-war budgets and incidence of taxation(£m.)

	Revenue	Expenditure Excl. transfer to capital account	Surplus	Transfer to capital account	Direct taxes on capital	Taxes on outlay	Subsidies	Taxes on outlay, less subsidies
1938	1,017	1,099	−82	9	78	410	32	378
1946	3,364	3,742	−378	552	143	1,282	350	932
1947	3,440	3,271	169	393	164	1,478	444	1,034
1948	3,985	3,323	662	219	215	1,703	542	1,161
1949	4,270	3,519	751	248	254	1,655	496	1,159
1950	4,323	3,513	810	160	190	1,722	455	1,267

The most serious conflict, however, appeared to exist between the anti-inflationary budget and what became the most controversial of Dr Dalton's financial policies, the policy of 'cheap money'. Low and steady interest rates had been in operation since 1932 and were one of the accepted weapons to counteract a threatened depression. The post-war Chancellor, however, maintained them in a period of full employment and inflation, which meant, in effect, that the monetary weapon could not be used until 'cheap money' was ended in 1951.[44] The policy was not, however, entirely without justification.

To begin with, full employment could by no means be taken for granted. The white paper had assumed an average of $1\frac{1}{2}$ million persons out of work, the insurance contributions were calculated on a basis of $8\frac{1}{2}\%$ unemployment, and there was substantial unemployment in several continental countries at the time. A cheap money policy at least removed that danger. It was only after the fuel crisis in 1947 that scarcity, rather than surplus, was generally taken to be the main problem,[45] and only in 1951 that the Insurance Scheme officially used lower unemployment figures as the basis for its actuarial calculations.[46]

Secondly, low interest rates kept down the cost of borrowing, not only of the Government, but also of the local authorities, mainly for house building, and of some of the basic industries after their nationalization. They also kept down the sums payable abroad, as Britain was a net short-term borrower. These reductions, apart from being desirable in themselves, helped the first reconstruction schemes to be concentrated in the basic industries and in the biggest export earners. Thirdly, the policy permitted the Government to preserve, for some years, the redistributive gains of the war years in favour of the lower incomes.[47]

Against this policy it was urged that it weakened and distorted economic incentives, that it was inflationary and that, therefore, thirdly, it made necessary the retention of many irksome and inhibiting controls.[48] As for the

[44] For the state of opinion on using monetary policy again at that time, see the discussion in *Bull. Oxf. Inst. Stat.*, vol. 14, Nos. 4, 5, 8, 1952.

[45] Especially *Economic Survey* (1947. Cmd. 7046).

[46] A. T. Peacock, *The Economics of National Insurance* (1952), pp. 27, 119–20; *Report on Social Insurance and Allied Services* (*Beveridge Report*) (1942. Cmd. 6404), Appx. A., para. 14.

[47] F. W. Paish, 'Cheap Money Policy', *loc. cit.*; W. Manning Dacey, pp. 116 ff.

[48] A. J. Youngson, *The British Economy, 1920–1957* (1960), pp. 159–61.

first of these, the weakened incentive was the concomitant of full employment, and while some of the critics were consistent enough to state that 'a moderate degree of unemployment would do a great deal of good – on the two conditions . . . that it does not exceed 5 to 7 per cent . . . and that the total does not contain many pockets of heavy or long-continued unemployment',[49] this was a policy which all the political parties were specifically pledged to avoid. The 'misdirection' of resources was a matter of opinion: many of the controls were specifically imposed to correct the undesirable allocations by market forces.[50]

The other two arguments, which were closely linked, had more substance. The lowering of the rate on Consols by $\frac{3}{8}$% to $2\frac{1}{2}$% in January 1947 involved a large-scale creation of new short-term debt and of additional liquidity: deposits of the 11 clearing banks rose by £900 million in this period, of which perhaps one-half was due to this operation. The serried ranks of Government paper, added to the balances and the outstanding short- and medium-term loans of the war years, which had to be renewed at a rate of £600–£1,000 a year, made financial control of the Money Market by the Government (other than keeping the rates down) quite impossible.

Basically, the institutions of the Money Market had not changed during or after the war. The Bank of England was nationalized in 1946, and the holdings of Government paper by the 'Departments' had increased, but any modicum of increased Government control that might have derived from these changes was more than counterbalanced by the dead weight of liquidity created. Investments of the clearing banks had fallen from the pre-war figure of 70% of deposits to 46·8% in 1948, the rest of the mounting deposits being covered largely by Government short-term paper. The total bill holdings of the London clearing banks increased from £369 million at the end of 1945 to £1,408 million at the end of 1950, or nearly four-fold, while the total of investments plus advances was allowed to rise only from £2,049 million to £3,175 million, or by 50%.[51] In these conditions, the withdrawal of cash from the banks by the authorities was not pyramided into a substantial restriction of credit: it merely led to the reduction (or a refusal to take up more) of the banks' holdings of Treasury Bills and, up to 1952, TDRs. Nor was any other 'credit squeeze' likely to be effective when so much surplus liquidity was left in the system.[52]

Institutions, like Insurance Companies or pension funds, had dutifully absorbed much Government paper during the war and after; but the risk of capital losses (i.e. the risk that low rates could not be indefinitely maintained) was beginning to make them also unwilling to absorb more and eager to increase their equity holdings instead, with prospects of capital gains in a period of inflation.[53]

[49] *Economist*, 4 June 1949, p. 1026. In terms of numbers, 5–7% meant 1–1$\frac{1}{2}$ million unemployed.

[50] PEP, *Government and Industry* (1952), p. 41.

[51] W, Manning Dacey, chapter 8; C. N. Ward-Perkins, 'Banking Developments', in *The British Economy, 1945–1950*.

[52] Sir Oliver Franks, 'Bank Advances as an Object of Policy', *Lloyds Bank Review*, NS, No. 59, 1961, pp. 5–6.

[53] *Radcliffe Report*, paras. 145–8, 162 ff., 185 ff., 252 ff., also chapters 5, 9; G. Clayton,

Recognizing, in practice, that Government paper, rather than the availability of cash as such, was the source of liquidity, 'there has been no attempt in the post-war period to operate on the banking position by limiting the supply of cash: the banks have always been automatically provided with whatever was necessary.'[54] The limit of the fiduciary issue was after 1939 raised without question according to the needs for cash,[55] and the inflationary pressures generated after 1945 ran up against no money barriers.

Hence 'the controls' had to stay, and in the prevailing boom conditions it seemed to each entrepreneur that only they stood between him and the opportunities for making much greater profits, even though he might, in reality, have been far worse off in the chaos of their removal. The pressure for their abolition may have come from a very small section of society only, but it was a powerful section, and, exactly as after the 1914–18 war, it forced the Government steadily and relentlessly to dismantle the apparatus of control inherited from the war.[56] The real accusation against the cheap money policy was that it slowed down this process of dismantling.

The controls surviving after 1945 were many and various. Consumer rationing of clothing, furniture, petrol, soap and many foodstuffs was abolished by 1950, but the main foodstuffs were still rationed and coal still 'allocated', and there were still restrictions on tourists' expenditure and on hire-purchase agreements. These provided cause for popular grumbling, but were not the main reason for the gathering campaign for economic 'freedom'. Rationed foods (and others) were, however, subsidized, and subsidies could be attacked as contributing to the high taxation which reduced incentives for the higher income earners. Sir Stafford Cripps drastically reduced food subsidies in 1949 from an estimated £568 million to a maximum limit of £465 million, and to £410 million in 1950.

In other sectors, price control of non-food goods, raw material allocation, including that of steel, control over labour (reimposed briefly and ineffectually in 1947) had all been repealed by 1950, timber only remaining to 1951; in October 1948, a veritable 'bonfire of controls' had been lit by the Board of Trade, and by 1951 most of the 'utility specifications' had lost their bite.[57] Apart from exchange restrictions under the Exchange Control Act of 1947, and import restrictions, therefore, there was very little to restrain private enterprise.

Controls were much more persistent in the capital investment field.[58] Building licences were still tightly controlled and attempts were still made to put into practice the war-time blueprints for the planned use of land;[59] the

'The Role of the British Life Assurance Companies in the Capital Market, *Econ. J.*, 61/241, 1951, pp. 91–2; G. Clayton and W. T. Osborn, 'Insurance Companies and the Finance of Industry', *Oxf. Econ. P.*, NS, 10/1, 1958.

[54] *Radcliffe Report*, para. 430.

[55] W. Manning Dacey, chapter 11.

[56] A. A. Rogow, *The Labour Government and British Industry 1945–1951* (Oxford, 1955), chapter 3, pp. 138–72; J. D. Stewart, *British Pressure Groups* (Oxford, 1958); S. E. Finer, *Anonymous Empire* (1958), pp. 8–10.

[57] Gilbert Walker, *Economic Planning by Programme and Control in Great Britain* (1957), p. 147; G. D. N. Worswick, 'Direct Controls', in *The British Economy, 1945–1950*.

[58] PEP, *Government and Industry*, chapter 2; Rogow, pp. 27 ff.

[59] See p. 231 above; also N. Rosenberg, *Economic Planning in the British Building Industry, 1945–1949* (1960).

vast profits realized by 'developers' since, explain in part the bitter opposition to these controls. Other powers survived after 1951, including the Town and Country Planning Act. The six 'Development Areas', extensions of the former 'Special Areas', were aided under the Distribution of Industry Acts of 1945 and 1950, by Government funds for the construction of factories to be let to light industry at pre-war rents, and by other inducements, including services, facilities and loans. It was the difficulty of obtaining labour, licences and facilities elsewhere that made the efforts to deal with the deep-set problems of these districts temporarily successful.[60]

Apart from the physical controls over building and siting, the Capital Issues Committee survived from the war years and its powers were extended by the Borrowing (Control and Guarantees) Act of 1946, which made Treasury sanction necessary for any new borrowing or raising capital by share issue of sums over £50,000, the CIC acting as adviser to the Treasury.[61] At the same time, banks were issued with memoranda of advice. Capital exports came under particularly severe scrutiny. To these negative measures was added positive aid. In 1946, the Industrial and Commercial Finance Corporation was set up by the Bank of England, the London clearing banks and the Scottish banks, in order to provide loans in the range of £5,000–£200,000, the 'Macmillan gap', while the Finance Corporation for Industry was established to finance larger schemes, particularly in rapidly expanding industries, which might for other reasons find a direct approach to the market difficult.[62] The Export Credits Guarantee Department provided insurance cover for exports, while 'in the early post-war years the discount market played an important part in absorbing offerings of short-dated bonds sold by industrial companies to finance reconversion.[63]

It was generally assumed that these various controls were the tools of an integrated Labour Party policy of economic 'planning'. The term, at one extreme, could be taken to mean little more than that the Government would determine the level of the total national expenditure, but would leave the detailed distribution to the decision of the market; this was the minimum programme of the coalition war-time white paper on employment. At the other extreme, it could imply complete control over all actual industries and services, an extension of the nationalization policy to the whole economy. In practice, the Government's policy of 'democratic planning' was to be somewhere in between, eclectic, varied, and changing rapidly in its brief years of office.[64]

The actual controls taken over from the Caretaker Government at the end of the war and continued by the Supplies and Services (Transitional Powers)

[60] Michael P. Fogarty, 'The Location of Industry', in *The British Economy, 1945–1950*, pp. 266, 275; *Distribution of Industry* (1948. Cmd. 7540), Parts II and III; *Town and Country Planning, 1943–1951* (1951. Cmd. 8204); Board of Trade, *The Development Areas Today* (1947); R. S. Edwards and H. Townsend, *Business Enterprise, its Growth and Organisation* (1959), chapter 16; also see p. 270 below.

[61] *Radcliffe Report*, paras. 272, 966, *passim*; *Memorandum of Guidance* (1945. Cmd. 6645).

[62] C. N. Ward-Perkins, 'Banking Developments', in *The British Economy 1945–1950*, pp. 218, 223; Raymond Frost, 'The Macmillan Gap 1931–53', *Oxf. Econ. P.*, NS, 6/2, 1954.

[63] Dacey, p. 65.

[64] The best account will be found in A. A. Rogow, *op. cit.*, esp. chapters 1 and 2.

Act of 1945 contained fiscal, financial and physical planning powers: 'the use of quantitative production programmes' has been called 'the outstanding feature of our war-time economic organization'.[65] They might have survived into the peace economy.

> The essence of planning and control by the State in relation to productive industry and commercial activity must be the same in war and peace [it was said in 1947],[66] . . . the essential elements are plans consisting of decisions of policy quantitatively expressed in the form of programmes and such measures as . . . may be necessary to ensure the performance of these programmes.

Such a policy appealed strongly to the Socialists among the Labour Government's supporters, but in fact it was not developed further.

Instead, with Germany and Japan out of the way as competitors, the dollar loans secured, and industrial output rising, Labour Ministers and officials were remarkably self-satisfied about their economic policy,[67] and many quantitative controls were allowed to lapse before the crises of early 1947 shocked the Government out of its complacency. Only in July 1947 were the membership and functions of the Economic Planning Board announced. In August, the exchange crisis occurred, but it was not until the end of September that economic policy was taken seriously enough to cause the appointment of Sir Stafford Cripps, hitherto President of the Board of Trade, to the newly created post of Minister of Economic Affairs, with the Economic Planning Staff, the Economic Information Unit and the surviving Economic Section of the Cabinet Secretariat to assist him. The relationship of this new Department to the Treasury was, however, never clarified, for almost at once Dr Dalton resigned from his post as Chancellor of the Exchequer, and Sir Stafford became Chancellor, taking most of his department with him.

With this chance event in its favour, and the general opposition of the business world and even of some Labour opinion[68] against physical controls, the Treasury found it easy to reassert its former authority by concentrating all power in the financial and fiscal weapons of control. 'The *Economic Surveys* became annually less ambitious. The "targets" of 1947 and 1948 became the "estimates" of 1949; in 1950 and 1951 the estimates became less detailed and more cautious; by 1952 they had almost disappeared.'[69]

With weak co-ordination, divided counsel and uncertain aim, the Government's post-war economic policy could not be said to have been a successful demonstration of the benefits of economic planning. But the picture drawn by some critics of a bureaucracy-ridden, atrophied planned economy, waiting with bated breath for a dash to economic freedom, bore little semblance to reality. In fact, the period 1945–50 was essentially one in which

---

[65] Sir Hubert Henderson, *The Uses and Abuses of Economic Planning* (Cambridge, 1947), p. 10.

[66] Sir Oliver Franks, *Central Planning and Control in War and Peace* (1947), p. 17.

[67] D. N. Chester, 'Machinery of Government and Planning', in *The British Economy, 1945–1950*, p. 341.

[68] E.g. W. A. Lewis, *The Principles of Economic Planning* (1949).

[69] A. J. Youngson, *op. cit.*, p. 264; Samuel H. Beer, *Treasury Control* (Oxford, 1956), pp. 79 ff.; Gilbert Walker, *op. cit.*, chapters 4, 5.

war-time controls were dismantled as fast as the highly vulnerable external position of the country and the need to preserve full employment would permit.

The evidence makes it equally difficult to sustain the charge that a misguided cheap money policy was responsible for continuing inflation. The inflation was world-wide and its progress in Britain not exceptional. In an economy in which prices and wages moved rigidly together,[70] rising import prices alone could fuel it in Britain. Significantly, the change to higher interest rates after 1951 did not end the inflation, despite the fact that the most adverse factor before 1951 was now reversed and import prices were falling. Inflation even after 1951 could only be temporarily halted at the cost of creating unemployment. Further, the actual policy followed was not entirely unsuccessful in reducing the weight of the suppressed inflation.[71]

Planning and the price level had a relatively low priority in the Government programme. Its economic policy should mainly be judged by its chief objectives of maintaining full employment, a rising output, and a high and socially desirable allocation of investment. The employment policy was successful beyond all hope: apart from the fuel crisis in February–March 1947, unemployment was generally below 400,000 of insured workers (i.e. under 2%), many of whom were either unemployable or waiting between jobs. Capital investment was also at a rate higher than many had believed possible: by 1948–52, net domestic capital formation was running at 6·61% of net national product, compared with only 4·13% in 1934–8, while an additional 0·2% was made available for foreign investment (compared with —0·5%).[72] There might be disagreement as to detail at the time,[73] but its general aptness and right proportions are in retrospect hardly open to doubt.[74]

Partly with the aid of this improved equipment, production as well as productivity showed a rise, despite the reduction in the average (actual) working week,[75] which compared well with any previous period in British history and with other countries, including those of Western Europe and North America. It was also bound to make the most effective contribution to the solution of the other major problems, including the foreign trade gap and the inflation. It is therefore not a little surprising that the period appears in much of the contemporary literature as a period of chaos and failure.

Much of this was no more than the normal bias of economic literature which regularly tends to portray periods of low profits as 'depressions' even though output and wage incomes are booming.[76] But something was also due

---

[70] J. C. R. Dow, 'Analysis of the Generation of Price Inflation. A Study of Cost and Price Changes in the United Kingdom 1946–1954', *Oxf. Econ. P.*, NS, 8/3, 1956, pp. 252–301.

[71] Cf. the figures on p. 244, Table 6·5 above.

[72] Based on C. H. Feinstein, *National Income, Expenditure and Output of the United Kingdom 1855–1865* (Cambridge, 1972), T. 6 and 106. Also see J. B. Jefferys and Dorothy Walters, 'National Income and Expenditure of the UK 1870–1952', *Income and Wealth*, Series 5 (1955), p. 19, Table VIII.

[73] E. Devons, 'The Progress of Reconversion', *Manchester School*, 15/1, 1947, pp. 12–17.

[74] Sir Dennis H. Robertson, *Britain in the World Economy* (1954), pp. 11–20; E. Nevin, 'Social Priorities and the Flow of Capital', *Three Banks' Review*, No. 19, 1953; Elliott Zupnick, *Britain's Postwar Dollar Problem* (New York, 1961), pp. 61–5.

[75] Dudley Seers, 'National Income, Production and Consumption', in *The British Economy, 1945–1950*, p. 38; figures on p. 251 below, Table 6·6.

[76] E.g. H. L. Beales, 'The "Great Depression" in Industry and Trade', *Ec. Hist. Rev.*, 5/1, 1934.

to genuine causes. One was that higher production was not fairly matched by higher incomes. On a rough calculation, of the £2,050 million increase in national output between 1938 and 1950 (£2,000 million at constant 1948 prices), £700 million was 'lost' by changes in world prices, £400 million by the need to increase exports to cover loss of foreign income, £100 million by a higher rate of capital investment, and £350 million by higher Government spending. The consumers were left with only a quarter of the increase, £500 million,[77] to share between an additional 6% of the population. Another calculation shows the real output per head in the United Kingdom to have risen, between 1937 and 1950, by about 25%, while the real income per head only rose by 7%.[78]

Secondly, there were the periodic crises and uncertainties, though it was external factors, particularly the erratic nature of American aid, that were largely responsible. Each critic believed that his own solution would have prevented any particular crisis, and rated Government policy accordingly, forgetting that meanwhile full employment was being maintained. 'If there is a lesson of the years 1945–50,' an observer summed up, 'it is that the recurrence of alternate periods of apparent austerity and apparent ease of supply is the price of stability of employment.'[79]

Lastly, there was the dissatisfaction with restrictions, with lack of choice, with continued shortages and high taxes. There was some substance in the complaints that there were too many resources devoted to manning the controls and to avoiding them, instead of to productive purposes. The gross unbalance of the late 1940s inevitably called for controls and austerity, but the solid foundations of reconstruction laid then could make an expansion possible which might well need greater freedom for enterprise, both public and private. Yet a doubt remains: for after decades of association, rationalization and control, British industry appeared to have lost the zest for enterprise,[80] and this lack, especially by comparison with businessmen of other advanced countries, constituted one of the major weaknesses of the 1950s.

3 Industrial Reconstruction

The most encouraging aspects of the post-war economy were undoubtedly the maintenance of a high level of employment, and of a high and rising level of output. These were achieved even though the capital equipment of the country was run down, there were raw material and fuel shortages, the hours of labour had been reduced, and the system of control and the high level of taxation were said to stifle enterprise, while full employment was said to be detrimental to industrial discipline. The high rate of production increase was, in fact, maintained well into the 1950s, and was then slowed down only by deliberate Government policies of deflation and restriction.

For this progress, science and technology claimed a growing share of the

---

[77] Seers, *loc. cit.*, p. 46.

[78] C. F. Carter, 'The Real Product of the United Kingdom 1946–1950', *London and Cambridge Economic Service*, 29/3, 1951.

[79] G. D. N. Worswick, 'Direct Controls', p. 311.

[80] Economist Intelligence Unit, *Britain and Europe* (1957), p. 62.

credit. Never before had the resources devoted to science been greater, yet never had there been so much criticism of their inadequacy.[81] There was some truth in the complaint that the traditions of British industry were against the use of academic knowledge and in favour of skill and experience learnt on the job, even on the part of senior management,[82] but this was less true for the new and now expanding industries.

With a population increase of barely 3% between 1938 and 1946 and another 3% in 1946–50, the rise in output per head was substantial.[83] (see Table 6·6) Manufacturing industry expanded the fastest; transport and the services expanded the least, being pulled down by actual declines in railway transport and domestic service.

Table 6·6:   The rise in industrial output

	Total production*	All industries**	Manufacturing industry only**
Average			
1936–8	86·0	97·5	95·6
1946	100	100	100
1947	97·8	105·4	105·8
1948	100·1	114·4	115·4
1949	103·9	121·0	122·7
1950	108·3	127·9	131·1

* At 1938 factor cost, recalculated to 1946 = 100. 1949 and 1950 recalculated from 1958 factor costs.
** 1946 = 100, recalculated from 1913 = 100.

Within manufacturing, again, the progress was very uneven. It was greatest in metals, engineering, chemicals and related industries. Unlike the post-war period 25 years earlier, the heavy industries, including shipbuilding and coal, as well as agriculture, were encouraged to continue their war-time expansion, instead of suffering a painful contraction; while others, like paper, printing, textiles, distribution and building, which had had to contract in the war years, were also urged to expand.[84] In general, however, recon-

[81] Sir F. H. Heath and A. L. Hetherington, *Industrial Research and Development in the United Kingdom* (1946), chapter 39; R. S. Edwards, *Co-operative Industrial Research* (1950); C. F. Carter and B. R. Williams, *Investment in Innovation* (1958), pp. 138–40, and *Industry and Technical Progress* (1957), chapters 1–3; R. L. Meier, 'The Role of Science in the British Economy', *Manchester School*, 18/2, 1950, pp. 101–2, 114–18; Duncan Burn, in *Structure of the British Economy*, vol. 2, pp. 436–40; Lord Hankey, 'Technical and Scientific Manpower', in Ministry of Labour and National Service, *The Worker in Industry* (1952).

[82] Stephen F. Cotgrove, *Technical Education and Social Change* (1958), chapter 7; *First Annual Report of the Advisory Council on Scientific Policy* (1948. Cmd. 7465), p. 15.

[83] C. H. Feinstein, *National Income, Expenditure and Output in the United Kingdom 1855–1965* (Cambridge, 1972), T. 16–17, 112–13. Also see *National Income and Expenditure, passim*, linked to pre-war figures according to A. R. Prest, 'National Income of the United Kingdom 1870–1946', *Econ. J.*, 58/229, 1948; N. H. Leyland, 'Productivity', in *The British Economy, 1945–1950*, p. 393; L. Rostas, 'Changes in the Productivity of British Industry, 1945–50', *Econ. J.*, 62/245, 1952.

[84] For employment statistics, see A. Beacham, *Economics of Industrial Organisation* (3rd ed., 1955) pp. 155 *passim*, and D. C. Marsh, *The Changing Social Structure of England and Wales, 1871–1951* (1958), chapter 6.

struction was dominated by the capital goods and the export industries,[85] largely because of deliberate policies designed to save imports, especially from the dollar area, to increase exports, and re-equip British industry.

There was also a marked shift from some of the older industries to some of the newer, accompanied by improved capital equipment and better techniques, including management techniques, in the latter. The industries which showed the most consistent expansion throughout, showed also the largest increase in labour productivity: 'large increases in output per head are associated with large increases in output, substantial declines in relative costs, and falling prices'.[86]

The course of industrial change may be summarized in the statistics of selected main industries shown in Table 6·7.[87]

Table 6·7:   Production and productivity changes in selected industries

	Index of industrial production (1924 = 100)			Average rate of productivity increase (%)*	
	Average 1936–8	1946	1950	1935–49	1949–55
Metal manufacture	139	157½	201½	1·2	3·3
Engineering, shipbuilding, electrical engineering	141	179	256	1·0	3·3
Vehicles	215	245	339	4·0	3·9
Chemicals	143	210	289	2·7	6·2
Textiles	118½	86½	128	2·0	1·4
Clothing	130	85	110	0·3	2·0
Food, drink, tobacco	141	163	181	1·6	0·5
All manufacturing	148	154	207	2·0	3·1
Building, contracting	174	132	157	− 3·6	3·6
Gas, water, electricity	206	290	372	3·7	4·5
Mining and quarrying	92	71	80	− 0·4	− 0·1
All industry	146	149	195	1·3	3·2

* Output per operative hour.

Among the main industries, the progress of coal was the most disappointing. Output crept up from the nadir of 175 million tons in 1945 to 204 m.t. in 1950, but this increase was largely due to an opencast output of 12 m.t. and an increased labour force, output per man-shift reaching the pre-war figure only in 1950, in spite of heavy investment in new equipment. As a result, a shortage of fuel remained one of the most serious brakes on recovery, and it culminated in the crisis of February–March 1947 when several million workers were kept idle for lack of power and export markets were disappointed also.

[85] E. Devons, 'The Progress of Reconversion', *Manchester School*, 15/1, 1947.

[86] W. E. G. Salter, *Productivity and Technical Change* (Cambridge, 1960), pp. 109, 144, 177–83. This is based on a study of 28 selected industries in the period 1924–50; cf. also Rostas, 'Changes in Productivity', pp. 23–4.

[87] Lomax, pp. 192–3, 203.

Coal mining was the first industry to be nationalized, but it was not until 1950 that the NCB published its long-term plan.[88] The tasks of the Board were indeed formidable, for the industry had much leeway in capital equipment to make up,[89] at a time when geological conditions tended to diminishing returns, and when the absolute coal shortage made the continuance of uneconomic pits essential.[90] It had also to deal with a militant work force expecting rapid improvements in wages and conditions under national ownership, while much of the old managerial class left. The obligation on the NCB to charge less than market prices (except for exports) gave the rest of industry cheap coal, but stimulated demand artificially, and deprived the NCB of reserve funds, for investment or as buffer to offset future losses. The coal problem survived to the end of the 1950s, when it was solved by the gradual fall in demand.[91]

The iron and steel industry also had much leeway to make up, but it found it easier to recruit additional labour, and it benefited more quickly from its capital investment. Its supervisory Board, appointed after the war, had on the request by the Government to prepare a five-year plan of expansion which was published in 1946.[92] The plan was criticized for 'patching' existing plants everywhere rather than proposing bold new construction in the low cost areas, and for reflecting the companies' fear of overproduction, by not being sufficiently ambitious. After some scrapping of obsolete plant, it proposed to increase the total steel capacity only to 15–16 million tons and pig iron capacity to $8\frac{1}{2}$–9 m.t. In the event the targets were raised again in 1948, but capacity continued to lag behind demand, though the average productivity was raised easily by the replacement of inefficient old plants by new works:[93] The index of output per man-year (1938 = 100) rose to 115 in 1947 and 139 in 1950. There was a large expansion of the output of basic open-hearth furnaces and of electric furnaces, and a beginning was at last made in the building of a large integrated plate mill at Margam, as well as in the replacement of the old pack mills by modern continuous tinplate mills.[94]

In engineering the centre of the picture came to be held by the motor-car industry. The pre-war peak output of 526,000 units (cars, commercial vehicles and tractors) in 1937 was almost reached in 1947 and exceeded in 1948, when 626,000 units were produced, and further large expansion

[88] NCB, *Plan for Coal* (1950); also A. Beacham, 'Planned Investment in the Coal Industry', *Oxf. Econ. P.*, NS, 3/2, 1951.

[89] *Coal Mining, Report of the Technical Advisory Committee (Reid Report)* (1945. Cmd. 6610); A. Beacham, 'Efficiency and Organisation of the British Coal Industry', *Econ. J.*, 55/218–19, 1945.

[90] Sir Hubert Houldsworth, 'The National Coal Board', in Institute of Public Administration, *Efficiency in the Nationalised Industries* (1952); *Report of the Advisory Committee on Organisation (Fleck Report)* (1955).

[91] G. C. Allen, *British Industries and Their Organisation* (3rd ed., 1951). pp. 56–9, 77–83; cf. also 4th ed. (1959). These volumes will also be found useful for the other staple industries.

[92] *Report of the British Iron and Steel Federation and the Joint Iron Council on the Iron and Steel Industry* (1946. Cmd. 6811).

[93] BISF, *Monthly Statistical Bulletin, passim*; Duncan Burn, *The Steel Industry 1939–1959* (Cambridge, 1961), chapters 3–5, and 'Steel', in *Structure of British Industry*, vol. 1; Anglo-American Council on Productivity, *Iron and Steel* (1952); H. G. Roepke, *Movements in the British Iron and Steel Industry, 1720–1951* (Urbana Ill., 1956), chapters 7 and 8; Cole, pp. 155–61.

[94] W. E. Minchinton, *The British Tinplate Industry* (Oxford, 1957), chapter 8.

schemes brought the output in 1950 up to 903,000 units, excluding motor cycles. In view of the delayed recovery of Western European production, the United Kingdom accounted for 66% of the European output of cars in 1946-8 and for 52% still in 1949-50, and since American cars were not generally available because of the dollar shortage, export markets were wide open and limited only by productive capacity. Instead of using the sellers' market to rationalize, British makers wasted their opportunity by making too many models, by building for the needs of British rather than of foreign roads, and by neglecting the vital aspects of service and spare parts, especially overseas.[95] There was some concentration in the industry, the 'big six' (reduced to five by the formation of the BMC) producing 85% of the cars and commercial vehicles by number, and 60% by value, in 1948.[96]

The aircraft industry, heavily subsidized by the taxpayer, was untypical in maintaining its technical lead and international competitive power. The ship-builders and marine engineers, by contrast, failed in 1945-50 to modernize the yards and works and were soon to be driven out of neutral markets by builders in Germany, Japan, Sweden, Holland and elsewhere. Their output rose only from 1,133,000 gross tons in 1946 to 1,315,000 in 1950.[97]

The machine tool industry, though still much inferior to the American in efficiency, maintained its high output of the war years: total production in the United Kingdom, by value, rose from £6½ million in 1935 to £47 million in 1951. Some of the most spectacular developments occurred in the electronics industry with the introduction of radar devices and of computers. The pre-war output of radio receivers was reached in 1947, when over ½ million television sets were produced also. Employment in the whole electronics industry fell from 98,000 in 1943-4 to about 80,000 in 1946-7, to reach 93,000 again in 1950, though it doubled afterwards in only five years. Like electrical engineering as a whole, it was dominated from the beginning by a few giant firms and agreements and associations between them.[98]

The chemicals and allied industries also continued to expand, even after the military stimulus was removed. The temporary eclipse of the main competitor, Germany, turned Britain from an importer into a large-scale exporter and permitted the industry to build up substantial markets abroad. At the same time, there occurred a phenomenal growth of demand for some of the industry's diverse products, notably plastics and pharmaceutical goods. Production of synthetic resin, for example, rose from 16,000 tons in 1941 to 25,000 in 1945 and 52,500 in 1950. The volume of output of the whole complex of chemical industries rose from an index number of 100 in 1946 to 120 in 1948 and 142 in 1950.[99] The industry remained dominated by a handful

---

[95] PEP, *Engineering Report II: Motor Vehicles* (1950), p. 25.

[96] Aubrey Silberston, 'The Motor Industry', in *The Structure of British Industry*, vol. 2.

[97] Ely Devons, 'The Aircraft Industry', and A. K. Cairncross and J. R. Parkinson, 'The Shipbuilding Industry', in *The Structure of British Industry*, vol. 2; L. Jones, *Shipbuilding in Britain* (Cardiff, 1957), chapter 9; Andrew Shonfield, *British Economic Policy Since* the War (Harmondsworth, 1958), pp. 41-8; *Economist*, 27.12.1952, pp. 901-2.

[98] M. E. Beesley and G. W. Troup, 'The Machine Tool Industry', in *The Structure of British Industry*, vol. 1; T. Wilson, 'The Electronics Industry', *ibid.*, vol. 2; S. G. Sturmey, *The Economic Development of Radio* (1958), pp. 181-5, 209-11.

[99] *Annual Abstract of Statistics*.

of very large firms and riddled by restrictive practices, but this did not impair either its rate of expansion or its technical efficiency.[100]

Particular mention must be made of oil refining, which Britain was driven to undertake in order to save dollars by substituting imports of crude Middle Eastern oil for refined American motor spirit. By large-scale projects, some of them built on virgin sites, rated capacity was increased seven-fold between 1938 and 1953, and the range of finished products and of by-products was greatly widened. Oil refining formed one of the prime examples of the substitution of capital for imports after the war.[101]

Among investment industries only building lagged behind, having by 1950 scarcely recovered its pre-war position. The typical building firm was still small: by 1949, only 6·5% of the skilled operatives and 20·6% of the others worked for very large firms employing over 1,000 employees each. Repair and maintenance accounted for about half the output of the industry, new building being shared between domestic and industrial or commercial building in the ratio of 3 : 2. By the end of 1949, one million houses had been built or reconstructed, and the ratio of houses to population was beginning to exceed the pre-war ratio, but unfulfilled demand remained as high as ever, because of smaller families and rising expectations of living standards.[102]

In contrast with the industries noted so far, most consumption goods industries showed relatively modest increases in output, not least because for many, domestic demand was still held down by rationing. Textiles were, perhaps, the outstanding example. War conditions had greatly reduced the output and the labour force of the traditional textile industries, and even in the post-war period they enjoyed a low priority. Employment in the cotton industry dropped by 42% between 1937 and 1945, and in the woollen and worsted industries it dropped by 37% between 1939 and 1945; much of the equipment was out of date and most firms were small.[103] After a brief post-war boom, exports of cotton goods were to slump again in 1952, though the woollen and worsted industries fared rather better, reaching by 1950 an output just below the pre-war level.[104] Man-made fibres on the other hand were being developed very rapidly. In 1952–3 nylon and rayon accounted for 80% of production of ladies' seamless hose, and for 90% of fully-fashioned ladies' hose. New fibres, such as 'Terylene', for which a pilot plant was set up

---

[100] W. B. Reddaway, 'The Chemical Industry', in *The Structure of British Industry*, vol. 1; C. J. Thomas, 'The Pharmaceutical Industry', *ibid.*, vol. 2; T. I. Williams, *The Chemical Industry* (1953), Part II; Association of British Chemical Manufacturers, *Report on the Chemical Industry, 1949* (1950) and *Supplement, 1953* (1954).

[101] Duncan Burn, 'The Oil Industry', in *The Structure of British Industry*, vol. 1; Richard Evely and I. M. D. Little, *Concentration in British Industry. An Empirical Study of the Structure of British Production 1935–51* (Cambridge, 1960), pp. 203–8; Institute of Petroleum, *The Post-War Expansion of the UK Petroleum Industry* (1954).

[102] Working Party Report, *Building* (1950); C. F. Carter, 'The Building Industry', and B. R. Williams, 'The Building Materials Industry', in *The Structure of British Industry*, vol. 1; Anglo-American Council on Productivity, Report on *Building* (1950).

[103] Working Party Reports: *Cotton* (1946), pp. 52 *passim*, *Wool* (1947), pp. 51 *passim*.

[104] G. W. Furness, 'The Cotton and Rayon Textile Industry', and G. F. Rainnie, 'The Woollen and Worsted Industry', in *The Structure of British Industry*, vol. 2; J. F. Brothwell, 'The 1951 Depression in the British Wool Textile Industry', *Yorkshire Bull.*, 4/2, 1952, and 5/2, 1953.

in 1950, 'Orlon' and 'Ardil' which went into production in 1951, were also being developed for other uses. The proportion of employment accounted for by nylon and rayon spinning was still quite small, being 2·8% of all textile employment in July 1946 and 4·9% in 1950,[105] but its growth rate was significant.

Among other consumer goods industries, the food industries were continuing to be transformed by canning and other methods of preservation and preparation; a section of the furniture industry came for the first time under the control of large firms using new methods of production, selling and branding; and the paper and printing industries experienced a remarkable post-war expansion in spite of the severe restriction in the supply of wood pulp.

Agriculture was urged to advance even beyond its war-time output after the war, in view of the shortage of foreign currency and the world shortage of grain. In 1946 bread had to be temporarily rationed – a measure which had not been necessary in either the First or the Second World War. The Agriculture Act of 1947 provided the framework for the official policy of 'stability and efficiency'. The former was to be achieved by annual price reviews and guaranteed markets for the most important farm products, which raised average farm incomes to six times their pre-war peak in 1949–50, and the latter by continued mechanization and the intelligent use of mixed farming techniques, encouraged by tax concessions and by the initiative of the County Agricultural Executive Committees.

The Government's 'plan' called for a 20% increase in output (to 150% of pre-war) in five years, especially of dollar-saving crops. By 1950–1 the quantum of output reached, in fact, 146% of the pre-war level, a result achieved by holding the employment figure and the arable acreage (except in the uplands more suited to cattle) to their high war-time levels.[106] Most food crops and farm animals shared in this increase, as illustrated in the comparative figures in Table 6·8.

Table 6·8:   Increase in agricultural output

	1938	1946	1950
Crops harvested in GB (m. tons):			
Grains	4·95	7·22	7·78
Potatoes	5·11	10·17	9·51
Fruit and vegetables	2·33	3·67	3·85
Animals on agricultural holdings in June (m.):			
Cattle	8·76	9·63	10·62
Sheep and lambs	26·77	20·36	20·43
Pigs	4·38	1·95	2·99
Poultry	74·25	67·12	96·11

[105] D. C. Hague, *The Economics of Man-made Fibres* (1957), p. 171, and 'The Man-made Fibres Industry', in *The Structure of British Industry*, vol. 2; G. C. Allen, *op. cit.*, 1951 ed., pp. 184–5; 1959 ed., pp. 208–10.

[106] A. J. Youngson, *op. cit.*, pp. 199–200; H. T. Williams, *Principles for British Agricultural Policy* (1960), pp. 44–58, 72 ff.; K. E. Hunt, *Changes in British Agriculture* (Oxford, dupl. 1952); PEP, *Agricultural Machinery* (1949), pp. 18–26, 95; H. C. Chew, 'Changes in Land Use and Stock over England and Wales, 1939 to 1951', *Geog. J.*, 122/4, 1956; John R. Raeburn, 'Agricultural Products and Marketing', in *The Structure of British Industry*, vol. 1; D. K. Britton, 'Agriculture', in *The British Economy, 1945–1950*; *Agriculture Bill: Explanatory Memorandum* (1946. Cmd. 6996); C. H. Blagburn, 'Import Replacement by British Agiculture', *Econ. J.*, 60/237, 1950.

In sum, British industry proved to be more adaptable than many observers had believed possible.[107] Its flexibility contrasted strongly with the tendency towards restriction and rigidity between the wars, and nowhere was the contrast more marked than in the attitude to monopoly.[108]

In this period it was no longer certain whether the average size of plant was still growing. Between 1935 and 1948, it is true, average employment in all manufacturing plants rose from 107 to 124,[109] and there was evidence 'consistent with the operation of a process of amalgamation and the concentration of some production in larger and more efficient plants'.[110] Such comparisons, however, by their very nature excluded the new industries which arose after 1935, and which would reduce the overall degree of concentration; they also exclude the fact that the opportunities of making and keeping high profits were often greater for small firms than for large during the war, so that in the 1940s the long-term tendency towards industrial concentration was, on balance, slowed up or perhaps even halted altogether.[111]

Irrespective of these trends, however, it was the full employment policies which demanded the release from artificial restrictions. The white paper on Employment Policy in 1944 already contained the first hint of the growing anti-restrictionist trend of public opinion.[112] It found expression in the Monopolies Act of 1948, which set up a Monopolies and Restrictive Practices Commission, with powers to inquire and to recommend action. By 1951 only two small industries had been reported on, but ultimately, it produced several valuable reports on individual industries and one general report,[113] and in 1956 an Act was passed giving power to curb restrictions which were deemed to be against the public interest. A separate Committee reported on resale price maintenance in 1949.[114]

By contrast, associations which were in the public interest were encouraged by the Government. In particular, the attention of economic policy makers turned to productivity, and to the enormous margin by which American productivity exceeded the British.[115] An Anglo-American Council on

---

[107] E.g. E. A. G. Robinson, 'The Changing Structure of the British Economy', *Econ. J.*, 64/255, 1954.

[108] S. R. Dennison, 'New Industrial Development and Exports', in University of London and Institute of Bankers, *The Industrial Future of Great Britain* (1948).

[109] P. Sargant Florence, *The Logic of British and American Industry* (1953), p. 31; J. B. Jefferys, *Retail Trading in Britain, 1850–1950* (Cambridge, 1954), chapter 3.

[110] Richard Evely and I. M. D. Little, *Concentration in British Industry* (Cambridge, 1960), pp. 173–4, also chapter 12.

[111] P. E. Hart and S. J. Prais, 'The Analysis of Business Concentration: A Statistical Approach', *J. R. Stat. S.*, 119/2, 1956; PEP, *Government and Industry* (1952), p. 186.

[112] Cmd. 6527 (1944); I. Bowen, *Britain's Industrial Survival* (1947), pp. 63–4; S. R. Dennison, 'Restrictive Practices and the Act of 1956', *Lloyds Bank Review*, NS, No. 59, 1961, pp. 36–7; Margaret Hall, 'Monopoly Policy', in *The British Economy, 1945–1950*; Cole, *op. cit.*, chapter 19.

[113] Monopolies and Restrictive Practices Commission, *Report on Collective Discrimination* (1955. Cmd. 9504).

[114] *Report of the Committee on Resale Price Maintenance* (Lloyd Jacobs Report) (1949. Cmd. 7696).

[115] E.g. L. Rostas, *Comparative Productivity of British and American Industry* (Cambridge, 1948); E. Rothbarth, 'Causes of Superior Efficiency of American Industry', *Econ. J.*, 56/223, 1946.

Productivity was set up in August 1948. It sent many teams selected from trade associations, trade unions and employers' federations to study American practices and publish their findings.

In the iron and steel industry a Board was set up in 1946 to steer the industry in the public interest. Elsewhere, it was decided in September 1945 to set up 'Working Parties' to inquire into individual industries and make recommendations. Seventeen were eventually appointed, and they reported in 1946–8, making many specific recommendations. One general result was the Industrial Organization and Development Act of 1947, which allowed the Government to set up Development Councils. However, in spite of the specific recommendation of most Working Parties for Councils of this kind, the results of the Act were disappointing: apart from the transformation of the existing Cotton Board into a Development Council, there were only three Councils formed and three other Orders made, for compulsory levies for research and exports.[116]

Much more significant than these schemes was the programme of nationalization, which formed one of the main platforms of the Labour Government. Apart from the minor measures which were little more than formalities, including the Bank of England Act, 1946, the Cable and Wireless Act, 1946, and the Civil Aviation Act, 1946, which set up British European Airways (BEA) and British South American Airways (the latter merged with BOAC in 1949), there were five major measures of nationalization: the Coal Industry Nationalization Act (1946), the Electricity Act (1947), the Transport Act (1947), the Gas Act (1948) and the Iron and Steel Act (1949). The Act nationalizing the steel industry was first held up by the House of Lords and its vesting date was further delayed until after the second post-war election, to 1951; by its provisions the firms were largely left intact and it was thus easy for the Conservative Governments to reverse the process of nationalization in the years after 1951 by selling the iron and steel firms back to private ownership. In the case of the other four major industries, the actual transfer took place in each case in the year following the passing of the Act.

This programme of nationalization was probably the most controversial part of the post-war Government's policy,[117] largely because of its political implications. On it were centred the hopes of Socialists, of whatever kind,[118] that the transfer of industry to public hands would alter the *rationale* of economic life by introducing production for use, in place of production for profit incidentally arising out of the process of production, and that it would remove the power of the capital-owning classes, and thus overturn the existing social and political structure and bring about a peaceful social revolution.

In retrospect it is clear that there was never any danger of such a

---

[116] N. H. Leyland, 'Productivity', in *The British Economy, 1945–1950*; P. D. Henderson, 'Development Councils: an Industrial Experiment', *ibid.*

[117] E.g. R. Kelf-Cohen, *Nationalisation in Britain. The End of a Dogma* (1959).

[118] Cole, *op. cit.*, chapter 9, also his *The Case for Industrial Partnership* (1957); H. A. Clegg, *A New Approach to Industrial Democracy* (1960), esp. chapters 1, 2, 4, 16; Austen Albu, 'The Organization of Nationalized Industries and Services', in W. A. Robson (ed.), *Problems of Nationalized Industry* (1952).

revolution,[119] and the heat and passion aroused by the controversy were largely misdirected. Industry was nationalized, the 'commanding heights' of the economy were occupied to the extent of 20%, not to dominate or transform the mainly profit-making industries composing the remaining 80% of the economy, but because it seemed a rational form of organization in each individual case, and to give the Government additional powers, besides those it already possessed in the fiscal, monetary and other spheres, to pursue its economic objectives. The measures of nationalization actually carried out are therefore best seen not as representing a revolutionary economic doctrine, but as lying well within a long tradition of the growth of Government responsibility, represented by the Employment white paper of 1944, on the one hand, and by the pre-war public corporations[120] on the other: 'British experience of nationalization shows once more how one control leads to another.[121] Some of the nationalized undertakings had, in fact, been public corporations (e.g. London Transport) or largely in the hands of local authorities (e.g. gas and electricity).

In line with tradition also was the fact that there was no 'pattern' of nationalization, but that the organization chosen for each industry differed fundamentally from all the others. Thus the National Coal Board began as a single unit controlling its numerous properties by a classic line-and-staff form of organization. In the electricity industry, by contrast, generation and bulk supply came under the (national) British Electricity Authority, while distribution was the preserve of the fairly autonomous Area Boards. The Gas Industry was split up entirely among 12 Area Gas Boards with very little co-ordination between them, and transport had the most complex organization of all, a Transport Commission controlling six main 'Executives', one for each of the operational sectors.[122]

This diversity was dictated by the diversity of the industries concerned, their differences in needs, structure and size. Their size compared 1950 as shown in Table 6·9.

Table 6·9: Comparative size of nationalized industries, 1950

	Employees (000)	Fixed assets (less depreciation) (£m.)	Gross revenue (£m.)
Coal	765	288	481
Electricity	170	548	214
Gas	141	211	192
Inland transport	888	1,341	560
Air transport	23	35	33
Grand total	1,988	2,443	1,480

[119] Cf. H. A. Clegg and T. E. Chester, *The Future of Nationalization* (Oxford, 1955), chapter 1; G. D. H. Cole, *Socialist Economics* (1950).

[120] See pp. 106–7 above.

[121] H. A. Clegg, 'Nationalized Industry', in *The British Economy, 1945–1950*, p. 246.

[122] Acton Society Trust, *Nationalised Industry. 9. Patterns of Organisation* (1951); D. N. Chester, *The Nationalised Industries* (2nd ed., 1951).

Even where some uniformity was desired, as in the principles of pricing,[123] different circumstances led to different results. In particular, the reluctance to allow the selling prices of nationalized industries to rise made it very much more difficult to break even in coal mining, where costs were rising exceedingly rapidly because of the rapid rise in miners' wages and the high proportion of wage costs to total costs, as compared, for example, with electricity generation, where rapid technical advance and advantages of scale allowed the industry to absorb many of the cost increases.

In the absence of any real intention of changing the structure of society, each separate act of nationalization has to stand on its own merits. On such a basis, the nationalization of coal mining and the railways was justifiable not only by such evident savings as the avoidance of overlapping or of illogical boundaries, but also by the necessity of raising the morale of the labour force and providing a source of finance for the very large capital schemes required after decades of neglect. The nationalization of gas and electricity supply, while partly justifiable as permitting economies of scale, and opportunity to bring the average up to the best practice,[124] as well as providing much necessary finance, would stand or fall much more with the possibility of planning energy supply as a whole.[125]

Under the Governments of the 1950s there was no hope of making nationalized industry a tool of economic planning in the national interest. With the sale of part of the road transport fleet to private ownership, and the independent control over passenger road transport, the attempt to plan and co-ordinate inland transport has been given up.[126] Elsewhere, as physical planning gave way, in the 1950s, to steering by fiscal and monetary methods and by exhortation, the nationalized industries, far from acting as instruments of controlling the rest of industry, were directed increasingly to become its servants, and to suffer the worst buffetings in their long-term investment plans with every change of wind of Government policy. Forced increasingly to deny the principle which they were established to promote, the principle of public service, and to justify themselves on the same commercial grounds as privately owned firms, the Boards of the nationalized industrial have been neither able to maintain consistent financial policies nor give adequate attention to consumers' interests, despite the safeguards of consumers' councils written into the Acts,[127] nor can they defend their

---

[123] A vast literature grew up on the theoretical principles of pricing (as well as other managerial decisions by nationalized industry), but it cannot be said to have had any effect on actual policy. J. Wiseman, 'The Theory of Public Utility Price – An Empty Box', *Oxf. Econ. P.*, NS, 9/1, 1957; D. N. Chester, 'Note on the Price Policy indicated by the Nationalization Acts', *ibid.*, NS 2/1, 1950; J. F. Sleeman, *British Public Utilities* (1953); D. H. Aldcroft, *British Railways in Transition. The Economic Problems of Britain's Railways since 1914* (1968), pp. 135–45.

[124] E.g. *Report on the Gas Industry* (Heyworth Report) (1945. Cmd. 6699); H. F. H. Jones, 'The Gas Industry', and Lord Citrine, 'Electricity Supply', in Institute of Public Administration, *Efficiency in the Nationalised Industries* (1952).

[125] Youngson, pp. 187–97; E. Stanley Tucker, 'Fuel and Power', in *The Industrial Future of Great Britain*.

[126] Gilbert Walker, *Road and Rail* (2nd ed., 1947), chapter 12.

[127] J. A. G. Griffith, 'The Voice of the Consumer', *Political Quarterly*, 21/2 1950; A. M. de Neumann, *Consumers' Representation in the Public Sector of Industry* (Cambridge, 1950); Frank Milligan, 'The Consumer's Interest', in Robson (ed.), *Nationalized Industry*; W. A. Robson, *Nationalized Industry and Public Ownership* (1960), chapter 10.

industries from the kind of public attacks which would be unthinkable in the case of the owners or managers of private industry.

4 Incomes and Work

The transition to peace involved a reduction in the numbers in the forces by $4\frac{1}{2}$ million persons and in the war industries by $3\frac{1}{4}$ million by the end of 1946, and their absorption into civilian industry or back into domestic duties.[128] The remarkable smoothness and absence of transitional unemployment with which this huge transfer of labour was carried through was due in part to Government planning, but was largely the result of the pressure of unfilled demands pervading all sectors of the economy. It was precisely the high level of demand for labour which preserved the flexibility of the British economy and permitted the rapid growth of some sectors at the expense of others.[129] By and large, labour was attracted to the expanding sectors by the offer of better wages and conditions, and this process contributed powerfully to the upward drive of wages.

Even without this additional element of 'bottleneck' wages, full employment was bound to contribute greatly to the bargaining strength of the trade unions. They could count on a friendly Government which passed, as one of its first measures, the Trade Disputes and Trade Unions Act of 1946, reversing the 1927 Act with its many cramping provisions. Their membership continued its upsurge of the war years, rising from 7,875,000 in 1945 to 9,243,000 in 1950, to embrace 43% of all employees (53% of the men, 23% of the women), including an increasing number of non-manual workers.[130] Trade union power was further increased by the extension of the Wages Council system under the Act of 1945,[131] which ensured that by 1950, 80% of employees were governed by statutory or voluntary forms of wage regulation; by the appointment of at least one former trade union officer to each of the Boards controlling the nationalized industries; by improved negotiating machinery in those industries; and by the continued Government consultation with trade union leaders on matters of economic policy, informally or formally through the National Joint Advisory Council, the Economic Planning Board, the Development Councils and elsewhere.[132]

On the whole, the trade unions used their increased political and economic power with a due sense of responsibility. The number of working days lost by disputes remained minute, averaging 2 million a year in 1945–50, nearly all in unofficial short strikes involving small numbers. 30% of working days lost were accounted for by transport workers, mainly dockers, and 25% by miners; there were also several flare-ups in shipbuilding and engineering, but

---

[128] Ministry of Labour and National Service, *Report fot the Years 1939–1946*, pp. 131–2, 151, 199–202, 225; T. Wilson, 'Manpower', in G. D. N. Worswick and P. H. Ady, *The British Economy, 1945–1950* (Oxford, 1952).

[129] G. D. N. Worswick, 'Personal Income Policy', in *The British Economy, 1945–1950*, pp. 320–4.

[130] G. D. H. Cole, *The Post-War Condition of Britain* (1956), chapter 30.

[131] See p. 224 above.

[132] Allan Flanders, *Trade Unions* (1952), p. 100; PEP, *British Trade Unions* (1948), pp. 50, 114.

the rest of industry experienced virtually no disputes at all. The war-time Order No. 1305 which made arbitration compulsory and made strikes without resort to arbitration illegal,[133] was operative throughout this period, and since the wage awards under it allowed wages to rise parallel with prices, it satisfied the leaders of most unions, particularly the weaker ones. The order did not, however, prevent unofficial strikes, in spite of some prosecutions, and when in 1951 the Government failed to secure the conviction of some dockers, a new Industrial Disputes Order was brought in.[134]

It would be erroneous to assume that the organic link of the Trade Union Movement with the Labour Party ensured that there was no friction between them. On the question of the control over the nationalized industries, it is true, the trade union leadership (with few exceptions, of which the Union of Post Office Workers was the most conspicuous) agreed with the Government view that the trade unions should have no direct representation on the Boards, but should be free to criticize and represent their members' views as independent bodies. But there were many grounds for disagreements over wages policy.

Those who advocated a genuine 'wages policy' had in mind the determination of the total available for wage increases in any given period from the national income estimates, and its division among the different groups of workers according to agreed principles. Such proposals generally hoped to curb wage increases and thereby reduce the rate of inflation, as well as using the wage structure as an instrument of economic planning.[135] But trade union leaders were too suspicious of Governments, and too jealous of their own powers, to sanction this, while experience in other countries showed that, whatever else might be said for it, a 'wages policy' would not cure an inflation.[136] A resolution proposing it was heavily defeated at the TUC in 1951.

Instead, wages were determined by free collective bargaining between unions and employers' organizations, and by statutory bodies such as Wages Councils, which tended, in so far as they had a consistent policy, to keep their awards in line with the wages of comparable trades arrived at by union bargaining.[137] Given the end of price control, rising prices, the labour shortage and union power began an upward push on wages which employers (including the nationalized industries) were unwilling to oppose, since they could easily recoup their higher costs by higher prices. In these conditions, only trade union restraint could prevent accelerating inflation. 1946 was the only year in which increases in wage rates (and earnings) exceeded the rise in the cost-of-living index; the restraint in personal income claims from 1947 onward is reflected in the index figures given in Table 6·10.

[133] pp. 223–4 above.

[134] D. F. MacDonald, *The State and the Trade Unions* (1960), pp. 177–8.

[135] E.g. Allan Flanders, 'Wages Policy and Full Employment in Britain', *Bull. Oxf. Inst. Stat.*, 12/7–8, 1950, pp. 235–42, and 'Can Britain have a Wage Policy?', *Scot. J. Pol. Econ.*, 5/2, 1958 (Symposium on Wages Policy); C. W. Guillebaud, 'Problems of Wages Policy', in Min. of Labour and National Service, *The Worker in Industry* (1952).

[136] H. W. Singer, 'Wage Policy in Full Employment', *Econ. J.*, 57/228, 1947; E. H. Phelps-Brown and B. C. Roberts, 'Wages Policy in Great Britain,' *Lloyds Bank Review*, NS, No. 23, 1952; B. C. Roberts, *National Wages Policy in War and Peace* (1958); T. L. Johnstone, 'Wages Policies Abroad', *Scot. J. Pol. Econ.*, 5/2, 1958.

[137] Barbara Wootton, *The Social Foundations of Wage Policy* (1955).

Table 6·10: Wage restraint and cost-of-living, 1945–50

	Average weekly earnings (M.o.Labour)	Wage rates (Bowley)	Cost of living (London and Cambridge Econ. S.)
1945 (1938 = 100)	180 (July)	154	148
1946 '' ''	190 (Oct.)	167	150
1946 (1946 = 100)	100 ''	100	100
1947 '' ''	107 ''	105	107
1948 '' ''	116 ''	$112\frac{1}{2}$	115
1949 '' ''	$120\frac{1}{2}$ ''	116	119
1950 '' ''	126 ''	118	123
1950 (1938 = 100)	240 ''	197	184

Wage *rates*, in fact, rose less than prices after 1946, and real incomes were kept up only by the inflation of earnings by overtime and piece-rate payments, or by the upgrading of workers. It could even be argued that the trade unions kept wages down: 'the fact that the employers are willing to pay more than the negotiated wage rates in order to obtain the labour they require points to a situation where wages are lagging behind the levels that they would spontaneously reach as a result of market pressures'. Therefore, it could be said, 'it is in no small measure the employers who have undermined the standard rates and made further wage claims from the unions almost inevitable'.[138]

The official wage restraint policy between 1947 and 1951 had several distinct phases. In January 1947 the Government in its *Statement on the Economic Considerations affecting Relations between Employers and Workers*,[139] a white paper issued with the endorsement of the National Joint Advisory Council, drew attention to the need to keep incomes and prices down in order to remain competitive in world markets. The convertibility crisis of the summer further emphasized the foreign trade aspects of inflation. As its earlier exhortation had met only a limited response, the Government felt compelled to issue the much sharper *Statement on Personal Incomes, Costs and Prices* in February 1948.[140] This white paper, after referring to the anti-inflationary effects of the Government's policy of high taxation, demanded a total standstill of profits and rents at their present levels, and a qualified limitation of wage increases. These were to be granted only where justified by increased productivity or by the national interest, e.g. in order to attract labour to undermanned occupations, and there was to be no unofficial 'wage drift'. The Government took care to bring its views to the attention of Wages Councils and other negotiating bodies.

Not unlike the white paper of 1941 in tone and effect,[141] this document

[138] B. C. Roberts, *National Wages Policy*, p. 16; C. W. Guillebaud, *loc. cit.*, p. 46; also A. T. Peacock and W. J. L. Ryan, 'Wage Claims and the Pace of Inflation', *Econ. J.*, 63/250, 1953.
[139] Cmd. 7018.
[140] Cmd. 7321.
[141] p. 226 above.

marked a turning point in wages policy. The General Council of the TUC fully endorsed the demand for wage restraint for the time being. A conference of trade union executives held in March 1948 also supported this, by a large majority, but it insisted on adding two further exceptions to the general wage standstill to the two permitted by the Government itself. One was the proviso to raise wages if they were found to be below a reasonable absolute minimum, and the other, to maintain differentials – a justification which the white paper had specifically rejected. These four grounds for exception would, between them, exempt from wage restraint virtually all the trade unions which voted for it, the others, a sizeable minority, voting against, so that the Government might be said to have won but a hollow victory. Yet it had committed the unions, at least on paper, to a policy in direct conflict with their reason for existence, and in practice they did observe restraint in a period of full employment.

After devaluation in September 1949, the General Council of the TUC again urged a wage standstill, until the end of 1950, provided the interim retail price index did not rise by more than 5%, and asked the trades whose wages were tied to sliding scales to forgo increases due to them. Put before another meeting of trade union executives in January 1950, these propositions could, however, muster such a narrow majority only (4,263,000 against 3,606,000) as to lose all their moral force.[142] The General Council itself abandoned its policy in June 1950 when it urged more 'flexibility' in wage negotiations. The impending crisis of 1951 led to a renewed attempt to peg wages with the help of enlarged subsidies, and Mr Gaitskell proposed a statutory dividend limitation, but the Labour Government fell before these measures could be given a trial.

Wages did not fall in the post-war years as a proportion of the national income, and as usual, in a period of industrial boom, the share of profits went up, though this was hidden by the widespread practice of heaping up undistributed profits in view of the penal rates of taxation and the powerful pressures to dividend restraint. In consequence, it was rents and salaries which had to bear the brunt of the necessary reductions.

Moreover, the proportion of wage-earners was falling: according to one calculation, wage-earners received 39·2% of the national income in 1938, when they formed 71·4% of the occupied population: in 1950 they received 41·9%, but by then they only formed 66·2% of the occupied population.[143] Conversely, the rising share of salaries has to be set against a rising number of salary earners: the growth of the 'salariat' interrupted or reversed during the war, was resumed with undiminished vigour after it.[144] In industry, the proportion of administrative, clerical and technical employees to operatives rose from 13·5% in 1935 to 18·6% in 1948. The 'middle classes' of managerial, professional and white-collar workers, as well as proprietors, numbered 10·4

[142] B. C. Roberts, *National Wages Policy*, p. 60; cf. also D. F. MacDonald, *The State and the Trade Unions* (1960), pp. 151 ff.; Allan Flanders, *Trade Unions* (1952), pp. 110–12.

[143] The figures are not quite on the same base. E. H. Phelps-Brown and P. E. Hart, 'The Share of Wages in National Incomes', *Econ. J.*, 62/246, 1952, p. 277.

[144] pp. 185–6 above. D. C. Marsh, *The Changing Social Structure of England and Wales, 1871–1951* (1958), pp. 105, 145, 194, *passim*.

million, or over 20% of the population, in 1951; of these, 'proprietors and managerial' numbered 4·3 million.[145]

Statistics of pre-tax incomes like those in Table 6·11 should be read with all these provisos in mind:[146]

Table 6·11: Composition of pre-tax income, 1938 and 1949

Proportion of Personal Incomes	1938	1949
Wages	37·8	41·9
Salaries	17·9	20·5
Other employment incomes	3·8	6·0
Self-employed	12·8	13·1
Rent, dividends, interest	22·3	11·4
Government transfers	5·4	7·1
	100	100

Whatever redistribution of incomes there had been, however, had largely occurred in the war period, not in the post-war years. Thus the share of rents, dividends and net interest in personal pre-tax incomes had fallen from 22·9% in 1938 to 14·4% in 1946 and 11·5% in 1950.[147] As a result of this downward pressure, tax evasion schemes abounded, but cannot be estimated. The inclusion of undistributed profits (including gains from stock appreciation) in the calculations does, however, confirm the general impression of the constancy of the main shares of personal incomes in the gross national product in the post-war years:[148]

Table 6·12: Proportions of personal incomes in the GNP, 1946 and 1950

Incomes of	1946	1950
Employees and Forces	57·2%	57·3%
Grants from public authorities	6·8	5·8
Self-employment	12·0	10·9
Property, including undistributed profits, additions to reserves	24·0	26·0

The statistics of savings showed again the concentration of 'small' savings in the hands of a small minority of the working classes and in those of the middle classes; the building societies, attracting mainly middle-class savers, showed by far the largest increases.[149]

[145] PEP, *Government and Industry* (1952), p. 171; Ministry of Labour and National Service, *Annual Reports*; C. W. McMahon and G. D. N. Worswick, 'The Growth of Services in the Economy', *District Bank Review*, No. 136, 1960; Cole, *op. cit.*, chapter 3.

[146] H. F. Lydall, 'The Long-Term Trend in the Size Distribution of Income', *J. R. Stat. S.*, 122/2, 1959, p. 17, Table 9. Cf. also pp. 226–7 above.

[147] C. H. Feinstein, *National Income, Expenditure and Production in the United Kingdom, 1855–1965* (Cambridge, 1972), T. 28.

[148] Based on *National Income and Expenditure, 1946–1952* (1953), Table 9, excluding incomes of public authorities and public corporations, and remittances abroad. Cf. also Worswick, 'Personal Income Policy', pp. 315–17.

[149] Kathleen M. Langley, 'The Distribution of Private Capital, 1950–1', *Bull. Oxf. Inst. Stat.*, 16/1, 1954; Esme Preston, 'Personal Savings through Institutional Channels (1937–1949)', *ibid.*, 1950.

Government still continued to restrict severely the spending of the higher income groups by rationing and restricting imports. Additionally, a large part of their income was in the form of undistributed dividends, and was as yet only potential spending power. The two largest reductions of personal expenditure (at constant, 1948, prices) occurred in the categories limited to the wealthier classes: expenditure on domestic service fell from £265 million in 1938 to £80 million in 1946 and £85 million in 1950, and private motoring from £250 million to £140 million and £160 million.[150]

The relative fall in salaries, as compared with wages, tended to level out earned incomes as a whole,[151] but there also took place a certain measure of levelling of wages during the war which was maintained in the post-war years. The differential of skill remained at about 20% of the unskilled wage, and women's and youths' wages were rising relatively to those of men. Above all, a large part of the bottom slice of the income pyramid, the population living in absolute poverty, was removed.

The virtual abolition of primary poverty in post-war Britain was caused mainly by two developments: full employment on the one hand, and the State welfare provisions on the other. B. S. Rowntree, visiting York in 1950 to conduct his third social survey there,[152] found the proportion of the working-class population living in poverty to have dropped from 31·1% in 1936 to 2·8% in 1950; of those living below the poverty line, nearly one-third gave unemployment as the reason in 1936, while not one was found in 1950; in that year 68% attributed their poverty to old age. At the same time, Rowntree and Lavers calculated that if the welfare provisions (including subsidies) in 1950 had been only those of 1936, the proportion of working-class families living in poverty would have been, not 2·8%, but 22·2%. It seems reasonable to conclude that for the majority of the population, who before 1939 had never been quite beyond the danger of want, the most important single development after 1945 was the creation of the 'Welfare State'.

5 The Welfare State

Among the most enduring achievements of the post-war Government was the 'Welfare State' which helped to consolidate the abolition of poverty. The limits of the 'Welfare State' are not easy to draw. At the centre, without a doubt, stood the Social Insurance scheme as proposed in the Beveridge Report,[153] and the National Health Service and the family allowances associated with it. The family allowances were enacted in 1945, providing 5s. a week for all children except the eldest; and in 1946 the National Insurance Act, the National Insurance (Industrial Injuries) Act and the National Health Service Act were passed, coming into operation together on the 'appointed day', 5 July 1948. In that year the National Assistance Act and the Children Act completed this group of reforms.

---

[150] Dudley Seers, 'National Income, Production and Consumption', in *The British Economy, 1945–1950*, p. 47.

[151] David Lockwood, *The Black-Coated Workers* (1958), pp. 67–8.

[152] B. S. Rowntree and G. R. Lavers, *Poverty and the Welfare State* (1951), pp. 30–5.

[153] pp. 229–31 above. Also, M. Bruce, *The Coming of the Welfare State* (1961), chapter 7.

In its detailed provisions, the Beveridge Report was followed remarkably faithfully. There were only two major departures from its principles. The first was caused by the rise in prices unmatched by increases in benefit rates, so that the principle of sufficiency was violated, and the National Assistance scheme, intended only as a 'safety net' for a small minority, became a necessary standby for large numbers of insured persons. Thus by the end of 1950, 1,350,000 persons were receiving weekly allowances from the Assistance Board, of whom no fewer than 873,000 were persons who were in need because the benefits under the insurance scheme were too low; 650,000 of them were old-age pensioners.[154] The National Assistance Board had to apply a needs test, and this threatened to bring back the old Poor Law under a new guise.

The other important departure from the war-time recommendations was the decision to apply increased retirement pensions at once, instead of after an interval in which the beneficiaries might have accumulated sufficient credits by their in-payments; indeed, higher pensions were paid as from October 1946, instead of waiting for July 1948, and the full rates were to come in after only 10 years instead of 20.[155] The numbers involved were 3.3 million persons in 1946 and 3.5 million in 1948.

This decision, made largely for political reasons, was doubly unfortunate from the point of view of the financial structure of the insurance scheme, since even at the less generous rates the growing number of retirement pensioners was certain to swallow a rapidly mounting share of its income. According to the available calculations, the number of people over 65 was expected to grow from 5 million in 1947 to around 8 million in the late 1970s. As a proportion of the total population, they would increase from 14% in 1951 to 18% in 1979. At the rates of the 1946 Act, the cost of the retirement pensions would then rise from £238 million in 1948 to £501 million in 1978, and the resulting deficit would fall entirely on the Exchequer, the contribution of which would grow quiet disproportionately from £36 million to £338 million.[156]

Although both the rates of subscription and the rates of benefits were raised the disproportion between the retirement pensions and the contribution rates remained, with the obligation on the Treasury to cover the widening gap. In strict logic, this took from the Insurance Fund the last vestiges of pretence of 'insurance'. Since the Treasury contributed a share of the normal income, adding sums at will or altering rates according to the short-term 'balance' of the Fund, as well as controlling the investment of the 'surplus' and finding most of the interest on it, the scheme was not run on insurance lines at all, but was a system of redistribution of incomes financed by three sets of taxes: a direct 'poll tax' on insured persons, an indirect tax in

---

[154] G. D. H. Cole, *The Post-War Condition of Britain* (1956), chapter 23; D. C. Marsh, *National Insurance and Assistance in Great Britain* (1950), chapter 12.

[155] *Report of the Ministry of National Insurance for the Period 17th November 1944 to 4th July 1949* (1950. Cmd. 7955), chapters 4, 12; Lord Beveridge, 'Epilogue', in W. A. Robson (ed.), *Social Security* (3rd ed., 1948).

[156] *Report of the Royal Commission on Population* (1949. Cmd. 7695), pp. 112–17; *Report of the Committee on the Economic and Financial Provisions for Old Age* (Phillips Report) (1954. Cmd. 9333), esp. Table IV, paras. 117–22, and Section IV.

the form of the employer's contribution (which in the prevailing sellers' market he could be expected to pass on to consumers in higher prices) and the total tax base in the form of the Exchequer contributions.[157] But more important than economic logic was the feeling of security an insurance scheme would bring to the members, the spirit in which they would claim its benefits, and the spirit with which it would be administered.

In other respects, the national insurance scheme followed the earlier proposals. It was compulsory and universal, the population being 'classified' into several separate classes of contributors and beneficiaries. The single insurance stamp provided unemployment, sickness and disablement benefits, and payments for retired persons, widows and orphans; there were also maternity benefits, death benefits (from July 1949) and associated schemes of family allowances (paid out of the Exchequer) and industrial injuries benefits (paid out of a separate fund), while the Insurance Fund also made an annual contribution to the Health Service. The total numbers insured rose from about $15\frac{3}{4}$ million to $21\frac{1}{2}$ million for unemployment insurance and from $24\frac{1}{3}$ million to 25 million for other benefits.

A comparison of the *real* values of the new scheme in 1948 with those of the earlier schemes before the war[158] shows that both contributions and benefits of single men remained below the pre-war level, but the family allowances raised the real value of the benefits for family men considerably above it, while old-age pensioners enjoyed the largest rate of increase. Because mass unemployment no longer existed, the social insurance budget, in spite of its rise in absolute terms, still fell short of its pre-war proportion of the total Government budget:[159]

Table 6·13:   The social insurance budget as a percentage of the total budget

	1938	1946	1950
Social Insurance contributions as % of total Government revenue	15·4	6·7	13·6
Social Insurance expenditure as % of total Government expenditure	13·6	3·9	11·3

The National Health Service, inaugurated on the same day, was also intended to be comprehensive, though a small proportion of the population elected to pay for private service.[160] It was to provide, free of charge, all medical services and needs, in so far as they could be met from existing resources, and it was to bring into a single organization the many different institutions that had grown up to form the existing variegated service. In practice, the scheme was greatly modified by the pressure of the BMA and other interests.[161] At the inauguration, the service had to overcome the handicap of much hostility, especially on the part of the medical profession;

[157] Alan T. Peacock, *The Economics of National Insurance* (1952); cf. Douglas Jay in *Hansard*, HoC, 26 April 1951, vol. 487, cols. 641–4; Walter Hagenbuch, *Social Economics* (Cambridge, 1958), pp. 265–7.

[158] E.g. D. C. Marsh, *op. cit.*, p. 116.

[159] Peacock, pp. 17–20.

[160] D. H. Hene, *The British Health Service* (1953), pp. 7–10.

[161] Harry Eckstein, *Pressure Group Politics* (1960), chapter 4.

it inherited a severe shortage of hospitals, of equipment and of staff, and a geographical maldistribution of doctors, none of which could be remedied in the short run. Further, there was an unexpectedly large backlog of hidden demand, especially for dentures and glasses, which created long waiting lists and other early problems. The service also became quickly the victim of many ill-judged economy drives. In 1949 a measure permitting charges for medicines and appliances was passed (held in reserve and imposed by the Conservative Government after 1951), in 1950 a ceiling on total expenditure of £400 million gross was imposed, leading to charges for spectacles and dentures, and capital expenditure on hospitals was cut to the derisory figure of one-third of the pre-war level.[162]

Nevertheless, the National Health Service became one of the most popular and successful measures of the post-war years.[163] The most sensitive public health index, the infant mortality rate, showed a welcome drop from 47·4 per 1,000 births in 1939 to 29·3 in 1949–50. The class differences still remained, however: in 1949–50, mortality ranged from 18·4 in the top (professional) class to 39·8 in the lowest (unskilled workers), while the differences in post-neo-natal deaths (at ages 4 weeks to 1 year), where environment counted for most, were greater still, ranging from 4·9 to 17·9.[164]

Housing standards had suffered perhaps more than any others from the war, both by the building backlog and the loss by enemy action of $\frac{1}{2}$ million houses. The total shortage, estimated officially at $1\frac{1}{4}$ million houses in 1945, would by the time of the completion of that number, be of the order of magnitude of 3 million dwellings. Thus the annual needs of building, for the next 10 years, were set at a minimum of 300,000 houses,[165] compared with a maximum pre-war building rate of 350,000 dwellings, when, however, the building labour force had been double the post-war size.

In the event, some 55,000 permanent buildings were completed in Great Britain in 1946, rising to 140,000 in 1947 and well over 200,000 a year for the next three years. In 1946–8, there were also 148,000 'temporary' prefabricated houses erected, financed by the Exchequer under the Act of 1944, so that at the time of the Census of 1951, the number of occupied dwellings, 13·3 million, exceeded the 1931 figure by over 3 million. Yet the number of households had been growing even faster, and in the Census year there were nearly $14\frac{1}{2}$ million married households. The number of houses per 1,000 of the population was higher than pre-war, but the shortage was worse than ever.

New houses and re-buildings for private owners amounted to only 158,000 in 1945–50 and most of the post-war houses were built by local authorities, subsidized by the Government under Bevan's 1946 Act, in order to ensure that the new houses went to those in greatest need. Rent restriction kept the rents of older houses at their 1939 levels, and was extended to about 1 million

[162] Brian Abel-Smith and R. M. Titmuss, *The Cost of the National Health Service in England and Wales* (Cambridge, 1956), pp. 137–8.

[163] Harry Eckstein, *The English Health Service* (Cambridge, Mass., 1959); J. S. Ross, *The National Health Service in Great Britain* (1952), Parts IV–VI.

[164] Cole. *op. cit.*, pp. 380–1.

[165] E.g. R. L. Reiss, *Municipal and Private Enterprise Housing* (1945), pp. 18–19; G. D. H. Cole, *Building and Planning* (1945), p. 150; Herbert Ashworth, *Housing in Great Britain* (1957), p. 43.

furnished houses by an Act of 1946 which set up Rent Tribunals. The Landlord and Tenant (Rent Control) Act of 1949 gave the Tribunals the additional powers to fix rents for unfurnished houses for the first time, but at no time did the price of houses come under control.[166] This legislation kept down rents for a large proportion of the population in the face of an acute housing shortage, at the price of making families immobile, but it could not cure the shortage, estimated, after the building of well over $1\frac{1}{4}$ million post-war houses by 1951,[167] to be still between 1 and 2 million houses, nor could it prevent it falling, as ever, mainly on the poorer families.

The planning powers of the Town and Country Planning authorities, the Counties and County Boroughs, were greatly extended by the Act of 1947 which ensured that, on paper at least, the whole country was covered by long-term development plans. A more ambitious approach to town planning was symbolized by the creation of 14 'New Towns', eight of them in the London region. These were to end the unco-ordinated urban sprawl of the inter-war years by creating complete self-contained and balanced communities, offering local employment as well as housing. The capital was provided by specially formed public corporations which were to act also as local authorities in the initial stages. Another significant attempt to realize the dreams of generations of reformers was the nationalization of the 'development value' of land, following the Uthwatt Report,[168] with the object of transferring to the community the additional values created by the community rather than the individual. The scheme, however, was badly designed, it proved unpopular and troublesome to administer and was quickly modified out of existence by the Conservative Government.[169]

In education, also, the brave post-war plans were held up by the shortage of buildings and teachers, in spite of the imaginative post-war Emergency Teacher Training Scheme. The raising of the school-leaving age to 15 under the Butler Act of 1944 had to be postponed to April 1947, and its planned extension to 16 was postponed further.[170] Total expenditure on education, at constant prices, rose from an index of 76 in 1937-9 to 83 in 1946 and 122 in 1950 (1948 = 100), but as the birth rate 'bulge' loomed ahead, most of this was devoted to increasing quantity rather than quality.[171]

The most important innovation of the post-war period was the creation of a universal and free secondary education system for children aged 11-15 and upwards. In practice, most authorities divided the children into three streams, grammar, technical and modern (not necessarily in separate schools), selected in most areas by an aptitude test taken at about the age of 11, the 'eleven-plus'. Though open in practice to many objections,[172] this

[166] F. W. Paish, 'The Economics of Rent Restriction,' in *The Post-War Financial Problem and Other Essays* (1950).

[167] Hagenbuch, *Social Economics*, p. 83; J. B. Cullingworth, *Housing Needs and Planning Policy* (1960), chapter 3.

[168] p. 231 above.

[169] G. D. H. Cole, *The Post-War Condition of Britain*, chapters 25, 26; Herbert Ashworth, chapters 17-19; Cullingworth, chapter 7; A. C. Duff, *Britain's New Towns* (1961).

[170] H. C. Dent, *Growth in English Education, 1946-1952* (1954), and *Secondary Education for All* (1949), chapter 4; Cole, *loc. cit.*, chapter 24.

[171] John Vaizey, *The Costs of Education* (1958), p. 70.

[172] E.g. Robin Pedley, *Comprehensive Education, a New Approach* (1956), also P. E. Vernon (ed.), *Secondary School Selection* (1957).

reorganization of secondary education did more than any other previous measure to make higher education available to capable children of all classes. It left untouched the privileged 'public school' system to those whose parents were able and willing to pay for it.

Besides social insurance, health, housing and education, there was also an expansion of many minor social services, for aged persons, for the blind, the mentally deficient, the problem families and others. In addition, there was still much scope for voluntary social work,[173] to fill the inevitable gaps left by national and local authorities. Finally, there were the provisions which involved no public expenditure, like Factory Acts, Food and Drug Acts, and rent control. Indeed, in its widest definition, the concept of the modern Welfare State was to focus much attention on intangible social improvements, such as the protection of personal rights including the prevention of neglect or cruelty to children, the fostering of the arts and recreational facilities, the abolition of ignorance and illiteracy, as well as of the grosser forms of inequality and privilege.[174]

Not all the welfare schemes necessarily favoured the poor at the expense of the rich, or the working classes at the expense of the middle classes. The public education system, for example, benefited the average child of middle-income families much more than it benefited the lower-income child, even if the heavier taxation of the wealthier families is taken into account.[175] The Health Service, likewise, was to benefit the middle classes more than the working classes, who were generally insured before 1948, though there was some justification for describing it as satisfying the quest for efficiency, always an important ingredient in Fabian and Labour Party doctrine, as much as the quest for social justice.[176] Whether the working classes as a whole gained from the social services, or whether the redistribution was merely 'horizontal', within classes, turned on definitions and assumptions. Working-class families certainly paid more in taxes and contributions than they received in social service benefits, but the question remains how much of the remainder of public expenditure should be assumed to be in their benefit and credited to them also, to set against their in-payments.[177] The major redistribution achieved by the social services was horizontal, e.g. from single and healthy men to large families, the sick, and the aged,[178] and this aspect of it met with widespread approval, for, after all, the net contributor and the net beneficiary was commonly the same person at different stages of his career.

It is also worth emphasizing that few of the post-war schemes were entirely novel: most of them developed naturally out of the older existing schemes. In

[173] G. Williams (ed.), *Voluntary Social Services since 1918* (1948); Lord Beveridge, *Voluntary Action* (1948); Hagenbuch, *op. cit.*, chapters 4, 7.

[174] W. A. Robson, *The Welfare State* (1957).

[175] Vaizey, *The Costs of Education*, p. 84.

[176] Eckstein, *The English Health Service*, esp. Introduction, and pp. 3 ff.

[177] Cf. pp. 243–4 above. Findlay Weaver, 'Taxation and Redistribution in the United Kingdom', *Rev. of Econ. and Statistics*, 32/3, 1950; A. T. Peacock and P. R. Browning, 'The Social Services in Great Britain and the Redistribution of Income', in Peacock (ed.), *Income Redistribution and Social Policy* (1954), esp. pp. 157–66; Asa Briggs, 'The Social Services', in G. D. N. Worswick and P. H. Ady, *The British Economy 1945–1950* (Oxford, 1952), p. 373.

[178] R. M. Titmuss, 'Social Administration in a Changing Society', *British Journal of Sociology*, 2/3, 1951.

spite of a widespread belief to the contrary, Britain did not spend significantly more on the social services after 1948 than she did before 1939, apart from the retirement pensions. The outlay on many services, in real terms or as a proportion of national income, had actually fallen. Comparisons are difficult and estimates differ widely. In terms of calendar years, the post-war growth, excluding capital expenditure, was of the order of magnitude shown in Table 6·14.[179]

Table 6·14:   Post-war growth in social services outlay (£m.)

	1946	1950
Subsidies (incl. local authorities)	387	475
Current grants to persons (incl. LAs)*	453	730
Net current Central Government expenditure on the Health Service	n.a.	401
Net current expenditure on social services by local authorities**	285	319
Totals	1,125	1,935

* Excluding Forces' allowances and pensions, grants for research and post-war credit payments.
** Incl. Northern Ireland.

A different classification, omitting subsidies and some other transfers, and couched in terms of financial years, yields the figures given in Table 6·15:[180]

Table 6·15:   Increase in social services expenditure (£m.)

	1938–9	1947–8	1949–50
Social security services	310·5	559·8	714·8
Education	111·8	222·8	228·5
Health	74·4	174·7	408·6
Housing	23·7	55·8	54·5
	520·4	1013·1	1406·4

Most of this increase was accounted for by rises in prices and by the Health Service.[181] In comparison with the pre-war years, the increases in the old-age pensions, the family allowances and the subsidies were counter-balanced in part by a reduction in unemployment benefits:[182]

[179] *National Income and Expenditure 1946–52* (1953), Tables 27, 30, 34, 35.

[180] Based on the *Monthly Digest of Statistics*; also John Vaizey, *The Cost of the Social Services* (Fabian Research Series, No. 166) (1954).

[181] Cf. other figures in A. J. Youngson, *The British Economy 1920–1957* (1960), p. 216; A. T. Peacock, *The Economics of National Insurance*, p. 24; Peacock and Browning, pp. 144–5; Hagenbuch, p. 213.

[182] Peacock and Browning, p. 151.

Table 6·16: Proportional growth in social services expenditure

	1937–8	1947–8	1950–1
Total expenditure on the social services as % of gross national income at market prices, plus transfers	9·8	14·8	16·9
Transfer payments, as % of personal incomes before tax, including transfers	5·4	5·4	5·7
Gross capital expenditure on the social services, as % of gross domestic capital formation	10·4	15·3	14·8

Of equal importance with the growth in quantity and extent of the welfare services, was the new spirit behind the provisions of the 'Welfare State', a spirit of communal responsibility and humanity. The war hastened its application by removing, temporarily, the usual barriers of administrative conservatism and the power of vested interests. The changes planned in the last years of war were forced through in the early years of peace by the Labour Government, which could rightly claim to have been an administration of social reform, even if not, as its programme implied, of Socialism.

7

Production and Incomes in the Years of Peace, 1950–1980

1 Industrial Growth and Decline

By 1950 the immediate after-effects of the war had been overcome, both in the United Kingdom and abroad, and the world could settle down to the peaceful creation of wealth which most of its citizens expected after the holocaust. The Korean War, it is true, was soon to shatter the precarious peace and to distort prices and production once again; but in retrospect it appears as the first violent clash within the uneasy world balance of forces which marked the peace, rather than as the last battle of the war. The economic disturbances it caused were not strong enough to interrupt the upward movement of output and productivity, which has become perhaps the most striking of all aspects of post-war economic history among the advanced Western nations.

In the United Kingdom, as elsewhere in the West, the rate of saving, the level of investment in scientific research and development, and the rate of application of technical progress were very high in comparison with any earlier period of history and in consequence there was a faster rate of economic growth than perhaps in any previous age. Industrial output, the key factor, rose, according to one calculation, by 3·7% a year in 1948–60, compared with 3·1% in the inter-war years, and 1·6% in 1877–1913. In 1962–79, though losing in importance in the national income, it still rose by 2·2% a year. In the disastrous years 1979–81, however, it fell by 15%. Physical output per head rose by 1·60% a year in 1924–50 and 1·84% in 1954–63; thereafter output per man-hour in manufacturing rose by as much as 3·1% a year in 1963–1979, but it then remained stagnant in 1979–81.[1] Productivity thus increased faster than ever in manufacturing in the 1960s and 1970s, although the growth in total output was slowing down because there were now fewer people employed in the manufacturing sector.

Extended over the economy as a whole, including all other sectors, the standard measure is the Gross Domestic Product (GDP). GDP *per head* rose by 40% in 1950–66 against 29% in the similar pre-war period, 1920–36.[2]

---

[1] K. S. Lomax, 'Growth and Productivity in the United Kingdom', *Productivity Measurement Review*, 38 (1964), p. 6; W. B. Reddaway, in W. E. G. Salter *Productivity and Technical Change* (2nd ed., Cambridge, 1966), p. 198; and calculations based on *National Institute Economic Review* (quarterly).

[2] (London and Cambridge Economic Service), *The British Economy, Key Statistics 1900–1966*, Table C. Also see Angus Maddison, *Economic Growth in the West* (1964), p. 37; *National Institute Economic Review* (quarterly).

Despite sharp annual variations, the growth in the gross domestic product was continuous throughout the whole period until 1979 (see Table 7·1).[3]

Table 7·1: GDP per head of the labour force, at constant prices

	1950	100·0
Average of years	1951–5	106·0
	1956–60	116·8
	1961–5	132·0
	1966–70	151·0
	1971–5	169·8
	1976–80	178·6

This amounted to an annual compound growth rate of GDP of 2·2% per head, or a growth of total product of 2·9%, between 1950 and 1966, and an annual compound growth rate of 2·6% in total and 2·3% per head in 1966–79, after which output began to fall.

Such an increase, superimposed on a complex industrial society, was necessarily accompanied by a substantial change in the industrial and geographical distribution of employment, by the introduction of new technology and new products, and by the replacement of some existing industries by others. Much was heard in this period about the conservatism and restrictionism of the British worker and manager, about their unwillingness to innovate or to accept change, and about their fondness for tradition, and it is true that, in comparison with otherwise similar Continental economies, British industry was less inclined to scrap the old and accept the new. Yet the changes in industrial structure were large by any standards.

On the whole, they followed, and in some cases completed, the structural transformation of the economy which had begun in the 1920s. Its main components were a relative and, in some cases, an absolute decline of the old 'staple' and export industries, including shipping; their replacement by others fulfilling the same functions; and the creation of altogether new industries, meeting new needs or using new materials and components. It was a significant feature of this transformation that improved technology and rising productivity were to be found both in the declining and in the expanding industries and occupations.

Agriculture was a good case in point. Its output doubled from an index number of 88 in 1950 to 178 in 1980, while its employment declined sharply by about one-third.[4] This increase in output was spread over all the main

---

[3] Ministry of Labour, *National Statistics on Incomes, Prices, Employment and Production.* Also Phyllis Deane and W. E. Cole, *British Economic Growth, 1688–1959* (2nd ed., Cambridge, 1967), Appx. Table 90, and *National Income and Expenditure* (annual). Series spliced around indices based on 1958, 1970, and 1975.

[4] *Key Statistics*; National Income and Expenditure. On another base (1975 = 100) at constant factor cost, the output of agriculture, forestry and fishing moved as follows:

1950	60·8
1960	75·7
1970	95·5
1980	120·5

products – grain, meat, dairy and market gardening. Land use, in fact, changed little over the period:[5]

Table 7·2: Land utilization, United Kingdom (million acres)

	1948	1965	1980
Tillage	13·2	12·0	12·4
Rotational grass	5·5	6·6	4·9
Arable	18·7	18·6	17·3
Permanent grass	12·4	12·1	12·7
Rough grazing	17·2	17·8	16·9
Total agricultural area	48·3	48·5	46·9

Since land remained constant and labour declined, the output increase was achieved largely by better equipment and better techniques. The equipment included the further extension of mechanization: the number of agricultural tractors licensed in 1951, 1966 and 1979 increased from 313,000 to 446,000 and 508,000. The new techniques included intensive breeding and better pest control. The stock of plant and machinery in agriculture, valued in constant (1958) prices at replacement cost, increased from £0·5 billion in 1951 to £0·8 billion in 1965, and gross capital at 1975 replacement cost, increased from £7·4 billion in 1970 to £9·7 billion in 1980.[6] The approximate calculations of annual percentage changes in Table 7·3 summarize the components of the output and productivity rise in agriculture:[7]

Table 7·3: Agricultural output and productivity

	1951–64	1965–80
Output	+ 2·6%	+ 2·1%
Labour	− 2·4%	− 1·7%
Capital	+ 1·5%	+ 3·0%
Labour productivity	+ 5·0%	+ 3·8%
Total factor productivity	+ 3·5%	+ 0·8%

This heavy programme of investment in an industry still made up of relatively small units[8] reflected the confidence of farmers in a continuing policy of agricultural support by the Government. This confidence was only to a small extent based on the Agricultural Act of 1947: it largely relied on the

[5] *Agricultural Statistics* (annual).

[6] *National Income and Expenditure*. Also see S. G. Hooper, *The Finance of Farming in Great Britain* (1955); M. T. Stewart, 'Capital in Scottish Agriculture', *Scottish Agricultural Economics*, 15 (1965); and literature quoted in K. E. Hunt and K. R. Clark, *The State of British Agriculture*, 6, 1965–6 (Oxford, 1966), pp. 20–1

[7] J. F. Wright, *Britain in the Age of Economic Management* (Oxford, 1979), p. 28; *Agricultural Statistics; National Income and Expenditure; Employment Gazette*; A. P. Power and S. A. Harris, *Agricultural Expansion in the United Kingdom with Declining Manual Labour Resources* (1973).

[8] In England and Wales, the average size of holdings increased from 66·4 acres in 1949 to 75·5 in 1964, and 188·4 in 1980, and the land in holdings of 500 acres and over, from 2,663,000 to 3,917,000 acres between 1949 and 1964, while the number of holdings over 500 acres rose from 5,747 in 1964 to over 9,000 in 1980. Hunt and Clark, p. 58; *Agricultural Statistics*.

assurance that in a highly protectionist country like post-war Britain agriculture, also, would have its particular security. After Britain joined the European Community in 1973, its common agricultural policy (CAP) strengthened the British farmer's feeling of security.

Agricultural policy, in fact, went through several phases. At first, under labour, the object was to secure higher production at all costs. This was continued up to the price review of 1952, when the saving of dollars was still stressed in a further expansion programme designed to raise output from 50% above pre-war, at which it stood then, to 60%. After this, policy changed sharply: the Government was no longer willing to 'plan' for specific quantities for any or all commodities, but, in parallel with its dismantling of food rationing and other controls, would undertake only to attempt to let supply and demand meet at acceptable consumer price levels. The actual mechanism of support was highly complex. Cereal and fatstock producers, who were in substantial competition with importers, were compensated by a set of 'deficiency payments' calculated retrospectively to meet the gap between the prices they obtained and the higher prices guaranteed by the annual review. From 1954, milk and potatoes, and from 1957, eggs, were sold by monopolistic official marketing boards which recovered and distributed the subsidies on behalf of the Government. After the Annual Review of 1962, it was the consumer, not the Government, who paid for the milk subsidy.[9] The system as a whole was designed both to give the consumer the benefit of (lower) world food prices, and to keep up efficiency incentives for farmers, while leaving the 'planning' of production to the farmer himself in the light of expected costs and prices and the variable subsidy.

In the mid-1950s the post-war world food shortage gave way to an incipient surplus in Western markets and it was largely due to the striking improvement in productivity and reduction in real costs that the subsidies declined in this period from the £382 million paid over in 1950 to an annual figure of around £250 – £300 in the mid-1960s to the early 1970s. They then rose about fivefold to a peak of £1,336 million in 1975, only to fall back again to £465 million in 1979 and £649 million in 1980 in current prices, or an index, in real terms, of 217 in 1975 and 81 in 1980 (1970 = 100). The Agriculture Act of 1957 attempted to allay the farmers' fears of drastic cuts in support by limiting the annual guaranteed price changes. In the 1965 annual price review, in a special white paper,[10] and in the National Plan for economic development of that year, the emphasis was again put on the increase in total output and on import savings. Various measures, including the Agriculture Act of 1966, were to help particularly the small farmer and the hill farmer, by advice, credit facilities and direct support.

The system has been criticized for giving greater support to the well-off farmer who needs it least, and less support to the farmer on poorer land or with less managerial ability; from the mid-1950s on, this was borne in mind when price subsidies were sharply reduced, but improvement grants extended

[9] E.g. Report on *Agricultural Marketing Schemes for the Years 1938–55* (1957); *Guarantees for Home-Grown Cereals*, Cmd. 8947 (1953); J. G. S. and Frances Donaldson, *Farming in Britain Today* (1969), pp. 41–8.

[10] *Annual Review and Determination of Guarantees*, Cmnd. 2621 (1965), *The Development of Agriculture*, Cmnd. 2738 (1965).

for capital investment under the Farm Improvement Scheme of 1957, and other direct grants to the small farmer under the Small Farm Scheme of 1959, the Horticulture Act of 1960 and the Agriculture and Horticulture Act of 1964. The system has also been criticized for attempting to achieve several, and partly contradictory aims:[11] the saving of foreign exchange, the improvement of home standards of nutrition, particularly milk consumption, and the provision of stable incomes and employment in agriculture. Certainly, over two-thirds of farmers' net income after the end of rationing has been provided by subsidies, which still left the average farmer's income at only £1,200 a year gross, or £900 net (i.e. after deducting interest on his capital), in 1960. Yet the gains were substantial. The increase in net output by 1960 was worth £300 m. a year, and more in foreign exchange, as higher British demand would have driven up world food prices, so that agriculture's claim for support on grounds of import-savings was very great. As a proportion of GNP, food imports fell from 8·9% in 1951 to 4·1% in 1976,[12] partly because of better terms of trade, partly because of the low income elasticity of food[13] and in part by greater efficiency. The strongest justification for the support which agriculture has received lies in its high rate of increase in output and, above all, in productivity; although, in turn, the reason for this success was its relative immunity from the repeated cuts and 'stops' by which Government policy prevented similar increases in the other sectors.[14]

The CAP which Britain had to accept on joining the European Community (EC) in 1973 had been inspired by similar objectives: rising efficiency, guaranteed regular supplies and stable markets with reasonable prices for consumers and fair incomes for the farming population. However, the latter was much larger than in Britain and self-sufficiency in food was much closer. Thus Britain supplied only three-quarters of her own meat and vegetables in 1974–5, two-thirds of her wheat and cheese, one-third of her rye and fresh fruit, one-fifth of her sugar and one-ninth of her butter, while the other members of the EC as a group were self-sufficient or had surpluses in all of these except the fresh fruit. Consequently, instead of holding prices down to world levels and paying subsidies to the farmers as in Britain, the CAP

---

[11] John R. Raeburn, 'Agricultural Production and Marketing', in Duncan Burn (ed.), *The Structure of British Industry* (2 vols., Cambridge, 1958), I, pp. 42–4; E. F. Nash, *Agricultural Policy in Britain: Selected Papers* (Cardiff, 1965).

[12] J. F. Wright, *Britain*, p. 10.

[13] It was calculated in 1968 that the income elasticities of demand for food in the United Kingdom were as follows:

Beef	0·71
Pigmeat	0·61
Mutton and lamb	− 0·10
Butter	0·60
Cheese	0·39
Margarine	− 0·49
Bread	− 0·76

T. E. Josling, 'The Future Demand for Food in Western Europe', in S. T. Rogers and B. H. Davey, *The Common Agricultural Policy and Britain* (Farnborough, 1973), p. 88.

[14] Peter Self and H. J. Storing, *The State and the Farmer* (1962), pp. 220 ff.; *Agriculture*, Cmnd. 1249 (1960); H. T. Williams, *Principles for British Agricultural Policy* (1960), pp. 64 ff., 167; Gavin McCrone, *The Economics of Subsidizing Agriculture. A Study of British Policy* (1962); OECD, *Agricultural Policies in 1966*.

allowed prices to rise to 'target' levels, suited to their own high farming costs, and levied duties on imports at a rate to bring them up to those prices. 'Intervention' prices were set somewhat below the target prices, and if prices fell below them, the CAP intervened, usually by buying up the surpluses. The system including export subsidies was financed through the European Agricultural Guidance and Guaranteed Fund, which in turn received its income from the import levies and from direct Government payments, the latter increasingly not by the home Government, but by the EC as a whole.[15]

CAP had a large number of disadvantages compared with the British system. First, it had no incentive to efficiency. Secondly, it produced surpluses which had to be stored at great expense or sold at give-away prices to third countries. Thirdly, it led to high prices. Thus in 1972–3, at the time of the British entry, typical prices compared as shown in Table 7·4.[16]

Table 7·4:   British and EEC agricultural prices, 1972–3

		EEC			UK
		Target	Basic Intervention	Guidance	Guaranteed
Soft Wheat,	£ per ton	47·41	43·65	—	34·40
Barley	£　″　″	43·44	39·88	—	31·20
Fat cattle,	£ live cwt.	—	—	15·63	13·20
Pig meat, £ score dw.		—	3·10	—	2·81
Milk, p. per gallon		23·00	—	—	20·60 (pool).

Fourthly, the CAP blocked the sale of foreign low-cost producers and was protectionist, while the British system was free. Fifthly, there was no upper limit set to the necessary support. Sixthly, by throwing part of the burden of inefficient farming, especially in France and Italy, onto other countries, mainly Germany and Britain, it led to annual recriminations, and has done more than any other element to sour relations among the European partners and divert them from building up the EC. Lastly, because of the shift in the value of currencies to each other, artificial units of account (the 'green pound') had to be used in the CAP to preserve the target and intervention rates which diverged increasingly from real prices and encouraged large-scale smuggling, totally contrary to the spirit in which the Common Market was designed. For Britain, with her highly efficient farms and high import needs, the system was particularly harmful, but had to be accepted as the price of entering.

The CAP also made provision for grants and payments; the basis was the notion of 'viability', which related farm incomes to locally current wage rates. In 1972 it was calculated that of 4·2 million farmers in the community, 3·5 million were 'non-viable'.[17] Payments are made for capital and other

---

[15] A. R. Prest and D. J. Coppock, *The UK Economy. A Manual of Applied Economies* (7th ed., 1978), pp. 175–8; T. Josling, 'Agricultural Policy' in Peter Coffey (ed.), *Economic Policies of the Common Market* (1979).

[16] B. H. Davey, 'Supplies, Incomes and Structural Change in UK Agriculture', in Rogers and Davey, p. 97.

[17] J. van Lierde, 'Recent EEC Decisions in Price and Structural Policy', in Rogers and Davey, p. 53.

improvements as formerly in Britain; but also for older people, aged over 55 and 60 respectively, to leave farming altogether – in direct contradiction to the bulk of the CAP which encourages them to stay.

The shifts within industry, and manufacturing in particular, are illustrated in Table 7·5, showing the changes from 1950 to 1980–81 in some major industrial sectors:[18]

Table 7·5:   Production and employment in industry

	Index of industrial production, 1980 (1964 = 100)	Index, employees in employment,		
		June 1950	June 1963	Sept.– Dec. 1981
Coal mining	59·7	136·2	100*	56·5*
Food, drink and tobacco	131·8	101·8	100	75·2
Coal and petroleum products	120·9	—	100**	57·0**
Chemicals and allied	190·4	92·9	100	75·5
Ferrous metals	49·6	92·5	100	52·4
Non-ferrous metals	55·8			
Mechanical engineering	115·3†	81·9	100*	59·0*
Electrical engineering	140·0	60·8	100*	71·1
Shipbuilding and marine engineering	72·3	150·1	100	66·3
Motor vehicles	75·7	111·1	100*	66·2*
Textiles	88·3	140·3	100	43·5
Clothing and footwear	111·4	129·3	100	53·8
Bricks, cement	92·1	73·9	100	59·9
Pottery, glass	139·6			
Timber, furniture	101·1	110·8	100	76·9
Paper, printing, publishing	115·6	83·5	100	77·7
All manufacturing	114·3	100·1	100	67·0
Construction	96·0	88·5	100	70·7
Gas, electricity, water	181·0	91·4	100	82·3
All industries other than construction	128·9	—	100	66·9
All industries	122·4	99·8	100	91·1††

* Base: March 1965 = 100
** Base: June 1970 = 100
† Mechanical and electrical engineering not separated out 1971–80.
†† All industries and services.

Two developments stand out. One was the divergence in the output statistics, particularly between the old staples, which actually declined sharply even in absolute terms, and the 'new' industries and others which recorded rises in output, although they were also shedding labour in substantial numbers. Thus the output of the chemical and allied industries has grown by over 90% in 16 years, and that of gas, electricity and water by over 80%. Electrical engineering as well as pottery and glass showed a 40% rise, food, drink and tobacco over 30%, coal and petroleum products 20% and paper, printing and publishing, together with mechanical engineering, still a rise of

[18] *Employment Gazette*, and Central Statistical Office. The Index of Industrial Production splices the index of weight 1970 with that of 1975, and is therefore only approximately correct.

some 15%. By contrast, the old staples of coal, iron and steel, shipbuilding and textiles showed actual declines. Motor vehicles, a leading growth sector of the 1930s, was now among the losers[19] and the sharp decline in iron and steel, compared with its relative stability in the inter-war period, may seem equally surprising.

The second development requiring an explanation is the steep fall in employment in all manufacturing industries, including those still supplying growing markets in real terms. That downward drift, which reverses the trend of at least two centuries and reflects one of the most significant changes of recent years, began only in the early 1970s. Up to then, employment in manufacturing industry had been stable, with a peak in 1965–6, and in 1970 was actually 145,000 above the level of 1963. Since then, the decline has been steady and seemingly irreversible. Falling at a rate of 1·1% in 1966–74, it then accelerated to over 3% a year. The decline in manufacturing *output* as a proportion of GNP at constant prices began just a little later, the turning point being 1972.[20]

The causes of this decline are made up of three main components. The first is the shift, worldwide and evident since the beginning of this century, from the manufacturing (as well as the agrarian) sector to employment in the tertiary, service sector.[21] Thus, while employment in manufacturing fell by almost 30% between 1970 and the end of 1981, employment in the service sector changed as shown in Table 7·6.[22]

Table 7·6: Changes in employment in the service sector (1970 = 100)

	June 1950	Sept. 1981	Average annual change, %
Transport and communication	113·9	90·4	− 0·7
Distributive trades	81·3	97·2	+ 0·6
Insurance, banking, finance, business services	46·0	127·9	+ 3·3
Professional and scientific services	51·7	125·3	+ 2·9
Miscellaneous services	95·6	130·0	+ 1·0
Public administration and defence	101·9	109·5	+ 0·2

In five of these services (excluding transport and communication) there worked, in September 1981, some 11·2 million employees, or 54% of all employed, and almost twice as many as in the workforce in manufacturing. These services have, therefore, in a real sense, become the determining sector in the labour market. These five services also accounted for the following shares in GDP:[23]

1950	35·1%
1960	36·3%
1970	40·6%
1980	49·5%

[19] See pp. 288–92 below.

[20] Ajit Singh, 'UK Industry and the World Economy: A Case of De-industrialisation?' *Cambridge Journal of Economics* 1, 1977, pp. 123–4.

[21] Colin Clark, *The Conditions of Economic Progress* (3rd ed., 1957).

[22] *Employment Gazette.*

[23] *National Income and Expenditure* (annual).

Inasfar as the switch to the services represents a necessary shift in the industrial structure, arising from differing demand elasticities for services, and from the success of mass production techniques in saving labour in the manufacturing sector, it has to be viewed as a natural phenomenon within a growing and modernizing economy.

In the same light has to be seen the rise in the public sector, which has been particularly singled out by some observers as being responsible for the choking off of British manufacturing. The negative effect here is alleged to be twofold, consisting not only in the diversion of resources from productive to unproductive activity, from making to administering, but also from the market sector, where demand is predominant and inefficiency is punished, to the non-market sector which need not fulfil any useful function, but can yet go on growing because of its inner dynamic in quest of jobs and personal aggrandizement. After declining as a share of national income to around 1965, giving rise to the criticism of 'private affluence and public squalor', the public sector has indeed grown since then despite repeated efforts to halt that growth. But apart from competing for a different type of labour, mostly low-paid female labour in place of the skilled male labour displaced in manufacturing,[24] the public sector has been expanding in all countries and thus cannot account for Britain's particular problems; nor can it be termed non-productive: it is frequently only political tradition which decides whether, say, the telephone system, education or steel production should be profit-making or public. It may well be that growing incomes, and the growing complexities of production necessary to produce them, demand an enlargement of just those sectors which tend to be public or non-market oriented.

There were, however, two other components in this significant decline in manufacturing employment, and they are not unconnected with each other. One is the successful penetration of the British market by foreign manufacturers, without an equivalent success of British manufacturers abroad; and the other is the rising unemployment, evident from the mid-1970s, but taking on disastrous dimensions only since 1979, and concentrated heavily on the manufacturing sector. Both have given grounds for concern, and together they have raised the spectre of the de-industrialization of Britain.

The high and rising level of unemployment, as far as it is connected with British and world problems of monetary dislocations and economic policies, will be considered in section 3 of this chapter and in chapter 9; here we turn to the falling competitiveness of British manufacturers. This is shown above all the falling share of British manufactured exports among the main suppliers of world markets, a fall which has been continuous since the war (see Table 7.7).[25]

---

[24] Alec Cairncross, 'What is De-Industrialisation?' p. 8 and C. J. F. Brown and T. D. Sheriff, 'De-Industrialisation, a Background Paper', p. 253, in Frank Blackaby (ed.), *De-Industrialisation* (1979); Robert Bacon and Walter Eltis, *Britain's Economic Problem: Too Few Producers* (1976).

[25] *National Institute Economic Review* (quarterly). Also see Sir Alec Cairncross, J. A. Kay and A. Silberston, 'The Regeneration of Manufacturing Industry', *Midland Bank Review*, Autumn 1977, p. 11–12.

Table 7·7: The fall in British manufactured exports

Averages of years	British exports of manufactures as percentage share of world total
1951–3	21·4
1959–61	16·5
1969–71	10·9
1975–7	9·1

This decline was not due, as in the 1920s, to an overvalued currency; with some delays and hiccups, the exchange rate had fallen at least in line with the rise in home inflation, and Britain was increasingly becoming a low-wage country. At current rates of exchange, average hourly wages in manufacturing had by 1981 (based on calculations in Deutschmark), with Britain as 100, reached 171·6 in Sweden, 156·4 in Germany, 156·1 in the USA and even 102·0 in Japan.[26] Nor was the decline due to adversely changing patterns of trade. The problem was, rather, inability to deliver on time or at the appropriate quality, in other words, a supply problem,[27] and this to some extent explains the remarkable ability of exports to keep up just when they might have been expected to fall most, in 1980–1, in the years when the pound was rising on the foreign exchanges and inflation in Britain was higher than in almost all competing countries. Similarly, the significant observation that with rising incomes, the United Kingdom had a very high elasticity of demand for imported manufactures, in many cases of a value of 2, while the world had a much lower income elasticity for British exports, in like cases a little over 1,[28] was not simply an Act of God, but was related to the failure of British manufacturers, in competition with others, to produce adequately what the world wanted.

Of equal concern in that period was the rise in import penetration. This had been noticeable earlier, but became acute in the second half of the 1970s, when imports from other members of the EC had to be permitted without hindrance, and rising unemployment at home made manufacturers everywhere look sharply to exports for compensation. This failure of British manufactures in the home market was particularly noticeable among some of the high-technology, high-growth industries, but also affected some of the older staples. Among the worst were those shown in Table 7·8.[29]

[26] On unit Labour costs, see p. 322 below.

[27] Brown and Sheriff, pp. 256–9; Michael Posner and Andrew Steer, 'Price Competitiveness and the Performance of Manufacturing Industry', p. 159, D. K. Stout, 'De-Industrialisation and Industrial Policy', pp. 176–7 and Thomas Balogh, 'Comment', pp. 179–9, in F. Blackaby, *De-Industrialisation*; Report in *Frankfurter Allgemeine Zeitung*, 19.6.1982; S. Pollard, *The Wasting of the British Economy* (1982), pp. 81–4; *Nat. Inst. Econ. Rev.*, 39, February 1967, p. 16.

[28] A. P. Thirlwall, 'The UK's Economic Problem: a Balance of Payments Constraint?' *National Westminster Bank Review*, February 1978, pp. 29–30, and 'The Balance of Payments Constraint as an Explanation of International Growth Rate Differences', *Banca Nazionale del Lavoro Quarterly Review*, 128, 1979, p. 51.

[29] *Annual Abstract of Statistics*.

Table 7·8: Imports as a percentage of home demand

	1971	1980
All manufacturing	17·1	25·4
Vehicles	15	39
Electrical engineering	18	37
Instrument engineering	37	61
Clothes and footwear	14	30

Some industries held their own, and others even enlarged their share. Moreover, there was also a substantial rise in manufacturing exports in those years as measured against GNP, but imports expanded faster,[30] and the gap widened significantly in 1980–1.

We now turn to individual industries. Coal mining remained a problem, but the issues had changed since the inter-war years. Because of the run-down state of the industry, and the efforts which had to be devoted simply to reorganization in the early years of the National Coal Board, coal mining was slow to show any improvements in output per manshift. Long-term improvement began with the plan of 1950[31] which proposed major reconstructions, the closure of 350–400 pits then working, new sinkings and general re-equipment to meet the estimated demand for coal for the next 15 years, until 1965. In the early years, however, all the efforts did little beyond countering the natural tendency of mining costs to rise with the age of the workings. Output per manshift refused obstinately to reach the magic figure of 25 cwt, and total saleable output similarly did not rise beyond the 210 m.t. level, while from 1953 onward the number of workers in the industry actually began to fall. Throughout this period, the supply of coal was well below the demand, the gap being variously estimated at between 15 and 20 million tons a year.[32] In one sense this 'gap' only existed because coal was seriously under-priced,[33] both in terms of costs and in terms of what the market would bear, and coal thus became a hidden means of subsidizing British industry, even to the extent of negative dumping, or selling at a higher price abroad than at home. But in fact, in the boom years of the 1950s, incredible as it might have seemed to another age, coal had to be imported, to the tune of 25 million tons all told, much of it from the dollar area. Because of the neglect of earlier investment in productive capacity, the booming demand led not just to full order books, full working, incentives to invest, and readiness thereby to meet the next expansion in demand, as it did elsewhere, but to imports of a commodity traditionally produced at home.

However, in the recession induced in 1957 and lasting until 1959, a major change-over to oil, fostered by the coal shortage itself, was superimposed on

[30] Clare Group, 'Problems of Industrial Recovery', *Midland Bank Review*, Spring 1982, p. 11.

[31] National Coal Board, *Plan for Coal* (1950); the revised plans were published as *Investing in Coal* (1956) and *Revised Plan for Coal* (1959). Cf. also A. Beacham, 'Planned Investment in the Coal Industry', *Oxf. Econ. P.*, 3/2 (1951) and K. S. Lomax, 'The Demand for Coal in Great Britain', *ibid.*, 4/1 (1952).

[32] PEP *Growth in the British Economy* (1960), pp. 99–103; Beacham, 'The Coal Industry', in Burn, *op. cit.*

[33] I. M. D. Little, *The Price of Fuel* (Oxford, 1953).

the long-term decline in demand. Coal consumption in the United Kingdom fell from 214 million tons in 1956 to 187 million tons in 1959, while oil consumption rose from 18 to 33 million tons (coal equivalent) and 0·5 m.t. equivalent was produced by nuclear energy. Coal stocks began to build up to 8·6 m.t. at the end of 1957, 19·7 m.t. in 1958, and 35·7 m.t. or about two months' output at the end of 1959. Ironically, it was precisely at this point that the investment and reorganization of earlier years began to bear fruit. Productivity increased, and over-production, as in the inter-war years, appeared on the horizon.[34] Calamity was averted by a massive programme of investment and reorganization. The plan of 1950 had involved the spending of £635 million in 1950–65. By 1956, the new plan envisaged a total of £1,350 million (or £500 million more, at 1955 prices) for a lower output target. The plan was changed again in 1959, in the light of the apparent permanent fall in demand, from the 1965 target of 240 m.t. to a target of 206 m.t., which was about the level of the actual 1959 production. This scaling down allowed the closing of high-cost pits to proceed even faster than had been intended, and the number of NCB mines in production in Great Britain fell from 901 at the beginning of 1951 to 438 in March, 1967. Output per manshift rose from 24·9 cwt in 1957 to 36·6 cwt in 1966–7, or by nearly one-half, and similarly output per man year stood at 293 t. in 1950 and 390 t. in 1966–7.

This striking success was reflected also in the accounts. In spite of the low-price policy, which deprived the National Coal Board of its own finance and forced it to increase its interest burden very heavily by outside borrowing, the rise in costs was kept below that of proceeds and in the mid-1960s it appeared that the Board might be permanently out of the red. The Board's chairman, Lord Robens, succeeded in reducing employment from a maximum of 711,000 in 1952 to 419,000 in 1967,[35] without arousing major opposition from the men. The care with which local closures and transfers of labour were prepared compared very favourably with the methods of some other industries in similar circumstances.

In November, 1967, a new white paper[36] announced a planned reduction of manpower to one-sixth, or a mere 65,000 by 1980 in the seven main regions, and an expected share of coal of only 120 m.t. out of a national total of 350 m.t. coal equivalent by 1975, a fall of 31% in output and 24% in the share of all fuels. This pessimistic forecast was justified in part by the relatively slow rise in fuel consumption, caused, in turn, by growing technical efficiency in the use of fuel, the slow growth of some large energy users like iron and steel, and the competition from oil, which turned out to be cheaper for all purposes; to this has to be added competition from natural gas from the mid-1960s onward. The output of the National Coal Board did indeed fall by − 4·3% a year in 1960–75, and employment by − 5·9%. Productivity rose by an annual + 1·7%, achieved in part by continuing mechanization. While 92% of coal was already mechanically cut in 1960, power loading increased

[34] E. S. Simpson, *Coal and the Power Industries in Post-war Britain* (1966), p. 16.

[35] National Coal Board, *Annual Report and Accounts*.

[36] *Fuel Policy*, Cmnd. 3438 (1967).

from 38% in 1960 to 93% in 1973, and coal from power-supplied faces, from 10% to 91%.[37]

An even greater fall in the demand for coal was prevented by the deliberate Government policy to keep coal-fired power stations going: these took 21·8% of coal supplies in 1957 and 62·9% in 1976. Meanwhile, however, the oil price rise of 1973–4 made coal competitive once more and transformed the industry's prospects. Re-expansion of output was planned, to add 42 million tons by 1980, and newly discovered fields were being developed at Selby in Yorkshire, and in Warwickshire. Output, having fallen from around 180 m.t. in the 1960s and 135 m.t. in 1970, stabilized around 110 m.t. saleable coal in 1971–81,[38] the share of coal in energy consumption staying around the 37% mark 1973–1980, while the share of petroleum fell from 46·5% to 36·8% and the share of natural gas rose from 12·5% to 21·5%. The number of miners also stabilized, being 230,000 in 1980–1, and this has allowed the men to return to their former position near the top of the wages league from which the temporary eclipse of coal had dislodged them.

Until 1973, oil was the fastest grower in the energy sector. Refining in Britain was furthered for strategic reasons and to save imports, but a home-based oil refining industry also provided some flexibility in varying the proportions of the product according to home needs and created a base for the petro-chemical industry. Beginning with the Shell plant at Stanlow (1947) and the Esso refinery at Fawley (1951), capacity in Britain increased from 29 million tons in 1953 to 88 million tons at the end of 1966 and 133 million tons in 1980. At the latter date, all but 3% of the refining was carried out in plants of over 1 million tons capacity, and three plants were at, or above, the 10 million ton optimum: Fawley (Esso), Kent (BP) and Shell Haven (Shell).[39]

The industry is highly capital intensive, and the small labour force showed one of the fastest rises in productivity per man in British industry. Larger throughput led to lower costs, so that a refinery of a capacity of 10 million tons had little more than one-third of the unit costs of a refinery of a half-million ton capacity. It is dominated by a handful of giants, British, American and Dutch, all with large international interests, forming one of the world's most powerful oligopolies.[40] Nevertheless, competition was fierce in certain areas and one form which it took after 1945, the buying up and tying in of the retail outlets, the petrol stations, was in striking parallel to the action of the brewers over half a century earlier. Opinion was divided on the value of this system to the customers, but the Monopolies Commission refused to condemn it outright.[41]

---

[37] National Economic Development Office, *A Study of the UK Nationalised Industries* (1976), p. 13; G. F. Ray and L. Uhlmann, *The Innovation Process in the Energy Industry* (Cambridge, 1979), p. 43.

[38] Prest and Coppock, p. 179. Actual output was 122·4 m. tonnes in 1979 and 130·1 m. tonnes in 1980. Department of Energy, *Digest of United Kingdom Energy Statistics*, 1981; NCB, *Plan for Coal* (1974).

[39] C. Pratten and R. M. Dean, *The Economics of Large-Scale Production in British Industry* (Cambridge, 1965), pp. 93, 97; Duncan Burn, 'The Oil Industry', in *Structure of British Industry*, I; E. S. Simpson, *op. cit.*, chapters 8 and 10; J. H. Dunning and C. J. Thomas, *British Industry, Change and Development in the Twentieth Century* (1961), pp. 89–92.

[40] Peter Odell, *Oil: The New Commanding Height* (Fabian Society, 1965), pp. 5–7.

[41] Monopolies Commission, *Petrol: A Report on the Supply of Petrol to Retailers in the*

In the 1970s, two dramatic developments affected the oil industry. The first was the sudden price rise engineered by OPEC, the organization of the leading oil exporters, following the Arab-Israeli war of 1973. From a stable level of £7–8 per tonne, held over the whole period 1950–72[42] in the face of a general inflation of world prices, the price was quadrupled to £33 per tonne by 1974, rose to £50–60 in 1976–8 and was increased substantially once more in 1979. The drastic cutback in consumption and switch to other fuels, with which all countries, including the United Kingdom, reacted to this sea-change, together with the rapid development of new oil fields in many parts of the world, could mitigate but not remove its catastrophic effects. In Britain, oil consumption, which had been rising at a rate of 8% a year, actually dropped from a maximum of 113 m. tonnes in 1973 to stabilize around 90 m.t. from 1975 onward; for Western Europe as a whole, where consumption had been growing much faster, the fall was from 749 m.t. in 1973 to around 700 m.t. thereafter. But despite these savings, the quantities involved were large enough to create unprecedented balance of payments difficulties for all importing countries, which included the major western industrial nations, and an unmanageable surplus for the oil exporters, estimated at $66 billion in 1974 and $42 billion in 1975. The earlier switch to oil and other fuels was everywhere reversed, and the worldwide technological search for fuel economy was boosted.

Equally dramatic was the impact of the discovery of oil in the North Sea, first confirmed as commercially viable in 1971. In November 1975 oil from the Forties field reached British shores, by 1976, one-eighth of consumption was met by the home field, by 1978 it was five-ninths, and by 1981 North Sea output was larger than home needs and provided a small net export surplus.

The effects of this turn-round were felt in all sectors of the economy. The oil payments deficit, which had risen in the early 1970s to around £3·5 billion a year, was kept up at first by the need to import much of the necessary heavy equipment, such as drilling platforms and pipelines; their imports peaked at £1·2 billion in 1976 and 1977. In the heavy investment years, 1976–9, the annual capital formation in North Sea gas and oil exceeded £2 billion and amounted to one-quarter of all British industrial investment and one-tenth of total gross fixed capital formation. Between one-third and two-fifths of this came from British companies, and to the extent that it relied on bank finance, it represented 4·4% of all advances of UK banks to UK residents by August 1978.[43]

On the positive side, the oil bonanza created at once new wealth and new jobs: 19,000 in Scotland in 1974 alone. Aberdeen became the centre of a boom region and the builders of the oil rig platforms also found lucrative, if fluctuating, employment. On a national basis, the flow of oil likewise reversed the age-old balance of payments threat into an easy surplus and the pound sterling rose on the foreign exchanges. Lastly, as the concessions of

United Kingdom (1965); Harry Townsend, 'Exclusive Dealing in Petrol: Some Comments', *Economica*, 32/128 (1965).

[42] D. I. MacKay and G. A. Mackay, *The Political Economy of North Sea Oil* (1975), p. 5.

[43] L. P. Tempest, 'The Financing of North Sea Oil 1975–1980', *Bank of England Quarterly Bulletin*, 19, March 1979, pp. 31–4; L. P. Tempest and R. J. Walton, 'North Sea Oil and Gas in the UK Balance of Payments since 1970', *ibid.*, September 1979, pp. 283–9.

the early years expired, a large and growing share of the oil revenue began to flow to the Government, in the form of royalties and petroleum revenue tax in addition to the normal corporation and profits taxes. This flow to the Exchequer is forecast to peak in the early 1980s. The oil boom thus helped both to explain and to compensate for the decline of manufacturing industry in the later 1970s: in 1977–9 it added 0·7% to the annual growth rate of GDP.[44] It remains to be noted that the earlier hopes for nuclear power to compensate for the exhaustion of other energy sources has not been fulfilled. In the 1970s its contribution stagnated at 12–14 m. tonnes coal equivalent, or 3–4% of British energy consumption.

Space does not permit a detailed treatment of each of the manufacturing industries. We must content ourselves with cursory accounts of some select examples, representing 'new' industries (motors, chemicals), mixed (steel) and the 'old staples' (cotton, shipbuilding).

The motor car was, in many respects, the symbol of the post-war prosperity: a product of advanced technology and mass production, a luxury which had become a necessity, international in its influence and markets, a 'consumer durable' which permitted a distinct widening of personal experiences, as well as an increase in the comforts of those possessing it, and not least, typical in often being bought before it could be afforded, by means of credit. It was a colourful proof that the austerities and privations of the war years were over; it was also a yardstick of the producing country's industrial power.

The products of the British motor industry were destined both for the home market and for export, and the change from the post-war shortages, when markets were almost unlimited and the problem was merely one of capacity, came, as in most other industries, around the early 1950s. In the home market, supply did not catch up with the eager demand, and the sellers' market did not end, until 1955 or even later.[45] Abroad, the motor vehicle came to belong to the group of complex manufactured products in which there was expanding trade among the industrialized countries.

On the face of it, Britain appeared to have done well in the early years, since her output rose 88% between 1955 and 1964 (or by 7·3% a year). But world production outside the USA rose from 4,331,000 to 12,762,000 vehicles, or by no less than 195%.[46] At first, the United Kingdom occupied an unnaturally favourable position which she owed to the destruction wrought in the rest of Europe. By the late 1950s or early 1960s, however, the leading competitors had not merely recaptured their share, but had overtaken the United Kingdom in the productivity of their plant and the skill of their salesmanship and presentation.

By the 1970s, the British lag had become disastrous. Output of vehicles per employee year, adjusted for certain incomparabilities, changed as shown in Table 7·9.[47]

[44] *National Institute Economic Review*, February 1978.

[45] G. Maxcy and A. Silberston, *The Motor Industry* (1959), pp. 18–19.

[46] A. Silberston, 'The Motor Industry 1955–1964', *Bull. Oxf. Inst. Stat.*, 27/4 (1965).

[47] *Ibid.*, p. 270; Central Policy Review Staff, (CPRS), *The Future of the British Car Industry* (1975), p. 80.

Table 7·9: Output of vehicles per employee year

	1950	1955	1959	1965	1973
USA	10·0	11·1	10·3	13·9	14·9
United Kingdom	3·3	4·2	5·2	5·8	5·1
France	3·2	3·6	5·7	6·1	6·8
West Germany	2·2	3·9	5·6	7·1	7·3
Italy	—	3·0	—	7·4	6·8
Japan	—	1·2	—	4·4	12·2

The differences were particularly striking in the case of identical cars assembled in similar plants (or where differences in plants could be allowed for). Thus in 1973, the British plant needed 67% more labour to produce a Ford Escort than the German, 87% more for the Cortina than the Belgians needed for the Taunus, and 132% more than the Belgians for a Mini.[48]

In the 1950s, the momentum of earlier successes and the sheer growth of the market for cars and other motor vehicles, continued to carry the British industry upward on a path of expansion, as perhaps the typical growth industry; thereafter it equally clearly typified the decline of manufacturing. The shrinking employment is tabulated on p. 280 above (Table 7·5). But even output fell off, as shown in Table 7·10.[49]

Table 7·10: Output of motor vehicles

	Output, 000 vehicles				% Exported		
	1951	1966	1972	1980	1951	1966	1981
Passengers cars	476	1604	1921	924	77	34	24
Commercial vehicles	258	439	408	389	53	36	37
Agricultural tractors	137	214	134	103·5	82	63	—

Yet registrations continued to increase, as in other countries, undeterred even by the rising fuel prices – which were in any case weakened in their effects by the high tax element in the consumer price for petrol which did not go up in line with OPEC increases. Thus private car registrations increased from $2\frac{1}{2}$ million in 1951 to over $9\frac{1}{2}$ million in 1966 and over 15 million in 1980, and commercial vehicles and tractors, from 1·4 to 2·2 and 3·6 million. The gap betwen shrinking output and rising registrations was filled by imports. Imports took 5% of the British car market in 1965, 14% in 1970, 49% in 1978 and 58% in early 1982.[50] The major car manufacturers, it is true, have in recent years tended to distribute their components production over different countries, so that the meaning of an 'imported' or 'home'-produced car is no longer clear-cut.[51] Nevertheless, the figures give a fair indication of the catastrophic market losses.

Why had British makers failed to improve their productivity in line with the others? One answer was too many makers and too many models. In the

---

[48] *Economist*, 20 December 1975.

[49] Ministry of Transport. There was some re-classification, especially of estate cars for export, between 1952 and 1953.

[50] See also p. 284 above.

[51] George Maxcy, *The Multinational Motor Industry* (1981), p. 233.

early post-war years, minimal costs might be reached by an output of half a million units a year; for the whole range, one million or more was needed in the 1970s.[52] No British model ever reached that figure even though the number of models in the cheaper classes was indeed reduced, and the runs much increased, particularly for the Mini. There also occurred a striking movement of amalgamation which, together with substantial American share purchases, turned the numerous firms of 1945 into little more than four large groups, of which one was British owned (Leyland-BMC), and the other three were subsidiaries of the three major US Companies, Ford, General Motors (Vauxhall) and Chrysler (Rootes). The latter was sold, in turn, to Peugeot-Citroen in 1978. Between them, they controlled over 90% of car and commercial vehicle output, and those left outside were mostly specialist sports or high-class car makers. British Leyland had to be saved from bankruptcy in 1974 and was nationalized in 1975; British Chrysler also received large subsidies to keep it in being in 1975–9.[53]

Among the main landmarks were the mergers of Standard and Triumph (1945), Austin and Nuffield (1952), Rootes and Singer (1955), Jaguar and Daimler (1960), Leyland and Standard-Triumph (1961) and Leyland and BMC (1968).[54] In the 1950s, at a time when the steel industry was unable to supply sufficient sheet steel to the British car industry, there was also a general scramble to link up with the body manufacturers, including Ford-Briggs Motor Bodies (1953), BMC-Fisher & Ludlow (1953), BSA-Car Bodies (1954), Standard-Mulliners (1958), and BMC-Pressed Steel. The motor industry, as an assembly industry, pays over about half its costs to components manufacturers, other than body builders, and these also became dominated by a few large firms which might secure even longer runs by standardizing output between rival car makers: Joseph Lucas for electrical equipment, S. Smith and Sons, and Champion for sparking plugs and other equipment and Dunlop for tyres.

Yet, having amalgamated, the companies were slow to undertake a thorough structural reorganization. British Leyland, for example, still operated on 60 different sites, and only the immediate renewed threat of bankruptcy from 1979 onward allowed its forceful chairman, Sir Michael Edwardes, to plan the necessary reorganization, together with new models and modern plant. In the 1970s Ford's rationalized by sharing their components manufacture among works in four countries (including Northern Ireland), and General Motors (Vauxhall) went even further, moving virtually all its car making to Germany, and its commercial vehicles to Britain. British Leyland began to assemble and market a Honda car in 1981.[55]

The Government contributed to the fateful dispersal of productive plant

[52] A. Silberston, 'The Motor Industry', in D. L. Burn, *op. cit.* II. p. 18; Krish Bhaskar, *The Future of the UK Motor Industry* (1979), pp. 25–6.

[53] Department of Industry, *The British Motor Vehicle Industry*, Cmnd. 6377 (1976).

[54] G. Maxcy, 'The Motor Industry', in P. Lesley Cook (ed.), *Effects of Mergers* (1958). In the BMC (or more correctly, BM Holdings) merger with Leyland, official support was forthcoming with an investment of £25 million by the Industrial Re-organization Corporation.

[55] Maxcy, *Multinational*, pp. 145–6, 189; Derek F. Channon, *The Strategy and Structure of British Enterprise* (1973), pp. 107–8; Richard Pryke, *The Nationalised Industries: Policies and Performance since 1968* (Oxford, 1981), pp. 218ff.

by forcing the industry to build its extensions, not next to the main works, but in regions lacking employment. In the early 1960s, in consequence, Rootes opened a plant in Linwood, Scotland, for the production of the 'Imp' model, Vauxhall's developed a unit in Ellesmere Port, Standard-Triumph in Speke (Liverpool), Fords at Halewood (Merseyside) and BMC in Llanelly. This necessarily raised costs, and in the long run did nothing to help the regions.[56] Weakened by inefficiency, labour troubles or just bad luck, several of these plants have had to be closed again, throwing large numbers of workers on the dole just when alternative employment was also disappearing.

A further cause was the failure to bring the capital equipment up-to-date: or in other words, inadequate investment. This was particularly striking in the case of British Leyland before the Edwardes reorganization, but it was evident among other British firms also, just as, on an international basis, those countries and firms did best which provided the most modern plant for their workers.[57]

The causes of this low investment rate are complex, but one major influence was undoubtedly the Government's periodic, yet unpredictable switches to restraint and cutback, the reign of 'stop-go', which disoriented, destabilized and penalized precisely those industrialists who had to make large lumps of costly investments. The motor industry was additionally harmed by the frightening frequency of further changes in purchase tax, VAT rates and HP regulations, each of which altered the market conditions for cars, threw all planning into confusion and was bound to create difficulties and to demoralize all those concerned with making and selling motor vehicles. There were no fewer than 18 such changes in 1961–74,[58] precisely the years when makers abroad moved unhindered into newly expanding mass markets.

Other failings which emerged clearly in international comparison were bad and slow workmanship; extremely poor maintenance work; and numerous labour disputes and strikes. In those years, the motor industry took over the lead from the miners in strike proneness, particularly harmful in an assembly industry where holdups in one sector quickly affected the output of others. The number of strikes was extraordinarily high also by international standards.

The motor industry may thus, by its early post-war rise in a sellers' market and its later failures, be taken as symbolic for much of British industry. It was, however, more than a symbol. Its own size, together with its impact on the suppliers of components, such as sheet steel, glass, tyres and electrical equipment, made it in itself a significant determinant of British industrial progress. Elsewhere, including Germany, Italy, Japan and even France, car

---

[56] C. Pratten, *Economies of Scale in Manufacturing Industry* (Cambridge, 1971), p. 132; The Society of Motor Manufacturers and Traders (SMMT). *The British Motor Manufacturing Industry – A Students' Guide* (1979), pp. 2·2–2·3.

[57] For some striking figures, see CPRS, *Car Industry*, p. 54; Bhaskar, *Motor Industry*, p. 88.

[58] CPRS, *Car Industry*, pp. 123–5; SMMT, p. 6·1; Bhaskar, *Motor Industry*, pp. 15–16; NEDC, *Industrial Report by the Motor Manufacturing EDC: Economic Assessment to 1972* (1970), p. 37; *idem, The Effect of Government Economic Policy on the Motor Industry* (1968); Maxcy and Silberston, pp. 44–5; J. C. R. Dow, *The Management of the British Economy* (Cambridge, 1965), pp. 275–82.

manufacture became a 'leading industry', pulling others up in its meteoric rise, easing wider policies by its healthy export surplus, and encouraging modern techniques at several levels. By the same token, the decline of the British motor industry had wider effects; above all, it was among the most significant causes of the persistent balance of payments weakness, which in turn induced the Government to pursue macro-economic policies that were bound to do grievous harm to all productive industries.

Chemicals, the second among our examples of 'new' industries, combined rapid technical progress with the opportunity of displacing older industries as well as creating new markets. The limits of the industry are ill-defined, and on some counts oil refining itself might be subsumed under it. A rough division into heavy chemicals and fine chemicals, such as pharmaceutical products, is often used, and there is also a dividing line between the production of intermediate raw materials and the production of finished or semi-finished goods such as paints, plastics or man-made fibres. Yet the processes used, if not commercial considerations also, impose much vertical and horizontal integration and the chemical industry, in Britain and elsewhere, remained in this period one of the most highly concentrated of modern industries. ICI alone employed about one-third of the labour force[59] and there have been several mergers among the other giants.[60] The major take-over bid, by ICI, was, however, beaten off successfully by Courtaulds's, the intended victim, in a dramatic battle in 1961, in which ICI had obtained as much as 38% of the Courtauld shares.[61]

Technical progress in this industry, also, though faster than in earlier periods, compared badly with the achievements of other countries. Britain, for example, delayed too long the switch from coal-based to gas-or oil-based technology, and fell behind in the production of plastics. While the chemical industry was among the fastest growers, averaging 5·39% a year in 1957–77, it formed a smaller share of manufacturing output than in all other comparable countries.[62] In this, as in other faster than average growth industries heavily based on science and technology like electronics and man-made fibres, for which reasons of space forbid more detailed treatment,[63] we find the same story of inadequate investment in new capacity and tardy adoption of new technology, so that the windfall technical lead acquired during the war and still held in 1950 was lost and competitive power suffered.[64] In boom years, not even the home market could be supplied because of shortage of capacity and, instead of rising exports, there were merely sharp increases in imports. The similarity in the development of these varied industries leads to

[59] W. B. Reddaway, 'The Chemical Industry', in *Structure of British Industry*, I, and C. J. Thomas, 'The Pharmaceutical Industry', *ibid.*, II.

[60] E.g. Charles Wilson, *Unilever 1945–1965* (1968), pp. 149ff.

[61] D. C. Coleman, *Courtaulds. An Economic and Social History. vol. 3. Crisis and Change 1940–1965* (Oxford, 1980), chapter 10.

[62] Prest and Coppock, pp. 172–3; Pratten, *Economies of Scale*, pp. 309, 319.

[63] E.g., Thomas Wilson, 'The Electronics Industry' and D. C. Hague, 'The Man-Made Fibres Industry', *Structure of British Industry II*.

[64] The mid-1960s did, however, see some massive investments and the ICI issue of £50 million in 1965 was the largest such private operation since the war. S. J. Wells, *Trade Policies for Britain* (1966), pp. 92–3.

the conclusion that the 'fault', if any, did not lie with them, but derived from the circumstances in which they operated.

Among industries of near-average growth, the iron and steel industry occupied an important place. It was representative in providing the raw material both for capital goods, such as machines, ships, buildings, vehicles and bridges, as also for many of the durable consumer goods, on which so much of the newly increased income was expended.

The first iron and steel nationalization was only temporary: the Iron and Steel Act of 1953 sold the industry back to private owners, but leaving 'an adequate measure of public supervision'[65] to be exercised by the Iron and Steel Board. A separate Iron and Steel Holding and Realization Agency was to dispose of the shares and by 1957 had sold 86%; after 1963 those of only one firm, Richard Thomas & Baldwin, were left, and were held by the State until the second nationalization act.[66]

By 1950 capacity had been raised to 16 million tons of steel and was still very much below demand, particularly since artificially low coal and scrap prices kept steel prices down. A second 'plan' in 1952 envisaged investment at around £60 million a year, to raise capacity to over 20 million tons, later revised to $22\frac{1}{2}$ million tons, by about 1957. This, however, was still well below national needs and forced Britain to spend foreign exchange on imports of sheet steel and other similar products in the 1950s.

A third development plan was published in 1957, envisaging an increase in capacity to 29 million tons by 1962, and it was under its provision that some of the most important new plants were built and others extended, including the continuous strip mills at Ravenscraig and in South Wales and the R.T.B. Spencer Works at Newport, while the Dorman-Long Lockerby plant, a universal beam mill, was opened in 1958. Conversions to electricity and to Oxygen processes, such as the LD or Kaldo furnaces, and extensions at Shotton, Appleby-Frodingham, Stocksbridge and elsewhere were also undertaken, though no complete new plant was put up. Fixed capital investment which had fluctuated around £60–80 million a year in 1947–55 (at constant, 1936 prices), rose to a peak of £207 million in 1961, only to drop back to *c.* £75 million by 1963–4.[67] A fourth plan, in April 1961, envisaged a further increase in capacity to 32 million tons in 1965, and a fifth plan, published under the shadow of nationalization in 1966, aimed at a capacity of 35·3 million tons in 1975, but the sellers' market had collapsed meanwhile and the plans were largely still-born, as was the 10-year development plan of 1972 that was to have raised capacity to 33–35 m.t. by the late 1970s and 36–38 m.t. by the early 1980s. The annual growth rate of 2·7% in 1950–69 compared with 6·4% in the Common Market and 34·0% in Japan (1952–1969),[68] but at least there was still a net addition. In the following

[65] Quoted in A. J. Youngson, *Britain's Economic Growth, 1920–1966* (1967), p. 217.

[66] Duncan Burn, 'Steel', in *Structure of British Industry*, I, pp. 298–300; G. W. Ross, *The Nationalization of Steel* (1965), pp. 153, *passim*.

[67] B. S. Keeling and A. E. G. Wright, *The Development of the Modern British Steel Industry* (1964), p. 129. See also J. C. Carr and W. Taplin, *History of the British Steel Industry* (Oxford, 1962).

[68] A. Cockerill, with A. Silberston, *The Steel Industry. International Comparisons of Industrial Structure and Performance* (Cambridge, 1974), pp. 9, 55; Department of Trade and Industry, *Steel*, Cmnd. 5226 (1973).

decade, crude steel production actually fell from 27·9 tonnes in 1970 to a catastrophic 11·4 m.t. in 1980 (imports then being 6·1 m.t. and exports 3·4 m.t.), to rise to 15·3 m.t. in 1981 (provisional figure). Within the general industrial decline, Britain had for the first time in modern times turned, between 1979 and 1980, into a net importer of steel.

To some extent, steel was a victim of the failure of the economy as a whole to grow as fast as expected after 1957, having been an important cause of that failure before 1957; technological changes, steel 'economies' and displacement by other materials also played a part.[69] But the import surplus showed that British steel was falling behind in general competitive power. Average furnace capacity, a good measure of technical efficiency,[70] increased three-fold in 1950–66, but was still low by international standards, and plant size failed to grow as fast as abroad. One 'efficiency ratio' of steel plants, which correlated well with export success, showed increases between the 1950s and the 1960s in Italy, Japan and the Netherlands, but a fall from 100 to 40 for Britain and France. Among the particular British handicaps were said to be: price controls, Government interferenec expecially on investment decisions, lack of working capital, delays in approval for closing high-cost plants, and endemic labour troubles. The British share of world output fell from 10% in 1950 to 5% in 1966 and 1·6% in 1980, and in 1967 crude steel output per man hour compared as follows:[71]

EEC, average 0·107 tons
USA   0·106
Japan   0·081
UK   0·037

By the Iron and Steel Act of 1967, the 14 major units of the industry were nationalized for the second time. After reorganization in 1970 into four major product divisions, general steels, special steels, strip mills and tubes, as well as constructional engineering and chemicals,[72] rationalization by concentration in certain plants was possible, and was aided by some support for redundancy by the European Coal and Steel Community (ECSC) to which Britain belonged by joining the EEC in 1973. Renewed efforts at modernization were made, and despite repeated stops imposed by Government in the interest of macroeconomic policies, gross capital formation rose, at 1975

---

[69] Keeling and Wright, pp. 95–7; British Iron and Steel Federation, *The Steel Industry, Stage I Report of the Development Co-ordinating Committee* (1966).

[70] The notional index of costs was as follows:
Blast furnace:

capacity of	Open hearth furnace size
100,000 t.p.a. 131	75 t. 131
200,000 t.p.a. 100	150 t. 100
1,000,000 t.p.a. 58	400 t. 85
1,500,000 t.p.a. 52	

Pratten and Dean, pp. 67, 70. Also see Cockerill, p. 82.

[71] Cockerill, pp. 32, 38, 94; D. L. Burn, *The Steel Industry 1939–1959* (Cambridge, 1961), p. 558; Wells, *op. cit.*, p. 99; L. Nabseth and G. F. Ray, *The Diffusion of New Industrial Processes. An International Study* (Cambridge, 1974), pp. 175–6, 193–5, 241, 247; Richard M. Duke *et al.*, *The United States Steel Industry and its International Rivals* (Washington, 1977), pp. 353, 438, 442.

[72] British Steel Corporation, *Third Report on Organisation*, H. of C. 60 (1969–70).

prices, from £316 million in 1970 to a peak of £600 million in 1976. But thereafter it collapsed, amounting only to £155 million in 1980.[73] The problem, under Mr Ian MacGregor, the new chairman appointed in 1980, was to reduce the vast annual losses by carrying through massive redundancies and the destruction of assets in order to halve the size of the industry. By mid-1982, the labour force had been reduced from 208,000 in 1977 to under 100,000.

Among the declining industries, cotton offers an important example. After a post-war boom in which all that could be made could be sold with ease at home and abroad,[74] the decline from 1951 onward was swift and would have been swifter still but for quotas and high protection including voluntary ceilings of exports to Britain from Commonwealth countries since 1958, and regulations for imports from low wage countries, laid down by GATT in 1962. After 1964, replacement by man-made fibres accelerated the downward trend in the cotton industry: Courtaulds had by then acquired one-third of Lancashire's spindles,[75] and they continued to convert more capacity towards artificial fibres in the following years, as did other firms, including ICI. In the 1950s and 1960s, labour moved out fairly smoothly, since there was a general high level of employment in the area, and in 1963–74 alone, employment in cotton was halved, but over-capacity in capital equipment was less easily dealth with. It was estimated in 1959 to have reached 30% in spinning, 60% in doubling, and 25–40% in finishing. The cotton industry thus appeared to be in an exceptionally unfavourable position in an otherwise booming Britain and the Government, in two minds whether to make grants for scrapping old plant or for installing new, was pressurized into doing both. The Cotton Industry Act, 1959, the first major post-war measure for aid towards the scrapping of obsolete plant, provided for the payment of two-thirds of the compensation by the Government, and one-third by an industrial levy. Displaced labour was also to obtain compensation; and the Government, in addition, was to make grants covering a quarter of the cost of any new machinery installed before 1962. The effectiveness of the Act was greater and speedier than had been anticipated. Plans were completed for spinning, doubling and weaving in 1959, and for finishing in 1960. By the end of March, the number of spindles had been cut by nearly half (12·4 million out of 25·3 million), and the number of looms by two-fifths (105,000 out of 259,000); 300 mills were closed completely in 1959–60 and a total of over £30 million was ultimately paid out for scrapping and for new plant.[76]

The result was a remarkable rise in productivity as total employment fell: it

[73] *National Income and Expenditure, 1981.* Figures deflated by the 'implied deflator' for gross domestic capital formation in the same volume.

[74] G. W. Furness, 'The Cotton and Rayon Textile Industry', in *Structure of British Industry*, II.

[75] William Lazonick, 'Industrial Organization and Technical Change: The Decline of the British Cotton Industry', *Bus. Hist. Rev.*, 1982; Franz Fabian, 'Der Konzentrationsprozess in der britischen Textilindustrie', in W. G. Hoffmann (ed.), *Textilwirtschaft im Strukturwandel* (Tübingen, 1966) pp. 81–120.

[76] P. D. Henderson, 'Government and Industry', in Worswick and Ady, *The British Economy in the Nineteen-Fifties* (1962), p. 351; *Reorganization of the Cotton Industry*, Cmnd 744 (1959); *Economist*, 2 April, 1960.

rose by 10% in 1956–61, and by 8% a year on average in 1963–74. Even so, this rise was much slower than the productivity rises abroad.[77]

Again, while large firms dominated one sector of the industry, family controlled firms continued to cling to independence; in 1968, there were still over 1,000 of them.[78] Similar comparisons could be made in other declining or stagnant industries, as in wool and worsted spinning and weaving, in the clothing industry and in leather and furs.

Finally, among declining manufacturing industries, shipbuilding deserves a special mention. Again, following the short-term post-war competitive advantage because of the destruction of shipyard capacity among other belligerents, and the inability of the rest of the world to buy tonnage launched in the dollar area, it is the relative British decline in competitiveness with the shipyards of other countries which is most striking. In the years 1949–51, the United Kingdom was still the leading producer for exports (i.e. foreign registration), selling 522,000 gross tons, or 38% of the world total; by 1956, she had become a poor third behind Japan and Germany, selling 435,000 g.t., or less than 14%; by 1967, sales were an exceptional 612,000 g.t. but in 1964–6 they had averaged only 186,000 g.t. a year.[79] Similarly, total merchant tonnage launched in 1950 was 1,325,000 g.t., compared with a world total of 3,489,000 g.t., and in 1966 1,084,000 g.t. out of a world total of 14,307,000. In that year, Britain slipped to fourth place among the world's producing nations. In 1977, launching 1·0 m.g.t., she produced 4% of the world's output, and by 1980 had slipped to eighth place. By 1980, output had fallen dramatically once more to less than half, 431,000 g.t. Export orders were falling also while imports approached 50% of British home demand. Once more, as in the early 1930s, the collapse of the shipbuilding industry was among the most devastating of all, though this time it was caused not by the failure of demand, but its pathetic inability to compete.

In the 1950s the chief competitors had been other European producers, such as Sweden and Germany, using mass production techniques on standardized vessels or standardized components, and a highly efficient technology. After that, Japan came to dominate the international market, defeating opposition both on cost grounds and on technological ability of building super-tankers measuring hundreds of thousands of gross tons. Any growth of this magnitude attracts to itself the further advantages of mass production. In recent years, even less likely low-wage countries have come to the fore: Taiwan, South Korea, Brazil, Poland and Yugoslavia.

As always, the basis of the British decline was the failure to invest in efficient, high-productivity equipment while the market was in Britain's favour.[80] The Geddes report of 1966 found fault with out-of-date equipment, poor sites, divided trade union allegiance leading to costly demarcation dis-

[77] Kenneth Keith, 'Finance and Structural Change in British Industry with Particular Reference to Cotton', *Moorgate and Wall Street* (Autumn, 1963), p. 26; Nabseth and Ray, p. 265.

[78] Pratten, *Economies of Scale*, p. 226.

[79] A. K. Cairncross and J. R. Parkinson, 'The Shipbuilding Industry', in *Structure of British Industry*, II, p. 102; Lloyd's Register, *Annual Summary of Merchant Ships Launched*.

[80] Andrew Shonfield, *British Economic Policy Since the War* (1958), pp. 41–8.

putes and relatively high costs of labour and raw materials in British yards. The proposed remedies included rationalization, standardization and amalgamation. Government support, totalling some £68 million in credit and compensation for losses, was to be made available to bring about the amalgamation of the 62 yards into three or four large combines, of which two were to be in the north-east and one or two on the Clyde. The 15 unions were similarly to amalgamate into five. In this way, the British share of the world market, which had fallen steadily to 10%, was to be raised to $12\frac{1}{2}$%.[81] Meanwhile, the Fairfield yard on the Clyde, one of the best equipped in the country, had to be rescued from bankruptcy by the Government, which reconstructed the firm in February 1966, a month before the Geddes Committee Report, and provided £$1\frac{1}{2}$ million of the £2 million of new capital required.

In the event, the industry remained racked by labour disputes, unable to deliver on time, technically backward. Without orders for oil rigs it would have fared worse still. As it was, it gained orders only by quoting at a loss, made up by heavy Government subsidies which caused resentment abroad. Finally, after an earlier amalgamation of Upper Clyde Shipbuilders and others into Govan Shipbuilders, the whole collection of some up-to-date but several ramshackle plants, some 27 companies, was taken over by the State under the Shipbuilding Industry Act of 1977, and several repair yards joined later. In the following year, 1978, 'British Shipbuilders' employed 86,000 and had sales of £548 million on which they made £108 million losses.[82] Closures, redundancies, and trade-union resistance to redundancies became the order of the day here also.

Lastly, the post-war years have seen important changes also in the provision of services. In transport, the outstanding development has been the progressive replacement of the railways and shipping by road and air transport, respectively. In consequence, the railways saw a yearly decline in the surplus out of which interest had to be paid; in 1956 they registered the first working deficit, i.e. before meeting central charges, and by 1958 the working deficit had rocketed to £48 million. As in the subsequent years the competitive position continued to deteriorate, all attempts to wipe out the deficit proved abortive, but meanwhile its existence led to a bewildering series of changes in policy,[83] which could only have increased the difficulties of those who had actually to manage the railway system.

The avalanche of conflicting advice which descended upon British Railways had two broad targets: organization and technical equipment and control. On the first, the Transport Act of 1953 made provision for returning the road haulage services to private ownership. In the event, only a proportion of vehicles was sold before 1956, when the sales ended, and by the Transport (Disposal of Road Haulage Property) Act, 1956, British Road Services were to keep not only the parcels service of the railways, but also to retain a main

---

[81] *Shipbuilding Inquiry Committee 1965–6, Report*, Cmnd. 2937 (1966).

[82] D. F. Channon, 'British Shipbuilders', in John M. Stopford, D. F. Channon, John Constable, *Cases in Strategic Management* (Chichester, 1980).

[83] Derek H. Aldcroft, *British Railways in Transition: the Economic Problems of Britain's Railways Since 1914* (1968), pp. 135–45.

trunk network. The Act of 1953, by abolishing the Railway Executive, left the British Transport Commission to supervise, rather than manage, a series of disparate enterprises, including a substantial proportion of road vehicles.[84] More usefully, many of the restrictive powers of the Transport Tribunal were abolished, giving greater pricing freedom to the railways. Following a white paper,[85] the Transport Act 1962 carried decentralization further, by abolishing the BTC and creating separate boards for railways, for London Transport, the docks, inland waterways and a holding company for the auxiliary services, such as British Road Services, buses, hotels and Thomas Cook and Son. Meanwhile, the Transport Tribunal, which had on several occasions considerably increased the losses of the railways by withholding or delaying rate increases, was to be shorn of its power, except for London.[86]

As for re-equipment, there was the common post-war delay. At last, a plan of 1955 envisaged the investment of £1,200 million (at 1954 prices) in 15 years, divided about equally between maintenance and modernization of track, the introduction of diesel and electric drive, etc., and proposed the closing of unprofitable branch lines.[87] But investment, which increased satisfactorily in the late 1950s, was soon cut down for reasons of short-term Treasury policy and because long-term prospects deteriorated. Actual traffic returns were to change as shown in Table 7·11.[88]

Table 7·11:   Changes in the distribution of passenger and freight traffic

| | Shares % | | | | Absolute terms | |
	1952	1960	1970	1980	1952	1980
Passengers:					Billion passenger-km	
Railways	21	15·6	8·7	6·9	38·8	36·0
Public road	45	27·7	13·7	9·8	80·6	51·0
Private road	34	56·4	77·1	82·8	61·0	433·0
Air	—	0·3	0·5	0·5	—	2·8
Freight:					Billion tonne-km	
Rail	54	38·0	24·0	14·6	36·0	17·6
Road	46	61·2	73·2	77·1	30·2	93·1
Inland waterways	—	0·4	0·1	0·1	—	0·1
Pipeline	—	0·4	2·6	8·2	—	9·9

In passenger traffic, the railways' share was to shrink to a fraction of its former size, but at least total numbers did not change very greatly. In goods traffic, the railways lost not only three-quarters of their share, but half their traffic. They were driven back essentially on to a small number of items which the roads could not or would not carry, such as coal or mail.

[84] *Transport Policy*, Cmnd. 8538 (1952); Gilbert Walker and C. I. Savage, 'Inland Carriage by Road and Rail', in *Structure of British Industry*, I.

[85] *Reorganization of the Nationalized Transport Undertakings*, Cmnd. 1248 (1960).

[86] Philip S. Bagwell, *The Transport Revolution from 1770* (1974), pp. 336–9; H. Pollins, *British Railways: An Industrial History* (Newton Abbot, 1971), pp. 175 ff.

[87] British Transport Commission, *Modernization and Re-equipment of British Railways* (1955), and *Proposals for the Railways*, Cmd. 9880 (1956); M. Beesley and A. A. Walters, 'Investment in British Railways', *Westminster Bank Review* (May 1955).

[88] *Annual Abstract of Statistics*.

In the 1950s, this transformation was visible but dimly. Indeed, in 1959 the earler plan was optimistically extended to a total of £1,500 million (at 1958 prices), much of it to be spent in the next four years, when investment was to run at £200 million a year,[89] and it was still hoped to turn the annual deficit into a surplus by these means. But 1959–60 proved to be a turning-point. There was to be a new policy not only in organization, but also in equipment. Investment was cut down to about £100 million p.a. in 1963–4. Dr Beeching, a leading industrialist, was called in in 1961 to advise, and while the 'Beeching Report', [90] which appeared in 1963, did not disagree fundamentally with the diagnosis of 1955, the remedy was now put on closures rather than on re-equipment. The only mention of the latter in the report was an estimate of new rolling-stock, liner trains, etc., of £250 million over an unspecified period. The main proposal was the closure of 5,000 miles of track, together with 2,363 out of 4,293 passenger stations. Against this, freight handling was to be rationalized and the trunk lines were to provide a faster and more efficient competitive service. Thus the reduction in the deficit was to be achieved largely by cutting costs, rather than by attracting new traffic, and the reduction in the labour force by 1966 was put at 70,000. These proposals were accepted in principle, and many of the closures were carried out quickly, while the benefits of the better rolling-stock and some important track improvement like the electrification of the London-Manchester line which derived from the earlier planned investment, also helped the management of the railways. Nevertheless, the deficits remained in 1963–8; only 1969 and 1970 showed small surpluses.

Preceded by a battery of white papers,[91] the Transport Act 1968 created a new National Freight Corporation, which included all the assets of the Transport Holding Corporation and all the road traffic assets. It was hoped to catch much of the developing container trade thereby, as also to co-ordinate road and rail traffic and limit long-distance heavy road traffic. Special funds were made available, as 'social service' grants, for keeping open unremunerative branch lines, and the capital burden on which interest was payable after 1969 was reduced to £300 million: £700 million of the original debt and £557 million of the commencing capital of 1962 were cancelled. Thereafter, however, no more Government capital was to be made available, and funds would have to be borrowed on commercial terms. Finally a National Bus Co. was created out of 93 companies and 21,000 vehicles, the Scottish group remaining separate. The Transport (London) Act of 1969 handed London transport over to the London Transport Executive, to be appointed by the Greater London Council, and another act of that year extinguished the LTB's debt, to allow London also a new start.[92]

In the 1970s, checked only slightly in 1974 by the sharp increase in petrol costs, growing car ownership affected both bus and rail revenues adversely

---

[89] British Transport Commission, *Reappraisal of the Plan for the Modernization and Re-equipment of British Railways*, Cmnd. 813 (1959).

[90] British Railways Board, *The Reshaping of British Railways* (1963); also D. L. Munby, 'The Reshaping of British Railways', *J. of Industrial Economics*, II/3 (1963).

[91] *British Waterways*, Cmnd. 3401; *Railway Policy*, Cmnd. 3439; *The Transport of Freight*, Cmnd. 3470; *Public Transport and Traffic*, Cmnd. 3481.

[92] Bagwell, pp. 350 ff.

and made a co-ordinated policy more necessary than ever. A consultative document of 1976[93] also stressed the problems of rural areas without access to any public transport after the closure of both railways and bus services; environmental problems; and the vast subsidies going especially to the railways. These had risen from £300 m. in 1968 to £630 m. in 1975, while the railways had had £3 billion of debt written off in 20 years. Suggestions included subsidies for buses, as they were more likely to benefit poorer people, increases in railway fares, and higher taxation of heavy road vehicles. A 1977 white paper[94] foreshadowed reduced rail subsidies, and reduced expenditure on the roads, but railway management has since then resolved itself into keeping the annual losses to a manageable size and persuading the unions to accept redundancies and more efficient working. The promising attempt in London in 1981 to relieve traffic congestion and halt the disintegration of London transport by a sharp reduction in fares, the increased deficits to be paid out of the rates, which showed some remarkably positive results, was declared illegal by the Courts. An answer to the problem of public transport in the age of the private car is as far off as ever.

On roads, curiously, new investment also lagged until the mid-1950s, but thereafter the momentum of the increase has been supported by powerful pressure groups and has been maintained. Even here, however, investment in major trunk road schemes and motorways has been too erratic to get the full economies of contractors' teamwork. Official figures of public expenditure on the roads (see Table 7·12) show the slow start of new building (as against repair, etc.) and its sharp increase in the late 1950s.[95]

Table 7·12: Expenditure on roads and public lighting (£m. current)

Average of years	Current	Capital formation	Total
1950–1	87	12	99
1955–6	115	28	143
1960–1	152	106	258
1964–5	209	212	421
1969–70	257	401	658
1974–5	550	673	1223
1979–80	1154	825	1979

Growing congestion as vehicle numbers increased much faster than road length was relieved to some extent by the building of motorways. After a long delay from the mooting of the first plans in 1939,[96] legislation in 1949 led to active preparation in 1955 and (apart from the short Preston by-pass in 1958) the opening of the first major stretch of motorway in 1959. Building continued apace in the following two decades, despite rising costs as the routes moved from rural stretches to costly suburban and urban properties. Since then, building has almost come to a halt, though the British mileage is well below that of other comparable countries. Growing environmental objec-

[93] Department of the Environment, *Consultative Document on Transport Policy* (1976).
[94] *Transport Policy*, Cmnd. 6836 (1977).
[95] *National Income and Expenditure*.
[96] Bagwell, pp. 367–72.

tions and the blight on all public capital expenditure have contributed to the petering out of the programme. The length of all types of public road open to traffic increased as shown in Table 7·13.

Table 7·13: Lengths of roads (OOO km)

	1962	1970	1980
Motorways	0·23	1·06	2·57
Trunk roads	13·4	13·4	12·5
Principal roads	31·8	32·5	34·2
Other roads	270·1	275·4	290·2
Totals	315·6	322·5	339·5

This cursory review of certain sectors of the economy cannot give a complete picture of the development of the productive equipment of the nation in 1950–80. It is intended merely as an illustration of some typical experiences of the primary, secondary and tertiary (service) industries in a period which began with much solid, if chequered expansion, then saw the beginnings of a long-term decline of the manufacturing sector, while the service sector still continued to expand, and finally, in the last two years, experienced a marked decline in all sectors.

This rise was essentially based on improved technology in its widest sense. This, by its nature, is likely to spread into most if not all fields. Where, however, new techniques were difficult to apply or were slow in appearance, e.g. in service trades like retail distribution, the rising real wages created by general productivity rises and transmitted by the pressures of the labour market and trade union power to the lagged sector, set up particularly strong incentives to save the now dearer labour by re-organization. The self-service revolution in retailing[97] typifies this reaction. Where, on the other hand, productivity rises were well above the average, then unless the industry was very small and in its early growth stages in this period, like oil refining, the general sluggishness of the growth of the economy as a whole held back the potential expansion of the favoured industry, and inhibited massive investment in new methods of the kind which could be absorbed by faster-growing economies like those of Germany or Japan.

2 Changes in Business Organization and Structure

The pre-war trend towards greater concentration of firms continued strongly in this period, particularly in manufacturing industry.[98] While the Bolton Committee[99] found that 'small firms', defined as having 200 employees or

[97] By 1966 it was estimated that 44% of grocery sales were in self-service stores or supermarkets, and the conversion rate was 150–200 stores per month.

[98] Alan Armstrong and Aubrey Silberston, 'Size of Plant, Size of Enterprise and Concentration in British Manufacturing Industry, 1935–1958', *J.R. Stat. S.*, 128/3, Series A (1965); K. D. George, 'Changes in British Industrial Concentration 1951–1958', *J. of Industrial Economics*, 15/3 (1967); W. G. Shepherd, 'Changes in British Industrial Concentration, 1951–1958', *Oxf. Econ. P.*, 18/1 (1966).

[99] *Report of the Committee of Inquiry into Small Firms*, Cmnd. 4811 (1971).

less, had dropped in numbers from 136,000 in 1935 to 60,000 in 1963, and their share of manufacturing output from 35% to 16%, the fastest growth was at the other end of the scale, among the largest firms. Plants also became larger, though not as decisively. Thus manufacturing plants employing under 200 accounted for 28% of net manufacturing output in 1958, and 10 years later, after an unprecedented number of mergers, they still had 25%.[100] Growth of firms occurred, in fact, largely by the acquisition or erection of additional plants, and only in part by the growth of the average individual plant. The 100 largest manufacturing companies had 27 plants per enterprise in 1958 and 72 in 1972, while the average employment of these enterprises rose from 20,300 to 31,180 in those years, and average plant size correspondingly diminished.[101]

The most detailed study of the largest 100 manufacturing firms showed that they were responsible for 21% of net manufacturing output in 1948, 38% in 1963 and 47% in 1976. In addition to more than doubling their share they were in this period also thoroughly transformed: whereas only 13% had a multidivisional structure in 1950, the proportion was 72% in 1970; and whereas 34% still made only a single product, and a further 41% one major dominant product in 1950, or a total of 75%, these proportions had shrunk to 6%, 34% and only 40% in 1970. Thus the large British firms allowed, if somewhat belatedly, the Chandler pattern of diversification, as they also advanced further along the road from family control to control by professional management. 54% of the 92 companies were still controlled by one family in 1950, but only 30% in 1970. On average, the boards of the 100 largest manufacturing firms held only 0·46% of the shares in 1972.[102] For individual industries, and invididual products, concentration showed itself in the growing share held by the top three or five firms in this period. Thus the share of the largest three firms in each average industry rose from 29% in 1951 to 42% in 1973; the share of the top five products rose from 53–55% in 1958 to 65–66% in 1975.[103]

The giant firm has thus become typical for manufacturing as a whole, and predominant in some sectors. Altogether, 45% of manufacturing employees worked in enterprises of 5,000 employees or over in 1972, compared with only 35% in enterprises employing 999 or under; and almost 60% worked in individual plants employing 500 or more. Nor was this trend confined to secondary industry. Even in building, perhaps the last stronghold of the small firm, large companies were increasing their share, and in the service industries, banks and insurance companies had been among the first to turn into

---

[100] Leslie Hannah, *The Rise of the Corporate Economy* (1976), p. 175.

[101] S. J. Prais, *The Evolution of the Giant Firm in Britain* (Cambridge, 2nd ed., 1981), p. 62.

[102] Hannah, *Corporate Economy*, pp. 172–4, 216; Derek F. Channon, *The Strategy and Structure of British Enterprise*, pp. 52 ff.; Alfred F. Chandler, *Visible Hand: the Managerial Revolution in American Business* (Cambridge, Mass., 1977) and *idem*, 'The Growth of the Transnational Industrial Firm in the United States and the United Kingdom: A Comparative Analysis', *Ec. Hist. Rev.*, 33/3, 1980; M. A. Utton, *Diversification and Competition* (Cambridge, 1979), pp. 3, 79; Prais, *Giant Firm*, p. xv.

[103] P. E. Hart and R. Clarke, *Concentration in British Industry 1935–1975* (Cambridge, 1980), pp. 1, 37; P. E. Hart, M. A. Utton, G. Walshe, *Mergers and Concentration in British Industry* (Cambridge, 1973), p. 25; G. C. Allen, *The Structure of Industry in Britain* (1970), pp. 41–4.

giants. In retail distribution, the 'multiples' or organizations having 10 establishments or more, raised their share of the trade from 22% in 1950 to 39% in 1971, while the giants, with 100 establishments or over (omitting the co-ops, grew from 12·9% in 1950 to 28·3% in 1971. In the latter year, in fact, the firms with 1,000 shops each or over had 7·9% of private retail trade and employed 8·1% of the work force. Large retailers further increased their share of the turnover to 54·2% in 1979 (including the co-ops), and grew by 81% between 1976 and 1980, compared with only 27% for small retailers.[104]

What was the cause of this remarkable drive towards concentration? Technical considerations seem to have played but little part. Economies of scale are, indeed, highly significant in many industries, but plant size where such economies should occur, grew very little; the significant growth was in the size of firms. The cause of the drive for expansion has to be looked for in the market rather than on the factory floor. From a larger base, outside services such as transport or communications might be obtained more cheaply, buying and selling agreements more favourably concluded, advertising more effectively driven home. Expansion into other fields reduced risks, particularly if secular decline or stagnation threatened the main activity of an industry, like tobacco because of health legislation, or natural textile fibres because of competition from man-made substitutes; diversification might also use resouces more fully or more efficiently.[105] At the same time, simple horizontal expansion into a growing share of sales would strengthen monopolistic powers over the market and monopsonistic powers over suppliers. There was also the possible hope of stronger leverage on Government, or within the employers' organizations, strengthened in 1965 by the formation of the Confederation of British Industry (CBI) out of the Federation of British Industries, the British Employers' Confederation and the National Association of British Manufacturers.[106] In expansion overseas, other motives, such as by-passing a tariff, access to cheap supplies or cheap labour might play a large part.[107]

Lastly, in companies in which ownership was wholly divorced from control, the purposes of directors and managers themselves might have dominated, quite irrespective of the interests of their shareholders: eliminating troublesome competition, sheer personal aggrandizement or prestige, the wish to keep the available and investible capital under direct control, may all have played a part. In more than a few mergers and battles for control the process of acquisition itself, rather than any long-term benefits at the end of it, seems to have been a major attraction among the contestants. Conversely, taxation and tax allowances which favoured managers rather than owners, unexpectedly large investment needs in order to

---

[104] A. R. Prest and D. J. Coppock, *The UK Economy* (7th ed., 1978), pp. 215–16; C. G. Powell, *The Economic History of the British Building Industry 1815–1979* (1980), p. 159; *Census of Distribution*, 1961 and 1971; Derek E. Channon, *The Service Industries: Strategy, Structure and Financial Performance* (1978), pp. 27–31, 58–63, 163, 170 ff.

[105] Prais, *Giant Firms*, pp. 50–9, 66–80; Channon, *Strategy and Structure*, pp. 220–1.

[106] Stephen Blank, *Industry and Government in Britain. The Federation of British Industries in Politics, 1945–1965* (Farnborough, 1973); W. Grant and David Marsh, *The Confederation of British Industry* (1977).

[107] See p. 309 below.

introduce new technology, and sheer failure of succession contributed to the willingness of some family owners to sell their companies.

For, although internal growth was significant, between one-third and one-half of the rise in concentration since 1950 has been accounted for by mergers and absorptions.[108] Firms grew largely by absorbing other firms. While mergers were found also in stagnant or declining sectors, they were particularly marked in expanding industries in their growth phase, including chemicals, electrical engineering, motor manufacture and finance companies, continuing the trend of the inter-war years. Large firms, themselves the products of mergers, seem to have been particularly prone to repeat the experience.[109] Of the largest 100 manufacturing companies in 1948, 48 had disappeared by 1968: 9 had been nationalized, 12 had fallen back to lower rankings, and no fewer than 27 had been acquired by other firms. After slowing down in the first post-war decade, compared with the pre-war years, merger activity was particularly intensive in the years 1959–73 (see Table 7·14).[110]

Table 7·14:   The scale of merger activity

	No. of firms disappeared by merger	Merger values as % total investment expenditure
1950–9	1,867	10
1960–9	5,635	28
1970–3	2,036	23

One particular technique which attracted much attention at that time was the 'takeover bid', in which one company was able to acquire control of another by offering to buy out its shareholders at prices much above market quotations, and was able to do so profitably because balance-sheet assets had been under-valued, or dividends had been kept unduly low in relation to earnings. Such a takeover represented a cashing in on hidden capital reserves and could be used to finance further acquisitions. Another method, particularly suitable in stores and offices, was to sell the premises or freehold, retaining a long lease, and use the capital thus freed to buy up similar property, to repeat the process in a snowballing series. Other entrepreneurs created holding companies in which their own limited holdings controlled large quantities of non-voting share capital. Some of the most spectacular post-war fortunes were made by these methods.[111] Additionally speculation

[108] Prais, *Giant Firm*, p. xvii; Hart, Utton and Walshe, pp. 101, 135.

[109] But acquisitions did not seem to increase with size. S. Aaronovitch and M. C. Sawyer, 'Mergers, Growth and Concentration', *Oxf. Econ. P.*, 27/1, 1975.

[110] Hannah, *Corporate Economy*, pp. 167, 214; Channon, *Service Industry, loc. cit.; idem, Strategy and Structure*, pp. 135, 161, 201; Graham Turner, *Business in Britain* (1969), pp. 84–8; G. Walshe, *Recent Trends in Monopoly in Great Britain* (Cambridge, 1974), pp. 25, 62; Hart, Utton and Walshe, p. 3; R. Evely and I. M. D. Little, *Concentration in British Industry* (1960); J. M. Samuels, 'Size and the Growth of Firms', *Rev. Econ. Studies*, 32/90 (1965).

[111] William Mennell, *Take-over: The Growth of Monopoly in Britain, 1951–1961* (1962); J. F. Wright, 'The Capital Market and the Finance of Industry', Worswick and Ady., *op. cit.*, pp. 464–73; *idem, Britain in the Age of Economic Management* (Oxford, 1979) pp. 71–2.

in urban land and city centre 'development' proved to be most profitable activities in the expansion years of the 1950s and in the early 1970s[112] and diverted much scarce capital from more productive employment.

Battles and bids of this kind caused much comment, some of it adverse. Whether they contributed to social welfare by using fully hitherto under-used resources, or whether they were merely the actions of power-hungry men in boardrooms, was one of the issues debated. One way of testing the answer would be to see whether the earning performance of companies improved after their merger, and this test has been applied in a number of cases. The results have been shown to be uniformly negative. While no doubt many individual examples could be found for improved returns after mergers, the large majority have been followed by falling profits and/or with poorer returns than a similar group of internal-growth firms.[113] Whatever marketing or technical gain there was to be had, was more than swallowed up by the additional costs of large organizations. There were in those cases few signs of rationalization, at least in the short run, but much friction between old and new personnel. Mergers, and particularly takeover bids, were thus to be explained by the hopes of quick promotional gains, and the quest for power, at least as much as by the quest for efficiency.

In the amalgamations of the giants the motives included the desire to occupy monopolistic positions of strength. This was the case, for example, in the amalgamations and takeovers in the motor trade noted above, in the abortive bid by ICI for Courtauld's in 1961, in the acquisition by Courtauld's of the Lancashire Cotton Corporation in 1964 and in the takeover of AEI by GEC in the electrical engineering field in 1967. In some cases the aim was near or total monopoly, as in the amalgamation of the aircraft industry into five units, of which two were to produce engines, two airframes, and one helicopters, all of which was engineered by the Government in 1959–60,[114] in the proposals of the Geddes Committee for the concentration of shipbuilding into three or four firms, or in the merger in 1968 of all British computer interests into a single combine, International Computer (Holdings) Limited, in which 10·5% was to be held by the Government.

Meanwhile, control in the public interest over restrictive practices was slowly being built up by the authorities. The Commission set up under the Monopolies and Restrictive Practices (Inquiry and Control) Act of 1948 produced in the early 1950s reports on individual industries which showed great variety in the methods used. It was not, however, always clear whether the public suffered, or whether, as in the report on electric cables and on insulin, the monopoly merely provided countervailing power against another monopoly, or, perhaps, used its large size and control over supplies to achieve greater technical efficiency.

Little positive action arose out of these detailed reports, but the general

---

[112] See p. 382 below.

[113] The most consistent study in the United Kingdom is that of 78 firms between 1961–1970 by M. A. Utton, 'On Measuring the Effects of Industrial Mergers', *Scot. J. Pol. Econ.*, 21/1 (1974); also see Hart, Utton and Walshe, p. 2; A. Singh, *Take-overs: Their Relevance for the Stock Market and the Theory of the Firm* (Cambridge, 1971), chapter 7; Channon, *Strategy and Structure*, pp. 224–5; Hannah, *Corporate Economy*, pp. 181–3.

[114] For a good account, see P. D. Henderson, in 'Government and Industry', pp. 361–9.

report, commissioned in December 1952 and published in May 1955, *Collective Discrimination: A Report on Exclusive Dealing, Collective Boycotts, Aggregate Rebates and other Discriminatory Trade Practices,*[115] was followed by an important new measure. The Restrictive Trade Practices Act of 1956 set up a Restrictive Trade Practices Court, of the status of a High Court, and inaugurated the change from inquiry to control.[116] All restrictive agreements were to be registered and well over 2,000 were registered at once, the total, by 1963, being 2,430 proffered voluntarily and about 100 others brought to light in other ways. About 100 of these were laid before the Court by the Registrar as contrary to the public interest under the Act and, while most were abandoned before the hearings were completed, only a few of those heard to the end were not condemned as failing to satisfy the limited clauses which might make them acceptable.[117] As a result of the early unfavourable judgements, over 1,500 agreements were abandoned or altered, and a further unknown number were abandoned in preference to registration.

In one respect, the Act allowed more restrictiveness than before: while prohibiting collective price fixing, it strengthened the power, hitherto very uncertain, of any individual firm to maintain the resale prices of its goods. When some firms actually used this power in a number of cases in order to force retailers to raise prices, it was shown up to be contrary to the spirit of the rest of the legislation, and in 1964 the Resale Prices Act aligned resale price maintenance with the other restrictive practices, by prohibiting it except in special cases where it could be shown to be necessary or in the public interest.

Thus, on paper, the anti-monopoly legislation had scored some formidable successes and, in some areas, particularly in retail trading, an unwonted freedom had by the mid-1960s replaced the earlier rigid price structure. Yet it was found to be easier to legislate against restrictive practices than to prevent them. For one thing, unofficial and unwritten agreements proved often as effectual as formal compacts. But secondly, the authorities were aware that mergers provided in certain critical cases the preconditions for rationalization and greater technical efficiency.

An attempt to discriminate more carefully between those restrictive actions that were in the public interest, and those which were not, was foreshadowed in a white paper prepared by the Conservative Government in 1964;[118] in the event, the proposals remained abortive, but the Monopolies and Mergers Act of 1965, passed by the new Government, gave the Board of Trade (and later the Department of Trade and Industry) authority to refer to the Monopolies

[115] Cmd. 9504 (1955).

[116] Catherine Brock, *The Control of Restrictive Practices from 1956* (1966); R. B. Stevens and B. S. Yamey, *The Restrictive Practices Court: The Judicial Process and Economic Policy* (1965); P. H. Guénault and J. M. Jackson, *The Control of Monopoly in the United Kingdom* (1960); Margaret Hall, 'The Consumer Sector', in Worswick and Ady, *op. cit.*, pp. 449–57; Alex Hunter, *Competitors and the Law* (1966); C. K. Rowley, *The British Monopoly Commission* (1966).

[117] In 29 cases and 42 issues decided in 1958–64, 29 Agreements were declared contrary to the public interest and 13 were not. A. Sutherland, 'Economics in the Restrictive Practices Court', *Oxf. Econ. P.*, 17/3 (1965), pp. 427 ff.

[118] *Monopolies, Mergers and Restrictive Practices*, Cmnd. 2299 (1964).

Commission any merger in which the assets acquired were valued at over £5 million, or which would give control over one-third of the market, reduced by the Fair Trading Act of 1973 to one quarter.

The new emphasis was thus on firms as criteria rather than on commodities or markets, but the effectiveness of this, as of the earlier legislation, depended on the strictness with which it was enforced. Altogether 833 mergers were considered in the first phase, 1965–73, by a Government panel, but only 20 of them were referred to the Monopolies Commission, and of those, seven were abandoned, seven were allowed and six were stopped, and while these included the merger of Barclays and Lloyds Banks, which might have created the largest banking combine in the world, and of Rank and De La Rue, the effects of the new Act were obviously circumscribed by the Government's hesitation to use it.[119] Of around 700 merger cases in the next phase, 1973–7, only 23 were referred. Similarly, the Restrictive Trade Practices Act 1968, which empowered the Board of Trade to enforce the registration of certain types of 'information agreements' was not likely to be very significant as long as knowledge of such agreements could effectively be kept from the Department.

The Act of 1973 extended to a moderate extent, and in several directions, the powers to curb market control. The market share test, reduced to one quarter, could now be applied to a local as well as a national market; uncompetitive practices adopted by firms as employers, restrictive labour practices, and uncompetitive practices by nationalized industries could also now be investigated; and legislation could be extended to services, and this was in fact implemented in 1976. By the end of 1977, 206 cases relating to the supply of services had been so registered.

Drawing a balance at that point, it could be stated that over 60 alleged monopolies had been investigated by the Commission, and several hundred merger cases screened. Twelve voluntary codes of practice to protect the consumer had been introduced, the Office of Fair Trading had exacted promises of good behaviour from numerous individual companies, and it had monitored the Consumer Act 1974 and carried out licensing under it. Well over 3,000 restrictive practices had been registered, of which almost 90% had been abandoned. Many practices harmful to the private consumer had been reformed.[120]

Yet there were misgivings about the effectiveness of the whole bundle of policies. They led to an Inter-Departmental Committee in 1978, but this in turn could do no more than suggest certain modest reforms.[121] As before, the two main problems were the effectiveness of stopping secret or unofficial collusive action, and the ambiguity about size and market control. For while the latter might help to exploit the public, it might also aid efficiency and enable British firms to stand up to foreign competition.

To some extent, the definition of what was British and what was foreign among large companies, in particular, was being obscured in this period by

---

[119] Hannah, *Corporate Economy*, pp. 175–6.
[120] Prest and Coppock, pp. 198–202.
[121] *A Review of Monopolies and Mergers Policy*, Cmnd. 7198 (1978).

the rise to prominence of the multinational (or transnational[122]) firm. It had existed in some form at least since the beginning of the century, but had grown particularly fast after the Second World War and if anything, even increased its share of capital and turnover in the 1970s.

The United Kingdom was still a net capital exporter, also in this 'direct', as well as in the more traditional 'portfolio' type of investment abroad, but foreign direct investments in Britain were growing apace – even if Britain was both housing and providing a declining share of the world's foreign direct investment (see Table 7·15).[123]

Table 7·15:   Stocks and flows of direct foreign investment

	Stocks ($ billion)		Flows (av. annual $ million)		
	UK assets abroad	Foreign assets in UK		Outflows	Inflows
1967	12·5	5·9	1967–9	− 1027	631
1974	23·8	15·9	1970–2	− 1600	965
(Market values)			1973–5	− 3428	1590
(1960)	(12·0)		1976	− 3379	1353
(1971)	(24·0)				
(1976)	(32·1)				

The foreign share of British capital investment flows in the UK fluctuated in those years between two-ninths and one-third. The stock of manufacturing capacity held in the United Kingdom by subsidiaries of foreign firms was particularly high (50% or over) in the manufacture of computers and electronics, typewriters, razor blades and electric razors, photographic equipment, spark plugs, sewing machines and boot and shoe machines, soap, detergents and cosmetic preparations, breakfast cereals, custard powder, cake mixes, instant coffee, frozen food, tractors, tyres and refrigerators. Most of them fell neatly into two groups: high-technology, or heavily advertised articles. Conversely, 22·9% of British direct investment abroad in 1965 was in petroleum and 4·5% in mining.[124] In the rapid internationalization of services which occurred in the 1970s, Britain kept a positive balance, in the sense of an excess of capital exports over imports in banking and insurance services, but was less successful among the large advertising agencies, which were also

[122] There is no agreement on the definitions of these terms, though some authors do use them to distinguish different types. E.g. Thomas G. Parry, 'The International Firm and National Economic Policy: A Survey of Some Issues', *Econ. J.*, 83/332, 1973, p. 1201; Neil Hood and Stephen Young, *The Economics of Multinational Enterprise* (1979), pp. 3, 117; J. E. S. Parker, *The Economics of Innovation* (1974), p. 159.

[123] James W. Vaupel and Joan P. Curhan, *The World's Multinational Enterprises* (Boston, Mass., 1973), pp. 66, 74; United Nations, *Multinational Corporations in World Development* (NY, 1973), pp. 130, 146, 161, 173; *idem*, Economic and Social Council, Commission on Transnational Corporations, *Transnational Corporations in World Development: A Re-examination* (NY, 1978), pp. 238–40.

[124] UN, *Multinational Corporations*, pp. 151, 166; Vaupel and Curhan, p. 50 and *passim*; Michael Hodges, *Multinational Corporations and National Government . . . 1964–1970* (Farnborough, 1974), p. 28.

crossing national frontiers.[125] Virtually all the foreign capital in Britain came from the advanced industrial countries, mostly from the USA, and about four-fifths of Britain's outward direct capital flows went there, with a tendency for the link with the members of the EC to strengthen after 1973.[126]

Naturally, it was the larger firms which were most likely to spawn subsidiaries abroad: the transaction costs of such operations were high and would be worth while only if the turnover could warrant it. Moreover, the giants were most likely to realize economies of scale of their technology and possibly their managerial abilities. Of the 41 largest manufacturing companies in Britain in 1976, 15 had more than half their sales abroad, and only two sold less than 5% of their turnover overseas. Conversely, the average numbers employed by the 49 largest British multinationals in 1973 was 82,244, or a total of 4 million.[127]

In small and backward countries, branches of multinationals were often feared because of their potentially disruptive and often actual overweening political power. In Britain, such fears would have been less realistic, while the benefits were often seen to be considerable. Apart from the obvious point that a local factory was an alternative to imports, thus affording work and income to British citizens and paying British taxes, foreign firms often introduced superior methods of management and technology. By 1970, sales per employee of multinationals in Britain were almost twice as high as among all firms, while the rapid rise of the share of patents granted to foreigners, from 40·1% in 1955 to 76·4% in 1972 largely reflected the technology transfer to Britain within the multinationals. There were numerous examples of foreign intruders who had forced British firms to modernize.[128] The 'product cycle', the mechanism which transmitted technological and other innovations from the advanced to the more backward economies, was in fact frequently a process which took place within the organization of the multinational firm. Moreover, this type of firm was most likely to foster an international division of labour and distribution of work among countries according to resources and relative factor prices.[129]

Yet there were misgivings in Britain too. Foreign firms, particularly the American firms which formed the largest contingent in the UK, were likely to import from their headquarters or from other branches rather than buy in Britain;[130] they would be managed in the interests of foreign owners, and, on

[125] UN, *Transnational Corporations*, pp. 46–8, 215–19; D. F. Channon, *British Banking Strategy and the International Challenge* (1977).

[126] J. M. Stopford, 'Changing Perspectives on Investment by British Manufacturing Multinationals', *Journal of International Business Studies*, 7/2, 1976.

[127] UN, *Transnational Corporations*, pp. 212–13; Hood and Young, pp. 17, 131.

[128] Thomas G. Parry, *The Multinational Enterprise. International Investment and Host-Country Impacts* (Greenwich, Conn., 1980) p. 111; Raymond Vernon, *Storm over the Multinationals. The Real Issue* (Cambridge, Mass., 1977), p. 8; Richard E. Caves, 'Industrial Organisation', and Edwin Mansfield, 'Technology and Technical Change', both in John H. Dunning, *Economic Analysis and the Multinational Enterprise* (1974).

[129] Hood and Young, pp. 60–2, 82–4, 149–50; John H. Dunning, *American Investment in British Manufacturing Industry* (1958), and 'Technology, United States Investment and European Economic Growth', in Charles P. Kindleberger (ed.), *The International Corporation* (Cambridge, Mass., 1970), p. 168.

[130] Curiously enough, British branches abroad did not. Thomas G. Parry, 'International

occasions, even to be put under duress by their home government to pursue the latter's political aims, by-passing the wishes of the British Government, as in the case of American sanctions against the Soviet Union in 1982. They could defeat taxation and pricing rules by internal price manipulation, and the trade unions feared their ability to escape abroad from excessive demands – though they were often also amenable and able to pay the highest wages. Others expressed unease that the multinationals would make Britain too dependent on foreign technology, and drive potential British winners out of the market.[131] The Industry Act 1975 included some provisions for restricting takeovers by non-residents, but otherwise Britain, unlike some other countries, placed few handicaps on British branches of foreign multinational companies.

The Government's attitude towards the task of providing a competitive environment for British industry was, in fact, vacillating and ambiguous. In spite of its elaborate provisions for 'fair trading' and against monopolies, it was at times itself enforcing or encouraging the monopolistic organization of industry, as in the case of British Leyland, the aircraft industry, shipbuilding, computer manufacture, cotton spinning and agricultural marketing noted above, not to mention the nationalized industries. Under the Labour government, the Industrial Reorganization Corporation of 1966–70 had been given the task of actually aiding and initiating mergers, including the spectacular creation of the GEC-AEI – English Electric combine[132] and British Leyland, all in the interest of efficiency and economy – while elsewhere mergers were blocked or treated with suspicion.

In the nationalized industries the problem of combining monopolistic powers with the obligation not to exploit them had been present from the start, but were aggravated in practice by the inability of most of them, including some of the largest, to operate at a profit, so that they required either regular or at least intermittent subsidies. The problem of the financial burden on the State within its overall economic stategy was thus superimposed on such questions as the size of the industries, the level of investment, and the criteria and the means of enforcement of economically efficient working. A further complication in these delicate decisions was the strength of unionization, and the particularly inflexible nature of the unions concerned, precisely in the least profitable industries of the nationalized sector. The earlier Socialist hopes that the nationalized industries would usher in a regime of better industrial relations, a motivation of unselfishness and a social purpose in industry, were soon disappointed.[133] Instead, there was an amalgam of social and commercial objectives.

Firm', pp. 1208–10, quoting W. B. Reddaway, *et al.*, *Effects of UK Direct Investment Abroad, Interim and Final Reports* (Cambridge, 1967, 1968); John H. Dunning, *The Role of American Investment in the British Economy* (1969); Hood and Young, p. 314.

[131] Mansfield, 'Technology', p. 170; S. Hymer and R. Rowthorn, *Multinational Corporation and International Oligopoly* (New Haven, 1969); Vernon, *Storm*, pp. 103–28; UN, *Multinational Corporations*, pp. 35, 46, 67 and *Transnational Corporations*, pp. 95, 141; Hodges, *Multinational Corporations*, pp. 40, 51–2, 220; Dunning, 'Technology', pp. 160–2.

[132] Robert Jones and Oliver Marriott, *Anatomy of a Merger: A History of GEC, AEI and English Electric* (1970); P. J. Curwen and A. H. Fowler, *Economic Policy* (1976), pp. 24–5.

[133] Herbert Morrison, Foreword to Institute of Public Administration, *Efficiency in the Nationalized Industries* (1952); also W. A. Robson, *Nationalized Industry and Public Ownership* (1962 ed.) pp. 460 ff.

The Coal Board is expected to keep down prices, and to make a profit, and to keep open a large number of uneconomic pits in Scotland, Wales and the northeast Coast. The Coal Board is, in fact, asked to act as a substitute for a proper national employment policy, and at the same time to meet commercial criteria.[134]

The industries were put into impossible dilemmas. If they made large surpluses, they were accused of abusing their monopoly powers: if small profits or losses, of being inefficient. For years low coal prices and low railway freight rates were used as a deliberate subsidy to industry, and then the two industries were derided for failing to make ends meet and to supply their own capital needs. It needed an outside Court of Inquiry into a labour dispute on the railways to lay down the obvious, but at that time startling, principle that 'having willed the end (of a nationalized public utility), the Nation must will the means', implying that employees of such a nationalized service should receive a fair and adequate wage, and that, in broad terms, the railwayman should be in no worse case than his colleague in a comparable industry.[135] The industries were not only attacked for ideological reasons by partisans of free enterprise, but also freely by press and public at large[136] in terms which, had they been used against a private firm, would have resulted in large damages against the libeller. Short-comings were put down freely to the fact of nationalization, while comparable shortcomings elsewhere were never blamed on private enterprise as such, but on weaknesses of individual firms. In fact, the main dilemma was that, far from becoming the spearhead of a Socialist economy, the nationalized industries remained anomalies in a private enterprise economy.

Most nationalized industries were exceptionally heavily capitalized. Between them they produced, in this period, a little over 10% of GDP, but swallowed almost 20% of United Kingdom investment. In addition to the industries taken over in the years after the war and the steel industry (1967),[137] the State also formed the British National Oil Corporation in 1976 and nationalized the aerospace and the shipbuilding firms in 1977. To these have to be added the individual firms taken over on behalf of the Government by the National Enterprise Board (NEB),[138] including Rolls Royce, Alfred Herbert, Ferranti and, in 1975–6, British Leyland. These additions did not alter the nature of the basket of the nation's industrial properties. It contains essentially two groups. One consists of some key sectors, especially in energy provision, transport and communications; the other is made up of lame ducks which could not be allowed, for various social reasons, to sink; and several fit both categories. It should perhaps be added that all comparable European countries have found it necessary to build up a similar list of socialized undertakings.

Neither the level of output, nor any long-term investment policy was at first laid down for these enterprises. They were merely required to break even, taking one year with another. Originally, their Boards had been given a

---

[134] Roy Jenkins, in Michael Shanks (ed.), *Lessons of Public Enterprise* (1963), p. 10.
[135] *Interim Report*, Cmd. 9352 (1955), p. 6.
[136] Robson, pp. 409–10, 447–8.
[137] See pp. 258–9 above.
[138] See pp. 399–400 below.

great deal of autonomy, but political realities, including the power of the Minister to dismiss members of Boards of Public Corporations, led to a substantial degree of political control over the management, all the more effective for being unofficial. The extent of that development was well documented in the reports of the Select Committee on Nationalized Industries, under Sir Patrick Spens and later Sir Toby Low, who, according to one critic, between 1957 and 1961 'documented the extent to which Whitehall has exercised power without responsibility, by exerting pressure on the Boards of these "independent" corporations, but in such a way as not to be accountable to the public, and so as to enable blame to be thrown onto the Boards. They have also documented the amateurishness and incompetence of the civil servants responsible for the major economic decisions.'[139] After 1955 this control was further tightened by obliging the Boards to borrow from the Treasury, instead of the market, even though the public clearly and increasingly showed its dislike of gilt-edgeds; the Treasury had increasing difficulty in placing its paper; and Local Authorities were, at precisely the same time, given the directly opposite instructions to borrow outside.[140]

If, as it was widely thought, this development was inevitable,[141] many observers agreed with the Herbert Committee, that the Ministers' ultimate power should be exercised openly and in specific cases only.[142] A white paper criticized the interference with long-term investment plans in the interests of short-term policy.[143] Further, it was seen to be incongruous that these industries received, not the capital they needed, but the capital which the Treasury could spare from year to year, and that the Treasury's naive aim of self-finance would lead to a wrong pricing policy.[144]

By the end of the decade, a new relationship began to crystallize. In 1961 a major white paper on the *Financial and Economic Obligations of the Nationalized Industries* laid down anew the divisions of power and the criteria of management. The Government, it stated, had the ultimate responsibility for seeing that the industries were administered economically and efficiently; further (in a passage begging all the main questions), 'although the industries have obligations of a national and non-economic kind, they are not, and ought not, to be regarded as social services absolved from economic and commercial justification.' More concretely, the industries were to accumulate adequate reserves, by depreciating at replacement, not historic cost; they were to plan to break even over five-year periods; and the rate of return expected from each of them was to be settled between the Minister and the Board and was to take account of any compulsory unprofitable activities.

---

[139] Select Committee, First Report, *Ministerial Control of the Nationalised Industries* H.C. 371-I (1967-8); D. L. Munby, 'The Nationalized Industries', in G. D. N. Worswick and P. H. Ady, *The British Economy in the Nineteen-Fifties* (1962), p. 384; also W. A. Robson, pp. 144, 160.

[140] Harrod, *British Economy*, pp. 105-8.

[141] E.g., A. H. Hansen, *Parliament and Public Ownership* (1961), pp. 210 ff.

[142] *Report of the Committee of Inquiry into the Electricity Supply Industry*, Cmd. 9672 (1956).

[143] *Public Investment*, Cmnd. 1203 (1960); also *Report of the (Plowden) Committee on the Control of Public Expenditure*, Cmnd. 1432 (1961), para. 23.

[144] Michael Shanks, p. 61.

As a consequence, Electricity Boards agreed to aim at $12\frac{1}{2}\%$ on net assets, the Gas Board at $10\frac{1}{4}\%$, and the Coal Board, to break even, on certain assumptions.[145]

New guidelines on prices and investment decisions were introduced in 1967.[146] 'Arms length rule', the freedom from direct interference by the politicians, was to be preserved, and the general instructions were to cover long-run marginal costs, with certain exceptions. It was a principle commending itself more to economic advisers than to people of practical experience, and apart from leading to some more refined peak period pricing for telephones in 1970 and for bulk electricity to areas (not consumers) in 1967–8,[147] it was quickly and mercifully forgotten. What remained was first, the obligation to meet costs in full together with a surplus to meet the financial targets, and secondly the principle that the consumer should pay 'the true costs of the goods and services he consumes in every case where these can be sensibly identified.'[148] The financial target consisted of a 'test discount rate' (TDR) of 8%, later raised to 10% in real terms and investment decisions were ordered to be governed by the net-present-value (NPV) principle.

The TDR was an attempt to align the nationalized industries with what was then thought to be the average rate earned in private industry, but it failed to have any rationing or allocation functions. Instead, the capital programmes tended to be justified as being simply necessary for expansion or replacement, or slashed to meet Government short-term panic demands. Some had the appearance of being little more than the results of Buggins's turn, or of the political muscle of the respective chairmen. The most that the TDR was called upon to do was to help to minimize costs of schemes already determined on.[149]

Whatever chance these policies might have had were lost by the industrial failures in the public sector. Of the nine major enterprises, four suffered declines in output and seven declines in employment between 1960 (1968 in the case of the British Steel Corporation) (BSC) and 1975. Meanwhile they gobbled up capital, much of which was soon lost, and thwarted successive governments' plans to cut public spending (see Table 7·16):[150]

[145] Cmnd. 1337 (1961); Pauline Gregg, *The Welfare State. The Economic and Social History of Great Britain from 1945 to the Present Day* (1967), p. 126.

[146] Treasury, *Nationalized Industries. A Review of Economic and Financial Objectives.* Cmnd. 3437 (1967); Michael G. Webb, *Pricing Policies for Public Enterprises*, pp. 79–82, and *idem, The Economics of Nationalised Industries* (1973), chapter 11; Prest and Coppock, pp. 184–91.

[147] R. L. Meek, 'The New Bulk Supply Tariff for Electricity', *Econ. J.*, 78/1, 1868.

[148] Cmnd. 3437, para. 18.

[149] David Heald, 'The Economic and Financial Control of UK Nationalised Industries', *Econ. J.*, 90/2, 1980, pp. 243–6; R. Rees, *Public Enterprise Economics (1976)*, pp. 18–19; National Economic Development Office, *A Study of UK Nationalised Industries. Their Role in the Economy and Control in the Future* (1976), pp. 9–10; Treasury (Working Paper No. 9), *The Test Discount Rate and the Required Rate of Return on Investment* (1979).

[150] *Nationalised Industries*, pp. 13, 19. PSBR = Public Sector Borrowing Requirement, for which see chapter 9 below.

[151] C. D. Foster, 'The Cost of Financing the Nationalized Industries', *Bull. Oxf. Inst. Stat.*, 22, 1960; R. Millward, 'Price Restraint, Anti-Inflation Policy and Public and Private Industry in the United Kingdom 1947–73', *Econ. J.*, 81/2, 1976; Graham Turner, p. 172; Richard M. Duke *et al., The United States Steel Industry and its International Rivals* (Washington, 1977), p. 353.

Table 7·16: Nationalized industries (£ billion)

	Capital needs	Total net impact on PSBR
Average of years		
1961–5	1·69	2·11
1966–70	3·48	3·19
1971–5	5·36	7·37

Some of the losses were caused by the obligation to keep prices down, compensated only in part by lower interest charged to them.[151] Nevertheless, the requests for ever more capital and current subsidies brought in political and bureaucratic interference and repeated switches of policy, which in turn led to uncertainty and demoralization among the managements. In 1976, cash limits were introduced and gave the Government further means of control, since ministerial assent was required to exceed them. They encouraged self-finance or, as in the case of BSC in 1977–8, savage reductions in capital programmes.

Following two further white papers,[152] the rules were changed once more in 1978, concentrating on prices, as in 1961, rather than investment criteria as in 1967. The new index was to be the Required Rate of Return (RRR) calculated on the whole of the new capital instead of, as the TDR, separately on each individual project. It was set initially at 5% before tax, again in alignment with private industry, the rate to be reviewed every three to five years. Individual prices and investment priorities were once more left to the industries themselves, subject to the requirement to relate the price structure to the cost structure. The existing capital was also made subject to financial targets, measured as a return on all assets after interest, but there was a different rate set for each industry,[153] and for persistent loss makers like British Rail the target might be set by the size of the subsidy. Industries which had some hopes of making a surplus or breaking even had in 1966 been given 'Public Dividend Capital' on which, as in private companies, no dividends need be paid in bad years, thus reducing the burden at critical times. This scheme was limited to British Airways, BSC, British Aerospace, British Shipbuilders and the Giro, and in 1978 it was decided not to extend it.[154] Instead, the Conservative Government, in office from 1979, proceeded to sell off some of the more profitable sectors of the nationalized industries to private owners, and to introduce privately-owned competition into others, including parts of the Post Office. By mid-1982 shares in four had been sold, of which British Aerospace was the largest, and several others, including British Airways, British Leyland and parts of the British National Oil Corporation, were under discussion.

The Price Commission was given authority in July 1977 to investigate most nationalized industry price increases.

[152] *Capital Investment Procedures*, Cmnd. 6106 (1975); *The Nationalized Industries*, Cmnd. 7131, (1978).

[153] E.g. Keith Hartley and Peter A. Watt, 'Profits, Regulation and the UK Aerospace Industry', *Journal of Industrial Economics*, 29/4, 1981, p. 418; Treasury, *Test Discount Rate*, pp. 12–13, 25.

[154] Cmnd. 7131, para. 88. Also Heald, pp. 247–62.

3 Incomes and their Distribution

The increases in output described in the first section of this chapter were reflected in increases in incomes over the same period, and consumers' expenditure showed a comparable rise (see Table 7·17).[155]

Table 7·17: Increases in income and expenditure

	Total domestic incomes			Consumers' expenditure		
	£ b.	Real domestic incomes per head		£ b.	Real consumers' expenditure per head	
		Index 1975 = 100	Av. annual growth %		Index 1975 = 100	Av. annual growth %
1950	12·0	57·8		9·5	61·7	
1955	17·0	64·6 } 2·0		13·1	67·4 } 2·0	
1960	22·9	70·5		16·9	75·4	
1965	31·6	74·4 } 1·7 } 2·1		22·9	82·8 } 1·8 } 2·0	
1970	45·1	83·5		31·8	90·0	
1975	99·1	100·0 } 2·6		64·7	100·0 } 2·1	
1980	202·0	107·5		135·4	110·3	

Thus in 30 years, both real incomes and consumers' expenditure almost doubled, rising at rates around 2% a year. The variations in the growth rates between the decades depend to some extent on the terminal years and should therefore not be used to read off a sequence of phasing: the phases and cycles of this period will be discussed in chapter 9.

The distribution of incomes showed some clear trends over the years 1950–1980:

Table 7·18: Percentage shares of domestic incomes before tax

	1950	1955	1960	1965	1970	1975	1980
Wages and salaries	65·0	67·7	66·4	64·9	63·9	62·8	59·5
Employers' contrib. to Nat. Ins. etc.	4·1	4·3	4·9	5·6	6·4	8·3	8·7
Total incomes from employment	69·1	72·1	71·3	70·5	70·3	71·1	68·2
Incomes from self-employment	12·6	10·6	9·4	8·4	8·8	8·9	9·2
Rents, divid., net interest Received by: Life Assurance and Superannuation schemes	1·3	1·6	2·1	2·7	3·1	2·8	3·5
Imputed rents from owner-occupied houses					3·0	3·5	3·8
Others	10·3	8·5	9·3	9·1	4·6	2·8	2·6
Nat. Insurance benefits etc.	6·9	7·1	7·8	9·2	10·0	10·7	12·7
Total personal incomes	100	100	100	100	100	100	100

Incomes from employment remained remarkably stable as a share of total incomes, but within this total, employers' contributions to national

---

[155] Based on *National Income and Expenditure*. Index of 1958 = 100 has been spliced into the 1975 = 100 index.

insurance more than doubled in what seemed like an inexorable rise of the social welfare state, and freely disposable wages and salaries correspondingly fell. Incomes from self-employment showed a sharp fall until the mid-1960s and thereafter rose again slightly, but this relative stability likewise hid a significant internal shift among the three major categories (see Table 7·19).

Table 7·19:   Shares among incomes from self-employment*

	1950	1965	1980
Professional persons	16·0	17·3	18·2
Farmers	25·0	23·9	15·5
Other sole traders and partnerships	59·0	58·8	66·3
	100	100	100

* Before tax, and before providing for depreciation and stock appreciation.

There was a marked fall in the income of farmers, but it was compensated by the rise in the incomes of sole traders and partnerships. Similarly, the stability of the share of incomes from property hides a rise in the share of imputed rents, and a near trebling of the incomes of insurance companies and pension funds, implying consequently a sharp drop in the property incomes of individuals, particularly in the 1970s. Finally, the share of national insurance and social welfare benefits doubled, and may be considered to be a counterpart of the growth of contributions recorded in the second line of Table 7·18.

Some of the implications of these shifts will be discussed in the following paragraphs, but the limitations of these statistics should be borne in mind. Above all they cannot be taken as an indication of relative income changes because of parallel changes in the numbers concerned. Among these were the fall in the number of farmers and the wholesale conversion of small businesses into companies leading to the conversion of the incomes of their owners from 'profits' to 'salaries'. Moreover, the growing skill in tax avoidance among larger companies and richer individuals may also not have been without significance.[156]

A better measure of the distribution of incomes is the share of total incomes taken by the top 1% or top 10% of income earners, and of each following decile (or 10%). This shows a marked, if not overwhelmingly strong levelling of incomes in the post-war period, visible in incomes both before and after tax (see Tables 7·20 and 21).[157]

Table 7·20:   Share of incomes before tax (UK)

	1949	1959	1973–4
Top 1%	—	8·4	6·5
Top 10%	33·1	29·4	26·8
Lowest 20%	5·4	5·3	6·2
Gini coefficient	—	39·8%	37·0%

[156] S. Pollard and D. W. Crossley, *The Wealth of Britain*, 1086–1966 (1968), p. 263.

[157] Royal Commission on the Distribution of Income and Wealth, *Report No. 4, Second Report on the Standing Conference*, Cmnd. 6626 (1976) pp. 12, 101–2. Distribution is the more equitable, the lower the Gini coefficient. Also Paolo Roberti, 'Income Distribution: A Time Series and a Cross-section Study', *Econ. J.*, 84/3, 1974, p. 635.

Table 7·21: Share of incomes after tax (UK)

	1949	1964	1973–4
Top 1%	4·6	5·3	4·5
Top 10%	27·1	25·9	23·6
2nd decile	14·5	16·1	15·5
9th and 10th deciles	—	6·5	7·5
Gini coefficient	35·5%	36·6%	32·8%
As % of median income:			
Top 1%	508	445	388
Top decile	208	212	201
Lower quartile	—	54	60

Calculated in tax units rather than incomes, the Gini coefficient of the income distribution fell similarly from 36·5% in 1948–9, to 30·2% in 1949–50, 29·1% in 1959–60 and 27·5% in 1973–4.[158]

For the top earners, the fall was more drastic. Thus the incomes of the highest-paid males, as a multiple of median incomes, dropped as shown in Table 7·22.[159]

Table 7·22: Highest incomes as a multiple of median incomes

		Highest decimillile	Highest millile	Highest centile
Before tax:	1959/60	21	10	4
	1972/3	15	8	$3\frac{1}{2}$
After tax:	1959/60	11	7	3
	1972/3	7	5	3

It will be noted that the tax system continued its function of redistributing incomes from the rich to the poor, although that levelling effect tended to become weaker rather than stronger in our period as shown in Table 7·23.[160]

Table 7·23: Effects of the tax system on redistribution

	Average taxes as % of incomes before tax			% of total taxes contributed		
	1959	1967	1974–5	1959	1967	1974–5
Top 1% incomes	43·2	43·3	47·1	34·5	23·3	15·8
Top 10%	23·5	24·5	29·1	64·9	50·0	42·2
Bottom 20%	0·1	0·8	1·0	—	0·4	0·3
All incomes	10·5	13·6	18·3	100	100	100

However, the influence of the State on income distribution reached further than the direct taxation system. In order to assess its full impact, indirect taxes, direct cash benefits and benefits in kind have to be calculated in as well,

[158] Royal Commission, *Report No. 4* p. 104.

[159] Chris Pond, 'The High Paid and the Crisis of Living Standards', in Frank Field (ed.), *The Wealth Report* (1979).

[160] *Ibid.*, p. 58.

and some of these went to the credit of the rich as well as that of the lower-income groups.

For 1970, some percentage change effects on the Gini coefficient (negative values mean a move in the direction of greater equality, positive values tend towards greater inequality) have been calculated as shown in Table 7·24.[161]

Table 7·24:   Percentage change effects on the Gini coefficient, 1970

Taxable pensions	− 3·58
Income tax	− 2·66
National health service	− 1·57
Education	− 0·63
Sickness benefit	− 0·58
Supplementary benefit	− 0·55
Housing subsidies	− 0·22
Indirect duties on oil	+ 0·15
Direct duties on oil	+ 0·16
Local rates (net)	+ 0·23
Duties on beer	+ 0·26
Duties on tobacco	+ 0·83

These are little more than guesses, and some benefits in kind, such as security and good government, cannot be allocated at all fairly. They have been omitted here. One estimate attempting to chart the redistribution resulting from State action in 1974 came to the results shown in Table 7·25 for the top two and the lowest two deciles of incomes:[162]

Table 7·25:   Income distribution, taxes and benefits, 1974, UK (£ per week)

		Top 10%	2nd decile	9th decile	Lowest decile
Average	original income	140·40	90·64	11·23	4·67
''	direct cash benefits	+ 2·06	+ 1·71	+ 12·21	+ 12·16
''	benefits in kind	+ 5·35	+ 4·79	+ 3·71	+ 5·10
''	direct taxes	− 32·20	− 19·54	− 1·50	− 0·43
''	indirect taxes	− 18·81	− 14·15	− 4·38	− 2·89
	final incomes	101·53	65·12	20·03	13·31
% Shares:	Original incomes	26·4	17·0	2·1	0·9
	Final incomes	23·7	15·2	4·7	3·1

The poorest 10%, and many in the next decile above them, were largely dependent on income redistributed by the State by means of Social Insurance and the Social Services, but the losses suffered in the redistribution by the top

[161] J. L. Nicholson, 'The Distribution and Redistribution of Income in the United Kingdom', in Dorothy Wedderburn (ed.), *Poverty, Inequality and Class Structure* (Cambridge, 1974), p. 80.
[162] Royal Commission, *Report No. 4*, p. 27. The totals do not add up because the mathematical operations were not always performed on the same incomes. In the original, direct taxes were deducted *before* benefits in kind were added, but the sequence has been altered here for more logical presentation.

earners were moderate. The middle groups including the better-paid wage earners largely covered their own needs supplied *via* the State; they were much affected by indirect taxes including those on alcohol and tobacco and by being pushed into higher tax brackets by the inflation.[163]

The taxes-cum-welfare system also tended to favour families and pensioners, at all levels of income. The effects in two not untypical income ranges worked out as shown in Table 7·26.[164]

Table 7·26: Net total state benefits received (+) less total taxes paid (−) for certain income ranges, 1971 (£ p.a.)

		Original income per annum (£)	
		816–986	987–1193
Non-retired households:	1 Adult	− 250	− 286
	2 Adults	− 18	− 139
	2 Adults, 1 Child	+ 45	− 122
	2 Adults, 2 Children	+ 99	+ 78
	2 Adults, 3 ''	+ 456	+ 213
Retired households:	2 Adults	+ 218	+ 45

Property or wealth, which was far more unevenly distributed than incomes, tended similarly towards greater equality in this period, and was considerably more egalitarian than before the war, but the levelling process slowed down in the 1960s. Definitions and valuations are even more difficult than in the case of incomes, and much depends on the assumptions made. Most, but not all, of the British estimates take the distribution revealed by the estate duty as their starting point and then make allowances for those dying without taxable estates and for other factors. Two sets of estimates, both derived from the 'estate' method, for the share of personal wealth held by the top 1% and the top 10% of wealth holders, are presented in Table 7·27.[165]

Table 7·27: Estimates of shares of personal wealth

	Royal Commission		Atkinson and Harrison		
	Top 1%	Top 10%	Top 1%	Top 5%	Top 10%
1936/8	56	88	54·6	77·2	85·3
1950	—	—	47·2	74·3	—
1954	43	79	45·3	71·8	—
1960	38·2	76·7	33·9	59·4	71·5
1970	29·0	70·1	29·7	53·6	68·7
1972	29·9	71·9	31·7	56·0	70·4
1975	23·2	62·4	—	—	—

[163] Dudley Jackson *et al.*, *Do Trade Unions Cause Inflation?* (1972), pp. 66–7; Geoffrey Stephenson, 'Taxes, Benefits and the Redistribution of Incomes', in Cedric Sandford, Chris Pond, Robert Walker (eds.), *Taxation and Social Policy* (1980), pp. 18–20.

[164] J. L. Nicholson, 'Distribution', pp. 76–8.

[165] A. R. Prest and D. J. Coppock, *The UK Economy* (1978), p. 238; A. B. Atkinson and A. J. Harrison, *Distribution of Personal Wealth in Britain* (Cambridge, 1978), p. 159; Louie Burghes, 'The Old Order', in Frank Field, *Wealth Report*, pp. 11, 20, 26; Peter Townsend, *Poverty in the United Kingdom* (Harmondsworth, 1979), p. 904.

The overall trend is unmistakeable, and it was matched by a slow increase among the smallest fortunes, the holdings of the bottom 80% rising from 4% in 1924–30 to 9% in 1960 and 13% in 1970.

Even if correctly evaluated, these comparisons would to some extent still be misleading, since the smaller wealth holdings consisted very largely of use values, such as dwellings, or of claims on insurance and pension funds, to be used up in later life, while among the very rich, ownership in shares, other securities and land, in other words, in property as a source of income tended to predominate. Thus in the wealth range of £10,000–£19,999 in 1974, 64% of assets were in the form of dwellings and household goods and $17\frac{1}{2}$% in the form of life policies, but these amounted to only 15% and $2\frac{1}{2}$% respectively in the case of the largest fortunes of over £200,000; against this, shares, other company securities and land figured at a negligible 3% of the smaller properties, but represented 64% of the larger. In line with the relative decline of the larger fortune, shares and other securities (but not land) fell sharply as a share of total assets in this period, whereas dwellings and life policies, the assets of the smaller fortunes, rose as rapidly (see Table 7·28).[166]

Table 7·28:   Personal wealth, asset composition (GB)

	1960	1974
Dwellings	20·7%	42·7%
Land	2·1	4·5
Life policies	11·9	14·9
Listed ordinary shares	15·2	6·8
Other company securities	7·8	4·0
Other assets	50·7	37·2
Debts (liabilities)	− 8·4	− 10·1
	100	100

At the other end of the scale, abject poverty, such as was still to be found among substantial groups of people between the wars, has practically disappeared in the post-war years. Applying the standards of 1971, for example, it fell from one-fifth of the population in 1953 to one-fortieth in 1973.[167] Yet it has been widely considered, above all among the poor themselves, that the definition of poverty must also contain a conventional or comparable element, that is to say the inability to afford, of suffering a deprivation of, items which were not considered necessary at an earlier period, but had in some sense become necessary in view of the rising standards achieved by the rest of the population. Taking another extreme definition, poverty might mean being among the poorest, say, 10% of the population: in that sense no society will ever be without poverty, and it will always affect every tenth person or family. Another, similar approach might be to take some arbitrary fraction of average or median income, say one half, and designate everything below it as 'poverty'. The problem is further complicated by differing basic

---

[166] Royal Commission, *Report No. 4*, Cmnd. 6626, pp. 52, 59; Thomas Stark, *The Distribution of Personal Incomes in the United Kingdom 1949–1963* (Cambridge, 1972), p. 72.

[167] Prest and Coppock, p. 259; for other estimates see Stark, *Distribution*, pp. 48 *passim*.

needs of different-sized families, the question of 'equivalence'.[168]

In post-war Britain, the tendency has been to take the National Assistance, and after 1966 the 'Supplementary Benefit' payments level as the threshold standard of poverty. This used as its base on the one hand family size and circumstances, such as rent payments, and on the other, tended to be raised, formally after 1959, year by year in line with the real wage level,[169] and thus paying tribute to the proportional or conventional element. Conversely, it might be said that the progressive abolition of abject poverty was achieved, on the one hand, by the absolute rise in the whole range of incomes, including the lowest, and on the other, by the payment of rising social security benefits.

The hopes of the Beveridge scheme of providing adequately for all conceivable causes of need were not fulfilled, and the gap between payments received as of right, and the minimal National Assistance/Supplementary Benefit scales was never closed. In recent years, the numbers on National Assistance/Supplementary Benefits have risen substantially, from 1 million in 1948 and $1\frac{1}{2}$ million in 1951 to almost 3 million in 1976, representing 5 millions including dependants, mostly because of the increase in the number of pensioners whose State pension has to be made up to that level, and the increase in the numbers of unemployed, but there have also always been those who were in employment and still not earning the officially fixed minimum. The number of families of those normally in full-time work or self-employed, with incomes below the Supplementary Benefit level rose from 130,000 to 290,000 between 1974 and 1976, and the number of persons involved, from 360,000 to 890,000.[170] Even those earning little above the minimal levels found themselves increasingly in a 'poverty trap' if they attempted to raise their earned incomes, as rising taxes and falling benefits then reduced the value of each additional pound earned to a few pence, and in certain critical ranges, even to a negative sum.

Among the causes of low pay continued to be handicaps such as repeated illnesses and frequent job changes, and undemanding, unskilled work. The old, the very young, and women, were additionally likely to be found in low-pay occupations.[171] Women's earnings in manufacturing as a proportion of male remained remarkably stable from pre-war years until 1970, fluctuating gently around the 50% mark, with a light rise in wartime and a subsequent return to the pre-war level. The Equal Pay Act of 1970, phased to come into full force in 1975, brought a dramatic change, and its momentum was continued by the Sex Discrimination Act of 1975 which prohibited non-pecuniary discrimination such as access to jobs or promotion. By 1975,

[168] Peter Townsend, *Poverty*, pp. 262 ff. G. Fiegehen, P. Lansey, A. Smith, *Poverty and Progress in Britain 1953-73* (Cambridge, 1977), pp. 15-17; P. Townsend, 'Poverty as Relative Deprivation: Resources and Style of Living', in Dorothy Wedderburn (ed.), *Poverty, Inequality and Class Structure* (Cambridge, 1974), p. 15.

[169] Department of Health and Social Security, *Low Pay* (1977), p. 9; Sir John Walley, *Social Security: Another British Failure?* (1972).

[170] Frank Field, 'Poverty, Growth and the Redistribution of Income', in Wilfred Beckerman (ed.), *Slow Growth in Britain, Causes and Consequences* (Oxford, 1979), pp. 86-8, 95; Department of Health and Social Security, *Social Security Statistics*.

[171] National Board for Prices and Incomes, *Report* No. 169: *General Problems of Low Pay*, Cmnd. 4648 (1971) pp. 36-63, 123.

women's wages had risen to $57\frac{1}{2}\%$ of men's and by 1978 to 61%, where they remained. Average hourly earnings for women, which had always been relatively higher, at around 60%, also rose by 11%, to 71%, and for non-manual earnings, the gap was reduced in similar manner: between 1970 and 1980, men's wages rose by 303%, but women's by 368%.[172]

Wage and salary earnings as a whole rose in line with total incomes, though diverging from time to time from the trend. Average real weekly earnings again just failed to double in the 30 years 1950–80 (see Table 7·29): (Total domestic real incomes are added for comparison from Table 7·17 p. 315 above.)

Table 7·29: The rise in earnings

	Average real weekly earnings		Total domestic real incomes per head	
	Index 1970 = 100	Av. ann. growth rate	Index 1975 = 100	Average annual growth rate
1950	65·3 ⎫		57·8 ⎫	
1955	73·4 ⎬ 2·5		64·6 ⎬ 2·0	
1960	83·8 ⎭		70·5 ⎭	
1965	94·6 ⎬ 1·8		74·4 ⎬ 1·7	
1970	100·0 ⎭		83·5 ⎭	
1975	115·8 ⎬ 2·0		100·0 ⎬ 2·6	
1980	122·4 ⎭		107·5 ⎭	

Again, not too much should be read into these figures for the purpose of phasing these changes.

Throughout this period, British wages rose considerably faster in relation to prices and to productivity than the wages in comparable countries abroad. The result was a more rapid rise in unit labour costs, which in turn contributed to the loss of markets für British goods.[173]

Table 7·30: Changes in unit labour costs

	1950–62 (whole period)	1963–80 (% per annum)
United Kingdom	+70%	+10·4
Germany	+48	+ 3·1
France		+ 5·8
USA	+27	+ 3·7
Japan	+ 9	+ 4·7

Particularly rapid was the rise of additional costs per employee in the form of national insurance contributions, taxes, etc., even after employment subsidies were deducted. Those rose in a steady progression from £6·25 per employee, or 21% of net earnings, to no less than £19·29, or 47% of net

[172] *Department of Employment Gazette.*
[173] Calculated from *Nat. Inst. Econ. Rev.* Also G. F. Ray, 'Labour Costs in OECD Countries 1964–1975', *ibid.*, 75, February 1976, pp. 60–1; OECD, *Economic Outlook*; UN, *Statistical Yearbook*.

earnings, between 1960 and 1980.[174] Some of the implications of these changes will be discussed in chapter 9 below.

Within wage and salary payments, the levelling up of the lower paid in relation to skilled wages that occurred in war time was very slightly reversed thereafter, and then stabilized. By the mid-1960s, in a number of representative industries, the true ratios of unskilled wage rates were around 85% of those of the skilled. In earnings the gap was wider, the unskilled rates averaging between 71% and 87% of skilled earnings. The income policies of the 1970s had a slight tendency to compress wages once more. More strongly in the same direction worked the inflation, in which, as on previous occasions, top incomes failed to keep pace with price rises.[175] In the later 1970s the trend was reversed again, however, and, taking the wage distribution in deciles, there was virtually no change over 1960–80, except for a very slight tendency of the top decile to rise against the median in 1979–80.[176]

Salaries drifted down against wages in the 1950s, and in the following two decades their decline was dramatic. Thus, taking annual earnings of adult men between 1960 and 1977, with skilled wages as 100 in each year, the incomes of higher professionals (doctors, lawyers), fell from 255 to 164, those of managers from 232 to 147, those of foremen and supervisors from 127 to 104, and those of clerks from 86 to 84. Measured against semi-skilled or unskilled wages, the drop would have been greater still. Only lower professionals (teachers, librarians) succeeded in raising their differential, from 106 to 131.[177] In their way, changes of that magnitude amount to a minor social revolution.

They were underlined by an equally dramatic collapse of the returns to capital over the same period. Crude measures of the rate of profit in quoted companies showed a fall from 25·2% in 1950–4 to 21% in 1960–4 and 12·1% in 1970. More accurate measures are available from 1960 on. Their precise meaning, however, is in dispute in view of the tax changes and the problems of inflation accounting and stock valuation. The simple calculation of returns on historic costs neglects the need to re-invest much higher sums to replace capital in an inflation, and several alternative measures to take account of this exist and have been revised from time to time. They all show, in their different ways, the same sharp downward trend. For industrial and commercial companies, excluding North Sea oil and gas, some typical rates of return are presented in Table 7·31.[178]

[174] *Nat. Inst. Econ. Rev.*, 98, November 1982, p. 11.

[175] William Brown, 'Incomes Policies and Pay Differentials', *Oxf. Bull. Econ. Stat.*, 38/1, 1976, pp. 44–5 and 'Engineering Wages and the Social Contract 1975–1977', *ibid.*, 41/1, 1979, pp. 51–2.

[176] L. C. Hunter and C. Mulvey, *Economics of Wages and Labour* (2nd ed., 1981), p. 76; *Annual Abstract of Statistics*.

[177] Hunter and Mulvey, p. 79; G. Routh, *Occupation and Pay in Great Britain 1906–60* (Cambridge, 1965), pp. 102–7, 150; A. R. Thatcher, 'The Distribution of Earnings of Employees in Great Britain', *J.R. Stat. S.*, 131/1 (1968); R. C. O. Matthews, C. H. Feinstein, J. C. Odling-Smee, *British Economic Growth 1856–1973* (Oxford 1982), p. 167.

[178] J. S. Flemming, L. D. D. Price, D. H. A. Ingram, 'Trends in Company Profitability', *B. of Eng. Qtly. Bull.*, March 1976, pp. 36–7, 42; 'Profitability and Company Finance: A Supplementary Note', *ibid.* 19, June 1979, pp. 183–5; *ibid.* 17, June 1977, p. 156; *Nat. Inst. Econ. Rev.*, 99, Feb. 1982, p. 23; John Black, *The Economics of Modern Britain* (1980), p. 81; *National Income and Expenditure*.

They show the most serious decline to have taken place between 1960 and the mid-1970s; following a slight recovery thereafter, there was a further collapse in 1979–80, which continued into the following year. It may be that these two downward phases had different causes.

The authors who first drew attention to the decline, associated it with the withdrawal of investment incentives by the Labour Government in the late 1960s.[179] Others, however, have pointed out that this fall amounted to a lowering of the costs of capital and was accompanied, on the contrary, by a considerable rise in productive investment in those years. Given constant supplies of labour and increasing supplies of capital, the returns on the latter may be expected to fall. Firms were then unable to compensate fully for their rises in costs by raising prices because of the then waxing strength and militancy of the trade unions, the price freeze, and sharpening competition from abroad. Also, companies were slow, especially in the early 1970s, to realize that they had to set aside larger sums for stock appreciation in order to compensate for the rise in replacement costs if they wanted to stay solvent.[180]

Several studies have emphasized the large part played in these calculations by the incidence of taxation and the actions over stock appreciation: a part of the rise in the costs of stocks, they point out, might on certain assumptions be considered to be profit, and firms were aided further in this respect by the tax changes of 1974 (see Table 7·31). In those terms, it could be shown that while profits before tax were falling in this period, profits after tax were not.[181]

Rising incomes, and the marked levelling of incomes, were reflected in the patterns of consumption. The motor car, once a middle-class status symbol, now became a leveller, as ownership extended yearly to lower income groups, and it was closely paralleled by radio and television sets, by other domestic electric and gas appliances, by furniture and furnishings in the home and even by clothes and fashion goods, particularly among the young. The ambitions and the tastes among the classes came much closer together, though there were still differences detectable by the statisticians in the purchase of household goods, beside the main outstanding ambition by the middle classes to own, rather than rent, their home, and the desire to pay for private, privileged schooling and aim for a University education. Differences in expenditure patterns were now often larger between differently constituted families, e.g. those with many small children as compared with those with children who were earners themselves, than between social groups.[182]

The raising of the bulk of the population above a subsistence standard was

[179] Andrew Glyn and Bob Sutcliffe, 'The Collapse of UK Profits', *New Left Review*, 66, March-April 1971.

[180] J. R. Sargent, 'Productivity and Profits in UK Manufacturing', *Midland Bank Review*, Autumn 1979, pp. 10–13; Flemming, Price and Ingram, pp. 43–4; *B. of Eng. Qtly. Bull.*, 17, June 1977, p. 156; J. F. Wright, *Britain in the Age of Economic Management* (Oxford, 1979), pp. 187–90.

[181] Mervyn A. King, 'United Kingdom Profits Crisis: Myth or Reality?' *Econ. J.*, 85/1, 1975; Frank Field, 'Private Capital's Blood Transfusion', in *idem, The Wealth Report*, pp. 98–101; M. Panić and R. E. Close, 'Profitability and British Manufacturing Industry' *Lloyds Bank Review*, April 1975.

[182] Ministry of Labour and National Service, *Report of an Enquiry into Household Expenditure in 1953–4* (1957); Ministry of Labour, *Family Expenditure Survey for 1963*.

Table 7·31: Rates of return for industrial and commercial companies

	1960	1965	1970	1974	1975	1976	1977	1978	1979	1980
Pre-tax historic cost returns	19·0	16·2	14·4	17·1	16·0	17·7	17·0	15·8	—	—
Pre-tax real rates of return, after revaluation of capital consumption and stock appreciation	13·4	11·2	8·1	5·4	4·6	4·9	6·0	5·9	4·1	0·2
Post-tax, real rates of return: forward looking	9·7	6·6	3·4	4·7	3·3	2·9				
do., excl. tax relief on stocks				0·2	0·5	0·2				
backward looking	8·3	6·1	4·2	4·3	2·8	2·4				
do., excl. tax relief on stocks				0·1	0·7	0·3				
Profit margin Net trading profits and rents,		21·1	16·9	13·5	11·4	12·4	15·2	14·9	10·9	5·8
All companies and financial institutions, as % net nat. product		10·6*	9·4	5·8	4·5	5·3	8·1	8·4	7·4	5·3

* 1968

reflected also in the national consumption statistics. In terms of quantity, the small increase in food and clothing contrasts with the sharp increase in 'luxuries', even though food rationing ended only in 1954 and coal rationing in 1958.[183] 'Expenditure elasticity' in the 1950s was found to be as high as 2·48 for transport and 1·57 for clothing, but only 1·05 for household expenses, 0·74 for drink and tobacco and 0·26 for food.[184] In terms of actual expenditure, however, because of the incidence of purchase tax and excise duties, and the increasing returns in the mass-production goods industries, the shares changed rather less, except for motor vehicles, which had still been held back by rationing in 1950, and among which increases in quantity greatly outweighed the relative reductions in costs. (See Table 7·32)[185]

Table 7·32:   Consumers' expenditure, 1950–1980

	Volume of consumption (1950 = 100)		% of consumers' expenditure, current prices		
	1965	1980	1950	1965	1980
Food	125·7	138·9	29·1	26·0	17·2
Drink, tobacco	129·8	183·1	16·5	12·8	11·1
Clothing	135·4	202·3	11·5	9·1	7·3
Housing and maintenance	137·3	190·3	8·6	11·1	14·6
Furniture, household goods	142·4	177·3	5·0	4·1	5·1
Radio, electrical	281·4	726·3	1·9	2·4	2·4
Motor vehicles and fuel	694·1	1199·4	1·9	7·6	10·4
Population (1950 = 100)	(108·5)	(111·5)	—	—	—

In the second phase, 1965–80, rationing and shortages played no part, and consumers' preferences had full play. The demand for food and for furniture was seen to have been largely sated by 1965, and rose but little with incomes; but drink, tobacco, clothing, housing, radio and electrical goods and motor vehicles proved highly income-elastic. Because of changing prices, however, the distribution of money expenditure shifted in a different way from the changes in volume. Thus housing, where real cost gains were low, rose disproportionately as a share of consumer expenditure; spending on radio and electrical goods, where cost reductions were particularly striking, rose hardly at all despite a sevenfold increase in the volume of sales between 1950 and 1980.

Further, with rising standards, there were 'luxury' elements even among necessities. Thus, richer people still spent more on food per head than poorer people, and with the general rise in incomes, there was also a substantial replacement of 'inferior' foods by 'superior' ones after the war. In some cases this trend continued after 1965, though in much weakened form (see Table 7·33).[186]

[183] Margaret Hall, 'The Consumer Sector', in Worswick and Ady, p. 439.

[184] I.e., the percentage increase in expenditure corresponding to an increase in income of 1%. W. Beckerman and Associates, *The British Economy in 1975* (Cambridge, 1965), p. 180.

[185] *National Income and Expenditure.*

[186] J. C. McKenzie, 'Past Dietary Trends as an Aid to Prediction', in T. C. Barker *et al.*, *Our Changing Fare* (1966), p. 136: *Annual Abstract of Statistics.*

Table 7·33: Consumption per head, UK

	1944	1965	1980
Liquid milk (litres)	139·7	141·7	129·3
Meat (kg)	51·7	69·1	71·4
Eggs (no.)	78·4	250	231
Butter (kg)	3·6	8·8	6·1
Vegetables, fruit and nuts (kg)	87·1	106·4	108·9
Margarine (kg)	8·2	5·4	7·1
Potatoes (kg)	124·8	100·9	105·4
Wheat, flour and other cereals (kg)	114·8	75·8	69·2

thus people ate even more meat, vegetables and fruit, and even less of the 'inferior' foods, wheat, flour and other cereals. But in the other items the trend was reversed, even if all changes were of a minor nature: thus the consumption of milk went down again, potatoes went up and butter and margarine seemed to switch roles, no doubt in part caused by the health scare over butter. All these post-war changes can without difficulty still be incorporated in a pattern of rising income and welfare. Interestingly enough, milk reached its maximum consumption in 1975, eggs in 1970 and potatoes their minimum in 1976, after which the trends changed direction.

The move towards uniformity, both of commodities available to the consumer and of the shops in which they were sold, which had been very evident between the wars, took further rapid strides forward, aided by the economies of mass-production and by advertising. Advertising, indeed, became one of Britain's most successful growth industries, particularly after the establishment of so-called Independent Television, and, after a temporary setback owing to the incidence of SET, resumed its growth in 1967–8. It rose from an estimated £102 million in 1950 to £2,562 million in 1980, the highest expenditure at constant prices being in 1973. It also called forth the consumers' countervailing power of self-protection by association and information. Consumer Co-operative Societies had performed this function in the nineteenth century, but in the mid-twentieth they were themselves producers, retailers and therefore competitors for the consumers' attention; besides, they were essentially working-class organizations. In 1957 the Consumers' Association, a middle-class body, began to publish *Which?*, reporting objective tests on articles and services of widespread sale, and registered immediate and lasting success, with a membership of 400,000 at their tenth anniversary. *Shoppers' Guide*, also dating from 1957, a similar publication linked with the Consumer Advisory Council of the British Standards Institute, was less successful, but some of its work was transferred to a new magazine, *Focus*. Following the report of the Molony Committee,[187] official interest was also known by the appointment of a national Consumer Council in 1963, and a tightening up of legislation protecting the consumers in the following years, culminating in the Trade Descriptions Act of 1968. Several cities, beginning with Sheffield, also appointed their own consumer protection officers. In one respect this movement simply made use of the possibilities provided by mass production and national chain stores to approach these problems nationally;

[187] *Final Report of the Consumer Protection Committee*, Cmnd. 1781 (1962); T. R. Nevett, *Advertising in Britain, a History* (1982), pp. 177, 188.

in another, it represented a new way of dealing with monopolistic traders and producers, and with a full-employment economy in which loss of custom was not as powerful a threat to the inadequate seller as it once had been.

One element affecting incomes could be largely ignored until the later 1960s: the impact of unemployment. In the first 20 years of peace it averaged 1·8%, or around 400,000, well within the limits of what were considered in a free society, to be justifiable numbers of those changing jobs and the temporarily or permanently unemployable, though some other economies managed with considerably fewer. In the later 1960s the numbers rose to 600,000 and reached a brief peak of 950,000, or 3·8% in 1972 before the Barber boom, but did not fall below 500,000 thereafter. In 1975 there was a second swell rising to a new level of one million, or 4%, and it stayed between 5·6 and 6·1% in the next five years, or around $1\frac{1}{2}$ million. Finally, in the second quarter of 1981 it jumped a third time to over 10%, or well over $2\frac{1}{4}$ million and by 1982 seemed to be settling around a level of three million registered unemployed.

With the exception of the last phase 1980–2, these trends were not dissimilar from those of other comparable economies (see Table 7·34)[188], and the deterioration of the 1970s must be brought into relation with the world economic recession released by the OPEC rise in oil prices. The particular causes responsible for the high level in Britain in 1981–2, connected with deliberate Government policies which added perhaps one million to the numbers of the unemployed, and for the concentration of much of the redundancies of the 1970s in the manufacturing sector, are discussed elsewhere;[189] here we are concerned with the relationship of unemployment to incomes.

Table 7·34:   Standardized rates of unemployment, %, US definition

	1960	1970	1979	1981
United Kingdom	2·2	3·1	5·8	11·4
U.S.A.	5·5	4·9	5·8	7·5
France	1·8	2·6	6·1	7·6
West Germany	1·1	0·8	3·0	4·5
Italy	3·8	3·1	3·9	8·2
Japan	1·7	1·2	2·1	2·5

Economists have not been wanting who have considered much of this unemployment to be voluntary, induced by over-generous State benefits. As a general statement this cannot be accepted, in view of the very low unemployment rates 1945–66 despite higher benefits than pre-war, and in view of the fact that British benefits as a proportion of incomes from employment were substantially below those of other countries.[190] But it is not impossible

---

[188] Constance Sorrentino, 'Unemployment in International Perspective', in Brian Showler and Adrian Sinfield, *The Workless State: Studies in Unemployment* (Oxford, 1981), p. 170; OECD, *Labour Force Statistics*. Problems of definition are discussed in G. D. N. Worswick (ed.), *The Concept and Measurement of Involuntary Unemployment* (1976), and *Unemployment Statistics. Report of an Interdepartmental Working Party*, Cmnd. 5157 (1972).

[189] Pp. 281–4 above and chapter 9 below.

[190] Sorrentino, p. 195.

that small minorities of workers have been induced by particular provisions to fall back on State benefits.

Two measures have mainly been held responsible. One was the Redundancy Payments Act 1965, which benefited older workers in particular, and it was indeed followed by a rise in the unemployment rates of older men; but in many cases, this had clear structural reasons. The other was the introduction of the Earnings Related Supplement (ERS), operating from 1966. Again, there appeared to be a not unreasonable mathematical relationship between the higher benefits and the higher numbers out of work: but in fact, only a small minority of the latter benefited from ERS. Thus in a comparison between 1965, before ERS, and 1972, while 467,000 additional men and 68,000 additional women were on unemployment benefit, only 129,000 of the former and 16,000 of the latter were on ERS and for some of them the benefits thus received were so low that they had to be made up by Supplementary Allowances. In May 1976, ERS recipients numbered 245,000, or one-sixth of the unemployed.[191] Combined tax and benefit changes actually reduced the 'incentive' to live on benefit in the 1970s.

As in the inter-war period, there were strong regional variations in the incidence of unemployment, but while the early post-war years showed a distribution not unlike the pre-war one, in the 1970s the West Midlands and the northwest suffered more than proportionately – a reflection of the contraction in textiles, engineering and motor vehicle manufacture. Particularly affected were also the young, the old, the unskilled and, as a newly emergent discriminated group, the coloured, who all had more than average rates of unemployment. For women the official figures of 'registered' unemployed are probably under-estimates, since many do not bother to register in adverse times.

What was further noticeable was the sharp increase in the duration of unemployment for each individual out of work, rather than the increase in the numbers affected.[192] It was a signal that in depressions cyclical, structural

---

[191] A. B. Atkinson and J. S. Flemming, 'Unemployment, Social Security and Incentives', *Midland Bank Review*, Autumn 1978, p. 8; Malcolm A. Sawyer, 'The Effect of Unemployment Compensation on the Rate of Unemployment in Great Britain: an Account', *Oxf. Econ. P.*, 31/1, 1979, p. 143. Also Z. A. Spindler and Dennis Maki, 'The Effect of Unemployment Compensation on the Rate of Unemployment in Great Britain', *ibid.* 27/3, 1975, and *idem*, 'More on the Effect of Unemployment Compensation on the Rate of Unemployment in Great Britain', *ibid.*, 31/1, 1979; J. S. Cubbin and K. Foley, 'The Extent of Benefit-Induced Unemployment in Great Britain: Some New Evidence', *ibid.* 29/1, 1977; K. Holden and D. A. Peel, 'The "Shake-Out" Hypothesis: A Note', *Oxf. Bull. Econ. Stat.*, 1967; D. Gujarati, 'The Behaviour of Unemployment and Unfilled Vacancies, Great Britain 1968–71', *Econ. J.*, 82/1, 1972; D. I. McKay and G. L. Reid, 'Redundancy, Unemployment and Manpower Policy' *ibid.* 82/4, 1972; S. Nickell, 'The Effect of Unemployment and Related Benefits on the Duration of Unemployment', *ibid.* 89/1, 1979; Brian Showler, 'Political Economy and Unemployment', in Showler and Sinfield, esp. pp. 44–5; J. K. Bowers and D. Harkess, 'Duration of Unemployment by Age and Sex', *Economica*, 46, 1979, pp. 255–7. Frank A. Cowell, 'Income and Incentive for the Working Poor', *Three Banks Review*, 122 (June 1979), 32–48; Jon Stern, 'Who Bears the Burden of Unemployment?' in W. Beckerman (ed.), *Slow Growth in Britain* (Oxford, 1979), pp. 70–82.

[192] Andrew Dean, 'The Labour Market in a Slow-Growing Economy', in Wilfred Beckerman (ed.), *Slow Growth in Britain*, pp. 45–7; Bowers and Harkess, pp. 239, 246; Showler and Sinfield, 'Introduction, pp. 12–3; T. F. Cripps and R. J. Tarling, 'An Analysis of the Duration of Male Unemployment in Great Britain 1932–73', *Econ. J.*, 84/2, 1974, p. 306.

and that novel phenomenon, 'capital-shortage' unemployment added more significantly to the total than frictional job-seeking:[193]

Table 7·35:   Estimate of causes of unemployment (% of labour force, UK)

	1974	1976
Cyclical unemployment	0·1	1·7
Frictional unemployment	2·0	2·4
Capital-shortage unemployment	0·1	0·9

Long spells of lack of employment were mostly strongly in evidence for those aged 60–4, who had the least hope of ever working again.

4 Trade Unions and Industrial Relations

After the momentous accession of strength to the trade-union movement in the war years, total union membership grew only very slowly for some years after 1950, from 9·3 million to just over 10 million in 1967, or rather less than the rate of growth of the labour force. There then followed a considerable boost in numbers, possibly encouraged by the favourable legislation of the Labour Government and the successful militancy of the unions which also extended the closed shop principle to Labour-controlled councils and other new fields. By 1979 there were 13·5 million members, or a rise from about 45% to 58% of the labour force.

Meanwhile, there were some significant amalgamations following the Trade Union (Amalgamations) Act of 1964, including the Society of Graphical and Allied Trades in printing, ASTMS among management and scientific staff and the Amalgamated Engineering and Foundry Workers' union in engineering in 1967. The number of unions continued to decline, even if only very slowly, and one of the most significant developments has been the increasing weight of the big union, which now dominates the trade-union world. There were nine unions with over a quarter of a million members each in 1968 and 11 of them in 1979, and their membership rose from 5·5 to 8·4 millions or 62% of the total. While there may have been some improvement in the competence of the bureaucracy as a result, there seemed little hope of changing the structure or the methods of working of the trade unions as a whole.[194] Also there are still great differences in provision: thus Donovan in 1968 counted a range of 1978 members (USDAW) to 6807 members (AEU) per full-time official. They were matched by over 10,000 personnel officers in firms.[195]

It is doubtful how far size led to efficiency in any sense – as distinct from political power and influence of the leadership. With the nominal widening

[193] OECD, *A. Medium-Term Strategy for Employment and Manpower Policies* (Paris, 1978), p. 126.

[194] H. A. Turner, 'British Trade Union Structure: A New Approach?' *British Journal of Industrial Relations*, 2/2 (1964). Also, TUC *Annual Report*, 1966, pp. 114 ff.; John Hughes, *Changes in the Trade Unions* (Fabian Society, 1964), pp. 14 ff.; Royal Commission on Trade Unions and Employers' Associations, *Report (Donovan Report)*, Cmnd. 3623 (1968), p. 181.

[195] *Report*, pp. 25, 188.

of the range of national negotiations there had ensued the use of a second, and usually more effective, system of negotiations at lower levels:

> Britain has two systems of industrial relations. The one is the formal system embodied in the official institutions. The other is the informal system, created by the actual behaviour of trade unions and employers' associations, of managers, shop stewards and workers.[196]

This second, informal system, was said to have weakened the impact of national incomes and wages policies, since actual plant earnings could move differently from nationally fixed levels and were at times 100% above them.[197] While Donovan undoubtedly exaggerated the significance of this dual system, being too prone to take conditions in some industries to be typical for all,[198] an enquiry some 10 years later showed that national or regional bargaining determined only one-quarter of money wages in 1977, while 'single-employer bargaining has become the important means of pay determination for two-thirds of manual workers'.[199] The wages-drift imparted an element of realism to the annual wage round.[200]

Donovan pronounced in favour of continuing voluntary bargaining, as well as of that peculiarly British institution, the 'closed shop'.[201] Affecting $3\frac{3}{4}$ million workers in 1962, equivalent to 39% of all trade unionists and of 51% of manual workers in the TUC, it rose to 4 million in 1974 and perhaps 7 million in 1975, after the legislation of 1975. Between 1962 and 1978 it had increased from 6% to 19% in clothing and footwear, 7% to 32% in chemicals and allied trades, 4% to 39% in food, drink and tobacco, and 44% to 67% in metals, vehicles, etc.[202] While it has been declared to be against human rights by the European Court and is viewed with misgivings in some quarters, especially when applied to public employment, it is welcomed by many employers and is likely to continue, whatever the legislation.

Particularly noticeable in this period was the growth of unionism among white-collar workers. These had largely held aloof from this form of organization before 1914 and even in the inter-war period had favoured trade unions only in certain occupations. It was in the post-war decades that their trade unions increased by leaps and bounds and they were largely responsible for the growth in the total numbers organized. Between 1948 and 1960 the membership of manual unions rose by + 0·6%, that of white-collar union by + 33·6%; density in 1960 was particularly high in local government (84% – up 16% from 1948) and in national government (83% – up 19% from 1948.[203]

[196] *Donovan Report*, p. 12, para. 46.

[197] *Ibid.* pp. 14–18.

[198] Kevin Hawkins, *Conflict and Change. Aspects of Industrial Relations* (1972), p. 88; Evans and Creight, pp. 10–11.

[199] William Brown (ed.), *The Changing System of British Industrial Relations. A Survey of Manufacturing Industry* (Oxford, 1981), p. 24.

[200] E. H. Phelps-Brown, 'New Wine in Old Bottles: Reflections on the Changed Working of Collective Bargaining in Great Britain', *British Journal of Industrial Relations*, 11, 1973, pp. 333–4.

[201] In most other countries it is outlawed, Stephen Milligan, *The New Barons. Union Power in the 1970s* (1976) p. 74.

[202] W. E. J. McCarthy, *The Closed Shop in Britain* (Oxford, 1964), pp. 28–35; John Burton, 'The Economics of the Closed Shop', in Lord Robbins *et al.*, *Trade Unions*, p. 43; Brown, *Changing System*, pp. 54–6.

[203] G. S. Bain, *The Growth of White Collar Unionism* (Oxford, 1970), pp. 25, 28; Kevin Hawkins, *Conflict*, pp. 138 ff.

There are two major causes for this expansion: the rapid growth in white-collar employment itself, and the relative loss in earnings and status vis-a-vis the manual workers which has accompanied this growth and has led to a radicalization of the attitudes of salaried personnel. It is significant that several of their organizations, which have in the past stood aloof from association with manual unions and the Labour Party, and have even shunned the term 'trade union', joined the TUC in these years, where they now form a large minority. Contrary to expectations they have not exercised a moderating influence there but, on the contrary, are to be found among all groups including the most militant: postmen, civil and local government servants, teachers and health workers have been among the strikers of recent years.

British trade unions have in the post-war years acquired a reputation of being unusually strike prone. The statistics do not bear this out, but the statistics are difficult to interpret; in any case, the impact of a disciplined strike, in, for example, the US motor industry in which several hundred thousand men stay out for some weeks while the works, having had due warning, are subject to planned total closure, is quite different from the impact of the same number of working days lost by several hundred unofficial and unprepared strikes, in component or transport undertakings, in which each group of strikers causes damage, hardship and lay-offs to groups several times their own size. British unions tended to specialize in the latter. One calculation – very much disputed – put the direct cost of strikes in 1976 at £6 billion, or 6% of GNP, not counting the indirect costs such as the cutting off of growth potential.[204]

Simple statistics are given in Table 7·36.[205]

Table 7·36:   Strikes in British industry

	Average of years:			
	1961–74	1975–8	1979	1980
Number of stoppages	2,575	2,368	2,080	1,330
Workers involved, 000	1,465	930	4,584	834
Working days lost, 000:				
All industries and services	7,351	7,211	29,474	11,964
Mining and quarrying	1,507	108	128	156
Metals, engineering, ship- building, vehicles	3,373	4,507	20,389	10,224

The leading post-war role of coal miners among the strikers (70% of all strikes in 1952–7 were in coal) was coming to an end in the 1960s, particularly after the National Power-Loading Agreement of 1966 and possibly also because of the decline in numbers and the end of the sellers' market in coal; instead, metal and especially car workers took on the mantle of strike leaders. By contrast, in 1971–3, 95% of plants in manufacturing had no stoppage at all. Around 95% of all strikes were unofficial, but the official ones tended to be larger and last longer. From the 1960s on, a larger proportion tended to be

[204] Lord Robbins, *et al.*, *Trade Unions: Public Goods or Public Bads?* (1978), pp. 50, 57.
[205] *Nat. Inst. Econ. Rev.*, 95, Feb. 1981, p. 12 and 97, August 1981, p. 28.

over pay, as simultaneously strikes tended to become more extensive. 1979 and 1980 stand out as major strike years, having several large rather than more numerous strikes.[206]

As in the case of the unemployed, the more generous benefits, including tax rebates to strikers, have been held responsible for the rising numbers of disputes from the 1960s on, and indeed, the concessions offered to British strikers on these two counts greatly exceeded those available in other countries. Yet the evidence is inconclusive,[207] and the influence of such factors, while real, is likely to be marginal. The Conservative Government of 1979 planned to abolish a number of these concessions.

In a strictly formal sense, there were few changes in this period in the Government's actions over wages and industrial relations. Some Wages Councils were abolished when the need for them had gone, including the one for chainmaking, one of the first four of 1909, and by the consolidating Wages Councils Act of 1959 the Minister of Labour was given power to order independent inquiries into industry and abolish Wages Councils on his own initiative. In the same year, the war-time method of compulsory arbitration, handled since 1951 by an Industrial Disputes Tribunal, was also abolished and any major breaches of agreement were to be put before the Industrial Court. By 1968, there were still 57 Wage Councils covering $3\frac{1}{2}$ million workers.

Powers of conciliation and of originating Courts of Inquiry or Committees of Investigation, however, remained and were used frequently. The latter were particularly important in cases in which relatively limited disputes might have widespread repercussions elsewhere, so that the public would clamour for intervention. There were many such in the 1950s and 1960s.[208] Industrial relations in the nationalized industries, in which it was quite often the Government's policy that was responsible for the employer's intransigence, were particularly fit subjects for official or semi-official enquiries. In this regard, Selwyn Lloyd's 'July measures' of 1961 formed a landmark, for they actually included a total standstill for wage increases (except for those already sanctioned) among all Government employees and employees of nationalized industries and a similar directive to the Wages Boards, backed by the power of the Ministry of Labour to refer back proposed increases. Against this, there were only general exhortations to private industry.

The real innovation of this period, however, was the growing interference with all collective bargaining by the Government in the interest of its own short-term policy. The justification, apart from the recurrent crises, was the inflationary framework in which, it was felt, employers were unable to provide a sufficient counterweight to trade union pressure and were likely,

---

[206] E. V. Evans and S. W. Creigh (eds.), *Industrial Conflict in Britain* (1977), esp. pp. 63–4, 80, 91–6, 127; R. Elliott, 'Industrial Relations and Manpower Policy', in F. T. Blackaby (ed.), *British Economic Policy 1960–74* (Cambridge, 1978), pp. 566–8.

[207] See discussion in *British Journal of Industrial Relations*, 12, 1974, John Gennard and Roger Lasko, pp. 1–25, J. W. Duncan and W. E. J. McCarthy, pp. 26–47 and Laurence C. Hunter, pp. 438–44; and John Gennard, *Financing Strikes* (1977).

[208] J. W. Grove, *Government and Industry in Britain* (1962), chapters 8, 17; W. E. J. McCarthy and B. A. Clifford, 'The Work of Industrial Courts of Inquiry', *British Journal of Industrial Relations*, 4/1 (1966).

instead, to raise prices against the public after conceding higher wages to their men.

We have noted in the last chapter the beginnings of voluntary wage restraint and its mixed success in the late 1940s. Little was heard of it in the early years of the Conservative Government, but in 1956 it was tried again. Trade union opinion was hostile and, when the engineering employers took the Government's exhortations seriously and determined to fight against a wage claim early in 1957,

> the Government was forced to beat a hasty and humiliating retreat, conceding to the railwaymen a bigger wage increase than had been awarded to them by an independent arbitration tribunal and putting severe pressure on the engineering employers and their shipbuilding allies to come to terms with their own unions.[209]

The experience was repeated later in the year by the dock employers. This retreat was, not unnaturally, resented by private employers, and under their pressure the Government then went to the opposite extreme of attempting to prevent at all costs pending wage rises in the public sector, to the extent of overruling a Whitley Council award by the Ministry of Health and a conciliation offer made in the London bus dispute, in 1957–58. The result was to discredit temporarily the official conciliation and arbitration machinery, and in the next two years, Government intervention swung back again to the pole of leniency and tended to favour wage increases for the sake of industrial peace.

Meanwhile, in August 1957, the Council on Productivity, Prices and Incomes (the 'Three Wise Men') had been set up to advise the Government on the criteria by which wage claims should be judged, or, as the trade unions alleged, to find respectable reasons for refusing wage increases. When the Council's first Report in 1958 seemed to confirm the unions' suspicions, with the suggestion that 'wage advances have chiefly been secured through the instrumentality of powerful trade unions',[210] that a wage standstill was desirable, and an effective level of unemployment might achieve it, 'the TUC virtually boycotted the Council ever after'.[211] In 1959 and 1960 official policy was again expansionist, and the Council's pronouncements became less rigid. Its influence, however, had much waned by that time, and any development of its attempt at a more discriminating incomes policy was rudely cut short by the more severe freeze introduced in 1961. The Council was dissolved in 1962, together with the still-born Economic Planning Board proposed in 1961, on the formation of the NEDC. In the same year the National Incomes Commission was set up to advise the Government on income claims. In due course the restrictionist policy of 1960–1 gave way to the easier conditions of 1962–3. Beginning with the severe crisis of late 1964, however, there was a further tightening up. Keeping wage incomes down to the low level of production increases achieved became a major aspect of policy.

The Declaration of Intent of December 1964 pledged the Government, the employers' organizations and the TUC, which was now once again amenable

---

[209] Michael Shanks, 'Public Policy and the Ministry of Labour', in B. C. Roberts (ed.), *Industrial Relations: Contemporary Problems and Perspectives* (1962), pp. 263–4.

[210] *Council on Prices, Productivity and Incomes, First Report* (1958), p. 52.

[211] K. G. J. C. Knowles, 'Wages and Productivity', in G. D. N. Worswick and P. Ady, *The British Economy in the Nineteen-Fifties* (Oxford, 1962), p. 511.

to steering by a Labour Government, to raise productivity, to keep income increases in line with output increases and hence to maintain a stable general price level. In February 1965 the agreement on the *Machinery for Prices and Incomes Policy* was published, which included the setting up of a National Board for Prices and Incomes (PIB), and an agreed white paper in April laid it down that all wage increases must be kept in line with the annual productivity rise, put somewhat optimistically at $3-3\frac{1}{2}\%$ p.a.[212]

The PIB, however, could look only at a few cases at a time, and neither the employers' organizations nor the unions were willing to operate a wider compulsory scheme themselves. There was also no effective scheme to hold price increases. In November 1965 the Government, therefore, instituted a voluntary notification scheme, whereby all wage claims were to be notified to the TUC and the Ministry of Labour, and all price increases to the appropriate Ministry for the industry concerned, and neither was to be granted without the Ministry's or the PIB's consent.[213] In the sterling crisis of July 1966 a complete wage standstill for six months was decreed, followed by six months of severe restraint, and thereafter a return to something like the notification scheme, with the difference that the TUC operated on a 'norm' of nil instead of $3-3\frac{1}{2}\%$, and the Government had power to delay any settlement for up to seven months. The result of this elaborate and demoralizing machinery was totally negative: in the 20 months before the 'freeze' (October 1964 to June 1966) earnings rose by $7\frac{1}{2}\%$, and in the 14 months from June 1966 to October 1967, which included the freeze, by just over $5\frac{1}{2}\%$.[214] Bearing in mind the rising unemployment and consequent short-term working in the second period, this rate of increase was no less, and may well have been more, than the rates in the more normal years before the restrictions.[215]

The Report of the Donovan Commission, a major investigation into collective bargaining, which had taken three years to complete, appeared in 1968. Its emphasis, as noted above, was on the localized and unofficial sources of most of the effective decisions on wages and conditions, and its tendency was therefore to question the wisdom of national policies and regulations. Nevertheless, it drew attention to the powers of the trade unions and proposed, *inter alia*, a Commission for Industrial Relations (CIR) which should work for some orderliness on the shop floor, essentially by voluntary means. The CIR was set up in March 1969.

The Report received a mixed reception, but there was general agreement on the need for trade-union reform. Barbara Castle, the responsible minister, whose Department had meanwhile been re-named from 'Ministry of Labour' to 'Department of Employment and Productivity' to emphasize the link between values created and incomes paid out, proposed her own set of reforms early in 1969 in a document, the title of which highlighted what troubled the legislators: *In Place of Strife*.[216]

---

[212] *Machinery for Prices and Incomes Policy*, Cmnd. 2577 (1965); *Prices and Incomes Policy*, Cmnd. 2639 (1965).

[213] *Prices and Incomes Policy: An Early Warning System*, Cmnd. 2809 (1965). Allan Fels, *The British Prices and Incomes Board* (Cambridge, 1972); Campbell Balfour, *Incomes Policy and the Public Sector* (1972).

[214] F. Blackaby and M. Artis, 'On Incomes Policy', *District Bank Review*, 165 (March 1968).

[215] See in general, Samuel Brittan and Peter Lilley, *The Delusions of Incomes Policy* (1977).

[216] *In Place of Strife: A Policy for Industrial Relations*, Cmnd. 3888 (1969).

In return for some additional legal privileges, including the power to force an employer to recognize a union, *In Place of Strife* proposed some curbs on the trade unions' freedom of action. They included compulsory ballots before a strike involving public interests or a serious threat to the economy; in the case of certain 'unconstitutional strikes', a conciliation pause of 28 days; the right of the Minister to impose a settlement in inter-union disputes; and financial penalties to back up these regulations. Owing to the opposition within the Labour Party, some of these provisions were weakened, and the requirement of a ballot dropped when the proposals were incorporated in an Industrial Relations Bill. Even so, it still displeased the trade unions, and they used their power over MP's to have it defeated in cabinet despite the support for it by Harold Wilson as well as Barbara Castle.[217] Instead, the General Council of the TUC who were willing enough to see unofficial actions curbed as long as their own were not, composed a 'Programme for Action' in May 1969 to assume more power to intervene in 'unconstitutional strikes' and inter-union disputes and in June they signed with the Government a 'solemn and binding contract' to implement this programme, whereupon the Government withdrew its bill. It must be assumed that, like the rest of the country, it knew that no undertaking by the TUC has any operative value.[218]

This overspill of trade-union power into the political sphere was to see its most remarkable demonstration in the following four years. Large-scale strikes in late 1969 drove up wages at unexpectedly fast rates[219] and, indeed, wage rises were to race ahead of price rises over the whole of the 1970s, except for the restrictionist period 1972–4. The newly elected Conservative Government abolished controls in 1970, but worked for lower pay settlements, and in the public sector, over which they had some influence, set out what in effect was the 'n-1' policy, i.e. each year's wage settlement to be 1% below that of the previous year. Its Industrial Relations Act of 1971 was to achieve the simultaneous aim of lowering the pressure of wage demands by weakening the bargaining powers of the trade unions. Central was the requirement for unions to register in order to keep their privileges; there was also a version of the cooling-off period and the secret ballot, beside other restrictions. The National Industrial Relations Court (NIRC) and the CIR were to supervise these provisions. They were to lead to an immediate boycott by the TUC – it suspended 32 unions in 1972 and expelled 20 in 1973 for registering under the Act – and to a continuing battle until 1974.

Among its more spectacular episodes was the defiance of the NIRC by the dockers, who were rescued by the Court of Appeal; the failure of the cooling-off period in the railway dispute; the freeing from prison of five unrepentant dockers, on a legal technicality, by the previously inconspicuous Official Solicitor; and the solution of a deadlock over a fine on the engineering union (AEUW) by its payment by an anonymous donor.[220] The miners meanwhile

---

[217] Peter Jenkins, *The Battle of Downing Street* (1970).

[218] Gerard A. Dorfman, *Government versus Trade Unionism in British Politics since 1968* (1979).

[219] Hugh Clegg, *How to Run an Incomes Policy and Why We Made Such a Mess of the Last One* (1971), pp. 60–1.

[220] For a brief account, see Peter Calvocoressi, *The British Experience 1945–75* (1978), pp. 76 ff.

won wage awards of 17–20% in 1972 after a national strike in January–February followed by the Wilberforce Court of Enquiry.

By mid-1972, it was clear that the inflation was getting out of hand with settlements in excess of 20% and that the Government's belief in the free market tempered by anti-union legislation had failed, as had the trial of a voluntary prices and incomes policy agreed between the TUC and the CBI. The Government therefore returned to a direct incomes policy, beginning in November 1972 with a total wages and prices freeze. For March-autumn 1973 Stage II of the statutory policy envisaged a maximum of £1 a week plus 4%, with £250 a year as the upper limit. A 'Pay Board' and a 'Prices Commission' were set up, and there appeared to be widespread support for this policy, as elaborated in a green paper.[221] Stage III relaxed conditions a little more, with a maximum of £7 a week or £350 a year, plus 1% flexibility allowance, plus additional pay for productivity rises and 'unsocial hours'.[222] While the latter allowed all the strong unions to ignore the limits set for the rest, a further provision of 40 p. per week for every 1% that prices rose over the threshold of 7% built in almost automatic inflationary settlements when the oil price explosion was added to domestic inflation. The miners, once more, refused to be bound by the general rules, though offered an award above the norm: their dispute led to a State of Emergency, a three-day week, power cuts and a general election early in 1974, lost by the Heath Government, before the Pay Board could find a face-saving formula to pay the miners more than the rest.

The new Labour Government, like the new Conservative one before it, began by abolishing the existing pay policy, and reimposed a new one shortly afterwards when prices and pay went through the roof: the 'Social Contract' of voluntary pay restraint had proved to be worth as little as all trade-union promises before, and between the second quarter of 1974 and the same period in 1975 average earnings were up by 28% and retail prices by 25%. The new policy limited pay increases to 6% a week, or £10–12 (Stage 1), and in 1976 to £2·50 to £4 or 5% within those limits (Stage 2). However, because of wages drift, average earnings rose, not by $4\frac{1}{2}$% as they should have done, but by 9%. In 1977 (Stage 3) the limitation consisted merely of putting in a single claim a year, with the interesting innovation of promising tax concessions contingent on low wage increases, and there was a 14% wage rise against a 10% target. 1978 had a 5% target, but as in the end of the unions refused to collaborate, a series of disputes made 1978–9 a 'winter of discontent', at the end of which the Government were defeated at the polls.[223]

In 1979 the new Conservative Government once more abolished the restraint policies of its predecessor, and reintroduced the discipline of the market instead. By engineering unheard-of rates of unemployment they did indeed induce lower pay claims after an initial wage explosion, at least in firms threatened by bankruptcy, but workers in the public services unaffected by unemployment were as militant as ever. As a result, the wages scissors between private and public employment opened in favour of the

[221] Treasury, *Price and Pay Code, Consultative Document*, Cmnd. 5247 (1973).

[222] Treasury, *Pay and Price Code for Stage 3. A Consultative Document*, Cmnd. 5444 (1973).

[223] For a brief review see Dermot R. Glynn, 'The Last 14 Years of Incomes Policy – a CBI Perspective', *National Westminster Bank Quarterly Review*, November 1978.

latter, having in earlier years worked for the former, and the Government introduced something that looked suspiciously like an incomes policy for public servants wherever they dared.

The effectiveness of incomes polices has been subject to much debate. After the experience of the 1960s and 1970s few observers were willing to credit it with the power to stop an inflationary drive on its own: too often after a temporary halt in incomes rises, their increase proceeded at an even faster rate. But as part of a larger package, incomes policy may have had an impact, and, in any case, there were few alternatives in sight.[224]

The growth in union power and militancy, to the point of defying legislation and challenging the courts as in 1972–3, had several causes. One lay in the favourable legislation passed by successive Labour Governments which indirectly strengthened the hands of the employees and their unions. Among these must be reckoned, beside the Redundancy Payments Act 1965 mentioned above,[225] the Employment Protection Act, the Health and Safety at Work Act and the Industry Act, all of 1975. The Trade Union and Labour Relation Act of 1976 more directly put the unions into an even more favourable position than they had been in before 1971. Ironically, these were part of the payment, together with higher social benefits, for the unions' promise to curb their demands in the 'Social Contract' which was then not kept. A second cause lay in the industrial and economic experience of the age: mounting inflation, stagnating living standards, and the climb into higher tax rates. A third lay in the structural changes among the unions themselves: local or shop steward bargaining,[226] productivity bargaining, sham or real,[227] the power of small groups to do intolerable damage to larger groups not concerned in the dispute,[228] all offered opportunities of driving up wages and earnings to well above prices or nationally settled rates. Finally, there was the opposition to the repeated policies of restraint themselves,[229] which provoked defiance by causing injustice and frustration, and by limiting the functions and powers of trade union leaders.

Industrial relations were therefore played out inside a tightening net of restrictions and enforceable guidelines, which reflected the immanent incompatibility of free bargaining and anti-inflationary policies in the given conditions. Did trade unions in this period contribute directly to the inflation, and in this sense abuse their powers so as to call forth the very countermeasure to curb them once more?

Up to the mid-1960s most observers trusted to the explanatory power of the 'Phillips Curve': this was the assumption, based on a study of British wage

[224] J. J. Fallick and R. F. Eliot, *Incomes Policies, Inflation and Relative Pay* (1982); R. G. Lipsey and Michael Parkin, 'Incomes Policy: A Reappraisal', *Economica*, NS 37/146 (1970), 115–38; Samuel Brittan and Peter Lilley, *The Delusions of Incomes Policy* (1977).

[225] P. 329 above.

[226] S. Lerner and J. Marquand, 'Regional Variations in Earnings, Demand for Labour and Shop Stewards Combined Committees in the British Engineering Industry', *Manchester School*, 31, 1963.

[227] J. E. Mortimer, *Trade Unions and Technological Change* (1971), pp. 35 ff.

[228] Charles K. Rowley, 'The Economics and Politics of Extortion', in Robbins *et al.*, *Trade Unions* pp. 91 ff.

[229] A. B. Tylecote, 'The Effect of Monetary Policy on Wage Inflation', *Oxf. Econ. P.*, 27/2, 1975.

rates for about a century, that wage changes depended on the state of aggregate demand, for which the level of unemployment was a good guide, however modified it might be by other influences, such as structural changes in the labour market or external trade.[230] Such a view gave unions, at best, only a transmission role in generating wage inflation. From 1964–5 on, however, wage rises were no longer held back by high unemployment: the presumed negative correlation between them had disappeared. A different explanation was needed, and interest returned once more to cost push and institutional factors, above all to trade union activity.[231]

A second explanation, once more based on the observation of several decades, but stressing supply rather than demand, was then offered in terms of union 'pushfulness', defined as membership growth and density. According to A. G. Hines, trade unions *did* influence wages. However, this relationship not only found many critics on theoretical grounds; it also failed to stand up to the test of British statistics in the period 1951–76.[232] Yet the role of the trade unions in the inflationary spiral was not thereby disproved, and pushfulness need not be reflected directly in membership figures.

Three linking mechanisms by which trade unions influence wages have been observed, and they need not coexist, but could operate at different times. There was, in the first place, the effect of a disjointed labour market, but one in which trade unions were in touch with and aware of each other. The result, observed particularly in years of high wage inflation, was that any group of workers who have achieved a rise in pay, no matter how justified by rising effort, poor recruitment, the need to catch up, or by whatever other acceptable cause, would in the competitive world of union politics be taken as a guideline and be followed by others, even if they had no justification other than the success of the first group.[233] Secondly, rises could sometimes be enforced by a new organization or a newly organized group, and would then be propagated throughout the system.[234] Lastly, it appears that in years of pressure, union wages did rise faster than those of the unorganized;[235] more conspicuously, the excess pay demands of a well organized group of workers were punished, not by their own unemployment, but by the loss of jobs of weaker groups elsewhere, so that the market sanctions, believed to hold all wage claims in check, did not operate in the way presumed. The share of the

[230] A. W. Phillips, 'The Relation Between Unemployment and the Rate of Change of Money Wage Rates in the United Kingdom, 1861–1957', *Economica*, 25/4, 1958; Prest and Coppock, pp. 273–81. There is a large critical literature.

[231] Milligan, *New Barons*, pp. 33–9.

[232] A. G. Hines, 'Trade Unions and Wage Inflation in the UK 1893–1961', *Rev. Econ. Studies*, 31, 1964; D. Dogas and A. G. Hines, 'Trade Unions and Wage Inflation in the UK. A Critique of Purdy and Ziz', *Applied Economics*, 7, 1975; D. L. Purdy and G. Zis, 'Trade Unions and Wage Inflation in the UK. A Reply to Dogas and Hines', *ibid.* 8, 1976; Wolfgang Fautz, 'Union Militancy, Excess Demand and Inflation in post-war United Kingdom, *ibid.* 12, 1980.

[233] J. Tobin, 'Inflation and Unemployment', *Amer. Econ. Rev.*, 62/1, 1972; J. R. Hicks, *The Crisis in Keynesian Economics* (Oxford, 1974), pp. 71–2, 80.

[234] Brian Griffiths: 'Economics of Labour Power: Can Unions Raise Real Wages?', in Robbins *et al.*, *Trade Unions*, p. 107; D. Metcalf, 'Unions, Incomes Policy and Relative Wages in Britain', *British Journal of Industrial Relations*, 15/2, 1977, p. 169.

[235] Ralph Turvey, 'Counter-Inflationary Policies', in Michael Posner (ed.), *Demand Management* (1978), p. 195.

trade unions and the industrial relations mechanism as a whole in causing the wage-price spiral and thus the destructive Government policies designed to stem it, is still obscure in part, but it cannot be written off altogether.

5 Economic Growth

In the years from 1950 to 1967 the population of the United Kingdom increased from 50·2 million to 55·4 million (mid-year figures), or by an average of around 270,000 a year. Thereafter the increase slowed down markedly, to turn into an actual decline in the years 1974–7. In 1973–81 the population remained virtually stationary at around 56 million, having fluctuated by less than 40,000 from one year to the next.

The growth, while it lasted, was based entirely on the excess of births over deaths. Annual births fluctuated around 800,000 in 1950–6, then rose in the second post-war baby boom to a peak of 1,015,000 in 1964, and gently declined thereafter to a low of 657,000 in 1977, with a slight upturn again in 1978–81. Deaths fluctuated much less and had a continuously rising tendency. Divided into 10-year periods, annual changes averaged as shown in Table 7·37.

Table 7·37:   Changes in UK population (000)

	Births	Deaths	Natural increase	Migration etc. (net)	Total change
1951–61	839	593	246	+ 6	+ 252
1961–71	962	638	324	− 44	+ 280
1971–81	745	678	67	− 29	+ 37

Migration, it will be seen, was a small and largely negative influence: only in the years 1951 and 1959–63 was there an actual net in-migration. Yet those relatively small net migration figures hide considerable losses, generally between 200–300,000 year by year by emigration, made up by somewhat smaller numbers of immigrants. While the emigrants went mostly to the white Commonwealth countries, Europe and the USA, there were important shifts among the immigrants. In addition to the Irish, arriving at a rate of 60–70,000 a year, the post-war wave from Europe, particularly into the service trades, continued in the 1950s but at a diminished rate. They were joined by Commonwealth immigrants from the West Indies, whose numbers rose to a peak of 30,000 in 1955–6, but then subsided because of the recession in Britain. The smaller numbers from India, Pakistan and Africa also declined in the later 1950s for the same reasons.

It was the threatened Commonwealth Immigrants Act, passed in 1962, which brought in a rush to beat the restrictions. In the 18 months from the beginning of 1961 to 30 June 1962, almost as many came (203,000) as had come in the six preceding years (219,000) from India, Pakistan and the Caribbean. Thereafter, only wives and children of those already in Britain were allowed in freely and the migration of men was strictly controlled: thus by December 1968, only 78,000 voucher holders from the New Commonwealth were admitted, compared with 257,000 dependants.

Estimates for 1966 put the total coloured population at 924,000 (or 1·7%) of the resident population) of whom 213,000 were born in Britain and 711,000 overseas. The total foreign-born population in Great Britain was 2,600,000, or 5%; of these the 739,000 born in the Irish Republic formed much the largest contingent.[236]

Since then immigration has been continuously more restricted, particularly by the Commonwealth Immigrants Act of 1968, but the birth rate of coloured immigrants is high, and the issue has become a bitterly controversial one: even the numbers concerned (and the definition) are in dispute. What is clear is that immigrants tended not only to settle in particular districts, but that they were younger than the resident population, their work participation rate was higher and they tended to concentrate in certain occupations – mostly those shunned by the natives. Among the men, the Irish had a particular interest in 1966 in the building industry, their proportion in it being far above the norm (30·7%), and an unusually high proportion of unskilled, and few among white-collar workers. Those from the Caribbean were concentrated in building, transport, engineering and catering, also mostly as unskilled or semi-skilled labourers, but with a higher ratio of skilled workers and a lower of non-manuals than the Irish. Indians were in transport and engineering, but had a higher ratio among professional and scientific workers than the British; and Pakistanis were concentrated in semi-skilled and unskilled jobs in textiles, metals and engineering. Among women, over half the Irish born were in services, especially hospitals, catering and distribution. Of those born in the West Indies, including Jamaica, 30–35% were in professional and scientific services, including nursing. Of the Indian women, over 60% were in similar 'non-manual' jobs; but there were very few Pakistani women in paid employment.[237] None of the immigrant groups had their full share of employers or managers, and only the Indians exceeded the average for professional workers. It is clear that their main flow had been into undermanned industries and services, a tendency strengthened by the immigration provisions.

For the population as a whole, in a period of generally full employment the proportion of males at work remained consistently high, but there was a significant increase in the proportion of females at work. Of those of working age (15–64), employment rose from 40·5% in 1950 to 47·9% in 1965 and 57·8% in 1979, reflecting the high demand for labour as well as continuing a long-term trend. Women and, in particular, married women did, in fact, become the elastic part of the labour supply. While the male labour force remained constant at around 15·9 million between 1951 and 1976, having risen to a peak of 16·2 million in between, and the number of unmarried women in the labour force fell from 4·3 million to 3·2 million, married women rose from 2·7 million to 6·7 million. The whole of the increase in the

---

[236] *Immigration from the Commonwealth*, Cmnd. 2739 (1965); E. J. B. Rose *et al.*, *Coloured Citizenship. A Report on British Race Relations* (1969), pp. 68–72, 83–88; Stephen Castles, Godula Kosack, *Immigrant Workers and Class Structure in Western Europe* (1973) pp. 4–5; also R. B. Davison, *Commonwealth Immigrants* (1964) and *Black British* (1966); Arnold M. Rose, *Migrants in Europe* (Minneapolis, 1969), pp. 15–21.

[237] Castles and Kosack, pp. 75–9; Rose, *Coloured Citizenship*, pp. 160 ff.; *Census of Population*, 1971.

working population of 3 million between those two dates was therefore furnished by women. According to the Census of Great Britain, the proportion of women in jobs or looking for jobs rose from 21·7% in 1951 to 42·2% in 1971. Many of those were part-time workers, whose numbers consequently also rose in those years.

Partly as a cause, and in part no doubt as a consequence, the technical facilities available to make paid work by married women possible, were greatly improved: gadgets in the home, pre-packed food, easy and quick shopping facilities near the place of work. Possibly the smaller number of children per family reduced the years when women were tied to the home; certainly society became more tolerant towards the working wife or mother. It seems that against a background of rising incomes and rising relative pay for women, the attractions of additional things, services or holidays, and perhaps even the attractions of the independence and the interests provided by an outside job, exceeded the increase in leisure preference.[238]

Actual weekly working hours remained at over 46 in the early 1950s and were still 44·3 in 1966–8 despite the decline of the official working week from an average of 44·6 hours in 1951 to 40·5 hours in January 1968, but in the squeeze of 1962–3 and again in 1966–8, reduced pressure also showed itself in more short-time, and less overtime worked. By 1976, normal hours were 40·0 a week, and actual hours worked, 42·6. The typical holiday probably doubled in length in those years[239]. Overtime work for men and female employment were the most sensitive to changes in demand for labour, though employment never fluctuated as much as total demand.[240]

A second secular trend of the inter-war period, the growth of the proportion of white-collar workers as against manual workers, also continued with undiminished force into the post-war decades. This was associated both with technical changes within industry and the growth of the service trades at the expense of extractive and manufacturing industries. White-collar employees formed 30·9% of the occupied population in 1951 and 35·9% in 1961. Among them, scientists and engineers increased in number from 71,000 in 1931 to 187,000 in 1951 and 378,000 in 1961, more than doubling in one decade; and draughtsmen and laboratory technicians increased from 70,000 to 199,000 and 277,000 in the same years, or by 39% in one decade.[241] In

[238] Roderick Floud and Donald McCloskey (eds.), *The Economic History of Britain since 1700*, vol. 2 (Cambridge, 1981), pp. 395–6; A. R. Prest and D. J. Coppock, *The UK Economy* (1978), pp. 225–30; J. F. Wright, *Britain in the Age of Economic Management* (Oxford, 1979), pp. 24, 92–3; A. R. Thatcher, 'Labour Supply and Employment Trends', in Frank Blackaby (ed.), *De-Industrialisation* (1978), pp. 27–9; R. McNabb, 'The Labour Force Participation of Married Women in Great Britain', *Manchester School*, 45/3, 1977; Christine Greenhalgh, 'Labour Supply Function of Married Women in Great Britain', *Economica*, 44/175, 1977.

[239] *Min. of Labour Gazette*; *Key Statistics*, Tables E and F; Beckerman, p. 83; *Statistics on Income, Prices, Employment and Production*, 24 (1968); E. G. Whybrew, *Overtime Working in Britain* (Research Paper No. 9 of the Royal Commission on Trade Unions and Employers' Associations) (1968); R. C. O. Matthews, 'Some Aspects of Post-War Growth in the British Economy in Relation to Historical Experience', *Transactions of the Manchester Statistical Society* 1964–5, p. 6.

[240] L. C. Hunter, 'Cyclical Variation in the Labour Supply: British Experience, 1951–60', *Oxf. Econ. P.*, 15/2 (1963); R. R. Neild, *Pricing and Employment in the Trade Cycle* (Cambridge, 1963), chapter 3; Harrod, *Economic Policy*, pp. 15–18.

[241] Paul Galambos, 'The Growth of the Employment of Non-Manual Workers in the British

manufacturing, white-collar employees grew further from 25·8% in 1968 to 30·0% in 1980. By 1971 the proportion had risen to 48·3% in all occupations measured in the same way, or 43·4% leaving out employers and proprietors. Among women the proportions had by then reached 54·1% (excluding employers), though most of these were in the lower-paid clerical, shop assistant and 'lower professions and technicians' ' grades, including teaching, and fewer in the higher professions and managerial grades.

In recent years attempts have also been made to measure the degree to which capital has been fully used, or left unemployed. The exercise bristles with difficulties, and the series produced often show contradictory results, but the broad movements do appear, as they do in the case of unemployed labour. One index of 'capital utilization measure' in manufacturing (1973 = 100) shows the changes indicated in Table 7·38, and is compared with the unemployment rate:[242]

Table 7·38: Capital utilization and unemployment

	Capital utilization index (1973 = 100)	Unemployment rate %
Averages of years:		
1960–2	86	1·6
1963–5	91	1·7
1966–8	93·3	2·1
1969–71	94·7	3·1
1972–4	96·7	3·0
1975–7	89·3	5·0
1978–80	85	6·0
First half 1981	72	10·0

Even if the measure could be relied on for accuracy, it shows only overall rates. As in the case of labour, local bottlenecks might inhibit output and growth even at times of under-use of resources; thus in October 1981, in the worst slump in British experienec for almost 50 years, 7% of CBI correspondents reported plant capacity, and 3% labour, as constraints on output.[243]

The labour input to provide the growth in the British economy may be said to have depended largely on factors outside the control of the economic policy makers. Inasmuch as it was, as in the case of working wives, British policy seems to have eased the supply position. Things were far otherwise in the case of capital. The rate of investment was much more amenable to steering by Government policy, but it was constantly being depressed, and the low rates of investment achieved in Britain compared with other countries is generally held to have had some connection with the low rate of economic

Manufacturing Industries, 1948–1962', *Bull. Oxf. Inst. Stat.*, 26/3 (1964); G. S. Bain, 'The Growth of White-Collar Unionism in Great Britain', *British J. of Industrial Relations*, 4/3 (1966); K. Prandy, *Professional Employees: A Study of Scientists and Engineers* (1965); *Scientific and Technological Manpower in Great Britain 1963*, Cmnd. 2146 (1963); R. M. Blackburn, *Union Character and Social Class: White-Collar Unionism* (1967).

[242] *Nat. Inst. Econ. Rev.*, 98, Nov. 1981, p. 13. Compare with it the Wharton measure, *ibid.*, and also *ibid.*, 39, Feb. 1967, p. 16.

[243] CLARE Group, 'Problems of Industrial Recovery', *Midland Bank Review*, Spring 1982, p. 16.

growth of the British economy in international comparison. The issue is a highly controversial one,[244] but we may briefly trace the consequences here.

Fixed capital formation, in absolute terms and as a proportion of GNP, changed as shown in Table 7·39 (absolute values in £ billion, at 1975 prices):[245]

Table 7·39:   Fixed capital formation

	Gross fixed capital formation		Capital consumption	Net fixed investment	
	£ b.	% GNP	£ b.	£ b.	% GNP
1950–2	4·8	14·7	2·7	2·1	5·9
1953–6	5·9	16·3	3·1	2·8	7·3
1957–9	10·5	17·6	5·2	4·5	8·6
1960–2	12·9	19·3	5·9	6·9	10·4
1963–5	15·1	20·4	6·7	8·4	11·3
1966–8	17·8	20·1	8·8	8·8	10·0
1969–71	19·3	20·3	9·0	10·3	10·8
1972–4	20·5	19·5	10·2	10·2	9·8
1975–7	20·4	19·0	11·4	9·0	8·3
1978–80	20·7	19·0	13·0	7·7	7·1

Investment thus started at a very low level in the early post-war years, rose rapidly in the 1960s to reach near European proportions, and fell back again in the 1970s. Since capital consumption continued to rise in line with the growing stock of capital, the key variable of net fixed capital formation, the actual increase in the productive apparatus, actually declined quite sharply in that decade, back to the levels of the early 1950s.

However, not all fixed capital formation was 'productive' in the narrow sense. About one-fifth was in the form of dwellings and of transfer fees (see Table 7·40), and this altered slightly in this period, being particularly high in the 1950s and in the mid-1970s:

Table 7·40:   Share of dwellings, transfer fees etc. in gross fixed capital formation

1950	21·9%
1955	24·3
1960	19·6
1965	21·5
1970	20·2
1975	23·4
1980	18·8

The rise of productive investment in the 1960s was thus rather steeper, and the drop in the later 1970s rather less, than the earlier table would imply.

It is time to pull together these various strands and to describe the overall growth in the economy in our period, as summarized by the rise in GDP

[244] S. Pollard, *The Wasting of the British Economy* (1982), chapter 2: 'First Causes'; pp. 380–1 and chapter 9 (below).

[245] *National Income and Expenditure.* Price indices of base 1958 have been spliced with those of 1975.

together with the factorial components that went into this growth. The total figures are very similar to those for incomes;[246] that is to say, they just failed to double over the 30 years. The broad division into periods and factors shows the results given in Table 7·41, with the inter-war years included for comparison:[247]

Table 7·41: Annual growth rates, per cent

	GDP	Labour	Capital	Labour productivity	Weighted inputs	Weighted total factor productivity
1924–37	2·2	1·5	1·7	0·7	1·5	0·7
1951–64	2·9	0·0	2·8	2·9	0·7	2·2
1964–73	2·7	−0·5	4·0	3·2	0·7	2·0
1973–80	0·6	−0·1	2·9	0·7	0·5	0·1

Another calculation splits the period 1951–73 into five phases, and distinguishes between a gross and a net capital input:[248]

Table 7·42: Annual growth rate of total factor productivity

	Gross capital	Net capital
1951–55	1·8	1·6
1955–60	2·1	1·7
1960–4	2·5	2·3
1964–8	2·5	2·4
1968–73	2·2	2·2

These rates confirm the impression given by other indicators that, measured by earlier phases, even by the relatively expansionary inter-war period, the three decades 1950–80 were remarkably successful in achieving that central economic variable, growth in the total domestic product. It was on this foundation that much of the improvement in economic welfare and social amelioration could be erected. Coupled with the fact of almost full employment, it should have given those years the character of an era of success, a golden age. To some extent it did; but widespread misgivings remained. They were largely connected with the fact that other, comparable economies achieved much faster growth and were able to provide more of the economic goods to their people than the British. Comparisons may be invidious, but looking at their example, the impression is strong that Britain must have missed her opportunity to do very much better than she did.

Comparatively slow growth in Britain may have two aspects: a slow growth rate per head, per worker or consumer, or a slow growth rate overall. We shall examine both. Some comparative figures from the major countries are given in Table 7·43.[249]

The abysmal relative performance of the United Kingdom stands out from these, or any comparable statistics. Nor does this depend on our selection. If

[246] P. 315 above.

[247] Wright, *Britain*, p. 26; *National Income and Expenditure*.

[248] A. Matthews, Feinstein and Odling-Smee, p. 208.

[249] Floud and McCloskey, vol. 2, p. 376; *UN Monthly Bulletin of Statistics*; Matthews, Feinstein and Odling-Smee, p. 31.

Table 7·43: Annual growth rates, percent

	Real domestic product						Output per person-hour in manufacturing			GDP per man-year
	1950-5	1955-60	1960-4	1964-9	1969-73	1970-80	1963-73	1973-76	1976-79	1951-73
UK	2·9	2·5	3·4	2·5	2·8	1·9	4·5	1·3	1·2	2·4
France	4·4	4·8	6·0	5·9	6·1	3·6	6·7	3·9	3·9	4·4
Germany	9·1	6·4	5·1	4·6	4·5	2·8	5·7	4·5	3·7	4·8
Italy	6·3*	5·4	5·5	5·6	4·1	3·0	7·0	2·3	3·0	5·5
Japan	7·1	9·0	11·7	10·9	9·3	4·9	11·2	2·0	7·7	7·9
USA	4·2	2·4	4·4	4·3	3·4	3·0	3·7	3·4	2·1	2·3

* 1952–55

we had taken the smaller advanced countries of Europe they would have shown rates similar to those of the larger economies listed. There was, in fact no advanced country anywhere with a record as poor as the British, except for the American in some phases; or, putting it differently, a rate of economic growth similar to that of the rest of the advanced world would have almost doubled the standard of living that obtained in the UK in the 1970s and would put Britain at the level of the richest countries in Europe, Sweden and Switzerland.

If we consider first the output per head or per worker, failure of labour productivity to grow adequately is likely to be connected with inadequate provision of capital.

> Physical investment in industry is a necessity of technical and even of social progress; new techniques of production, new commodities and changing tastes of consumers require new equipment. Hence it is difficult to achieve a high rate of technical advance without a high level of investment. Conversely, a high level of investment tends to stimulate technical progress since it gives rise to increased opportunities to introduce improved techniques and to experiment with new ideas. In short, a high level of investment and rapid technical progress go hand in hand and it is not practicable to answer the question what would happen to one in the absence of the other.
>
> It is a more useful approach to regard technical progress and investment as different aspects of the same process, namely the application of new ideas to industry and the adaptation of industry to a changing environment.
>
> All new methods require investment outlays before they can be utilized, irrespective of whether they are more mechanized or not. . . The relevant concept is gross investment; all investment expenditures increase productivity, either by bringing the capital stock up to date or by increasing the degree of mechanization.[250]

Of course, there is no precise correlation between productivity increases and investment, for some investment may be misplaced; there are periods and industries in which a high incremental capital/output ratio must prevail, and some 'investment', like technical education, may not appear in any official statistics at all. Moreover, productivity increases come about partly by more intensive or more intelligent use of existing equipment, by smoother organization, by more rapid adaptations to market demands or the use of different raw material inputs. Yet, on the whole, it is only by investment that new methods of production can be introduced; it is only by a high level of investment that a high proportion of the total capital stock can be kept up to date; and given a similar structure of industry and a similar stage of technology, the country with a higher investment rate will cash in more on technical advance, while the country whose investment plans are brusquely cut by

---

[250] Tibor Barna, *Investment and Growth Policies in British Industrial Firms* (Cambridge, 1962), p. 1; W. E. G. Salter, *Productivity and Technical Change* (Cambridge, 1966), p. 145. For obvious technical reasons, there was no correlation *as between industries* between investment and speed of productivity growth. R. J. Nicholson, 'Capital Stock, Employment and Output in British Industry 1948-1964', *Yorkshire Bulletin*, 18/2 (1966), p. 83; also W. B. Reddaway and A. D. Smith, 'Progress in British Manufacturing Industries in the Period 1948-1954', *Econ. J.*, 70/277 (1960).

decisions originating outside industry, will find it particularly difficult to gain the full advantages of any new technology.[251]

The provision of capital, though difficult to measure, did indeed bear a strong correlation to annual growth in output. Japan, the fastest grower, did invest the highest proportion of her national income. Britain and the USA, the slowest, invested the least; and other countries ranged between these extremes.[252] (See Table 7·44.)

Table 7·44:   Investment as a proportion of GNP

| | Gross domestic investment 1950–60, %GNP | Fixed capital less residential | | Gross domestic investment 1980, %GDP |
		1956–63 %GNP	Rate of growth of stock per man-hour 1950–76	
UK	15·4	6·9	4·2	18·3
France	19·1	12·1	5·7	21·8
Germany	24·0	14·7	6·4	22·4
Italy	20·8	13·7	(5·6)*	20·2
Japan	—	21·4	8·7	31·9
USA	—	9·7	3·4	16·8

* Gross Stocks only.

Richer countries will invest more absolutely at a similar percentage of GNP: absolute quantities of capital equipment per worker in manufacturing are equally clearly related to output and their growth is related to the growth of output.[253] (See Table 7·45.)

Table 7·45:   Gross fixed capital formation per head of employed labour in manufacturing ($)

	1960	1965	1970	1975
UK	334	460	604	1006
France	—	905	1439	2682
Germany	—	—	—	1707 (1974)
Italy	332	367	751	1469 (1974)
Japan	492	760	1317	1768
USA	—	1675	2145	2947

The United Kingdom showed both a slow growth and a low investment rate. In productive industry, the British capital equipment became particularly dangerously antiquated. By the end of 1961, it was calculated, 60%

[251] This phenomenon is also well known in historical instances, e.g. P. Temin, 'The Relative Decline of the British Steel Industry, 1880–1913', in H. Rosovsky (ed.), *Industrialization in Two Systems: Essays in Honour of Alexander Gerschenkron* (New York, 1966). Also Kenneth Hilton, review of Beckerman, in *Bankers Magazine*, 203/1 (1967); T. P. Hill, 'Growth and Investment in International Comparison', *Econ. J.*, 74/294 (1964); and the general tenor of Richard E. Caves and Associates, *Britain's Economic Prospects* (Washington, DC, 1968).

[252] Angus Maddison, *Economic Growth in the West*, pp. 76, 81; and 'The Long-Run Dynamics of Productivity Growth', in Wilfred Beckerman (ed.) *Slow Growth in Britain* (Oxford, 1979), p. 203; OECD, *National Accounts*; J. Carrington and G. Edwards, *Financing Industrial Investment* (1978), p. 72.

[253] Frank Blackaby (ed.), *De-Industrialisation* (1978), p. 247.

of the buildings and 38% of plant and machinery in manufacturing and construction dated from before 1948. In some industries the proportion was much higher: 50% of the plant and machinery of the metal-using industries, 39% in textiles and 43% in paper and printing was built in 1947 or earlier. Similarly, 32% of all fixed capital in mining and quarrying, 78% of railway capital, 87% of docks and harbours and 71% of the capital sunk in roads, dated from before 1948.[254]

The relationship between investment and production increases, however, is by no means simple. There are no constant returns to scale on investment, no constant incremental capital-output ratios. Much ingenuity has been shown in recent economic literature, beginning with Solow's seminal essay,[255] in the exploration of the relationships between investment, technology and productivity changes in advanced economies. As far as concrete observation was concerned, two main phenomena have emerged in recent years in Britain and elsewhere.[256] The first is that the post-war increases in output were larger than the increases in the inputs of capital, labour and other factors. The second is that this 'extra' was the larger, the larger the addition to capital and the higher the growth rate, so that it grew more than proportionally with investment: 'there is . . . clear evidence that the residual is correlated with the growth rate'.[257]

Neither of these observations should occasion much surprise. The first confirms that one kind of technological progress consists precisely in the creation of increased output per unit of capital-and-labour input. The second confirms that it is only by re-equipment and by investment in new methods, new organizations and new locations that this 'residual' can be created. Even with a similar technology, there are economies of scale in individual enterprises, which fast-growing economies, pressing against their capacity, reach more quickly.[258]

The close relationship between faster growth of output and faster growth of productivity applies essentially to manufacturing. In a comparison of the growth rates of different industries in Britain in 1924–63, Salter showed that

[254] G. A. Dean, 'The Stock of Fixed Capital in the United Kingdom in 1961', *J.R. Stat. S.*, 127/3, Series A (1964), pp. 338–9, 343.

[255] R. Solow, 'Technical Change and the Aggregate Production Function', *Rev. of Econ. and Statistics*, 39/3 (1957). Also see Solow, 'Investment and Technological Progress', *Mathematical Methods in Social Science 1959* (Stanford, 1960), and literature quoted in J. C.R. Dow, *The Management of the British Economy 1945–1960* (Cambridge, 1965), p. 394; B. R. Williams, 'Investment and Technology in Growth', *Manchester School*, 32/1 (1964); P. A. David and Th. van der Klundert, 'Biased Efficiency, Growth and Capital-Labour Substitution in the US, 1899–1960', *Amer. Econ. Rev.*, 55/3 (1965); National Bureau of Economic Research, *Output, Input and Productivity Measurement* (Princeton, 1961).

[256] B. Williams, 'Research, Development and Economic Growth in the United Kingdom', *International Social Science Journal*, 18/3 (1966); United Nations, Economic Commission for Europe, *Some Factors in Economic Growth in Europe during the 1950s* (Geneva, 1964).

[257] W. Beckerman and Associates, *The British Economy in 1975* (Cambridge, 1965), p. 42, and Table 1·12 on p. 41. Also pp. 256–7. Cf. also T. P. Hill, 'Growth and Investment According to International Comparison', *Econ. J.*, 74/294 (1964).

[258] One recent study of the comparative growth of Britain and Germany attributes more of the difference to economies of scale than to technology – but the latter ('advance in knowledge') is an artificial and quite arbitrary figure, derived from the experience of the USA, and is in this context quite indefensible.

most of the extreme cases ran true to type and that the correlation coefficient of the rise of output with the rise of output per head was + 0·81 for the years 1924–50 and + 0·69 for 1954–63. The 'fit' was better for the faster than the slower growing industries.[259] This relationship, sometimes knows as 'Verdoorn's Law', showed up less clearly in the more turbulent years after 1966, but by no means disappeared altogether.[260] It has no significance in non-manufacturing sectors, other than possibly agriculture, but there is widespread agreement that in economies like the British it is manufacturing that has to supply the mainspring of growth.

Beside inadequate investment, poor management and poor industrial skills have also been blamed for the low rate of British economic growth. In particular, the amateurism and lack of technical understanding of British directors and managers, their bias towards finance rather than production, their conservative attitude to practical training, to changing their firms, to risk taking and competition[261] have been held responsible for many of Britain's economic ills. Yet these alleged failings did not apparently prevent British industry from performing magnificently in wartime, nor did they prevent British banks and other service industries from maintaining their world lead, nor yet all British industry from being more productive, even if slower growing, than the Continent for many years after the war. It would be fairer to state that in view of the repeated discouragement and actual penalty received by enterprise and investment at the hands of an all-powerful Government economic policy since 1947, the caution of British industrialists is perhaps not entirely surprising.[262] Certainly, it is in the Government service that scientists and technologists have been severely discriminated against.[263]

Sources of Growth, Annual growth rates, %

		UK		W. Germany	
Input of factors:	Labour	0·35		0·94	
	Capital	0·80		1·57	
Due to factor inputs			1·15		2·51
Other causes:	Advance of knowledge	0·76		0·76	
	Contraction of agriculture and self-employment	0·09		0·66	
	Economies of scale	0·43		1·25	
	Other	0·16		0·21	
Due to other causes			1·12		2·88
Total observed growth in National Income			2·27		5·39

It is significant that Germany was assumed to operate at full capacity, while in Britain it was assumed that 0·54% p.a. or nearly one-fifth of total annual growth of capacity, had been wasted. Edward Dennison, *Why Growth Rates Differ* (1968).

[259] Salter, *Productivity*, pp. 82, 123, 206–7.

[260] P. J. Verdoorn, 'Verdoorn's Law in Retrospect: A Comment', *Econ. J.*, 90/2, 1980: A. P. Thirlwall, 'Another Interpretation of Verdoorn's Law, *ibid.*; Nicholas Kaldor, *Causes of the Slow Economic Growth of the United Kingdom* (Cambridge, 1966), p. 25; P. Stoneman, 'Kaldor's Law and British Economic Growth 1800–1970', *Warwick Economic Research Papers* No. 93 (1976).

[261] E.g. Richard E. Caves, 'Market Organization, Performance and Public Policy', in *idem, Britain's Economic Prospects* (1968), pp. 301–5; Roger Betts, 'Characteristics of British Company Directors', *Journal of Management Studies*, 4, 1967.

[262] Pollard, *Wasting*, pp. 102–6.

[263] Select Committee on Science and Technology, *2nd Report* (1969), pp. xxviii–xxxii, 263–5.

Labour, similarly, is said to have been too traditional in its training and the trade unions to have been more restrictive in relation to technical progress than those of other countries. Both are justifiable observations, and not even the extensive efforts following the Industrial Training Act of 1973[264] could modernize some of the more antique apprenticeship schemes. Yet here, too, the experience under 30 years of Government economic policy may seem an adequate explanation for the stance of trade union leaders.[265]

Unless the falling behind in productivity[266] is matched by falling exchange rates or by willingness to accept lower incomes, it will lead to loss of international competitiveness (see Table 7·46). Over much of the period, until 1971, exchange rates remained fixed, to be changed only in large belated lurches. However, after the devaluation of 1967 and once more in the 1970s, price competitiveness improved with the downward trend in the pound sterling, to be reversed only from 1979 onward as the result of the oil flow and of deliberate policy.[267]

Table 7·46: Manufactures: export competitiveness and trade performance, United Kingdom

	Index of competitiveness (1970 = 100)	Share of 'world' trade %
1964	104·1	14·4
1966	107·2	13·4
1968	98·1	11·6
1970	100	10·8
1972	103·7	10·0
1974	93·4	8·8
1976	94·3	8·7

But this relative rise in 'competitiveness' or fall in prices, could not hold up the steady decline in the United Kingdom share of world manufacturing exports based as it was on poor quality, poor delivery and other non-pecuniary inferiority. In the task of securing economic growth at a level of that of other countries, there seemed to be no substitute for productive efficiency at home.

[264] Ian Jones, 'The New Training Initiative – An Evolution' *Nat. Inst. Econ. Rev.*, 99, Feb. 1982, pp. 68–70; Treasury and Department of Industry, *An Approach to Industrial Strategy* Cmnd. 6315 (1975), p. 5.

[265] Pollard, pp. 102–6.

[266] C. F. Pratten, *Labour Productivity Differentials Within International Companies* (Cambridge, 1976).

[267] C. J. F. Brown and T. D. Sheriff, 'De-Industrialisation, a Background Paper', in Blackaby, *De-Industrialisation*, p. 257; Ajit Singh, 'UK Industry and the World Economy: A Case of De-Industrialisation?', *Cambridge Journal of Economics*, 1, 1977, pp. 130–1.

8
Trade and Finance in Transformation

1 Trade and the Balance of Payments

Traditionally, Britain had been an open economy in which exports of manufactured goods and services, together with incomes from earlier foreign investments, were large enough to pay for all necessary imports of food and raw materials as well as manufactures, generally leaving a comfortable margin for further net investments abroad. These ratios were disturbed in the war years, in the crisis years 1931–2, and, as we have seen, in the immediate post-war years 1945–50 with all their particular problems. Normally, however, the United Kingdom had had no difficulty in balancing her international accounts.

This changed fundamentally in the post-war decades. Until the oil flow of the late 1970s dramatically reversed Britain's fortunes, the economy suffered from a persistent tendency to import more than could be paid for or, in other words, to run a balance of payments deficit. In those years, a large part of the Government's economic policies was devoted, year by year, to rectifying this apparent underlying unbalance and since, as we shall see,[1] its policy measures gravely damaged Britain's productive capacity, while it was the very failure in productivity which in turn lay behind the balance of payments deficit, a vicious circle was set up which was at the very heart of Britain's disappointing economic performance since the war. Foreign trade and payments thus occupied a key role in the fortunes of the British economy after 1950.

One of the outstanding characteristics of that period was the failure of Britain to maintain the share of her exports in world markets. Her share of manufactured exports, which had been 21·3% in 1937, fell dramatically from 25·4% in 1950 to 16·2% in 1961, 10·8% in 1970 and 8·8% in 1981.[2] Significantly, the expansion of foreign exports at the expense of the British was fastest in the boom; in the 1970s, British exports hardly lost any ground at all.

Britain's poor export performance was not due, as it had been in the 1920s, to her concentration on stagnant, rather than on growth industries: on the contrary, her switch to new industries had been very successful, and in the post-war years Britain had a higher share of trade in the expanding industries than any of her leading competitors, except Germany.[3] Her area pattern, it is

[1] Chapter 9 below.
[2] London and Cambridge Economic Service, *Key Statistics*, 1966, Table N; *Nat. Inst. Econ. Rev.*
[3] M. Panic and T. Seward, 'The Problem of UK Exports', *Bull. Oxf. Inst. Stat.*, 28/1 (1966),

true, was slightly less favourable, since traditionally Britain was geared to supplying the underdeveloped areas of the world which grew more slowly in these years, rather than the European market which grew fastest,[4] but this was not of great significance and Japan, the most successful exporter, had an even less favourable area distribution from a growth point of view. Moreover, by the end of our period a significant switch in the direction of exports had taken place. The share of exports to the expanding EEC market jumped from 26·7% in 1968 to 35·6% in 1976 and 43·4% in 1980, and the share going to the oil producing nations from 5·7% to 12·4% and 10·1% in the same years. By contrast, the share going to the rest of the less developed world and the centrally planned economies fell from 22·6% to 16·6% and 15·5%.[5] What was significant was that Britain's exports did substantially less well than her competitors' in each main market separately. There may, perhaps, also have been a failure in salesmanship, though this is difficult to prove, and is in any case a part of economic efficiency.

The basic causes of the lag in exports are not in any doubt. There was, first, the inability to deliver at the right quality and on time.[6] Secondly, there was the change in prices. Compared with the price level of all world imports, UK export prices rose, i.e. deteriorated competitively, by 14·5% in 1953–63; compared with total import prices into the Common Market, they rose 15·5% more; and compared with other imports into the USA, their excess was 22·9%. Only US export prices rose to the same extent as the British.[7]

The reason for both these factors was the same: exports were affected by the relative decline in British productivity, or the rise in real costs, relative to those of the chief competitors which tended to price British goods out of the competitive world markets. Nevertheless, the main lines of British policy were to have a succession of incomes restraints, rather than efforts to raise productivity;[8] in other words, they were attempts to make prices reflect the relative impoverishment of Britain, rather than to remedy the causes of that impoverishment, and they were unsuccessful even on their own misguided terms.

In 1967 Britain devalued the pound sterling from $2·80 to $2·40 or by 14·3% after the Government had attempted to hold the pound to its parity at increasing cost to the economy[9] in the preceding years. The result, however,

p. 26; also H. Tyszynski, 'World Trade in Manufactured Commodities, 1899–1950', *Manchester School*, 19/3 (1951); S. Spiegelglass, 'World Export of Manufactures, 1956 vs. 1937', *ibid* 27/2 (1959); PEP, *Growth in the British Economy* (1960), p. 166.

[4] S. J. Wells, *Trade Policies for Britain. A Study in Alternatives* (1966), p. 127.

[5] Peter Maunder (ed.), *The British Economy in the 1970's* (1980), p. 250; *United Kingdom Balance of Payments*.

[6] E.g. Lawrence A. Krause, 'British Trade Performance', in Richard E. Caves (ed.), *Britain's Economic Prospects* (1968), pp. 218–26; D. K. Stout (NEDO), *International Price Competitiveness, Non-Price Factors and Export Performance* (1977); Michael Posner and Andrew Steer. 'Price Competitiveness and the Performance of Manufacturing Industry', in Frank Blackaby (ed.), *De-Industrialisation* (1978); pp. 345–51 above.

[7] H. B. Junz and R. R. Rhomberg, 'Prices and Export Performance of Industrial Countries, 1953–1963', IMF *Staff Papers*, 12/2 (1965), pp. 235 *passim*.

[8] See p. 420 below.

[9] W. Beckerman (ed.), *The Labour Government's Economic Record: 1964–1970* (1972), especially the introductory essay by Andrew Graham and Wilfred Beckerman; B. Gould, J. Mills and S. Stewart, *Monetarism or Prosperity?* (1981), pp. 85–7; H. Brandon, *In the Red: the Struggle for Sterling 64/66* (1966).

was not a simple return to more competitive British export prices and thus to an improved payments balance. At first, exports declined not only in value terms, as might be expected: there was even a decline in volume and a lengthening of delivery dates to certain key foreign markets.[10] In due course, there was indeed a substantial improvement in the balance of payments in 1969–70, but significantly, it was much more marked among 'invisibles', that is to say in services, than among commodities.[11] As far as goods were concerned, in practice, exporters did not lower their foreign prices to the full amount of the devaluaion but absorbed some of the gap in higher unit profits and lower sales, while importers, similarly, did not pass on all the price increases. Home prices then began at once to rise until they had returned to something like their former parity with prices abroad.[12]

After the collapse of the Bretton Woods system in 1971, sterling exchange rates were allowed to float from July 1972, and in those conditions the pound sterling drifted down steadily, more or less in line with British productivity and comparative prices, from 115·5% in 1967 (1975 = 100) to 66·1 in 1976. 'Export competitiveness' thus remained stable in 1968–77, fluctuating only gently between a maximum of 104·1 (1972) (at 1970 = 100) and a minimum of 94·3 (1976); thereafter relative export prices rose sharply, from 101·8 in 1977 (1975 = 100) to 134·6 in the last quarter of 1980.[13] Between 1970 and 1980, unit values of exports of manufactures rose by 253% in the UK, but by only 193% in the six leading industrial nations, giving the other five, on average, a price advantage of 21% over the United Kingdom in 1980, compared with 1970.[14]

The hardening of the pound after 1978 was in part deliberate policy, but it was made possible by the oil flow from the North Sea, which rose from almost nothing in 1975 to add *c.* £8·5 b. a year to the current balance in 1979–80.[15] It will be noticed that while there was no obvious association on a year-to-year basis between price 'competitiveness' and export performance, since quality, delivery and other non-price effects played an important part, in very broad outline they did agree: Britain's losses of markets *c.* 1950–70 coincided with loss of competitiveness, while in the 1970s both indices tended to stabilize.

[10] R. L Mayor, 'The Competitiveness of British Exports Since Devaluation'. *Nat. Inst. Econ. Rev.*, 48 (1969), pp. 31–4.

[11] According to one estimate, of the £425m improvement in the balance of payments by 1970, £295m was due to the invisible balance and only £130m to visible trade. Nat. Inst. of Economic and Social Research, 'The Effects of the Devaluation of 1967 on the Balance of Payments', *Econ. J.*, 82, Special Issue (March 1972); G. D. N. Worswick, 'Trade and Payments', in Sir Alec Cairncross (ed.), *Britain's Economic Problems Reconsidered* (1971), p. 87. In services themselves, the British share of world transactions was also falling, but not as fast: J. R. Sargent, 'UK Performance in Services', and T. M. Rybczynski, 'Comment', in Blackaby, *De-Industrialisation.*

[12] W. Robinson, T. R. Webb and M. A. Townsend, 'The Influence of Exchange Rate Changes on Prices. A Study of 18 Industrial Countries', *Economica*, 46/181 (1979); J. Odling-Smee and Nicholas Hartley, *Some Effects of Exchange Rate Changes* (Government Economic Service Working Paper No. 2, 1978).

[13] Michael Posner (ed.), *Demand Management* (1978), pp. 88, 105; *Nat. Inst. Econ. Rev.*

[14] *Nat. Inst. Econ. Rev.* Also p. 351 above.

[15] L. P. Tempest and R. J. Walton, 'North Sea Oil and Gas in the UK Balance of Payments since 1970', *B. of Eng. Qtly. Bull.*, 19 (1979), pp. 383–4.

As in other countries, exports grew faster than output, so that the share of exports in final total expenditure continued to expand, rising in absolute volume (at 1975 prices from £13·1 b. in 1960 to £33·3 b. in 1980, or by 154%, and as a proportion of total final expenditure exports increased from 14·9% in 1960 to 18·2% in 1970 and 22·5% in 1980. This did represent some measure of success of the export industries and services, but essentially these figures show the growing integration of the world economy, particularly among the advanced countries, since imports grew at a comparable pace. They rose from £15·8 b. to £34·1 b. at constant prices of 1975, or by 115%. and as a proportion of total final expenditure, from 18·0% to 20·1% and 23·1% in the same years.

All advanced countries were in fact returning to the development pattern of the pre-1914 era, when their mutual trade had increased faster than their output. Trade among the developed nations formed a growing share of this expansion, and consisted increasingly of similar, mainly manufactured, goods crossing the frontier in both directions. This could be associated with the 'variety hypothesis', i.e. the assumption that with rising incomes, consumers were prepared to pay higher transport charges in order to have a wider variety of choice of commodities.[16] Among exports, engineering products continued to increase somewhat, from 36% of the total in 1955 to a maximum of about 45% around 1970, to drop to below 40% in 1980, and chemicals also expanded steadily, to reach 11·5% of exports by value in 1977. Textiles, metals and basic materials declined, oil more than making up the decline of coal among 'fuels' in 1955–75. In imports there was a more remarkable switch still, food, beverages and tobacco falling from 36·2% of imports in 1955 to 12·4% in 1980, and industrial materials from 47·9% to 35·6%, and in their place finished manufactures increased their share from 5·1% to 35·6%.[17] The frightening import penetration, threatening some of Britain's key industries,[18] accelerated at the end of the decade, and in 1980 for the first time there was an excess of the import of road vehicles over their export value.

It is easy to see that for commodities with a marginal 'propensity to import' of 0·30 or over and a very high income elasticity of demand of 2 or 3, almost the whole of additional incomes will be spent on imports.[19] This could be generalized and could, when combined with a low export elasticity for British goods, for which again examples could be found in some bad export years, be used to show that Britain faced an inevitably increasing adverse trade gap that no manipulation of exchange rates could cure, as soon as she went in for economic growth bringing rising incomes.[20] In those terms, Britain's balance

[16] T. Barker, 'A Priori Restrictions on Income and Price Elasticities' (1975), quoted by Jim Hibberd and Simon Wren-Lewis, *A Study of UK Imports of Manufactures* (Government Economic Service Working Paper No. 6, 1978), p. 10.

[17] A. R. Prest and D. J. Coppock, *The UK Economy* (1978), p. 127; *Overseas Trade Statistics*.

[18] Pp. 289, 292 above.

[19] Hibberd and Wren-Lewis, p. 10; A. D. Morgan, 'Imports of Manufactures into the UK and other Industrial Countries 1955–69', *Nat. Inst. Econ. Rev.*, 56 (1971).

[20] A. P. Thirlwall, 'The UK's Economic Problem: A Balance-of-Payments Constraint?', *National Westminster Bank Quarterly Review* (Feb. 1978), pp. 24–32; J. J. Hughes and A. P.

of payments difficulties could be presented as being no one's fault, but the result of unfortunate 'elasticities'.

As a matter of fact, however, other calculations showed the demand elasticities for British exports to have been much higher, around 2, and thus neither dissimilar from the import elasticities, nor from the export elasticities of other countries.[21] But even if they were not, even if a high propensity to import were peculiarly adverse in Britain, this would be 'not so much an explanation as a reformulation of the problem'.[22] These elasticities were not God-given, but the result of real factors, above all the growing inability of Britain to produce competitively, particularly in booms.[23] The emphasis on elasticities instead, illustrates the growing tendency of modern economics to objectify ratios that are by their nature tenuous, temporary and derived. Had Britain been able, say, to produce cars as cheaply and as well as Japan, she would have found her foreign and home markets, just as elastic as the Japanese car makers.

For most of the time, in periods of restriction, output was at less than capacity, preventing the full use of home resources for such objectives as improving Britain's productive potential:[24] when the brakes were taken off, capacity was then found to be too inelastic and too low.

The NEDC Inquiry of 1965 investigated in detail the general rise of imports in 1954–64, and the sharp rise in 1962–4, of eight groups of manufactures. In three cases (chemicals, textiles, especially man-made fibres, and electrical household goods), shortage of capacity was given as the main reason; in three others, it was given as one of the main reasons (paper and board, iron and steel, building materials); and in the remaining who (engineering products, motor vehicles) performance and consumer preference were put to the fore.[25] Once again in the 1960s it was the shortage of machine-tool capacity which imperilled all hopes of faster growth, and its inadequacy was explained by the low and irregular demand it had met in the past.[26] Moreover, the progressive deterioration of British technical competitiveness meant that at each crisis, the dependence on imports increased and when the tide receded, left them at a higher level than before. This 'ratchet effect' was noted among all advanced countries, but in the United Kingdom it was particularly powerful in the case of machinery and other capital goods.

Thirlwall, 'Trends and Cycles in Import Penetration in the UK', *Oxf. Bull. Econ. Stat.*, 39 (1977), pp. 301–17; C. J. F. Brown and T. D. Sheriff, 'Background Paper', in Blackaby, *De-Industrialisation*, p. 259.

[21] R. M. Stern, J. Francis, B. Schumacher, *Price Elasticities in International Trade* (1976); Gould, Mills and Stewart, p. 91.

[22] Gould, Mills and Stewart, p. 91.

[23] W. A. Eltis, 'Economic Growth and the British Balance of Payments', in D. H. Aldcroft and Peter Fearon (eds.), *Economic Growth in Twentieth-Century Britain* (1969), pp. 197–9. See also Youngson, *Britain's Economic Growth 1920–1966* (1967), pp. 232–5; J. R. Parkinson, 'The Progress of United Kingdom Exports', *Scot. J. Pol. Econ.*, 13/1 (1966); M. FG. Scott, *A Study of United Kingdom Imports* (Cambridge, 1963); Lynden Moore, 'Factors Affecting Demand for British Exports', *Bull. Oxf. Inst. Stat.*, 26/4 (1964), p. 347.

[24] W. A. H. Godley and J. R. Shepherd, 'Long-Term Growth and Short-Term Policy', *Nat. Inst. Econ. Rev.*, 29 (1964).

[25] *Loc. cit.*, paras. 19, 26, 34, 48–50, 58, 61, 77–9, 82.

[26] E. W. Evans, 'Some Problems of Growth in the Machine Tool Industry', *Yorkshire Bulletin*, 18/1 (1966), pp. 43, 47–8.

It was therefore in the United Kingdom, where the threat to home industry by foreign imports appeared first, that voices demanding the raising of tariff barriers were heard most loudly. As early as October 1964, the Labour Government had attempted to correct the threatened adverse trade balance by a so-called 'import surcharge', a thinly disguised tariff of 15%; an export rebate, involving a refund of certain indirect taxes, amounting to about 2% on exports, also became operative from 1964. Both were unpopular with the members of the trade agreement, GATT, the former being almost certainly in breach of the undertakings entered into by Britain, and they were repealed in 1966 and 1968 respectively. They were followed by an 'import deposit' scheme in November 1968, penalizing importers by making them deposit with the Government for six months a sum equal to half the value of the imports. This scheme never had much effect, and after being gradually reduced in amount, was ended in December 1970.

From the mid-1970s on, protection was demanded not only by manufacturers under threat, but also by economists such as the Cambridge Economic Policy Group. The cry to 'buy British' was taken up in various quarters, and attempts were made to negotiate limitations of imports such as Hongkong textiles and Japanese cars,[27] since international agreements inhibited direct protectionist policies. As the slump spread throughout the advanced world from 1979 on, the practices of hidden subsidies, as for steel, and disguised protection were taken up by one nation after another, an echo, albeit a very soft one, of the reactions to the slump of the 1930s.

Among the 'invisibles', the returns from property, etc., abroad showed an increasing trend in monetary terms, though they declined in real terms. The other 'invisibles', however, showed a sad decline from their former importance in Britain's balance of payments. Civil aviation showed a small surplus year by year, but shipping, once a very large net earner of foreign currency, was a net loser by the 1960s: Britain paid more in shipping services to foreigners than she received in return. Much of this was due to a negative balance on tankers, some of it also to the growing competition from Third World countries and flags of convenience. The Merchant Shipping Act of 1974 permitted some retaliation against the latter and by 1980 the balance was positive again. Travel and private transfer were negative items in the 1960s, but after 1968 they became increasingly net earners, achieving a surplus of around £1,000 million a year in the late 1970s, aided by the falling value of sterling.

Only financial and other services, the work of the City of London, were positive throughout, and if it is borne in mind that the official statistics may slightly under-state the rise in these earnings,[28] these may have kept pace with prices and thus kept their real value. The growth of international banking services from the late 1950s onward, discussed in section 3 of this chapter, and in which London played a leading part, contributed to this buoyant

---

[27] Peter Maunder, 'International Trade' in *idem*, *British Economy*, pp. 256–8.

[28] A. E. Holmans, 'Invisible Earnings', *Scot. J. Pol. Econ.*, 13/1 (1966), pp. 56–7. Also, British National Export Council (William M. Clarke, Director of the Study), *Britain's Invisible Earnings* (1967); F. N. Burton and P. Galambos, 'The Role of Invisible Trade in the United Kingdom's Balance of Payments, 1952–1966', *National Provincial Bank Review*, 82 (1968); Peter Maunder, 'International Trade', pp. 260–77; *The Times*, 4 August 1982.

increase. Overall, the earning power of invisibles held up well in international competition. Their net surplus could pay for 6–8% of total imports at the beginning of our period, and 8–10% at its end.

It is important to note that criss-crossing the changes in relative prices caused by currency alterations, there were significant changes also in the terms of trade, i.e. the world prices of goods bought and sold by the UK. We have seen that an adverse movement in the terms of trade hampered the recovery in the years 1945–50, but thereafter their improvement aided the British balance of payments. It was partly the end of this favourable shift which made the devaluation of 1967 necessary, and by the late 1970s the terms were back at the low levels of the Korean War,[29] adding to the difficulties of that decade (see Table 8·1).

Table 8·1:   Terms of trade (1970 = 100)

1938	98
1950	83
1955	82
1960	93
1965	98
1970	100
1975	81
1980	84

It is time now to consider the actual trade balance and some aspects of the balance of payments in the decades 1950–1980 (Table 8·2)[30]. Two features stand out at once. One is the wide margin of fluctuations from year to year in the private series. The other is the basic stability in the relationships nonetheless, with commodity trade showing a substantial deficit in most years, invisibles showing a substantial surplus, and net Government transactions representing a large and increasing negative item. In some respects, that appearance of stability is misleading, for it is an *ex-post* result, having been achieved only by dint of deliberate policies to maintain an overall balance, some of which were costly in growth and prosperity. The fluctuations underlying these policies will be discussed in chapter 9 below. But the main ratios are real enough. Private current transactions were adequate to keep Britain in balance and even leave a fairly regular surplus for foreign investment, as in former times; in many years the British surplus was as high, or higher, than those of the most successful exporting nations, Germany and Japan. Yet the country was in almost constant balance of payments difficulties. How can this be explained?

There have been two main causes for the pressure on the balance of payments. One has been the sum of overseas capital transactions, or net foreign investment. The other has been the sum of Government activities. Between them they have repeatedly imposed a burden on the British economy beyond its powers to bear. We shall examine them in turn.

---

[29] Sir Alec Cairncross, 'The Postwar Years 1945–77', in R. Floud and D. McCloskey (eds.), *The Economic History of Britain since 1700* (Cambridge, 1981), vol. 2, pp. 389–90; *Economic Trends*, Annual Supplement.

[30] *UK Balance of Payments; B. of Eng. Qtly. Bull.*

Table 8·2: United Kingdom Current Balance of Payments 1950–80 (£m.)

	Private sector					Government sector		
	Exports f.o.b. £b.	Imports f.o.b £b.	Visible balance of trade	Invisible balance	Total private balance	Services and transfers (net)	Interest profits divid's.	Total current government balance
1950	2·3	2·3	(−51)	(+433)*		−136	*	
1951	2·7	3·4	(−689)	(+330)*		−150	*	
1952	2·8	3·0	−279	(+355)*		−61	*	
1953	2·7	2·9	−244	(+398)*		−66	*	
1954	2·8	3·0	−204	(+406)*		−131	*	
1955	3·1	3·4	−313	(+283)*		−138	*	
1956	3·4	3·3	+53	(+309)*		−175	*	
1957	3·5	3·5	−29	(+328)*		−144	*	
1958	3·4	3·4	+29	(+285)*		−219	*	
1959	3·5	3·6	−118	(+190)*		−227	*	
1960	3·7	4·1	−408	(+59)*		−283	*	
1961	3·9	4·0	−153	+554	+401	−332	−164	−496
1962	4·0	4·1	−102	+730	+628	−360	−146	−506
1963	4·3	4·4	−80	+719	+639	−382	−133	−515
1964	4·5	5·0	−519	+688	+169	−432	−119	−551
1965	4·8	5·1	−223	+775	+552	−446	−132	−578
1966	5·2	5·3	−66	+783	+717	−470	−156	−626
1967	5·1	5·7	−557	+886	+329	−462	−168	−630
1968	6·3	6·9	−659	+1091	+418	−466	−230	−696
1969	7·1	7·2	−143	+1407	+1046	−467	−324	−791
1970	8·2	8·2	−34	+1612	+1578	−486	−269	−755
1971	9·0	8·9	+190	+1658	+1849	−520	−204	−724
1972	9·4	10·2	−748	+1698	+950	−561	−142	−703
1973	11·9	14·5	−2586	+2573	−13	−769	−199	−968
1974	16·4	21·5	−5351	+3272	−2079	−842	−352	−1194
1975	19·3	22·7	−3333	+3266	−67	−940	−541	−1454
1976	25·2	29·1	−3929	+5151	+1222	−1455	−648	−2103
1977	31·7	34·0	−2248	+4815	+2567	−1839	−733	−2572
1978	35·1	36·6	−1542	+5497	+3955	−2401	−615	−3016
1979	40·7	44·1	−3458	+6028	+2570	−2857	−576	−3433
1980	47·4	46·2	+1178	+5306	+6484	−2623	−655	−3278

* The invisible balance figures contain the negative element for the Government sector interest, profits and dividends which cannot be separated out. Without these, the private invisible balance would show larger positive figures.

The actual annual sums invested abroad may seem large (see Table 8·3)[31] but a substantial proportion of them were derived from retained earnings overseas, and they were matched by similar figures of inward investment in private British assets, so that net outflow has remained relatively limited. Although capital exports have come under attack from time to time as being greater than the economy could afford,[32] their economic case is a strong one. Given a surplus on current account which obtained throughout, and which was maintained until 1959 even when Government expenditure was included, it was in the interest of world trade and prosperity, particularly of less developed countries hit by the adverse terms of trade which so helped Britain,

[31] *UK Balance of Payments.*
[32] E.g. A. R. Conan, 'The Unsolved Balance of Payments Problem', *Westminster Bank Review* (Nov. 1963), p. 11; F. W. Paish, 'Britain's Foreign Investment: the Post-War Record' (1956), in *Studies in an Inflationary Economy. The United Kingdom 1948–1961* (1962), chapter 9.

to use Britain's trading surplus precisely in this traditional way. Moreover this expenditure was productive and contributed to the growing 'invisible' surpluses on current account.[33]

Table 8·3:   UK Long-term private foreign investment (£m.)

Average of years	Foreign capital invested in the UK	UK capital invested abroad	Net investment
1958–61	+ 258	– 342	– 84
1962–4	+ 224	– 320	– 97
1965–7	+ 313	– 376	– 63
1968–70	+ 653	– 745	– 92
1971–3	+ 1095	– 1341	– 246
1974–6	+ 1935	– 1595	+ 341
1977–9	+ 3538	– 4508	– 970
1980	+ 4646	– 6891	– 2245

In concrete terms, many of these investments opened out and developed British markets and supply areas, mainly in the earlier years of the period. In the later years, they represented, in part, the necessary attempts of British firms to establish themselves behind tariff barriers. Private capital abroad, estimated at £3,300 million at the end of the war, rose to around £9,300 million in 1957 and to £11,800 million in 1961 according to one calculation.[34] Capital assets abroad are notoriously difficult to value, and official figures put private long-term investment abroad at £7,855 million at the end of 1962, at £9,600 million at the end of 1966 and at £48,300 million in 1980.[35]

In these totals, portfolio investments showed some increases, but the largest growth was registered in direct investment in non-financial companies, and particularly in oil. According to Revell, these two items grew from £6,080 million in 1957 to £7,387 million in 1961, or by £325 million a year, and according to the official figures, direct investment rose from £3,755 million in 1962 to £6,880 million in 1970 and £31,700 million in 1980, and oil investment from £1,100 million in 1962 to £2,700 million in 1974 and £7,350 million in 1980. Even more striking was the change in direction. Before 1960 most of British overseas investment went to areas like Canada and Australia, but since then it was made increasingly in Western Europe, both in the Common Market and the EFTA countries as well as the USA. As the return on investment was scarcely higher abroad than at home (7·8% as against 7·6% by 1960–2),[36] it was likely that many of these investments were made to

[33] W. B. Reddaway *et. al.*, *Effects of UK Direct Investment Overseas: Interim Report* (Cambridge, 1967) and *Final Report* (Cambridge, 1968).

[34] Jack Revell, *The Wealth of the Nation. The National Balance Sheet of the United Kingdom, 1957–1961* (Cambridge, 1967), Table 12·3, pp. 268–9, taking 'Private' and 'Direct Investments', less 'Cash and Short-Term Assets' and Bank 'Advances', which still overstates the long-term holdings.

[35] *UK Balance of Payments; B. of Eng. Qtly. Rev.* Also 'An Inventory of UK External Assets and Liabilities: end 1978', *ibid.* 19 (June 1979), pp. 160–5 and Alexander G. Kemp, 'Long-Term Capital Movements', *Scot. J. Pol. Econ.*, 13/1 (1966), pp. 143–9.

[36] J. H. Dunning, 'Does Foreign Investment Pay', *Moorgate and Wall Street* (Autumn, 1964); Wells, pp. 59–60; W. Beckerman and Associates, *The British Economy in 1975* (Cambridge, 1965) pp. 116–19.

enlarge markets rather than to find profitable outlets for capital.

Within the Sterling Area[37] there were no limitations on foreign investment, apart from the closure of the 'Kuwait gap' in July 1957 through which sterling funds had escaped, but there were restrictions on raising new money in London; in 1966–72 investment in the white Commonwealth Sterling Area countries was however made subject to some restraints. To the outside world, foreign investment was strictly limited through exchange control until 1969, when there was some liberalization. After sterling was allowed to float in 1972 conditions were eased outside the Sterling Area and tightened within it, so that the distinction between them almost disappeared. It is not clear that these restrictions ever had much effect, but it seems that after the liberalization, funds withdrawn from the Sterling Area in 1972–3 were invested outside.[38] Entry into the EEC brought further easements and in the course of 1979 all exchange controls limiting outward investments were removed.

The growth of real overseas long-term assets was in part matched by foreign investment in Britain. Inward investment grew from around 20% of outward capital flows in the early 1950s to 70–80% from the mid-1960s onwards, and in 1961 and 1967 as well as the years after the oil crisis of 1973 the balance was actually positive. The main component of capital imports, was direct investment, particularly by American firms, in subsidiaries to beat the British tariff or to form bases for covering British and European markets. American investment in Britain was estimated at $847 million in 1950 and $1,420 million in 1955, of which 80% was in oil and manufacturing; by 1967, it was estimated to have reached $7,000 m. Total private foreign-held capital was estimated at £3,150 million in 1957 and £5,750 million in 1961 by one calculation, and by another to have risen from £3,160 million in 1962 to £7,280 million in 1970 and by an enormous jump to £33,150 million in 1980. The inward investments of the 1970s were boosted by the billions of OPEC funds seeking investment opportunities abroad, by foreign investment in North Sea oil, and by the foreign borrowings of the nationalized industries. The net sum of private long-term capital investment in favour of Britain thus rose in money terms from £5·9 b. in 1962 to £15·1 b. in 1980; but in real terms this represented scarcely any change at all.[39]

American capital introduced into Britain the advantages of American systems of management, as in the building of the Esso Fawley refinery, or American technical know-how, as in the motor and other engineering firms, and the American-owned plants were often much concerned with exports or with import-saving.[40] In the long run, however, these investments burdened the economy with a flow of annual service charges to match the in-payments from British investments abroad.

These sums were swamped in the annual statistics by the growth in the

[37] See pp. 362–4 below.

[38] J. H. B. Tew, 'Policies Aimed at Improving the Balance of Payments', in F. T. Blackaby (ed.), *British Economic Policy 1960–74* (Cambridge, 1978), pp. 325–37.

[39] *UK Balance of Payments*; Revell, *loc. cit.*; J. McMillan and Bernard Harris, *The American Take-Over of Britain* (1968); *B. of Eng. Qtly. Bull.*

[40] J. H. Dunning, *American Investment in British Manufacturing Industry* (1958), pp. 290–310, and 'US Manufacturing Subsidiaries and Britain's Trade Balance', *District Bank Review*, 115 (1955); and discussion on multinationals, pp. 308–10 above.

overseas assets and liabilities of the banking and commercial sector, arising largely from the rise of the Euro-currency system, to be discussed below.[41] However, while the assets concerned rose more than fifty fold from £2–3 b. in 1962 to £158–60 b. in 1980, they largely balanced out year by year, being essentially book entries within the banking system.

In addition to these private capital transfers, there were also official investments, of which the 'sterling balances' were the most important in the early post-war years. Created first in wartime by the expenditure of British forces in such countries as India and Egypt, they had become almost as large as British investment overseas in the immediate post-war years. After 1950 the total never moved far from the £3,500 million mark, of which 20–25% was held by countries not in the sterling area; but within this total, India, Pakistan, Ceylon and Egypt used up most of their holdings and those of Australia, New Zealand and South Africa also declined, while, by contrast, the oil countries of the Middle East, and some Far Eastern areas like Malaysia and Hong-Kong, the surplus economies of the sterling area, greatly increased their holdings in London.[42]

The concept of the 'Sterling Area' itself underwent considerable changes.[43] The level of the sterling balances proved that London was still favoured by many countries, mainly those in the Commonwealth, as a place to hold their reserves, and the high and rising interest rates payable in London, a reflection of the increasing weakness of sterling, helped to continue them in their resolve. On the other hand, the Commonwealth received a small and falling share of British investments and a falling share of British trade, as tariff preference margins were, on the whole, not increased, while the attractions of other markets grew.[44] Sterling's role as an international currency also declined with British trade, British shipping and the importance of the London Money Market: by the mid 1960s, well under one-third of world transactions was left to be made in sterling.[45]

Yet even with this diminished responsibility, the burden on the British reserves were far greater than they could bear. The sterling balances of almost £4,000 million in the mid-1960s were far larger than the reserves or the annual surplus or deficit of the payments balances, and hung there as a threat, inhibiting the British Government repeatedly from necessary remedial action to safeguard the British economy. Above all, they were a major reason for the costly postponement of devaluation, which nevertheless had to be submitted to in the end, in 1967. Here was a prime example of how the historical burden

[41] P. 389 below.

[42] Beckerman, p. 113; Bank of England, *Quarterly Bulletin*; S. Strange, *The Sterling Problem and the Six* (PEP, European Series No. 4, 1967), Table 6, p. 68.

[43] C. W. McMahon, *Sterling in the Sixties*; Symposium in *Bull. Oxf. Inst. Stat.*, 21/4 (1959); J. M. Livingstone, *Britain and the World Economy* (Pelican, 1966), chapter 2; David Williams, 'The Evolution of the Sterling System', in C. R. Whittlesey and J. S. G. Wilson (eds.), *Essays in Money and Banking in Honour of R. S. Sayers* (Oxford, 1968).

[44] G. D. A. MacDougall and R. Hutt, 'Imperial Preference: Quantitative Analysis', *Econ J.*, 64/254 (1954); Wells, pp. 18 ff; G. Arnold, *Economic Cooperation in the Commonwealth* (1967), pp. 57–67.

[45] P. M. Oppenheimer, 'Monetary Movements and the International Position of Sterling', *Scot. J. Pol. Econ.*, 13/1 (1966).

of Empire and of former economic strength led to particular policies which were bound severely to curtail British prosperity.[46] The enforced devaluation may be taken as a major step, albeit a belated one, in the slow recognition on the part of British Governments that their political ambitions based on past glories were beyond the capability of the economy to sustain and were inflicting an intolerable level of damage on it.

True, in the preceding 10 years, outside countries, which tended to vary their sterling holdings more frequently, had reduced them, while members of the Sterling Area had increased theirs, thus adding to the overall stability, but the devaluation hit the remaining holders hard in 1967 by diminishing the value of their reserves. Not surprisingly, there followed in 1968 a massive withdrawal of funds from London by the overseas sterling countries in search of safety, which Britain, significantly, could stem only by internationalizing the burden. Under the Basle Group Agreement of that year, 12 central banks together with the Bank for International Settlements extended a credit of $2 billion to Britain, to allow her to meet the drain of these withdrawals and to guarantee the dollar value of a large proportion of the remaining official sterling holdings. In the event, the sterling balances, both official and other, increased again in the following years, and the Agreement was ended in 1974, not before having involved Britain in large compensation payments arising from the loss of value of sterling against the dollar in 1972-4. Thereafter, the sterling balances rose once more, in 1974-5, largely with OPEC funds, though by then the oil prices were expressed in dollars. But they remained a highly volatile element, as soon as the value of sterling was threatened, unless compensated by exceptionally high interest rates in London: thus in 1976 another Basle Agreement was negotiated, but did not have to be activated. Meanwhile the accession of Britain to the EEC increased the pressure on London to relinquish the role of sterling as a reserve currency, for which it no longer had the resources.

A glance at Table 8·2 on p. 359 will show that there was one burden on the external balance of the UK far larger than the two we have considered so far, foreign investment and the constraints imposed by the Sterling Balances: this was the overseas expenditure of the Central Government itself. Year by year, a large and increasing Government deficit wiped out the surpluses achieved by the rest of the economy and kept it in an almost continuous state of crisis. The deficit up to the devaluation of 1967 was, in fact, larger than appears from the table, since in addition to the current items shown here, a substantial and rapidly rising proportion of capital investment, amounting to a net £386 million for the four years 1963-6, was also on Government account. Even omitting these large sums, the net expenditure[47] of Government abroad rose eightfold in monetary terms in this period, and the purely military (net) expenditure within it rose even more sharply from £12 million in 1952 to £313 million in 1966. This item alone, therefore, was sufficient to wreck the delicate balance of payments of the United Kingdom since 1950, and to account for the worsening imbalances, in spite of the progressively improved

[46] S. Strange, *Sterling and British Policy* (Oxford, 1971).

[47] Gross expenditure rose less, it was the collapse of counterbalancing in-payments which caused the multiplication of the net figure.

trading accounts. Whether expenditure of this order of magnitude was wise or justifiable, or whether it contributed to the political strengthening of the United Kingdom, are political questions outside the purview of this book.[48] It may, however, be of interest to compare the Government foreign balances of payments and receipts of nine major countries in 1966[49] (see Table 8·4).

Table 8·4: Net Governmental foreign balances of payments and receipts

	$ million
USA	− 6,385
UK	− 1,288
Belgium/Luxembourg	− 46
Sweden	− 45
Netherlands	− 42
Italy	− 9
France	− 1
Japan	+ 315
Germany	+ 339

With the exception of the USA, which at least achieved superpower status on the basis of her expenditure, Britain was clearly in a class of her own. Given the unwillingness to impose overseas trading and payments restrictions which might have permitted Britain to incur this kind of expenditure without repeated deflation at home, the real cost-benefit analysis of British foreign policy would have to count the cost of Government activities abroad not merely in the hundreds of millions annually spent, but in the billions annually lost in output and income because of the restrictions made necessary to maintain it.

The deficit on Government transactions continued to grow in money terms after 1967, though it declined in real terms with the reductions in military and other commitments 'East of Suez', but meanwhile Government overseas transactions were swamped by the need of the central monetary authorities to raise large credits, mainly from the IMF and from other central banks, to cover the periodic British balance of payments deficits. Britain became a regular debtor in need of aid on the world's money markets, subject to control and inspection by her foreign creditors, even though her own non-Governmental economic transactions left her normally in healthy surplus, and her private citizens were still year by year investing heavily abroad. These official loans required interest payments which further burdened the external balance, and when restrictions, devaluations and similar actions on the part of the Government had created temporary surpluses as in 1969-71, these could not be used fully to expand the economy, but had to be devoted to repaying the foreign loans.

An indication of the sums involved and the yearly fluctuations is provided by Table 8·5.

---

[48] For other politically inspired burdens on the British economy, see R. N. Gardner, *Sterling-Dollar Diplomacy* (1956).

[49] W. A. P. Manser, *Britain in Balance* (1971), p. 31.

Table 8·5: UK balance of payments – official financing, 1964–1980*

Net transactions with overseas monetary authorities		Foreign currency borrowing		Alloc. of spec. drawing rights £m.	Gold subscr. to IMF £m.	Official reserves** £m.	Total official financing £m.	Outstanding official borrowing abroad end-year† $m.
IMF £m.	Other £m.	By HM Gov't £m.	By other public bodies £m.					
1964 +357	+216					+122	+695	1,604
1965 +489	+110					−246	+353	3,282
1966 +15	+610††				−44	−34	+547	3,542
1967 −339	+895††					+115	+671	4,356
1968 +506	+790					+114	+1410	7,464
1969 −30	−669		+56			−44	−687	5,803
1970 −134	−1106			+171	−38	−125	−1287	3,406
1971 −554	−1263		+82	+125		−1536	−3146	1,447
1972 −415	+864			+124		+692	+1265	266
1973			+999			−228	+771	2,982
1974		+644	+1017			−105	+1646	7,092
1975		+423	+387			+655	+1465	8,921
1976 +1018	−34		+1791			+853	+3628	14,160
1977 +1113		+871	+242			−9588	−7362	18,042
1978 −1016		+191	−378			+2329	+1126	15,847
1979 −596			−250	+195		−1059	−1710	14,585
1980 −140		−629	−312	+180		−291	−1192	11,991

* *UK Balance of Payments; Bank of Eng. Qtly. Bull.* Plus signs indicate borrowings, minus signs repayments.
** Plus signs mean drawings, minus signs additions.
† Short and medium term borrowings.
†† Includes transfer of dollar portfolio to reserves.

The British economy thus proceeded in its foreign transactions in heavy lurches and ever-deepening dependence on foreign credits, which in the 1970s involved even the nationalized industries. By 1980 also over £6 billion of UK Government stock was held abroad, almost £4 billion of it outside the central banks.[50] Until Britain was rescued by the flow of North Sea oil at the end of the decade, each of the shocks to her economy was caught and buffered by a smoothly functioning system of international credit provision. This network of international economic and financial agreements to deal with just such imbalances stood in sharp and remarkable contrast to the chaos and disruption of the 1930s. To its creation and evolution we must now turn.

2 International Economic Co-operation

Among the institutions devised in the early post-war years to prevent a repetition of the economic warfare of the 1930s[51] was GATT, the General Agreement on Tariffs and Trade. It came into operation at the beginning of 1948, after the more ambitious Havana Charter of 1948 to set up an International Trade Organisation (ITO) had failed to get support, and it offered some hope of limiting obstacles to international trade. Its objective was the lowering of tariffs and other trade barriers and the elimination of discrimination, and one of its main instruments was to be the most-favoured-nation clause.

[50] *B. of Eng. Qtly, Bull.*, 21/2 (June 1981), pp. 203–5.
[51] See chapter 5, section 6 above.

The great hopes set on it in the beginning were to be largely disappointed. After some initial reductions in tariffs on individual commodities which no country thought vital, it soon found its success diminishing when it attempted to tackle those which members held to be important. It therefore turned, instead, to across-the-board percentage cuts. Some of these were negotiated on a multilateral basis in the 'Kennedy Round' of 1964-7, but they were limited in extent. The 'Tokyo Round', lasting from 1973-9 was even less productive of direct cuts. It did, however, lead to some significant agreements on customs valuation, on the removal of technical barriers and of export subsidies and countervailing duties, all of which could make further concessions easier in the future. Even if not very effective in lowering barriers, GATT has been fairly successful in inhibiting member states from raising them too blatantly. As in the case of the British 'surcharge' of 1964, it lacked the enforcing power to hold its members to the spirit of the agreement when they felt themselves to be under pressure, but it still represented a considerable moral force in that direction. This has become more important in the late 1970s, when mounting unemployment led Britain as well as other major trading countries to 'manage' their foreign trade.[52]

The less developed countries of the world saw their share of trade decline under the liberalized post-war regime, and brought about in 1964 the United Nations Conference on Trade and Development (UNCTAD) for the purpose of obtaining particularly favourable terms, the right to impose unilateral restrictions, and aid from the richer nations. Some aid has flowed in their direction as a result, though Britain has never reached the target of 1% of its national income to be provided for the poorer countries, as recommended then, nor has any other advanced nation. However, the Integrated Programme for Commodities, agreed to by UNCTAD in 1976, led to the establishment of the first agreement, for natural rubber, in 1979 and in the same year Britain agreed to relieve 17 of the poorest countries of their debt repayments. The independent Brandt Report of 1980, part of the 'North-South dialogue', showed however that in spite of these and similar measures on the part of other developed nations the gap between the poor and the rich world has not been narrowed.

Much more significant than these attempts to foster trade on a world-wide basis were the regional agreements which sprang up in Europe. The European Economic Community, or Common Market, deriving from the earlier Coal, Iron and Steel Community among the 'Six' (Germany, France, Belgium, Holland, Italy and Luxemburg), was set up by the Treaty of Rome, signed in 1957. It came into operation in 1958 with a 12-year programme of gradual removal of all barriers to trade among the members and the erection of a unitary tariff to the outside world. In the event, not only were the customs union provisions speeded up, but it proved possible to 'harmonize' many other economic activities, from social welfare provisions and agricultural protection to taxation, much faster than most observers had thought possible.[53]

---

[52] S. A. B. Page, 'Management in International Trade, in R. Major (ed.), *Britain's Trade and Exchange Rate Policy* (1979).

[53] M. Camps, *Britain and the European Community, 1955-1963* (1964) and *European*

The United Kingdom attempted to gain associate status at the foundation, offering an internal free-trade area without full economic integration, but this was turned down. In the event, the EEC countries made immense economic progress in the years after the signing of the Treaty, although it is open to doubt how far this was as a result of it or how far they merely continued their earlier fast growth.[54] The large and expanding market among the 'Six' not only stimulated trade among the members, but even offered a market to British exporters which, in spite of the increasing tariff discrimination implicit in the Treaty, grew faster and became more important than any other.[55] The temptation to apply for full membership proved irresistible in the United Kingdom, despite many misgivings expressed in various quarters, but two attempts to join, in 1961–3 and in 1966–7, were turned down by French veto.

Meanwhile, after refusing to sign the Rome Treaty, the United Kingdom proceeded with her own proposal of a free-trade area, involving the abolition of tariffs and trading restrictions among the members, but not the harmonization of their tariffs against others, or of any other economic or social policies. In 1959 she was instrumental in setting up the European Free Trade Area, the 'Seven', by the Stockholm Convention. The other members were the three Western Scandinavian countries, Switzerland and Austria, both of whom were reluctant to imperil their status of neutrality by joining the EEC, and, somewhat incongruously, Portugal.[56] Finland became associated with them in 1961. The political and geographical viability of EFTA was much less obvious than that of the EEC. The 15% surcharge on imports imposed by the United Kingdom in 1964 without prior consultation caused grave offence, and it was clear that the United Kingdom and some other members were prepared to jettison EFTA as soon as the British attempts to enter the EEC succeeded. Nevertheless, the internal tariff reductions were kept in line with those of the EEC to advance to full free trade by the end of 1966 instead of 1969, and, given the existence of one trading block, the members found clear advantages in belonging to another block with a population of nearly 100 million, a large proportion of whom enjoyed a very high standard of living.[57] There was some mutual adjustment of trade, some specialization and some investment among the members which possibly might not have come about without EFTA's existence. In the first 10 years 1959–69, intra-EFTA trade rose by 186% (exports f.o.b.) compared with a rise of 108% of imports and 111% of exports from and to non-EFTA countries. Britain's overall export figures, it has been estimated, were 2% higher than they would otherwise have been owing to EFTA.[58] For

Unification in the Sixties. From the Veto to the Crisis (1967); U. Kitzinger, *The Politics and Economics of European Integration* (1962); J. F. Deniau, *The Common Market. Its Structure and Purpose* (1960); Sidney Dell, *Trade Blocs and Common Markets* (1963).

[54] A. Lamfalussy, 'Europe's Progress: Due to Common Market?', *Lloyds Bank Review*, 62 (1961).

[55] S. J. Wells, 'Trade with Europe', *Scot. J. Pol. Econ.*, 13/1 (1966).

[56] F. V. Meyer, *The Seven* (1960); EFTA, *A Free Trade Area in Europe* (Geneva, 1966).

[57] *EFTA Trade 1959–1966* (Geneva, 1968); S. J. Wells, 'EFTA – The End of the Transition', *Lloyds Bank Review*, 82 (1966).

[58] M. A. G. van Meerhaege, *International Economic Institutions* (2nd. ed., 1971), p. 355; EFTA Secretariat, *The Effects of EFTA on the Economies of the Member States* (Geneva, 1969), p. 162.

the time being, the United Kingdom tariff level against outside countries remained not only considerably higher than the common EEC tariff, but even exceeded that of the protectionist United States.

Nevertheless, despite the two earlier rejections, Britain began in 1969 a renewed series of negotiations which ultimately led to her accession to the EEC as from 1 January 1973. With her also joined Denmark and the Irish Republic; Norway, which had also been accepted, withdrew as the result of an adverse referendum. The Six thus became the Nine (increasing to the Ten with the accession of Greece in 1981) while only a rump of EFTA remained in being linked by special treaties in an industrial free-trade system with the EEC.[59] By the Treaty of Accession signed in 1972, Britain became simultaneously a party of EURATOM, and a decision of the Council of Ministers also made her a member of the European Coal and Steel Community.

In the midst of her negotiations for entry, the Community itself attempted to strengthen its bonds by a progressive harmonization of the one major economic sphere still left outside its purview, the monetary sphere. It agreed to a locking of the members' currencies to each other within a much narrower band of variation than had been fixed by the Smithsonian agreement of December 1971 (the 'snake in the tunnel', April 1972) with a view to a complete monetary union by 1980. Britain was unable to keep the weakened pound within the snake for more than a few weeks, and also stayed outside the renewed attempt at fixing the European exchange rates to each other, the European Monetary System (EMS) of 1979.[60] In trade matters, tariffs on industrial goods were progressively adjusted over four years, so that Britain obtained completely free trade with the EEC and a common tariff to the outside world by 1977; the agricultural policies were similarly progressively adjusted,[61] and by 1979 the full adjustment to the Community budget had been achieved.

The effects of joining the Common Market have been much disputed. They are not easy to establish, in part because of the other major simultaneous jolts suffered by the British economy since 1973, and in part because it must forever remain unknown how Britain would have fared had she stayed outside.

It was understood from the beginning that linking up with the western European economies represented for Britain a major switch from the centuries-old position as the intermediary between the colonial and overseas world on the one hand, and the continent on the other, on which British wealth and power had been built up. It meant an end to cheap food, drawn from the extensive agriculture of Australia, New Zealand and the Americas, in favour of dear food, produced by the European peasantry, it meant a loss of old-established preferences overseas and in consequence a forced

[59] Victoria Curzon, *The Essentials of Economic Integration* (1974), pp. 226 *et seq.*

[60] R. Jenkins, 'European Monetary Union', *Lloyds Bank Review* (Jan. 1978); Michele Fratianni and Theo Peeters, *One Money for Europe* (1978); Dennis Swann, 'The European Community Dimension', in W. P. J. Maunder (ed.), *The British Economy in the 1970s* (1980), pp. 284 ff.

[61] See pp. 278–80 above.

diversion of industrial exports and probably also capital exports from their wonted extra-European destinations into the bitterly competitive markets within the EEC. At the same time the highly efficient industries of Western Europe would obtain free access to the British home markets. The immediate effects of all this would undoubtedly be a decline in living standards, a deterioration of the current account balance and possibly also of the capital account balance, with various other associated adverse effects; but it was hoped that these would be more than counterbalanced in the longer run by the faster growth and the dynamic atmosphere of the EEC and the economies of scale which almost 200 million additional consumers would provide. Efficient firms would benefit, inefficient ones would go to the wall, and this would jog many firms out of their current inefficiency.[62]

In the event, the diversion of trade was less than had been assumed: it seems that most of the adjustment effects had been exhausted by the Six before the British entry, by which time they had raised the share of their mutual trade from one-third in 1958 to one-half. Moreover, even before entry, trade with the EEC had been growing at the expense of trade within the Commonwealth. Nevertheless, while British exports to the EEC had been rising by an average of 12·5% a year in 1969–73 and imports thence by 17·7%, in the years of adjustment to full internal free trade they rose by 25·7% and 28·5% a year respectively. Also, European food prices were rising less fast than world prices, so that here, too, the effects were less than had been feared.[63] British trade flows were in any case disturbed in the later 1970s by the impact of North Sea oil.

Moreover, internal tariff-free trade within the Community did by no means mean the removal of all trade barriers, as the queues of trucks at all European frontier posts will testify, and 'harmonization' was far from perfect.[64] Subsidies and other obstructions, including preferences in public tendering, more or less hidden, persisted. Official complaints about non-tariff barriers numbered 70 in 1970, 114 in 1974 and topped 300 by the end of the decade.[65] VAT rates remained different, and a complex 'destination system' had to be devised to eliminate distortions arising therefrom.[66] There was much illicit traffic across the intra-EEC frontiers to cash in on these anomalies. In some cases, industry erected its own barriers: possibly the best-known case was that of the motor manufacturers, who by the early 1980s

[62] *Britain and the European Communities: An Economic Assessment*, Cmnd. 4289 (1970); *The United Kingdom and the European Communities*, Cmnd. 4715 (1971); Robert L. Pfaltzgraff. Jr, *Britain Faces Europe* (Philadelphia, 1969), chapters 4, 7, 8; (Overseas Development Institute), *Britain, the EEC and the Third World* (New York, 1972); Douglas Evans (ed.), *Destiny or Delusion: Britain and the Common Market* (1971); A. D. Morgan, 'Commercial Policy', in F. T. Blackaby (ed.), *British Economic Policy 1960–74* (Cambridge, 1978).

[63] A. R. Prest and D. J. Coppock, *The UK Economy* (1978), pp. 156–7.

[64] C. C. Twitchett (ed.), *Harmonisation in the EEC* (1980).

[65] Fratianni and Peeters, p. 14; EEC Commission, *Programme of the Commission for 1977* (Brussels, 1977); Alexis P. Jacquemin, 'European Industrial Policy and Competition', in Peter Coffey (ed.), *Economic Policies of the Common Market* (1979); D. L. McLachlan and D. Swann, *Competition Policy in the European Community* (1967), chapters 3 and 4.

[66] Dennis Swann *loc. cit.*, p. 283; Alan R. Prest, 'Fiscal Policy', in Peter Coffey, *op. cit.*, pp. 69–97; A. E. Walsh and John Paxton, *The Structure and Development of the Common Market* (1968), chapter 6.

were maintaining new car prices in Britain about one-third above prices elsewhere in the EEC.

On the other hand, there were plans to have the corporation tax system of the member countries aligned; the EC law on monopolies was given precedence over the legislation of individual countries, as was the legislation on labelling, design and composition; and in 1977–9 the UK abolished all restrictions on capital movements. As far as movement of labour across the frontiers was concerned, restrictions had been dismantled in the early years of the EEC so that there was no discrimination in access to jobs or social security benefits. Yet some disadvantages of the immigrant worker inevitably remained: access to subsidized housing depending on length of residence, knowledge of legal entitlement, the language barrier. Moreover, discrimination on grounds of public health, public order, or within the State service was permitted. By 1976 a start was made on easing the migration of the self-employed by recognizing professional qualifications gained abroad: thus doctors wholly trained within the EEC were allowed to practice anywhere within it from 1977, dentists from 1978 and nurses from 1980.[67]

The EEC has also taken common action on economic relations with the outside world, notably the USA, Japan and the former colonial possessions of its member states, and on political issues, such as the 1975 Helsinki Conference on Security and Co-operation in Europe and on the Arab-Israeli conflict.[68] The impact of this collaboration is difficult to quantify, though there can be no doubt that at least diplomatically, a unit comparable in size with the USA or the Soviet Union must carry more weight than the several member states would do individually.

In the public debate in Britain, however, what appears to have weighed most heavily was the effect of the EC budget, for here the figures are clear-cut and easily intelligible. Here, after an initial period of adjustment, the UK was to take her full share from 1979 onward. The income of the Community is made up of 90% of the proceeds of the common external tariff and of the levies on food imports (the remainder being held back as costs of collection), plus the equivalent of 1% of VAT receipts.[69] Of the expenditure, Britain stood to gain by net inward payments from the Regional Fund, of the order of £60 million in 1975–7 (compared with £500 million spent out of home funds for the same purpose) and by net inward payments to the Social Fund, of a similar order of magnitude. There is also the Investment Bank which has loaned Britain about £2 billion in 1973–81. These, and some minor items, were however wholly swamped by the EEC expenditure on agriculture. Ratios in 1978 were as follows:[70]

Agriculture	73·87%
Social sector	4·52%
Regional sector	4·25%

[67] C. C. Twitchett, 'The EEC and European Co-operation', in K. J. Twitchett (ed.), *European Co-operation Today* (1980), p. 67; Peter Coffey, 'Social Policy', in *idem, op. cit.* pp. 52–68.

[68] Kenneth J. Twitchett (ed.), *Europe and the World: the External Relations of the Common Market* (1976); Ph. P. Everts, *The European Community in the World* (Rotterdam, 1972).

[69] Peter Maunder, 'International Trade', in *idem, British Economy*, p. 275.

[70] C. C. Twitchett, 'EEC', p. 63.

Agriculture had become the tail to wag the EEC dog and it was here, because of her high imports, and her small but efficient agriculture, that Britain stood to pay in much more, and get back far less than her 'fair' share.

As early as 1977, the Treasury had forecast *net* outpayments, by 1980, of £830 million; before long it was clear that, if uncorrected, they would be well over £1,000 million a year by then. The Dublin summit of 1975 had agreed to a 'corrective mechanism' to provide refunds to members paying in more than their share of the budget, but it was of a minor nature only. The main problem remained: only Germany and the UK made net in-payments, and the UK, as one of the poorest members of the Community, felt this imposition to be particularly unjust. In 1980 it was agreed once more to reduce the British net contribution for 1980 and 1981, but the basic problems of the bottomless pit of agricultural payments, and of the inequitable share of the UK, have not been solved.

The OEEC, having been formed to distribute the Marshall Plan funds, remained as a permanent organization of the Western, mainly industrialized nations. In its early days it helped to set up the EPU (see below) and to liberalize trade among the member states. Re-named Organization for Economic Co-operation and Development (OECD) in 1960, its economic functions remained limited to the co-ordination of information, the harmonization of economic policies in such fields as foreign aid and exchange of scientific information, and generally the provision of a forum for discussion.[71]

More significant was the European co-operation in the monetary sphere. Bretton Woods had ushered in a long period of stable or fixed exchange rates, to be changed only rarely under great pressure,[72] as in the case of the sterling devaluations of 1949 and 1967, and had provided a buffer of international credit to maintain them; however, the effective reality then had been a severe dollar shortage in Europe[73] which caused each country to hoard its 'hard' currencies and thus to restrict international monetary transactions even with countries whose currency was not in short supply. In 1950 the European Payments Union (EPU) was formed to get round this problem by setting up what was in effect a form of European clearing, in which all the debits and credits of each country with all the others were settled as a single monthly sum, in US dollars or 'credits' with the Bank for International Settlements. Trade between them could therefore expand irrespective of the general shortage of American or Canadian dollars.

Rapid recovery in Europe and the positive balances of payments of most OEEC countries soon made such limitation unnecessary. In 1958 the EPU

---

[71] Meerhaeghe, pp. 203, 213; D. Mallet, 'The History and Structure of OEEC', *European Yearbook*, 1 (1955), pp. 62–70; A. S. Miller, 'The Organisation for Economic Co-operation and Development', *Yearbook of World Affairs*, 17 (1963), pp. 80–95; OECD, *OECD – History, Aims, Structure* (Paris, 1971); Henry G. Aubrey, *Atlantic Economic Co-operation: The Case of the OECD*, (New York, 1967); Michele Fratianni and John C. Pattinson, *The Economics of the OECD* (Amsterdam, New York, 1976), pp. 75–140.

[72] See pp. 232–3 above.

[73] Donald McDougall, 'A Lecture on the Dollar Problem', in *Studies in Political Economy*, vol. 2 (1975), pp. 81–98, and *The World Dollar Problem* (1957).

was dissolved and foreign payments liberalized: the UK too, made non-resident sterling officially convertible into US dollars, and the regulations applying to hard and soft currency areas coalesced. But as the world boom developed in the 1950s and 1960s, as trade greatly expanded and prices rose, the ever mounting sum of monetary transactions had to be pyramided on what was basically a fixed metallic reserve, the gold in the IMF and in the banks of member countries, and the US dollar, also tied to gold. The strains which arose therefrom[74] were greatly aggravated by the fact that the system was designed, at best, to deal with temporary unbalances, but had in practice also to accommodate the payments problems of countries that were permanently or structurally out of balance, the United Kingdom being the leading example.

This world monetary reserve problem was dealt with in two ways. The first was what turned out to be a continuous balance of payments deficit of the United States, caused by her vast military and 'political' expenditure in excess of the surpluses earned in her trading activities. At first the mounting annual outflow of dollars was eagerly absorbed everywhere and by the end of the 1950s it had ended the dollar shortage. It then continued into the 1960s with undiminished force, so that not only dollars, but also the gold reserve began to leave America and be redistributed among the central banks of other countries. As the American holdings of gold fell from $20 billion in 1958 to $11·9 billion in 1969,[75] other countries could expand their gold holdings accordingly and increase the quantity of their own currency on the base of their added gold and dollar reserves, while the USA had no fewer dollars circulating than before.

The world reserve problem was eased thereby, but concern grew regarding the position of the USA. The outflow was ultimately to overwhelm the United States and topple the dollar from its gold parity. Meanwhile, however, the dollar kept up its value, and the United States had to live with an increasingly overvalued currency, in spite of the ever larger quantities of dollars in the world's banking vaults, precisely because it continued to be sought after as reserve currency (sterling having lost that role) and as a store of value. These demands helped to keep up both its exchange rate and the belief in its further stability in a mutually reinforcing market opinion – until both were to collapse in the early 1970s. Until then, the falling value of the dollar against gold on the open markets forced the eight 'gold pool' countries to confine their action to hold the dollar to $35 per ounce to that part of the metal held by central banks; gold elsewhere was allowed to appreciate in what became in effect a two-tier system.[76]

The other remedy was the increasing willingness of the major states to come to the aid of deficit countries. In 1961 10 leading members of the IMF, the 'Group of Ten' (11 in 1963 with the addition of Switzerland) offered to

[74] There is a large literature. See, e.g. H. G. Grubel, *World Monetary Reform* (1964); R. Triffin, *The International Monetary System* (New York, 1968); *idem, Gold and the Dollar Crisis* (New Haven, 1960) and *The World Money Maze* (New Haven, 1966).

[75] Brian Tew, *The Evolution of the International Monetary System 1945–81* (1982), pp. 52, 104; US Department of Commerce, *Survey of Current Business* (Monthly).

[76] Robert Solomon, *The International Monetary System, 1945–1976: An Insider's View* (New York, 1977), pp. 114–19.

make additional quotas of $6 billion available to the IMF for temporary credits in the General Agreement to Borrow (GAB). The IMF itself raised its quotas in 1959 and 1966, so that, with the aid of the quotas granted in the same period to new members, its total rose from $9·2 billion at the end of 1958 to $21·3 billion at the end of the 1960s. There was also the 'swap' agreement between the USA and 14 other countries to make available lines of credit to each other of up to $20 billion for up to three months. In 1969 the IMF devised its 'Special Drawing Right' (SDR) scheme to extend the credit facilities for deficit countries by $3·5 billion in 1970 and $3 billion each in 1970 and 1971, to be more readily available than the standard credits. Finally, by the Jamaica Rules of 1976, effective from 1978, there was a further increase of one-third in all IMF quotas. Within the EEC short-term as well as medium term credit facilities were developed in the early 1970s.

Yet none of this could help the ailing dollar, and in 1971 the Bretton Woods system finally collapsed. Following exceptional balance of payments deficits of the USA of $10 billion in 1970 and $30 billion in 1971,[77] and concomitant increases in official US liabilities to foreign holders of $8 billion and $27 billion respectively,[78] America went off gold in August 1971 and the world was once more without a metallic standard. In order to avert the threat of uncontrolled fluctuations, the major countries concluded the 'Smithsonian Agreement' in Washington in December of that year to keep their currency fluctuations within a narrow band of each other after taking into account the fall of the dollar from $35 to $38 per ounce of gold, or by 8·6%. The EEC was more ambitious, narrowing the percentages within which its currencies could fluctuate even more, and thus, as noted above, aiming for what was picturesquely called the 'snake in the tunnel'.

Neither scheme held for very long. The dollar, once more under pressure in 1972, was further devalued in February 1973 from $38 to $42·2 per ounce (the commercial value being by then more like $100) and in a further crisis in the following month, all the major currencies floated away from it. The 'snake', which Denmark, Ireland and the UK had joined in May 1972, was left by the latter only a month later, when sterling was allowed to float. The other weaker members also left and re-joined in bewildering sequence, so that at the start of the EMS in 1979[79] only Germany, Denmark, Norway and the Benelux countries were still in membership. The attempt by the 'Committee of Twenty' in 1972–4 to re-establish some kind of firm new monetary standard also failed in the midst of a major phase of world inflation.[80]

As the world's major currencies were thus afloat, held in some reasonable stability to each other only by the unilateral action of individual monetary authorities, they were hit by the OPEC oil price increases which sent shock waves of hitherto unimaginable dimensions through the system. By a fourfold price rise in 1973–4 ($2\frac{1}{2}$-fold if measured against the soaring inflation of industrial goods prices) and a further doubling, measured against

---

[77] Of this latter figure, the genuine deficit amounted to only $10 billion or so. The rest was caused by panicking speculators.

[78] Tew, pp. 142–3.

[79] Above, p. 368.

[80] John Williamson, *The Failure of World Monetary Reform, 1971–4* (Sunbury, 1977).

other prices, in 1979–80, the hitherto poor oil exporters acquired almost overnight far more financial resources than they could possibly absorb in imports
of goods and services. Estimates of the quantities involved are given in Table
8·6.[81]

Table 8·6:   Oil exporters, annual balances, $ billion

				Identified deployment of cash surplus			
	Trade balance	Services and transfers	Current balance	UK	USA	Other, incl. international organizations	Total
1973	19	− 13	6				
1974	84	− 17	67	21·0	11·7	20·5	53·2
1975	54	− 25	29	4·3	9·6	21·3	35·2
1976	64	− 29	35	4·5	12·1	19·2	35·8
1977	65	− 38	27	3·8	7·3	20·6	31·7
1978	44	− 45	− 1	− 1·8	0·9	15·5	14·6
1979	112	− 46	66	17·2	6·8	36·6	60·6
1980	160	− 54	106	17·6	14·5	54·4	86·5

Expressed in a different form, the price rise of 1974 was the equivalent of a
tax of 2% of GNP of the whole of the OECD and exerted a deflationary pressure not unlike the inter-war reparations.[82] It will be seen that just when the
world had, remarkably, learnt to absorb these vast deficits in 1978, it was
floored once more by the increases of 1979–80.

In barely seven years, 1974–80, a total of over $300 billion in the hands of
the oil producers had thus had to be absorbed or 'recycled'. Its distribution
has been estimated as follows ($ billion):

Bank deposits	147
US and UK Government securities	28
Finance supplied to IMF and International Bank for Reconstruction and Development	14
Finance supplied to developing countries	47
Other capital flows	81
	317

Much of this forms an enormous volatile and inflationary mass, threatening
by speculative attack any currency or any money market that shows any sign
of weakness, and similarly boosting currencies considered 'safe', like the
pound sterling as soon as the North Sea oil had begun to flow. That the world
monetary system was capable of absorbing two such shocks shows a remarkable stability and willingness to collaborate among the individual monetary
authorities, a practice no doubt acquired in the boom years after the Second
World War, and in sharp contrast to the inter-war experience. But they did it

[81] Tew. pp. 177—9, based on Bank of England, *Quarterly Bulletin*.
[82] Solomon, p. 292; Thomas Balogh and Andrew Graham, 'The Transfer Problem Revisited:
Analogies between the Reparations Problem and the Problem of the OPEC Surplus', *Oxf. Bull.
Econ. Stat.*, 41/3 (1979), 183–91.

at a price: industrial decline and mass unemployment, especially after the second OPEC increase, on a scale not seen since the 1930s.

3 Finance and the Banking System

Thanks to the heroic efforts of the later 1940s, the immediate danger posed by the high post-war financial liquidity in the British economy had been overcome by the end of the decade. Clearing bank deposits, which had risen nearly tenfold from pre-war days to 1950, were then held steady for three years, and rose by only 50% to 1967, much less than prices; the ratio of net bank deposits to GDP, which had been around 50% in the late 1930s and had risen to a maximum of 65% in 1947, fell steadily to a mere 30% in 1966. Currency circulation was also held at the same level over 1945–50, and afterwards rose less than incomes, and although deposits with acceptance houses and overseas banks rose much faster, these were not large enough to affect appreciably the general liquidity position.[83]

One of the main factors which helped to end the over-heating of the economy was the reduced pressure from the Government, whose borrowing had so much weakened the hands of the monetary policy makers in the 1920s and again in the 1940s. On current account, the Government achieved annual surpluses averaging £450 million a year, and while this was more than counterbalanced by heavy Government capital formation, so that on combined revenue and capital account there was still an annual deficit, it was so small that over much of the period it could be covered by the growth in the net National Savings. The decline of the latter in the mid-1960s, when they increased by only £175 million in the three years to the end of 1967, was not enough to weaken the Government's monetary control, which in any case depended on many other factors. As for short-term borrowing, 'the value of tender Treasury bills outstanding in 1965 was less than the sum of tender bills and Treasury deposit receipts outstanding in 1948', so that there was no floating debt increase either, to weaken monetary control.[84]

It was this more 'normal' money supply situation which allowed the Conservative Government to re-introduce monetary policy, including the bank rate, as the major innovation of the 1950s. After 20 years of a 2% Bank Rate, cheap money ended in 1951 and changes in the rate began to be used vigorously to support Government policies. However, as the long-term position of Britain worsened from 1956 on, the general tendency for the Bank Rate was upward. It never fell below 4% and the crisis rate of 7% was used with increasing frequency, but this medicine (like all the other dosages of restrictiveness) became ever less effective with increasing use.

The Radcliffe Committee Report,[85] one of the most thorough and intelligent examinations of the British Monetary System, was in this respect

---

[83] *Financial Statistics*; London and Cambridge Economic Service, *Key Statistics 1900–1966*, Table M; G. L. Bell and L. S. Berman, 'Changes in the Money Supply in the United Kingdom, 1954 to 1964', *Economica*, 33/130 (1966), p. 149.

[84] W. B. Reddaway, 'Rising Prices for Ever?', *Lloyds Bank Review*, 81 (1966), p. 3; Bell and Berman, p. 163.

[85] *Committee on the Working of the Monetary System*, Cmnd. 827 (1959).

very much a document of the 1950s. The Committee totally failed to see both the slow erosion of the United Kingdom's positive balance of payments, and her failure to keep up competitively with production and productivity increases abroad. Instead, its attention (like that of Montagu Norman in the 1920s) was largely concentrated on protecting the reserve and on suppressing inflation, still thought to be the main danger. Their particular concern was the monetary mechanism by which these aims could be accomplished, particularly in the crisis years of high pressure. In this field they made one of their most valuable contributions by showing that the traditional braking mechanism, the reduction of the 'liquidity' of the banks which forced them, in turn, to restrict their credit, was no longer working efficiently.

One of the main reasons for this was the transactions of the Government itself. Even when the Government finances were in balance, the high level of the floating debt requiring periodic renewal, and the large sums to be borrowed for the capital programme of the nationalized industries, could not be switched off at will when the authorities wished, on general grounds, to reduce the creation of credit. The banking system therefore could compensate for any reduction of liquidity engineered by the authorities, by simply reducing its holdings of Government short-term debt, particularly Treasury Bills, and thus, in effect, force the authorities to restore its former liquid position. Particularly clear cases of this process in the restrictions of 1955 and 1957 were very much in the forefront of the Committee's mind to support their analysis.[86]

Put differently, the Committee were concerned to extend the concept of the 'supply of money', by which the authorities hoped to regulate demand, beyond the cash and bank deposits to which it used to be limited, to a much wider range of alternatives and to 'the state of liquidity of the whole economy'.[87] In those terms, restricting the money supply could always be circumvented by substituting other forms of money. The velocity of circulation was thus practically unlimited, and there was no stable ratio between the quantity of money and the price level.[88] The Committee were also concerned to evolve a mechanism which would limit the effect on home activity of fluctuations caused by changes in the foreign balance, and in general they were aiming for stability rather than, as in recent years, for restriction. For all these reasons they recommended operating on interest rates rather than on the money supply.[89] For a time the Committee's ideas carried all before them.[90] A more passive monetary policy was pursued, and interest rates remained at the centre of the picture for the time being.[91] From the mid-1960s

[86] Charles Kennedy, 'Monetary Policy', in G. D. N. Worswick and P. H. Ady (eds.), *The British Economy in the Nineteen-Fifties* (1962), pp. 310–11; Edward Nevin and E. W. Davis, *The London Clearing Banks* (1970), pp. 261–2.

[87] *Radcliffe Committee*, para. 981.

[88] E. Victor Morgan, 'The Radcliffe Report in the Tradition of Official British Monetary Documents', in D. R. Croome and H. G. Johnson (eds.), *Money in Britain 1959–1969. The Radcliffe Report Ten Years After* (1970), pp. 10–11; *Radcliffe Report*, Para. 391.

[89] *National Institute Economic Review*, No. 99 (Feb. 1982), p. 62.

[90] E.g., W. Manning Dicey, *Money Under Review*, and literature quoted in Worswick and Ady, p. 545.

[91] Douglas Fisher, 'The Objectives of British Monetary Policy, 1951–1964', *Journal of Finance*, 23 (1968) 821–31; Croome and Johnson, p. v.

onward, the restrictive rather than the stabilizing element in monetary policy began once again to become dominant. Moreover, while the problems of 1964-7 were seen to be essentially those of balancing the foreign balance of payments, in the 1970s the target became increasingly to hold back the rate of inflation. The response of Government policy to this was twofold: a gradual, but clearly marked turning away from Keynesian policies towards monetarism, with the control (i.e. reduction in the rate of growth) of the quantity of money as the main target, and linked with this, an emphasis on reducing the Government's deficits, which were once more on the increase.[92]

The move toward monetarism was a world-wide phenomenon, not unconnected with the world-wide acceleration of inflation in the 1970s. Indeed, its acceptance by Britain was speeded up by the monetarist obligations imposed on the British Government by the IMF and other foreign bankers as the price for their loans, and accepted as early as 1967 in the 'letter of intent' by the then Chancellor of the Exchequer in which he promised that the growth of the money supply in 1968 would not exceed its expected growth in 1967. The doctrine itself had been propounded with great verve by the American economist Milton Friedman, on the basis of the experience of the USA: in Britain even its supporters had difficulty in finding proof without complex manipulation of a relationship between the supply of money and the price level.[93] However, a number of British economists embraced the new ideas with enthusiasm and they also came to dominate the economic policies of the Labour Government implicitly after 1976, and those of the Conservative Government explicitly after 1979. A variant or extension of that policy, 'supply side economics', which made use of the weakening of the unions in a period of mass unemployment to raise labour productivity, sell off all that was profitable in the public sector into private hands and generally give market forces a free run,[94] was essentially a feature of the years after 1980. Since, by 1982, the monetarists were claiming success because the inflation rate was down almost to as low a level as they found when thay took over, while the Keynesians pointed to the devastation in the industrial districts and the $3\frac{1}{2}$ million unemployed as signs of failure, any agreement between them on the direction of policy seemed as far distant as an agreement on theory.

With the change in the dominant theory as to how the economy worked and how it could be influenced, there also came a change in the intermediate instrumental targets. Incomes policies, operative until the later 1970s, were finally abandoned.[95] Discussions on whether inflation was due to demand-

[92] Bank of England and Treasury, 'The Operation of Monetary Policy since Radcliffe', in Croome and Johnson, p. 214; Clare Group: 'Macroeconomic Policy in the UK: Is There an Alternative?' *Midland Bank Review* (Autumn-Winter 1981), pp. 7-9.

[93] David Laidler and Michael Parkin, 'The Demand for Money in the United Kingdom 1956-67: Preliminary Estimates', *Manchester School*, 38 (1970), 187-208; also see C. D. Cohen, *British Economic Policy 1960-1969* (1971), p. 135; David Williams, C. A. E. Goodhart, D. H. Gowland, 'Money, Income and Causality: The UK Experience', *Amer. Econ. Rev.*, 66 (1976), 417-23.

[94] David F. Lomax, 'Supply Side Economics: The British Experience', *National Westminster Bank Quarterly Review* (August 1982), 2-15; John Burton, 'The Varieties of Monetarism and their Policy Implications', *Three Banks Review*, 134 (1982) 14-31.

[95] See p. 338 above.

pull or cost-push,[96] the former caused by excessive demand throughout the economy and the latter by price rises of individual factors of production, particularly of labour, came to take second place to the debate about the role of the monetary sphere. Interest switched from the concern over the impact of Government income and expenditure on the national quantities of these flows, typical for the 1960s,[97] to domestic credit expansion (DCE) and ultimately to the money supply and its key subsidiary, the Government's deficit or, more precisely, the Public Sector Borrowing Requirement (PSBR).

On the assumption that the velocity of circulation did not change, and that the massive switches of funds in and out of the country[98] could be ignored, it seemed a reasonable proposition that the quantity of 'money' made available in one phase would determine prices (total transactions[99] divided by quantities) at some time in the future, if only all that was embraced under 'money' could be included in the calculation. Since several alternatives presented themselves, such as M1, M3, or PSL2, each moving in a different way,[100] they gave the monetary authorities, which had begun to announce targets in 1976, the opportunity to switch in their targetry from whichever showed inconvenient results to that which, for the time being, provided a better fit. As for the 'Medium Term Financial Strategy', it 'was born only to be buried (for the time being) under an avalanche of borrowing and its targets were tumbled into the dust'.[101]

A major factor in every monetary expansion was the public authorities' deficit, which had indeed begun to expand in the 1960s, and was growing very rapidly in the 1970s.[102] Control of the PSBR thus became another prime target within the overall monetary strategy.

Yet, in spite of these switches in theory and professed mechanism, the

---

[96] J. C. R. Dow, *The Management of the British Economy 1945–60* (Cambridge, 1965), chapter 13; Thomas Wilson, *Inflation* (Oxford, 1961); P. A. Samuelson and R. M. Solow, 'Analytical Aspects of Anti-Inflation Policy', *Amer. Econ. Rev.*, 50 (1960); Wynne A. H. Godley, *Inflation in the United Kingdom* (University of Cambridge, Department of Applied Economics, Reprint No. 18, 1978), and criticism by Michael Parkin, pp. 476 ff.

[97] E.g. R. W. R. Price, 'Public Expenditure', in F. T. Blackaby (ed.), *British Economic Policy 1960–74* (Cambridge, 1978), pp. 105–7; *Nat. Inst. Econ. Rev.*, 96 (May 1981), 12.

[98] Thus sharp rises in interest rates would attract foreign funds away from the Government to the banks, and force the Government to borrow more from the home banks, thereby *increasing* the money base. K. K. F. Zawadski, *Competition and Credit Control* (Oxford, 1981), pp. 29–30. Also see A. A. Walters, 'The Radcliffe Report – Ten Years After. A Survey of Empirical Evidence', in Croome and Johnson, p. 62.

[99] J. S. Cramer, 'The Volume of Transactions and of Payments in the United Kingdom, 1968–1977', *Oxf. Econ. P.*, 33/2 (1981), 234–55.

[100] % Changes p.a.

	1972–9	1980	1981/I	1981/II	1981/III	1981/IV
PSL2	13·75	13·5	13·5	13·5	14	11 (est)
£M3	14·5	19	18	16·5	16·5	13 (est)
M1	13·5	4	13·5	10·25	12	8 (est)

Nat. Inst. Econ. Rev., 99 (Feb. 1982), 8; also A. R. Prest and D. J. Coppock, *The UK Economy* (1978), p. 105; G. E. J. Dennis, 'Money Supply and its Control', in Peter Maunder (ed.), *The British Economy in the 1970s* (1980), pp. 49–53.

[101] 'Annual Monetary Survey No. 32 – 1980', *Midland Bank Review*, (1981), p. 22; also see *Nat. Inst. Econ. Rev.*, 99 (Feb. 1982), 63.

[102] Below, pp. 396–7.

practical measures taken within the sphere of monetary policy showed very little change, except that, as time went on, the periods of 'restraint' and 'restrictions' became longer, the expansion periods between them shorter, and the squeeze to be exerted, stronger. This was so even though the end of fixed exchange rates in 1972 gave the authorities considerably more freedom of manoeuvre. Tighter policies meant that there had to be created a whole battery of measures to stiffen the traditional policies of choking off demand for credit by higher interest rates, and the supply of funds, by open market operations. Moreover, even in the early 1960s the need to manage the Government's debt operations made it advisable to supplement interest rate policy with other weapons. To this new armoury we must now turn.

Before the concept of 'money' had been widened by Radcliffe and in subsequent experience, the authorities' main concern was to control the London clearing banks, together with the Scottish and Northern Irish equivalent institutions. To ensure that traditional central bank measures would work, there had to be some stability in the reserve ratios. The long-established cash ratio of 8% was accepted in the 1950s as appropriate, and would give the authorities some control over short-term rates. For total reserves, the Bank of England had in 1951 named 28–32% as the expected ratio, with 25% as exceptional minimum. By 1955, 30% was regarded as the normal minimum, but in 1963, when the banks were under liquidity pressure at a time when the authorities did not want to restrict credit, the minimum was lowered to 28%.[103]

Meanwhile a new method of control, the 'Special Deposit', was introduced in 1960. This gave the authorities the power to require the clearing banks to deposit a certain proportion of their gross deposits with the Bank of England, thus reducing their liquidity ratio by an equal amount, and reducing their power to lend, by a multiple of that sum. Imposed in 1% and $\frac{1}{2}$% rates at a time, Special Deposits quickly reached an early peak of 3% in September 1961, and later peaks of $3\frac{1}{2}$% in October 1970 and 6% in November 1973. The rapid changes in the rates showed that the authorities used them as an important part of their armoury, but in 1967 the Bank announced that it would use them more flexibly rather than as a crisis measure. However, the joint-stock banks were able greatly to weaken its impact by selling their investments and continuing their advances,[104] so that the Chancellor soon had to revert to exhortations, directives and the crude upper ceilings for bank lendings[105] when he wanted to reduce the amount of credit in the economy.

There were also periods of restrictions of new issues by the Capital Issues Committee, and the occasional restriction on Building Society lending, a rapidly growing mechanism of finance. Insurance funds, another important source of finance, could not be controlled. Curiously, one of the most effective means to be discovered in this period was the restriction of

---

[103] J. E. Maycock, 'Monetary Policy and the Clearing Banks', in Croome and Johnson, pp. 164–5.

[104] J. E. Wadsworth, 'Bank Ratios Past and Present', in C. R. Whittesley and S. S. G. Wilson (eds.), *Essays in Money and Banking in Honour of R. S. Sayers* (Oxford, 1968), pp. 244–5.

[105] J. H. B. Tew, 'Monetary Policy I', in Blackaby, *op. cit.*, pp. 219–224, 237; M. J. Artis, 'Monetary Policy II', *ibid.*, p. 261; J. C. R. Dow, *op. cit.*, p. 240.

hire-purchase terms, partly because of the rapid growth of this method of finance, and partly since it took effect much more quickly and directly than any of the other methods:[106] 'If we look at the actual experience of the 1950s . . . we come to the conclusion that the really quick substantial effects were secured by hire-purchase controls, just those which have the most concentrated directional effects.'[107] Further, while the other methods largely cut investment, hire-purchase control largely cut consumption, though it also affected the finance of smaller firms, and it was thus the one method which did no long-term damage to the economy. In the 1950s and 1960s, every major 'package' of restrictive or relaxing measures contained statutory changes in hire-purchase provisions. The advantages of such methods, which both worked at once and hit the right section of the economy, were evident, but on the whole the Treasury preferred to stick to controls which worked through the City rather than 'directly'.

Altogether, there was thus built up in the 1950s and 1960s an impressive array of monetary weapons, grouped around the Bank Rate, with which the authorities could hope to determine their alternating policies of squeezes and relaxations. Yet in spite of it, control seemed always to slip out of the Treasury's grasp, as the money market developed new methods and institutions and as market conditions changed. Examples quoted above[108] show some of the ways in which traditional methods of control became counterproductive. It did not help much – though it afforded a certain amount of relief – that the quantity of Treasury Bills in the hands of the market rapidly declined in the 1960s, to be replaced by commercial bills, and that the gilt-edged market constantly 'slid downwards'.[109] Moreover, the more comprehensive and efficient the restrictions on the clearing banks, the more rapidly business by-passed them by turning to other institutions where it would escape control, and which were by then expanding rapidly above all in what became known as parallel money markets. Thus between 1958 and 1968, the share of deposits held by the clearing banks (including the Scottish and Northern Irish equivalents) had shrunk from 43·5% to a mere 27·4% of the total, whereas the share of British overseas, Commonwealth and foreign banks had risen in the same years from 4·7% to 26·4% or from little more than a tenth of the former, to virtual equality.[110]

It was therefore becoming clear that new operational methods were needed to allow the Government's monetary policy to remain effective within an

[106] J. K. S. Gandhi, 'Estimates of Hire Purchase and its Finance, 1948–1957' *Bull. Oxf. Inst. Stat.*, 28/4 (1966); Dow, pp. 246–8; J. H. B. Tew, *loc. cit.*, pp. 226, 251; M. J. Artis, *loc. cit.*, p. 267.

[107] *Radcliffe Committee*, para 472.

[108] P. 376. Also Douglas Fisher, 'The Instruments of Monetary Policy and the Generalized Trade-Off Function for Britain, 1955–1968', *Manchester School*, 38 (1970), 209–22; N. J. Gibson, 'Special Deposits as an Instrument of Monetary Policy', *ibid.* 32/3 (1964); C. D. Cohen, pp. 119–25; 'Annual Monetary Survey No. 32 – 1980', *Midland Bank Review* (1981), p. 10; F. P. R. Brechling and R. G. Lipsey, 'Trade Credit and Monetary Policy', *Econ. J.*, 73/4 (1963), 618–41.

[109] Nevin and Davis, *op. cit.*, p. 273; Maycock, p. 184; E. R. Shaw, *The London Money Market* (1978), pp. 20–1.

[110] I. R. J. Clark, 'The UK Financial Sector Since Radcliffe', in Croome and Johnson, p. 134.

evolving money market. The most important step in that direction was taken by the Bank of England in 1971 with a peckage of new practices summarized in a consultative document entitled *Competition and Credit Control*.[111] Its object was simultaneously to further a 'more competitive and innovatory attitude',[112] and to strengthen the Government's control over the market. To this end, the 'cartel' of interest rates among the banks was to be cancelled, and banks were to be free to vary their rates and thus also to gain some initiative as against the rest of the London Money Market. At the same time the official ceilings on bank lendings were to be abolished, but the banks were to hold $12\frac{1}{2}\%$ of 'eligible reserves' and the finance houses 10%, with an additional $1\frac{1}{2}\%$ for the London clearing banks held at the Bank of England. In other respects all financial institutions were to be treated alike. In a further set of innovations, the members of the London Discount Market agreed to keep at least 50% of their borrowed funds in public sector debt (altered later to an obligation not to extend their *non*-public sector debt beyond 20 times their capital plus reserves); they would continue to take all Treasury Bills offered, but at individual instead of syndicated prices; and for this, the Bank of England would continue as lender of last resort to them.[113]

It was the hope of the authorities that by these means they could regain full control over interest rates and over funds available, and it was certainly the case that they made the Special Deposits more effective thereby. In 1973 the Bank of England added a further special deposits scheme, known popularly as the 'corset'. Under this, the Bank specified a target rate of growth for interest-bearing 'eligible liabilities', suitably defined, for a given period, and any growth beyond this was subject to progressively higher calls for supplementary interest-free special deposits. This made expansion of the 'eligible liabilities' unprofitable, and clearly, in practice, was responsible for limiting their expansion in the following years: in fact a maximum of 14 institutions out of 360 were ever under penalty at any one time. However, the total effect on the money market was more doubtful. The scheme was abolished in 1980.[114]

Meanwhile, it was also intended that the market should benefit by its greater freedom. The cash reserve limit of 8% for the clearing banks had been abolished[115] and in 1972 the Bank Rate was transformed into the Minimum Lending Rate (MLR), fixed no longer by the Bank, but derived from the average rate of discount of Treasury Bills, plus $\frac{1}{2}\%$ rounded upwards to the nearest $\frac{1}{4}\%$ figure. That experiment, however, was ended in 1978, the control

[111] *B. of Eng. Qtly. Bull.*, 11/2 (1971), 189.

[112] Sir Harold Wilson (Chairman), *Committee To Review the Functioning of Financial Institutions* (henceforth: *Wilson Committee*), *Evidence*, vol. 5, Bank of England written evidence, p. 219.

[113] Zawadzki, pp. 33 ff.; M. J. Artis and J. M. Parkin, 'Competition and Credit Control: A General Appraisal', *The Bankers' Magazine* (September 1971); European Communities, Monetary Committee: *Monetary Policy in the Countries of the European Economic Community*. Supplement 1974: Denmark, Ireland, United Kingdom (II/213/74), Part III: *Monetary Policy Instruments of the United Kingdom*, pp. 12 ff.

[114] Zawadzki, pp. 108–26.

[115] M. D. K. W. Foot, C. A. E. Goodhart, A. C. Hotson, 'Monetary Base Control', *B. of Eng. Qtly, Bull.*, 19/2 (1979), 150.

over the MLR reverted to the directors who again led, rather than followed, the market.

That the bounds of freedom had perhaps been drawn too widely was suggested also by the scandal of the property boom, ending in the so-called 'secondary banking crisis' of 1971–5. It began in 1971 when the expansion fostered by the authorities largely flowed into a highly speculative and basically unsound property market. In 1972 the banks withdrew their direct support, but a number of less sound fringe companies took their place, in turn supported within the inter-bank market, and large profits were made by some speculators. By 1973, however, the international currency crisis and the new 'corset' began to limit liquidity, and a number of the less sound companies involved in the speculation were threatened with collapse, which in turn would have led to widespread havoc in the City. The situation was saved only by the Bank of England which stepped in and with the help of the clearing banks mounted a 'lifeboat operation' in which up to £1,200 million were committed (equal to 40% of the capital and reserves of all the English and Scottish clearing banks) plus additional funds by the Bank of England alone. By 1975 the worst was past. Several property companies went under and some finance companies made large losses, but a major crash was averted.[116] The ease with which city firms, no matter how unsound, had access to banking funds compared with the alleged difficulties of productive industry to obtain finance, attracted much unfavourable comment,[117] but a repetition is unlikely as long as Governments continue to shun expansions and maintain only restrictive practices.

We must now turn to the sources of the savings on which the financial markets were ultimately built up. In the normalization of the monetary system in the 1950s one of the most important developments was the startlingly rapid recovery of personal savings. Their virtual disappearance in the post-war years had been most perturbing and their re-emergence was not only a symbol, but also part cause, of more normal peaceful conditions: the post-war buying spree, the excessive velocity of circulation, had given way to a more balanced disposal of resources. In 1949–51, personal savings were still only 1–2% of GNP, but they jumped almost at once to 5%, and soon after rose to 6–7%.[118] The pressure was at once relieved on Government savings, which fell *pari passu*, while the savings of Companies and of Public Corporations remained at about the same level, the former showing a falling, and the latter a welcome rising tendency.

As Table 8·7 shows, personal savings took a further astonishing upward turn in the course of the 1970s. The average for 1978–80 hides a further rising tendency: measured as a share of all savings, the proportions of personal savings were 47·4% in 1978, 52·6% in 1979 and 60·3% in 1980. Measured as a percentage of real disposable personal incomes, the rates rose as follows:

[116] 'The Secondary Banking Crisis and the Bank of England's Support Operations', *B. of Eng. Qtly. Bull.*, 18/2 (1978), 230–9; *Wilson Committee, Second Stage Evidence*, vol. 4, Bank of England, pp. 97–8.

[117] E.g. *Wilson Committee Progress Report* (1977), p. 13.

[118] Richard Stone, 'Private Saving in Britain, Past, Present and Future' *Manchester School*, 32/2 (1964); *National Income and Expenditure*; R. C. O. Matthews, C. H. Feinstein, J. C. Odling-Smee, *British Economic Growth 1856–1973* (Oxford 1982), pp. 145, 150–1.

Table 8·7: Percentage share in total savings*

	1950	Average 1954–6	Average 1959–61	Average 1970–2	Average 1978–80
Persons	− 2·8	16·5	28·6	27·7	53·4
Companies	53·0	56·5	50·2	41·7	44·3
Public corporations	5·1	6·3	6·5	8·2	10·7
Central and Local Government	42·2	18·3	16·0	29·5	− 5·7
Residual error	2·5	2·5	− 1·3	n.a.	n.a.
Overseas	n.a.	n.a.	n.a.	− 7·1	− 2·8
	100·0	100·0	100·0	100·0	99·9

* *National Income and Expenditure*; W. Beckerman and Associates, *The British Economy in 1975* (Cambridge, 1965), p. 278. The figures refer, with slight variations, to gross savings adjusted by capital transfers and increases in the value of stocks and work in progress, but *before* deduction of gross capital formation.

Average	1962–4	7·7%
	1966–8	8·5
	1970–2	9·3
	1976–8	12·8
	1979	14·7
	1980	15·8

The highest point was in fact reached in the third quarter of 1980, after which the ratio began to decline.[119]

This behaviour on the part of the general public has caused some surprise, since it had been assumed that in times of inflation individuals would try to buy goods rather than hold assets expressed in money terms. The explanation of the increased willingness to save may lie either in the need to hold more liquid assets in line with the price level, a transaction cost argument, or in the ultimate purpose of saving, such as provision for old age, which also requires the accumulated sums to keep pace with inflation.

It is useful in this context to distinguish between contractual savings such as insurance or pension funds, which remained stable in the 1970s, and discretionary savings, which rose from around 40% of the total in the mid-1960s to 60% in the mid-1970s and further still in the later years of the decade. Yet in 1970–7, the inflation loss on liquid assets was actually larger than the discretionary savings of houatholds, so that there was a net loss, but it was more than balanced by the acquisition of housing, pensions and insurance. As a share of personal assets, land, buildings and other physical assets rose from 50·2% to 67·8% between 1966 and 1976, and liquid assets fell correspondingly from one-half to one-third of the total.[120]

[119] Prest and Coppock, p. 289; K. Cuthbertson, 'The Measurement and Behaviour of UK Savings Ratio in the 1970s', *Nat. Inst. Econ. Rev.*, 99 (Feb. 1982), 77; *Economic Trends*. Also see *Wilson Report, Progress Report* (1977), p. 7; Peter Falush, 'The Changing Pattern of Savings', *National Westminster Bank Quarterly Review* (August 1978), 47.

[120] K. Cuthbertson, *passim*; M. E. Blume, *loc. cit.*, pp. 292–8; Richard J. Briston and Richard Dobbins, *The Growth and Impact of Institutional Investors* (1978), p. 124.

There was also a substantial shift in the liquid assets held by the personal sector. The 1950s were marked by a revulsion against Government securities, though this might have been no more than a wish to return to normal after the long years when the Government had absorbed most of the voluntary and involuntary savings made in the economy. The trend was then towards equities and away from all fixed interest securities. This lasted for about 10 years and was followed by a drastic reversal. For the decade 1966-76, the flight out of shares on the part of individuals has been estimated at a net £1·1 billion a year. The shares were largely bought up by insurance and pension funds and other institutional investors (see Table 8·8).[121]

Table 8·8:   Ownership of company shares, in % of market values

	1957	1963	1969	1975
Persons	65·8	54·0	47·4	37·5
Overseas sector	n.a.	7·0	6·6	5·6
UK institutions: Insurance cos.	8·8	10·0	12·2	15·9
Pension funds	3·4	6·4	9·0	16·8
Others	22·0	22·6	24·8	24·2
	100	100	100	100
£ billion	11·6	27·5	37·8	44·6

Meanwhile the companies' internal sources of funds declined, largely because of the decline in trading profits, from 94% in 1952-5 to 84% in 1961-5 and 80% in 1971-6, or, by another calculation, from 64·6% in 1964 to 36·1% in 1974, the gap being made up by recourse to the banks and the capital market, as well as from abroad.[122]

The contribution of the new capital market remained modest. In 1965-6, UK share issues represented only 12·4% of new capital, and by 1975-6 this had dropped to 8·7%. The once popular preference share had virtually disappeared in this total. Equally striking was the collapse of the contribution of loans and mortgages in the capital raised. Instead, joint-stock companies turned to the banks, particularly in the high inflation and interest years of 1973 and 1974, when no less than 41% of their capital needs were raised in that way, but even in 1975-6 this amounted to 13·5% compared with 8·3% in 1965-6. In addition, a newly significant source was the foreign sector, whose share rose steadily from 7·4% to 19·7% in the same years. As a result, the 'gearing' of outside funds over own funds rose rapidly from 0·01 in 1952-4 to 0·16 in 1961-3 and 0·24 in 1974-6 and began to approach the ratios of other countries. The development may be summarized in the figures given in Table 8·9[123] and 8·10.[124]

[121] W. A. Thomas, *The Finance of British Industry 1918-1976* (1978), p. 144; *Wilson Committee, Progress Report* (1977), p. 21; Briston and Dobbins, pp. 122, 139; Blume, p. 294.

[122] Thomas, p. 218; 'Capital Requirements and Industrial Finance', *Midland Bank Review* (February 1976), p. 12; *Wilson Committee, Evidence*, vol. 2 (1977), CBI evidence, p. 10; Matthews, Feinstein and Odling-Smee, pp. 348-9.

[123] *Wilson Committee, Evidence*, vol. 2, p. 21, vol. 5, pp. 53, 61; W. A. Thomas, pp. 155, 311; J. S. Flemming, L. D. D. Price, S. A. Byers, 'The Costs of Capital Finance and Investment', *B. of Eng. Qtly. Bull.*, 16 (June 1976), 202, also *ibid.* 17 (June 1977), 158-9, 19 (June 1979), 185.

[124] T. M. Rybczynski, 'Structural Changes in the Financing of British Industry and their Implications', *National Westminster Bank Quarterly Review* (May, 1982) p. 35.

Table 8·9: Industrial and commercial companies: market valuation of liabilities, %

	1960	1976
Ordinary shares	78·9	59·0
Preference shares	6·7	0·7
Debentures	6·6	6·6
Bank advances	7·8	33·7
	100·0	100·0
Total values, £ billion	25,496	68,563

Table 8·10: Industrial and commercial companies, % share of funds

Averages of cycles	Capital issues at home	Capital issues overseas	Bank borrowings	Other loans and mortgages
1965–9	46·7	2·3	43·2	7·8
1970–3	10·4	2·8	75·4	11·4
1974–9	17·7	0·3	73·8	8·2

The reliance on bank advances posed particular problems for new and small firms, as had been recognized since the days of the Macmillan Committee. In the expansionary decades of the 1950s and 1960s they had little difficulty in raising bank loans, and the Government was also offering aid through the Industrial and Commercial Finance Corporation (ICFC),[125] but in the tougher 1970s they once again complained of discrimination. In particular, banks required more stringent security and charged higher rates, while the small individual investor was discouraged by high tax rates. For longer-term capital, even medium-sized companies found it hard to float new issues. Equity Capital for Industry (1976), supported by 350 financial institutions provided some support, and several new schemes were founded in 1980–2,[126] but the main problem was that the institutional investors were not interested in small companies; yet it was precisely the institutional investors who had come to dominate the capital market in those years.

Among the most significant of them were the insurance companies, as will be evident from Table 8·8. In the 1950s, they reflected the switch into equities and away from gilt-edgeds. According to one calculation, while their total assets rose from £3,108 million in 1950 to £6,610 million in 1960, Government securities held by them increased by only 30% from £1,034 million to £1,332 million, but loan capital (much of it on mortgage secured on real estate) rose from £924 million to £2,285 million, and ordinary shares grew more than fourfold, from £338 million to £1·417 million. In 1964 their equity holdings were up to £2,253 million, and preference shares to £409 million, out of total assets of just over £10,000 million.[127]

[125] P. 400 below, and *Wilson Committee, The Financing of Small Firms*, Cmnd. 7503 (1979).

[126] *Wilson Committee, Progress Report* (1977), pp. 22, 33–7, vol. 3, p. 89, *Evidence*, vol. 2, 110–22, vol. 5 p. 20; Mike Jarrett and Mike Wright, 'New Initiatives in the Financing of Small Firms', *National Westminster Bank Quarterly Review*, (August 1982), 40–52.

[127] Jack Revell, *The Wealth of the Nation* (Cambridge, 1967), pp. 218–19, *passim*; E. V. Morgan, *The Structure of Property Ownership in Great Britain* (Oxford, 1960); *Annual Abstract of Statistics*.

By 1969 their assets had reached £14·2 billion, by 1974, £24·4 billion in book values and £46·8 billion in market values, and at the end of 1979, market values were £52·8 billion. While their holdings of preference shares declined steadily, their heavy buying of ordinary shares reached a peak in 1972, and was replaced by mortgages and loans in 1973 and Government securities in 1975. With an annual net acquisition of £2·5 billion of British funds in those years, they had a substantial influence on capital markets. Their asset distribution changed as shown in Table 8·11.[128]

Table 8·11: Asset distribution of insurance companies

	1966	1979
British government securities	22%	25·6%
Local authority securities	4	1·4
Ordinary shares: British	} 21	{ 23·6
other		{ 4·4
Other shares	20	4·8
Unit trusts	—	1·6
Loans and mortgages	16	6·5
Land, property, ground rents	10	21·4
Other assets, including short term	7	10·7
	100	100

It is noteworthy that around 40% of their business originated abroad, directly or through subsidiaries.

Beside insurance companies, it was Pension Funds that registered the most rapid expansion in the capital market. Together those two groups absorbed £478 million from the personal sector in 1955, £1,173 in 1965 and 10 times that sum, £11,113 in 1980. Assets held by the Pension Funds rose from £4·6 billion in 1963 to £41·3 billion in 1979; those of private funds alone from £4·7 billion in 1970 to £31·5 billion in 1980. They concentrated even more than insurance companies, in fact to the extent of one-half, on ordinary shares, and in the 1970s they became the most important buyers in the market. From 1974 on, following the property collapse, they spread more widely into other securities.[129]

Investment Trusts, among the largest institutional investors at the beginning of our period, expanded more slowly, from £2·8 billion in 1963 to over £7 billion in 1980, of which 39% was held overseas. Unit Trusts provided an alternative mechanism for the public to spread their risks of shareholding: they grew much faster, from £0·35 billion to £6 billion, of which over 15% was held abroad, over the same years. In both cases, around 90% of their assets were in the form of (mostly ordinary) shares, and the rest in Government securities and short-term assets. In 1975 they held 10·3% of the shares of British-registered companies between them.[130]

[128] CSO, *Financial Statistics; B. of Eng. Qtly. Bull.*, 10/4 (1970), 419–22; *Wilson Committee, Evidence* vol. 3, pp. 67–9, *Second Stage Evidence*, vol. 2, pp. 13–17.

[129] *B. of Eng. Qtly. Bull.*, 10/4 (1970), p. 429; Briston and Dobbins, p. 139; *Wilson Committee*, vol. 3, pp. 140–2; and Table 8·8 on p. 384 above.

[130] Briston and Dobbin, pp. 146–7; Wilson Committee, *Second Stage Evidence*, vol. 4, p. 36.

The rising proportion of these large institutions in the ownership of British companies, amounting to 25% in 1966 and 40% in 1975, has given some cause for concern. In view of the dispersal of ownership, often among many thousands of shareholders in the larger companies, an individual institutional shareholder controlling perhaps no more than 1% or 2% of the capital, was in a position to exercise a disproportionate influence; still more decisive would be the action of several of them combined. It has, indeed, become clear that takeover bids, mergers and reconstruction schemes normally need the backing of the institutional investors before they can be undertaken.

The traditional facilities for the small saver have been in decline: thus the Post Office Savings Bank and National Savings between them dropped from 28·5% of all deposits in 1958 to a mere 13·8% 10 years later,[131] but the Government recovered some ground with new offers, including lotteries and index-linked bonds. Nevertheless, their share in savings continued to decline (Table 8·12):[132]

Table 8·12:   Distribution of small savings (%)

	1950	1960	1970	1977
National savings	46	42	29	21
Banks	45	41	35	32
Building societies	9	17	35	47
	100	100	100	100
£ billion	13·4	16·6	28·5	66·3

Altogether in May 1981 National Savings totalled £17 billion and the Trustee Savings Banks, after a drastic phase of amalgamations which reduced their numbers from 67 in 1975 to 16 in 1981, held £5·7 billion of deposits.

Finally, the Building Societies resumed their pre-war triumphant advance immediately after the war, with assets worth under £800 million in 1939, £2,400 million in 1957 and £54 billion in 1980, lending by then at the rate of £10 billion a year in new mortgages. The astonishing expansion in their role as recipients of savings is evident from Table 8·12, but in recent years other institutions, including the banks, have shown an increasing interest in this profitable business. In 1970 the personal sector borrowed a net £158 million, or under 13% for house purchases from institutions other than Building Societies; by 1980 that sum had risen tenfold, to £1,570 million, and represented over 21%.[133]

Housing was in fact, the only private sector which continued to attract finance at the traditional rate by the end of our period, as the huge needs of Government borrowing swamped the capital market. The summary of these changes in Table 8·13 compares 1966 and 1979:[134]

[131] I. R. J. Clark, *op. cit.*, p. 134.

[132] *Wilson Committee*, vol. 3, p. 9 and *Second Stage Evidence*, vol. 3, p. 9.

[133] Margaret Wray, 'Building Society Mortgages and the Housing Market', *Westminster Bank Review* (February 1968), 31, 38; *National Income and Expenditure*.

[134] *Financial Statistics*.

Table 8·13:   Sources and uses of funds, non-bank financial institutions, select major items (£m.)

		1966	1979
Sources:	Deposits in building societies	724	5,769
	Net inflow, life and pension funds	1,241	8,969
	Deposits in trustee and savings banks	} 221	522
	National Savings Bank investment account		326
Uses:	British Government securities	110	6,264
	Local authorities, long-term debt	—	− 130
	UK ordinary shares	} 804	1,824
	Overseas ordinary shares		563
	Loans and mortgages for house purchase	728	5,532
Totals, sources and uses (including other items)		2,340	18,064

In the face of these and other developments it was nevertheless, as we have seen, the joint-stock banks which bore the brunt of the Government's periodic restrictive measures, at least until 1971, while having to adapt at the same time to a rapidly changing environment. They reacted with remarkable flexibility in their practice as well as with organizational changes. Among these a further merger movement stands out. Following the Report No. 34 of the National Board for Prices and Incomes (PIB), *Bank Charges*, in 1967,[135] which stated that the authorities would not object to some bank amalgamations, the National Provincial and the Westminster merged, and soon after the National Commercial Bank (itself a merger of three banks) with the Royal Bank of Scotland. Meanwhile the major English banks had acquired stakes in the Scottish and Irish banks, and the four big clearing banks between them owned the Yorkshire Bank. However, the proposed merger of Lloyds, Barclays and Martins which would have combined nearly 50% of clearing bank deposits was vetoed and only the combination of the last two allowed. The number of London clearing banks was thus reduced from 11 to 6. The large banks also broke with tradition by entering new or expanding types of business, usually by means of subsidiaries, including HP finance, leasing, factoring, Unit Trusts, insurance broking and merchant banking, and were then said to have become more like the 'universal banks' of the continent.

After the war, the transfer from Government to private business had meant a substantial rise of advances as against investments among clearing banks. Among English and Welsh Banks, investments fell from 32·6% of assets (31·3% in Government paper) in 1949–52 to 12·5% (11·2%) in 1964–6, while non-Government loans and discounts rose from 27·3% to 52·3%. By 1980, over two-thirds of their resources were committed to lending (compared with one-third in 1957), but instead of using almost entirely the form of the overdraft, they had developed 'contractual term lending'. As for their sources, these had been expanded far beyond the deposits of their customers by tapping the expanding 'wholesale' inter-bank markets.[136] An

[135] Cmd. 3292 (1967).

[136] *Wilson Committee, Evidence*, vol. 2, pp. 75 ff., vol. 5, pp. 103 ff., vol. 6, pp. 18 ff.; Nevin and Davis, Table 14; T. M. Rybczynski, pp. 31 ff.; Tew, 'Monetary Policy', pp. 241–3; David K. Sheppard, *The Growth and Role of UK Financial Institutions 1880–1962* (1971), pp. 118–19.

interesting new instrument here was the 'Certificate of Deposit' (CD) available from a minimum value of £50,000 upwards, carrying a rate of interest and running for a fixed term, which had several advantages from the point of view of the banks as also of the lender. First used in 1966, the CD's were shown in the balance sheets from 1971 onward and had reached a total of £6 billion by 1973.

Yet these innovations were not able to hold up the rise of a whole new parallel or secondary banking sector to trench into much of the traditional business of the clearing banks. It was made up of the branches of foreign banks in London, of Finance Houses and of other institutions which began to proliferate in the 1960s. While in 1959–65 the deposits of the joint-stock banks rose by 5% a year, those of overseas banks registered 25% and Accepting Houses 20% a year increases. The numbers of overseas banks represented in London rose only from 53 in 1950 (of which 12 were American) to 77 (15) in 1960, but then jumped to 255 (61) in 1976 and 360 in 1981. Their market share of deposits rose from a mere 1·6% in 1958 to 20·2% in 1968. Acceptance Houses concentrated on short-term finance of which they provided £2$\frac{1}{2}$ billion (much of it in non-sterling currencies) and £1 billion as acceptance credit in January 1977, plus £1 billion in medium-term credits of up to 5–7 years within a total of £7$\frac{1}{2}$ billion credit managed by them.[137]

This 'parallel money market', outside the traditional banking and discount markets, developed as shown in Table 8·14.[138]

Table 8·14:   Liabilities outstanding at year-end (£ million)

	1965	1970	1977
Inter-bank market	366	1,694	11,496
Markets in sterling CDs	—	1,089	4,641
Discount market, borrowed funds	1,381	2,259	3,610
Finance house deposits	654	688	809
Local authority temporary debt	1,740	1,879	3,013

Within these growing totals, the business in foreign currencies and with foreign borrowers and lenders, was growing fastest, explaining, in turn, the growing number of foreign banking institutions in London. The most spectacular development here was that of the 'Euro-currencies' in general. The trade in Euro-dollars first became possible on the basis of dollars flowing to Europe as a result of the Marshall plan and the American payments deficit. It developed around 1957 because of the high bank rate and other financial constraints in London in the sterling crisis on the one hand, and because of tax legislation, minimum liquidity provisions and legal interest limitation ('Regulation Q') in the USA. All these could be circumvented by the Euro-dollar trade. Since then it has spread to many other centres, though London has retained perhaps half the total business, it has taken in other currencies, and there has also developed a market in long-term securities, or 'Euro-bonds'.

---

[137] Nevin and Davis, p. 214; *Wilson Committee, Evidence*, vol. 3, p. 75, vol. 5, pp. 1 ff., vol. 8, p. 31; I. R. J. Clark, p. 134, and T. Rybczynski, p. 154, both in Croome and Johnson, *op. cit.*

[138] *Wilson Committee, Second Stage Evidence*, vol. 2, p. 118. Also see E. R. Shaw, p. 80.

The essence of a Euro-dollar deposit (which is generally of a minimum amount of $1 million) as distinct from a ' "national" dollar deposit is that it is the liability of a bank located outside the USA'.[139] As such it can be transferred between foreign (e.g. in the case of the US dollar, non-American) banks and between foreign lenders and borrowers. While at first particularly attractive because it got round irksome restrictions, the system has continued to expand even after 1974 when most of them had fallen away, because it offers favourable rates. It has helped to ease American balance of payments pressure in 1968–9 and to absorb the billions of OPEC surplus petrodollars but at the same time added to the volatility and instability of international speculative switches between currencies, especially in the years 1969–70.

Estimates of its extent are difficult to make, since multiple transfers may lead to double counting to an unknown degree. Widely accepted estimates put the business at $2 billion in 1960, $38 billion in 1970 and $67 billion in 1976. In the 1970s, central banks also entered this market, and the British Government itself borrowed $2·5 billion in the Euro-dollar market in 1973 and $1·5 billion in 1974.[140]

Overseas business liabilities among all the United Kingdom banks together increased from $2 billion in 1964 to £115 billion in 1977; between 1972 and 1976 alone, the share of foreign currency to total deposits rose from $\frac{1}{5}$ to $\frac{1}{3}$. The enormous size of the financial balances, as well as of long-term investments abroad, compared with actual trade in the later 1970s, will be evident from Table 8·2 on p. 359 above. The decline in investment in British industry, in particular, was matched by a sharp rise in direct investment abroad which amounted to £6·4 billion in 1969, excluding oil and insurance, but had risen to £24 billion in 1981 (net asset value); foreign holdings here exceeded £5 billion by then.[141] British currency holdings abroad totalled £10 billion and institutional investors were putting over £1·5 billion a year, or one-fifth of their new money, overseas. Some key annual figures are presented in Table 8·15.[142]

Table 8·15:

	1965	1970	1975	1980
Overseas investment in UK private sector	+238	+725	+1527	+4081
UK private investment overseas	−368	−773	−1367	−6891
Foreign currency borrowing and lending abroad by UK banks (net)	−22	+472	+253	+2024

More striking still was the recourse of the public authorities to foreign markets. Overseas holders of United Kingdom Government stock expanded their holdings as shown in Table 8·16.

[139] Brian Tew, *The Evolution of the International Monetary System 1945–77* (1977), p. 154.

[140] George W. McKenzie, *The Economics of the Euro-Currency System* (1976), pp. 69, 89; *Wilson Committee, Second Stage Evidence*, vol. 2, 117–18, and vol. 4, 33–4; W. Clendenning, *The Euro-Dollar Market* (Oxford, 1970); P. Einzig, *The Euro-Dollar Market* (1973); E. R. Shaw, pp. 94–100; Geoffrey Bell, *The Euro-Dollar Market and the International Financial System* (1973).

[141] T. M. Rybczynzki, 'Structural Changes', p. 27; *Wilson Committee, Evidence*, vol. 3, p. 91, vol. 5, p. 13; *Bank of Eng. Qtly. Bull.*, 21/2 (1981), 203–5.

[142] *Annual Abstract of Statistics*.

Table 8·16:   Market values of UK Government stocks
held overseas at year-end (£ million)

	1977	1980
Held by central monetary inst's	1,341	2,234
Other holders	2,490	3,939
	3,831	6,173

The nationalized industries were similarly urged to borrow abroad, and all the major Public Corporations did so, especially from 1974 onward. Borrowings by the nine Corporations rose as shown in Table 8·17.[143]

Table 8·17:   Borrowings abroad by Public Corporations (£ million)

Total of 5 years	1968–72	281
	1973	64
	1974	1,063
	1975	646
	1976	676
	1977	1,345

By 1978, some £4·3 billion was outstanding from the Public Corporations abroad, plus £0·5 billion by the Local Authorities.

The picture that emerges, then, is a remarkable acceleration in international financial interdependence in the later 1970s. This closer link-up with overseas money markets represents a major departure for the British banking and financial system within a world market in which it is no longer a dominant, though it still remains an important, component.

---

[143] 'An Inventory of UK External Assets and Liabilities: End 1978', *B. of Eng. Qtly. Bull.*, 19 (1979), 163; W. A. Thomas, p. 303.

9

The Government and the Economy

1 Taxation and Fiscal Policy

In the midst of the emergence of new weapons and new techniques of monetary policy, such as were described in the last chapter, the Budget still retained its central importance. The budget speech, yearly at first and, as economic crises forced Governments to have emergency budgets more often, several times a year, provided the keynote of Government plans, indicators of their strategic thinking, and statistics to back them up. The budget retained the traditional roles, such as providing finance for public expenditure, and contributing to such social aims as fairer distribution of incomes and social security. But now its substantive role was to ensure that the call on resources was matched up with the resources available in any one year, both in the economy as a whole and in the separate sectors such as labour, investment or consumption, while at the same time supporting all the other goals of Government economic policy, including full and stable employment, stabilization of the value of the currency at home and of its foreign exchange rate, economic growth and the preservation of the framework and the incentives for private enterprise.[1]

Several technical innovations were introduced into the budget, generally reflecting either immediate needs or long-term changes in policy. Income tax, among the most buoyant and prolific taxes during the two world wars, was largely left alone, the standard rate varying only marginally around the 8 s. in the £ mark. A radical change abolished the 'standard rate' from 1972–3 onward and with it the system of charging lower income bands at lower rates, and substituted the 'basic rate', which dropped correspondingly to 30% from the last standard rate of 38·75%. It rose to a high of 35% in 1975–7, but then declined again to 30% from 1979–80 on. In that year, the top rate was reduced from its high level of 83% to 60% as part of the redistributive trend of Sir Geoffrey Howe's first budget; meanwhile, a lower rate of 25%, 5% below basic, had been introduced again for the bottom band in 1978–9.

The actual impact on incomes of these rates depended, in part, on the allowances, which were raised as inflation eroded their value, but not always fully. Family size and circumstances further altered the picture. The significance of these allowances becomes clear when it is considered that in a typical year, 1973/4, only 45% of aggregate gross income was subject to tax. Over the long term, falling real thresholds, caused by inflation and deliberate

---

[1] I. M. D. Little, 'Fiscal Policy', in G. D. N. Worswick and P. Ady, *The British Economy in the Nineteen-Fifties* (Oxford, 1962), pp. 233–4.

policy, tended to be compensated by lower rates. Table 9·1 provides data for a married couple with two children:[2]

Table 9·1: Impact of tax rates on incomes

	Tax threshold as % of average earnings	Standard/Basic Rate start, as % of average earnings	First rate payable (p. in £)
1955/6	96·0	179·3	9
1965/6	70·5	109·8	15
1979/80	46·8	62·6	25

In view of these complications, it is not easy to determine exactly the movement of the income tax burden on equivalent real incomes over time, but the general trend is clear. Tax rates fell steadily from the early 1950s to a low in the early 1960s, and rose again thereafter erratically, to reach their initial levels in the mid-1970s. In the later 70s they fell again, experiencing a sharp drop in the budget of 1979/80.[3] 'Unearned income' continued to be taxed at higher rates throughout, but with differences in detail. Proposals for what was sometimes termed 'negative income tax', combining social payments with the tax allowance system, or alternatively for expenditure in place of income taxes, were made from time to time,[4] but were not adopted.

Profits taxes were used more flexibly and changed more drastically than taxes on incomes. The gap between distributed and undistributed profits was widened to 50%:10% in Gaitskell's budget of 1951, forming one of the main props of his deflationary policy. In 1952 rates were reduced and henceforth they changed frequently, but the gap remained until 1958, when a single flat rate of 10% was imposed. This equality in tax rates lasted for eight years. In April 1965 a new corporation tax was announced, to come into operation after a year, which had the practical effect of higher rates of taxation on both distributed and undistributed profits, but implied a differential of 24·75% in favour of retention. In 1973 the basis of the corporation tax was changed once more to the 'imputation system', in which all profits, whether distributed or not, were subject to the same tax, which was then deemed to have been paid by the shareholders on their dividends, so that additional taxes were payable by them only to the extent that they were liable to more than the basic rate.

While the differential lasted, it penalized equities as against loans and debentures, it penalized investment by shareholders in new ventures as

[2] David Piachaud, 'Taxation and Social Security', p. 69; also Chris Pond, 'Tax Expenditure and Fiscal Welfare', p. 54, both in Cedric Sandford, Chris Pond and Robert Walker (eds.), *Taxation and Social Policy* (1980).

[3] F. W. Paish, 'Inflation, Personal Incomes and Taxation', *Lloyds Bank Review*, 116 (April 1975), Table 4, p. 14; Joseph A. Pechman, 'Taxation', in Richard E. Caves and Lawrence B. Krause (eds.), *Britain's Economic Performance* (Washington, 1980), Table 10, p. 247.

[4] J. E. Meade (Chairman), *The Structure and Reform of Direct Taxation* (1978); Nicholas Kaldor, *An Expenditure Tax* (1955); *Proposals for a Tax Credit System* (Green Paper), Cmnd. 5116 (1972); David Collard, 'Social Dividend and Negative Income Tax', in Sandford, Pond and Walker, *op.cit.*, pp. 190 ff.; *Report of the Committee on Turnover Taxation*, Cmnd. 2300 (1964).

against capital accumulation in existing companies and it penalized risky investments. The lowering of the tax in 1952 and the abolition of the differential in 1958 were followed by quite significant upward jumps in the proportions of profits distributed in 1953 and in 1959, and thus became significant influences on the post-war patterns of distribution.[5]

Matching the relatively high tax rates, Britain developed a particularly favourable system of investment allowances. 'Initial allowances', permitting accelerated depreciation of capital installed and thus a delay in taxation and a consequent gain in interest charges, had been introduced in 1945 as a method of helping to finance investment. They were suspended in 1951, in the budget which was perhaps the most damaging of all to long-term investment, but reintroduced in 1953.[6] They were subsequently varied frequently with changes in policy, but they were temporarily replaced in 1954 by 'investment allowances', which were true tax exemptions rather than delays, and thus amounted to a direct subsidy. Both have since been used at varying rates. In 1970 'first year allowances' were added in place of investment grants, and from the budget of November 1974 on, substantial allowances on stock appreciation were granted to deal with the distortions caused by the inflation.

A 30% capital gains tax was enacted in 1965, modified substantially in 1971; it was to be levied at the point of disposal of most types of assets. The effects of this tax have been much disputed, but it is widely believed that it discouraged saving and investment.[7] In 1978–9, a special tax was placed on land development gains over £160,000 in lieu of the capital gains tax.

National insurance contributions may be considered as a form of payroll tax. To it was added the Selective Employment Tax (SET) of 15% on payrolls in 1966. It was intended to perform a double function. In addition to the main objective which was to make labour more expensive and encourage labour-saving investment,[8] the tax had a distributional objective which largely cancelled out the first. Only the 'service industries' were to pay the tax effectively; some selected employments (e.g. hospitals) were to have the tax refunded after some delay; but manufacturing firms were in fact to gain more than they paid in. This discriminatory and arbitrary division into productive and unproductive employment ignored the fact that economic progress in general is accompanied by a decline in the primary and secondary industries and a growth of the tertiary occupations, both of which were penalized by the tax, and that in the British circumstances in particular, a penalty on high (labour) costs would have been especially valuable in manufacturing industries working for exports.[9] However, it was based on the notion that the expansion of the labour force in industry was a mainspring of the rise of productivity.[10] The effects of the tax have remained uncertain. To some

[5] Little, p. 237 (footnote); *Royal Commission on the Taxation of Profits and Income, Final Report*, Cmd. 9474 (1955), esp. chapter 20.

[6] Changes are summarized in J. C. R. Dow, *The Management of the British Economy, 1945–1960* (Cambridge, 1965), p. 206; and in Pechman, Table 14, p. 251.

[7] A. R. Prest and D. J. Coppock, *The UK Economy* (1978), pp. 94–5.

[8] J. R. Sargent, *Out of Stagnation* (Fabian Society, 1959).

[9] J. P. Hutton and K. Hartley, 'The Selective Employment Tax and the Labour Market', *British J. of Industrial Relations*, 4/3 (1966).

[10] See pp. 349–50 above.

extent, the distributive impact was met by the budget of 1968, which extended the effective range of the tax to all employees, but exempted the Development Areas. It was abolished in 1973 as part of the major tax reform which included the introduction of the Value Added Tax (VAT).

Expenditure taxes fell into two broad categories. One consisted of items of mass consumption, such as tobacco, alcoholic drinks and fuel oils,[11] all very regressive in their incidence, and all (except for the special oil surcharge following the closing of the Suez Canal in 1956) showing a strong upward 'ratchet' effect, perhaps inevitable under rising prices when duties are specific. By contrast, purchase tax on a broad range of other items, calculated *ad valorem*, moved up and down much more freely. In 1960 the right was granted to the Chancellor to vary during the year, and therefore free from the artificial timing of the budget proposals, purchase tax and excise duties by up to 10% either way. This was estimated to make, at its maximum, a difference of £200 million to revenue. A 10% surcharge was imposed almost at once, and since it was consolidated next year, it left the Chancellor free to use his powers again. The VAT of 1973 replaced the former purchase tax with the difference that it was also levied on services and thus ended the discrimination against commodities, while it had the further advantage that it was easier to remit on exports. Its main purpose, however, was to align the British system with that of the EEC.

There were thus numerous changes affecting the distribution of the tax burden among sections of the community,[12] but in the debate on macro-economic policy, it has been the overall weight of the 'burden' of taxation which has been given importance. Modern Governments have many sources of income beside taxation; further, their range of expenditure, including for example capital investment and subsidies to the nationalized industries, is also much wider than was traditionally the case. These items cannot genuinely be kept apart, so that it has become the practice to include them in the Government sector, distinguishing only between resources used and transfer payments. The items actually included in the literature do, however, differ frequently in detail and comparisons should therefore be made with care.

In general the Second World War had seen a rise in the share of Government expenditure as a proportion of GNP from which, as after the First World War, it did not quite fall back to its pre-war level. This 'ratchet effect' did not apply to local government, which returned after the war to the position of the late 1930s.[13] The total share of both local and central government in the country's economic activity then stayed fairly level, but with a slightly rising tendency which became more pronounced only in the 1970s, to rise to a peak in 1975 and the fall thereafter[14] (see Table 9·2).

---

[11] J. C. R. Dow, 'Fiscal Policy and Monetary Policy as Instruments of Economic Control', *Westminster Bank Review* (August 1960).

[12] See discussion pp. 317–9 above.

[13] Alan T. Peacock and Jack Wiseman, *The Growth of Public Expenditure in the United Kingdom* (1967), pp. 107, 166.

[14] *National Income and Expenditure*; Prest and Coppock, pp. 86–7. Also R. W. R. Price, 'Public Expenditure', in F. T. Blackaby (ed.), *British Economic Policy 1960–74* (Cambridge, 1978), pp. 94 ff.

Table 9·2:   General government expenditure as % of GNP at market prices

	Expenditure on goods and services	Total government expenditure**
1950*	17·7	39·3
1958*	18·6	37·0
1966	21·4	37·7
1970	22·2	40·2
1975	26·7	49·3
1980	23·9	46·0

* Not strictly comparable with the later figures.
** The difference between these two columns is made up of transfer payments.

These shares were very similar to those of other western and industrialized countries, whereas the burden on employers of social payments to be added to their wage roll were in Britain well below the average of others. Nevertheless, the high level of public expenditure (which might, on the part of some critics, include the public corporations) has been repeatedly made responsible for the poor British economic performance.[15] It should be noted that the weight of the National Debt fell sharply because of the inflation, above all in the 1970s, precisely when its increase caused so much public concern: as a proportion of GNP it dropped from 300% in 1945 to 40% in 1975, to rise slightly thereafter. Government, in fact, was a net saver throughout this period, imparting a deflationary bias to the economy, right up to the later 1970s when the deficits predominated. Even then the returns show that while real Government expenditure had been rising by 4·9% a year in 1961–73, it rose by only 0·4% a year in 1973–8, when complaints were loudest.[16]

Table 9·3:   Public authorities income and expenditure (as % of GNP)

	Central government receipts		Public authorities current expenditure, of which:		
	Taxes on income and capital (inc. net insurance contributions)	Taxes on expenditure	Social services	Defence	Debt interest
1950	20·8	14·7	13·6	7·1	4·7
1951	20·0	14·7	12·5	8·6	4·6
1964	18·1	11·5	16·1	6·8	4·4
1965	19·3	12·2	17·1	6·8	4·4
1970	24·3	16·7	23·1	5·6	4·6
1971	23·0	16·0	22·5	5·5	4·2
1979	22·5	18·1	27·1	5·4	5·3
1980	23·8	19·3	28·6	5·9	5·8

[15] E.g. David Smith, 'Public Consumption and Economic Performance', *National Westminster Bank Quarterly Review* (November 1975); Sir Alec Cairncross, 'The Postwar Years 1945–77', in Roderick Floud and Donald McCloskey, *The Economic History of Britain Since 1700*, vol. 2 (Cambridge, 1981), pp. 409–12; Michael Beenstock, 'Taxation and Incentives in the UK', *Lloyds Bank Review*, 134 (October 1979), p. 4; Pechman, pp. 206, 243–5; Robert Bacon and Walter Ellis, *Britain's Economic Problem: Too Few Producers* (1976).
[16] David Higham and Jim Tomlinson, 'Why Do Governments Worry About Inflation?',

Table 9·3[17] shows the major items of income and expenditure. The ratio of taxes on income to taxes on expenditure moved slowly in favour of the latter, but perhaps less than one might have assumed after all the budgetary changes. Among expenditure items, it is the social services that are clearly responsible for the rise overall; defence expenditure came down and debt interest also drifted downward, only to jump in the later 1970s with renewed borrowing and high interest rates.

Fiscal policy was, throughout, one of the instruments with which the authorities sought to 'steer' the economy, in year-to-year or even more frequent changes. Within this sphere of economic management the general assumption until 1963/4 was that taxation was too high, having a negative effect on incentives,[18] so that the budget should be used only in expansionary policies by lowering taxation, whereas if restrictive policies were required, they should operate *via* the financial mechanism only.[19] In the later 1960s and in the mid-1970s, this liberal attitude to the budget was overlaid by the need to raise revenue, but it reappeared to determine Conservative policy in 1970-4. There was thus in existence a medium-term policy enveloping the yearly or shorter switches, quite apart from the fact that fiscal changes tended in any case to work too slowly for the Government's demand management. Besides, their effect could not be gauged precisely,[20] even though towards the end of the period quite sophisticated calculations were made to determine the fiscal 'stance', in other words, to work through what the total effect of tax changes was on employment and the economy in general.[21] Nevertheless, overall the budgets were destabilizing, increasing fluctuations instead of smoothing them out, as indeed was the Government's investment policy for the public sector by itself.[22]

The frequent disturbances of the budget for the sake of short-term policy switches necessarily did damage to the Government's power to perform its remaining tasks of raising revenue and redistributing incomes. It might even reasonably be held that 'it should be regarded as a confession of failure when changes in the level of public expenditure. . . . are made and then reversed on a countercyclical basis', and that changes in public expenditure for the purpose of managing the economy should be used only as a last resort.[23] At the same time, it is worth noting that economic policy, including the 'stop-go' sequence, did in fact largely concern itself with marginal quantities and

National Westminster Bank Quarterly Review (May 1982), p. 4; Andrew Glyn and John Harrison, *The British Economic Disaster* (1980), p. 128; R. C. O. Matthews, 'Why Britain Had Full Employment Since the War', *Econ. J.*, 78 (1968), 556; C. V. Downton, 'The Trend of National Debt in Relation to National Income', *B. of Eng.Qtly.Bull.*, 17/3 (1977), 320.

[17] *National Income and Expenditure.*

[18] Such an effect has never been objectively established. E.g. Pechman, pp. 218 ff.

[19] J. M. Buchanan, 'Easy Budgets and Tight Money', *Lloyds Bank Review*, 64 (April 1962), 17–30.

[20] Prest and Coppock, p. 29; R. W. R. Price, 'Budgetary Policy', in F. T. Blackaby, *Economic Policy*, pp. 139–41.

[21] E.g. *Nat.Inst.Econ.Rev.*, 63 (February 1973), 13 and 96 (May 1981), 12.

[22] C. D. Cohen, *British Economic Policy, 1960–1969* (1971), pp. 82–3; Price, 'Public Expenditure', p. 126. Also see note 111 below.

[23] Ninth Report of the Expenditure Committee, *Public Expenditure, Inflation and the Balance of Payments*, H. C. 328 (1974), para. 19, p. xi.

formed, in the long view, little more than ripples on the gently upward slope of production and incomes. Even the most drastic budget 'package' of all, the measures of 1968, were intended to cut consumption by less than £1 billion in a full year, or 3% of national income. This should be compared with unemployment rates of up to 22% in the 1930s and 12–15% in the early 1980s.

2 Forms of Direct Intervention

Much of the Government's initiative in economic affairs took the form of indirect influence by means of taxation and subsidies, for example, by redistributing incomes through the social services, by tariffs, by controlling financial markets or by maintaining control over the foreign exchanges. The more important measures among these have been described in the preceding sections. In addition, the Government also intervened directly in industry and in other spheres of economic activity. The most immediate form was the control over nationalized industry, discussed in section 2 of chapter 7 above. But there were innumerable other means, many of which were expanded or transformed in our period. This section will deal with a representative sample of them.

After the preference shown for State initiative and economic planning under the Labour Governments of 1945–51, the Conservative administration of the following 13 years emphasized the market and private initiative for industry, and gave industry its 'freedom' in the 1950s. Some innovations of the Labour Government, such as the Development Councils, were allowed to lapse. Direct intervention, such as the titanium agreement with ICI or the decision on the two new steel rolling mills in 1959–60, remained rare and a matter of isolated actions. But by the early 1960s, the signs of weakness of British industry under that regime, such as its slow growth and substantial loss of export markets, could no longer be ignored, and Government turned once again to more direct forms of action. Partly designed to deal with the repeated balance of payments crises, the National Economic Development Council (NEDC, or 'Neddy') began working in 1962 as a common forum on which management, labour and Government and some independents could meet. As such it has been valued by all the participants; prime ministers and chancellors of the exchequer have attended its meetings, and it has survived the economic vicissitudes of the following 20 years to the present. Yet its exact functions and powers have never been clear.[24]

Its first task was to consider obstacles to quicker growth or greater efficiency, and a major report, published within one year, *Growth of the United Kingdom Economy 1961–6*[25] studied the implications of a 4% growth rate (compared with a 3% rate assumed by the Treasury). In December 1963 approval was given for the appointment of specialist industrial Economic Development Committees ('little Neddies'), and 21 of them have been set up, engaged mainly in activities such as economic forecasting, studying the

[24] Richard Bailey, *Managing the British Economy. A Guide to Economic Planning in Britain Since 1962* (1968), pp. 9–36.
[25] Published in February 1963. See also NEDC, *The Growth of the Economy* (1964).

effects of such changes as decimalization, taxation and devaluation, and disseminating and exchanging information of various kinds.

NEDC itself, however, lacked executive powers, and when the incoming Labour Government in 1964 wanted to improve industrial performance and growth, it established a new department under a senior minister, the Department of Economic Affairs (DEA). Behind the founding of the DEA lay the belief that growth had not only not been furthered, but had actually been inhibited by deliberate Government action in the interest of short-term policies, and that a ministry responsible for all economic policies, and therefore superior to the Treasury which was concerned only with fiscal and financial matters, was needed to make long-term growth plans stick. It did, indeed, publish a plan in 1965[26] for a 4% annual growth over five years, but in spite of the enthusiasm of the minister, George Brown, the DEA soon fell victim to the logic of balance of payments deficits and the inherent power of the Treasury.[27] With it fell the only real chance since the war of making growth, expansion and efficiency the major Government economic goal, as the foundation of other economic objectives.

In the month in which the DEA was set up, October 1964, the Ministry of Technology was also created as part of the same drive and it began work in 1965. Among its first objects was the sponsoring of four technological industries: computers, machine tools, electronics and communications. It also took over from the Ministry of Aviation all the functions relating to aircraft production and design. These critical and vulnerable growth industries received the repeated attentions of Government thereafter.

In part, Government support took the form of offering finance and sponsoring reconstruction. In December 1966, following a white paper[28] the Labour Government established the Industrial Reorganization Corporation (IRC) with a capital of £150 million to encourage mergers on grounds of efficiency, and by the Industrial Expansion Act of 1968 it took general powers to finance industrial investment schemes without having to ask for legislation each time. The incoming Conservative Government dissolved the IRC and emasculated the Industrial Expansion Act, but was soon forced once more to commit large sums to rescuing the shipbuilding companies on the Upper Clyde in the form of the reorganized Govan Shipbuilders, and to nationalizing the Rolls Royce company, both having been in danger of bankruptcy. Further, it sponsored the Industry Act of 1972 which included provisions for tax incentives for investment as well as specific grants for capital expenditure in assisted areas and elsewhere.

Labour's Industry Act of 1975 extended these provisions and set up the National Enterprise Board (NEB). This was given large financial means, of up to £1,000 million, to continue the policy of awarding specific assistance and to extend public ownership not only to firms on the point of collapse, but also to profitable companies – a policy of 'backing winners'. It was

[26] *The National Plan*, Cmnd. 2764 (1965).

[27] George Brown, *In My Way* (1971), pp. 95–6, 113, 119; Jacques Leruez, *Economic Planning and Politics in Britain* (1975), pp. 48–9; Roger Opie, 'Economic Planning and Growth', in Wilfred Beckerman (ed.), *The Labour Government's Economic Record 1964–1970* (1972), p. 171.

[28] *Industrial Reorganisation Corporation*, Cmnd. 2889 (1966).

instructed to further industrial democracy in the firms it sponsored and to remain profitable overall, but hopes nursed in some quarters that it would become part of a wider industrial strategy[29] have not been realized. However, some specific influence through the 'Accelerated Projects Scheme' of 1975 to encourage firms to bring investment projects forward in depression years, and the 'Selective Investment Scheme' for projects that would benefit the national economy but would not be undertaken without Government assistance, did remain. Also, so-called 'planning agreements' from 1974 on encouraged firms to exchange information with the Government in return for favourable treatment in assistance measures.

The result of this legislation was a wide net of investments in and subsidization of industrial firms in the 1970s.[30] Approval for the action taken under it was not, however, universal. The Conservative administration of 1979 set out to weaken the role of the NEB and transfer its portfolio to private hands as circumstances permitted, though it found it impossible in practice to keep to its intention of denying further support to old or newly emerging 'lame duck' companies, especially if they were large. In 1979–80, financal aid provided by the Department of Industry totalled £1,060 million, including £540 million for regional and general support, £140 million for scientific and technological assistance and £380 million for manufacturing directly sponsored by the Department, but excluding the nationalized industries.

Finance of a semi-official nature also continued to be available through the Finance Corporation for Industry and the Industrial and Commercial Finance Corporation; these were merged in 1973 to form Finance for Industry (FFI), which was provided by the Bank of England and the Clearing Banks with funds of up to £1,000 million. The Bank of England was also instrumental in setting up a so-called equity bank, Equity Capital for Industry, in 1976, which channelled insurance and pension funds into equities.

As far as policy on industrial location was concerned, the post-war legislation, based on assumptions of massive unemployment, was used less and less in the 1950s when that assumption proved wrong, though northeast Lancashire was added to the Scheduled Development Areas in 1953. Control was further reduced when building licensing was abolished in 1954, but then the recession of 1957–8 provided a new impetus. This was enhanced by the increasing traffic strangulation of London, the South-East and the Midlands, which made location policy necessary for the sake of the congested as well as the depressed areas. By the Distribution of Industry (Industrial Finances) Act, the powers of the Treasury to grant loans or grants for industrial buildings were extended to all forms of business, and to places outside the Development Areas with persistently high unemployment rates of over 4%. A major, consolidating measure in 1960, the Local Employment Act, provided for a new list of localities (Development Districts), based on actual

---

[29] *The Regeneration of British Industry*, Cmnd. 5710 (1974); *An Approach to Industrial Strategy*, Cmnd. 6315 (1975).

[30] Michael C. Fleming, 'Industrial Policy', in Peter Maunder (ed.), *The British Economy in the 1970s* (1980), pp. 145–6; Alan Whiting (ed. for Department of Industry), *The Economics of Industrial Subsidies* (1976); also see pp. 311–2 above.

and potential unemployment of 4·5% or above to qualify for the privileges; some 160 Districts were designated and the list varied from time to time. Grants and loans were to be more freely available also. Among the early successes was the setting up of branches of the main motor manufacturers in those areas.[31]

In the Depression of 1962–3 a Secretary of State for Industry, Trade and Regional Development was appointed to deal with the disturbingly high unemployment figures in the traditional problem areas in Scotland, Wales and northern England. Regional reports worked on the assumption that the solution lay in bringing work to these areas, rather than moving people out of them, and stressed the need for positive incentives and for amenities,[32] but in fact mobility was fairly high, and in 10 years 18% of the population had moved outside their towns, and nearly 7% into another region, mostly to London and the South-East.[33] The real watershed in post-war legislation came with the Local Employment Act of 1963, which provided for grants of 10% for machinery, 25% for buildings, an option of 'free' depreciation, and a more stringent use of Industrial Development Certificates (IDC) in congested areas.[34] Its effectiveness was also increased by the higher total incidence of unemployment.

In July 1965, Regional Planning Councils were set up to co-ordinate industrial and social policies with the needs of whole regions in mind:[35] the object was now 'balanced regional growth' as part of overall planning, rather than curative action after the damage was done. It is doubtful if they had much effect.

The Industrial Development Act of 1966 substituted Development Areas for Development Districts, increasing the coverage to some 20% of the working population; in 1969, following the report of the Hunt Committee,[36] subsidies were extended to the so-called 'Intermediate Areas' with less severe structural and unemployment disadvantages. Finally, in this legislative period, the Regional Employment Premium (REP) was created in 1967, amounting to a subsidy of 5–7% on wages in the favoured areas, in addition to preferential rebates under the SET, which brought the subsidy up to perhaps 8%. The Local Employment Act 1970 designated two new types of area, 'Intermediate (Gray) Areas', and 'Derelict Land Clearance Areas'.[37]

In contrast to the Labour Government of 1964–70, which had seen locational policy as an aid to national economic planning,[38] the Conservative

[31] P. D. Henderson, 'Government and Industry' in Worswick and Ady, pp. 337 *passim*.

[32] See also Colin Clark, 'Industrial Location and Economic Potential', *Lloyds Bank Review*, 82 (1966).

[33] A. J. Harris and R. Claussen (Government Social Survey), *Labour Mobility in Great Britain, 1953–1963*, S. S. 333(1966), pp. 10–3.

[34] A. P. Thirlwall, 'The Local Employment Acts 1960–1963: A Progress Report', *Yorkshire Bulletin*, 18/1 (1966).

[35] Ministry of Labour Gazette; Michael Stewart, *Keynes and After* (Penguin, 1967), p. 157; Paul Burrows, 'Manpower Policy and the Structure of Unemployment in Britain', *Scot.J.Pol.Econ.*, 15/1 (1968), pp. 75–7; G. McCrone, *Regional Policy in Britain* (1969).

[36] Department of Economic Affairs, *The Intermediate Areas*, Cmnd. 3998 (1969).

[37] P. J. Curwen and A. H. Fowler, *Economic Policy* (1976), p. 165.

[38] J. Hardie, 'Regional Policy', in W. Beckerman, *Labour Government*.

administration of 1970–4 was both averse to planning in general, and to supporting individual firms in particular. Investment grants were abolished in the mini-budget of October 1970 and replaced by allowances. IDC and Office Development Permit controls (first brought in in 1964 for London) were relaxed, and the financial grants reduced in total. The depression of 1971–2, however, forced a re-examination of the issue[39] and a return to the broad policies of the late 1960s by means of grants. Thus the Industry Act of 1972 extended the designated Intermediate Areas, so that altogether 44% of the population came under one or other special status;[40] the REP, which it had been intended to abolish in 1974, would now stay; and investment tax allowances in the budget of 1972 were given a strong regional bias.

The Labour Government that followed not only held to that commitment, but actually doubled the rate of subsidy under it. It also gave more power to the regional offices of the Department of Trade and Industry established earlier, extended the designated Development and Special Development Areas, and decided to disperse more Government Departments to the regions. In 1975 and 1976 the Scottish and Welsh Development Agencies, respectively, were set up, to deal with the high unemployment as well as to assuage the apparently growing nationalism of those regions.

Meanwhile, the problems of regional inequality were taking on new, or rather, additional forms, The Census of 1971, the results of which were becoming known in 1976, showed not only the beginning of an overall decline of manufacturing labour, but in particular the migration of industry out of the large cities leaving a pool of unskilled and unemployed labour in the city centres, not only in traditional black spots like Glasgow and Liverpool, but also in formerly prosperous urban communities like Birmingham.[41] The Government reacted in 1977 by a reversal of its previous policies, intending to channel both offices and the vulnerable small workshop industries back to the centres of conurbations, but in fact made little financial provision for this.[42] Since then the social consequences of the economic decay of the inner city areas have become more evident.

Added to this particular problem was the decline, in the later 1970s, of the motor and other engineering industries, causing a more than average rise of unemployment in precisely the formerly most prosperous regions, the West Midlands and the South-East. While this development would in any case have led to weakening support for the traditional recipients of favours, the industrial North and West, two further factors hastened that trend. The first was the greater emphasis on cost cutting employment, which worked against the high-cost Development Areas; and the second was the strong regional policy of the EEC which frowned on the REP as incompatible with its principles, and as keeping alive low-productivity firms. The new Conservative

---

[39] Department of Trade and Industry, *Industrial and Regional Development*, Cmnd. 4942 (1972).

[40] T. Nuttall, 'The Industry Act and Regional Policy', *National Westminster Bank Quarterly Review* (November 1973), 55–68.

[41] Kenneth J. Button, 'Spacial Economic Policy', in Maunder, *British Economy*, p. 178.

[42] Department of the Environment, *A Policy for the Inner Cities*, Cmnd. 6845 (1977); J. S. Foreman-Peck and P. A. Gripaios, 'Inner City Problems and Inner City Policies', *Regional Studies*, 11 (1977).

Government of 1979 added its dislike of all subsidies and of semi-independent 'quangos' which had mushroomed under the numerous regional policies. Thus it announced in 1979 that by means of boundary changes the proportion of the employed population in favoured areas would be cut from over 40% to 25%, and the planned traditional regional aid programme would be cut from £609 million to £376 million by 1982-3. Meanwhile the United Kingdom has received considerable payments from the EEC Regional Fund. They have tended to be for specific projects, and to favour investment rather than subsidizing operating costs.

The new towns legislation should also be mentioned here. Some 20 towns have been built on the basis of the New Towns Act of 1946 and the Town Development Act of 1952, and others enlarged. The object was essentially to relieve the pressure on large conurbations, above all on London, and they have had some success in drawing industry out to the New Towns with the population.

The effectiveness of these regional policies as a whole is hard to gauge. Significant moves of manufacturing industry from the South-East and the West Midlands did take place, but not always to the real deficit regions, and the motives were mixed.[43] Some elements, such as the IDC's and direct subsidies, were undoubtedly effective in locating new factories,[44] but almost by definition they were high-cost units and often among the first to suffer or even close in depressions. The effects of REP were less clear-cut.[45] The principle, taken over from the 1930s, of bringing jobs to people rather than encouraging migration, in order to preserve the social capital of established communities, was no doubt responsible for lowering overall British efficiency, but the likelihood is that apart from certain significant exceptions, these cost effects of location were small.[46] On the other hand, the advantages offered have been largely on investment, which encouraged capital-intensive industries in the favoured areas and thus did little to create jobs. Large differences in regional levels of unemployment remained, and widened as rates rose (see Table 9·4), though it is not possible to say what they would have been had the battery of policies not been adopted.

Finally, a further area of direct Government intervention was the promotion and support of scientific and technological research and training. These had been much boosted by the war and became again a method of improving the poor industrial performance of the 1960s. Government expenditure on

[43] A. J. Brown, *The Framework of Regional Economics in the United Kingdom* (Cambridge, 1972), pp. 250 ff.

[44] J. K. Bowers and A. Gunarwardena, 'Industrial Development Certificates and Regional Policy', parts 1 and 2, *Bulletin of Economic Research*, 29 (1977) 112-22 and 30 (1978) 3-13; B. Ashcroft and J. Taylor, 'The Movement of Manufacturing Industry and the Effect of Regional Policy', *Oxf.Econ.P.*, 29/1 (1977).

[45] K. J. Button, pp. 188-9; also see A. Beacham and T. W. Buck, 'Regional Investment in Manufacturing Industries', *Yorkshire Bulletin*, 22/2 (1970); B. C. Moore and J. Rhodes, 'Evaluating the Effects of British Regional Employment Policy', *Econ.J.*, 83/1 (1973) and *idem*, 'Regional Employment Policy and the Scottish Economy', *Scot.J.Pol.Econ.*, 21/3 (1974); Gavin McCrone, *op.cit.*, pp. 151 ff., C. H. Lee, *Regional Economic Growth in the United Kingdom Since the 1880s* (Maidenhead, 1971), pp. 147 ff.

[46] A. R. Prest and D. J. Coppock, *The UK Economy* (1978), pp. 205-8; A. J. Brown, *op. cit.*, p. 302.

Table 9·4:   Unemployment in UK regions, per cent

	December 1958–March 1961*	
London and South-East	1·21	
Central (Midlands & Yorks.)	1·21	
East and South	1·40	
South-West	1·87	
North-West	2·23	
Wales	2·70	
North	2·85	
Scotland	3·81	
Great Britain	1·83	

	1970	1980
South-East	1·6	4·8
East Anglia	2·1	5·7
East Midlands	2·2	6·4
South-West	2·8	6·7
West Midlands	1·9	7·8
Yorkshire & Humberside	2·8	7·8
North-West	2·7	9·3
Scotland	4·2	10·0
Wales	3·8	10·3
North	4·6	10·9
Northern Ireland	6·8	13·7
United Kingdom	2·6	7·4

* P. C. Cheshire, 'Regional Unemployment Differences in Great Britain', NIESR, *Regional Papers II* (Cambridge, 1973).

civil research and development rose from £6·6 million in 1945–6 and £30 million in 1950–1 to an estimated £295 million in 1967–8, growing at a rate of 13% per annum.[47] By 1981–2, total Government expenditure on research and development (R and D) was estimated at £3,000 million, of which above one half, £1,683 million, went to the Ministry of Defence, £788 million to the Department of Education and Science, including the funds for the Universities and Research Councils, and the rest to other Departments with research interests, including Industry (£305 million), Energy (£234 million), and Agriculture, Fisheries and Food, including Scotland (£112 million). The distribution of funds and actual R & D work changed as shown in Table 9·5.

Table 9·5:   Distribution of funds and R & D work

Sources of funds:	1958/9	1964	1968	1978
Government	66·9	53·6	48·6	47·0
Private industry	28·5	41·1	40·2	36·9
Other	4·6	5·2	11·2	16·6
Carrying on the work:				
Government: defence	}		11·5	9·4
other	}	27·6	13·5	12·2
Private industry		63·7	59·1	58·7
Other		8·7	15·6	19·7
Total, £ million	477·8	768·0	986·0	3510·3

[47] Council For Scientific Policy, *Report on Science Policy*, Cmnd. 3007 (1966), para. 9 and p. 20, and *Second Report on Science Policy*, Cmnd. 3420 (1967), para. 10.

The share of Government, both in providing funds and in carrying out research, therefore fell substantially in those years, whereas private industry, and particularly 'other' institutions, including the universities and other centres of higher learning, have increased their contribution. The overall rising totals were caused by inflation rather than expansion. At constant (1970) prices, intramural R & D rose by only 7·5% from 1964 to 1978, and the R & D performed by the Government actually fell, from £608 million to £511 million, or by 16%.[48]

Official support for scientific research took mainly two forms: the work of the Scientific Civil Service and of Government-sponsored research institutions, and Government support for independent bodies.[49] The former were largely concerned with defence, but some, like the research activities of the Atomic Energy Authority, had important economic and industrial aspects and applications. The National Research Development Corporation, set up in 1948, had the task both of supervising the commercial exploitations of patents derived from public sponsored research and of supporting promising research which could not find industrial backers. Among the latter the development of the hovercraft was perhaps the most spectacular.

In the support of outside civil research, the Department of Scientific and Industrial Research, strengthened by a new Act in 1956, was the main agency. It subsidized research associations formed by industries and also supported research in the Universities and similar institutions. Following the Trend Report it was abolished[50] and, after an electoral campaign in 1964 emphasizing the expansion of technological research and development,[51] a Ministry of Technology was set up. By the Science and Technology Act of 1965 the former DSIR was divided among two authorities, the Science Research Council and the National Environment Research Council, both under the Department of Education and Science. Apart from the continuing Medical and the Agricultural Research Councils and the Road Research Laboratory which went to the Ministry of Transport, most other Government research and development activity came under the new Ministry, which began by promising massive support to the British computer industry, the NRDC undertaking to invest £5 million in International Computers and Tabulators (ICT). The Atomic Energy Authority was also permitted to engage in research outside the nuclear field. In 1967 the Ministry of Technology added the R & D functions of the Ministry of Aviation, its first real operative Sections and in 1969 those of the Ministry of Power, to its competence.[52]

Under the Conservatives from 1970 on, the coolness towards Government initiatives applied to the field of sponsored research also, though the distribution of funds hardly slackened in practice. In the administrative reorganization of that year, the Department of the Environment was created as also

---

[48] *Annual Abstract of Statistics*; Philip Gummett, *Scientists in Whitehall* (Manchester, 1980), pp. 39, 57.

[49] J. W. Grove, *Government and Industry in Britain* (1962), chapter 11.

[50] *Report of the Committee of Enquiry into the Organization of the Civil Service*, Cmnd. 2171 (1963); Ian Varcoe, *Organizing for Science in Britain. A Case Study* (1974), pp. 4, 78, 81.

[51] Norman J. Vig, *Science and Technology in British Politics* (Oxford, 1968), pp. 34 ff.

[52] P. Mottershead, 'Industrial Policy', in F. T. Blackaby (ed.), *British Economic Policy 1960–74* (Cambridge, 1978), pp. 442 ff.; Vig, pp. 146 ff.; Gummett, p. 45.

the Department of Industry and Trade, which combined the Ministry of Technology (less some aviation) with much of the Board of Trade. In February 1974, in turn, the DTI was split again into Departments of Trade, of Industry and of Prices and Consumer Protection. Meanwhile, the newly constituted 'think tank', or Central Policy Review Staff, came out in favour of applied R & D on a customer-contractor basis, the customer stating his requirements to the scientists. Specialist 'Requirement Boards' were to bring supply and demand together. These proposals were adopted in principle, and a share of the funds allocated to the Research Councils were switched to 'customer' Government Departments.[53]

To judge the effects of the Government's involvement in industrial R & D, individual industries have to be examined in detail.[54] By such means as direct subvention, enforced amalgamation, the provision of orders and of scientific information, the Government undoubtedly helped certain firms in such sensitive industries as aircraft, electronics and machine tools, in which the bulk of the R & D expenditure occurred[55] to stay alive and remain up-to-date. Yet several of them remained ailing and vulnerable, and had to be rescued repeatedly at the taxpayer's expense.

The sums devoted in Britain, by Government and other sources together, to R & D seemed large by the standards of most other countries, but these totals were in some sense misleading, since an unusually high proportion in Britain was spent on defence, or else on defence-related objects, such as that prominent loss-maker, Concorde. Further, while Britain had an unusually low ratio of scientists and technologists among its higher civil service, most of those she had were, once again, engaged in defence work and unlike France, she has never been able to develop a 'science policy'.[56] In any case, the gap was rapidly narrowing in the 1970s (Table 9·6).[57]

In view of the widely acknowledged shortcomings of British technical and scientific education, it was not surprising that it should receive particular attention when lagging British industrial performance began to be debated in the late 1950s and early 1960s. The rising demand for more education of this type was superimposed on an existing upward curve of demand for all kinds of higher education, described most fully by the Robbins Report.[58] In 1956

[53] Civil Service Department, *A Framework for Government Research and Development*, Cmnd. 4814 (1971); *Framework for Government Research and Development*, Cmnd. 5046 (1972); Gummett, pp. 57, 132, 197, 201.

[54] Several such studies will be found in Mottershead, *loc. cit.*

[55] The leading recipients were (in % of the total):

	1972–3	1978
Electrical engineering	26·5%	32·1%
aerospace	25·2	18·2
chemical and allied	16·7	18·4
motor vehicles	6·7	5·6
mechanical engineering	6·5	7·8

No other industry received more than 4%. Prest and Coppock, p. 212; *Annual Abstract of Statistics*.

[56] S. C. on Science and Technology, *2nd Report* (1969), pp. xxvii–xxix; Gummett, pp. 215, 233–5.

[57] B. R. Williams, *Technology, Investment and Growth* (1967); Prest and Coppock, p. 213.

[58] *Report of the Committee on Higher Education*, Cmnd. 2154 (1963), and Appendices.

Table 9·6: Expenditure R & D

	Total spent on R & D % of GNP	Public sector R & D. % of GNP		Industry-funded R & D % of GDP of manufacturing	
	1965	1970	1975	1967	1975
United Kingdom	2·3	1·25	1·18	3·3	2·7
W. Germany	1·3	0·96	1·22	2·2	2·7
France	1·5	1·24	1·16	n.a.	2·0
Italy	—	0·46	0·40	—	—
Netherlands	1·8	—	—	3·5 (1969)	3·6
USA	2·8	1·56	1·33	3·5	4·2

the Government announced a five-year plan, estimated to cost £100 million, to expand the Technical Colleges both in their full-time and their part-time courses.[59] At a higher level, in addition to the foundation of seven new Universities a number of Technical Colleges became Colleges of Advanced Technology and ultimately full Universities in the early 1960s, and others were elevated into a hierarchy of Polytechnics or Regional Colleges (which also offered degree courses), Area Colleges, and others. In 1964, the new Department of Education and Science was established to combine the lower and higher levels of education under one administrative control.

At a lower level, the Industrial Training Act of 1964 broke new ground.[60] Under it the Minister of Labour was given statutory power to set up Industrial Training Boards in individual industries which would be authorized to make compulsory levies from all firms and distribute them to those offering formal training facilities, thus providing a direct financial incentive to each firm to enlarge its own training activities in order to recoup its levy. By 1969, 27 Boards has been formed. In the midst of the general redistribution of costs and benefits that this scheme implied, there seemed to be indeed a greater willingness on the part of firms to spend money on training. Totals under vocational training rose from 4,000 in 1962 to 18,000 in 1971 and under the Training Opportunity Scheme to 40,000 in 1973; the planned total then became 100,000 a year.[61] The later phasing out of the Industrial Training Scheme may be taken as a sign of success rather than failure.[62]

At the beginning of 1974 the Manpower Services Commission (MSC) was set up in place of the Central Training Council. The Training Services Agency was created at the same time. The MSC had little influence on industrial training – its main concern turned out to be employment problems – and it reported in 1980 that in spite of the emphasis of the Employment and Training Act, 1973, 'in traditional crafts, it is still the passage of time rather than objectively assessed performance standards, which decide whether a trainee is accepted as skilled.'[63] However, more worrying was the fact that,

[59] *Better Opportunities in Technical Education*, Cmnd. 1254 (1961).

[60] *Industrial Training. General Proposals*, Cmnd. 1892 (1962).

[61] *Capital Investment Procedures*, Cmnd. 6106 (1975), p. 4.

[62] R. Elliott, 'Industrial Relations and Manpower Policy', in F. T. Blackaby, *Economic Policy*, pp. 606, 612.

[63] Manpower Services Commission, *Review of the Employment and Training Act 1973* (1980), para. 4.16.

compared with the leaders, Britain lagged badly in vocational apprenticeship of all kinds (see Table 9·7).[64]

Table 9·7: Activities of young people after compulsory school period (%)

	Year	Full-time general education	Full-time vocational education	Appren-ticeship	Work or unem-ployed
West Germany	1980	25	18	50	7
Switzerland	1978/79	20	9	52	19
Great Britain	1977	32	10	14	44

As a proportion of GNP, education as a whole had grown from 2·5% in the 1930s to 3% in the 1950s, 5% by the mid-1960s[65] and 6%, or £11,880 million, in 1980.

3 Macro-economic Policy: Stop-go

In several of the earlier sections, the evolution of Government economic policies has been traced in broad sweeps, showing changes in emphasis, aims and methods over a 30-year period (especially chapter 8, sections 2 and 3, and chapter 9, sections 1 and 2). We have also had occasion to examine the medium-term changes in direction that arose from the replacement of one governing party by another, in 1951, 1964, 1970, 1974 and 1979. Such an approach brings out some specific aspects of British economic development and of the role of the State in economic life. But it would be wrong to suggest that behind these wide movements there lay some consistent long-term strategy, and still more misleading to imply that whatever strategy there had been, had exercised much effect on the actual unfolding of events.

On the contrary, as noted in numerous specific instances above, British economic policy was dominated by short-term expedients reacting to short-term crises. Whatever major movements occurred were the result of the sum of short-term policies impinging on the underlying trends in a catastrophic rather than a clearly planned manner, and in the end, and without exception, sacrificing long-term aims for immediate needs. Among the long-terms aims were full employment, dominating the early post-war years, and economic growth and structural change, which occupied the leading place from the late 1950s onward. The short-term crises, which repeatedly disrupted their attainment, were caused by failures to achieve balance, above all in the foreign balance of payments, which led to the failure to keep up the international value of the pound sterling until the flow of North Sea oil had solved that problem, and failure to match home supply and demand for money, which led to inflation. At the very end of the period, crisis measures to deal with inflation appeared to have blotted out any other economic aim for material well-being whatever.

---

[64] Ian Jones, 'The New Training Initiative – An Evaluation', *Nat.Inst.Econ.Rev.*, 99 (February 1982), 70.

[65] John Vaizey and John Sheehan, *Resources for Education. An Economic Study of Education in the United Kingdom, 1920–1965* (1968), pp. 2, 139.

The repeated zig-zag course with which successive Governments reacted to the temporary imbalances became known, not inaptly, as 'stop-go', designating alternate phases of permitted expansion and enforced contraction. The attempted mechanism was macro-economic throughout, informed by Keynesian thinking in the earlier phases and monetarist thinking increasingly in the 1970s: that is to say, imbalances, no matter where they occurred and how limited their impact, were to be cured by subjecting the whole economy to a regime of contraction or expansion. The sequence in which this occurred will itself help to explain how the mechanism worked and why it was bound to continue without solution in an ever deteriorating cycle.

We begin with the year of 1951 which saw a sudden deterioration of the balance of payments.[66] The largest part of this deficit was caused by a sharp decline of the terms of trade,[67] to their trough of the post-war years, precipitated by the Korean War and the stockpiling of imported raw materials in expectation of further price rises, which made inventories one of the most volatile of factors. Finally, the sudden rearmament programme, decided on in August 1950 at the request of the Americans, had dangerously extended the home economy,[68] at a time when stocks had been already run down. Sharp restrictions were called for, but when Gaitskell's April budget was announced, the full extent of the deterioration in the balance of payments from the surplus of 1950 was not realized. Since the pressure was to come from rearmament, consumption cuts were not very relevant, and taxes on consumption were raised by £150 million only. The real cut was to fall on investment by such means as the suspension of 'initial allowances' and there was a hint of re-examining the merits of monetary policy shunned by Dr Dalton.

As the crisis of 1951 turned out to be one of the foreign balance, a swing of £700 million from a surplus of £300 million in 1950 to a deficit of £400 million, the incoming Conservative Government proceeded almost at once to drastic import cuts and cuts in tourist allowances, in sharp reversal from a liberalizing trend before. A rise in the bank rate to $2\frac{1}{2}\%$ in November was to be followed by a further rise to 4% in March, 1952, accompanied by money market operations to make them effective, ushering in the new 'monetary' policy.[69] The budget of 1952 continued the policy of keeping consumption level and cutting investment in order to free resources for rearmament, but it also fulfilled some election pledges by a cut in subsidies and increases in indirect taxation, as well as cuts in income and profits taxes, all designed to redistribute income to the rich and to 'enterprise'. An excess profits levy was to prevent war profiteering.

[66] The year-by-year account of the following paragraphs is heavily indebted to J. C. R. Dow, *The Management of the British Economy, 1945-1960* (Cambridge, 1965); I. M. D. Little, 'Fiscal Policy', in G. D. N. Worswick and P. Ady, *The British Economy in the Nineteen-Fifties* (Oxford, 1962); the Annual Review in *Nat.Inst.Econ.Rev.*; *Bank for International Settlements, Report 1967-8*, pp. 3-16; R. J. Ball and T. Burns, 'Stabilization Policy in Britain 1964-81', in Michael Posner (ed.), *Demand Management* (1978); W. Beckerman (ed.), *The Labour Government's Economic Record 1964-1970* (1972); F. T. Blackaby (ed.), *British Economic Policy 1960-74* (Cambridge, 1978); W. P. J. Maunder, (ed.), *The British Economy in the 1970s* (1980), esp. Tony Westaway, 'Stabilization Policy and Fiscal Reform'.

[67] Roy Harrod, *The British Economy* (New York, 1963), pp. 133-5.

[68] Joan Mitchell, *Crisis in Britain* (1963), pp. 33-4, 106-7.

[69] A. J. Youngson, *Britain's Economic Growth, 1920-1966* (1967), p. 176.

The fall in import prices, some running down of stocks and the measures taken, together afforded gratifying relief to the balance of payments in 1952.[70] Home industrial output was cut by 3%, more sharply than had been intended, and tax revenue was also cut thereby, but the other indicators were more promising by the time of the 1953 budget. Butler, however, was still uncertain of the foreign balance, and the only concessions to expansion were the restoration of the initial allowances and some reduction in income and purchase taxes, calculated to add £100–150 million to consumption. As a controlled boom got under way, some import and other restrictions were removed in 1953, and the bank rate was reduced by $\frac{1}{2}$%. The most encouraging aspect was the buoyancy of exports, so that the boom was allowed to continue into 1954, when the economy again reached full employment. The budget of 1954 made no important changes apart from turning 'initial' into 'investment' allowances to encourage investment, but food rationing and building controls were abolished. Things seemed to be getting better every year and it was at this time that Mr Butler announced his hope for a doubling of the standard of living in 25 years – the first important statement of concrete long-term growth as a major policy objective.

By the end of 1954 the boom was beginning to endanger the balance of payments, as consumption and imports exceeded the ability to produce and export. Measures early in 1955 including the raising of the bank rate in two steps from 3% to $4\frac{1}{2}$%, and some hire-purchase restrictions. But in his budget, the Chancellor, misled perhaps by an improvement of sterling exchange rates rather than of the true balance and no doubt conscious of the impending election,[71] added to the expansion by an income tax cut of £150 million. By the summer, the economy was in crisis again, and the first cycle of the 1950s was completed. An autumn budget became necessary to rectify the balance of payments and to stop the speculation anticipating another devaluation. The *de facto* return to sterling convertibility about this time did not make the control of the economy any easier. There were sharp tax increases, and early in 1956 investment allowances were exchanged for the less valuable initial allowances, the bank rate was raised to $5\frac{1}{2}$%, and there were hire-purchase restrictions. This crisis also saw some of the most savage cuts of the investment plans of nationalized industries, though Macmillan's budget speech had declared for increased production, rather than for cutting demand.[72]

On the whole, this credit squeeze was effective. The Budget was neutral, but contained Macmillan's best-known innovation, the premium bond to encourage saving. Output stagnated in 1956 and 1957, and so did investment, and imports actually fell, helped by a reduction in inventories. Exports showed an encouraging rise, and it is likely that in normal circumstances slow growth might have been resumed soon after, but instead the attack on Suez supervened at the end of 1956. The economic effects proved less destructive than might have been expected, though petrol was rationed once more, but it

---

[70] Joan Mitchell, chapter 9.

[71] E.g. Michael Pinto Duschinsky, 'Bread and Circuses? The Conservatives in Office 1951–1964' in Vernon Bogdanor and Robert Skidelsky (eds.), *The Age of Affluence 1951–1964* (1970), pp. 64–6.

[72] Samuel Brittan, *Steering the Economy: The Role of the Treasury* (1969), p. 125.

led, in September 1957, to a sharp speculative attack on sterling. The crisis of 1957 was thus not based on 'real' factors, nor did it reflect the performance of the economy which was reasonably healthy in that year. Nevertheless, it had to be met by the normal battery of squeeze measures, superimposed on a stagnant economy, and these prolonged the stagnation for another year. It was significant that the great price rise, which contributed to the sterling crisis, was based on a smaller than normal wage rise, but one which was not justified by a large enough increase in output. Further, the budget of 1957 had encouraged consumption by cuts in direct taxes, but failed to encourage investment, except in ships.

Thus the crisis of 1957 showed itself in a drain of the reserve, rather than a payments shortfall. It was precipitated by a number of circumstances: a *de facto* devaluation of the franc, the refusal of Germany to revalue the Mark even though large quantities of gold had moved into that country, the decision to wind up the EPU, and by an attack launched from the City, led by the Governor and Deputy Governor of the Bank of England, recalling some aspects of the summer of 1931, on the alleged recklessness of the British Government in permitting credit expansion and wage increases. The Council on Prices, Productivity and Incomes, the 'Three Wise Men', had been set up in July 1957, and all seemed set for ever more drastic restrictions, but in fact Mr Thorneycroft was not prepared to go much further than raise the bank rate to a sensational 7%, asking the banks to stop lending and arranging for cuts in Government spending and in the investment plans of the nationalized industries.

By early 1958 it was clear that the economy was in depression, and the budget laid the basis for only a slow expansion, since there were still fears of wage rises and another attack on the reserves. Heathcoat Amory raised 'initial' allowances, and made some moderate cuts in indirect taxes. Production stagnated but, owing to a substantial improvement in the terms of trade, Britain had the highest favourable trade balance of the post-war era, and the fall in import prices also kept home price level increases down to a low figure. Unemployment, at 2·8% in January 1959, was the highest since the war, and on this basis, Heathcoat Amory felt justified in introducing substantial boosts into the budget of 1959. Already during 1958, the ceiling on bank advances had been abolished, and hire-purchase restrictions taken off. Also sterling was made fully convertible at what looked to be an auspicious time. Now the intention was to return to full employment. Among the considerable tax cuts, purchase tax was reduced by one-sixth, the duty on beer cut, the standard income tax cut by 9*d*., and the investment allowance reinstated. Altogether, £300 million was to be added to consumers' spendable incomes in a full year, plus £70 million in a once-for-all post-war credit repayment.

For a while output increased without exceeding the labour supply, though some bottlenecks, e.g. sheet steel, began to develop. During the year, industrial output rose 10%, national output 3–4%, and final expenditure, 6%. The external balance was less favourable, though still positive, and full capacity was being reached by the end of the year. In the budget of 1960 the changes were only minor, but the bank rate had been put up to 5% in January and went up to 6% in June, and the first 1% 'Special Deposits' was called for. In consequence, the consumption rise was held back, but the reduction was greater in production and exports, while imports and investment continued strongly. In February, Macmillan as Prime Minister had resisted the clamour of the Treasury and the Bank of England to put on the 'brake'.[73] By now, policy makers had also become conscious of the very much faster rate of expansion sustained on the Continent, and for once, the attempt was made *not* to let the inevitable squeeze fall on investments. The total result of all these influences was a sharp deterioration in the balance of payments in 1960, marking the end of the second cycle, in a form very similar to the crisis of 1955.

The budget of 1961 thus inaugurated another period of restriction and decline. There were tax increases, but these were of a kind to raise costs, and the balance of payments, while improving, was still weak. The large deficit of 1960 had been met, not by a drain of the reserves, but by more short-term loans, and now, in 1961, these turned against sterling, repeating the experience of a monetary, or speculative crisis of 1957, but this time much closer to the real deficit period, only some months earlier, which had caused it. The attack on sterling was beaten off with the help of large loans, including £323 million from the European Central Banks, and a £178 million standby credit, plus £535 million from the IMF, all of which weakened sterling still further in the long run. Meanwhile, the measures of July 1961, the 'Little Budget', included a rise of the bank rate from 5% to 7%, another 10% surcharge on customs, excise and purchase tax, a further 1% special deposit, and promises of major Government cuts in expenditure as insisted on by the IMF, heralded by an immediate attempt to stop wage rises of employees in the public sector. These were sufficient to turn the modest expansion of the first half of 1961 into a sharp decline. The losses in economic growth now began to be considered more seriously, but the simultaneous (and partly contradictory) criticism was made that the collapse had come because expansion had been allowed to proceed too quickly.

The first type of criticism was perhaps best formulated by Harold Wilson, when moving the Amendment in the House of Commons.[74] The July measures, he alleged, were designed to keep the 'hot money' in London and, since a loan from the IMF was necessary, to statisfy the international banking community by 'massive, masochistic and irrelevant cuts in our standard of living, harmful restrictions on our production, and needless increases in our cost and price structure (in the belief that speculators are impressed only by actions which in the long term harm the economy). The Government's policies are so bankrupt that 16 years after the war we have to go for international aid. We will be a magnet again for hot money all over the world.'

The budget of 1962 showed only minor changes as the Treasury overestimated the rise in demand, needlessly prolonging the depression.[75] The economy recovered only slowly, while more strenuous exhortations were uttered to hold down wages, and the NEDC began working on its long-term growth plan. A world economic boom allowed exports to increase slowly and to improve the balance so that a cautious reflationary policy could begin. By

[73] Harold Macmillan, *Pointing the Way 1959–1961* (1972), pp. 220–6.
[74] *H. of C. Debates*, vol. 645, cols. 441–2, 26 July 1961.
[75] Brittan, *Steering*, pp. 161–7.

the end of the year indirect taxes had been reduced, the Special Deposits released, and investment allowances increased. However, the recovery was disappointing, industrial investment was still declining and unemployment was still substantial. For 1963 it was expected that the economy would move towards fuller capacity, and output would rise in line with the NEDC 4% target overall.[76] Maudling's Budget was openly expansionary, and tax remissions, including income tax concessions, together with the abolition of 'Schedule A' tax were estimated to amount to £269 million. There was also greater assistance to the Development Districts. Wage increases, however, were to be limited, mainly by exhortation, to the 'guiding light' of $3\frac{1}{2}$%. In the event, the recovery was substantial, output rose by 5–6%, but private investment was still depressed and there was still spare capacity, but at least the foreign balance had stood up well to the reflation and exports were rising.

1964 became the crisis year, marking the peak of the third cycle since 1951. The budget was still hopeful. It gambled on rising output, investment and productivity to break through the export price barrier to keep up a reasonable foreign balance; this, in turn, would permit expansion to continue at the existing rate, which was no more than the NEDC and others considered a minimum. The slight deflationary indirect tax increases were intended to hold expansion down to 4%, and if there had been any intention to impose tighter restrictions and cut short the boom, it was resisted in view of the coming General Election. In the event, the gamble failed. With the rise in consumption and investment, the foreign balance collapsed, and the balance-of-payments deficit was the largest ever, reaching nearly £700 million.

The new Labour Government announced a number of crisis measures in October almost immediately on taking office,[77] including a 15% surcharge on all imports of manufactures and semi-manufactures, which raised a storm of protest abroad, and some export rebates. In November a second budget increased petrol taxes at once, and announced an income tax increase and a new Corporation Tax, from April 1965, estimated to yield £215 million in a full year. Meanwhile, to stem the panic sterling outflow, the Bank Rate went up again to 7%, and an emergency credit of $3,000 million was raised abroad.

Callaghan's April budget of 1965 was only mildly deflationary, since he still hoped to increase exports by encouraging production rises at home. Foreign central bankers, satisfied with the tough British policies, bought sterling in September to 'squeeze the bears' among the international speculators who had banked too early on a devaluation, and by February the relief, as the hot money flowed back, allowed Britain to repay a large part of the loans raised abroad.[78] However, while incomes and imports rose in the United Kingdom, exports stayed down and by the end of the year the balance was still adverse. The budget in 1966 was delayed until May because of the General Election, but when it came, its most important deflationary provision, the SET, which was calculated to bring in £315 million in the first year and to be equivalent to a £200 million purchase tax, could take effect only

[76] NEDC, *The National Plan*, Cmnd. 2764 (1965).

[77] Prime Minister's Office, *The Economic Situation* (1964).

[78] Robert Solomon, *The International Monetary System, 1945–1976. An Insider's View* (New York, 1977), pp. 90–1.

slowly. Meanwhile, the first half of the year had seen not only the drain on the reserves continuing, but some special features aggravating it, including the seamen's strike and a particularly heavy capital outflow matched by an unusually small inflow. There was thus a renewed run on sterling, which caused an even more severe application of the brake in the shape of the 'July measures'. They included severe hire-purchase restrictions; a 10% surcharge on purchase tax, petrol, and excise duties, except tobacco; savage cuts in Government spending, including investment by nationalized industries; tighter building controls; a 10% surcharge on surtax and various other measures, which together were calculated to reduce the pressure by £340 million in the current year and £516 million in a full year. The brief attempt to hold on to growth was abandoned; henceforth, the only reply to a sterling weakness would be further deflation and further squeezes.

The most controversial measure, perhaps, was the total wage freeze for six months, affecting even firms in which increases were to be paid for by increases in productivity, to be followed by a further six months of 'severe restraint'.[79] On its own premise, which was that incomes have to be cut to match productivity and not production raised to match incomes, it was a reasonable approach, though its effect was temporary, wage rises were postponed rather than abandoned and the damage done to industrial relations was incalculable. But the most significant result was that despite these most savage cuts, and five budgets in 20 months, the drain and the imbalance continued. Growth was duly slowed down, but exports did not thereby pick up. To some extent, again, there were special factors in 1967. World trade declined somewhat, while UK imports remained high and rising interest rates abroad weakened sterling; there were dock strikes in London and Liverpool; Mr Wilson's application to join the EEC renewed fears of a sterling devaluation; and the Middle East War in June again increased costs by closing the Suez Canal. This time the drain of funds out of London, particularly by speculative owners weary of three years' continuous crisis, could not be stopped by any amount of foreign lending, and in November the pound was devalued by one-seventh from $2·80 to $2·40.[80]

As noted above, the flight from sterling was not stopped by devaluation but continued, and Britain required further large foreign loans. The measures taken at once in 1967, and the full budget of March 1968, exceeded all previous cuts and tax increases in extent, and surprised even foreign bankers. Among others, SET relief was withdrawn, except for Development Areas, purchase tax, customs and excise and petrol duties increased, and Bank Rate raised from $6\frac{1}{2}$% to 8% (down to $7\frac{1}{2}$% in March). No less than £923 million, or 3% of GNP, was to be diverted from consumption, one half to wipe off the foreign payments deficit and the other to build up an annual positive balance, to pay off the debts accumulated since 1964, and resume economic growth. It is worthy of note that of the total negative foreign balance of £3·6 billion accumulated 1964–8, which had led to such humiliating borrowing abroad

[79] F. Blackaby and M. Artis, 'An Incomes Policy', *District Bank Review*, 165 (1968); Harold Wilson, *The Labour Government 1964–1970. A Personal Record* (1971), pp. 258–9.

[80] *B. of Eng.Qtly.Bull.*, 7/4 (1967), 335 and 8/1 (1968), 4–8. *Midland Bank Review* (February, 1968).

and destructive deflation at home, the actual current account deficit amounted to only £1·3 billion, or just over one-third; the rest of the deficit was caused by speculative moves of sterling holders, and by British capital exports.[81] Further, throughout these financial disasters, in which the confidence of overseas bankers and speculators had become at least as important as the real situation of the British economy,[82] some growth in output had continued, though the 4% target had long since been abandoned.

Contrary to widespread expectations, the devaluation with its associated savage deflationary measures, offered no immediate relief to the adverse balance of payments. Apart from the well known 'J-curve' effect, caused by an early loss of foreign currency after devaluation owing to lower export unit prices before the greater quantity could outweigh the loss per unit, there were particular features distinguishing the British case. The most important of these was that Britain was near full employment and there was thus no spare capacity to divert to exports; but further, one major export market, the Sterling Area, was hit by the loss in value of its sterling reserves, and/or devalued with the United Kingdom, while the other major export market, the advanced industrial nations, was not very price-elastic.[83] British exports did indeed rise by $6\frac{1}{2}$% in dollar value, but those of all industrial countries rose by 13%, so that Britain continued to fall behind, and her foreign drain went on. In the September Basle Group Arrangement, foreign central banks offered credits to repay the holdings of Sterling Area countries, and thus remove that millstone from British necks, but a further speculative attack on sterling followed in the belief that the Deutschmark would be revalued.

So the Squeeze continued. In November 1968 HP restrictions were tightened, and the April 1969 budget increased corporation tax, SET and purchase tax. The effect on demand was to be £200–250 million, but the total Government surplus was estimated at £800 million. Unemployment continued to rise, while inflation received a boost by the devaluation.

The 1969 budget added further burdens, totalling £130 million, and the Bank Rate had been raised in February to 8%, but at last devaluation had begun to work and the foreign balance had turned positive. Wages and earnings, it is true, were rising faster, in the face of the Government's inability to hold the unions to either a statutory or a voluntary incomes policy, but the budget of 1970 set the signals to 'go', even if hesitantly. The new Conservative Government inherited a comfortable foreign surplus, but also the obligation to repay a large loan, and faced a threatened wages explosion. It reacted by asking the banks in July 1970 to limit lending, and keeping the October 1970 budget neutral.

In 1971 the combination of rising unemployment and rapidly rising prices and incomes confused the policy makers, who had hitherto looked upon these two movements as incompatible. The budget, which included some

---

[81] C. D. Cohen, *British Economic Policy 1960–1969* (1971), p. 181.

[82] 'The British Government had it brought home in no uncertain terms in late 1964, that it should not only steer the economy in what it thinks to be the right direction, but also in what foreign governments think to be the right direction.' A. R. Prest, 'The British Economy, 1945–1960', *Manchester School*, 33/2 (1965), 144.

[83] F. V. Meyer, D. C. Corner, J. E. S. Parker, *Problems of a Mature Economy* (1970), pp. 572–7.

major tax reforms, was inflationary to the extent of £500 million, but of this sum only £160 million had immediate effect in the form of increased child allowances. Further relaxation followed later in the year, including tax cuts, the ending of HP restrictions, the lifting of lending ceilings, two Bank Rate cuts of 1% each, public works programmes and the repayment of the last post-war credits. Conditions were set for the great property boom. Meanwhile there was an unprecedented £1 billion surplus on foreign current account, superimposed on a £1·8 billion influx of capital, of which £1 billion had gone into private industry. The dollar was devalued as a consequence of American payments deficits and the world began its move towards floating exchange rates.

Thus the budget of 1972 could afford to try and deal positively with the unemployed, now at a temporary peak of $3\frac{1}{3}$% of the labour force. It was strongly reflationary. There were tax reductions and national and regional incentives: a total of £960 million in taxes plus £135 million in purchase tax were given away. The foreign balance was still positive, but a brief attempt to join the European currency 'snake' had to be given up, and the pound was floated in July. The budget of 1973 was neutral in effect, but included many changes in detail. The aim was to increase output and absorb the unemployed, still at 650,000. But while the pound sterling drifted down at the foreign exchanges, attention turned increasingly to the home inflation. After its *laissez-faire* attitude in 1970-2, the Government had some temporary success here with its incomes policy in 1972-3, only to end in failure in 1974.

The Conservative Government fell early in 1974, and Labour entered office committed not to impose restraints on the unions; the result was the most devastating wages explosion in British history. In the year between the second quarter of 1974 and the second quarter of 1975, average earnings were up by 28% and retail prices by 25%. With the foreign balance still precarious and rapidly being undermined by the OPEC oil price increases of 1973-4, inflation at home joined it at the centre of the stage. Policy now had to battle with these two dangers simultaneously, and in the process sacrificed all else, including in particular employment and economic growth, by measures of unprecedented severity. This was in marked contrast to 1970-4, when relaxed, if inflationary conditions, building on the investment and improved technology of the late 1960s, had seen the most sustained period of expansion in post-war history, real disposable income growing at the rate of 4·2% a year.

There were three budgets in 1974. The first, in March, was very slightly deflationary and largely distributional, taking from the rich in favour of the poor, by increasing pensions and food subsidies, and raising corporation taxes while cutting tax relief. The two later budgets reversed most of these trends, being slightly inflationary as well as favouring industry, by measures which included the relief on taxation of stock appreciation. In terms of prices also these three budgets were 'distinctly erratic. Changes in indirect taxes and subsidies tended to raise prices in March, lower them in July, and raise them again in November.'[84] What was clear was that the tendency for favouring investment and expansion, noticeable in the preceeding years, was coming to

[84] David Savage, 'Fiscal Policy, 1974/5-1980/1: Description and Measurement', *Nat.Inst.Econ.Rev.*, 99 (February 1982), 85.

an end, and in the budget of 1975, Mr Healey for the first time openly jettisoned Keynesian policies. Though unemployment was high and rising, he abstained from expansionary policies, for fear of worsening the foreign balance and above all the Government deficit, conventionally described as the Public Sector Borrowing Requirement (PSBR). So taxes were increased in 1975, public expenditure was to be cut in 1976 and meanwhile a tough incomes policy was to bridle inflation at home.

The quite exceptional inflation rate of 1974–5 had fallen back to a still disturbing 14% by the time of the 1976 budget, and output was stagnating for the fourth year running, while unemployment reached a new high, averaging 5·76% for the year. In a somewhat bizarre move the Chancellor offered income tax reductions in return for wage restraint, but could not offer other positive incentives because the adverse foreign payments balance remained critical. The pound was allowed to drift down from $2·02 to a final $1·71, a 15% loss, to help employment at the expense of making inflation worse, thus operating directly against all the rest of the current policy package, which attempted to curb inflation at the expense of employment. Higher indebtedness abroad became necessary in the sterling crisis of 1976, when the Bank of England MLR reached 15%. There had to be a $5 billion standby loan from the central banks of the Group of Ten, plus Switzerland and the bank for International Settlements (BIS) in June, but the $3·9 billion credit, granted towards the end of the year by the IMF, carried as one of its conditions a limitation of domestic credit expansion (DCE). This helped to complete the switch to monetarist thinking which had already taken a big step forward with the announcement of monetary targets at the time of the budget earlier in the year. Budgets were now geared to medium-term DCE with limits on public expenditure, and progressive cuts in the PSBR as the main instruments. There were savage cuts in public expenditure in July, and yet again in December 1976, when there were also tax increases.

Although the foreign balance was now moving into equilibrium, there were but moderate reliefs in the three budgets of 1977. MLR moved down briskly to $12\frac{7}{8}$% in January and a low of 5% in October. By April 1978, inflation and the foreign drain had eased, whereas output and employment had stayed down: the opportunity was thus ripe for some substantial tax cuts worth £2 billion in 1978–9 and £2·5 billion in a full year, and all signals were set to 'go', but no effort was made to ensure that this benefited investment rather than consumption. The monetary quantity (sterling M3) became a six-months 'rolling target' to offer greater flexibility and perhaps quicker reactions in Government spending. Real disposal income rose by 8·3% in the year, having actually declined for three years running before,[85] but by the end of the year the trade unions rejected all further forms of pay policy, and in the 'winter of discontent' strikes and rising inflation ruined the chances of the Callaghan Government's re-election. After a neutral Labour budget in April, the new Conservative Government set out to enforce major changes of direction in its budget of June 1979.

---

[85] S. Brittan, 'A Transformation of the English Sickness', in Ralf Dahrendorf (ed.), *Europe's Economic Crisis* (1982), p. 95.

Within a framework that was ideologically committed to reducing Government intervention, Sir Geoffrey Howe determined to cut the public sector deficit, even though the economy was clearly sliding into recession, unemployment was rising and output was actually expected to drop. The cuts were to fall mainly on investment, and it is worthy of note that at least a part of the reduction in the PSBR was to be achieved, not by genuine savings, but by the sale of national assets into private hands. In a separate move, income tax, especially for the top incomes, was cut substantially, and to make up the loss of revenue, VAT was raised from 8% to $12\frac{1}{2}$% to a standard 15%. This redistribution, switching benefits from the poor to the rich, was likely to and did indeed boost inflation directly by 4–5% and indirectly by much more, in startling contradiction to the Government's declared main target, which was to *reduce* inflation. The package was completed by the plan announced in November to cut a further £3·5 billion from future public expenditure and sell an additional £1·5 billion of national assets.

By now it was clear that the monetary targets and indicators used by the Government, including M1, M3, Sterling M3, DCE and PSL 1 and 2 were too contradictory to be of much practical use. Thus in 1978–9, while £M3 had actually fallen, helping to add to the severe depression in Britain, DCE was simultaneously sharply rising, sustained in the absence of home money supplies by borrowing abroad; in 1976–7 both had moved in exactly contrary directions and were thus equally opposite to each other.[86] Far from abandoning these indicators, however, the authorities used their erratic behaviour to switch between them, according to which looked best for the time being from their point of view. Yet in the final analysis this nimble targetry was of little account. What mattered was the solid reality of classic deflationary or 'stop' policies, applied with remarkable and unflinching consistency, and reminiscent of nothing so much as the Britain of the 1920s or the German Government after 1930.

The effects were broadly as expected. Between 1979 and 1980 total output fell by 3%, manufacturing output by 9%, investment by 9% and total employment by 2%: 418,000 jobs were lost in manufacturing alone in one year. Meanwhile, the North Sea Oil, now about to come on full stream, had almost overnight solved two of the most intractable problems of the past 30 years, the balance of payments and the international value of sterling. At that point, with employment and output still falling and the foreign balance safe, all previous chancellors would have welcomed the opportunity to stop damaging the productive side of the economy further and would have reflated. Sir Geoffrey Howe however held fast to his classic deflationary strategy. The budget of 1980 brought additional increases in excise duties, petrol tax and income tax (by abolishing the reduced rate), further spending cuts and further sales of assets. The pay of employees in the public service was also to be more tightly controlled, and there were to be minor distributional changes, such as provisions to tax the unemployed and the strikers, and to reduce benefits to the latter. As the overall targets, now projected for no less than four years ahead, were once again not being met, further spending cuts

---

[86] Bryan Gould, John Mills and Shaun Stewart, *Monetarism or Prosperity?* (1981), pp. 39–40. Also p. 378 above.

and an increase in the employers' contribution to national income were imposed in November 1980. The balance of payments meanwhile had swung heavily in Britain's favour and the pound rose by a further 10% against the dollar and 9% against all currencies in the course of the year.

This depressing story of 30 years may at first sight appear confusing and without order. Closer inspection shows however that the periodic changes affecting the British economy were clearly of a cyclical nature. The cycles, which had an average duration of just under five years, were strongly influenced if not caused by the measures imposed by the authorities, which were, in turn, based on reactions to immediate crises. In the process, the repeatedly announced intentions of Governments to hold to long or medium-term plans were regularly and systematically thwarted by these needs of short-term 'management'.

It is possible to construct a typical or model cycle for this period, in which all these factors come into play.[87] Let us start with the upswing from the bottom of the trough. In that position, some resources would be unemployed and imports would be low because of low incomes and possibly some protectionist measures such as the import surcharge. Exports, encouraged by poor sales at home, would hold up better, despite the high unit costs ruling at less than full employment, and would benefit by better delivery dates, since inability to deliver at the right quality or price had helped to thwart exports in the boom. Thus there would be spare capacity and a positive balance of payments.

At this point, expansionary Government measures would gradually bring the spare capacity into play. Output could rise fairly fast and prices could stay low or rise but little as fuller use of resources reduced real costs. But to the extent that the 'go' phase brought on economic growth, the imports of the necessary raw materials would rise, and early bottlenecks would develop and become more frequent the closer full employment was approached, for it was of the essence of the preceding 'stop' phase that few additional investments had been undertaken to allow future expansion. Bottlenecks, also, had to be met by increasing imports while export delivery dates would lengthen because of capacity limitation. Thus the foreign balance would turn adverse and would lead, at once under fixed exchange rates and after some depreciation under 'floating' rates, to a drain on the reserves.

This would be the signal for panic on the part of the Bank of England and the Treasury, and all systems would go into reverse to bring the economy once more to a 'stop': Government spending cuts, incomes policies, tax rises, interest rate increases, credit curbs and import restrictions, among others, would combine to make incomes and output decline, imports drop, speculative hot money flow back, the balance of payments improve and spare capacity open up once more. The cycle was ready to begin once again *da capo*.[88]

The 'stops', imposed as the means to solve the temporary crises, became at the same time the cause of the long-term conversion of the cycle into a secular

---

[87] See S. Pollard, *The Wasting of the British Economy* (1982), pp. 47–55.

[88] Samuel Brittan, *Steering the Economy: the Role of the Treasury* (1969), p. xv.

downward spiral. For it was of the essence of the 'stop' policies that it was above all investment that was held back, not personal incomes or consumption, and it was, in turn, the consequent relative decline in British productivity, or the rise in real costs, relative to those of the chief competitors which tended to price British goods out of the competitive world markets and kept exports from expanding. This tendency could, in theory, have been counteracted by a policy of deflating the British price-level parallel with Britain's inability to keep pace with the efficiency of her rivals, but neither of the two methods of doing this, lowering foreign prices by devaluation, or lowering home prices by a severe incomes policy, were open to the United Kingdom.

Devaluation was not permitted at all under the Bretton Woods system, and later, under floating rates, when it was brought into use, it could not be pursued to the extent necessary to match Britain's failure to reduce her real costs, because it had several adverse side effects, including accelerated inflation induced by higher import prices.[89] Incomes policies, the other means, were indeed tried, but could never be sustained for long; in any case, they were based on fundamentally mistaken assumptions, since as Table 9·8 shows strikingly, British wage rises were, if anything, below those of most other countries until the 1970s. Moreover, it came to be increasingly clear that there was an 'institutional' element in a free society enjoying full employment and strong trade unions, which raised wages by around 5% a year as a matter of course and correspondingly more in the inflationary years of the 1970s.[90] The difference between British and foreign experience was not that money wages rose here; but that these increased costs were absorbed by rising productivity elsewhere, but not in the United Kingdom. Both the devaluation of 1967 and the incomes policies were attempts to make prices reflect the relative impoverishment of Britain, rather than to remedy the causes of that impoverishment, and neither was successful even on its own misguided terms.

Table 9·8:   Hourly earnings, annual percentage growth rates[91]

	Manufacturing	All labour	Manufacturing	
	1948–63	1963–7	1967–75	1975–80
France	9·7	6·2	13·5	13·2
W. Germany	8·0	6·7	9·4	6·2
Italy	6·3	8·0	16·0	21·2
Japan	7·7	11·1	19·2	7·3
Netherlands	6·9	10·7	12·4*	—
UK	6·0	5·4	14·0	15·2
USA	4·2	3·6	6·9	8·6

* 7 years to 1974

[89] M. V. Posner, 'The Main Issues', in *idem, Demand Management* (1978), pp. 129–30.

[90] A. G. Hines, 'Trade Unions and Wage Inflation in the United Kingdom, 1893–1961', *Rev.Econ.Studies*, 31/88 (1964); Colin Clark, 'An International Comparison of "Overemployment" Trends in Money Wages', *Oxf.Econ.P.*, 9/2 (1957); E. V. Morgan, 'Is Inflation Inevitable', *Econ.J.*, 76/301 (1966), 6; Dow, *Management*, pp. 355–6; L. A. Dicks-Mireau and J. R. C. Dow, 'The Determinants of Wage Inflation: United Kingdom, 1946–56', *J. R. Stat.S.*, 122/2, Ser.A. (1959); K. G. J. C. Knowles, 'Wages and Productivity', in Worswick and Ady, pp. 520 ff.

Thus, given common variations in input prices, like imports and wage rates, and given fixed exchange rates, Britain's failure to achieve the real cost reductions of other countries was bound to mean a relative rise in her export prices. Given the high demand elasticity, or in other words, the strongly competitive conditions in export markets, there is no alternative but to place the reponsibility for the relative decline in British exports squarely on increasingly non-competitive price and quality, i.e. on a failure to keep up productive efficiency.[92] The circle is thus complete: failure in productivity led to losses in exports; these led to balance of payments difficulties, and these, in turn, led to Government short-term measures which were certain, in the long term, to make the productivity failures worse and start the circle up again, in less favourable conditions, as soon as the restrictions were taken off.[93] All this was in addition to the sheer inability, noted above, of increasing output and exports in booms because of the physical limitations of existing plant.

In the case of imports, the mechanism was even simpler. The fear had been often expressed in the late 1940s that expansion of incomes would lead to a proportionate increase in imports of raw materials, food and goods that could not be produced at home according to a calculable 'propensity to import'. In the event, it was true that every expansion after 1950 led to an immediate sharp import rise; but just as the failure of exports to rise steeply was not simply due to the attractions of home demand, with which the negative correlation was weak,[94] but to a failure to produce, so this sharp rise in imports was not in commodities in which other countries enjoyed natural advantages in production, but on the contrary, the increase was greatest in machinery, steel and other capital goods, and in manufactures generally. For the economy in general in 1948–68 it was found that the elasticity of imports relative to home activity was higher for manufactures than for food.[95] Excess imports were thus largely due to non-necessities or to 'bottlenecks', i.e. failure to create sufficient capacity from home sources. To a varying extent, it was also due to a parallel sharp increase in inventories.[96] This may be put

[91] UN *Statistical Yearbook;* OECD, *Main Economic Indicators.*

[92] See also Youngson, *Britain's Economic Growth 1920–1966* (1967), pp. 232–5; J. R. Parkinson, 'The Progress of United Kingdom Exports' *Scot.J.Pol.Econ.*, 13/1 (1966); M. FG. Scott, *A Study of United Kingdom Imports* (Cambridge, 1963); Lynden Moore, 'Factors Affecting Demand for British Exports', *Bull.Oxf.Inst.Stat.*, 26/4 (1964), p. 347.

[93] R. W. Bacon and W. A. Eltis, 'Stop-Go and De-Industrialization', *National Westminster Bank Quarterly Review* (November 1975), 31–43.

[94] R. J. Ball, J. R. Eaton and M. D. Steuer, 'The Relationship between United Kingdom Export Performance in Manufactures and the Internal Pressure of Demand', *Econ.J.*, 76/301 (1966).

[95] Klein, Ball, Hazlewood and Vandome, *An Econometric Model of the United Kingdom* (Oxford, 1961), p. 97. Also Marc Nerlove, 'Two Models of the British Economy', *International Economic Review* 6/1 (1965), p. 165.

[96] See, e.g., NEDC, *Imported Manufactures: An Enquiry into Competitiveness* (1965); M. F. W. Hemming and G. F. Ray, 'Imports and Expansion', *Nat.Inst.Econ.Rev.*, 2 (1959); A. Maizels, *Industrial Growth and World Trade* (Cambridge, 1963); S. J. Wells, *Trade Policies for Britain. A Study in Alternatives* (1966), p. 92; PEP, *Growth in the British Economy* (1960), pp. 143 ff.; K. S. Lomax, 'Growth and Productivity in the United Kingdom', *Productivity Management Review*, 38 (1964), p. 14; Roy Harrod, *Towards a New Economic Policy* (Manchester, 1967), p. 25; P. M. Oppenheimer, 'Is Britain's Worsening Trade Gap due to bad Management of the Business Cycle', *Bull.Econ. and Stat.* (formerly *Bull.Oxf.Inst.Stat.*), 27/3

differently. Investment, the creation of productive capacity, was at no time undertaken in a quantity to sustain a higher growth rate, so that if income growth occurred at a rate approaching the average Continental experience, it expressed itself in an import surplus rather than a commensurate growth in output. This import surplus, as noted above, resulted in measures which injured the creation of productive capacity still further. For most of the time, in periods of restriction, output was at less than capacity, preventing the full use of home resources for such objectives as improving Britain's productive potential:[97] when the brakes were taken off, capacity was then found to be too inelastic and too low.

Moreover, the progressive deterioration of British technical competitiveness meant that at each crisis, the dependence on imports increased, and the gap widened. While there is no clear trend in the amplitude of the swings of the post-war cycles, the overall deterioration will be clear enough from the sample series in Table 9·9.[98]

Table 9·9:

Reference cycles in quarter years		changes in industrial production, %		changes in unemployment rate, in % of total employment	
Peaks	Troughs	P→T	T→P	P→T	T→P
I 1951		—		+0·5	
	III 1952		+21·4		−0·8
IV 1955		−1·2		+1·1	
	III 1958		+13·3		−0·5
III 1960		−0·4		+0·9	
	I 1963		+18·3		−1·1
I 1965		+2·6		+1·0	
	III 1967		+8·6		0·0
I 1969		−2·4		+1·6	
	I 1972		+13·7		−1·2
II 1973		−10·1		+1·4	
	III 1975		+16·5		+1·3
II 1979		(−14·1)*		(+5·0)*	
	II 1981		—		—

* Estimated

The basic difference between Britain and the other industrial nations and the causes of Britain's relative decline lay therefore not so much in the existence of cycles as such, for these were found among all of them, including even the fastest growers like Germany and Japan,[99] but in the particular form

(1965). M. FG. Scott, 'The Volume of British Imports', in Worswick and Ady, *op. cit.*, though published in 1962, is still wholly couched in the terms of the immediate post-war problems, and is witness to the delay in recognizing the long-term post-war trend.

[97] W. A. H. Godley and J. R. Shepherd, 'Long-term Growth and Short-term Policy', *Nat.Inst.Econ.Rev.*, 29 (1964).

[98] D. J. O'Dea, *Cyclical Indicators for the Postwar British Economy* (Cambridge, 1975), p. 39; *Nat.Inst.Econ.Rev.*, 96 (May 1981), p. 9 and 98 (November 1981) p. 7.

[99] E.g. A. Whiting, 'An International Comparison of the Instability of Economic Growth', *Three Banks Review*, 109 (March 1976); T. Wilson, 'Instability and Growth: An International Comparison 1950–65', in D. H. Aldcroft and Peter Fearon (eds.), *Economic Growth in Twentieth-Century Britain* (1969), pp. 184–95.

taken by these cycles. While elsewhere the downward phases were caused by temporary shortfalls in market demand and were used, with the strong encouragement of Government, to invest in building up the productive capacity ready for the next expansion, in Britain they were caused by the enforced deflation or *reduction* in investment, so that the next expansionary phase was condemned from the start to be throttled almost at once by inadequate capacity to sustain it. Whereas in Britain upswings were often shorter than downswings, abroad the trend was up, with but short, sharp downs to shake out the inefficient. The damage inflicted on the British economy by successive phases of Government policy thus worked essentially through cutting back the possibility and the urge to invest, and the urge to use the capital once it was installed. Inadequate investment[100] thus plays a part in all explanations of the unsatisfactory course of British economic development, though different authors assign to it differing degrees of importance.

Each of the cycles had well marked characteristics of its own. The first, covering approximately the years 1951–5, was still largely dominated by a seller's market and by the Korean War, and its price rises were superimposed on the price rises following from the devaluation of 1949.[101] Capacity was still stretched to the full, and demand on resources was balanced with supply by deliberately cutting investment, in order to make the particularly scarce engineering products available first for export, and secondly for rearmament.[102] Policy was concerned mainly with liquidity, the price level at home and the payments balance abroad, and long-term growth was not a major issue, since British growth was satisfactory by historical standards. North American growth was slow, and Continental growth could be safely dismissed as a mere catching-up process after war damage.[103]

The second phase, 1955–60, which began with two years' stagnation ending in a purely financial crisis, saw substantial real income growth in its last three years. It saw the ending of controls, particularly over sterling convertibility and capital movement, which the economy could not possibly sustain without major structural alteration, and it saw the peak and decline of the belief in 'monetary' means of economic control. In this period, Continental countries caught up with British absolute levels of output and income, and the first stirrings of disquiet about the slow British growth were heard.[104] Productive investment was less single-mindedly attacked by

[100] E.g. M. E. Blume, 'The Financial Markets'. in R. E. Caves and L. B. Krause (eds.), *Britain's Economic Performance* (1980), pp. 263–4; F. T. Blackaby (ed.), *De-Industrialisation*, pp. 247–9; R. C. O. Matthews, C. H. Feinstein, J. C. Odling-Smee, *British Economic Growth 1856–1973* (Oxford, 1982), pp. 492–3; United Nations, Economic Commission for Europe, *The European Economy from the 1950s to the 1970s* (New York, 1972), pp. 12–4.

[101] Harrod, pp. 21–6; also 147–8, 165–9.

[102] 'In the long run our industries must have the equipment they need for expansion and efficiency. At the present time, however, some of them must needs be sacrificed because of the overriding importance of increasing exports of precisely those goods for which investment demand is heaviest. The Government has therefore taken steps to divert resources on a large scale from supplying engineering goods to the home market to production for exports.' *Economic Survey 1952*, Cmd. 8509 (1952), paras. 30–1; Joan Mitchell, *Crisis in Britain* (1963); PEP, *Growth*, pp. 139 ff.; R. Nurkse, 'The Relation between Home Investment and External Balance in the Light of British Experience, 1945–1955', *Review of Economics and Statistics*, 38/2 (1956).

[103] PEP, *Growth*, pp. 2–3.

[104] 'The Government is pledged to foster conditions', the white paper on the *Economic*

short-term policymakers than in 1951–5,[105] investment in a real sense replaced exports,[106] and, taking the long view, the failure was less one of hitting investment thoughtlessly, but rather of allowing it too much freedom to turn into fields such as overseas companies or city centre properties which could not benefit British industrial competitiveness.

The third phase, 1960–5, was the most growth-conscious. It saw the setting up of the National Economic Development Council at the end of 1961 and its brave attempts to clear the path for a 4% growth rate.[107] The squeezes were designed to hit investment and production as little as possible, and various new encouragements to use resources productively were designed. Yet the massive backlog of investment, particularly in public utilities and capital-intensive basic industries, could not be made up in so short a space of time. Indeed, capital formation was still lower than in any other comparable country and Great Britain's productivity fell behind more and more.

The balance of payments deficit of 1964 was the largest ever, and the years 1965–9 formed one long squeeze, punctuated by several financial crises. There was no period when the balance of policy was not deflationary, and over much of it new records in deflationary pressures were set up. Any plans for future growth gave way to current panic measures. NEDC and its 'Little Neddies', and the Department of Economic Affairs, both of which were dedicated to expansion and to a strengthening of the real industrial base, were effectively disarmed by the Treasury. Nevertheless, though all was sacrificed to it, the balance of payments remained obstinately negative, and year by year the burden of short-term debt and the annual interest payable on it had to be increased to finance it. When confidence fell away in the autumn of 1967, the second devaluation of sterling became inevitable, for although its immediate cause was speculative and financial, its underlying reality was that Britain's prices and costs had been left too high in relation to others by her failure to maintain similar increases in productivity. When most of the foreign private short-term capital had left, by early 1968, the total of official foreign lending (and the burden of its servicing and repayment) showed the extent to which Britain had been living beyond her means, by sustaining a quantity of foreign investment and Government expenditure abroad for which her economic strength had provided no justification. (See Table 9·10) To this $3·2 billion has to be added an estimated $2 billion undisclosed debt, bringing the total to $5·3 billion, matched by a reserve of $2·8 billion,

---

Implications of Full Employment declared somewhat hesitantly, 'in which the nation can, if it so wills, realize its full potentialities for growth in terms of production and living standards.' Cmd. 9725 (1956), quoted in *Radcliffe Committee Report*, para. 58.

[105] 'A check to the expansion of investment was necessary, but it was also desirable to curb consumers' expenditure, so as to make room for a healthy growth of investment and a surplus in the balance of payments.' *Economic Survey 1956*, Cmd. 9278 (1956), para. 69. Nurkse, pp. 135 ff.

[106] W. Beckerman and Associates, *The British Economy in 1975* (Cambridge, 1965), Table 9·2, p. 271.

[107] E.g., 'The "Neddy" Experiment', *Midland Bank Review* (February 1968); Basil Taylor, 'The NEDC after Six Years', *Westminster Bank Review* (February 1968); Sir Robert Shone, 'Problems of Planning for Growth in a Mixed Economy', *Econ.J.*, 75/297 (1965); also M. FG. Scott, 'The Balance of Payments', in P. D. Henderson, *Economic Growth in Britain* (1966), pp. 85, *passim*.

Table 9·10: Disclosed debt, repayable by 1975* ($ million)

US and Canadian Government, US Eximbank (part of loans, repayable by 1975)	1,245
Bank for International Settlements	250
IMF (loans of 1965 and 1966)	1,521
Swiss, German and Portuguese banks	193
	3,210

* Well over half of this was repayable in 1970 or before. *Economist*, 23 March 1968, p. 70 and 30 March, 1968, p. 62.

not all of which was owned by Britain, so that the crude deficit was some $2·5 billion, or over £1 billion.

The following cycle 1969–73 saw the last attempt to break out of the downward spiral by positive means. The strategy of Barber's 'dash for growth' was the basically sound one of using the temporary payments surplus and the reserves to sustain a high rate of growth for long enough to allow sufficient investment to be built up to maintain a self-reinforcing high growth and investment rate thereafter; this, after all, had been the successful recipe of all the other industrial economies. The experiment foundered on two major obstacles. The first was the inadequacy of the reserves for the long haul, or at least, the loss of nerve on the part of the policy makers when the drain began to assume threatening proportions. The other, which would have in any case sealed the fate of the experiment, was that the freedom granted to the economy was used, not so much to invest in productive and cost reducing plant in Britain, but in property and financial speculation at home or in investment abroad. Investors had ceased to trust the promises of expansion policies, having learnt to their cost that they would be followed by contraction measures, including high interest rates and shrinking markets, just when the new plant was most vulnerable.[108] Real investment was lower than in the preceding cycle.[109] It was much easier and safer to speculate in currency or in land.

Here was indeed the apotheosis of British Keynesian 'management', which had worked in macro-quantities only, without considering *what* it was that the additional purchasing power released in expansion phases should be spent on. The difference between consumption and investment was neglected, and in this it was quite unlike the policy decisions abroad where pure theory was less strongly anchored and economic policy makers were therefore less inhibited in applying common sense to growth policies. At the same time, Keynesian policies were also being undermined from quite a different direction, by a growing emphasis, especially by the foreign bankers on whom Britain now depended, on the supply of money as a steering mechanism, and inflation as the major problem.

The monetarists had certainly put their finger on one increasingly troublesome phenomenon, the accelerating inflation in spite of high and rising unemployment. Expectations of ever rising prices were without a doubt

[108] E.g., CBI evidence to *Committee to Review the Functioning of Financial Institutions* (Wilson Committee), Evidence vol. 2 (1977), p. 8.
[109] Matthews, Feinstein and Odling-Smee, pp. 126, 133, 320.

beginning to play a part in the growing militancy and unreasonableness of organized labour; but even more significant was the general exasperation with increasingly tough but clearly ineffective incomes policies and other restraints.

This unruliness spilled over into the final cycle of 1973–9, and tended to dominate most phases of it. For although the Labour Government succeeded in enacting a quite remarkable range of reforms in favour of the trade unions and the poor which transformed the labour market in a significant way, practically everything else went wrong for them. Inflation got out of hand, unemployment rose, output and investment stagnated, manufacturing declined, foreign indebtedness increased with ever more humiliating terms imposed by foreign lenders, and the growing deficits of the public authorities at home worsened all other troubles and hampered the Government's freedom of action. Between 1973 and 1980 output per person-hour in British manufacturing increased by no more than 6%, compared with 20% in the USA, 23% in Germany, 25% in Italy, 31% in France and 40% in Japan.[110] It was clear that without the godsend of the oil, Britain would have sunk even further and faster below the levels of her European partners.

Thus, on the face of it, British economic policy, the attempt to control the economy as a whole, proved to be astonishingly unsuccessful, particularly by comparison with other countries similarly placed. It failed to maintain stability or the value of the currency. It led to a lower rate of growth than technological improvements would have warranted. It demoralized employers and workers by periodic squeezes, discouragements to expansion and enforcements of breaches of collective agreements. It failed to preserve the Sterling Area and proved incapable of staying within the European currency agreements. And at the end of the period, it left Britain with a litter of industrial dereliction and a contrived level of unemployment, large enough to dismay even the most sanguine.

Not surprisingly, therefore, British policy came under repeated and varied attack in this period. How far has the criticism been justified? Much of the criticism was directed towards the technical handling of short-term crises, and in particular, it has frequently been alleged that the Government permitted expansion to proceed too rapidly, thus exhausting spare capacity too quickly and creating bottlenecks by-passed by high imports. It may also be said that most of the measures taken operated too slowly, so that the squeezes came only when the economy was already depressed, and the expansion effects appeared only when the resources were already over-extended.[111]

Much of this criticism seems misplaced. In technical terms, the Treasury did as well as could be expected in dealing with *ad hoc* crises and usually had the financial and economic press on its side.

The principal fault lay in ignoring long-term benefits for the sake of solving short-term problems, and this, in turn, raises the question whether

[110] *Nat.Inst.Econ.Rev.*, 101 (August 1982), 78.

[111] E.g. F. Brechling and J. N. Wolfe, 'The End of Stop-Go', *Lloyds Bank Review*, 75 (1965); P. D. Henderson, *Economic Growth in Britain* (1966), pp. 17–9; Youngson, pp. 259 ff.; Lomax, 'Growth and Productivity', pp. 14 *passim*; G. D. N. Worswick, 'Fiscal Policy and Stabilization in Britain', in A. K. Cairncross (ed.), *British Economic Prospects Reconsidered* (1971).

there was anything inherent in the British situation to tend towards this particular failure. Was the British relative decline, was the heartbreaking succession of crises when all our neighbours enjoyed prosperity and growth, really inevitable? Had Britain, in other words, inherited a predisposition to decline from her long-established position of economic leadership?

There were indeed several relevant unfavourable factors that were not, or not to the same extent, operative in other countries. Each of them alone might have been overcome, as they were overcome from time to time elsewhere. All of them together proved too powerful to withstand.

We may begin with the victory in the war itself. Whereas defeat and destruction on the continent and in Japan had led to low income expectations there and the unhindered devotion of large resources to reconstruction, and whereas the USA and Canada on the other side had enough resources to satisfy both a growth of incomes and of investment, in Britain the victorious outcome had induced expectations of a high standard of living[112] without the means to sustain it. The British problem, whether it appeared in the guise of an income inflation or an import surplus, may throughout be seen as pressure, not only by labour but by all income earners, to take more out of current output than their productivity warranted, and in view of the immunity or stickiness of other items, such as Government expenditure or foreign investment, the cuts fell regularly on the remaining item, productive investment at home. Secondly, arising from the same victory and preceded by a long and successful imperial tradition, Britain took on the burdens of a Great Power, including actual fighting in Korea and in several colonies before their independence, for which she no longer had the resources. Her politicians and generals failed for too long to realize to what extent Britain's earlier world leadership had depended on her economic power rather than the skills of her diplomats or field commanders. It is a sombre reflection that throughout all the crises, cuts and humiliations Britain's economy had worked up a larger and healthier surplus than even her most successful rivals, Germany and Japan; it was only the Government's expenditure abroad, to a large extent of a military nature, that turned it into a long-term deficit[113] with all its fateful consequences. The Sterling Area, another imperial burden of the past, was instrumental in enforcing similarly costly restrictions on the British economy before it finally faded away.

Thirdly, Britain was uniquely saddled with a complex of financial interests, the 'City', which were not directly dependent on the welfare of industry, as were financiers in other countries, and with an all-powerful Treasury with inadequate access either to economic science or to industry, so that it was totally subservient to the doctrines and the appraisals of the City, transmitted by the Bank of England. Only this one-sided influence upon the Treasury can explain its failure to learn from British and other experience that growth need not mean inflation; that a 'stop' need not mean stability; and that the policy of the post-war years has led to a galloping deterioration,

---

[112] C. F. Carter, 'The International and Domestic Financial Policy of the United Kingdom', *Public Finance*, 8 (1953), p. 229.

[113] W. A. P. Manser, *Britain in Balance* (1971); A. Shonfield, *British Economic Policy Since the War* (Harmondsworth, 1959), p. 91.

without even a theoretical model, let alone any practical example, that could lead one to hope for a break out of the vicious circle if more of the same medicine were continued.[114] After all, the information must have been available to the Treasury, as it has been to the public at large, that it was in 'stop' periods specifically designed to hold down prices, that prices rose fastest (see Table 9·11).[115]

Table 9·11: Stop-go and key indices

	Expansion periods (1953–5, 1958–60, 1962–4, 1967–9, 1972–3, 1975–9)	Stagnation periods (1955–8, 1960–2, 1964–7, 1969–72, 1973–5, 1979–80)
Annual growth rate in UK industrial production	4·9%	0·1%
Annual rise in prices:		
retail	6·6	7·5
manufactures	6·4	7·4
Annual growth in volume:		
exports	6·8	2·6
imports	7·5	1·5

It is surely very irrational indeed to tolerate 'stop' measure, lasting two years or more, causing a loss of output of perhaps 3% of the national income in the first year and 6% in the second year, merely to correct a deficit amounting to 0·85% of national income . . . it is positively wrongful in relation to economic welfare.[116]

For similar reasons, protective policies never had a chance. In May 1968 even the mere suggestion by the Institute of Economic and Social Research that preparations for possible import curbs might be advisable drew at once a sharp rebuke from Mr Jenkins, the Chancellor of the Exchequer. The policy remained that of ever sharper and ever less effective credit squeezes. It could be only a financier's mind, unfamiliar with the workings of industry, that could have thought, after 20 years of consistent failure, of responding to the problem of inadequate productivity, not with 'produce more', but with 'consume and invest less'.

Fourthly, Britain suffered not only from a higher Civil Service largely innocent of Mathematics, Technology or Economics, but also from an excess of remarkably brilliant and well trained economists who tended, for different reasons but with the same ultimately disastrous effects, to ignore the problems of productive industry in their search for satisfying macro-economic solutions.[117] Less theoretically inclined economists elsewhere, where business studies enjoyed a higher prestige, could hardly have sustained such long years

[114] Harrod, pp. 189–206; Samuel Brittan, *The Treasury under the Tories 1951–1964* (Pelican, 1964).

[115] W. A. Eltis, 'Economic Growth and the British Balance of Payments', *District Bank Review*, 164 (1967); all figures based on *Key Statistics* and *Annual Abstract of Statistics*. See also Harrod, *Towards a New Economic Policy*, p. 13; Michael Shanks, *The Stagnant Society* (Penguin, 1961), chapter 2; Norman MacRae, *Sunshades in October* (1963).

[116] Harrod, *op. cit.*, p. 30.

[117] S. Pollard, *Wasting*, pp. 143–50.

of practical failure without questioning the bases of their assumptions. Nor did matters improve when monetarists supplanted Keynesians as official advisers.

This intellectual failure was also sustained, fifthly, by the long tradition of British economic and technical leadership, going back some 200 years to the industrial revolution. While British businessmen, technologists or civil servants were, as we have seen, willing to learn from the USA after the war, the arrogance towards the rest of the world, founded on history, survived almost to the end of our period when it had long since lost its justification, and prevented Britain not only from obtaining useful lessons from across the channel, but also from even questioning her own progress, as a first step to altering course.

Sixthly, several of the ways in which the world was changing around Britain, worked to her ultimate disadvantage. Possibly the most powerful effect here was the advance of the industrial world as against the 'third world', and the benefits which the advanced countries derived from growing mutual trade and an ever more detailed international division of labour. In this way the traditional economic role of Britain as mediator between the two worlds was weakened, though it should be stressed that Britain lost ground in *all* markets and cannot therefore put much blame on the relative weakening of her traditional trade partners.

Lastly, there was necessarily a cumulative trend, or learning process, in the sum of these adverse factors. Entrepreneurs and trade unionists learned to accommodate to stagnation and shied away from, if they were not actively hostile to, innovation. Engineers and technologists, whose quality was certainly not inferior to that of the continentals and who were frequently but somewhat unjustly blamed for the British ills, had fewer opportunities to stretch their wings by planning new schemes. Growth itself generates growth. To be sure, the argument that slower growth in Britain goes back to 1900 or even beyond, though true, is of little relevance, since all countries jumped after the war from a 1–2% annual rate to a 4–5% rate, and in the last pre-war decade British economic growth was in fact faster than most, so that the continuation of earlier trends should have favoured Britain. But it is true that it is easier to sustain a high rate, once it is started, than to switch over to it, and the recovery from lower levels in the immediate post-war years may have helped some other countries by setting them on a fast growth course.

Thus the inheritance of the past had saddled the British economy with some undeniable burdens; but it also provided her with immense initial advantages after the war. Among them was a fairly intact productive apparatus, bettered only by Sweden and Switzerland in Europe, with strength in some of the key growth sectors, like vehicles, aircraft and electronics. There was also a high reputation for quality, compared, say, with German, let alone Japanese products. There was high morale at home, prestige abroad, and a degree of social and political cohesion that most other industrial countries would envy. Britain had a firm footing in many of the world's leading markets, strengthened in the later 1940s when most of her rivals were still too weak to compete. Lastly, she still had her resources advantage of location, iron ore, coal and, lately, natural gas and oil.

Perhaps all this was not enough to outweigh the long list of disadvantages.

But the disadvantages became fatally operative only because policy makers chose to react repeatedly in a certain way to them, and it is difficult to believe that these reactions were, indeed, wholly inevitable.

4 Into the 1980s

The story of the post-war development of the British economy is one of immense progress compared with any previous period, but one of disappointing relative decline when measured against the achievements of other, comparable countries. Towards the end of our period, the relative falling back turned into an absolute decline in certain sectors, above all in manufacturing. What of the immediate future?

Two trends have dominated the general development of the British economy in the early 1980s. One is the flow of North Sea oil, which has maintained a comfortable balance of payments surplus and made it easy to stabilize the external value of sterling, and the other is the world economic recession marked by high rates of unemployment and stagnation of production in the face of inflation in every major economy, but above all in the American.

Deflationary policies in the USA, which included the use of high interest rates, kept rates high in the rest of the world, but their reduction towards the end of 1982 did not lead to a noticeable upswing. On the contrary, in the course of 1981 and 1982 the forecasts of future trends, gloomy enough to begin with, were repeatedly revised downwards, towards lower growth and higher unemployment, in one country after another.

The methods of keeping the major exchange rates stable were running fairly smoothly, occasional devaluations (French franc) or revaluations (Deutschmark) being made in formally announced steps. Against this comparative success, a rising threat was posed by the rapidly mounting indebtedness, especially of the less developed, the Latin American and the Eastern European countries. Since the western industrialized creditor nations in recession could not absorb increasing imports, even if the debtors had been capable of providing them, the inability to service the debt led debtors to ask for rescheduling (a euphemism for partial default) to an ever increasing extent, with the threat of complete default not far in the background. Just as the exports without immediate payments to these countries had helped to fuel the uncertain boom of the later 1970s, default now would cause losses and even collapse among the mixed consortia of banks, central banks and governments who had provided the funds in the first instance. Meanwhile the growing State indebtedness within the western countries themselves was a potent force helping to prevent Keynesian spending as a solution to the depression, as on earlier post-war occasions.

Against this background, the trends begun by the Conservative budget of 1979 continued very strongly in Britain. Unemployment grew with inexorable force, each pessimistic forecast being overtaken by even more sombre events, to reach an official figure of $3\frac{1}{3}$ million by the end of 1982 (corresponding to perhaps 4 million in fact) with further increases forecast for 1983. Particularly heartbreaking was the high ratio of unemployment among young school leavers, above all the coloured, and, as always in longer depression, the rise in the numbers of the long-term unemployed: those out of work for one year, two years, or even longer.[118]

Much was made of the fact that labour productivity was up quite substantially, rising by perhaps 10% in 1981 alone. But this result was not at all due to greater technical efficiency, but to the closure of less efficient units and possibly to greater effort on the part of each man employed; also, it seems that as the depression deepened, employers tended to let go of their labour reserves kept in more optimistic days for possible future orders.[119] No gain was achieved by the economy, for the resources thus freed became immediately idle, while even those left at work put in fewer hours each. Between 1971 and the third quarter of 1981, manufacturing employment fell by 24%, but operative hours worked fell by 28%; since 1962 they had fallen by over 42%.[120] Unlike other Governments, the British Government had still not realized that ultimate re-employment, the creation of jobs, involved a substantial investment per worker, and it continued to turn down proposals for providing funds from one source or another for this purpose. Since profit rates and orders were also still declining, it was difficult to see on what their expectation of an upturn in employment could have been based. They were in tune with other governments at least to the extent of also periodically revising downward their estimates of future output or employment.

Inflation and the PSBR, however, came down sharply in the latter part of 1982, ahead of expectations. This broadly favourable development may have taken the Government by surprise, in part because according to their own theories it should not have happened. The expansion of the PSBR and of M3, among others, was particularly high 18–24 months before, M3 for example increasing by 18·6% in 1979–80 and by 13·6% in 1980–1, so that inflation should have been kept up at a high level according to the monetarist doctrine. All this certainly helped to maintain the confusion in monetary targetry.[121] It is not clear how much longer, therefore, the Government will continue to use monetary 'targets' to justify a classic deflationary policy, nor whether the expected turnround in policy will be timed, as in the past, with an eye on election dates.

If inflation can be held down, this may reflect on savings and investment habits of the general population, as well as on the policies of specialist financial firms. 1980–2 saw a remarkable increase in private borrowing from the banks, and an even more striking rise in bank lending for house purchases, from £30 million in the first quarter of 1980 to £870 million in the last quarter of 1981.[122] British financial institutions clearly continued their ability to react quickly to changed circumstances.

In longer term, British de-industrialization is set to continue, but it is by no means certain that this, by itself, must be considered an unmitigated disaster. The trend everywhere is for employment in manufacturing industry to

[118] *Employment Gazette* (Monthly).

[119] Douglas Jones, 'Great Productivity Mirage'. *Observer*, 2 May 1982; Treasury, *Recent Trends in Labour Productivity*, Economic Progress Report, No. 141 (1982).

[120] *Nat.Inst.Econ.Rev.*

[121] See, e.g., Sir Alec Cairncross, 'Two Years Without Cheers', *Three Banks Review*, 129 (March 1981), 11.

[122] *Midland Bank Review* (Summer 1982), 14.

decline and employment in the tertiary sectors to increase,[123] just as, some 200 years ago, employment in agriculture began to decline in favour of industry. Britain may thus be one step ahead of most others in a switch towards the service economy, which has traditionally been a sector of British strength.

However, the adaptation to the 'post-industrial economy' is not achieved by closing down firms and then throwing the workers on the dole: it is achieved by providing efficiently run, competitive jobs in the expanding sectors and fitting the workforce to them. There is no sign, at present, that this is understood by British policy makers. Still less is it understood that future prosperity will depend on providing adequate and sophisticated capital equipment for a workforce not only highly skilled, but trained to be flexible, adaptable and forward looking. There has been a change in economic development itself: it is now faster, less predictable and more far-reaching than ever before.

[123] Daniel Bell, *The Coming of Post-Industrial Society* (New York, 1973).

Further Reading

This bibliography contains only a few titles of general works which the reader may find useful. For the rest of the recommended reading, students are referred to the Preface, pp. v–vii.

The only work covering most of the period considered here is A. J. Youngson, *Britain's Economic Growth 1920–1966* (1967). This is essentially a series of essays, mostly on economic policy, and requires some knowledge of the economic controversies of these years. Comprehensive volumes of statistics are now available in B. R. Mitchell and Phyllis Deane, *Abstract of British Historical Statistics* (Cambridge, 1962), and R. C. O. Matthews, C. H. Feinstein and J. C. Odling-Smee, *British Economic Growth 1856–1973* (Oxford, 1982).

For the years up to 1939, an elementary introduction will be found in M. W. Thomas (ed.), *A Survey of English Economic History* (1960 ed.), and a more advanced treatment in W. Ashworth, *An Economic History of England 1870–1939* (1960). For the inter-war years specifically, W. A. Lewis, *Economic Survey 1919–1939* (1949), and Sean Glyn and John Oxborrow, *Interwar Britain: A Social and Economic History* (1976) are strongly recommended.

The best account of the years of the Second World War is in the main volume of the official series of war histories, W. K. Hancock and M. M. Gowing, *British War Economy* (1949). The most comprehensive study made to date, of the immediate post-war years in the collective work, edited by G. D. N. Worswick and P. H. Ady, *The British Economy 1945–1950* (Oxford, 1952). This contains a valuable bibliography, as do most of the other works mentioned here.

For the years since 1950, see G. D. N. Worswick and P. H. Ady (ed.), *The British Economy in the Nineteen-Fifties* (1962); W. Beckerman and Associates, *The British Economy in 1975* (Cambridge, 1965); J. C. R. Dow, *The Management of the British Economy 1945–60* (Cambridge, 1965); F. T. Blackaby (ed.), *British Economic Policy 1960–74* (Cambridge, 1978); W. Beckerman (ed.), *The Labour Government's Economic Record 1964–1970* (1972); W. P. J. Maunder (ed.), *The British Economy in the 1970s* (1980); A. R. Prest and D. J. Coppock, *The UK Economy. A Manual of Applies Economics* (latest edition).

Index